Preliminary Edition

Reconceptualizing Mathematics

Reasoning About Numbers and Quantities
Reasoning About Algebra and Change
Reasoning About Shapes and Measurement

Judith Sowder
Larry Sowder
Susan Nickerson

San Diego State University

© 2008
W.H. Freeman & Company
New York, New York

Reconceptualizing Mathematics:
Reasoning About Numbers and Quantities
Reasoning About Algebra and Change
Reasoning About Shapes and Measurement

by Judith Sowder, Larry Sowder, and Susan Nickerson

This is a preliminary edition of *Reconceptualizing Mathematics*, to be published
by W.H. Freeman & Company in 2009.

Senior Acquisitions Editor: Terri Ward
Associate Editor: Laura Capuano
Development Editor: Elka Block, Twin Prime Editorial
Executive Marketing Manager: Jennifer Somerville
Director of Market Research and Development: Steven Rigolosi

ISBN: 1-4292-2427-4

For more information about this title:
WHFreemanMathematics@whfreeman.com
www.whfreeman.com/sowderpreview

W.H. Freeman & Co.
41 Madison Avenue
New York, NY 10010
www.whfreeman.com

About the Text

These materials were developed by a team of mathematics educators at San Diego State University, including Professors Judith Sowder (Project Director), Larry Sowder, Alba Thompson (now deceased), Patrick Thompson, Janet Bowers, Joanne Lobato, Nicholas Branca (now deceased), and Randolph Philipp. Graduate students Jamal Bernhard, Lisa Clement, Melissa Lernhardt, Susan Nickerson, and Daniel Siebert assisted in the development of the materials. The original text materials have been extensively revised and edited by the author team.

Note: The materials in this book were developed at San Diego State University in part with funding from the National Science Foundation Grant No. ESI 9354104. The content of this book is solely the responsibility of the authors and does not necessarily reflect the views of the National Science Foundation.

About the Authors

JUDITH SOWDER is a Professor Emerita of Mathematics and Statistics. Her research has focused on the development of number sense and on the instructional effects of teachers' mathematical knowledge at the elementary and middle school level. She served from 1996 to 2000 as editor of the *Journal for Research in Mathematics Education* and served a three-year term on the National Council of Teachers of Mathematics Board of Directors. She was an author of the middle school content chapter of the Conference Board of Mathematical Sciences document *The Mathematical Education of Teachers,* published in 2001 by the Mathematical Association of America. She has directed numerous projects funded by National Science Foundation and the Department of Education. In 2000 she received the Lifetime Achievement Award from the National Council of Teachers of Mathematics.

LARRY SOWDER taught mathematics to preservice elementary school teachers for more than 30 years, before his retirement as a professor in the Department of Mathematics and Statistics at San Diego State University. Work in a special program in San Diego elementary schools also shaped his convictions about how courses in mathematics for preservice teachers should be pitched, as did his joint research investigating how children in the usual grades 4–8 curriculum solve "story" problems. He served on the National Research Council Committee that published *Educating Teachers of Science, Mathematics, and Technology* (NRC, 2001).

SUSAN NICKERSON was involved in the development of these materials as a graduate student and has taught both pre-service and in-service teachers using these materials. Also a faculty member of San Diego State University's Department of Mathematics and Statistics, she is presently undertaking research focused on long-term professional development of elementary and middle school teachers with an emphasis on increasing teachers' knowledge of mathematics and mathematics teaching. She recently directed a state-funded professional development program for middle school teachers.

All three authors consider themselves as having dual roles—as teacher educators and as researchers on the learning and teaching of mathematics. Most of their research took place in elementary and middle school classrooms and in professional development settings with teachers of these grades.

Message to Prospective and Practicing Teachers

This course is about the mathematics you should know to teach mathematics to elementary and middle school students. Some of the mathematics here may be familiar to you, but you will explore it from new perspectives. You will also explore ideas that are new to you. *The overall goal of this course is that you come to understand the mathematics deeply so that you are able to participate in meaningful conversations about this mathematics and its applications with your peers and eventually with your students.* Being capable of solving a problem or performing a procedure, by itself, will not enable you to add value to the school experience of your students. But when you are able to converse with your students about mathematical ideas, reasons, goals, and relationships, they can come to make sense of the mathematics. Students who know that mathematics makes sense will seek for meaning and become successful learners of mathematics. Of course, you as the teacher must make sense of the mathematics before you can lead your students to do so. Sense-making is a theme that permeates all aspects of this course. Thus, although the course is about mathematics rather than about methods of teaching mathematics, you will learn a great deal that will be helpful to you when you start teaching.

One avenue to understanding mathematics deeply enough to hold conversations about it and make sense of it is to develop an orientation to look for "big ideas"—to realize that mathematics is not just about getting answers to questions but rather about developing insight into mathematical relationships and structures. For example, our base-ten numeration system is a big idea that is fundamental to understanding how to operate on numbers in meaningful ways. A solution to a sophisticated or complex problem emerges from understanding the problem rather than meaninglessly applying procedures to solve it, often unsuccessfully. This course focuses on the big ideas of the mathematics of the elementary school.

The following suggestions are intended to assist you in developing a conceptual orientation to the mathematics presented here, that is, understanding the big ideas behind mathematical procedures we use. With this orientation you are far more likely to be successful in learning mathematics.

How to Write Your Reasoning

You will have opportunities to write your reasoning when you work on assignments and on exams, and frequently when you work through classroom activities. Writing your reasoning begins with describing your understanding of the situation or context that gives meaning to the present task. Do not take this aspect of writing lightly. Many difficulties arise because of initial misunderstandings of the situation and of the task being proposed to you. Another way to look at this aspect of writing is that you are making your tacit assumptions explicit because, with the exception of execution errors (such as "2 + 3 = 4"), most difficulties can be traced back to tacit assumptions or inadequate understandings of a situation.

Focus on the decisions you make, and write about those decisions and their reasons. For example, if you decide that some quantity has to be cut into three parts rather than five parts, then explain what motivated that decision. Also mention the consequences of your decisions, such as "this area, which I called '1 square inch,' is now in pieces that are each 1/3 square inch." When you make consequences explicit, you have additional information with which to work as you proceed. Additional information makes it easier to remember where you've been and how you might get to where you are trying to go.

You will do a lot of writing in this course. The reason for having you write is that, in writing, you have to organize your ideas and understand them coherently. If you give incoherent explanations and shaky analyses for a situation or idea, you probably don't understand it. But if you do understand an idea or situation deeply, you should be able to speak about it and write about it coherently and conceptually.

Feel free to write about insights gained as you worked on the problem. Some people have found it useful to do their work in two columns—one for scratch and one for remarks to yourself about the ideas that occur to you. Be sure to include sketches, diagrams, and so on, and write in complete, easy-to-read sentences.

Learn to read your own writing as if you had not seen it before.

> ➤ Is what you wrote just a sequence of "things to do"? If so, then someone reading it with the intention of understanding why you did what you did will be unable to replicate your reasoning. There is an important distinction between reporting what you did and explaining what you did. The first is simply an account or description of what you did, but the latter includes reasons for what you did. The latter is an explanation; the former is a report.

> ➤ Does your explanation make sense? Do not fall into the trap of reading your sentences merely to be reminded of what you had in your mind when you wrote them. Another person will not read them with the advantage of knowing what you were trying to say. The other person can only try to make sense of what you actually wrote. Don't expect an instructor to "know what you really meant."

> ➤ Are sentences grammatically correct?

Assignments will contain questions and activities. You should present your work on each question logically, clearly, and neatly. Your work should explain what you have done—it should reflect your reasoning. Your write-up should present more than an answer to a question. It should tell a story—the story of your emerging insight into the ideas behind the question. Think of your write-up as an assignment about how you present your thinking. Uninterpretable or unorganized scratch work is not acceptable.

How to Participate in Class

> ➤ Have the attitude that you want to understand the reasoning behind what anyone (the instructor or a classmate or a student) says.

> ➤ Don't have the attitude that "maybe it will make sense later." It will make more sense later if you have a basic understanding of a conversation's overall aims and details. A conversation will probably not make sense later if it makes no sense while you are listening.

> ➤ It is not necessary that you remember verbatim what transpires in class. Instead, try to understand classroom discussions and activities as you would a story's plot: motives, actors, objectives, consequences, relationships, and so on.

> ➢ At the moment you feel you are not "with it," raise your hand and try to formulate a question. Don't prejudge the appropriateness of your question. If the instructor judges that your question requires a significant digression, he or she will arrange to meet you outside of class. Make sure you keep the appointment so that you don't fall behind.

How to Read Others' Work (the Instructor's or a Classmate's or the Textbook)

> ➢ Make sure you are clear about the context or situation that gives rise to an example and its main elements. Note that this is not a straightforward process. It will often require significant reflection and inner conversation about what is going on.

> ➢ Interpret what you read. Be sure that you know what is being said. Paraphrasing, making a drawing, or trying a new example may help.

> ➢ Interpret one sentence at a time. If a sentence's meaning is not clear, then do not go further. Instead,

> > • Think about the sentence's role within the context of the initial situation, come up with a question about the situation, and assess the writer's overall aims and method.

> > • Rephrase the sentence by asking, "What might the writer be trying to say?"

> > • Construct examples or make a drawing that will clarify the situation.

> > • Try to generalize from examples.

> > • Ask someone what he or she thinks the sentence means. (This should not be your initial or default approach to resolving a confusion.)

How to Use This Textbook

The first step toward using a textbook productively is to understand the structure of the book and what it contains. This textbook is separated into two volumes, each with two parts. The first volume contains *Part I: Reasoning About Numbers and Quantities* and *Part II: Reasoning About Algebra and Change*. The second volume contains *Part III: Reasoning About Shapes and Measurement* and *Part IV: Reasoning About Chance and Data*.

Each part includes several chapters, each with the following format:

> ➢ A brief description of what the chapter is about.

> ➢ Chapter sections that contain the following elements:

> > • An introduction to the section.

> > • Prose that introduces and explains the section's content. This prose is interspersed with activities, discussions, and reflective questions called "think abouts."

> > • *Activities* intended to be worked in small groups or pairs and to provide some hands-on experiences with the content. In most instances they can be completed and discussed in class. Discussion on activities is worthwhile because other groups many times will take a

different approach. (See the above sections on how to participate in class and how to read others' work.)

- *Discussions* intended primarily for whole class discussion. These discussions provide more opportunities to converse about the mathematics being learned, to listen to the reasoning of others, to voice disagreement when that is the case. (Remember to disagree with an idea, not with the person. Read the above sections on participation in class and reading the work of others.)

- *Think Abouts* intended to invite you to pause and reflect on what you have just read, or extend your thinking about an idea presented. (See the section above on how to read other's work.)

- *Definitions* that are concise ways of describing important ideas. They need to be considered very thoughtfully to fully understand them. Examples are provided to help you make sense of them. If you don't understand a definition, ask your instructor or discuss it with another student.

- *Take-Away Messages* summarizing the overriding messages of the section.

- *Examples* provide needed clarification and opportunities to explore meanings and demonstrate procedures.

- *Learning Exercises* to be used for homework and sometimes for classroom discussion or activities. Note the term "learning" used here. Although the exercises provide opportunities for practice, they are intended primarily to help you think though the section content, note the relationships, and extend what you have learned. *Not all problems in the exercises can be solved quickly.* Some are challenging and make take more time than you are used to spending on a problem. By knowing this, you should not become discouraged if the path to an answer is not quickly apparent. (Be sure to read the section above on how to write your reasoning.)

➤ For many chapters there is a section called *Issues for Learning*, which most often contains a discussion of some of the research about children's learning of topics associated with the content of the chapter. Reading about these issues will help you understand some of the conceptual difficulties children have in learning particular content, and will help you relate what you are learning to the classroom and to teaching.

➤ A *Check Yourself* section at the end of every chapter that will help you organize and consolidate what you have learned in that chapter. This list can serve to organize review of the chapter for examinations.

In addition to chapters you will find the following in each book:

➤ A *Summary of Formulas* for Measurement

➤ A *Glossary* of important terms

➤ *Answers (or hints) for Many Learning Exercises.* Space does not permit each answer to include all of the rationale described above in writing about your reasoning, but you should provide this information as you work through the exercises.

➢ *Appendix A: A Review of Some Rules* provides a review of some basic arithmetic skills that you are expected to have when beginning this course but may have forgotten.

➢ For Part I only, an appendix (**Appendix B**) that provides a website for *video clips* that show student thinking, and questions for reflection and discussion about what you see in these clips.

➢ **Master Pages** with dot paper and templates to be copied as needed.

Also available online at www.whfreeman.com/sowderpreview, you will find:

➢ *Supplementary Learning Exercises with Answers* that will provide more examples and learning experiences if you need additional help to understand the content.

Finally, you will see that this text includes a large margin on the outside of each page so that you can freely write notes to help you remember, for example, how a problem was worked, or to clarify the text, based on what happens in class. These materials are produced at the lowest possible cost so that you can mark up the text, keep it, and use it to help you review mathematics needed to plan lessons when you begin teaching.

Contents

This book, comprising Parts I, II, and III, is a preliminary, abridged, black-and-white version of the forthcoming *Reconceptualizing Mathematics* text by Judith Sowder, Larry Sowder, and Susan Nickerson. The final color textbook will be available from W.H. Freeman & Co in 2009. The complete contents will be as follows (table of contents subject to change):

PART IV   Reasoning About Chance and Data

Chapter 27   Quantifying Uncertainty

*Supplementary Exercises with Answers in Appendices C and E are available at www.whfreeman.com/sowderpreview.

Part I

Reasoning About Numbers and Quantities

Much of what you see in these first eleven chapters will look familiar. However, you will be asked to begin understanding the mathematics of arithmetic at a more fundamental level than you may now do. Knowing *how* to compute is not sufficient for teaching; a teacher should understand the underlying reasons we compute as we do.

An important focus of these chapters is on *using* numbers. We do this by helping you develop the skill of quantitative reasoning. This reasoning is fundamental to solving problems involving quantities (such as the speed of a car or the price of chips). You may recognize such problems as *story problems*. In Chapters 1, 8, and 9 you will learn how to approach such problems, using quantitative reasoning.

Our base ten system of numbers, introduced in Chapter 2, is the foundation for all of the procedures we use for computing with whole numbers. A teacher must acquire a dccp understanding of the base ten system and the arithmetic procedures, which is the focus of Chapters 3, 4, and 5. We then turn to the study of fractions, decimals, and percents in Chapters 6 and 7. Many people in our society do not know how to compute with these numbers, or how these numbers are related. The emphasis on understanding these numbers and how to operate on them will give you a foundation to teach fractions, decimals, and percents well. Your students will benefit if they do not develop the belief that they cannot "do" fractions. Teachers who can teach arithmetic in a manner that students understand will better prepare their students for the mathematics yet to come.

Chapter 10 expands the type of numbers we used in previous chapters to include negative numbers, and discusses arithmetic operations on these numbers. Again, the focus is on understanding. Chapter 11, on number theory, provides different ways of thinking about and using numbers. Topics such as factors, multiples, prime numbers, and divisibility are found in this chapter.

An underlying theme throughout these chapters is an introduction to children's thinking about the mathematics they do. You will be surprised to learn the ways that children do mathematics, and we think that knowing how children reason mathematically will convince you that you need to know mathematics at a much deeper level than you likely do now. Prospective teachers are often fascinated with these glimpses into the ways children reason, particularly if they have a good foundation in their work with numbers.

Chapter **1**

Reasoning About Quantities

We encounter quantities of many kinds each day. In this chapter you will be asked to think about quantities and the manner in which we use them to better understand our lives. In particular, you will encounter "story problems" and learn how to solve them using a powerful reasoning process, most likely aided by a drawing of some sort.

1.1 | What Is a Quantity?

Consider the following questions:

How long do humans live?

How fast is the wind blowing?

Which is more crowded, New York City or Mexico City?

How big is this room?

How far is it around the earth?

The answer to each of these questions involves some quantity.

> A **quantity** is anything (an object, event, or quality thereof) that can be measured or counted. The **value** of a quantity is its measure or the number of items that are counted. A value of a quantity involves a number and a unit of measure or number of units.

For example, the length of a room is a quantity. It can be measured. Suppose the measurement is 14 feet. Note that *14* is a number, and *feet* is a unit of measure: 14 feet is the value of the quantity, length of the room. The number of people in the bus is another example of a quantity. Suppose the count is 22 people. Note that *22* is a number, and the unit counted is *people*, so 22 is the value associated with the quantity "number of people on the bus."

A person's age, the speed of the wind, the population density of New York City, the area of this room, and the distance around the earth at the equator are all examples of quantities.

THINK ABOUT . . .

What are some possible values of the five quantities mentioned above? Notice that population alone will not be sufficient to address the question of how crowded a city or a country is. Why?

Not all qualities of objects, events, or persons can be quantified. Consider *love*. Young children sometimes attempt to quantify love stretching their arms out wide when asked, "How much do you love me?," but love is not a quantity. Love, anger, boredom, and interest are some examples of qualities that are not quantifiable. Feelings, in general, are not quantifiable—thus, they are difficult to assess.

THINK ABOUT . . .

Name some other "things," besides feelings, that are not quantities.

The fact that a quantity is not the same as a number should be clear to you. In fact, one can think of a quantity without knowing its value. For example, the amount of rain fallen on a given day is a quantity, regardless of whether or not someone measured the actual number of inches of rain fallen. One can speak of the amount of rain fallen without knowing how many inches fell. Likewise, one can speak of a dog's weight, a tank's capacity, the speed of the wind, or the amount of time it takes to do a chore (all quantities) without knowing their actual values.

Discussion 1   Identifying Quantities and Measures

1.   Identify the quantity or quantities addressed in each of the following questions.
     a.   How tall is the Eiffel tower?   *Eiffel tower's height*
     b.   How fast does water come out of a faucet?   *waters speed*
     c.   Which country is wealthier, Honduras or Mozambique?   *The countries amounts of $*
     d.   How much damage did the earthquake cause?   *Amount wrecked by the earthq*

2.   Identify an appropriate unit of measure that can be used to determine the value of the quantities involved in answering the questions in Problem 1. Is the wealth of a country measured the same way as the wealth of an individual? Explain.

Discussion 2   Easy to Quantify?

1.   Many attributes or qualities of objects are easily quantifiable. Others are not so straightforward. Of the following items, which are easy to quantify and which aren't?
     a.   The weight of a newborn baby   b.   The gross national product
     c.   Student achievement   d.   Blood pressure
     e.   Livability of a city   f.   Infant mortality rate
     g.   Teaching effectiveness   h.   Human intelligence
     i.   Air quality   j.   Wealth of a nation

2. How is each item in Problem 1 typically quantified?

3. What sorts of events and things do you think primitive humans felt a need to quantify? Make a list. How do you think primitive societies kept track of the values of those quantities?

4. Name some attributes of objects (besides those listed in Problem 1) that are not quantifiable or that are hard to quantify.

5. Name some quantities for which units of measure have been only recently developed.

> TAKE-AWAY MESSAGE . . . In this introductory section you have learned to identify quantities and their values and to distinguish between the two. This understanding is the basis for the quantitative analyses in the next section. ♦

1.2 Quantitative Analysis

In this section you will use what you have learned about quantities in Section 1.1 to analyze problem situations in terms of their quantitative structure. Such analyses are essential to being skillful at solving mathematical problems.

> For the purposes of this course, to **understand a problem situation** means to understand the quantities embedded in the situation and how they are related to one another.

Understanding a problem situation "drives" the solution to the problem. Without such understanding, the only recourse a person has is to guess at the calculations that need to be performed. It is important that you work through this section with care and attention. Analyzing problem situations quantitatively is central to the remainder of this course and other courses that are part of your preparation to teach school mathematics.

Activity 1   The Hot Dog Problem

♦ Albert ate $2\frac{3}{4}$ hot dogs and Reba ate $1\frac{1}{2}$ hot dogs. What part of all the hot dogs they consumed did Albert eat? ♦

This fairly simple problem is given here to illustrate the process of using a quantitative analysis to solve a problem. We first analyze the situation in terms of the quantities it involves and how those quantities are related to one another: its **quantitative structure**. To do so productively, it is extremely important to be specific about what the quantities are. For example, it is not sufficient to say that "hot dogs eaten" is a quantity in this problem situation. If you indicated "hot dogs eaten" as one of the quantities and specified no more, then someone could ask: Which hot dogs? The ones Albert ate? The ones Reba ate? The total number of hot dogs eaten?

Continue on the next page.

Continuation of Activity 1

To understand the quantitative structure of this problem situation, you can do the following:

1. Name as many quantities as you can that are involved in this situation. Be aware that some quantities may not be explicitly stated although they are essential to the situation. Also, just because the value of a quantity may not be known nor given, the quantity is still part of the situation's quantitative structure.

2. For each quantity, if the value is given, write it in the appropriate space. If the value is not given, indicate that the value is unknown and write the unit you would use to measure it. You may need more space than provided here. (*Reminder:* There should be no numbers appearing in the Quantity column.) Compare your list with those of others in your class.

Quantity	Value
a. Number of hot dogs eaten by Albert	$2\frac{3}{4}$
b.	
c.	etc.

3. Make a drawing that illustrates this problem. Here, the outer rectangle indicates the total number of hot dogs eaten, and the parts show the portions eaten by each person. (Note that drawings such as this one need not be drawn to scale. Here, the number of hot dogs eaten by Albert is shown only to be more than the hot dogs eaten by Reba.)

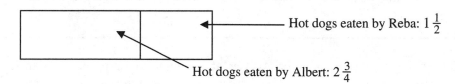

Hot dogs eaten by Reba: $1\frac{1}{2}$

Hot dogs eaten by Albert: $2\frac{3}{4}$

4. Finally, use the drawing to solve the problem. The drawing shows that the total number of hot dogs eaten is $2\frac{3}{4} + 1\frac{1}{2}$ or $4\frac{1}{4}$. What part of the total was eaten by Albert? $\dfrac{2\frac{3}{4}}{4\frac{1}{4}}$ hot dogs, which simplifies to $\frac{11}{17}$ of the hot dogs. This value is about two-thirds of the hot dogs, a reasonable answer to this question.

The purpose in Activity 1 is to illustrate how one must **analyze** a situation **in terms of the quantities and the relationships present in the situation** in order to gain an understanding that can lead to a meaningful solution. **Such an activity is called a quantitative analysis**. On problems such as this one, you may find that you don't really need to think through all four steps. However, more difficult problems, such as those in the next two activities, are more easily solved by undertaking a careful quantitative analysis. You will improve your skill at solving problems when you engage in such analyses because you will come to a better understanding of the problem.

Activity 2   Sisters and Brothers

Try this problem by undertaking a quantitative analysis before you read the solution. Then compare your solution to the one shown here.

♦ Two women, Alma and Beatrice, each had a brother, Alfred and Benito, respectively. The two women argued about which woman stood taller over her brother. It turned out that Alma won the argument by a 17-centimeter difference. Alma was 186 cm tall. Alfred was 87 cm tall. Beatrice was 193 cm tall. How tall was Benito? ♦

First, name the quantities involved in the problem.

a. Alma's height
b. Beatrice's height
c. Alfred's height
d. Benito's height
e. The difference between Alma's and Alfred's heights
f. The difference between Beatrice's and Benito's heights
g. The difference between the differences in the heights of the sister and brother pairs

Next, identify the values of the quantities.

a. Alma's height   186 cm
b. Beatrice's height   193 cm
c. Alfred's height   87 cm
d. Benito's height   not known
e. The difference between Alma's
    and Alfred's heights   not known
f. The difference between Beatrices's
    and Benito's heights   not known
g. The difference between the differences
    in the heights of the sister and brother pairs   17 cm

(Quantity g is a given quantity and crucial to solving the problem.)

Draw a picture involving these quantities. Here is one possibility:

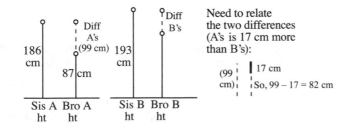

Need to relate the two differences (A's is 17 cm more than B's):

(99 cm) | 17 cm
So, 99 – 17 = 82 cm

Or, perhaps this alternative drawing would help clarify the problem. Next to each quantity, place its value if known, and use these values known to find values unknown.

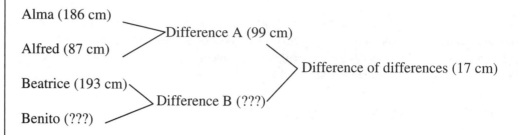

Alma (186 cm)

Alfred (87 cm)

Difference A (99 cm)

Difference of differences (17 cm)

Beatrice (193 cm)

Difference B (???)

Benito (???)

Finally, use the drawing and/or diagram to solve the problem. Notice that in this case the solution is shown in the first drawing, and can easily be found in the second drawing. But note that the question asked was Benito's height. According to the drawings, it is 193 cm – 82 cm = 111 cm.

Often students begin a problem such as the one in Activity 2 by asking themselves "What operations do I need to perform, with which numbers, and in what order?" Instead of these questions, you would be much better off asking yourself questions such as the following.

Quantitative Analysis Questions

- What do I know about this situation?

- What quantities are involved here? Which ones are critical?

- Are there any quantities that are related to other quantities? If so, how are they related?

- Which quantities do I know the value of?

- Which quantities do I **not** know the value of? Are these related to other quantities in the situation? Can these relationships enable me to find any un- known values?

- Would drawing a diagram or acting out the situation help me answer any of these other questions?

And so on.

The point is that you need to be specific when doing a quantitative analysis of a given situation. How specific? It is difficult to say in general, because it will depend on the situation. Use your common sense in analyzing the situation. When you first read a problem, avoid trying to think about numbers and the operations of addition, subtraction, multiplication, and division. Instead, start out by posing the questions such as those listed above and try to answer them. Once you've done that, you will have a better understanding of the problem, and thus you will be well on your way to solving it. Keep in mind that understanding the problem is the most difficult aspect of solving it. Once you understand the problem, *what to do to solve it* often follows quite easily.

Activity 3   Down the Drain

Here is another problem situation on which to practice quantitative analysis.

◆ Water is flowing from a faucet into an empty tub at 4.5 gallons per minute. After 4 minutes, a drain in the tub is opened, and the water begins to flow out at 6.3 gallons per minute. ◆

a. Will the tub ever fill up completely without overflowing?
b. Will it ever empty completely?
c. What if the faucet is turned off after 4 minutes?
d. What if the rates of flow in and out are reversed?
e. What assumptions do we have to make in order to answer these questions?

When you carry out a quantitative analysis of a situation, the questions you ask yourself should be guided by your common sense. A sense-making approach to understanding a situation and then solving a problem is much more productive than trying to decide right away which computations, formulas, or mathematical techniques you need in order to solve the problem at hand. Using common sense may lead you to make some sort of a diagram. Never be embarrassed to use a diagram. Such diagrams often enhance your understanding of the situation, because they help you to think more explicitly about the quantities that are involved. Deciding what operations you need to perform often follows naturally from a good understanding of the situation, the quantities in it, and how those quantities are related to one another.

> TAKE-AWAY MESSAGE . . . You should be able to determine the quantities and their relationships within a given problem situation, and you should be able to use this information, together with drawings as needed, to solve problems. These steps are often useful: (1) List the quantities that are essential to the problem. (2) List known values for these quantities. (3) Determine the relationships involved, which is frequently done more easily with a drawing. (4) Use the knowledge of these relationships to solve the problem. This approach may not seem easy at first, but it becomes a powerful tool for understanding problem situations. This type of quantitative analysis can also be used with algebra story problems, and thus, when used with elementary school students, prepares them for algebra. ◆

Learning Exercises for Section 1.2

1. Some problems are simple enough that the quantitative structure is obvious, particularly after a drawing is made. The following problems are from a fifth-grade textbook.[i] For each problem given, make a drawing and then provide the answer to the problem.

   a. The highest elevation in North America is Mt. McKinley, Alaska, which is 20,320 feet above sea level. The lowest elevation in North America is Death Valley, California, which is 282 feet below sea level. What is the change in elevation from the top of Mt. McKinley to Death Valley?

b. The most valuable violin in the world is the Kreutzer, created in Italy in 1727. It was sold at auction for $1,516,000 in England in 1998. How old was the violin when it was sold?

c. Two sculptures are similar. The height of one sculpture is four times the height of the other sculpture. The smaller sculpture is 2.5 feet tall. How tall is the larger sculpture?

d. Aiko had $20 to buy candles. She returned 2 candles for which she had paid $4.75 each. Then she bought 3 candles for $3.50 each and 1 candle for $5.00. How much money did Aiko have then?

e. In Ted's class, students were asked to name their favorite sport. Football was the response of $\frac{1}{8}$ of them. If 3 students said football, how many students are in Ted's class?

f. The first year of a dog's life equals 15 "human years." The second year equals 10 human years. Every year thereafter equals 3 human years. Use this formula to find a 6-year-old dog's age in human years.

2. These problems are from a sixth-grade textbook[ii] from a different series. This time, undertake a full quantitative analysis to solve each of the problems.

a. At Loud Sounds Music Warehouse, CDs are regularly priced at $9.95 and tapes are regularly priced at $6.95. Every day this month the store is offering a 10% discount on all CDs and tapes. Joshua and Jeremy go to Loud Sounds to buy a tape and a CD. They do not have much money, so they have pooled their funds. When they get to the store, they find that there is another discount plan just for that day—if they buy three or more items, they can save 20% (instead of 10%) on each item. If they buy a CD and a tape, how much money will they spend after the store adds a 6% sales tax on the discounted prices?

b. Kelly wants to fence in a rectangular space in her yard, 9 meters by 7.5 meters. The salesperson at the supply store recommends that she put up posts every 1.5 meters. The posts cost $2.19 each. Kelly will also need to buy wire mesh to string between the posts. The wire mesh is sold by the meter from large rolls and costs $5.98 a meter. A gate to fit in one of the spaces between the posts costs $25.89. Seven staples are needed to attach the wire mesh to each post. Staples come in boxes of 50, and each box costs $3.99. How much will the materials cost before sales tax?

3. *All Aboard!* Amtrail trains provide efficient, non-stop transportation between Los Angeles and San Diego. Train A leaves Los Angeles headed towards San Diego at the same time that Train B leaves San Diego headed for Los Angeles, traveling on parallel tracks. Train A travels at a constant speed of 84 miles per hour. Train B travels at a constant speed of 92 miles per hour. The two stations are 132 miles apart. How long after they leave their respective stations do the trains meet?

4. My brother and I walk the same route to school every day. My brother takes 40 minutes to get to school and I take 30 minutes. Today, my brother left 8 minutes before I did.[iii]

a. How long will it take me to catch up with him?

b. Part of someone's work on this problem included $\frac{1}{30} - \frac{1}{40}$. What quantities do the two fractions in $\frac{1}{30} - \frac{1}{40}$ represent?

c. Suppose my brother's head start is 5 minutes instead of 8 minutes. Now how long does it take for me to catch up with him?

5. At one point in a Girl Scout cookie sales drive, region C had sold 1500 boxes of cookies, and region D had sold 1200 boxes of cookies. If region D tries harder, they can sell 50 more boxes of cookies every day than region C can.

   a. How many days will it take for region D to catch up?

   b. If sales are stopped after eight more days, can you tell how many total boxes each region sold? Explain.

6. The last part of one triathlon is a 10K (10 kilometers, or 10,000 meters) run. When runner Aña starts this last running part, she is 600 meters behind runner Bea. But Aña can run faster than Bea: Aña can run (on average) 225 meters each minute, and Bea can run (on average) 200 meters each minute. Who wins, Aña or Bea? If Aña wins, when does she catch up with Bea? If Bea wins, how far behind is Aña when Bea finishes?

7. Research on how students solve word problems contained the following incident.[iv] Dana, a seventh grader in a gifted program in mathematics, was asked to solve the following problem:

   ◆ A carpenter has a board 200 inches long and 12 inches wide. He makes 4 identical shelves and still has a piece of board 36 inches long left over. How long is each shelf? ◆

   Dana tried to solve the problem as follows: She added 36 and 4, then scratched it out, and wrote 200 × 12, but she thought that was too large so she scratched that out. Then she tried 2400 − 36 which was also too large and discarded it. Then she calculated 4 × 36 and subtracted that from 200, getting 56. She then subtracted 12, and got 44.

   Dana used a weak strategy called "Try all operations and choose." She obviously did not know what to do with this problem, although she was very good at solving one-step problems.

   Do a quantitative analysis of this problem situation, and use it to make sense of the problem in a way that Dana did not. Use your analysis to solve the problem.

Notes

8. The problems listed below, and in Exercise 9, are from a Soviet Grade 3 textbook[v]. Solve the problems and compare their conditions and solutions:

   a. Two pedestrians left two villages simultaneously and walked towards each other, meeting after 3 hours. The first pedestrian walked 4 km in an hour, and the second walked 6 km. Find the distance between their villages:

   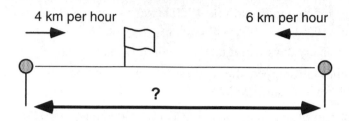

   b. Two pedestrians left two villages 27 km apart simultaneously and walked towards each other. The first one walked 4 km per hour, and the second walked 6 km per hour. After how many hours did the pedestrians meet?

   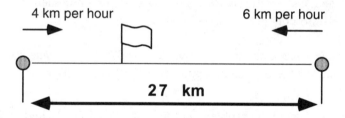

   c. Two pedestrians left two villages 27 km apart simultaneously and walked towards each other, meeting after 3 hours. The first pedestrian walked at a speed of 4 km per hour. At what speed did the second pedestrian walk?

   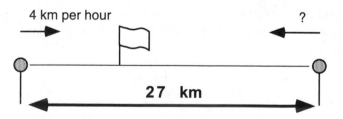

9. Two trains simultaneously left Moscow and Sverdlovsk, and traveled towards each other. The first traveled at 48 km per hour, and the second at 54 km per hour. How far apart were the two trains 12 hours after departure if it is 1822 km from Moscow to Sverdlovsk?

1.3 | Values of Quantities

The value of a quantity may involve very large or very small numbers. Furthermore, since the value is determined by counting or other ways of measuring, it can involve any type of number—whole numbers, fractions, decimals.

> **THINK ABOUT . . .**
>
> Consider the following quantities. Which ones would you expect to have large values? Small values?
>
> **a.** The distance between two stars
> **b.** The diameter of a snowflake
> **c.** The weight of an aircraft carrier
> **d.** The national deficit
> **e.** The thickness of a sheet of paper

Discussion 3   Units of Measure

1. What determines the appropriateness of the unit chosen to express the value of a quantity?

2. For each quantity listed in parts (a)–(e) above, name a unit of measure that would be appropriate to measure the quantity.

3. Explain how you would determine the thickness of a sheet of paper.

4. What determines the "precision" of the value of a quantity?

In a particular book the height of the arch in St. Louis is reported to be 630 feet. In another book the height is 192 meters. Why are the numbers different?

> **THINK ABOUT . . .**
>
> What determines the magnitude of the number that denotes the value of a given quantity? Can we measure the speed of a car in miles per day? Miles per year? Miles per century? Is it convenient to do so? Explain.

Unless one has some appreciation and understanding of the magnitude of large numbers, it is impossible to make judgments about such matters as the impact of a promised five million dollars in relief funds after a catastrophic flood or earthquake, the level of danger of traveling in a country that has experienced three known terrorist attacks in a single year, the personal consequences of the huge national debt, or the meaning of costly military mistakes. For example, people are shocked to hear that the Pentagon spent $38 for each simple pair of pliers bought from a certain defense contractor, yet they pay little attention to the cost of building the Stealth fighter or losing a jet fighter during testing.

Notes

Activity 4   Jet Fighter Crashes

In the 1990s, a west coast newspaper carried a brief article saying that a $50 million jet fighter crashed into the ocean off the California coast. How many students could go to your university tuition-free for one year with $50 million?

Discussion 4   What Is Worth a Trillion Dollars?

Suppose you hear a politician say "A billion dollars, a trillion dollars, I don't care what it costs, we have got to solve the AIDS problem in this country." Would you agree? Is a billion dollars too much to spend on a national health crisis? A trillion dollars? How do the numbers one billion and one trillion compare?

Reminder: Values of quantities, like 16 tons or $64, involve units of measure—ton, dollar—as well as numbers.

> ### THINK ABOUT . . .
>
> Name several units of measure that you know and use. What quantities are each used to measure? Where do units come from?

Units can be arbitrary. Primary teachers have their students measure lengths and distances with pencils or shoe lengths, or measure weights with plastic cubes. The intent of these activities is to give the children experience with the measuring process so that later measurements will make sense. As you know, there are different systems of **standard units**, like the English or "ordinary" system (inches, pounds, etc.) and the **metric system** (meters, kilograms, etc.), more formally known as **SI** (from Le Système International d'Unités).

Virtually the rest of the world uses the metric system to denote values of quantities, so many are surprised that the United States, a large industrial nation, has clung to the English system so long. Although the general public has not responded favorably to governmental efforts to mandate the metric system, international trade efforts are having the effect of forcing us to be knowledgeable about, and to use, the metric system. Some of our largest industries have been the first to convert to the metric system from the English system.

Discussion 5   Standard Units

Why are standard units desirable? For what purposes are they necessary? Why has the public resisted adopting the metric system?

Scientists have long worked almost exclusively in metric units. As a result, you may have used metric units in your high school or college science classes. Part of the reason for this is that the rest of the world uses the metric system because it is a sensible system. A basic metric unit is carefully defined (for the sake of permanence and later reproducibility). Larger units and smaller sub-units are related to each other in a consistent fashion, so it is easy to work within the system. (In contrast, the English system unit, *foot,* might have been the length of a now-long-dead king's foot, and it is related to other length units in an inconsistent manner: 1 foot = 12 inches; 1 yard = 3 feet; 1 rod = 16.5 feet; 1 mile = 5280 feet; 1 furlong = $\frac{1}{8}$ mile; 1 fathom = 6 feet. Quick!—how many rods are in a mile? A comparable question in the metric system is just a matter of adjusting a decimal point.

To get a better idea of how the metric system works, let's consider something that we frequently measure in metric units—length. Length is a quality of most objects. We measure the lengths of boards and pieces of rope or wire. We also measure the heights of children; height and length refer to the same quality but the different words are used in different contexts.

> *THINK ABOUT . . .*
> What are some other words that refer to the same quality as do "length" and "height?"

The basic SI unit for length (or its synonyms) is the **meter**. (The official SI spelling is **metre**. You occasionally see "metre" in U.S. books.) The meter is too long to show with a line segment here, but two sub-units fit easily, and illustrate a key feature of the metric system: Units larger and smaller than the basic unit are multiples or sub-multiples of powers of 10.

0.1 meter ──────────────────────────

0.01 meter ───

Furthermore, these sub-units have names—decimeter, centimeter—which are formed by putting a prefix on the word for the basic unit. The prefix "deci-" means one-tenth, so "decimeter" means 0.1 meter. Similarly, "centi-" means one one-hundredth, so "centimeter" means 0.01 meter. You have probably heard "kilometer;" the prefix "kilo-" means 1000, so "kilometer" means 1000 meters. On reversing one's thinking, so to speak, there are 10 decimeters in 1 meter, there are 100 centimeters in 1 meter, and 1 meter is 0.001 kilometer.

Another feature of SI is that there are symbols for the basic units—m for meter—and for the prefixes—d for deci-, c for centi-, and so on. By using the symbol for meter together with the symbol for a prefix, a length measurement can be reported quite concisely: for example, 18 cm and 2.3 dm. The symbols, cm and dm, do not have periods after them, nor do the abbreviations in the English system: ft, mi, etc., except that for inch (in.).

If you are new to the metric system, your first job will be to familiarize yourself with the prefixes so you can apply them to the basic units for other qualities. The

Notes

table below shows some of the other metric prefixes. Combining the symbol k for kilo- and the symbol m for meter gives km for kilometer.

Prefix	Symbol	Meaning of Prefix		Applied to Length
kilo-	k	1000	or 10^3	km
hecto-	h	100	or 10^2	hm
deka-	da	10	or 10^1	dam
no prefix		1	or 10^0	m
deci-	d	0.1	or 10^{-1}	dm
centi-	c	0.01	or 10^{-2}	cm
milli-	m	0.001	or 10^{-3}	mm

Activity 5   It's All in the Unit

1. Measure the width of your desk or table, in decimeters. Express that length in centimeters, millimeters, meters, and kilometers.
2. Measure the width of your desk or table, in feet. Express that length in inches, yards, and miles.
3. In which system are conversions easier? Explain why.

TAKE-AWAY MESSAGE . . . The value of a quantity is expressed using a number and a unit of measure. Commerce depends upon having agreed-on sets of measures. Standard units accomplish this. The common system of measurement in the United States is the English system of measurement. We use the metric system, another measurement system, for science and for international trade. Most countries of the world use only the metric system. The metric system is based on powers of ten and on common prefixes, making the system an easier one to use. ♦

Learning Exercises for Section 1.3

1. Name an appropriate unit for measuring each given quanitity.
    a. the amount of milk that a mug will hold.
    b. the height of the Empire State Building.
    c. the distance between San Francisco and New York.
    d. the capacity of the gas tank in your car.
    e. the safety capacity of an elevator.
    f. the amount of rainfall in one year.

2. a. What does it mean to say that "a car gets good mileage?"
    b. What unit is used to express gas mileage in the United States?
    c. How could you determine the mileage you get from your car?
    d. Do you always get the same mileage from your car? List some factors that influence how much mileage you get.

   e. How would you measure gas consumption? Is gas consumption related to mileage? If so, how?

3. Explain how rainfall is quantified. You may need to use resources such as an encyclopedia or the internet.

4. a. Calculate an approximation of the amount of time you have spent sleeping since you were born. Explain your calculations. Express your approximation in hours, in days, in years.

   b. What part of your life have you spent sleeping?

   c. On the average how many hours do you sleep each day? What fractional part of the day is this?

   d. How does your answer in part (b) compare to your answer in part (c)?

5. Name an item that can be used to estimate the following metric units:

   a. a centimeter   **b.** a gram   **c.** a liter

   d. a meter   **e.** a kilometer   **f.** a kilogram

6. There are some conversions from English to metric units that are commonly used, particularly for inch, mile, and quart. What are they?

1.4 Issues for Learning: Ways of Thinking About Solving Story Problems

In solving story problems, how do children decide what to do? In one study[vi] students were found to use the following seven different strategies. The first six strategies are based on something other than understanding the problem.

1. Find the numbers in the problem and just do something to them, usually addition because that is the easiest operation.

2. Guess at the operation to be used, perhaps based on what has been most recently studied.

3. Let the numbers "tell" you what to do. (One student said, "If it's like 78 and maybe 54, then I'd probably either add or multiply. But if the numbers are 78 and 3, it looks like a division because of the size of the numbers.")

4. Try all the operations and then choose the most reasonable answer. (This strategy often works for one-step problems, but rarely does for two-step problems.)

5. Look for "key" words to decide what operation to use. For example, "all together" means to add. (This strategy works sometimes, but not all the time. Also, words like "of" and "is" often signify multiplication and equals, but some students confuse the two.)

6. Narrow the choices, based on expected size of the answer. (For example, when a student used division on a problem involving reduction in a photocopy machine, he said he did because "it's reducing something, and that means taking it away or dividing it.")

7. Choose an operation based on understanding the problem. [Often students would make a drawing when they used this strategy. Unfortunately, though, few of the children (sixth and eighth graders, of average or above average ability in mathematics) used this strategy.]

Only the last strategy was considered a mature strategy. These children understood the problem because they had undertaken a quantitative analysis of the problem, even though not so formally as introduced in this chapter.

Making drawings or mental pictures can play an essential role in coming to understand a problem. Here is an excerpt from one interview with one of the children in this study:

Emmy: I just pictured the post, how deep the water was . . . Sometimes I picture the objects in my mind that I'm working with, if it's a hard problem . . .

Interviewer: Does that help?

Emmy: Yeh, it helps. That's just one way of, kind of cheating, I guess you'd say.

Unfortunately, too many students seem to believe that making drawings is cheating, or is juvenile, yet making a drawing is a valuable problem-solving process.

In another study,[vii] two researchers compared how drawings are used in U.S. textbooks and in Japanese textbooks. They found that many elementary school students in the United States are not encouraged to make drawings that will help them understand a story problem. However, even just flipping through the pages of Japanese textbooks shows that drawings are used throughout. Teachers say to students, "If you can draw a picture, you can solve the problem."

> **THINK ABOUT . . .**
>
> In what ways have drawings helped you so far with solving the problems in this first chapter?

All too often adults try to avoid making a drawing because they think that the need for drawings is childish. But this is *not* the case. The ability to represent a problem with a drawing is an important component of problem solving, no matter what the age of the problem solver is. Young children often draw a picture to help them understand a problem. For example, for the problem "There are 24 legs in the sheep pen where two men are shearing sheep. How many sheep are there?", one child might draw something similar to this:

Yet another child might represent this problem as:

II II   IIII IIII IIII   IIII IIII

There are, of course, multiple ways this problem could be represented with a drawing, but here perhaps the first is more appropriately called a picture, and the second would more appropriately be called a diagram. Students will quite naturally evolve from pictures to diagrams. "A diagram is a visual representation that displays information in a spatial layout."[viii] Although diagrams are very useful in understanding the structure of a problem, students are often unable to produce an appropriate diagram without some assistance. Whether or not a picture or a diagram is appropriate depends on how well it represents the structure of the problem. A diagram is more abstract than a picture in that it often does not contain extraneous information. It takes less time to draw, but it continues to represent the problem.

In the sheep problem, the objects are discrete, that is, they can be counted. But not all problems about discrete quantities need to be represented by individual objects because diagramming large numbers can become a chore, and pictures would take far too long to produce. Thus we often use lines or boxes to represent the problems, even those involving discrete quantities.

Discussion 6   Drawings and Diagrams

1. A fourth grader was asked to solve some story problems you saw in the Learning Exercises for Section 1.2. Two problems are shown here. Before looking at the student's solutions, go back and see how you solved the problems.

2. Discuss the types of drawings used by this student. How did they help her visualize the problems leading to solutions?

Problem 1. (Modified from Section 1.2, Learning Exercise 1c)

♦ Two sculptures are similar. The height of one sculpture is two and one-half times the height of the other sculpture. The smaller sculpture is 3 feet tall. How tall is the larger sculpture? ♦

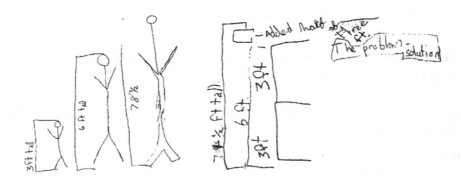

Problem 2. (From Section 1.2, Learning Exercise 7)

♦ A carpenter has a board 200 inches long and 12 inches wide. He makes 4 identical shelves and still has a piece of board 36 inches long left over. How long is each shelf? ♦

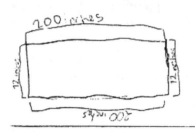

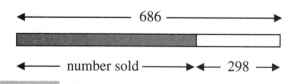

Drawing diagrams to represent and then solve problem situations are common in Singapore textbooks. They use diagrams they call strip diagrams. S. Beckmann[ix] has provided the following problems as examples.

EXAMPLE 1 is from a third grade textbook (*Primary Mathematics,* Volume 3A, p. 20, Problem 4):[ix]

♦ Mary made 686 biscuits. She sold some of them. If 298 were left over, how many biscuits did she sell? ♦

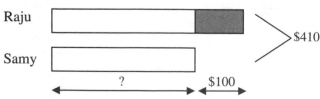

EXAMPLE 2 is from a fifth grade textbook (*Primary Mathematics,* Volume 5A, p. 23, Problem 1):[ix]

♦ Raju and Samy share $410 between them. Raju received $100 more than Samy. How much money did Samy receive? ♦

Raju

Samy

>$410

? $100

Continue on the next page.

2 units = $410 – $100 = $310
1 unit = $____
Samy received $____

THINK ABOUT . . .

Can the sheep problem be represented with a strip drawing?

In this chapter we have used diagrams rather than pictures to represent problems. Analyzing situations quantitatively, which may include making drawings, can help one understand the problems being solved. "Quantitative reasoning is more than reasoning about numbers, and it is more than skilled calculating. It is about making sense of the situation to which we apply numbers and calculations." [x]

Learning Exercises for Section 1.4

Use a mature strategy and a strip diagram to work each of the following:

1. Kalia spent a quarter of her weekly allowance on a movie. The movie was $4.25. What is her weekly allowance?

2. Calle had five times as many stickers as Sara did, and twice as many as Juniper. Juniper had 25 stickers. How many stickers did they have altogether?

3. Nghiep gave his mother half of his weekly earnings, and then spent half of what was left on a new shirt. He then had $32. What were his weekly earnings?

4. Zvia's sweater cost twice as much as her hat, and a third as much as her coat. Her coat cost $114. How much did her sweater cost?

5. One number is four times as large as another number, and their sum is 5285. What are the two numbers?

6. Jinfa, upon receiving his paycheck, spent two-thirds of it on car repairs and then bought a $40 gift for his mother. He had $64 left. How much was his paycheck?

7. Rosewood Elementary School had 104 students register for the fourth grade. After placing 11 of the students in a mixed grade with fifth graders, the remaining students were split evenly into 3 classrooms. How many students were in each of these 3 classrooms?

8. Jacqui, Karen, and Lynn all collect stamps. Jacqui has 12 more stamps than Karen, and Karen has three times as many as Lynn. Together they have 124 stamps. How many does each person have?

9. Jo-Jo has downloaded 139 songs on his iPod. Of those songs, 36 are jazz, twice that are R & B, and the remaining are classical. How many classical songs has he downloaded?

1.5 | Check Yourself

In this first chapter, you have learned about the role quantities play in our lives and the ways we express quantities and their values. You have learned about dealing with problem situations by analyzing the problem in terms of its quantities and their relationships to one another. Quantitative analysis helps solve a problem in a meaningful, sense-making way. The same kind of analysis can be applied to arithmetic problems and to algebra problems.

You also learned how quantities are measured in terms of numbers of units, and how to express values of quantities in standard units, including metric units.

You should be able to work problems like those assigned and to meet the following objectives.

1. Identify the quantities addressed by such questions as, How much damage did the flooding cause?

2. Name attributes of objects that cannot be quantified.

3. Distinguish between a quantity and its value.

4. Given a problem situation, undertake a quantitative analysis of the problem and use that analysis to solve the problem.

5. Determine appropriate units to measure quantities.

6. Discuss reasons why the metric system is used for measurement in most countries.

7. Discuss some incorrect ways that children solve story problems.

8. Discuss the importance of appropriate drawings in problem solving.

9. Make strip diagrams to represent simple arithmetic and algebraic problems.

REFERENCES FOR CHAPTER 1

[i] Maletsky, E. M., Andrews, A. G., Burton, G. M., Johnson, H. C., Luckie, L., Newman, V., Schultz, K. A., Scheer, J. K., & McLeod, J. C. (2002). *Harcourt Math.* Orlando, FL: Harcourt.

[ii] Lappan, G., Fey, J. T., Fitzgerald, W. M., Friel, S. N., & Phillips, E. D. (1998). *Connected mathematics: Bits and pieces II: Using rational numbers. Teachers Edition.* Menlo Park, CA: Dale Seymour Publications.

[iii] Krutetskii, V. A. (1976). *The psychology of mathematical abilities in schoolchildren* (J. Teller, Trans.). Chicago: University of Chicago Press.

[iv] Sowder, L. (1995). Addressing the story problem problem. In J. Sowder & B. Schappelle (Eds.), *Providing a foundation for the teaching of mathematics in the middle grades* (pp. 121–142). Albany, NY: SUNY Press.

[v] *Russian Grade 3 Mathematics.* (1978). Translated by University of Chicago School Mathematics Project.

[vi] Sowder, L. (1988). Children's solutions of story problems. *Journal of Mathematical Behavior, 7,* 227–239.

[vii] Shigematsu, K., & Sowder, L. (1994). Drawings for story problems: Practices in Japan and the United States. *Arithmetic Teacher, 41* (9), 544–547.

[viii] Diezmann, C., & English, L. (2001). Promoting the use of diagrams as tools for thinking. In A. C. Cuoco & F. R. Curcio (Eds.), *The roles of representation in school mathematics* (pp. 77–89). Reston, VA: NCTM.

[ix] Beckmann, S. (2004). Solving algebra and other story problems in simple diagrams: A method demonstrated in grade 4–6 texts used in Singapore. *The Mathematics Educator, 14,* 42–46.

[x] Thompson, P. (1995). Notation, convention, and quantity in elementary mathematics. In J. Sowder & B. Schappelle (Eds.), *Providing a foundation for the teaching of mathematics in the middle grades* (pp. 199–221). Albany, NY: SUNY Press.

Notes

Chapter 2

Numeration Systems

Contrary to what you may believe, there are many ways of expressing numbers. Some of these ways are cultural and historical. Others are different ways of thinking about what the digits of our conventional number system mean. For example, you probably think of 23 as meaning two tens and three ones. We think this way because we use a base ten system of counting. (How many fingers do you have?) But why not base five (using only five fingers)? What would 23 mean then? You are about to find out.

2.1 Ways of Expressing Values of Quantities

The need to quantify and express the values of quantities led humans to invent numeration systems. Throughout history, people have found ways to express values of quantities they measured in several ways. A variety of words and special symbols, called **numerals**, have been used to communicate number ideas. How one expresses numbers using these special symbols makes up a **numeration system**. Our Hindu-Arabic system uses ten **digits**: 0, 1, 2, 3, 4, 5, 6, 7, 8, 9. Virtually all present-day societies use the Hindu-Arabic numeration system. With the help of decimal points, fraction bars, and marks like square root signs, these ten digits allow us to express almost any number and therefore the value of almost any quantity.

> ***THINK ABOUT . . .***
>
> Why are numerals used so much? What are advantages of these special symbols over using just words to express numbers? What are some exceptions to representing numbers with digits?

Activity 1   You Mean People Didn't Always Count the Way We Do?

A glimpse of the richness of the history of numeration systems lies in looking at the variety of ways in which the number twelve has been expressed. In the different representations shown on the next page, see if you can deduce what each individual mark represents. Each representation expresses this many:

□□□□□□□□□□□□

Continue on the next page.

Notes

II	ιβ	XII	**‹II**
Old Chinese	Old Greek	Roman	Babylonian

⋮⋮ (Mayan symbol)	◇⋮	12	30
Mayan	Aztec	Today, base ten	Today, base four

THINK ABOUT . . .

How would ten have been written in each of these earlier numeration systems?

Some ancient cultures did not need many number words. For example, they may have needed words only for "one," "two," and "many." When larger quantities were encountered, they could be expressed by some sort of matching with pebbles or sticks or parts of the body, but without the use of any distinct word or phrase for the number involved. For example, in a recently-discovered culture in Papua New Guinea, the same word "doro" was used for 2, 3, 4, 19, 20, and 21. But by pointing also to different parts of the hands, arms, and face when counting and saying "doro," these people could tell which number is intended by the word. This method of pointing allows the Papua New Guineans to express numbers up through 22 easily.[i] It was only when this culture came into contact with the outside world and began trading with other cultures that they needed to find ways of expressing larger numbers.

THINK ABOUT...

Why do you think we use ten digits in our number system? Would it make sense to use twenty? Why or why not?

Discussion 1   Changing Complexity of Quantities Over Time

What quantities, and therefore what number words, would you expect a caveman to have found useful? (Assume that the caveman had a sufficiently sophisticated language.) A person in a primitive agricultural society? A pioneer? An ordinary citizen living today? A person on Wall Street? An astronomer? A subatomic physicist?

TAKE-AWAY MESSAGE . . . Mathematical symbols have changed over the years, and they may change in the future. Symbols used for numbers depend upon our need to determine the value of the quantities with which we work. ♦

Learning Exercises for Section 2.1

1. Based on what you have seen of the old counting systems such as Greek, Chinese, Roman, Babylonian, Mayan, and Aztec, which systems make the most sense to you? Explain.

2. Symbols for five and for ten often have had special prominence in geographically and chronologically remote systems. Why?

3. Numbers can be expressed in a fascinating variety of ways. Different languages, of course, use different words and different symbols to represent numbers. Some counting words are given below.

English	*Spanish*	*German*	*French*	*Japanese*	*Swahili*
zero	cero	null	zero	zero	sifuri
one	uno	eins	un	ichi	moja
two	dos	zwei	deux	ni	mbili
three	tres	drei	trois	san	tatu
four	cuatro	vier	quatre	shi	nne
five	cinco	fünf	cinq	go	tano
six	seis	sechs	six	roku	sita
seven	siete	sieben	sept	shichi	saba
eight	ocho	acht	huit	hachi	nane
nine	nueve	neun	neuf	kyu	tisa
ten	diez	zehn	dix	ju	kumi

Which two sets of these counting words most resemble one another?

Why do you think that is true? Do you know these numbers in yet another language?

4. Roman numerals have survived to a degree, as in motion picture film credits and on cornerstones. Here are the basic symbols: I = one, V = five, X = ten, L = fifty, C = one hundred, D = five hundred, and M = one thousand. For example, CLXI is $100 + 50 + 10 + 1 = 161$. What numbers does each of these represent?

   a. MMCXIII　　　　　**b.** CLXXXV　　　　　**c.** MDVII

5. How would each of the following be written in Roman numerals? For example, one thousand one hundred thirty would be MCXXX.

   a. two thousand sixty-six　　**b.** seventy-eight　　**c.** six hundred five

6. Other systems we have seen all involve addition of the values of the symbols. Roman numerals use a **subtractive** principle as well; when a symbol for a smaller value comes before the symbol for a larger value, the former value is subtracted from the latter. For example, IV means 5 – 1 = 4, or four; XC means 100 – 10 = 90; and CD = 500 – 100 = 400. Note that no symbol appears more than three times together, because with four symbols we would use this subtractive property. What number does each of these represent?

     a. CMIII   **b.** XLIX   **c.** CDIX

7. Even within the same language, there are often several words for a given number idea. For example, both "two shoes" and "a pair of shoes," refer to the same quantity. What are some other words for the idea of two-ness?

2.2 | Place Value

What does each 2 in 22,222 mean? The different 2s represent different values because our **Hindu-Arabic numeration system** is a **place-value system**. This system depends upon the powers of ten to tell us the meaning of each digit. Once this system is understood, arithmetic operations are much easier to learn. Understanding of place value is a fundamental idea underlying elementary school mathematics.

But first, what does it mean to have a place-value system?

> In a **place-value** system, the value of a digit in a numeral is determined by its position in the numeral.

EXAMPLE 1

In 506.7, the 5 is in the hundreds place, so it represents five hundred. The 0 in 506.7 is in the tens place, so it represents zero tens, or just zero. The 6 is in the ones place, so it represents six ones, or six. And the 7 is in the tenths place, so it represents seven-tenths. The complete 506.7 symbol then represents the sum of those values: five hundred six and seven-tenths.

Notice that we do not say "five hundred, zero tens, six and seven-tenths," although we could. This is symptomatic of the relatively late appearance, historically, of a symbol for zero. The advantage of having a symbol to say that nothing is there is apparently a difficult idea, but the idea is vital to a place-value system. Would 506.7 mean the same number if we omitted the 0 to get 56.7? The 0 may have evolved from some type of round mark written in clay by the Babylonians to show that there are zero groups of a particular place value needed.

THINK ABOUT . . .

In the Hindu-Arabic place-value system, how many different places (positions) can you name and write numerically? (Don't forget places to the right of the decimal point.)

Before the use of numerals became widespread, much calculation was done with markers on lines for different place values. The lines could be on paper, or just drawn in sand, with small stones used as markers. (Our word "calculate" comes from the Latin word for "stones.") One device that no doubt was inspired by these methods of calculating is the **abacus**, which continues to be used in some parts of the world.

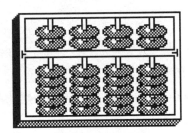

A Chinese Abacus

Notice that we have often used words to discuss the numbers instead of the usual numerals. The reason is that the symbol "12" is automatically associated with "twelve" in our minds because of our familiarity with the usual numeration system. We will find that the numeral "12" could mean five or six, however, in other systems! (If no base is indicated, assume the familiar base ten is intended.)

In our *base-ten* numeration system, the whole-number place values result from *groups of ten*—ten ones, ten tens, ten hundreds, etc. The digits 0, 1, 2, 3, 4, 5, 6, 7, 8, 9 work fine until we have ten of something. But there is no single digit that means ten. When we have ten ones, we think of them as one group of ten, without any leftover ones, and we take advantage of place value to write "10," one ten and zero leftover ones. Similarly, two place values are sufficient through nine tens and nine ones, but when we have ten tens, we then use the next place value and write "100." It is like replacing ten pennies with one dime, and trading ten dimes for a dollar.

EXAMPLE 2

If I want to find the number of ten dollar bills I could get for $365, the answer is not just 6, it is 36.

If I want to know how many dollar bills I could get from $365, the answer is 365.

If I want to know the number of dimes I could get from $365, the answer is 3650.

But if I want to know how many tens are in 365, I could say either 36 or 36.5, depending on the context.

Continue on the next page.

If I have 365 bars of soap and I want to know how many full boxes of 10 I could pack, the answer would be 36.

If I am buying 365 individual bars of soap priced at $6 per 10 bars, then I would have to pay 36.5 times $6.

With a good understanding of place value, the problems like those in Example 2 can be easily solved without undertaking long division or multiplication by 10 or powers of 10. Children who do not understand place value will often try to solve the problem of how many tens are in 365 by using long division to divide by 10, rather than observing that the answer is obvious from the number.

Discussion 2   Money and Place Value

Explain your answers to each of the following:

1. How many ten-dollar bills does the 6 in $657 represent? The 5?

2. How many tens are in 657?

3. How many one-hundred dollar bills can you get for $53,908?

4. How many one-hundreds are in 53,908?

5. How many pennies can you get for $347? For $34.70? For $3.47?

6. How many ones are in 347? In 34.70? In 3.47?

The decimal point indicates that we are beginning to break up the unit *one* into tenths, hundredths, thousandths, etc. But the number *one*, not the decimal point, is the focal point of this system. So 0.642 is 642 thousandths of *one*. Put another way, 0.6 is six tenths of *one*, while 6 is six *ones*, and 60 is six tens, or 60 *ones*. But just as 0.6 is six tenths of one, 6 is six tenths of 10, 60 is six tenths of one hundred, and so on up the line. Or starting with smaller numbers, 0.006 is six tenths of 0.01, while 0.06 is six tenths of 0.1. Likewise, 6000 is 60 hundreds, 600 is 60 tens, 60 is 60 ones, 6 is 60 tenths, 0.6 is 60 hundredths, 0.06 is 60 thousandths, and so on.[ii] While this at first might seem confusing, it becomes less so with practice and thought.

> TAKE-AWAY MESSAGE . . . Our base ten place-value numeration system is adequate for expressing all whole numbers and many decimal numbers. The value of each digit in a numeral is determined by the position of the digit in the numeral. Digits in different places have different values. Finally, the number 1, not the decimal point, serves as the focal point of decimal numbers. ◆

Learning Exercises for Section 2.2

1. a.   How many tens are in 357? How many whole tens?
   b.   How many hundreds are in 4362? How many whole hundreds?

   c. How many tens are in 4362? How many whole tens?

   d. How many thousands are in 456,654? How many whole thousands?

   e. How many hundreds are in 456,654? How many whole hundreds?

   f. How many tens are in 456,654? How many whole tens?

   g. How many tenths are in 23.47? How many whole tenths?

   h. How many thousandths are in 23.47? How many whole thousandths?

   i. How many ones are in 23.47? How many whole ones?

   j. How many hundredths are in 23.47? How many whole hundredths?

   k. How many tenths are in 2347? How many whole tenths?

   l. How many tenths are in 234.7? How many whole tenths?

2. In 123.456, the hundre*d*s place is in the third place to the <u>left</u> of the decimal point; is the hundred*th*s place in the third place to the <u>right</u> of the decimal point? In a long numeral like 333331.333333, what separates the number into two parts that match in the way hundreds and hundredths do?

3. **a.** Is the statement "For a set of whole numbers, the longest numeral will belong to the largest number" true or false? Why?

   b. Is the statement "For a set of decimals, the longest numeral will belong to the largest number" true or false? Why?

4. Pronounce 3200 in two different ways. Do the two pronunciations have the same value?

5. Write in words the way you would pronounce each:

   a. 407.053   **b.** 30.04   **c.** 0.34   **d.** 200.067   **e.** 0.276

6. Each of the following represents work of students who did not understand place value. Find the errors made by these students, and explain their reasoning.

   a.   **b.**   **c.**   7
       15   55   4^{1}8
    +95   + 48   − 2 6
   1010   913   1 1

   d.   **e.**
     36   36
   7⟌43   × 8
   42   2448
   22
   21

7. In base ten, 1635 is exactly ___1635___ *ones,* is exactly ___163.5___ *tens,* is exactly ___16.35___ *hundreds,* is exactly ___1.635___ *thousands;* it is also exactly ___.1635___ *tenths,* or exactly ___.01635___ *hundredths.*

8. In base ten, 73.5 is exactly ___73.5___ *ones,* is exactly _____ *tens,* is exactly _____ *hundreds,* is exactly _____ *thousands;* it is also exactly _____ *tenths,* or exactly _____ *hundredths.*

9. Do you change the value of a whole number by placing zeros to the right of the number? To the left of the number?

2.3 | Bases Other Than Ten

Too often children learn to operate on numbers without having a deep understanding of place value, the lack of which leads them to make many computational errors. The purpose of this section is to provide experiences with base numeration systems other than ten so you understand the underlying structure of the base ten system of numeration. You are not expected to become fluent in a base other than ten. Rather, you should be able to calculate in different bases to the extent that is needed to understand the role of place value in calculations.

> **THINK ABOUT ...**
>
> We use a base ten system of counting because we have ten fingers. Other cultures have used other bases. For example, some Eskimos were found to count using base five. Why would that be? What other bases might have been used for counting?

Cartoon characters often have three fingers and a thumb on each hand, a total of eight fingers (counting thumbs) instead of ten. Suppose that we live in this cartoon land and instead of having ten digits in our counting system (0, 1, 2, 3, 4, 5, 6, 7, 8, 9) we have only eight digits (0, 1, 2, 3, 4, 5, 6, 7). Using this new counting system we write the number eight as 10_{eight}, meaning 1 group of eight and 0 ones. Thus, we would write as we count in base eight:

$$1, 2, 3, 4, 5, 6, 7, 10, 11, 12, 13, 14, 15, 16, 17, 20, 21, ...$$

We read this list of numbers as: one, two, three, ... , one-zero, one-one, one-two, ... , two-zero, ...

Activity 2   Place Value in Cartoon Land

1. Show the value of each place in base eight by completing this pattern:

...	8^5	8^4	8^3	8^2	8^1	8^0
	?	?	?	sixty-fours	eights	ones

2. What would follow 77 in base eight? 80

3. What would each digit indicate in the numeral 743 in base eight?

Notice that the base-eight numeration system has eight digits, 0–7. Writing 6072 in base eight would require the use of the first four places to the left of the decimal point and represents 2 ones (8^0), 7 eights (8^1), 0 sets of eight squared (8^2), and 6 sets of eight cubed (8^3). The digits 6, 0, 7, and 2 would be placed in the Activity pattern in the four places to the left of the decimal point. We call this number "six zero seven two, base eight" and write it as 6072_{eight}.

THINK ABOUT . . .

If you had 602_{eight} chairs in an auditorium, how many chairs would you have, written in base ten?

Discussion 3   Place Value in Base Three

What are the place values in a base three system? What are the digits, and how many do we need? (Rather than invent new symbols for digits, let's use whichever of the standard symbols we need.) Study the chart below. What should be in place of the question marks?

Items	Name in base ten	Name in base three	Base three symbol
	zero	zero	0_{three}
□	one	one	1_{three}
□ □	two	two	2_{three}
□ □ □	three	???	???10_{three}

one-zero base three

Naming *three* in base three is a key step in understanding base three. Since there are three single boxes above, they will be grouped to make *one group of three*, and the base three symbol is 10! Notice that in base three "10" does not symbolize *ten* as we think about ten. In base three, "10" means "one group of three and zero left over." Since it does not mean ten, we should not pronounce the numeral as "ten." The recommended pronunciation is "one zero, base three," saying just the name for each digit and for the base. Notice how this chart differs from the one above.

Items	Name in base ten	Name in base three	Base three symbol
	zero	zero	0_{three}
□	one	one	1_{three}
□ □	two	two	2_{three}
□□□	three	one-zero	10_{three}
□□□ □	four	one-one	11_{three}

If there are four boxes, as in the last line of this table, we can make one group of three, and then there will be one left-over box, so in base three, four is written "11". Because we have the strong link between the marks "11" and eleven from all of our base ten experience, the notation 11_{three} is often used for clarity to show that the symbols should be interpreted in base three. Recall that 11_{three} should be pronounced "one one, base three," and not as "eleven."

Activity 3   Count in Base Three and in Base Four

Continue to draw more boxes and to write base three symbols. What do you write for five boxes? (Now you see why the symbol 12 might mean five.) Six? Seven? Eight? And, at another dramatic point, nine? Did you write "100_{three}" for nine? What would 1000_{three} mean?

Check your counting skills by following along with counting in base four: 1, 2, 3, 10, 11, 12, 13, 20, 21, 22, 23, 30, 31, 32, 33, 100, 101, 102, 103, 110, 111, 112, 113, 120, 121, 122, 123, 130, 131, 132, 133, 200 . . .
What does 1000_{four} mean?

Discussion 4   Working with Different Bases

1. What are the place values in base five? What digits are needed? How would thirty-eight (in base ten) be expressed in base five? Record the first fifteen counting numbers in base five: 1, 2, . . .

2. What are the place values in a base b place-value system? What digits are needed?

3. What are the place values in a base-two place-value system? How would eighteen (in base ten) be written in base two? The inner workings of computers use base two; do you see any reason for this fact?

4. Perhaps surprisingly, there is a Duodecimal Society, which promotes the adoption of a base twelve numeration system. What are the place values in a base twelve system? What new digits would have to be invented?

With several numeration systems possible, there can be many "translations" among the symbols. For example, given a base ten numeral (or the usual word), find the base six (or four or twelve) numeral for the same number, and vice versa, given a numeral in some other base, find its base ten numeral (or the usual word). In each case, the key is knowing, and probably writing down, the place values in the unfamiliar system. (Recall that any nonzero number to the 0 power is 1. Example: $5^0 = 1$.)

EXAMPLE 3

Changing from a non-ten base to base ten: What does 2103_{four} represent in base ten?

SOLUTION

1. 2103_{four} has four digits. The first four place values in base four are written here, and the given digits put in their places:

2	1	0	3
of four sixteens, or sixty-four, or 4^3	of four fours, or sixteen, or 4^2	of four ones, or four, or 4^1	ones, or 4^0

2. What does the 2 tell us? The 2 stands for two of 4^3 which is $2 \times 64 = 128$ in base ten.

3. What does the 1 tell us? The 1 stands for one 4^2 which is $1 \times 16 = 16$ in base ten.

4. What does the 0 tell us? The 0 stands for zero of 4^1 which is $0 \times 4 = 0$ in base ten.

5. What does the 3 tell us? The 3 indicates 4^0 is used three times, $3 \times 1 = 3$ in base ten.

6. Thus $2103_{\text{four}} = (128 + 16 + 0 + 3)_{\text{ten}} = 147_{\text{ten}}$
    that is, $2103_{\text{four}} = 147_{\text{ten}}$.

EXAMPLE 4

Suppose instead we want to change a number written in base ten, say 236, to a number written in another base, say base five. We know that the places in base five are the following:

1	4	2	6
... one-hundred-twenty-fives (5^3)	twenty-fives (5^2)	fives (5^1)	ones (5^0)

SOLUTION

(You may find these steps easier to follow by dropping the ten subscript for now, for numbers in base ten.)

1. Look for the highest power of 5 in the base ten number; here it is 5^3 because 5^4 is 625_{ten} and 625_{ten} is larger than 236_{ten}. Are there any 5^3s in 236_{ten}? Yes, just one 5^3 because $5^3 = 125$, and there is only one 125 in 236. Place a 1 in the first place above to indicate one 5^3. Now you have "used up" 125, so subtract: $236_{\text{ten}} - 125_{\text{ten}} = 111_{\text{ten}}$.

2. The next place value of five is 5^2. Are there any twenty-fives in 111_{ten}? There are 4, so place a 4 above 5^2. Now four twenty-fives, or 100, have been "used," and $111_{\text{ten}} - 100_{\text{ten}} = 11_{\text{ten}}$.

Continue on the next page.

3. The next place value is 5^1 which is 5. How many fives are in 11_{ten}? It has two fives, so place 2 above 5^1. There is 1 one left, so place a 1 above 5^0. Thus $236_{ten} = 1421_{five}$.

Working with different bases can be easier when one can physically move pieces that represent different values in a base system. Often, after doing physical manipulation, one can mentally picture the manipulation and work without physical objects. Multibase blocks are manipulatives that have proven to be extremely useful in coming to understand any base system, but primarily base ten in elementary school. Multibase blocks are wooden or plastic blocks that can be used to demonstrate operations in different bases. For base ten, a centimeter cube can be used to represent a unit or one; a long block one centimeter by one centimeter by ten centimeters (often marked in ones) would then represent ten; ten longs together form a flat that is one cm by ten cm by ten cm and that represents one hundred, ten flats form a ten cm by ten cm by ten cm cube that represents thousands. If the long is used for the unit, then the small cube would represent one-tenth, the flat would represent ten, and so on. The multibase blocks can be used to strengthen place value understanding.

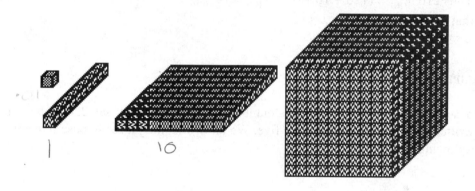

If the multibase blocks are not available, then they can easily be sketched as shown below:

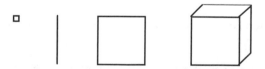

The materials are often called "small cube, long, flat, big cube." Any size of the multibase blocks can be used to represent one unit. Familiarize yourself with the multibase blocks by doing this section's Learning Exercises and making up more problems until you feel you are familiar with the blocks and their relationships.

EXAMPLE 5

The sketch below represents numbers with bases larger than five because there are five flats. If the little cube represents the unit one, the number here is 520 for any base larger than five. If the long represents one, then the number represented here is 52 in any base larger than five. If the flat represents one, then the number represented here is 5.2 in any base larger than five.

Discussion 5   Representing Numbers with Multibase Drawings

1. Here is a representation of a number:

    Which bases could use this representation if it is in the final form, with no more "trades" possible? Why? What are some possible numbers that can be represented by this drawing?

2. In base eight, how many small cubes are in a long? How many in a flat? How many in a large cube? How many longs in a flat? How many flats in a large cube? Answer the same questions for base ten; for base two.

One can also represent decimal numbers with base ten blocks or drawings. You must first decide which block represents the unit. If the unit is the long, then the small block is one-tenth, the flat is ten, and the large block is 100. Thus 2.3 in base ten could be represented as:

Activity 4   Representing Numbers with Multibase Blocks

For these problems, use your cutout blocks (from the appendix) or use drawings such as shown above. Note that the drawings do not show the markings of the base that appears in the picture of the blocks, and thus do not clearly indicate the base in the way that multibase blocks do.

1. Represent 2.3 in base ten using the long as one unit. Represent 2.3 using another size of block as the unit. Compare your representation with a neighbor.

2. Use the base five blocks to represent 2.41_{five} in two different ways. Be sure to indicate which piece represents the unit in each case.

TAKE-AWAY MESSAGE . . . We could just as easily have based our number system on something other than ten, but ten is a natural number to use because we have ten fingers. By working in bases other than ten, you have probably gained a new perspective on the structure and complexity of our place value system, particularly the importance of the value of each place. This understanding underlies all of the procedures we use in calculating with numbers in base ten. As teachers, you will need this knowledge to help students understand computational procedures. ♦

Learning Exercises for Section 2.3

1. If you have access to the internet, go to http://nlvm.usu.edu/en/nav/ and find Virtual Library, then Numbers and Operations, then 3-5, then to Base Blocks. You cannot choose numbers to represent, but you can set the base and you can set the number of decimal points. Practice doing this with the following:

   a. whole numbers in base ten,

   b. decimal numbers in base ten,

   c. whole numbers in base five,

   d. "basimal" numbers in base five.

2. Write ten (this many: 🍎🍎🍎🍎🍎🍎🍎🍎🍎🍎) in each given system.

   a. base four   b. base five   c. base eight

3. Write each of these.

   a. four in base four   b. eight in base eight
   c. twenty in base twenty   d. b in base b
   e. b^2 in base b   f. $b^3 + b^2$ in base b
   g. 29_{ten} in base three   h. 115_{ten} in base five
   i. 69_{ten} in base two   j. 1728_{ten} in base twelve

4. Write the numerals for counting in base two, from one through twenty.

5. How do you know that there is an error in each statement?

   a. ten = 24_{three}

   b. fifty-six = 107_{seven}

   c. thirteen and three-fourths = 25.3_{four}

6. Write each of these as a base ten numeral with the usual base ten words. For example, $111_{two} = (1 \times 2^2) + (1 \times 2) + (1 \times 1) = 7_{ten}$ and $31.2_{four} = (3 \times 4) + (1 \times 1) + \frac{2}{4} = 12 + 1 + \frac{5}{10} = 13.5$, or thirteen and five-tenths.

   a. 37_{twelve} b. 37_{nine} c. 207.0024_{ten}
   d. 1000_{two} e. $1,000,000_{two}$ f. 221.2_{three}

7. For a given number, which base—two or twelve—will usually have a numeral with more digits? What are the exceptions?

8. In what bases would 4025_b be a legitimate numeral?

9. Compare these pairs of numbers by placing < or > or = in each box.

   a. 34_{five} ☐ 34_{six} b. 4_{five} ☐ 4_{six} c. 43_{five} ☐ 25_{six}
   d. 100_{five} ☐ 18_{nine} e. 111_{two} ☐ 7_{ten} f. 23_{six} ☐ 23_{five}

10. On one of your space voyages, you uncover an alien document in which some "one, two, . . ." counting is done: obi, fin, mus, obi na, obi obi, obi fin, obi mus. What base does this alien civilization apparently use? Continue counting through twenty in that system.

11. Hints of the influence of other bases remain in some languages. What base could have led to each of these?

    a. French for eighty is *quatre-vingt*.

    b. The Gettysburg Address, "Four score and seven years ago . . ."

    c. A gross is a dozen dozen.

    d. A minute has 60 seconds, and an hour has 60 minutes.

12. What does 34.2_{five} mean? What is this number written in base ten?

13. In each number, write the "basimal" place values and then the usual base ten fraction or mixed number.

    Example: $10.111_{\text{two}} = (2 + 0 + \frac{1}{2} + \frac{1}{4} + \frac{1}{8})_{\text{ten}} = 2\frac{7}{8}$ (Recall: $4 = 2^2$ and $8 = 2^3$.)

    a. 21.23_{four} b. 34.3_{twelve}

14. Write each of these in "basimal" notation.

    Example: three-fourths in base ten is *what* in base two?
    $$(\tfrac{3}{4})_{\text{ten}} = (\tfrac{1}{2} + \tfrac{1}{4})_{\text{ten}} = 0.11_{\text{two}}$$

    a. one-fourth, in base twelve

    b. three-fourths, in base twelve

    c. one-fourth, in base eight

15. Give the base ten numeral for each given number.

    a. 101010_{two} b. 912_{twelve} c. 425_{six}

    d. 41.5_{eight} e. 1341_{five}

16. Write this many ♦♦♦♦♦♦♦♦♦♦♦♦ in each given base. (Note that there are 12_{ten} diamonds.)

    a. nine   b. eight   c. seven   d. six   e. five   f. four   g. three   h. two

17. Write 100_{ten} in each given base.

    a. seven   b. five   c. eleven   d. two   e. thirty-one

18. Complete with the proper digits.

    a. $57_{\text{ten}} = \underline{\hspace{1cm}}$ five   b. $86_{\text{nine}} = \underline{\hspace{1cm}}$ ten

    c. $312_{\text{four}} = \underline{\hspace{1cm}}$ ten   d. $237_{\text{ten}} = \underline{\hspace{1cm}}$ eight

    e. $2101_{\text{three}} = \underline{\hspace{1cm}}$ ten   f. $0.111_{\text{two}} = \underline{\hspace{1cm}}$ ten

19. Represent 34 in base ten, with the small block as the unit; with the long as the unit.

20. **a.** Represent 234_{five} with the small cube as the unit. (Notice that 234 does not mean two-hundred thirty-four here.)

    b. Represent 234_{six} with the small cube as the unit.

(If you have only base ten blocks available, then sketch drawings for these exercises.)

21. In base six, 5413 is _____ *ones*, is _____ *sixes*, is _____ *six²s*; is _____ *six³s.*

22. Represent 2.34 in base ten with the flat as the unit.

23. Decide on a representation with base ten blocks for each number.

    a. 3542   **b.** 0.741   **c.** 11.11

24. Represent 5.4 and 5.21 with base ten blocks, using the same block as the unit. (What will you use to represent one?) Many school children say that 5.21 is larger than 5.4 because 21 is larger than 4. How would you try to correct this error using base ten blocks?

25. Someone said, "A number can be written in many ways." Explain that statement.

2.4 | Operations in Different Bases

Just as we can add, subtract, multiply, and divide in base ten, so can we perform these arithmetic operations in other bases. The standard algorithm for addition, depicted first below, is commonly used and is probably known to all of you. The expanded algorithms make the processes easier to understand. Once it is well understood, an expanded algorithm is easily adapted to become the standard algorithm. Not all standard algorithms in this country are used in other countries, so the word "standard" is a relative one.

In base ten we could add 256 and 475 in these two ways, as shown here. (There are other ways, of course.) The first way is called an *expanded* algorithm, and the second, called the standard algorithm, is probably the one you were taught.

$$
\begin{array}{r}
256 \\
+\,475 \\
\hline
11 \quad \text{(thinking } 6 + 5) \\
120 \quad \text{(thinking } 50 + 70) \\
\underline{600} \quad \text{(thinking } 200 + 400) \\
731
\end{array}
\qquad
\begin{array}{r}
11 \\
256 \\
+\,475 \\
\hline
731
\end{array}
$$

The expanded algorithm is now being taught in some schools as a preparation for the standard algorithm. Note how place value is attended to in the expanded algorithm: add the ones $6 + 5$, then add the tens $50 + 70$, then add the hundreds, $200 + 400$, then add the resulting sums, $11 + 120 + 500$. In the standard algorithm, each "column" is treated the same: 6 + 5 in the column on the right, 5 + 7 +1 in the middle column, and 2 + 4 + 1 in the column to the left. Although the standard algorithm leads to the correct answer, students frequently do not know why each step is taken. But when the expanded algorithm is understood, it can be condensed into the standard algorithm as shown above.

We can also use either method for adding in other bases, but the expanded algorithm is sometimes easier to follow until adding in another base is well understood.

EXAMPLE 6

Here is an example using both the standard and expanded algorithms to add the same two numbers in base ten and base eight. Make sure you can understand each way in each given base.

$$
\begin{array}{r}
1 \\
351_{\text{ten}} \\
+\ 250_{\text{ten}} \\
\hline
601_{\text{ten}}
\end{array}
$$

$$
\begin{array}{rl}
351_{\text{ten}} & \\
+250_{\text{ten}} & \\
\hline
1_{\text{ten}} & \text{thinking } (1 + 0) \\
100_{\text{ten}} & \text{thinking } (50 + 50) \\
500_{\text{ten}} & \text{thinking } (300 + 200) \\
\hline
601_{\text{ten}} & \text{thinking } (1 + 100 + 500)
\end{array}
$$

$$
\begin{array}{r}
1 \\
351_{\text{eight}} \\
+\ 250_{\text{eight}} \\
\hline
621_{\text{eight}}
\end{array}
$$

$$
\begin{array}{rl}
351_{\text{eight}} & \\
+\ 250_{\text{eight}} & \\
\hline
1_{\text{eight}} & \text{thinking } (1 + 0)_{\text{eight}} \\
120_{\text{eight}} & \text{thinking } (50 + 50)_{\text{eight}} \\
500_{\text{eight}} & \text{thinking } (300 + 200)_{\text{eight}} \\
\hline
621_{\text{eight}} & \text{thinking } (1 + 20 + 100 + 500)_{\text{eight}}
\end{array}
$$

Activity 5   Adding in Base Four

Add these two numbers in base four in both expanded and standard algorithms: 311_{four} and 231_{four}. (Drawings of base four pieces may be helpful.)

If we can add in different bases, we should be able to subtract in different bases. Here is an example of how to do this.

EXAMPLE 7

Find $321_{\text{five}} - 132_{\text{five}}$.

One way to think about this problem is to regroup in base five just as we do in base ten, then use the standard way of subtracting in base ten.

Continue on the next page.

SOLUTION: 321

    $- 132$

Step 1:   We cannot remove 2 ones from 1 one, so we need to take one of the fives
from 321_{five} and trade it for five ones:

$$321_{five} \rightarrow 300_{five} + 20_{five} + 1_{five} \rightarrow 300_{five} + 10_{five} + 11_{five}$$

Step 2:   We can now take 2 ones from 11 ones (in base five) leaving 4 ones.
(Notice how 321 has changed with 3 five squared, then 1 five, then 11
ones, from Step 1.)

$$\begin{array}{r} 1 \\ 3 \ \ \cancel{2} \ \ ^1 1_{five} \\ -1 \ \ 3 \ \ 2_{five} \\ \hline 4_{five} \end{array}$$ means 3 (five squared) + 1 five + 11 ones as in Step 1.

Step 3:   In the fives place: We cannot subtract 3 fives from 1 five, so we must
change one five squared to five sets of five. This, together with the one
five already in place, gives us 11 fives (or six fives).

That is: $300_{five} + 10_{five} \ \ \rightarrow 200_{five} + 110_{five}$, so

$$\begin{array}{r} 2 \ \ 11 \\ \cancel{3} \ \ \cancel{2} \ \ ^1 1_{five} \\ 1 \ \ \ 3 \ \ 2_{five} \\ \hline 1 \ \ 3 \ \ 4_{five} \end{array}$$ means 11 fives, not 11 ones, so the 11 stands for 110
and 11 fives minus 3 fives is 3 fives, or $110 - 30$ is 30)

We now have 2 (five squared) from which 1 (five squared) is subtracted,
leaving 1 (five squared). The answer is 1 five-squared plus 3 fives plus 4
ones which is 134_{five}.

Activity 6   Subtracting in Base Four

Subtract 231_{four} from 311_{four} in base four.

Subtracting in base four is similar to adding in base four. However, for both operations we can use base materials to help visualize adding and subtracting in other
bases. We will do that next. You can cut out and use materials from an appendix on
bases. As you use the base materials, notice how they support the symbolic work you
did earlier in this section.

EXAMPLE 8

Suppose we want to add 231_{four} and 311_{four} using base four blocks, using the small
block as the unit. We could first express the problem as

We have too many longs (in base four), so trade four longs for a flat. Now we have too many flats (each representing four squared). Trade four flats for a large cube (which represents four cubed).

Represents the answer, which is 1202_{four}

The blocks represent one four cubed, two four squared, and two ones.

EXAMPLE 9

Suppose we want to subtract 23_{four} from 32_{four}. This time let us use the *long* as the unit. 32_{four} is represented:

I cannot remove 3 longs (ones) until I change a flat to four longs (which means change one four into four ones).

Remove two flats; three longs

To take away 23_{four} we must remove three longs (three ones), and 2 flats (2 fours), and we are left with 3_{four} as the difference.

> **THINK ABOUT . . .**
>
> If we had used the small block as the unit in the above subtraction example, would the numerical answer be different? Try it.

Activity 7   Subtracting in Base Four

Once again, subtract 231_{four} from 311_{four} in base four, this time using drawings.

We can also multiply and divide in different bases. However, the intent here is to introduce you to different bases so that you have a better understanding of our own base ten system, and that you understand why children need time to learn to operate in base ten. Thus there are no examples or exercises provided here for multiplication and division in different bases, although it is certainly possible to carry out these operations.

Notes

TAKE-AWAY MESSAGE . . . Arithmetic operations in other bases are undertaken in the same way as in base ten. However, because we have less familiarity with other bases, arithmetic operations in those bases take us longer than operations in base ten. For children not yet entirely familiar with base ten, time needed to complete arithmetic operations takes longer than it does for us. ◆

Learning Exercises for Section 2.4

1. Add 1111_{three} and 2102_{three} without drawings and then with drawings in the ways illustrated above. Which way did you find it easier?

2. Do these exercises in the designated bases, using the cardboard cutouts in an appendix, or with drawings.

   a. $\begin{array}{r} 341_{five} \\ +\ 220_{five} \end{array}$ **b.** $\begin{array}{r} 101_{two} \\ +\ 110_{two} \end{array}$ **c.** $\begin{array}{r} 321_{four} \\ -\ 123_{four} \end{array}$ **d.** $\begin{array}{r} 296_{ten} \\ -\ 28_{ten} \end{array}$

3. Go to http://nlvm.usu.edu/en/nav/ on the internet and find Virtual Library, then Numbers and Operations, then 3-5. Go to Base Blocks Decimals. You cannot choose numbers to add and subtract, but you can set the base and you can set the number of decimal points. Do the following:

   a. Practice adding and subtracting numbers in base ten using whole numbers.

   b. Practice adding and subtracting numbers using one decimal place.

   c. Practice adding and subtracting numbers in base four using whole numbers.

   d. Practice adding and subtracting numbers in base four using one "decimal" place.

4. Add the following in the appropriate bases, without blocks unless you need them.

   a. $\begin{array}{r} 2431_{five} \\ +\ 223_{five} \end{array}$ **b.** $\begin{array}{r} 351_{nine} \\ +\ 250_{nine} \end{array}$ **c.** $\begin{array}{r} 643_{seven} \\ +\ 134_{seven} \end{array}$ **d.** $\begin{array}{r} 99_{eleven} \\ +\ 88_{eleven} \end{array}$

5. Subtract in different bases, without blocks unless you need them.

   a. $\begin{array}{r} 351_{nine} \\ -\ 250_{nine} \end{array}$ **b.** $\begin{array}{r} 643_{seven} \\ -\ 134_{seven} \end{array}$ **c.** $\begin{array}{r} 2431_{five} \\ -\ 223_{five} \end{array}$ **d.** $\begin{array}{r} 772_{eleven} \\ -\ 249_{eleven} \end{array}$

6. Do you think multiplying and dividing in different bases would be difficult? Why or why not?

7. Use the cut-outs from the appendix for the different bases to act out the following. As you act each out, record what would take place in the corresponding numerical work.

   a. $\begin{array}{r} 232_{four} \\ 13_{four} \\ 113_{four} \end{array}$ **b.** $\begin{array}{r} 232_{five} \\ 13_{five} \\ +\ 113_{five} \end{array}$ **c.** $\begin{array}{r} 232_{eight} \\ 13_{eight} \\ +\ 113_{eight} \end{array}$ **d.** $\begin{array}{r} 101_{two} \\ 11_{two} \\ +\ 111_{two} \end{array}$

8. Use the cut-outs from an appendix for the different bases to act out the following. As you act each out, record what would take place in the corresponding numerical work.

   a. 200_{four} **b.** 200_{five} **c.** 200_{eight} **d.** 100_{two}

       -13_{four} -13_{five} -13_{eight} -11_{two}

9. Describe how cut-outs for base six would look. For base twelve.

2.5   Issues for Learning: Understanding Place Value

The notion that ten ones and one ten give the same number is vital to understanding the usual numeration system, as are the later rethinking of ten tens as one hundred, ten hundreds as one thousand, etc. Understanding place value is considered to be foundational to elementary school mathematics.

But base ten for children might be as mysterious as base b may have been for you. (Admittedly, your extensive experience with base ten also gets in the way!) By working with other bases, you have had the opportunity to explore what it means to have a place-value system where each digit has a particular meaning, and thus come to a better understanding of our base ten system of writing numbers and calculating with numbers.

One activity-centered primary program incorporates many activities involving grouping by twos, by threes, and so on, even before extensive work with base ten groupings, to accustom the children to counting not just one object at a time, but groups each made up of several objects. Ungrouping needs to be included also. That is, 132 could be regarded as one one-hundred, three tens, and 2 ones. Or, it could be regarded as one one-hundred and 32 ones. Here, the 3 tens are "unbundled" to make 30 ones. Regarding a group made up of several objects as one thing is a major step that needs instructional attention.

The manner in which we vocalize numbers can sometimes cause problems for students. For example, some young U.S. children will write 81 for eighteen, whereas scarcely any Hispanic children (diez y ocho = eighteen) or Japanese children (ju hachi = eighteen) do so. (Some wishfully think we should say "onetyeight" for eighteen in English.) What other numbers can cause the same sort of problem that eighteen does?

Place value instruction in schools is often superficial and limited to studying only the placement of digits. Thus, children are taught that the 7 in 7200 is in the thousands place, the 2 is in the hundreds place, a 0 is in the tens place, and a 0 is in the ones place. But when asked how many hundred dollar bills could be obtained from a bank account with $7200 in it, or how many boxes of ten golf balls could be packed from a container with 7200 balls, children almost always do long division, dividing by 100 or by 10. They do not read the number as 7200 ones, or 720 tens, or 72 hundreds, and certainly not as 7.2 thousands. But why not? These are all names for the same number, and the ability to rename in this way provides a great deal of flexibility and insight when working with the number. (It is interesting that we later expect students to understand newspaper figures such as $3.2 billion. What does .2 billion mean here?)

Over the years many different methods have been used to teach place value. An abacus with nine beads on each string is one type of device used to represent place value. The Base Ten Blocks pictured in Section 2.3 have been extensively used to introduce place value and operations on whole numbers and decimal numbers. One problem with these representations, however, is that students do not always make the connections between what is shown with the manipulative devices and what they write on paper.

Our place value system of numeration extends to numbers less than 1 also. The naming of decimal numbers needs special attention. The place value name for 0.642 is six hundred forty-two thousandths. Compare this to reading 642, where we simply say six hundred forty-two, not 642 ones. This is a source of confusion that is compounded by the use of the ten*ths* or hundred*ths* with decimal numbers, the use of te*n* or hundre*d* with whole numbers, and the additional digits in the whole number with a similar name. The number 0.642 is read 642 thousand*ths*, meaning 642 thousand*ths* of one, while 642,000 is read 642 thousand, meaning 642 thousand ones. That tens and ten*ths*, hundreds and hundred*ths*, etc., sound so much alike no doubt causes some children to lose sense-making when it comes to decimals. Some teachers resort to a digit-by-digit pronunciation—"two point one five" for 2.15—but that removes any sense for the number; it just describes the numeral. Plan to give an artificial emphasis to the -th sound when you are discussing decimals with children. (You can also say "decimal numeral two and three-tenths" and "mixed numeral two and three-tenths" to distinguish 2.3 and $2\frac{3}{10}$.)

To compare 0.45 and 0.6, students are often told to "add a zero so the numbers are the same size." (Try figuring out what this might mean to a student who does not understand decimal numbers in the first place!) The strategy works, in the sense that the student can then (usually) choose the larger number, but since it requires no knowledge of the size of the decimal numbers, it does not develop understanding of number size. Instead of annexing zeros, couldn't we expect students to recognize that six-tenths is more than forty-five hundredths because 45 hundredths has only 4 tenths and what is left is less than another tenth? But for students to do this naturally, they must have been provided with numerous opportunities to explore—and think about—place value. Comparing and operating on decimals, if presented in a non-rule oriented fashion, can provide these opportunities. If teachers postpone work with operations on decimals until students conceptually understand these numbers, students will be much more successful than if teachers attempt to teach computation too early. Some researchers[iii] have shown that once students have learned rote rules for calculating with decimals, it is extremely difficult for them to relearn how to calculate with decimals meaningfully.

2.6	**Check Yourself**

In this chapter you have explored the ways we express numbers. Historically, many numeration systems were used to express numbers in different ways. A place value numeration system such as the modern world now uses provides a far more efficient way to express numbers than ancient systems, such as the Roman numeral system. Our use of base ten is probably due to the fact that we have ten fingers. Other bases could be used. Because we are so familiar with base ten, however, working with other bases is useful in appreciating the difficulties children have in learning to use base ten, particularly when learning to operate with numbers in base ten.

Understanding place value and its role in the elementary school mathematics curriculum is crucial. Too many teachers think that teaching place value is simply a matter of noting which digit is in the ones place, which is in the tens place, etc. But it is only when students have a deep understanding of place value that they can make sense of numbers larger than 10 and smaller than 1, and understand how to operate on these numbers. Most arithmetic errors (beyond careless errors) are due to a lack of understanding of place value. Unfortunately, the algorithms we teach usually treat digits in columns without attending to their values, and students who learn these algorithms without understanding the place value of each digit are far more likely to make computational errors.

You should be able to work problems like those assigned and to meet the following objectives.

1. Discuss the advantages of a place value system over other ancient numeration systems.

2. Explain how the placement of digits determines the value of a number in base ten, on both sides of the decimal point.

3. Explain how the placement of digits determines the value of a number in any base, such as base five or base twelve and answer questions such as: What does 346.3 mean in base twelve? Convert that number to base ten.

4. Given a particular base, write numbers in that system beginning with one.

5. Make a drawing with base materials that demonstrates a particular addition or subtraction problem, e.g., 35.7 + 24.7 or 35.7 − 24.7 in base ten.

6. Write base ten numbers in another base, such as 9 in base nine, or 33 in base two.

7. Add and subtract in different bases.

8. Understand the role of the unit, one, in reading and understanding decimal numbers.

9. Discuss problems that children who do not have a good understanding of place value might have when they do computation problems.

Notes   **REFERENCES FOR CHAPTER 2**

[i] Saxe, G. B. (1981). Body parts as numerals: A developmental analysis of numeration among the Oksapmin in
      Papau New Guinea. *Child Development, 52,* 306–316.

[ii] Sowder, J. T. (1997). Place value as the key to teaching decimal operations. *Teaching Children Mathematics,
      3*(8), 448–453.

[iii] Hiebert, J., & Wearne, D. (1986). Procedures over concepts: The acquisition of decimal number knowledge.
      In J. Hiebert (Ed.), *Conceptual and procedural knowledge: The case of mathematics* (pp. 199–223).
      Hillsdale, NJ: Erlbaum.

Chapter 3

Understanding Whole Number Operations

There are two major ideas interspersed in this chapter. The first is that an arithmetic operation such as subtraction can be modeled by many different situations. Teachers need to know what these situations are in order to understand and extend children's use of the operations. The second is that the kind of procedures that children can develop for computing, when they have not yet been taught the usual standard algorithms, can demonstrate a deep conceptual understanding that might be lost if standard algorithms are introduced too soon. The examples of student work given in this section are all taken from published research, although in some cases the numbers have been changed. Most of the examples of nonstandard algorithms come from students who have been in classrooms where there is a strong emphasis on building on intuitive knowledge and on place value understanding. The students demonstrate that they are able to compute with ease. Some of the examples are from classrooms where the students have calculators always available. However, they tend not to use calculators if they can do the calculation easily themselves using paper and pencil and/or mental computation. The use of calculators introduced these students to new ways of using numbers, including, in some cases, using negative numbers to help them in their computation.

3.1 | Additive Combinations and Comparisons

When does a problem situation call for adding? When does it call for subtracting? Both types of situations are considered in this section. At times, knowing when and what to add or subtract is not at all easy. To solve more difficult problems, we turn once again to undertaking quantitative analyses of problems.

Activity 1   **Applefest**

Consider the following problem situation:

♦ Tom, Fred, and Rhoda combined their apples for a fruit stand. Fred and Rhoda together had 97 more apples than Tom. Rhoda had 17 apples. Tom had 25 apples. [i] ♦

Continue on the next page.

Notes

Perform a quantitative analysis of this problem situation with these four steps.

1. Identify as many quantities as you can in this situation, including those for which you are not given a value. Can you make a drawing?

2. What does the 97 stand for in this situation?

3. How many apples did Fred and Rhoda have together? How many apples did all three of them have combined?

4. How many apples did Fred have?

_____

Note in the Activity 1 problem that when Fred and Rhoda combined their apples, they had 97 *more* apples than Tom. The 97 apples does not refer to Fred and Rhoda's combined total, rather it refers to the *difference* between their combined total and Tom's number of apples.

Consider the following drawing that represents the applefest problem.

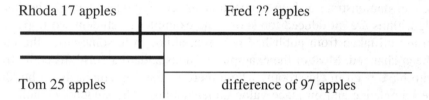

Rhoda 17 apples   Fred ?? apples

Tom 25 apples   difference of 97 apples

Quantities are often ***combined additively*** (put together) and the new quantity has the value represented by the sum of the values of the quantities being combined. The sum of the number of Rhoda's apples and the number of Fred's apples is the value of the number of apples belonging to the two. Quantities can also be ***compared additively***. In the applefest problem, the quantities consisting of the value of the quantity represented by Rhoda's and Fred's combined apples is compared to the value of the quantity represented by Tom's apples.

When quantities are combined additively, they are joined together, so the appropriate arithmetic operation on their values is usually addition. This operation is called an **additive combination**. The result of an additive combination is a **sum** of the values combined. Any time we compare two quantities to determine how much greater or less one is than the other, we make an **additive comparison**. The **difference** of two quantities is the quantity by which one of them exceeds or falls short of the other. The appropriate arithmetic operation on their values is usually subtraction.

The reason this comparison in this problem is called additive is that two quantities can also be compared multiplicatively. We will study multiplicative comparisons in a later section.

Typically, subtraction is the mathematical operation used to find the difference between the known values of two quantities. We can think of the difference as the amount that has to be added to the lesser of the two to make it equal in value to the greater of the two. Thus, rather than use *additive/subtractive comparison* we use the shorter *additive comparison*. The following diagrams illustrate how one might think of a situation as either a difference of two quantities or as a combination of two quantities (even when, in the latter case, the value of one of the quantities being combined is unknown).

EXAMPLE 1

♦ Julian wants to buy a bicycle. The bike costs $143.95. Julian has a total of $83.48 in cash and savings. How much more does he need? ♦

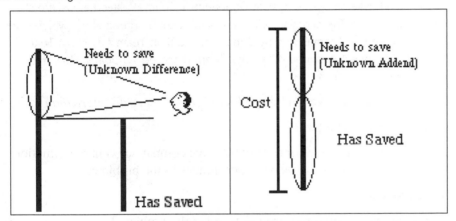

Two ways to conceive the situation

The drawings help in seeing how the quantities are related in this situation.

Although typically subtraction is the operation used to find a difference, this is not always the case. Consider the following example.

EXAMPLE 2

♦ Jim is 15 cm taller than Sam. This difference is five times as great as the difference between Abe and Sam's heights. What is the difference between Abe and Sam's height? ♦

SOLUTION

The difference between Abe's and Sam's heights is 15 ÷ 5 cm, or 3 cm.

THINK ABOUT . . .

What would the diagram for Example 2 look like?

Example 2 illustrates that the additive comparison of two quantities does not automatically signal that one must subtract. How the quantities in a situation are related to each other determines the mathematical operations that make sense. Understanding the quantitative relationships is essential to being able to answer questions reliably involving the values of quantities in the given situation. Without such an understanding one has no recourse but to guess what mathematical operations are needed, as was illustrated in the last chapter. In the absence of real understanding it is the unreliability of the guessing games that students often play that makes story problems difficult for many of them.

Activity 2   It's Just a Game

Practice doing a quantitative analysis to solve this problem:

♦ Team A played a basketball game against Opponent A. Team B played a basketball game against Opponent B. The captains of Team A and Team B argued about which team beat its opponent by more. Team B won by 8 more points than Team A won by. Team A scored 79 points. Opponent A scored 48 points. Team B scored 73 points. How many points did Opponent B score? ♦

1. What quantities are involved in this problem? (*Hint: there are more than four.*)

2. What does the 8 points refer to?

3. There are several differences (results of additive comparisons) in this situation. Sketch a diagram to show the relevant differences in the problem.

4. Solve the problem.

5. What arithmetic operations did you use to solve the problem?

6. For many students this is a difficult problem. Why do you suppose this is the case? Is the computation difficult? What is difficult about this problem?

7. Suppose you are the teacher in a fifth-grade class. Do you think telling your students that all they need to solve this problem is subtraction and addition, will help them solve it? Explain.

TAKE-AWAY MESSAGE . . . The problems undertaken in this section involved additive combinations (which can be expressed with an addition equation) and additive comparisons (which can be expressed with a subtraction equation). What makes these problems difficult is the complexity of the quantitative structures of the problems, not the arithmetic. The problems involve only addition and subtraction. Understanding the quantitative relationships in a problem is what's crucial. Once again, these problems illustrate how undertaking a quantitative analysis by listing quantities and using diagrams to explore the relationships of the quantities can help one understand a complex problem situation. ♦

Notes

Learning Exercises for Section 3.1

To develop skill in analyzing the quantitative structure of situations, work the following tasks by first identifying the quantities and their relationships in each situation. Feel free to draw diagrams to represent the relationships between relevant quantities.

1. **a.** Bob is taller than Laura. Suppose you were told Bob's height and Laura's height. How would you calculate the difference between their heights?

    b. Bob is taller than Laura. Suppose you were told the difference between Bob's height and Laura's height. Suppose you were also told Laura's height. How would you calculate Bob's height?

2. Kelly's mom timed her as she swam a 3-lap race in 1 minute 43 seconds. Her swimming coach timed Kelly only on her last two laps. Describe how Kelly might calculate how long it took her to swim the first lap using the information from her mom and the coach.

3. Metcalf School has two third-grade rooms (A and B) and two fourth-grade rooms (C and D). Together, rooms C and D have 46 students. Room A has 6 more students than room D. Room B has 2 fewer students than room C. Room D has 22 students. How many students are there altogether in rooms A and B?

4. In Exercise 3, what quantities are combined? Which quantities are compared?

5. Following are two variations of the activity "It's Just a Game," from the last Activity, but the captain of Team B still wins the argument by 8 points in each case.

    a. **Variation #1:** Team A scored 79 points. Opponent A scored 53 points. Fill in the blanks with scores for Team B and Opponent B so that the specified conditions are met.

    Team B _____   Opponent B _____

    b. **Variation #2:** Team B scored 75 points. Opponent B scored 69 points. Give possible scores for Team A and Opponent A so that the specified conditions are met.

    Team A _____   Opponent A _____

    c. Compare your response to Variation #1 with those of classmates. Are they correct? How many possible responses are there?

    d. What did you find out after thinking through Variation #2? State your conclusion and explain why it is the case.

6. Connie bought several types of candy for Halloween: Milky Ways, Tootsie Rolls, Reese's Cups, and Hershey Bars. Milky Ways and Tootsie Rolls together were 15 more than the Reese's Cups. There were 4 fewer Reese's Cups than Hershey Bars. There were 12 Milky Ways and 14 Hershey Bars. How many Tootsie Rolls did Connie buy?

7. **a.** One day Annie weighed 24 ounces more than Benjie, and Benjie weighed $3\frac{1}{4}$ pounds less than Carmen. How did Annie's and Carmen's weights compare on that day?

    b. Why can't you tell how much each person weighed?

8. You have two recipes which together use a pound of butter. One recipe takes $\frac{1}{4}$ pound more than the other one. How much butter does each recipe use?

9. A hospital needs a supply of an expensive medicine. Company A has the most, 1.3 milligrams, which is twice the difference between the weight of Company B's supply and Company C's, and 0.9 mg more than Company C's supply. How many milligrams can the hospital get from these three companies?

10. A city spent about $\frac{1}{4}$ of its budget on buildings and maintenance, which was about $\frac{1}{8}$ of the total budget less than it spent on administrative personnel. The amount spent on administrative personnel was about $\frac{1}{8}$ of the budget more than was spent on public safety. About what part of the budget was left for other expenses?

11. All of the problems in the previous exercises involve the quantitative operations of combining and comparing quantities. Choose two of them and for each state one additive combination or one additive comparison that is involved.

3.2 Ways of Thinking About Addition and Subtraction

Although the idea of combining two or more quantities additively seems quite simple, situations involving additive combinations can vary in difficulty for young children. Situations involving subtraction are quite varied, and when only one type of situation is taught (for example, take away), children can have difficulty with other situations (for example, comparing) that also call for subtraction. In this chapter we consider two types of situations calling for addition and three calling for subtraction.

A problem situation that calls for addition often describes one quantity being *physically*, or *actively*, put with another quantity, as in Example 3.

EXAMPLE 3

♦ Four girls were in the car. Two more got in. How many girls were in the car then? ♦

Another type of problem situation that calls for addition involves *conceptually* (rather than physically or literally) placing quantities together, thus leading to another view of what addition means.

EXAMPLE 4

♦ Only 4 cars and 2 trucks were in the lot. How many vehicles were there altogether? ♦

Even though both problems involve the additive combination of two quantities, and they both call for the mathematical operation of addition, many research studies have shown that the second problem is more difficult for young children. They may not yet understand concept relations as "cars and trucks are simply two different kinds of vehicles."

Addition can describe situations that involve an **additive combination of quantities**, either literally (as in the first example) or conceptually (as in the second example). Numbers added together are called **addends**. The number that is the result of an addition is called the **sum**.

In either of the problems given in Examples 3 and 4, the numbers being added (2 and 4) are addends, and the result is called the sum (6).

An important distinction calling for awareness by the teachers is this: The calculation one does to solve a problem may be different from that suggested by the action described in the problem or by the problem's underlying structure. The following illustrates this important point.

EXAMPLE 5

♦ Josie needs to make 15 tacos for lunch. She has made 7 already. How many more tacos does she have to make? ♦

You would probably regard this as a subtraction problem, because one can calculate the solution from the number sentence $15 - 7 = n$. Yet, when young children have solved similar problems, perhaps with the aid of concrete materials, they often count out 7 blocks, and then put out additional blocks, one at a time, until they have 15. Their actions are a reenactment of the problem's story. The action of the problem suggests addition of an unknown number of tacos to the 7 tacos, to give a total of 15. Mathematically this problem can also be described by the sentence $7 + n = 15$, where the sum and one addend are known, but the other addend is missing. If the numbers were larger, say $1678 + n = 4132$, you would probably *want* to subtract to find n. Such **missing-addend** (or **missing-part**) situations, then, can be solved by subtraction, and missing-addend story problems may be in a subtraction section of an elementary textbook. Note the potential confusion for students due to the mismatch of the joining action suggesting addition and the calculation which uses subtraction. The classification of such problems as "missing addend" problems serves to point out this connection.

A problem situation that can be represented as $a + ? = b$ is called a **missing addend problem**. Although the action suggests addition, the missing value is $b - a$. It is therefore classified as a subtraction problem.

THINK ABOUT . . .

♦ Ana has to practice the piano for 15 minutes every day. Today she has practiced 7 minutes. How many more minutes does she have to practice today? ♦

Why is this problem a missing-addend problem calling for subtraction?

In the typical elementary school curriculum, missing-addend situations are not the first ones students encounter when dealing with subtraction. Usually *take-away* situations are the first introduced under subtraction. In fact, the minus sign (–) is often read as "take away" instead of as "minus," a reading that can limit one's understanding of subtraction.

Contrast the following story problem with the missing-addend given in the above Think About problem:

♦ Josie made 15 tacos for her friends at lunch. They ate 7 of them. How many tacos did they still have? ♦

THINK ABOUT . . .

How do you suppose children would act out this story problem using counters?

In situations like the problem above, children typically start with 15 counters, and then they **take-away** or **separate** 7 counters. The remaining counters stand for the uneaten tacos. This enables them to answer the question. In a take-away situation, it is natural to call the quantity that is left after the taking away is done, the **remainder**.

A situation in which one quantity is removed or separated from a larger quantity is called a **take-away subtraction situation**. What is left of the larger quantity is called the **remainder**.

As in the case of addition, one can distinguish between two types of situations: one in which there is a physical taking-away, and ones in which there is no "taking-away" action as such, but there is a missing part, given a whole.

THINK ABOUT . . .

How would you classify the following problem situation?

♦ Of Josie's 15 tacos, 7 had chicken and the rest had beef. How many of the tacos had beef? ♦

Because the discussion of missing addends is fresh in your mind, you may be saying to yourself, "I think I can see both of the last two taco problems as missing-addend problems."

[number of tacos eaten (7)] + [number still to eat (?)] = total number (15)

[number of chicken tacos (7)] + [number of beef tacos (?)] = total number (15)

This similarity of structure is one reason that some textbooks emphasize the missing-addend view when dealing with subtraction.

EXAMPLE 6

One can think about 7 − 3 = ? as 3 + ? = 7.

Familiarity with 3 + 4 = 7 enables one to see 7 − 3 = 4. Some curricula build considerably on this view and may at some point teach *families of facts*. The family of (addition and subtraction) facts for 3, 4, and 7 would include all of these: 3 + 4 = 7, 4 + 3 = 7, 7 − 3 = 4, and 7 − 4 = 3. Do you see what might be some advantages to families of facts?

A third type of subtraction comes from the additive comparison idea. This type of situation is also found in elementary school curriculum. Consider the following situation:

♦ Josie made 15 tacos and 7 enchiladas. How many more tacos than enchiladas did Josie make? ♦

Two *separate* quantities, the number of tacos and the number of enchiladas, are being compared in a how-many-more (or how-many-less) sense.

> A problem situation involving an additive comparison is referred to as a **comparison subtraction** situation.

Subtraction can tell how many more, or less, there are of one than of the other. The result of the comparison is the **difference** between the values of the two quantities being compared. Comparison subtraction usually appears in the curriculum after take-away subtraction.

> When one number is subtracted from another, the result is called the **difference** or **remainder** of the two numbers. The number from which the other is subtracted is called the **minuend** and the number being subtracted is called the **subtrahend**.

EXAMPLE 7

In 50 − 15 = 35, 50 is the minuend, 15 is the subtrahend, and 35 is the difference (or remainder).

Notes

In all of the previous examples, the objects under consideration were separate, disconnected objects, like tacos. But there are other situations in which we combine or compare things such as distances, areas, volumes, and so forth.

> Quantities being considered are called **discrete** if they are separate, non-touching, objects that can be counted. Quantities are **continuous** when they can be measured only by length, area, and so on. Continuous quantities are measured, not counted.

EXAMPLE 8

The following problem situation is also a comparison subtraction problem. Height is a *continuous* quantity. The heights given are only approximations of the real height of each. One cannot *count* an *exact* number of inches.

♦ Johann is 66 inches tall. Jacqui is 57 inches tall. How much taller is Johann than Jacqui? ♦

EXAMPLE 9

The following problem situation is a comparison problem calling for subtraction of discrete quantities. One can count siblings; one cannot have parts of siblings.

♦ Johann has 5 siblings and Jacqui has 4 siblings. How many more siblings does Johann have than Jacqui? ♦

Activity 3   Which Is Which?

Pair up with someone in your class and together classify each of the following problem situations.

1. Velma received four new sweaters for her birthday. Two of them were duplicates, so she took one back. How many sweaters does she have now?

2. Velma also received cash for her birthday, $36 in all. She has an eye on some software she wants, which costs $49.95. Her dad offered to pay her to wax and polish his car. How much does she need to earn to buy the software?

3. Velma also received two mystery novels and three romance novels for her birthday. How many novels did she receive?

4. There were six boys and eight girls at her birthday party. How many more girls than boys from class were at the party? How many friends were at the party?

Activity 4   Writing Story Problems

1. Pair up with someone in your class. Write problem situations (not necessarily in the order given) that illustrate these different views of addition and subtraction:

   a. Addition that involves putting two quantities together

   b. Addition that involves thinking about two quantities as one quantity

   c. Take-away subtraction

   d. Comparison subtraction

   e. Missing addend subtraction

2. Share your problems with another group. Each group should identify the types of problems illustrated by the other group, and discuss whether each group can correctly identify the problem situations with the description. In each problem, identify whether the quantities are discrete or continuous.

Discussion 1   Identifying Types of Problem Situations

If there are any disagreements in the story problems written for the last activity, discuss these as a class.

TAKE-AWAY MESSAGE . . . Addition is called for in problems of two different generic types: combining actively or implicitly. Subtraction is called for in three different generic types: taking away, comparing, and finding the missing addend. Missing addend problems are sometimes called additive comparison problems, but they are solved by subtracting. If a teacher illustrates subtraction only with take-away situations, then that teacher should not be surprised if his or her students cannot recognize other types of subtraction situations. Also, if students are presented only with discrete objects when they add or subtract, they will not necessarily be able to transfer this knowledge to situations in which the quantities are continuous.

One might ask how children cope with the diversity of situations that call for addition or subtraction. The manner in which they act out the story usually shows how they have conceived the situation. The physical situations can be quite different even though the symbolic mathematics may be the same. ♦

Learning Exercises for Section 3.2

1. Illustrate the computation $8 - 5$ with both continuous and discrete drawings for each of the three generic situations for subtraction.

   a. take-away   b. comparison   c. missing-addend

   Notice how the drawings differ.

2. a. The narrative in this section has neglected story problems like this one: "Jay had 60 pieces of clean paper when she started her homework. When she finished, she had 14 clean pieces. How many pieces of paper did she use?" What mathematical sentence would one write for this problem? Notice that

the action here is take-away, but the correct sentence *for the action* would be $60 - n = 14$, not $60 - 14 = n$ (one could calculate $60 - 14$ to answer the question though). Such complications are usually avoided in current K–6 treatments in the United States, but several other countries give considerable attention to these types! Are we "babying" our children intellectually?

   b. Make up a story problem for this "missing-minuend" number sentence: $n - 17 = 24$.

3. Teachers sometimes emphasize "key words" to help children with story problems. For example, "altogether" suggests addition, "left" suggests subtraction. The intent is good: Have the children think about the situation. But unfortunately children often abuse the key words. They skim, looking just for the key words, or they trust them too much, taking what is intended as a rough guide as a rule. In the following, tell how the italicized key words could mislead a child who does not read the whole problem or who does not think about the situation.

   a. Dale *spent* $1.25. Then Dale had 55 cents. How much did Dale have at the start?

   b. Each classroom at one school has 32 children. The school has 12 classrooms. How many children are at the school *altogether*?

   c. Ben *divided* up his pieces of candy evenly with Jose and Cleveland. Each of the three boys got 15 pieces of candy. How many pieces did Ben start with?

   d. Flo has 3 *times* as much money as Lacy does. Flo has 84 cents. How much does Lacy have?

   e. Manny's mother bought some things at the grocery store. She gave the clerk $10 and got $1.27 in change. *In all*, how much did she spend at the store?

   f. Each package of stickers has 6 pages, and each page has 12 stickers on it. What is the *total* number of stickers in 4 packages?

4. Consider this comparison subtraction situation: "Ann has $12.85 and Bea has $6.43. How much less money does Bea have than Ann?" Note that the question is awkward. This is believed to be one explanation of why young children have more trouble with comparison story problems than with take-away problems. When story problems are phrased less awkwardly, children tend to do much better. For example, "There are 12 bowls and 8 spoons. How many bowls do not have a spoon?" is easier for the children than, "There are 12 bowls and 8 spoons. How many more bowls are there than spoons?" This may be due to the fact that the phrasing in the former case is suggestive of an action (matching bowls with spoons) that enables students to obtain an answer.

Re-phrase the questions to make these problems easier.

   a. The baseball team has 12 players but only 9 gloves. How many more players are there than gloves?

   b. There are 28 children in the teacher's class. The teacher has 20 suckers. How many fewer suckers are there than children?

5. Give the families of facts for these:

    a.   2, 6, 8

    b.   12, 49, 61

    c. x, m, and p, where $m - p = x$

6. Choose a family of facts in 5 above; write one addition word problem and three subtraction word problems, one of each type, for that family of facts.

7. In a first-grade class the teacher gave the following problem:[ii]

    ♦ There are 12 boys and 8 girls. How many more boys than girls? ♦

    A majority of the children answered "four more boys" correctly, but 5 children chose to add and gave "20 children" as their answer. One of these 5 children insisted that subtraction could not be used because it is impossible to **take away** 8 girls from 12 boys. None of the other children could respond to this child's claim. In light of what you have learned in this section, describe how you would handle this situation if you were the teacher, in order to help this child understand that subtraction is the appropriate operation in this situation. Note that simply telling a student "the right way" does not necessarily help him/her understand.

8. Tell which type of subtraction is indicated in each of these story problems, with an explanation of your choice.

    a.   Villi is running a 10-kilometer marathon. He has run 4.6 kilometers. How far does he have yet to go?

    b.   Diego is saving up for a car. He needs $2000 to buy one from his uncle. Thus far he has $862. How much more does he need?

    c.   Laresa just got paid for the week. She received $200. She owes her mother $185 for some clothes. Once she pays it, what will she have left?

    d.   Laresa's friend works at a different place and is paid $230 a week. How much more does she make per week than Laresa?

    e.   Bo just bought gas for $2.79 per gallon. Last week he bought gas for $2.72. How much more did he pay for gas this week than he did last week?

9. Make up a word problem for each of the two different types of addition situations; make one for the three different types of subtraction situations.

10. Mr. Lewis teaches second grade. He has been using "take-away" problems to illustrate subtraction. A district text contained the following problem:

    ♦ Vanessa's mother lost 23 pounds on a diet last year. Vanessa herself lost 9 pounds on the diet. How many more pounds did Vanessa's mother lose? ♦

    Most of Mr. Lewis's students were unable to work the problem, and he was very discouraged because he had spent so much time teaching subtraction. Do you have any advice for him?

11. For each of the following problems, name the quantities, their values, note the relationships among the values, make a drawing for the problem, then compute the answer.

Notes

EXAMPLE

♦ JJ earned $2.50 an hour for helping a neighbor. JJ worked 5 hours. Then JJ bought a T-shirt for $7.35. How much money did JJ have left?   ♦

SOLUTION

Quantities with values are: Amount JJ earns per hour: $2.50. Number of hours JJ works: 5. Cost of T-shirt: $7.35. Amount of money left after purchase of T-shirt: unknown.

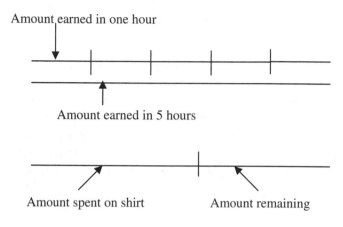

Amount earned in one hour

Amount earned in 5 hours

Amount spent on shirt   Amount remaining

To find the amount earned, I would multiply her wage per hour by the number of hours she worked or add five $2.50s. Then I would subtract the amount she spent on the shirt because that cost is taken away from the total earned.

$2.50 \times 5 - \$7.35 = \$5.15$

a. A post 12 feet long is pounded into the bottom of a river. 2.25 feet of the post are in the ground under the river. 1.5 feet stick out of the water. How deep is the river at that point?

b. At one school $\frac{3}{5}$ of all the eighth graders went to one game. $\frac{2}{3}$ of those who went to the game traveled by car. What part of all the eighth graders traveled by car to the game?

c. A small computer piece is shaped like a rectangle which is 2.5 centimeters long. Its area is 15 square centimeters. How wide is the piece?

d. Maria spends two-thirds of her allowance on school lunches and one-sixth for other food. What fractional part of her allowance is left?

e. On one necklace, $\frac{5}{8}$ of the beads are wooden. There are 40 beads in all on the necklace. How many beads are wooden?

f. A painter mixes a color by using 3.2 times as much red as yellow. How much red should he use with 4.8 pints of yellow?

3.3	**Children's Ways of Adding and Subtracting**

Children who understand place value and have not yet learned a standard way to subtract often have unique ways of undertaking subtraction.[iv] Prepare to be surprised!

Activity 5   Children's Ways

1. Consider the work of nine second-graders, all solving 364 – 79 (in written form, without calculators or base ten blocks).

   Identify:

   a. which students clearly understand what they are doing;

   b. which students might understand what they are doing; and

   c. which students do not understand what they are doing.

2. Pick out places where errors were made, and try to explain why you think the errors occurred.

In Activity 5 the solutions of Students 2, 3, and 5 are all based on the *standard algorithms* that are taught in school. Student 3 correctly uses the "regrouping" algorithm taught in most U.S. schools.

Describe in writing the steps followed when one uses the standard regrouping algorithm for subtraction.

Activity 6   Making Sense of Students' Reasoning

1. Justify, using your knowledge of place value and the meanings of addition and subtraction, the procedure used in Solution 3 of the activity called Children's Ways. Make up some other problems, and talk them through, using the language of "ones, tens, hundreds" etc.

2. Discuss what you think happened in the solutions of Students 2 and 5.

3. The procedure used by the fourth student is called the "equal additions" method. Figure out how this algorithm works, and the mathematical basis for it. Hint: Because 9 cannot be taken from 4, ten was added to both numbers, but in different places.

Sometimes teachers dismiss solutions that do not follow a standard procedure. Yet sometimes these solutions show a great deal of insight and understanding of our base ten numeration system and how numbers can be decomposed in many helpful ways. But there are times that a solution that is "different," such as the equal additions method of subtraction, may not demonstrate any insight. Rather, any procedure can be learned as a sequence of rules. In the United States, subtraction is usually taught by a "regrouping method" (see Student 3's method in Activity 5) but in some other countries children are taught the "equal additions" method (see the work of Student 4). Either can be taught rotely or meaningfully.

Activity 7   Give It a Try

Go back over the solutions of students 1, 6, 7, 8, and 9. Make sure you understand the thinking of each student. You can do this by thinking through each method as you try 438 – 159.

The other students appear to have used "nonstandard algorithms" or "invented algorithms," that is, procedures they have developed on their own, or perhaps as a class, for solving subtraction problems. In Activity 7, you should have thought about place value understanding for each of the methods here.

> ### THINK ABOUT . . .
>
> If you were (or are) a parent, what would you say to your child if he or she subtracted like Student 1? or Student 9? What about Student 4? Have you ever seen this subtraction method before? If so, tell your instructor so that your method might be shared with others.

Discussion 2   Is One Way Better?

Is any one method of subtraction (from the ones illustrated at the beginning of this lesson) better than others? Why or why not? Which methods do you think could be more easily understood? Are there any methods that should not be taught (rather than invented by a student)? Why or why not?

TAKE-AWAY MESSAGE . . . Children do not think about mathematics in the same way that adults do. Part of the reason for this is that adults are more mature and have a wider variety of experiences with numbers. But also part of the reason is that we have had limited opportunities to explore numbers and the meaning of operations on numbers. When children enter school they are often inquisitive and willing to explore in ways that they often lose in later grades, unfortunately. But when children are given numerous opportunities to think about numbers and come to understand the place value system we use, and then apply that understanding in a variety of situations, they often come up with novel ways of approaching problems. The ways they invent for undertaking addition and subtraction are useful to them, and often can be generalized. This knowledge can also help them understand and remember any traditional algorithms they are taught. This has the advantage that they are unlikely to make the common errors that result when place value is not well understood. ♦

Learning Exercises for Section 3.3

1. Make up some new subtraction problems and try solving them by each of the methods illustrated in the activity, Children's Ways. Try inventing some other ways you think a child might approach your subtraction problems.

2. Here are several cases of addition and subtraction problems solved by other first and second graders in classrooms where the standard algorithms were not taught. Some procedures are more sophisticated than others, based on the individual student's understanding of numeration. Some were done mentally; others were written down. Study each method until you understand the thinking of the student, and then do the problem given using the same strategy.

   Case A. Teacher: What is 39 + 37?

   Student 1: 30 and 30 is 60, then 9 more is 69, then 7 more is 70, 71, 72, 73, 74, 75, 76.

   You do: 48 + 59.

   Case B. Teacher: What is 39 + 37?

   Student 2: 40 and 40 is 80, but then you need to take away. First 1, and get 79, then 3, and get 76.

   You do: 48 + 59.

   Case C. Teacher: What is 39 + 37?

   Student 3: 40 and 37 is, let's see, 40 and 30 is 70, and 7 more is 77, but you need to take away 1, so it's 76.

   You do: 48 + 59.

   Case D. A student talks aloud as he solves 246 + 178:

   Student 4: Well, 2 plus 1 is 3, so I know it's 200 and 100, so now it's somewhere in the three hundreds. And then you have to add the tens on. And the tens are 4 and 7. . . .Well, um. If you started at 70; 80, 90, 100. Right? And that's four hundreds. So now you're already in the three hundreds because of this [100 + 200], but now you're in the four hundreds because of that [40 + 70]. But you've still got one more ten. So if you're doing it 300 plus 40 plus 70, you'd have 410. But you're not doing that. So what you need to do then is add 6 more onto 10, which is 16. And then 8 more: 17, 18, 19, 20, 21, 22, 23, 24. And that's 124. I mean 424.[iii]

You do: 254 + 367.

Case E. Teacher: What is 65 – 7?

Student 5: 65 take away 5 is 60, and take away 2 more is 58.

You do: 58 – 9.

Student 6: 65 – 7. 7 and 8 is 15, and 10 is 25, and 10 is 35 and 10 is 45 and 10 is 55 and 10 is 65. Five tens is 50, and 8 is 58. (Uses fingers to count tens.)

You do: 58 – 9.

Case F. Written solution for 654 – 339.

Student 7: 6 take away 3 is 3 and you make it into hundreds so 300. Then you add 50—>350–30 and it comes to 320, +4 is 324, –9 is first –4 is 320 then –5 is 315.

You do: 368 – 132.

Case G: Oral solution for 500 – 268.

Student 8: 2 to get to 270, then 30 more to get to 300, then 200 more, so 232.

You do: 800 – 452.

3. Discuss the procedures used in Exercise 2 in terms of how well you think the student understands the procedure, how long you think it took for the student to develop and understand the process being used; and how robust the procedure is, that is, can it be used on other problems?

4. Discuss the procedures used in Exercise 2 in terms of whether the procedure would be difficult for students to remember. Do you think the student, when faced with another subtraction problem, will be able to use his or her procedure? Why or why not?

5. In many European countries and in Australia, addition and subtraction are taught using an "empty" number line that is not marked with 0 and 1. Here are two examples for addition, with 48 + 39:

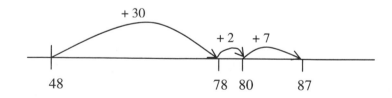

or

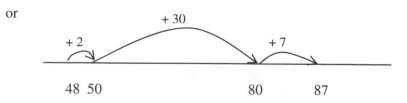

Notes

Subtraction is done similarly. Consider 364 – 79, a problem you saw earlier.

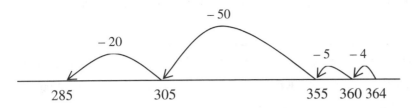

or

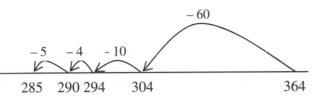

Try the following computations using the empty number line method.

a. 62 + 49   **b.** 304 – 284   **c.** 72 – 38   **d.** 253 – 140

3.4 | Ways of Thinking About Multiplication

Just as there are different ways of thinking about addition and subtraction, depending upon the quantities involved and the type of situation involved, there are different ways of thinking about multiplication and division. Many children learn to think of multiplication *only* as repeated addition, which limits the type of situations in which they know to multiply.

Discussion 3   When Do We Multiply?

How would you solve these two problems?

1. One kind of cheese costs $2.19 a pound. How much will a package weighing 3 pounds cost?

2. One kind of cheese costs $2.19 a pound. How much will a package weighing 0.73 pound cost?

If you even hesitated in deciding to multiply to solve the second problem, you are not alone. Researchers across the world have noticed that success on the second problem is usually 35 to 40% *less* than success on the first problem, even among adults! Many solvers think they should divide or subtract on the second problem. Why does this happen? This section will offer a possible reason: Each of multiplication and division, like addition and subtraction, can represent quite different situations, but solvers may not be aware of this fact.

Just as there are different ways of thinking about subtraction, there are several ways to think about multiplication and division. We begin with different meanings of multiplication.

> When a whole number n of quantities, each with value q, are combined, the resulting quantity has value $q + q + q + \ldots$ (*n* addends), or $n \times q$. This is called the **repeated addition view of multiplication**.

EXAMPLE 10

♦ Karla invited 4 friends to her birthday party. Instead of receiving gifts, she gave each friend a dozen roses. How many roses did she give away?
$4 \times 12 = 12 + 12 + 12 + 12$. ♦

Some critics say that repeated addition receives attention for so long (grade 2 or 3 on) that it restricts children's attention when other situations that use multiplication appear. Nonetheless, this view does build on the children's experience with addition, and it does fit many situations.

Using the notion of repeated addition, 3×4 means the sum of 3 addends, each of which is 4: $3 \times 4 = 4 + 4 + 4$. Notice the order; 3×4 means 3 fours, not 4 threes. At least that is the case in every U.S. text series; the reverse is the case in some other countries (British or British-influenced countries, for example), which can cause confusion. Of course, you know from commutativity of multiplication that $3 \times 4 = 4 \times 3$, but as a teacher, you would want to model the standard meaning, even after the children have had experience with commutativity. In contrast with commutativity of addition, commutativity of multiplication is much less intuitive: It is not obvious ahead of time that 3 eights (3×8) will give the same sum as 8 threes (8×3).

> The numbers being multiplied are called **factors**, and the result is called the **product** (and sometimes a **multiple** of any factor). The first factor is sometimes referred to as the **multiplier**, and the second the **multiplicand**. In some contexts, **divisor** is used as a synonym for factor, except divisors are not allowed to be 0 (but factors may be).

Note that under the repeated-addition view of multiplication, the first factor must be a whole number. Under this view, 2.3×6 cannot be interpreted; it is meaningless to speak of the sum of 2.3 addends. However, the commutative property of multiplication (which children should know by the time they are solving problems with decimal numbers) tells us that 2.3×6 is the same as 6×2.3. Overall, any story situation in which a quantity of any sort is repeatedly combined could be described by multiplication. 6×2.3 could be used, for example, for "How much would 6 boxes of that dog treat weigh? Each box weighs 2.3 pounds."

> **THINK ABOUT . . .**
>
> Read again the cheese problems in Discussion 3. Does the idea of multiplication as repeated addition fit both problems?

An emphasis on multiplication only as repeated addition to the exclusion of other interpretations of multiplication appears to lead many children into the unstated and dangerous over-generalization that the product is always larger than the factors, expressed as: *Multiplication always makes bigger.*

> **THINK ABOUT . . .**
>
> When does multiplication NOT "make bigger"?

A second type of situation calling for multiplication is a rectangular array with n items across and m items down, for a total of $m \times n$ items. Or we could generate a rectangle of n squares across and m squares down for a total of $m \times n$ squares. (This is, of course, what we use to find the area of a rectangle.)

> The **array (or area) model of multiplication** occurs in cases that can be modeled as a rectangle n units across and m units down. The **product** is $m \times n$.

Note: When the factors are represented by letters, we often use a dot or drop the multiplication symbol: $m \times n = m \cdot n = mn$.

If n and m are whole numbers, this could be considered a special case of repeated addition. One attraction of this model is that for continuous quantities the n and the m do not have to be whole numbers. Another feature of this model is that commutativity of multiplication is easily seen: Length times width (or number of rows times number in each column) is just reversed if the array or rectangle is turned sideways.

> **THINK ABOUT . . .**
>
> Draw a rectangle that is $3\frac{1}{2}$ inches across and $2\frac{1}{4}$ inches high. What is the total number of square inches shown? Find the answer first by counting square inches and parts of square inches, and then by multiplying. Did you get the same answer?

There is a third way to think about multiplication.

> The **fractional part of a quantity model** of multiplication occurs when we need to find a fractional part of one of the two quantities. This is sometimes referred to as the **operator view of multiplication**.

With this model we can attach a meaning to products such as $\frac{2}{3} \times 17$ (pounds, say), meaning two-thirds *of* 17 pounds, or to a product of 0.35×8.2 (kilograms), meaning thirty-five hundredths *of* eight and two-tenths kilograms.

> ### THINK ABOUT . . .
>
> Suppose you are dealing with cookies. How could you "act out" $6 \times \frac{1}{2}$? How could you "act out" $\frac{1}{2} \times 6$? How are these different? Do you get the same answer for both? What is the "unit" or the "whole" for the $\frac{1}{2}$ in each case?

You should have said that the unit or whole for the $\frac{a}{b}$ in the second situation, $\frac{1}{2} \times 6$, is the amount represented by the second factor, 6 cookies. We want one-half of *six cookies*. The reason this is referred to as the operator view is because the $\frac{a}{b}$ acts on, or operates on, the amount represented by the second factor. The operator view will be treated in more detail later, but you now have the background to consider the following question.

> ### THINK ABOUT . . .
>
> Using the part-of-an-amount way of thinking about multiplication by a fraction, tell what 0.4×8 or 0.7×0.9 might mean. Does that help you locate the decimal point in the 0.4×8 (= 3.2) and 0.7×0.9 (= 0.63) products?

> ### THINK ABOUT . . .
>
> If you buy 5.3 pounds of cheese costing \$4.20 per pound, could this be represented as a repeated addition problem?

> ### THINK ABOUT . . .
>
> What is meant by 5.3×4.20, as in finding the cost of buying 5.3 pounds of meat at \$4.20 a pound?

There are other situations in which ordered "combinations" of objects, rather than sums of objects themselves, are being counted and which can be described by multiplication. This fourth type of situation uses what is commonly called the **fundamental counting principle**. These situations show that, mathematically at least, multiplication need not refer to addition at all. The next activity leads to a statement of that principle.

Activity 8   Finding All Orders with No Repeats Allowed

You hear that Ed, Fred, Guy, Ham, Ira, and Jose ran a race. You know there were no ties, but you do not know who was first, second, and third. In how many ways could the first three places in the race have turned out?

If you were successful in identifying all 120 possible orders for the first three finishers, you no doubt used some sort of systematic method in keeping track of the different possible outcomes. One method which you may encounter in elementary school books is the use of a tree diagram. Here is an example, for a setting that is often used in elementary books:

♦ You have 3 blouses and 2 pairs of pants in your suitcase, all color-compatible. How many different blouse-pants outfits do you have? ♦

At the start, you have two choices to make—a choice of blouse, and a choice of pants. A **tree diagram** records these choices this way:

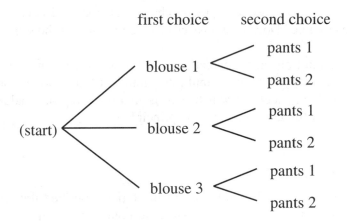

Notice that after a blouse is chosen, both possibilities for the choice of pants make the next "branches" of the tree. You make a choice by going through the tree. For example, blouse 1 and pants 2 would be one choice. You make all possible choices by going through the tree in all possible ways. Do you find 6 different outfits? What would the tree diagram look like if you chose pants first? Would there be 6 choices then also?

With a situation as complicated as the 6-racers problem in Activity 8, making a tree diagram is quite laborious (try it). Although it is good experience to make tree diagrams, there is an alternative. Notice that in the outfits example, the first act, choosing a blouse, could be done in 3 ways and then the second act, choosing pants, could be done in 2 ways, no matter what the choice of blouse was. And, $3 \times 2 = 6$, the number of possible outfits. Situations which can be thought of as a sequence of acts, with a number of ways for each act to occur, can be counted efficiently by this principle:

> In a case where two acts can be performed, if Act 1 can be performed in m ways, and Act 2 can be performed in n ways no matter how Act 1 turns out, then the sequence Act 1-Act 2 can be performed in $m \cdot n$ ways. This is the **fundamental counting principle view of multiplication**.

The principle can be extended to any number of acts. For example, the racers problem has three "acts": finishing first (6 possibilities), finishing second (5 possibilities after someone finished first), and finishing third (now 4 possibilities). The number of possible first-second-third outcomes to the race can then be calculated by the fundamental counting principle: $6 \times 5 \times 4$, or 120, without having to make a tree diagram. Notice that here the unit for the end result is different from any unit represented in the factors. (As an aside, notice also that the tree diagram here is not the same as the "factor tree" that you may remember from elementary school.)

> *THINK ABOUT . . .*
>
> At an ice cream shop, a double-decker ice cream cone can be ordered from two choices of cones, 12 choices for the first dip, 12 for the second dip, and 8 kinds of toppings. How many choices of double-decker ice cream cones are possible? Does your answer include two dips of the same flavor?

A later section on multiplicative comparisons (not additive comparisons) will give a fifth important way of thinking about multiplication. Until then, when you use multiplication for a problem, identify which way is involved: repeated addition, array, part-of-a-quantity, or fundamental counting principle.

Activity 9   Merrily We Multiply

Devise a multiplication problem for each of the types described thus far: repeated addition, array, part-of-a-quantity, or fundamental counting principle. If you do this in pairs or groups, compare your problem situations with those of a neighboring group.

Earlier we referred to the **commutative** property of multiplication, that is, for any numbers m and n, $mn = nm$. This property tells us we can treat either m or n as the multiplier. You should also remember the **associative** property of multiplication, that is, for numbers p, q, and r, $(pq)r = p(qr)$. This property tells us that when multiplying, we do not need parentheses, because it does not matter which product we find first.

EXAMPLE 11

$$(3 \times 2) \times 8 = 3 \times (2 \times 8) \text{ or } 6 \times 8 = 3 \times 16$$

Thus we could write the product as $3 \times 2 \times 8$. Parentheses tell us which operation to do first, but the associative property tells us that when multiplying, it does not matter which multiplication we do first.

The **distributive property of multiplication over addition** (often just shortened to *the distributive property*) is a particularly useful property: for numbers c, d, and e, $c(d + e) = cd + ce$.

Notes

EXAMPLE 12

Here is an illustration of this property, showing that $2 \times (4 + 3) = (2 \times 4) + (2 \times 3)$. (The right side could have been written without parentheses because in a string of operations, all multiplication must be done before addition.)

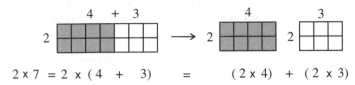

$$2 \times 7 = 2 \times (4 + 3) \quad = \quad (2 \times 4) + (2 \times 3)$$

Learners often wonder, in the symbolic form, where the other 2 came from. The drawing shows it was there all the time.

TAKE-AWAY MESSAGE . . . Problem situations that call for multiplication can be categorized in different ways, including the following:

1. Finding the sum when a whole number of like quantities is combined is called the repeated addition view of multiplication. In the United States, finding mn means $n + n + n \ldots$ with n as an addend m times. Using this form consistently makes understanding easier at first. Later, when commutativity is understood, students recognize that the addend and the number of addends could be reversed.

2. Finding the area of a rectangle or the number associated with a rectangular array, is called the array (or area) model of multiplication. This view highlights commutativity of multiplication and the distributive property of multiplication over addition.

3. Finding the fractional part of a quantity is sometimes called the operator view of multiplication because it appears that the multiplier is "operating" on the multiplicand. This third type of situation can involve a product that is smaller than one or both of the factors, which causes difficulty for students who have only thought about multiplication as repeated addition. The misconception that "multiplication makes bigger" is common and needs to be countered during instruction.

4. In situations where finding the number of ways in which one act follows another, the fundamental counting principle view of multiplication applies. Tree diagrams help to illustrate this principle. ♦

Learning Exercises for Section 3.4

1. **a.** Make sketches for 6×2 and for 2×6 and contrast them.

    b. Make sketches for $5 \times \frac{1}{2}$ and for $\frac{1}{2} \times 5$ and contrast them.

    c. Make a systematic list of possible names for this problem:

    ♦ Janice is ordering ice cream. There are 5 kinds available: vanilla, strawberry, chocolate, mocha, and butter pecan. There are also five kinds of sprinkles to put on top: M&Ms, coconut, Heath bar pieces, chocolate chips, and walnut bits. If she orders one scoop of ice cream and one kind of sprinkles, how many choices does she have? ♦

Notes

2. A teacher quite often has to make up a story problem on the spot. For *each* view of multiplication, make up *TWO* story problems that you think children would find interesting. Label them for later reference (e.g., array model). Use a variety of sizes of numbers. You might want to share yours with others.

3. Will multiplying a whole number (>1) by *any* fraction always result in a product smaller than the whole number we started with? When *does* multiplication make bigger?

4. Does repeated-addition make sense for $4 \times {}^-2$? For ${}^-2 \times 4$? For $8 \times \frac{2}{3}$?

   For $\frac{2}{3} \times 8$? Explain your thinking for each case.

5. In terms of repeated addition and/or part-of-an-amount, what does $6\frac{1}{2} \times 12$

   mean? (Here is a context which may be helpful: $6\frac{1}{2}$ dozen eggs.)

6. For each, make up a story problem which could be solved by the given calculation.

   a. 32×29 **b.** 4×6.98 **c.** 0.07×19.95

   d. $12 \times \frac{3}{8}$, about pizza   **e.** $\frac{2}{3} \times 6$, about pizza   **f.** $40\% \times 29.95$

7. Here are the ingredients in a recipe that serves 6:

   6 skinned chicken breast halves   1 tablespoon margarine

   1 cup sliced onion $1\frac{1}{2}$ cups apple juice

   1 tablespoon olive oil $2\frac{1}{2}$ tablespoons honey

   2 cups sliced tart apples $\frac{1}{2}$ teaspoon salt

   a. You want enough for 8 people. What amounts should you use?

   b. You want enough for 4 people (and no leftovers). What amounts should you use?

8. The fact that $m \times n$ and $n \times m$ are equal is a very useful idea for, say, learning the basic multiplication facts. For example, if you know that $6 \times 9 = 54$, then you automatically know that $9 \times 6 = 54 \ldots$ if you believe that $m \times n = n \times m$. Text series may use the array model to illustrate this idea. An array for 3×5 would have 3 rows with 5 in each row (rows go sideways in almost every text series, and in advanced mathematics).

A 3 × 5 array   With a quarter-turn,
of square regions   becomes a 5 × 3 array

Since the two arrays are made up of the same squares, even without counting you know that $3 \times 5 = 5 \times 3$.

a. Make an array for 4×7 and turn the paper it is on $90°$. What does the new array show?

b. Use a piece of graph paper to show that $12 \times 15 = 15 \times 12$.

c. Show how this idea works in verifying that $6 \times \frac{1}{2} = \frac{1}{2} \times 6$.

9. a. Show with a drawing that $5 \times (6 + 2) = 5 \times 6 + 5 \times 2$. What is the name of this property?

b. How could you illustrate, without a drawing, the associative property of multiplication? [*Hint:* $(a \times b) \times c = a \times (b \times c)$]

c. Show with a drawing that $3 \times 6.5 = 6.5 \times 3$.

10. Make a tree diagram or a systematic list for three of these, and check that the fundamental counting principle gives the same answer. Tell how many you found.

a. You flip a spinner that has four differently-colored regions (red, white, blue, green) all equal in area, and toss one die and count the dots on top (1 through 6 possible). How many color-dot outcomes are possible?

b. A couple is thinking of a name for their baby girl. They have thought of 3 acceptable first names and 4 acceptable middle names (all different). How many baby girls could they have without repeating the whole name!?

c. In a sixth-grade election, Raoul, Silvia, Tien, Vena, and Wally are running for president; Angela and Ben are running for vice-president; and Cara and Von are running for treasurer. In how many ways could the election come out?

d. In a game you toss a red die and a green die, and count the number of dots on top of each one, for example, R2, G3. (The numbers of dots are *not* added in this game.) In how many different ways can a toss of the dice turn out?

11. A hamburger chain advertised that they made 256 different kinds of hamburgers. Explain how this claim is possible. [*Hint:* One can choose 1 patty or 2, mustard or not, etc.]

12. An ice-cream store has 31 kinds of ice cream and 2 kinds of cones.

a. How many different kinds of single-scoop ice-cream cones can be ordered at the store?

b. How many different kinds of double-scoop ice-cream cones are there? (Decision: Is vanilla on top of chocolate the same as chocolate on top of vanilla?)

13. You have become a car dealer! One kind of car you will sell comes in 3 body styles, 4 colors, and 3 interior-accessory "packages," and costs you, on average, $12,486. If you wanted to keep on your lot an example of *each* type of car (style with color with package) that a person could buy, how much money would this part of your inventory represent?

14. License plate numbers come in a variety of styles.

a. Why might a style using 2 letters followed by 4 digits be better than a 6-digits style?

b. How many more are there with a style using 2 letters followed by 4 digits than the 6-digits style? How many times as large is the number of license plates possible with a style using 2 letters followed by 4 digits as is the number possible with a 6-digits style? (Ignore the fact that some choices of letters could not be used because they would suggest inappropriate words or phrases.)

c. Design a style for license plate numbering for your state. Explain why you chose that style.

15. Locate the decimal points in the products by thinking about the part-of-an-amount meaning for multiplication. Insert zeros in the product, if needed.

a. $0.6 \times 128.5 = $ 7 7 7 (Where does the decimal point go?)

b. $0.8 \times 0.95 = $ 7 6

c. $0.75 \times 23.8 = $ 1 7 8 5

d. $0.04 \times 36.5 = $ 1 4 6

e. $0.328 \times 0.455 = $ 1 4 9 2 4

f. $0.65 \times 0.1388 = $ 9 0 2 2

3.5 | Ways of Thinking About Division

Next we turn to division. There are two common types of situations that call for division, and they both appear in virtually every curriculum. A third view, which you may recognize from your earlier coursework, is more encompassing and mathematically includes the first two views. Under any of these views, this vocabulary applies:

> In a division situation that can be described by $a \div b = q$, the a is called the
>
> **dividend**, b is called the **divisor**, and q is called the **quotient**. In a division
>
> situation in which b is not a factor of a, the situation can be described as $a \div b$
>
> $= q + \frac{r}{b}$, the quotient is $q + \frac{r}{b}$, and the quantity r is called the **remainder**. This
>
> situation is also written as $a \div b = q$ remainder r. Note that the divisor can never
>
> be 0.

EXAMPLE 13

In $28 \div 4 = 7$, 28 is the dividend, 4 is the divisor, and 7 is the quotient. In the usual U.S. calculation form, $divisor\overline{)dividend}$, the quotient is written on top of the dividend. There may also be a remainder, as in $13 \div 4 = 3$ R 1, or $3\frac{1}{4}$. Division calculations that have a remainder of 0 are informally said to "come out even."

One basic view of the division $a \div b$ is called the **measurement view**. This follows from the question, "How many measures of b are in a?" Because the answer can often be found by repeatedly subtracting b from a, this view of division is also sometimes referred to as the **repeated-subtraction view** of division. This view is also called the **quotitive view** of division.

You will find that different textbooks use different terms.

EXAMPLE 14

When asked what $12 \div 4$ means, one would say it means "How many 4s are there in 12" or "How many measures or counts of 4 are in 12" and the answer can be obtained by repeatedly subtracting 4 until the 12 are gone, resulting in a quotient of 3. When asked what $13 \div 4$ means, we can repeatedly subtract 4 three times again, resulting in a partial quotient of 3, but this time there is a remainder, 1, because it was not possible to again subtract 4.

THINK ABOUT . . .

What is meant by $\frac{3}{4} \div \frac{1}{2}$, using the measurement view? How can one think of using repeated subtraction to find the quotient? What is meant by $0.6 \div 0.05$?

Using the measurement view of division one could ask, "How many measures of $\frac{1}{2}$ are in $\frac{3}{4}$?"

THINK ABOUT . . .

Suppose a child has this problem situation: "Danesse has 3 friends. She has 12 cookies to share with them. How many cookies does each of the four people get?" How do you suppose a child who does not yet understand division might model this situation?

Another basic view of division is **sharing equally**. When one quantity (the dividend) is shared by a number of objects (the divisor), the quantity associated with each object is the quotient. This sharing notion of division is also called **partitive division**.

EXAMPLE 15

Danesse probably shared her cookies by saying one for you, one for you, etc. Thus the 12 cookies are shared equally by four people, and each gets three cookies. Or, you might say that the 12 cookies have been partitioned into four sets of the same size.

Activity 10   Highway Repair

Are these two problems the same? Which view of division is represented in each? Would you make the same drawing for each?

1. The highway crew has several miles of highway to repair. Past experience suggests that they can repair 2.5 miles in a day. How many days will it take them to repair the stretch of highway?

2. The highway crew has the same stretch of highway to repair. But they must do it in 2.5 days. How many miles will they have to repair each day to finish the job on time?

Discussion 4   Practicing the Meanings

Tell what the following could mean with each view of division.

1. $85 \div 7$

2. $22.5 \div 2$

3. $\frac{7}{8} \div \frac{1}{8}$ (repeated subtraction view only)

4. $1.08 \div 0.4$ (repeated subtraction view only)

A more general way of thinking about division is the **missing-factor view of division** in which a question is asked about a missing factor that, when multiplied by the divisor, would result in the dividend. That factor is the quotient.

EXAMPLE 16

$12 \div 4 = n$ would be associated with $n \times 4 = 12$ (with repeated subtraction in mind) or $4 \times n = 12$ (with sharing in mind). Indeed, the common way to check a division calculation is to calculate divisor $\times$ quotient, and see whether the product is the dividend.

A missing-factor view could replace the earlier two views of division, once they are understood. Because our emphasis is on mathematics for the elementary school, our attention will center on the repeated subtraction and sharing views. Keep them in mind.

Discussion 5   Dividing by Zero

"You can't divide by 0." An elementary school teacher should know why this is not the case. Perhaps the easiest way to think about the issue is to think of checking a division calculation: the related multiplication, divisor $\times$ quotient, should equal the dividend. So $12 \div 4 = 3$ is true because $3 \times 4 = 12$. Do the following:

1. "Check" $5 \div 0 = n$. What number, if any, checks?

2. "Check" $0 \div 0 = n$. What number, if any, checks?

3. A child says, "Wait! Last year my teacher said, 'Any number divided by itself is 1.' So isn't $0 \div 0 = 1$?" What do you reply?

Thus, either *no* number checks (as in $5 \div 0$) or *every* number checks (as in $0 \div 0$) when dividing by zero. Either is clearly a good reason to say that division by zero is undefined, or "You can't divide by zero."

TAKE-AWAY MESSAGE . . . Just as with other operations, there are different contexts that can be described by division:

1. Finding the number of times a particular value can be repeatedly subtracted from another value. This view of division has different labels: repeated subtraction division, measurement meaning of division, and quotitive meaning of division.

2. Finding the number in each share if a quantity is shared equally by a number of objects. This view of division is called sharing equally division, or partitive division.

3. Finding the missing factor that, when multiplied by another known factor, would result in a known product. This view of division is called the missing-factor view of division. Mathematically, this view can encompass the first two views, but we depend on the first two views when helping children to understand division.

4. When one value (the dividend) is divided by another (the divisor, which cannot be 0), the result is a value called the quotient. In situations where the quotient must be expressed as a whole number, there is sometimes a value remaining, called the remainder.

5. For good reasons, division by zero is undefined. That is, one cannot divide by zero. ♦

Learning Exercises for Section 3.5

1. For the repeated-subtraction (also called measurement or quotitive) view of division, make up *TWO* story problems that you think children would find interesting. Do the same for the sharing (partitive) view of division.

2. Illustrate $12 \div 3$ with drawings of counters using the repeated-subtraction view and then the sharing view. Notice how the drawings differ.

3. Write story problems that could lead to the following equations.
   a. $150 \div 12 = n$ (partitive)
   b. $150 \div 12 = n$ (repeated-subtraction)
   c. $3 \div 4 = n$ (partitive)
   d. $3 \div 4 = n$ (repeated-subtraction)

4. After years of working with division involving whole numbers, children often form the erroneous generalization, *division makes smaller.* Give a division problem which shows that division does not always make smaller.

5. Consider the following situation:

◆ Mount Azteca is 1.3 km high. There are 3 different trails from the starting place at the bottom to the top of the mountain. One trail is 4.5 km long, another is 3.5 km long, and the most difficult is 2.4 km long. ◆

For each computation indicated below, finish the story problem started above so that your problem could lead to the computation described. As always, it may be helpful to make a drawing of the situation and think about the quantities involved.

a. 3×2.4

b. $(4.5 + 3.5) - (2 \times 2.4)$

c. $4.5 \div 3$ (partitive)

d. $4.5 \div 3$ (repeated subtraction)

e. $10 \div 2.4$

6. a. A national test once used a question like "The bus company knows that after a ball game, 1500 people will want to catch a bus back to the main bus terminal. Each bus can hold 36 people. How many buses should the company have ready?" What is your answer to the question?

b. There will be 300 children singing in a district songfest. Each singer gets a sash. Sashes come in boxes of 8. Calculate $300 \div 8$, and then answer the following from your calculation.

1. How many boxes of sashes should the district order?

2. If the district orders only 37 boxes, how many children would not get a sash?

7. Analyze the quantities in this setting to generate some questions you can answer:

◆ One company plans to open 505 acres around an old gold-mining site and to process the ground chemically. The company hopes to extract 636,000 ounces of gold from 48 million tons of ore and waste rock, over a $6\frac{1}{2}$-year period. The company expects to get about $200 million for the gold. ◆

8. The six problems below were taken from elementary school mathematics textbooks. Discuss the meaning or interpretation of division in each problem and explain how you would help students visualize the action in the problem and connect it to a meaning of division. Identify the quantities in each and tell how to use them to draw a diagram for each problem.

a. The park bought 900 kg of seal food. The food comes in boxes of 12 kg each. How many boxes did the park buy? (Fourth grade)

b. The dolphins ate 525 kg of food in 3 weeks. What is the average number of kilograms of food they ate each day? (Fourth grade)

c. A salesperson drove about 34,500 km in 46 weeks. What was the average distance the salesperson drove each week? (Fifth grade)

d. The art teacher has 128 straws in the supply room. Each student needs 16 straws for an art project. How many students can do the art project? (Fifth grade)

e. A strange coincidence. Six hens each weighs the same. Their total weight is 35 lbs. How much does each hen weigh? (Sixth grade)

f. It takes 1 minute to make a gadget. How many gadgets can be made in 14 minutes? (Sixth grade)

9. What is $24 \div 3$? $240 \div 30$? $2400 \div 300$? $24,000 \div 3000$? $2.4 \div 0.3$? Formulate a rule for finding quotients such as these.

10. **Reflect on:** If you were not taught by a teacher who clarified the meanings of operations, how did this affect your ability to solve, and develop an attitude toward, story problems?

| 3.6 | **Children Find Products and Quotients** |

When students can analyze situations that involve finding a product or a quotient, they might use novel methods for computing, perhaps not even realizing that they are multiplying or dividing. In this section you will see a variety of ways that children think about multiplication and division problems.

Discussion 6   Indian River Oranges

In a third-grade classroom the focus had been on understanding problem situations and the children knew that multiplication can be thought of as repeated addition. They were working on this problem.^{v}

♦ Every Christmas my father gets big boxes of fruit, like Indian River oranges, from his company. We get so many pieces of fruit that we have to give some away. This year we ended up making 24 grocery bags of fruit with 16 pieces in each bag. How many pieces did we bag altogether? ♦

Discuss what you think each child was thinking about in each case below.

Student 1

$20 \times 10 = 200$
$20 \times 6 = \underline{120}$
$\qquad 320$

$4 \times 10 = 40$
$4 \times 6 = \underline{24}$
$\qquad 64$
$\qquad \underline{320}$
$\qquad 384$

Student 2

(continued
24 times)

Student 3

80
$\underline{16}$
96

96
$\underline{96}$
192
$\underline{192}$
384

Student 4

$16 \times 12 = 10 \times 12 = 120$
$\qquad\qquad\quad 6 \times 12 = \underline{\ 72}$
$\qquad\qquad\qquad\qquad\quad 192$
$\qquad\qquad\qquad\qquad\quad \underline{192}$
$\qquad\qquad\qquad\qquad\quad 384$

(Note: Student 2 actually wrote the number 16 twenty-four times.)

Discussion 7   What Were They Thinking?

1. Justify, using your knowledge of place value and multiplication, *each* of the methods used in Discussion 6.

2. Discuss the relative clarity and the relative efficiency of the four methods.

3. Another child (Student 5) was asked to find 54×62 and wrote: "First I did 50×60 wich (*sic*) came to 3000. Then I did 60×4 and then I added it on to 3000 wich (*sic*) came to 3240. Then I did 50×2 which came to 100 and this I added it on to the 3240 which came to 3340 then I did 4×2 which came to eight and that's how it came to 3348." Work through this thinking to see whether it is correct.

Discussion 8   Thinking About Division

Here is some children's work[vi] on what we typically regard as division problems. None of these children had learned the standard division algorithm but coped quite well without it. You are to study each method and tell what you think each child is thinking. The first child was about 7 years old and had not learned about division, but he knew how to multiply using the calculator. The second child, also about 7, knew simple division facts and used them to his advantage. Note the way he deals with remainders.

Student 1

How many cups containing 160 ml are in 2200 ml?

$10 \times 160 = 1600$

$13 \times 160 = 2080$

$14 \times 160 = 2240$

So 13 cups, 120 ml left over.

Student 2

What is 78 divided by 3?

$20 + 20 + 20 = 60$

$8 \div 3 = 2 \text{ R } 2$

$10 \div 3 = 3 \text{ R } 1$

$2 + 1 = 3$

$3 \div 3 = 1$

So $78 \div 3 = 26$

The next two solutions were from children in fourth grade who had been solving problems requiring division. The teacher had not yet taught them a particular method for dividing. However, they knew that division could be thought of as repeated subtraction. $12 \div 3$ could be found by asking how many times 3 could be subtracted from 12; the answer is 4 times.

Student 3

$$280 \div 35$$

$$
\begin{array}{r}
280 \\
-70 \\
\hline
210 \\
-70 \\
\hline
140 \\
-70 \\
\hline
70 \\
-70 \\
\hline
0
\end{array}
$$

So four 70s is eight 35s.

Student 4

$$
\begin{array}{r}
27\overline{)3247}
\end{array}
$$

2700	100
547	
270	10
277	
270	10
7	120

So $3247 \div 27 = 120 \text{ R } 7$.

The fourth way is the Greenwood or "scaffold" algorithm, dating back to the seventeenth century.

The next child was in first grade and knew a few simple division and multiplication facts. Hc also knew what division meant, and in his head he made up a story that he explained after he had given the method that appears here.[vii]

Student 5

What's 42 ÷ 7? Well, 40 divided by 10 is 4, and 3 times 4 is 12, and 12 and 2 is 14, and 14 divided by 7 is 2, and 2 plus 4 is 6, so it's 6.

Do you understand the thinking of each student? (The last one may be difficult.) What knowledge of place value did these students have?

_____

TAKE-AWAY MESSAGE . . . When young children can work problems such as "Amelia has 6 vases and 24 roses. She wants to put the same number of roses in each vase. How many roses will she put in each vase?" or "Amelia has 24 roses and some vases. If she wants to place 4 roses in each vase, how many vases will she need?," they are doing division. They may find the quotient in each case by acting it out. As the numbers in each situation become larger, the methods they use may seem more complex because we find it more difficult to follow their reasoning. In actuality, they are using one of the three different views of division to solve each problem. They deal with the situation at hand, solving the problem in a sense-making manner. Student-devised methods may help them to later develop and understand algorithms for finding quotients. ♦

Learning Exercises for Section 3.6

Exercises 1 through 5 refer to the children's work in Discussion 8.

1. How is the first student's method related to estimating?

2. The second student shows remarkable facility in dealing with remainders. Try this method yourself on 56 divided by 4.

3. Student 3 solved the division problem by repeatedly subtracting. What are advantages and disadvantages of this method?

4. Student 4's method of dividing is sometimes called the *scaffolding* method, and in some schools it is taught as a first algorithm for doing division. Compare it to the standard division algorithm in terms of advantages and disadvantages.

5. Student 5's method for dividing is perhaps the most difficult one to understand. Suppose you start by telling yourself you have 42 candies to share among 7 people, and since you don't know how many each person should get, you begin with 10 piles. When you have figured this method out, try it on 63 ÷ 9.

6. The problem given on the next page was written by a third grader who was challenged by her father to make up some story problems for him to solve. How much of the information given is used to solve the problem? What would you ask this child about this problem (in addition to: Where did you learn the word "heedless?")?

Notes

♦ Alicia was a heedless breaker, and she broke 24 lamps in one week. Her parents paid $7.00 for every light-bulb she cracked to replace it. Her parents only paid for 5 bulbs in a week, like Monday–Friday. How much money did her parents pay for one week, not counting the week-end? ♦

3.7 Issues for Learning: Developing Number Sense

The idea of developing number sense in the elementary grades is a crucial one. Too often, when focusing just on answers rather than on both reasoning and answers, children do not try to make sense of mathematics as shown by contrasting the two elementary classrooms described by Howden.[viii] She asked students in one first-grade classroom in a very transient neighborhood to tell what came to mind when she said twenty-four. The children immediately gave a variety of answers: two dimes and four pennies, two dozen eggs, four nickels and four pennies, take a penny away from a quarter, the day before Christmas, my mother was 24 last year, when the hand (on a grocery scale hanging in the room) is almost in the middle of twenty and thirty. When she asked this question in a third-grade classroom in a professional community, 24 was just a number that is written in a certain way, that appears on a calendar or on a digital watch. Howden claimed the students in the first-grade class had more *number sense*. She said:

> Number sense can be described as a good intuition about numbers and their relationships. It develops gradually as a result of exploring numbers, visualizing them in a variety of contexts, and relating them in ways that are not limited by traditional algorithms. Since textbooks are limited to paper-and-pencil orientation, they can only suggest ideas to be investigated, they cannot replace the "doing of mathematics" that is essential for the development of number sense. No substitute exists for a skillful teacher and an environment that fosters curiosity and exploration at all grade levels (p. 11).

There has been a great deal written about number sense in the past two decades. Educators have come to realize that developing good number sense is an important goal in the elementary school. In fact, an important document from the National Research Council,[ix] called *Everybody Counts,* contains the statement: "The major objective of elementary school mathematics should be to develop number sense. Like common sense, number sense produces good and useful results with the least amount of effort" (p. 46).

Research has shown that children come to school with a good deal of intuitive understanding, but that for many this understanding is eroded by instruction that focuses on symbolism and does not build on intuitive knowledge. Many educators now recognize that we can introduce symbols too soon and that students need to build an understanding of a mathematical phenomenon before we attempt to symbolize it.

Unfortunately, many teachers believe that while an emphasis on understanding is good for some students, others, particularly those in inner-city schools and in remedial programs, need a more rigid approach to mathematics. Yet a very large research study[x] of academic instruction for disadvantaged elementary school students showed that mathematics instruction that focused on understanding was highly beneficial to the students. "By comparison with conventional programs, instruction that emphasizes meaning and understanding is more effective at inculcating advanced skills, is at least as effective at teaching basic skills, and engages children more extensively in academic learning" (p. i).

Number sense is a way of thinking about numbers and their uses, and it has to permeate all of mathematics teaching if mathematics is to make sense to students. It develops gradually, over time. All of the instruction in these pages focuses on helping you develop number sense and recognize it when it occurs. For example, mental computation and computational estimation both build on number sense and continue to develop it. The examples of children's methods of operating on numbers demonstrate, in most cases, a good deal of number sense on the part of the students.

TAKE-AWAY MESSAGE . . . Students exhibit good number sense when they can find ways to tackle problems, such as subtraction, multiplication, and division, even though they have not been taught procedures to solve these types of problems. Teachers must have good number sense if they are going to be successful in helping their students develop it. Do *you* have good number sense? Do you think you are developing better number sense? ◆

Learning Exercises for Section 3.7

The first five Learning Exercises will, like the earlier children's work, give you a better idea of what number sense means.

1. In each pair, choose the larger. Explain your reasoning (and use number sense rather than calculating).

    a. $135 + 98$, or $114 + 92$ **b.** $46 - 19$, or $46 - 17$

    c. $\frac{1}{2} + \frac{3}{4}$, or $1\frac{1}{2}$ **d.** 0.0358, or $0.0016 + 0.313$

2. Is 46×91 more, or less, than 5000? Is it more, or less, than 3600? Explain.

3. Suppose you may round only one of the numbers in 32×83. Which one would you choose, 32 or 83, to get closer to the exact answer? Explain with a drawing.

Notes

4. Without computing exact answers, explain why each of the following is incorrect.

	a.		b.		c. $27 \times 3 = 621$

a.		b.
	310	119
	520	46
	630	137
	150	940
+	470	+ 300
	2081	602

     c. $27 \times 3 = 621$

     d. $36 \div 0.5 = 18$

5. Suppose that the sum of 5 two-digit whole numbers is less than 100. Decide whether each of the following must be true, false, or may be true. Explain your answers.

 a. Each number is less than 20.

 b. One number is greater than 60.

 c. Four of the numbers are greater than 20, and one is less than 20.

 d. If two are less than 20, at least one is greater than 20.

 e. If all five are different, then their sum is greater than or equal to 60.

6. Look for *compatible numbers* to estimate these:

 a. $36 + 47 + 52 + 18 + 69$ b. 39×42

 c. $1268 - 927$ d. $34{,}678 \div 49$

 e. $19 + 26 + 79 + 12 + 74$ f. $4367 \div 73$

7. a. A quick estimate of $56 \div 9.35$ is 5.6, from $56 \div 10$. A better estimate would adjust the 5.6 up. Explain why, using a meaning for division.

 b. A quick estimate of $715 \div 10.2146$ is 71.5. A better estimate would adjust the 71.5 down. Explain why, using a meaning for division.

8. Consider 150.68×5.34. In estimating the product by calculating 150×5, one has ignored the decimal part of each number. In refining the estimate, which decimal part (the 0.68 or the 0.34) should be the focus? Explain.

9. In multiplying decimals by the usual algorithm, the decimal points do not need to be aligned (in contrast to the usual ways of adding and subtracting decimals). Why not?

3.8 | Check Yourself

This very full chapter focused on how children can come to understand the four arithmetic operations on whole numbers. As teachers, either now or in the future, you need to be able to reason through a child's solution that is different from one you may have seen before. Of course, this cannot always be done quickly, but children should not be told their work is incorrect when it is not. Sometimes a student has

Notes

a unique and wonderful way of using knowledge of number structure to find a solution—such a child has good number sense. At other times the answers are wrong because of a lack of understanding of the underlying place value structure of the numbers.

You should be able to work problems like those assigned and to meet the following objectives.

1. Identify the operations and the view of that operation that fits a problem situation involving any of the four operations.

2. Write story problems that correctly illustrate any specified view of an operation; for example, write a story problem with the missing addend view of subtraction.

3. Provide reasons why some views of operations are more difficult than others.

4. Explain why using "key words" is not a good strategy for answering story problems (see Section 3.2, Learning Exercises).

5. Study students' arithmetic procedures and explain how the students are reasoning.

6. Describe why, in many countries, the empty number line is a popular way of beginning addition and subtraction of multiple digit numbers.

7. Describe how you would explain to someone that "multiplication makes bigger" is not always true.

8. Describe what is meant by "number sense" and how you would recognize it.

REFERENCES FOR CHAPTER 3

[i] Thompson, P. W. (1996). Imagery and the development of mathematical reasoning. In L. P. Steffe, B. Greer, P. Nesher, & G. Goldin (Eds.), *Theories of learning mathematics* (pp. 267–283). Hillsdale, NJ: Erlbaum.

[ii] Hatano, G., & Inagaki, K. (1996). *Cultural contexts of schooling revisited: A review of* The Learning Gap *from a cultural psychology perspective.* Paper presented at the Conference on Global Prospects for Education: Development, Culture and Schooling. East Lansing, MI.

[iii] Carpenter, T. P. (1989, August). *Number sense and other nonsense.* Paper presented at the Establishing Foundations for Research on Number Sense and Related Topics Conference, San Diego, CA.

[iv] Shuard, H., Walsh, A., Goodwin, J., & Worcester, V. (1991). *Primary initiatives in mathematics education: Calculators, children and mathematics.* London: Simon and Schuster.

[v] Kamii, C., & Livingston, S. J. (1994). Classroom activities. In L. Williams (Ed.), *Young children continue to reinvent arithmetic in 3rd grade: Implications of Piaget's theory* (pp. 81–146). New York: Teachers College Press.

[vi] Shuard, H., Walsh, A., Goodwin, J., & Worcester, V. (1991). *Primary initiatives in mathematics education: Calculators, children and mathematics.* London: Simon and Schuster.

[vii] Harel, Guershon. Personal conversation with a child he interviewed.

[viii] Howden, H. (1989). Teaching number sense. *Arithmetic Teacher, 36*(6), 6–11.

[ix] National Research Council. (1989*). Everybody counts: A report to the nation on the future of mathematics education.* Washington, DC: National Academy Press.

[x] Knapp, M. S., Shields, P. M., & Turnbull, B. J. (1992). *Academic challenge for the children of poverty* (Summary LC88054001). Washington, DC: U.S. Department of Education.

Chapter 4

Some Conventional Ways of Computing

The previous chapter introduced you to some of the ways children invent for carrying out arithmetic operations. The procedures you yourself use are probably the standard ones you learned in elementary school. Contrary to what some believe, these algorithms, or procedures, took centuries to evolve, and other algorithms are standard elsewhere. In this section we will look at those procedures for carrying out arithmetic operations more carefully, and come to understand how and why they work.

4.1 Operating on Whole Numbers and Decimal Numbers

The arithmetic operations on whole numbers or on decimal numbers are similar since the same base-ten structure underlies both of these forms. The computations are highly dependent on this base-ten structure. Developing sensible step-by-step procedures, or **algorithms**, to carry out the arithmetic operations of addition, subtraction, multiplication, and division demands understanding our base ten system. When students have difficulty with computational algorithms, many errors they make can be traced back to a lack of understanding of our base-ten system.

THINK ABOUT . . .

Are the algorithms you use for the four arithmetic operations based on right-to-left or left-to-right procedures? Can all be undertaken working from left-to-right?

Some children understand algorithms better when they are illustrated with base ten materials or drawing.

EXAMPLE 1 Use base ten drawings to illustrate 174 + 36.

SOLUTION Step 1: Represent the problem, using the small cube as 1.

174
+ 36

Continue on the next page.

Step 2: Place all cubes together; replace 10 small cubes with one long.

$$\begin{array}{r} 1 \\ 174 \\ +36 \\ \hline 0 \end{array}$$

Step 3: Place all longs together; replace 10 longs with one flat.

$$\begin{array}{r} 11 \\ 174 \\ +36 \\ \hline 10 \end{array}$$

Step 4: Put like blocks together to represent the sum.

$$\begin{array}{r} 11 \\ 174 \\ + 36 \\ \hline 210 \end{array}$$

Activity 1

Act out the following calculations using base ten blocks or drawings, whichever is appropriate. Then re-do each and record numerically at each step. It is important that one writes down the steps as the procedures are undertaken, with the numerical work linked to the work with the blocks, software, or drawings. When you use base ten blocks or drawings, be sure you specify which block or drawing is being used to represent one whole.

1. $312 - 124$
2. 3×21
3. $123 + 88$
4. $12.3 + 88$
5. $12.3 + 8.8$
6. $12.3 + 0.88$
7. Describe what new blocks would be needed to compute $235.42 + 6.345$.

Multiplication and division algorithms are more difficult to understand than addition and subtraction algorithms. In the last section you saw some multiplication algorithms that could easily lead to the standard algorithm that you use. If children understand place value and use that to multiply, they will understand the process. The first example on the next page shows all six partial products. The second example is a shortened way to find the product using just two partial products. If children first learn to write all partial products, they will understand where the partial products come from in the condensed algorithm. Note the use of decomposing 348 as 8 + 40 + 300 and then using the distributive property.

```
  348                              348
× 26                            × 26
   48   = 6 × 8               2088 = 6 × 348
  240   = 6 × 40             6960 = 20 × 348
 1800   = 6 × 300            9048
  160   = 20 × 8
  800   = 20 × 40        (Note that 348 = 300 + 40 + 8.)
 6000   = 20 × 300
 9048
```

We can also use all partial products to make sense of multiplying by decimal numbers.

```
  3.48                           3.48
× 2.6                          × 2.6
  .048   = .6 × .08           2.088 = .6 × 3.48
  .240   = .6 × .4            6.960 = 2 × 3.48
 1.800   = .6 × 3             9.048
  .160   = 2 × .08
  .800   = 2 × .4
 6.000   = 2 × 3
 9.048
```

Activity 2   **Your Turn**

Multiply 1.3 × 2.4, showing all partial products.

Here is an example of a series of division algorithms for 472 ÷ 37 that leads to the standard algorithm that you probably use. In the first example, 37s are subtracted 10 at a time or 1 at a time. In the second, we subtract other multiples of 37 (in this case 2). In the third, we simply move the 10 and 2 to the top. In the last, we do not write 10, but only the first digit of 10, aligned with the tens place in the dividend, and thus leaving room for a digit in the ones place so that the 2 can be filled in. Notice that the standard algorithm you learned is just a condensed version of subtracting 37s.

```
                                        12
                                         2
                                        10             12
  37)472          37)472          37)472         37)472
     370    10       370    10       370            37
     102             102             102            102
      37     1        74     2        74            74
      65             28     12        28            28
      37     1
      28    12
```

Thus 472 divided by 37 is 12 with a remainder of 28. Notice that each successive time the division problem is worked, it becomes a little more condensed, so that the final illustration matches the way most of us learned to divide. However, the previous three illustrations show that the problem can be thought of as how many 37s are in 472, and subtracting multiples of 37 until no more can be subtracted. While this is happening, we keep count at the side or on top of the number of 37s that have been subtracted and record them. Studying this series of algorithms will help you understand the last one, which is the one most widely used in the United States but often never understood.

Activity 3   Why Move the Decimal Point?

As you know, the first step in using the usual algorithm for calculating, say, 56.906 ÷ 3.7 is to move the decimal point in the divisor to make a whole number (37) and to move the decimal point in the dividend that number of places (giving 569.06).

1. Use a calculator to find answers to the following:
    a.   56.906 ÷ 3.7
    b.   (56.906 × 10) ÷ (3.7 × 10)
    c.   1.728 ÷ 1.44
    d.   (1.728 × 100) ÷ (1.44 × 100)
2. What insights into the "move the decimal point in the divisor" rule does this activity suggest?

Activity 4   Now I Know How to Divide Decimal Numbers

Try dividing 0.18 by 1.5 using each of the techniques demonstrated for 472 ÷ 37. Use knowledge gained from the previous activity to account for "moving the decimal point."

TAKE-AWAY MESSAGE . . . Undertaking the fundamental arithmetic operations using the standard procedures is easier when you can first see them "unpacked," with each step along the way clarified by using properties and thinking about the meaning of the operation involved. This work can lead to an understanding of where all the numbers come from and how the algorithm can then be condensed into the procedures we all know and probably all use. ♦

Learning Exercises for Section 4.1

1. Work through the following problems, thinking about each step you perform, and why. If you have used base ten blocks or sketches of base ten blocks, you can use them to help you with these problems. *In each case, specify what you decide to use as your unit.* For example, if the flat is used to represent 1, then 34.52 can be represented as follows:

    a. 56.2 + 34.52

    b. 4 × 0.39

    c. 345.6 − 21.21

    d. 2912 ÷ 8 (Think of this as a sharing problem.)

2. Work through the following problems in the base indicated. Write down your procedure, and *specify what you use as your unit in each case.*

    a. 231 + 342 in base five

    b. 1000 − 555 in base six

    If you feel at all uncertain about these problems, make up and try some of your own.

3. Show how you could use a series of algorithms, such as those in this section, to teach another person to understand the standard algorithms for multiplication and division: 35 × 426; 14910 ÷ 426.

4. There have been, in the past, many different algorithms developed for carrying out computation. Here are two such algorithms for computing 36 × 342. The first is called the **lattice method** for multiplication, used by the Arabs in the 1600s and carried to Europe. The method depends on knowing the multiplication facts, but not much on place value. The factors are written across the top and right, and the answer, 12,312, is read off going down on the left and around the bottom. Compare this method to showing all partial products.

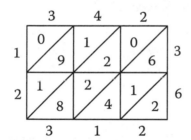

The second is called the **Russian peasant algorithm**. One number is successively halved until 1 is reached (if it is odd, 1 is subtracted before halving) and the other number is doubled the same number of times the first is halved. Numbers in the second column are crossed out when the corresponding number in the first column is even, and the remaining numbers are added. Reread the preceding steps as you study this calculation of 36 × 342.

36	~~342~~
18	~~684~~
9	1368
4	~~2736~~
2	~~5472~~
1	<u>10,944</u>
	12,312

Try these algorithms on 57 × 623. They are not magic! Each can be justified mathematically.

5. Use your understanding of division to complete each equation.

If $4000 \div 16 = 250$, then

a. $8000 \div 16 =$ _____   b. $16,000 \div 16 =$ _____

c. $2000 \div 16 =$ _____   d. $4000 \div 32 =$ _____

e. $4000 \div 64 =$ _____   f. $4000 \div 8 =$ _____

g. $4000 \div 4 =$ _____   h. $4000 \div 0.4 =$ _____

4.2 Issues for Learning: The Role of Algorithms

In Section 4.1 we focused on the methods used in carrying out the arithmetic operations on whole numbers and decimal numbers, methods that are likely to be already familiar to you. By learning well one algorithm for each operation, traditional long division for example, that skill becomes automatized and allows one to think about other things, for example, the problem at hand that led to the division.

Discussion 1   What Do You Remember?

What do you remember about learning algorithmic procedures in school? Did you understand these procedures? Were they easy or painful to learn? Were they easy or difficult to remember? Do you use them often now? How important is it to be able to carry out operations rapidly with paper and pencil?

The standard algorithms are called "standard" because children are taught to do them the same way. The evolution of these algorithms began in the 1600s, with the demise of the use of the Roman numeral system due to the hard-won acceptance of the Hindu-Arabic decimal system of numeration (our place-value system). The algorithms came into existence as people attempted to become as efficient and speedy as possible in their calculations. Even so, some of the algorithms we use here are not standard in other parts of the world. For example, our subtraction algorithm was selected for teaching in U.S. schools because a research study[i] in 1941 showed it to be "slightly better" than the equal-additions method of subtraction you saw in Chapter 3, a method that is taught in many other countries. Those who learned the equal-additions algorithm find the algorithm used in the United States to be strange.

Many mathematics educators say that there should be less emphasis on teaching pencil-and-paper algorithms because students can use calculators to compute. But they do not argue that we should therefore *not* teach methods of calculating that are independent of calculator use. One reason for teaching calculation methods is because calculation is a useful tool. Another reason is that it may lead to a deeper understanding of numbers and number operations. Students make better sense of standard algorithms when they have had opportunities to explore arithmetic operations and find their own ways of operating on numbers, exemplified by those children whose work you have studied in the last chapter. Students can then learn standard algorithms as required, because in most states and school districts they are required. If they learn standard algorithms with an understanding of why the procedures lead to correct answers, they are more likely to remember them and use them correctly.

> *THINK ABOUT . . .*
>
> Do you have a better understanding of the multiplication and division algorithms after seeing, in the previous section, how longer algorithms can be used to show why standard algorithms work?

What, then, is the role of calculators in elementary school? Calculators are ubiquitous, and are much faster than any human calculator. Will calculators someday completely replace paper-and-pencil calculations? Not likely. But efficiency and automaticity should be reconsidered as valid reasons for teaching arithmetic skills. This does not mean that people should not have these skills, but rather that finding an answer using paper and pencil may no longer need to be rapid (except in some testing situations). There are times when pencil-and-paper computing should be preferred, and times when calculators should be used.

Discussion 2   What Is the Role of Calculators?

What is the role of calculators in school mathematics? A newspaper cartoon showed parents and grandparents sitting at desks using calculators for computing, while the 12-year-old son was sitting at his desk doing worksheets of long-division practice. What do you think was the message?

Contrary to what is believed by many, research has shown that calculators do not hinder the learning of basic skills and can, in fact, enhance learning and skill development when used appropriately in the classroom.[ii,iii,iv] The National Assessment of Educational Progress (NAEP) from years 1990 to 2003 shows no difference in scores for fourth-grade students in classrooms where calculators were frequently used and where calculators were not used.[v] (The NAEP test in mathematics is administered nationally at grades 4, 8, and 12 every 2–4 years.) In eighth grade, students who frequently used calculators scored significantly higher than students who did not. Keep in mind that students often do not understand enough about arithmetic operations to be able to choose appropriate operations to solve real problems, and in such cases a calculator is useless. If understanding algorithms leads to less need for practice, more time can be devoted to learning which operations are appropriate and when.

In the next chapter you will be given opportunities to consider a third option using standard algorithms or calculators. In many cases an exact answer is not needed. What should be done then?

4.3 | Check Yourself

By now you should be able to explain the multiplication and division algorithms to someone else who does not understand the processes. You should know the pros and cons of the standard algorithms and student-invented algorithms, and provide a cogent argument defending your view of what is important for children to learn about the procedures for carrying out arithmetic procedures.

You should also be able to do problems like those assigned and to meet the following objectives.

1. Explain each step of the addition (e.g., for 378 + 49) and subtraction algorithms (e.g., for 378 – 49) and show how renaming is used.

2. Explain each step of whole number multiplication (e.g., 375 × 213) using partial products.

3. Explain division of whole numbers (e.g., 764 ÷ 46) using a series of algorithms that leads to the standard algorithm.

4. Recognize the role of place value in the algorithms.

5. Discuss the role of both nonstandard and standard algorithms.

REFERENCES FOR CHAPTER 4

[i]Brownell, W. A. (1941). *Arithmetic in grades I and II: A critical summary of new and previously reported research.* Durham, NC: Duke University Press.

[ii]Shuard, H., Walsh, A., Goodwin, J., & Worcester, V. (1991). *Primary initiatives in mathematics education: Calculators, children and mathematics.* London: Simon and Schuster.

[iii]Kloosterman, P., & Lester, F. K., Jr. (Eds.). (2004). *Results and interpretations of the 1990 through 2000 mathematics assessments of the National Assessment of Educational Progress.* Reston, VA: National Council of Teachers of Mathematics.

[iv]Kilpatrick, J., Swafford, J., & Findell, B. (Eds). (2001). *Adding it up.* Washington, DC: National Research Council, National Academy Press.

[v]Kloosterman, P., Sowder, J., & Kehle, P. (2004). *Clearing the Air About School Mathematics Achievement: What Do NAEP Data Tell Us?* Presentation at the April 2004 American Educational Research Association, April, 2004, San Diego.

Chapter 5

Using Numbers in Sensible Ways

People who are comfortable working with numbers have many ways to think about numbers and number operations. For example, they use "benchmarks," that is, numbers close to particular numbers that are easier to use in calculating. Thinking about numbers in various ways allows them to estimate answers, do mental arithmetic, and recognize when answers are wrong. This chapter will help you acquire a better *number sense*, that is, the ability to recognize when and how to use numbers in sensible ways.

5.1 | Mental Computation

When people hear the word "computation" they usually think of paper-and-pencil computation using the methods they learned in school. But computation can take many forms, and an individual with a good understanding of numbers will choose the most appropriate form of computation for the problem at hand. Today, this often means using a calculator because it is fast and efficient. Often, though, one can mentally compute an answer faster than one can compute with paper and pencil or even a calculator. At other times, one might wish to compute mentally simply because it is more convenient than finding pencil and paper or a calculator. To become skilled at mental computation takes some practice. Number properties must be understood and used, although you may not even be aware of the properties because they are so natural for you to use. One important advantage of practicing mental computation, for children and for adults, is that it helps develop flexibility of use of numbers and properties of operations and gives them a sense of control over numbers.

Consider some of the following ways of mentally computing 12×50:

1. 12×50 can be thought of as $12 \times 5 \times 10 = 60 \times 10 = 600$. This required decomposing 50 into 5×10, and then using the associative property of multiplication: $12 \times (5 \times 10) = (12 \times 5) \times 10 = 60 \times 10$.

2. 12×50 can be thought of as $(10 + 2) \times 50 = (10 \times 50) + (2 \times 50)$ (using the distributive property of multiplication over addition), which is $500 + 100 = 600$.

3. $12 \times 50 = (6 \times 2) \times 50 = 6 \times (2 \times 50) = 6 \times 100 = 600$ (using the associative property).

Remember that addition is also commutative and associative, giving a great deal of flexibility in adding numbers.

There are also several ways of thinking about how to mentally compute a difference. For example:

1. $147 - 66$ could be found by adding 4 to each number: $151 - 70$ is $151 - 50 - 20 = 101 - 20 = 81$.

2. $147 - 66$: Count up 4 to 70, then 30 to 100, then 40 to 140, then 7 to 147. This is $4 + 30 + 40 + 7$ which is 81.

3. $147 - 66$ is $140 - 60$ which is 80, plus 7 is 87, minus 6, is 81.

And of course there are other ways . . .

Activity 1   I Can Do It in My Head!

Before reading ahead, do the following calculations in as many ways as possible.

1. $152 - 47$ **2.** $1000 - 729$ **3.** 25×24

4. $38.6 + 27.2 + 4.8 - 38.6$ **5.** $12 \div \frac{1}{4}$ **6.** $6 \times 43 + 6 \times 7$

Many times the ease of mental computation depends on the numbers used, and on familiarity with properties of operations. The computation should not begin before looking over the numbers and thinking of different ways of reorganizing or rewriting the numbers. Consider Problem 4 in Activity 1. Many people would begin by trying to add 38.6 and 27.2 mentally, a challenge but certainly possible. But as one becomes more adept at mental computation, the knowledge that the numbers could be reordered, allowing the $38.6 - 38.6$ to be the first operation, makes this a much easier problem to compute mentally: $27.2 + 4.8$ is $31 + 1$ is 32.

Now consider Problem 3, which is 25×24. One way to think about this problem is as $(5 \times 5) \times (4 \times 6) = (5 \times 4) \times (5 \times 6) = 20 \times 30 = 600$. Notice that you have really done the following, but without writing it all:

$$
\begin{aligned}
25 \times 24 &= (5 \times 5) \times (4 \times 6) \\
&= 5 \times (5 \times 4) \times 6 \text{ using the associate property of multiplication,} \\
&= 5 \times (4 \times 5) \times 6 \text{ using the commutative property of multiplication,} \\
&= (5 \times 4) \times (5 \times 6) \text{ using the associative property again.}
\end{aligned}
$$

When 25 is a factor, it could also be thought of as $\dfrac{100}{4}$. Now 25×24 becomes

$$
\frac{100}{4} \times 24 = \frac{100}{4} \times 4 \times 6 = 100 \times 6 = 600.
$$

For Problem 6, the arithmetic is easy if we use the distributive property:

$$(6 \times 43) + (6 \times 7) = 6 \times (43 + 7) = 6 \times 50 = 300.$$

For Problem 2, which is 1000 – 729, the mental computation by counting up is actually easier than using the standard algorithm, which, because of the zeros, often leads to errors. Add 1 to 730, 70 to 800, then 200 to 1000, 1 + 70 + 200 is 271. Notice that this is based on the missing-addend view of subtraction.

In Problem 5, think of how many quarters are in $12. Too often, people give the answer 3. Why do you think this happens?

Discussion 1   Becoming Good at Mental Computation

Try these individually, and then together discuss different ways of undertaking these mental computations.

1. Mentally compute $50 \times 35 \times 2 \div 5$
2. Mentally compute 19×21 (Is this the same as 20×20?)
3. Mentally compute $5,400,000 \div 600,000$
4. Mentally compute $3476 + 2456 - 1476$
5. Mentally compute 50×340
6. Mentally compute $24 \times 38 + 24 \times 12$
7. Mentally compute $8 \times 32 \times 4$ (Hint: You can use powers of 2.)
8. Mentally compute $35 \times 14 + 35 \times 6$

Mental calculation with some percents is not difficult. Here are some hints about calculating with percents.

1. 10% of a number is $\frac{1}{10}$ or 0.1 times the number.

    10% of 50 is 5.   10% of 34.5 is 3.45.

2. Multiples of 10% can be found using the 10% calculation:
    20% of 50 is twice 5, or 10.
    20% of 34.5 is 3.45 twice, or 6.90.
    70% of 20 is 10% seven times, or 14.
    (Or think: 10% of 20 is 2, and $2 \times 7 = 14$ is 70% of 20.)

3. 15% is 10% plus half that again. 15% of 640 is 64 + 32 or 96.

4. 25% is a quarter of an amount, and 50% is half an amount. Thus 25% of $360 is $90 because one quarter of 360 is 90. Or, you could say 10% is 36, 10% more is 36 more, then 5% is half of 10%, and half of 36 is 18. Finally, 36 + 36 + 18 is 90.

Notes

Activity 2   I Can Do Percents in My Head

Determine the following mentally. Does a mental drawing like the one here help in some cases?

a.   What is 25% of 40?

b.   Twelve is 20% of what number?

c.   Thirteen is 50% of what number?

d.   Ten percent of what number is 10?

e.   What is 30% of 55?

f.   What percent of 66 is 22?

TAKE-AWAY MESSAGE . . . There are many ways to mentally compute if one knows the properties of operations on numbers. As people become more comfortable using numbers, they are more likely to mentally compute answers when this is easy to do. Computing mentally leads to greater facility with numbers and more confidence in one's ability to work with numbers. ♦

Learning Exercises for Section 5.1

1.   How can the following computations be done mentally using the distributive property? Write out your solutions.

    a. 43×9 **b.** $23 \times 98 + 23 \times 2$ **c.** 72×30

2.   Tell how you could mentally compute each of the following.

    a. $365 + 40 + 35$ **b.** $756 - 28$ **c.** $2391 + 431 - 1391$

    d. $499 - 49$ **e.** 124×25 **f.** $42 - 29$

    g. 44×25 **h.** 75×88 **i.** 8×32

3.   Compute each of the following mentally.

    a. 25% of 60   **b.** 10% of 78   **c.** 30% of 15

    d. 80% of 710   **e.** 15% of $40   **f.** 100% of 57

    g. 125% of 40   **h.** 20 is 20% of ?   **i.** 5% of 64

4.   Compute each of the following mentally.

    a. 24 is 20% of what number?   **b.** 38 is 10% of what number?

    c. 89 is 100% of what number?   **d.** 50 is 125% of what number?

5. The figure shown below is 120% of a smaller figure. Can you show 20% of the smaller figure? Shade 100% of the smaller figure.

6. If you wish, shade a grid to help you find the **fractional equivalent** in simplest form for each of the following percents.

50% = _____ $33\frac{1}{3}$% = _____   75% = _____

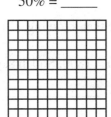   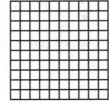   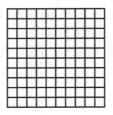

$66\frac{2}{3}$% = _____   12.5% = _____   20% = _____

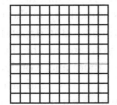   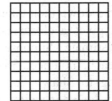   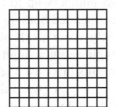

| 5.2 | **Computational Estimation** |

Many times an estimate rather than an exact answer to a calculation may be sufficient. Estimates are used not only when an exact answer could be found but is not needed, but also when an exact answer is not possible, such as when you make a budget and estimate how much your total utilities bills will be each month. Mental computation is used in computational estimation, but when you estimate, you are looking only for an approximate answer. However, estimation is sometimes considered more difficult because it involves both rounding *and* mental computation.

> ***THINK ABOUT . . .***
>
> Think back on the times you have needed a numerical answer to a computation in the past week. How many times did you need an exact answer? How many times did you need just an estimate?

Discussion 2   Is One Way Better Than Another?

1. Estimate 36×55 alone before discussing this problem.
2. Carefully read these students' solutions to the first exercise. Be sure you understand the thinking behind each one. Then discuss them in terms of whether each way is a good way to estimate. Did you use one of these ways?

> Shawn: Round to 40 and 60. $40 \times 60 = 2400$.
>
> Jack: First round down: $30 \times 50 = 1500$. Then round up: $40 \times 60 = 2400$. So it's about in the middle, maybe a little past. So I'd say 2000.
>
> Maria: Rounding both up would make it too big, so I'll round 36 to 40 and 55 to 50. $40 \times 50 = 2000$.
>
> Jimmy: A little more than 36×50, which is $36 \times 100 \div 2$ and that's $18 \times 100 = 1800$. It's about 5×36 more, or about 180 more, so I'll say 1980.
>
> Deb: Rounding both up gives $40 \times 60 = 2400$. Since that's too big, I'll say it's about 2200.
>
> Sam: A little more than $6 \times 6 \times 50$, which is $6 \times 300 = 1800$. So I'll say 1900.

Each of the above ways provide good estimates, but some are better than others because they are efficient and/or because they are more accurate. For example, Shawn rounded both numbers up to the closest multiple of 10. Rounding up gives a high estimate. Jack rounded both up and down then takes something in the middle. His way takes slightly more work but gives a closer estimate. But depending on the context, you might want a high estimate. Suppose you are at the hardware store buying drawer pulls that cost 55¢ each. You need 36 of them and wonder if you have enough cash with you. According to Shawn you need $24, and according to Jack, you need $20. Before you reach for your wallet, which estimate would you use? Why?

Activity 3   Now I'll Try Some

1. Try each of the strategies from the above discussion (if appropriate) to estimate 16×48. Which estimates do you think are better? Why?
2. If a city's property tax is $29.87 per $1000 of assessed value, what would be an estimate of the tax on property assessed at $38,600?
3. Estimate 789×0.52.
4. Estimate $148.52 + 49.341$.

THINK ABOUT . . .

In a research study[i] many middle school students were asked to estimate 789×0.52. Some students rounded 0.52 to 1, rounded 789 to 800, and said their answer was $800 \times 1 = 800$. Is 1 a good substitute for 0.52? Why or why not? Suppose something cost $0.52, and you bought 789 of these objects. Would $800 be a good estimate of the price? Why do you think students rounded 0.52 to 1?

THINK ABOUT . . .

In the same study the students were asked to estimate 148.52 + 49.341. Some students said, "148 is almost 150 and 49 is almost 50. And 0.52 is almost 0.6, and 0.341 is almost 0.3. And 0.6 + 0.3 is 0. 9. So the answer is 200.9." Find the flaw in this argument. (Hint: Is the 148 being rounded up to 150, or is the 148.52 being rounded up to 150?)

Research has shown that good estimators use a variety of strategies and demonstrate a deep understanding of numbers and of operations. They are flexible in their thinking and are disposed to make sense of numbers. A good estimator uses the rounding of numbers a great deal, but seldom uses the formal rounding procedures often taught in schools.[ii] Proficiency in flexible rounding requires that an individual has an intuitive notion of the magnitude of the number in question, and this intuition is acquired through practice in comparing and ordering numbers and using benchmarks, especially for fractions and decimals. For example, to estimate 257 + 394 + 2 + 49, a good strategy (but not the only one) would be to round 257 to 250, 394 to 400, 49 to 50, and drop the 2 since it is insignificant here (or think of rounding it to 0). School students who are inflexible in their rounding will insist that 257 must be rounded to 300, or perhaps 260 if rounding to the nearest 10, but not to 250. In another example, if you want to estimate the quotient of 6217 ÷ 87, you might find it more convenient to round to 6300 and 90 rather than 6000 and 90, since 70×90 is 6300. The activity below is intended to provide you with practice in estimating.

Activity 4   Finding "Just About"

Be sure to check your solutions and methods with others. You may be surprised to find many good ways of doing these estimations.

1. Estimate $\dfrac{71 \times 89}{8}$

2. Estimate 42×34

3. Estimate $5.8 \div 12$

4. If 34×86 is estimated as 30×86, then the estimate is 2580. The exact answer is 2924. The difference between these two numbers is 344. If 496×86 is estimated as 500×86, then the exact answer is 42,656 and the estimate is 43,000. Again, the difference is 344. Which of these would you choose: (a) the first estimate is better; (b) they are the same; (c) the second estimate is better. Why?

5. 18×86 can be estimated as (a) 20×90; or (b) 20×86; or (c) 18×90. Which of these three ways gives the closest estimate?

6. If you estimate 53×27 by saying 50×30 is 1500, is the exact answer less than, equal to, or more than your estimate?

By now you know that when multiplying two numbers, rounding both up gives a high estimate, and rounding both down gives a low estimate. Thus a more accurate estimate of a product could be found by rounding one number up and one number down.

Discussion 3   Rounding Up and Down

If you are adding two numbers is it usually best to round both numbers up? If not, what is the better thing to do? What about subtraction? What about division?

Estimating with percents is very common. When you shop and see a sale at "30% off" you need to know what you have to pay. Here are some hints about estimating with percents, building on the earlier mental computation with percents.

1. Estimating 10% of 34.5 could be 10% of 35 which is 3.5.

2. If you estimate 20% of 34.5, it is 3.5 twice, or 7. An estimate of 30% of 50.3 is 10% of 50 three times: $3 \times 5 = 15$.

3. 15% is 10% plus half that again. 15% of 642 is 64.2 + 32.1 or 96.3. But if you are estimating, such as for a tip, you could say 15% of 640 is 64 + 32, or 96, or even 100.

4. 25% is a quarter of an amount. 25% off of $350 is about 25% of $360 which is $90. (Note that 1/4 of 360 is 90.) Or, you could say 10% is 35, 10% more is 70, half of 35 is about 18, and 35 + 35 + 18 is 88.

5. When estimating a discount on price, it may be easier to estimate the sale value. Thus, if a vase is regularly priced at $140 and is 20% off, then the actual price is 80% of $140. 50% of 140 is 70. 10% of 140 is 14 and so 30% of 140 is 3×14, or 42. So the actual price is $70 + $42 = $112. To estimate, 80% of $150 would be 8 $\times$ $15 or 4 $\times$ $30 or $120. In this case, finding the actual value was probably as easy as estimating it.

Activity 5   What Does It Cost? Estimate.

1. A coat is 30% off. It was originally $150. How much is it now?

2. A dress, marked as $90 before the sale, is 40% off. What percent of the original price must one pay to buy it? What is the discounted cost?

3. A jacket cost $45 after the 50% discount. How much was it originally?

An eighth-grade teacher of a low-ability class told one of the authors that she spent the last 8 weeks of math classes on mental computation and estimation because her students were so weak in this area, and she wanted them to better understand how to operate with numbers. Her students did extremely well. She said that they came to feel very confident, mathematically, and were no longer afraid of numbers.

TAKE-AWAY MESSAGE . . . Computational estimation builds a greater facility with numbers but at the same time reinforces facility. Estimation plays a major role in our daily lives.

Learning how to make better estimates can be a valuable skill, one we want to pass on to students. You should be estimating calculations throughout this course. ♦

Learning Exercises for Section 5.2

1. Estimate 0.76×62.

2. You buy 62 tablets at 76¢ each. You want to estimate the price before you get to the cash register to make certain you have enough money with you. Do you estimate differently than in Exercise 1? Discuss times when an estimate should be an overestimate, and times when an underestimate is preferable.

3. Which is greater (without calculating): 0.21×84.63 or $84.63 \div 0.21$? Explain your answer.

4. Your restaurant bill is $27.89. What should you leave as a tip if you want to tip 15%?

5. Reflect in writing on the six ways of estimating the product of 36 and 55 used in the first discussion in this section. Can all be done mentally? Are some better than others? Why or why not? Are some easier than others? Which ones show a better "feel" for numbers?

6. Estimate the following products using whatever strategies you prefer.
   a. 49×890 b. 25×76 c. 16×650
   d. 341×6121 e. 3×532

7. Explain how you would estimate the cost of the following items with the discounts indicated.
   a. a dress marked $49.99 at a 25% discount
   b. a CD marked $16.99 at 15% off
   c. a blouse at 75% off the $18.99 clearance price
   d. a suit at 60% off the already marked-down price of $109.99

8. Use your "close to" knowledge to *estimate* the following. The first one is done for you.
   a. 0.49×102 is about of half of 100, or 50
   b. 32% of 12
   c. 94% of 500
   d. 0.52×789
   e. 23% of 81
   f. 35% of 22
   g. 76% of $210

9. Return to the activities in this section and once again work though each part on your own.

5.3 | Estimating Values of Quantities

Many times when people talk about estimation, they mean estimating numerosity rather than estimating calculations, for example, the crowd at some big event. Perhaps you have at some time entered a contest where you had to guess the number of jelly beans in a large jar and found it very difficult to do. Numerosity refers not just to guessing, but to making intelligent guesses. If you went home and found a similar jar that you filled with jelly beans, then counted them, you might make a better guess than had you not done so. For a long time you will be able to make pretty good judgments concerning the number of jelly beans in jars. Although that may not be a skill worth developing, there are other contexts where estimating skills can be useful. Skill in estimating values of quantities, whether discrete counts (like jelly beans) or continuous measures (like the height of a tree) require practice.

Money is certainly one area in which understanding estimates can be useful. A recent news report recommended that those speaking about social security legislation speak only about numbers in the millions, because people don't know what a trillion means. Perhaps large numbers will make more sense to you after this section.

Activity 6   Developing a "Feel" for the Size of Quantities

1. How big is a crowd of 100 people? Of 1000 people? Of 10,000 people? Do you have a sense for how large each of these groups would be?
    a. Would 100 people fit in a typical classroom? If so, how crowded would the room be?
    b. Would 1000 people fit in a typical classroom? Inside your home? Where would it be natural to find a group this size? Are there enough seats in a standard movie theater for 1000 people?
    c. Where would you expect to see 10,000 people? Do you have a feel for how large a group this would be? If exactly this many people were in attendance at your local stadium, would it be completely full? Half full? How full?
2. How long is 10 feet? 100 ft? 1000 ft? 10,000 ft? Do you have a sense for how long each of these lengths is?
    a. Name at least five objects whose typical length or height is approximately 10 feet. (Think of the length of your bedroom. Is it more or less than 10 feet?)
    b. Do the same for 100 feet. Think about a point or object in the environment surrounding you that is approximately 100 feet away from you, 100 feet tall, or 100 feet long. If necessary, go outside and find something that will help you make sense of 100 feet.
    c. Name some things that you could use as a reference for a length, height, or distance of 1000 ft. (One way—a mile is 5280 feet, so 1000 feet is about. . . . ?)

Having good number sense requires having some sense not only of the relative size of a number (e.g., the relative size of 3 and 30, or of $\frac{1}{3}$ and $\frac{1}{2}$) but also of the absolute size of a number. (For example, how much is a million? Could you reasonably ask a third-grade class to bring in their pennies until they reached a million?) To develop a "feel" for the size of numerical amounts it is helpful to compare them to some reference amount with which you are familiar. Such a reference amount is often called a *benchmark.* A benchmark is a personally meaningful and recognizable amount that can be used to make size estimates. Benchmarks are particularly useful when we want to have a feel for very large or very small numerical amounts. Benchmarks can involve money, population, time, distance, height, weight, a collection of objects, or any other physical or nonphysical attributes.

EXAMPLE 1

♦ It is 250,000 miles from the earth to the moon. How far is that? ♦

If you know that it is approximately 25,000 miles around the earth along the equator, you could think that traveling 10 times around the earth would be comparable in distance to traveling to the moon.

Or

You could think of a place that is roughly 100 miles away from where you live and imagine traveling there back and forth 1250 times!

Or

You could think of a place that is roughly 10 miles away from where you are and imagine covering that distance 25,000 times!

> *THINK ABOUT . . .*
>
> Does the example above give you a "sense" for how far away the moon is? Is it farther away than you thought? Or closer? How long would it take you to walk to the moon?

Having one's own benchmarks can be very helpful. If these referents are to be useful to you they must be personalized. This means that you are the one who needs to be familiar with the amount. For example, if you attend games at the local stadium and you know its capacity, you can use that as a benchmark for that many people. In one city, the football stadium holds more than 60,000 people. Such a reference can give you a feel for that many people. Having a feel for 60,000 people, however, does not necessarily help you have a feel for how far 60,000 miles is, or how much $60,000 can buy. Therefore, the nature of the quantity, not just its numerical value, is important in deciding the usefulness of a reference amount.

TAKE-AWAY MESSAGE . . . Many people have little "feel" for the size of numbers unless they practice, within some context. For example, a builder can easily estimate the height of a building and its square footage. Having some benchmarks for numbers as they are used in different contexts is an important aspect of living with numbers every day. ♦

Learning Exercises for Section 5.3

1. Think of a personal referent that will give you a feel for each of the following distances:

   a. 3 miles　　　　**b.** 30 miles　　　　**c.** 300 miles

   d. 3000 miles　　　**e.** 30,000 miles

2. How long would it take you to travel each of the distances in Exercise 1 if you were to drive your car?

3. Find personal benchmarks for at least five large numbers (groups) of people. For example, you might say that 1000 people is about the number of students that attended your high school; your university has about 25,000 students; the city you live in has a population of about half a million people, and so on. (These are estimates of numerosity.)

   Do the same thing for amounts of money. For example, my car is worth about $10,000; the salary of a beginning teacher in my city is about $35,000; the average price of a home in my city is $250,000, and so on. But find your own!

4. A congressman once said, "I don't care how much it costs—a billion, a trillion. We need to solve the AIDS problem." Can the United States afford to spend one million dollars to fund AIDS research? One billion dollars? One trillion dollars? Why or why not? The population of the United States is now about 300 million. What would each of these amounts mean for each person in this country, in terms of a person's share of the national debt?

5. Write a children's story (not a school lesson) that uses at least five quantities with large values in ways that will help children understand how big the values really are. Include references to places, things, and events that will make sense to them. The story should have between 500 and 1000 words. (Do you have a feel for how many pages that is?)

As you develop your own personal referents, make a list of them so that you can refer to them at any time. In a later study of measurement, you will again be asked to prepare a list of personal referents.

5.4 Using Scientific Notation for Estimating Values of Very Large and Very Small Quantities

Most very large and very small numbers are actually estimates. For a 12-digit number, the digit in the ones place is not going to matter. Indeed, for a large number, only a few digits to the far left really matter.

Many people do not even know the names of numbers past one trillion, even though uses for very large numbers exist. Very small numbers also need to be expressed in some standard way that can be shared. We can express very large and very small numbers using scientific notation.

> A number is written in **scientific notation** when it has the form $a \times 10^b$ where
>
> a is a number between 1 and 10, and b is an integer.

EXAMPLE 2

a. 50 million is 50,000,000, and in scientific notation this is 5×10^7.

b. For small numbers, scientific notation requires the use of negative integers. 10^{-3} means $\dfrac{1}{10^3}$. We formalize this by saying that for any nonzero c and any d,

$$c^{-d} = \frac{1}{c^d}.$$

c. 6 ten-thousandths is .0006 or $\frac{6}{10,000}$, which in scientific notation is 6×10^{-4}. Sometimes we write .0006 as 0.0006 so that the decimal point is more obvious.

d. $350,000,000 = 3.5 \times 100,000,000$, which in scientific notation is 3.5×10^8.

e. $0.00052 = 5.2 \times 0.0001$, which in scientific notation is 5.2×10^{-4}.

Note that both the 3.5 and the 5.2 are between 1 and 10, and that the second part of the numerals have ten to a power.

Operating on numbers in scientific notation requires knowing how to use exponents to your advantage. Recall that $5^3 \times 5^4$ means $(5 \times 5 \times 5) \times (5 \times 5 \times 5 \times 5)$ which is $5 \times 5 \times 5 \times 5 \times 5 \times 5 \times 5$ or 5^7, and that $5^3 \div 5^4$ means $\dfrac{5 \times 5 \times 5}{5 \times 5 \times 5 \times 5}$ which is $\dfrac{1}{5}$ or 5^{-1}.

In general, we have:

> **Two laws of exponents useful in scientific notation:**
>
> $$a^m \times a^n = a^{m+n} \qquad \text{and} \qquad a^m \div a^n = a^{m-n}$$

EXAMPLE 3

$(3.5 \times 10^8) \times (5.2 \times 10^4) = (3.5 \times 5.2) \times (10^8 \times 10^4) = 18.2 \times 10^4$. But this is not in scientific notation because 18.2 is larger than 10. $18.2 \times 10^4 = 1.82 \times 10^5$.

EXAMPLE 4

$(3.5 \times 10^8) \div (5.2 \times 10^4) = (3.5 \div 5.2) \times (10^8 \div 10^4) \approx 0.67 \times 10^{12}$. But this is not in scientific notation because 0.67 is smaller than 1. $0.67 \times 10^{12} = 6.7 \times 10^{11}$.

EXAMPLE 5

♦ Light travels 186,000 miles in a second. A light-year is the distance that light travels in one year, even though it might sound like a time unit. About how many miles are in a light-year? ♦

SOLUTION

$$1.86 \times 10^5 \, \frac{\text{mi}}{\text{s}} \times 60 \, \frac{\text{s}}{\text{min}} \times 60 \, \frac{\text{min}}{\text{h}} \times 24 \, \frac{\text{h}}{\text{day}} \times 365 \, \frac{\text{days}}{\text{year}} \approx 5.87 \times 10^{12} \, \frac{\text{mi}}{\text{year}}$$

so a light-year is about 5.87×10^{12} miles. (Is this a meaningful number?)

Activity 7   Do You Agree?

Write out two very large numbers and two very small numbers and give them to a partner to write in scientific notation. Your partner should do the same with you. Check the numbers to see if you agree with the ways in which these numbers are written in scientific notation. Make certain that you are using the notation. Then write other numbers in scientific notation and give them to one another to write in full notation. If you have questions, seek clarification.

TAKE-AWAY MESSAGE . . . Scientific notation provides an efficient way to express and operate on very large and very small numbers, using powers of ten and laws of exponents. ♦

Learning Exercises for Section 5.4

1. **a.** What is $(6.12 \times 10^4) \times (3 \times 10^2)$?

    b. What is $(6.12 \times 10^4) \div (3 \times 10^2)$?

    c. What is $(6.12 \times 10^2) \div (3 \times 10^4)$?

2. Why is $(3 \times 10^4) \times (4 \times 10^6)$ *not* 12×10^{10} in scientific notation?

3. **a.** Write $45,000,000 \times 220,000,000,000$ in scientific notation, then compute and be sure the answer is in scientific notation.
    b. Do the same for $6,900,000 \div 23,000,000,000$.
    c. Do the same for $0.0000000000056 \div 70,000$.
    d. Do the same for $0.0084 \div 0.000004$.

4. **a.** Write 1.5 billion in scientific notation.
    b. Write 4.27 trillion in scientific notation.

5. Find $(3.14 \times 10^6) + (2.315 \times 10^4)$. Write a sentence about the role of scientific notation in addition and subtraction.

6. Experiment with scientific notation on a scientific calculator. Where does the power of ten appear on the calculator? Do the computations in Exercises 1, 3, and 5 using a scientific calculator. Think about how to enter and read the numbers.

7. Choose some number to be *n*, and then find $2n$; 2^n; n^2; 10^n. As *n* gets larger, describe how the results change in each case. Does the result grow faster when *n* is an exponent, or when it is a base?

8. How long is 1 billion seconds in hours? In days? In years?

9. A googol is 10^{100}. Have you ever heard this term used? If so, where?

10. Not all large numbers are commonly expressed in scientific notation. Computer memory is expressed in powers of two. A kilobyte is 2^{10} (kilo means 1000, and $2^{10} = 1024$); a megabyte is 2^{20}; a gigabyte is 2^{30}. Which of these is close to 1 billion?

5.5 | Issues for Learning: Mental Computation

In a research study[iii], fourth- and sixth-grade students received almost daily instruction on mental computation that always allowed students to discuss a variety of strategies for mental computation problems. At the beginning, these students wanted to perform the mental analogue of the paper-and-pencil procedure, that is, they would say (when asked to add 38 and 45 mentally) "I put the 45 under the 38. Then I add 5 and 8 and that's 13 and I write down a 3 and carry the 1. Then I add 1 and 3 and 4 and I get 8, so the answer is 83." When asked to add 345 and 738 these students could not mentally remember the steps and made frequent errors. By the end of the research study, students would have other methods of mental computation that did not depend on trying to remember all the numbers from the standard algorithms. For example, they would add 38 and 45 by saying "Thirty and 40 is 70, and 8 and 5 is 13, and 70 and 13 is 83." Now they were using place value. Instead of adding 3 and 4, they were adding 30 and 40. They could now mentally compute with skill and accuracy.

Mental computation is used in many cultures by people who need to do frequent calculations. For example, in studies[iv] of the Diola people of the Ivory Coast, unschooled children who worked with their parents in the marketplace developed excellent mental computation skills that showed deep insight into the structure and properties of the whole number system.

Mental computation can play an important role in developing number sense through explorations that force students to use numbers and number relations in novel ways that are likely to increase awareness of the structure of the number system. Unfortunately some teachers view mental computation as a skill to be practiced very rapidly. In such cases instruction tends to focus on drill using chain calculations (e.g., 4 + 15; –9; × 2; × 3, –15, ÷ 5 is 9) and on learning "tricks" such as those for multiplying by 9 or by 11. Although such skills are valuable and could have a place in the curriculum, it is questionable whether they should be emphasized at the expense of instruction that could lead children to better number sense.

5.6 | Check Yourself

The power of mental computation and computational estimation skills is that they both cause and result from number flexibility. As you develop these skills you will feel more comfortable with numbers. This is true for elementary school children as well. By providing them opportunities to work with numbers in this personal way, you will allow them to develop a comfort with numbers that can permeate their study of numbers and operations.

You should be able to work problems like those assigned and to meet the following objectives.

1. Perform mental calculations when appropriate, depending on the numbers involved, and do so in a variety of different ways.

2. Identify the associative and commutative properties of addition and multiplication, and the distributive property of multiplication over addition when they are used in a mental computation.

3. Estimate calculations in a variety of ways, for a variety of forms of numbers.

4. Evaluate computational estimations in terms of what they reveal about the number understanding of the person doing the calculations.

5. Use personal benchmarks to estimate, at the least, numerosity and distance.

6. Determine when a number is in scientific notation, and what it means.

7. Discuss why scientific notation makes it easier to express large and small numbers.

8. Express given numbers or do calculations involving scientific notation.

REFERENCES FOR CHAPTER 5

[i] Threadgill-Sowder, J. (1984). Computational estimation procedures of school children. *Journal of Educational Research, 77,* 332–336.

[ii] Sowder, J. T. (1992). Making sense of numbers in school mathematics. In G. Leinhardt, R. Putnam, & R. Hattrup (Eds.), *Analysis of arithmetic for mathematics education.* Hillsdale, NJ: Erlbaum.

[iii] Markovits, Z., & Sowder, J. T. (1994). Developing number sense: An intervention study in grade seven. *Journal for Research in Mathematics Education, 25,* 4–29.

[iv] Ginsburg, H. P., Posner, J. K., & Russell, R. L. (1981). The development of mental addition as a function of schooling and culture. *Journal of Cross-Cultural Psychology, 12*(2), 163–178.

Chapter **6**

Meanings for Fractions

The symbol $\frac{2}{5}$ can be interpreted in several ways. In this chapter, we discuss two such ways, and we make the connections between the different meanings of the fraction symbol.

Discussion 1   Which Is Greater?

1. In which of the following descriptions is the teacher referring to the largest part of her or his class? Be prepared to defend your answer.

   a. $\frac{3}{5}$ of the class   **b.** $\frac{18}{30}$ of the class

   c. 0.6 of the class   **d.** 60% of the class

2. Which represents the greatest quantity of cheese? Be prepared to defend your answer.

   a. $1\frac{3}{4}$ pounds   **b.** $\frac{7}{4}$ pounds   **c.** 1.75 pounds   **d.** 28 ounces

These questions illustrate an especially important idea: The value of a quantity may be expressed in many ways. When a part of a quantity is involved, there is an especially rich variety of forms that the numerical value can take: fractions, decimals, mixed numbers, and percents.

In general, the term "fraction" includes all of the following:

$$\frac{\sqrt{3}}{4} \qquad \frac{3+\sqrt[3]{7}}{5} \qquad \frac{9}{10} \qquad \frac{2}{3} \qquad \frac{1.382}{0.94} \qquad \frac{12\frac{3}{4}}{1\frac{5}{6}} \qquad \frac{2.3\times 10^{3}}{1.7\times 10^{-2}} \qquad \frac{a^{2}}{b}$$

For now, however, the term *fraction* will usually be limited to the form most prominent in elementary school: $\frac{\text{whole number}}{\text{nonzero whole number}}$. You may recall the terms **numerator** and **denominator**, which can be used with any fraction: $\frac{\text{numerator}}{\text{denominator}}$.

6.1 | Understanding the Meanings of $\frac{a}{b}$

There are different meanings associated with a fraction in the usual elementary school curriculum. The first one introduced to the children is the *part-whole* meaning of a fraction, then the *division* meaning (although sometimes not made explicit), and later the *ratio* meaning of the symbol $\frac{a}{b}$. The part-whole and division meanings are the focus of this section. Ratio is considered in Chapter 8.

> The **part-whole** meaning for the fraction $\frac{a}{b}$ has these three elements:
>
> $\frac{a}{b}$
>
> 1. The unit, or whole, is clearly in mind. (What = 1?)
> 2. The denominator tells how many pieces of equal size the unit is cut into (or thought of as being cut into).
> 3. The numerator tells how many such pieces are being considered.

There are two basic kinds of wholes, depending upon whether the unit is *discrete* or *continuous*. Recall from Chapter 3 that quantities that are separate, countable objects are **discrete**. For example, we might say "one half of the team is boys," when each of the two subsets of the team, one subset being girls and the other boys, has the same number of children. In this case the *size* of the part is measured by a **count** of the objects in the whole. If there are 6 players on the team (the whole), then $\frac{1}{2}$ of the team is 3 boys. But not all fractions make sense in a given discrete setting. It would not make much sense to talk about $\frac{1}{7}$ of a team of 6 players, for example.

Quantities are **continuous** when they can be **measured** by length, area, and mass, and so on. Continuous quantities cannot be counted, rather, they are measured. Even though we might say something is 5 inches long, this is only approximate. With lengths, it *is* possible to talk about $\frac{1}{7}$ of a quantity, no matter what that quantity is. This second kind of whole, like a pizza, can be thought of as cut up or marked off into *any* number of equal-sized pieces. (Notice that we cannot do this with a quantity such as number of people.) A pizza (the whole) can be cut up into (approximately) 6 equal-sized pieces, each of which is $\frac{1}{6}$ of the whole pizza, or 13 equal-sized pieces, each being $\frac{1}{13}$ of the whole pizza. We say that such a whole is continuous. The size of a continuous whole and its equally-sized parts can be measured, for example, by length, area, volume, weight, or other noncount measures, depending on its nature. The equally-sized pieces of pizza have the same area on top.

Whether the whole is continuous or discrete, it should be clear that the denominator can never be 0. There will always be *at least one piece* in a continuous unit, or whole, or *at least one object* with a discrete unit, or whole. Note that "equally-sized" is an ideal. In real life the pieces can be only approximately equal.

Activity 1   What Does $\frac{3}{4}$ Mean?

Explain how each of the following diagrams could be used to illustrate the part-whole meaning for $\frac{3}{4}$, making clear what the unit, or whole, is in each case. In which diagrams does $\frac{3}{4}$ refer to a part of a continuous length or region? In which diagrams does it refer to a discrete unit?

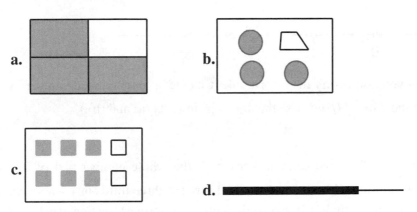

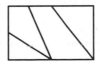

Depending on the context, what the word *size* refers to may vary. If the whole is continuous, say area, or length, or volume, then the part-whole interpretation requires that the pieces have equal sizes: For example, the phrase "3 out of 4" is not good all-purpose language; instead, use the phrase "3 pieces when the whole has 4 *equal pieces*." In a discrete situation the parts do not have to be equal in size, but all the pieces must belong to some set of objects for which it makes sense to talk about parts of the whole, such as in the case of "3 of the 4 pieces of fruit are apples."

In the early grades, the pieces of continuous quantities are most often the same size and shape, but having the same shape is not a requirement. It is only necessary that the unit be in pieces with the same length or area or volume or count, for example, or that the unit can be thought of in terms of such pieces.

Discussion 2   When Are the Parts Equal?

Explain how you know that the pieces are or are not the same size.

 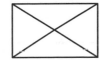

Careful use of drawings, making certain the pieces are the same size, can help develop an understanding of fractions.

Activity 2   What Do the Rules Say? What Do They Mean?

One rule often taught for changing a mixed number like $2\frac{1}{3}$ to a fraction, is multiply the 2 and 3, add the 1, and then write this result over 3, that is, $2\frac{1}{3} = \frac{7}{3}$. Explain how to make that rule sensible, starting with these drawings.

a.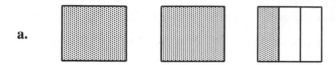

b.

c.   Can you also justify the reverse rule: Change $\frac{7}{3}$ into a mixed number by dividing the 7 by 3? (*Hint:* Use the drawings in parts (a) and (b).)

Note that in the first two parts of Activity 2, the whole number part of $2\frac{1}{3}$, the 2, needs to be considered in terms of thirds. There are three thirds in 1 whole and therefore six thirds in 2 wholes. If you begin with an "improper fraction" such as $\frac{7}{3}$ to be replaced by a mixed number, then you first need to find out how many wholes there are. In this case, because each of the 3 of the 7 pieces makes a whole, there are 2 wholes. What is left over?

Likewise, $\frac{7}{3}$ can be seen as $\frac{3}{3} + \frac{3}{3} + \frac{1}{3} = 2\frac{1}{3}$.

Under the **part-whole view**, $\frac{5}{6}$ means 5 one-sixths and requires only 1 whole. However, there are other meanings for a fraction. An important meaning is that a fraction can denote **division**: $\frac{5}{6}$ can tell how many 6s are in 5, for example.

The fraction $\frac{a}{b}$ can be interpreted to mean **sharing equally division** (or *partitive division*), denoted by $a \div b$, in which case a wholes would be partitioned into b equal parts, each part being an equal "share." The fraction $\frac{a}{b}$ can also be interpreted to mean **repeated subtraction division** (*measurement* or *quotitive division*): How many of b are in a? If the fraction can be represented as $\frac{1}{n}$, or $1 \div n$, it is called a **unit fraction**.

In contrast to the part-whole view, when $\frac{5}{6}$ is interpreted in terms of division, $5 \div 6$, we mean that 5 wholes could be partitioned into 6 equal parts, each of which is an equal "share." This interpretation requires a quite different display from that under the part-whole view.

Activity 3   What Does $\frac{5}{6}$ Mean?

Show that the part-whole $\frac{5}{6}$ is indeed the same amount as $5 \div 6$ (using a partitive, that is, sharing interpretation). Use the square region as the unit in each case.

a.   Show $\frac{5}{6}$.

b.   Show $5 \div 6$
         (partitive).

(For $\frac{5}{6}$, think: "One person gets $\frac{5}{6}$ of a brownie." How can this be shown? For $5 \div 6$, think (for example): "Five brownies are being shared by 6 people." How much does each person get?)

> ### THINK ABOUT . . .
>
> Suppose one wants to show what 0.6 means by using drawings. One could begin with one unit rectangle as the unit whole, or with ten unit rectangles. In each case, how would 0.6 be shown? How do the representations differ?

TAKE-AWAY MESSAGE . . . The fraction symbol can mean different things, but if it is interpreted within a context, one usually knows what the symbol means. The two most common uses in the elementary grades are as part of a whole, and as a way to indicate division. Any time you use fractions in the part-of-a-whole sense, you should be clear about *what unit or whole a given fraction is a fraction of*. Not doing so is frequently a source of many errors in work with fractions. Even in a given situation involving several fractions, not all the fractions have to refer to the same whole. The same pertains to decimals. ◆

Learning Exercises for Section 6.1

1.   In how many ways can you "cut" a square region into two equal pieces?

2.   Using a rectangular or circular region as the whole, make sketches to show each of these:

   a. $\dfrac{2}{3}$ **b.** $\dfrac{7}{4}$ **c.** $2\dfrac{3}{8}$ **d.** $\dfrac{0}{4}$ **e.** $\dfrac{3}{1}$

Notes

3. a. Mark this representation of 4 feet of a licorice whip to show $\frac{3}{4}$ of the licorice whip. ▄▄▄▄▄▄▄▄▄▄▄▄▄▄▄▄▄▄▄▄▄

   b. Mark $\frac{3}{4}$ on the number line.

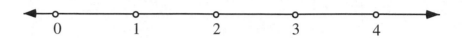

   c. Explain the difference in parts (a) and (b) by referring to the unit.

4. It is important to keep in mind what the unit or whole is for a particular fraction. Make a drawing for this situation: John ate $\frac{1}{4}$ of a cake. Maria ate $\frac{1}{4}$ of the remaining cake. What was the unit or whole in John's case? In Maria's case? How much of a full pan was there in each case?

5. With a square region as unit, show $\frac{3}{2}$ under

   a. the part-whole view.   **b.** the division view.

6. (Pattern Blocks) Using pattern blocks, take the yellow hexagon, the red trapezoid, the blue rhombus, and the green triangle. (Cutouts of the pattern blocks are included in an appendix. Depending upon the colors used, they may or may not be the colors indicated here.)

   a. Let the hexagon = 1. Give the value for each of the other three pieces. (*Note:* = means *represent*.)

   b. Let the trapezoid = 1. Give the value for each of the other three pieces.

   c. Let a pile of two hexagons = 1. Give the values for the hexagon and each of the other three pieces.

7. (Pattern Blocks) In how many different ways can you cover the hexagon? Write an addition equation for each way.

8. Using drawings of circular regions, justify that each of these is true.

   a. $\dfrac{5}{8} > \dfrac{1}{2}$ **b.** $\dfrac{5}{8} < \dfrac{3}{4}$ **c.** $2\dfrac{5}{6} > \dfrac{5}{2}$

9. Use drawings of rectangular regions to find the larger of

   a. $\dfrac{2}{3}$ and $\dfrac{3}{4}$ **b.** $\dfrac{1}{2}$ and $\dfrac{4}{7}$ **c.** $\dfrac{1}{8}$ and $\dfrac{1}{9}$

   Using the part-whole meaning of a fraction, find the larger of each. Write down your explanation.

   d. $\dfrac{12}{17}$ and $\dfrac{12}{19}$ **e.** $\dfrac{10}{9}$ and $\dfrac{11}{9}$ **f.** $\dfrac{62}{101}$ and $\dfrac{62}{121}$

10. You are in charge of the Student Education Association cake sale. As you leave to buy some paper plates, you ask someone you do not know to cut all the cakes.

When you return and look at the cakes (see the diagrams below), you gasp! The plan had been to charge $5 for a whole cake, and you had thought that each piece could be priced by dividing $5 by the number of pieces if necessary.

a. For each cake, is it fair to charge the same amount for each piece? (Do not worry about how the icing is spread, or whether a piece close to an edge might be a little smaller in height.)

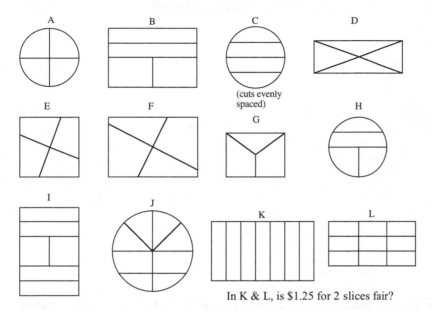

(cuts evenly spaced)

In K & L, is $1.25 for 2 slices fair?

b. Cut your own cake *creatively*, but so that every piece is worth the same amount.

c. Which of your fair/not fair decisions in diagrams A–L would change if the price of a whole cake changed from $5 to some other amount?

d. What does part (a) (A–L) have to do with fractions?

11. Can you say what fraction of the second rectangular region is shaded?[i] Explain.

12. a. If you were offered a piece of cake from one of the following, which cake would give you a piece with more cake?[i]

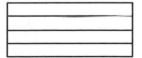 

b. It is interesting that until about grade 3 or 4, children often believe that one cake or the other will give a larger piece. If you have access to a young child, see what he or she says. (First make sure that the child agrees that the cakes are the same size.)

13. $\frac{5}{6}$ of an amount is represented here. How many marks would there be in $\frac{2}{3}$ of the same amount? Explain how you get your answer.

```
                              *                          *      *

                   *                      *      *

                                    *      *      *      *

                          *     *          *      *

                              *         *                          *

                       *      *            *
```

14. Children were asked in one class to show what $\frac{3}{4}$ means in as many ways as possible. Here is the work of three children. How would you evaluate the understanding in each case? (Make certain that you first understand what the child is thinking.)[ii]

Sally:

Sam:

1. $\frac{3}{4}$ is bigger than $\frac{5}{8}$

2. $\frac{3}{4}$ is smaller than 1 whole

3. $\frac{4}{4}$ is bigger than $\frac{3}{4}$

4. $\frac{13}{16}$ is bigger than $\frac{3}{4}$

5. $\frac{32}{16}$ is $\frac{20}{16}$ bigger than $\frac{3}{4}$

Sandy:

1	$\frac{1}{2}$	$\frac{1}{4}$	$\frac{1}{9}$	$\frac{1}{16}$
–	–	–	–	12
–	–	–	1	10
–	–	–	2	8
–	–	–	3	6
–	–	–	4	4
–	–	–	5	2
–	–	–	6	–
–	–	1	–	8
–	–	1	1	6
–	–	1	2	4
–	–	1	3	2
–	–	1	4	–
–	–	2	–	4
–	–	2	1	2
–	–	2	2	–
–	–	3	–	–
–	1	1	–	–
–	1	–	2	–
–	1	–	1	2
–	1	–	–	4

Sandy claimed to have "found them all." What do you think he meant by
that? (Note that this is a table, and that the first row contains headings for
each column.)

15. The region below shows $\frac{3}{4}$ of a candy bar.

   a.   Show how large the original candy bar was. Write down your reasoning.

   b.   Show how large $2\frac{1}{6}$ of the original candy bar would be.

16. The piece of carpet runner below is $2\frac{2}{3}$ units long (the units are usually yards or feet). Drawing as accurately as you can, show each of these. (Trace the piece below to make a separate drawing for each part.)

a. $\frac{3}{4}$ unit   **b.** 4 units   **c.** $1\frac{1}{3}$ units

d. If the $2\frac{2}{3}$ unit piece was for sale for $4.80, what would be a fair price for 1 unit? Write down your reasoning.

17. Pretend that the piece of expensive wire below is 1.25 decimeters long.
    a. Show how long 1 decimeter of wire would be (without using a ruler).

b. If the 1.25-decimeter piece cost $1.60, what would you expect the 1-decimeter piece to cost?

18. Here is part of a number line, with only two points labeled.

```
◄────────┼──────────────┼────────►
         0             1.5
```

Drawing as accurately as you can, locate the points for 2 and for $-\frac{3}{4}$. Explain your reasoning.

19. Use the part-whole notion to explain why $\frac{1}{7} > \frac{1}{8}$; why $\frac{7}{10} > \frac{7}{11}$.

20. A second grader announced to his father that $\frac{2}{7}$ was smaller than $\frac{1}{3}$ but bigger than $\frac{1}{4}$. When asked how he knew, he said "You take 7 sevenths, and you know that 7 divided by 3 is bigger than 2, but 7 divided by 4 is smaller than 2." Can you explain his thinking?

21. Which label, discrete or continuous, applies to each of these "wholes"?
    a. the number of fans at a ball game
    b. the mileage traveled by a wagon train
    c. the amount of Kool-Aid drunk at a third-graders' party
    d. the number of cartons of milk ordered for snack time in kindergarten

22. Make a sketch to show each unit. Then use shading or some sort of marks to indicate the fractional part. Be sure that the thirds are clear.

   a. $\frac{2}{3}$ of the 6 children in the play were girls.

   b. $\frac{2}{3}$ of the 6 yards of cloth were needed for the play.

   c. $\frac{2}{3}$ of the 6 cartons of ice cream were chocolate.

   d. $\frac{2}{3}$ of each of the 6 cartons of ice cream were eaten.

   e. $\frac{2}{3}$ of the 6 moving vans were painted red.

   f. $\frac{2}{3}$ of each of the 6 moving vans were painted red.

   g. The store had 6 cartons of paper towels and used $\frac{2}{3}$ of them.

   h. The store had 6 cartons of paper goods and used $\frac{2}{3}$ of each of them.

6.2 | Equivalent (Equal) Fractions

At times fractions that look different can refer to the value of the same quantity. For example, the symbols $\frac{2}{3}$ and $\frac{100}{150}$ certainly look different to children, but as you know these two fractions are **equivalent**, or **equal** (elementary school textbooks use both terms). For example, $\frac{3}{4} = \frac{6}{8} = \frac{9}{12}$ is reasonable to conclude from these drawings because the same amount of the unit is shaded in each drawing:

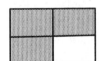 

Starting with $\frac{3}{4}$, each of the original four pieces is cut into two equal pieces, giving $4 \times 2 = 8$ equal pieces all together in the second drawing, of which 6 are shaded: thus $\frac{6}{8}$ is shaded. If each of the original four pieces is cut into three equal size pieces, then 9 of the 12 pieces are shaded: $\frac{9}{12}$ is shaded.

Activity 4   More About $\frac{3}{4}$

Give a similar analysis to show that $\dfrac{3}{4} = \dfrac{3 \times 4}{4 \times 4}$, and make drawings to show

$\dfrac{3}{4} = \dfrac{3 \times 5}{4 \times 5}$.

As a general principle,

$$\frac{a}{b} = \frac{a \times n}{b \times n},$$

as long as n is not 0.

Notice that the above equation can be read in reverse: $\dfrac{a \times n}{b \times n} = \dfrac{a}{b}$. This understanding is also important because it shows that a **common factor** of both the numerator and the denominator, like n, can be "ignored" to give a simpler-looking fraction. (You may recall that a **factor** of a number divides the number leaving no remainder. For example 3 is a factor of 6, 2 is a factor of 6, but 4 is not a factor of 6.)

Thus $\dfrac{12}{30} = \dfrac{6 \times 2}{15 \times 2} = \dfrac{6}{15}$. Also, $\dfrac{6}{15} = \dfrac{2 \times 3}{5 \times 3}$, so $\dfrac{6}{15} = \dfrac{2}{5}$. Because 2 and 5 have no common factors (except 1), we say that $\dfrac{2}{5}$ is the **simplest form** of $\dfrac{12}{30}$. Alternatively, we say $\dfrac{12}{30}$ in **lowest terms** is $\dfrac{2}{5}$.

Note that we could have done this in one step: $\dfrac{12}{30} = \dfrac{2 \times 6}{5 \times 6} = \dfrac{2}{5}$

Finding a simpler form for a fraction is often difficult for children because the common factor is not visible; the common factor must be arrived at by thinking about factors of the numerator and denominator. The common phrase *reduced fraction* is potentially misleading. *Reduce* usually means to decrease in size, but a *reduced* fraction still has the same value as the original. *Simplest form* does not carry any incorrect ideas.

The **greatest common factor (GCF)** of two (or more) whole numbers is the largest number that is a factor of the two (or more) numbers. For example, 2, 3, and 6 are all common factors of 12 and 18, and 6 is the *greatest* common factor of 12 and 18. The GCF is sometimes also called the **greatest common divisor (GCD).**

TAKE-AWAY MESSAGE . . . The ability to recognize equivalent fractions is fundamental to operating with them. The focus in this section was to find a meaning for the ways we used to find equivalent fractions. Of next importance is being able to compare fractions: which of two fractions is larger or smaller. ◆

Learning Exercises for Section 6.2

1. **a.** Write ten fractions that are equivalent to $\frac{2}{3}$ and ten fractions that are equivalent to $\frac{5}{8}$.

   b. Do any of your twenty fractions have **common denominators**?

   c. When would having common denominators be useful?

2. Use sketches of regions or number lines to show each of the following.

   a. $\frac{2}{3} = \frac{10}{15}$
   b. $1\frac{4}{10} = 1\frac{2}{5}$
   c. $\frac{5}{4} = \frac{15}{12}$

3. Find at least one equivalent fraction for each of the following and demonstrate with a diagram that the two fractions are equivalent.

   a. $\frac{3}{5}$
   b. $\frac{3}{4}$
   c. $\frac{0}{2}$

4. Suppose a school committee is made up of 6 girls and 4 boys. What fraction describes the part of the committee that is girls? How would you show, through a diagram, that $\frac{3}{5}$ also describes that part? (*Hint:* GGGGGGBBBB can be organized as GG GG GG …)

5. Write the simplest form for each. For efficiency's sake, try to find the greatest common factor of the numerator and denominator.

   a. $\frac{450}{720}$
   b. $\frac{24 \cdot 45 \cdot 17}{64 \cdot 12 \cdot 17}$
   c. $\frac{225}{144}$

   d. $\frac{x^2 y^3 z^6}{xy^4 z^3}$
   e. $\frac{\left(4.2 \times 10^7\right) \times \left(1.5 \times 10^8\right)}{4.9 \times 10^4}$

6. For the following pairs, place <, >, or = between the two fractions. Use your knowledge of fraction size to complete this exercise.

   a. $\frac{3}{4}$ _ $\frac{3}{5}$
   b. $\frac{102}{101}$ _ $\frac{75}{76}$
   c. $\frac{8}{9}$ _ $\frac{40}{45}$
   d. $\frac{8}{9}$ _ $\frac{9}{10}$
   e. $\frac{13}{18}$ _ $\frac{29}{62}$

7. With the discrete model, choosing the unit to illustrate given equivalent fractions takes some thought. Just any number of objects may not fit the fractions well; a set of 4 objects would not work for showing $\frac{2}{4} = \frac{3}{6}$, for example. Describe a usable unit for showing that each of the following pairs of fractions are equivalent. Then show each fraction on a separate sketch of the unit, in such a way that the equivalence is visually clear. If a context is given, make your sketch to fit that context.

a. $\dfrac{4}{5} = \dfrac{8}{10}$ Context: popsicle sticks

b. $\dfrac{6}{9} = \dfrac{4}{6}$ Context: marbles (Do you have the smallest unit?)

c. $\dfrac{2}{3} = \dfrac{4}{6}$ Context: children

d. $\dfrac{2}{3} = \dfrac{12}{18}$ Context: Choose your own.

8. Sometimes a textbook or a teacher will refer to *reducing* a fraction like $\dfrac{9}{12}$.
   What possible danger do you see in that terminology?

9. Each letter on this number line represents a number. Match the numbers to each operation shown *without doing any calculation*. Use good number sense.

a. $\dfrac{3}{4} \times \dfrac{4}{3}$ b. $2 \times \dfrac{2}{3}$ c. $\dfrac{3}{4} \times \dfrac{1}{2}$

d. $2 \div \dfrac{2}{5}$ e. $\dfrac{1}{3} \times \dfrac{2}{5}$

10. In each case, use number sense rather than equivalent fractions to order these fractions and decimals. Use only these symbols: < and =. Explain your reasoning.

a. $\dfrac{2}{5}$ $\dfrac{2}{3}$ $\dfrac{40}{80}$ 0.60 $\dfrac{7}{10}$

b. $\dfrac{3}{15}$ $\dfrac{1}{10}$ 0.4,   0.1 $\dfrac{1}{5}$ 0.2

11. Go to http://illuminations.nctm.org/, then to **Activities**. Place check marks in the box before 3–5 and another in the box 6–8 and click on **Search**. Scroll down to **Equivalent Fractions** and click to open. Click on the box to the left of **Instructions**. Do several sets of problems, as directed in the instructions, sometimes using circles, sometimes squares.

12. In the same activity given in Exercise 11, use the circle choice. Ignore the red circle. Use only the blue and green circles to find which is the larger. Use the <, >, and = symbols as appropriate. You may need to use the number line below the circles.

a. $\dfrac{2}{3}$ $\dfrac{1}{2}$ b. $\dfrac{3}{5}$ $\dfrac{7}{11}$ c. $\dfrac{3}{10}$ $\dfrac{5}{12}$

d. $\dfrac{2}{5}$ $\dfrac{5}{16}$ e. $\dfrac{3}{4}$ $\dfrac{7}{11}$ f. $\dfrac{5}{14}$ $\dfrac{5}{16}$

6.3 | **Relating Fractions, Decimals, and Percents**

When children in a research study[iii] were asked to find the sum $5 + 0.5 + \frac{1}{2}$, many said it could not be done because they thought fractions and decimals could not be combined. But as you know, fractions and decimals (and percents) are very closely related even though they look different. All fractions can be expressed as decimals, using a division interpretation of a fraction, and many decimals can be expressed as fractions in a $\frac{\text{whole number}}{\text{nonzero whole number}}$ form. And both fractions and decimals can be represented as percents.

> ### THINK ABOUT . . .
>
> In the last chapter you practiced estimating with percents. How are percents related to fractions and to decimals?

Activity 5   Reviewing Something I Learned Long Ago

Write the following as percents:

a. $\frac{3}{4}$ **b.** $\frac{1}{2}$ **c.** 0.37   **d.** 1.45   **e.** 0.028   **f.** 43.21

Write the following as decimals and as fractions:

g. 32%   **h.** 123%   **i.** 0.01%   **j.** 43.2%

Activity 6   Can Every Fraction Be Represented as a Decimal?

Write an exact decimal equivalent for each fraction in a–h. Be sure to discuss any that cause difficulty, and to reach consensus.

a. $\frac{2}{5}$ **b.** $\frac{2}{3}$ **c.** $\frac{2}{40}$ **d.** $\frac{1}{7}$

e. $\frac{23}{800}$ **f.** $\frac{16}{250}$ **g.** $\frac{3}{12}$ **h.** $\frac{24}{35}$

i. Which of these decimals terminate? What can be said about the denominators in each of the fractions? (Hint: Rewrite the denominators as products of 2s and 5s. If this cannot be done, see if you can first simplify the fraction.)

j. Which decimals did not terminate? Can you find a part of each of these decimals that repeats?

When the denominator of a fraction is a power of 10, changing the fraction to a decimal representation is easy: for example, $\frac{3}{100} = 0.03$. Note that any power of 10 can be written as a product of 2s and 5s. For example, $100 = 2^2 \, 5^2$ and $1000 = 2^3 \, 5^3$. When a denominator has factors of only 2s and 5s, we can rewrite the fraction so that it has an equal number of 2s and 5s in the denominator. Doing so allows us to easily change the fraction to a decimal number.

EXAMPLE 1

$$\frac{7}{40} = \frac{7}{2^3 5} \times \frac{5^2}{5^2} = \frac{175}{1000} = 0.175$$

EXAMPLE 2

$$\frac{16}{250} = \frac{8}{125} = \frac{8}{5^3} = \frac{8 \times 2^3}{5^3 \times 2^3} = \frac{64}{1000} = 0.064$$

THINK ABOUT . . .

$\frac{3}{12}$ yielded a terminating decimal representation, but 12 cannot be factored as a product of only 2s and 5s. Why did this happen? Why did $\frac{3}{12}$ give a terminating decimal?

From Examples 1 and 2 and the previous Think About, we can conclude the following.

A fraction $\frac{a}{b}$ in simplest form can be represented with a terminating decimal when the denominator has only 2s and 5s as factors, because we can always find an equivalent fraction with a denominator that is a power of 10.

Discussion 3   Remainders That Repeat

1. What are the possible remainders when you divide a whole number by 7? How many possible remainders are there? Test your conclusion by calculating 1 divided by 7. When a remainder repeats, what happens when you continue the division calculation?

2. How many possible remainders are there when you divide a whole number by 11? Test your conclusion on $\frac{3}{11}$ and revise your conclusion if necessary.

Nonterminating, repeating decimals, like those you get for $\frac{1}{7}$ and $\frac{3}{11}$, are often abbreviated by putting a bar over the repeating part.

EXAMPLE 3

$4.333333.... = 4.\overline{3}$ and $1.7245245245245...... = 1.7\overline{245}$

THINK ABOUT . . .

How many repeating digits *might* there be in the decimal equivalent for $\dfrac{n}{73}$, for different whole number values for *n*?

We now can conclude one more fact about a fraction in simplest form.

> In general, a fraction $\frac{a}{b}$ in simplest form can be represented with a non-terminating, repeating decimal if the denominator has factors other than 2s and 5s.

The reverse question can now be considered: *Can every decimal be represented as a fraction?*

Activity 7   From Decimals to Fractions

For each of the following decimals, can you write the number as a fraction?

a. 0.62   **b.** 1.25   **c.** $0.\overline{6}$ **d.** 0.125   **e.** $0.\overline{5}$

You may remember that $\frac{2}{3} = 0.6666\ldots = 0.\overline{6}$. But you probably had difficulty with changing $0.\overline{5}$ to a fraction. Here is a way to think about repeating decimals.

Think of $0.\overline{5}$ as $0.5555\ldots$ and multiply by 10:

$$10 \cdot 0.\overline{5} \quad = \quad 10 \cdot (0.5555\ldots)$$

which gives

$$10 \cdot 0.\overline{5} \quad = \quad 5.5555\ldots$$

but

$$\underline{\qquad 0.\overline{5} \quad = \quad 0.5555\ldots}$$

$$\underbrace{10 \cdot 0.\overline{5} - 0.\overline{5}}_{9 \cdot 0.\overline{5}} \quad = \quad 5.0000\ldots \qquad \text{Subtract on both sides.}$$

$$9 \cdot 0.\overline{5} \quad = \quad 5 \qquad \text{Now divide both sides by 9.}$$

$$0.\overline{5} \quad = \quad \frac{5}{9}$$

If you try dividing 5 by 9 on a calculator, the quotient will appear as a terminating decimal (0.555556) only because there are a finite number of places on the screen. Thus, the calculator generated quotient for 5 divided by 9 is really only an estimate of $\dfrac{5}{9}$, albeit a very close one.

Activity 8   Your Turn

Find fraction equivalents for

a. $0.\overline{4}$ **b.** $18.\overline{2}$ **c.** $0.\overline{1}$

Notes

THINK ABOUT . . .

1. To find the fractional equivalent of $0.\overline{4}$ you multiplied by 10. Could you multiply by 100 and get the same result? Consider $0.\overline{35}$. Would multiplying by 10 help find its fractional equivalent? Why not? Would multiplying by 100 help? Why?

2. What is $0.\overline{9}$?

3. Write 0.24 as a fraction, and 0.240 as a fraction. Are the fractions equal? What does this result imply about placing zeros after a decimal number?

The decimals we have considered thus far all terminate or repeat. All can also be represented as fractions.

> A **rational number** is a number that can be written as a terminating or repeating decimal or its fractional equivalent.

The word rational comes from the word *ratio,* which is one way of interpreting a fraction symbol.

Nonterminating, nonrepeating decimals cannot be represented as fractions with whole numbers as the numerator and as the denominator, so they are not rational numbers. They are called **irrational numbers**. For example, $\sqrt{3}$ is an irrational number. It cannot be written as a fraction in which the numerator and denominator are whole numbers, and its decimal is nonterminating and nonrepeating. The set of rational numbers together with the set of irrational numbers form the set of **real numbers**. All numbers used in this course are real numbers, and they are sufficient for all of elementary and middle school mathematics. Below is a Venn diagram showing how some sets of numbers are related. (If you remember enough about integers, place them correctly in this Venn diagram.)

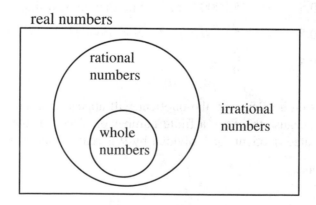

THINK ABOUT . . .

$\sqrt{3}$ on a calculator may give 1.7320508. But $1.7320508 = \frac{1732508}{10000000}$, so why is $\sqrt{3}$ said to be irrational?

TAKE-AWAY MESSAGE . . . All fractions of the form $\frac{a}{b}$ with whole numbers a and b where $b \neq 0$ can be written in decimal form; some terminate and some repeat. Vice versa, decimals that terminate or repeat can be written as fractions. These numbers are known as rational numbers.

If a nonterminating decimal does not repeat, it names an irrational number. Together the rational numbers and the irrational numbers make up the set of numbers we call real numbers. ♦

Learning Exercises for Section 6.3

1. Determine which of the following fractions have repeating decimals. Then write each fraction as a terminating or as a repeating decimal.

   a. $\frac{3}{8}$ **b.** $2\frac{3}{10}$ **c.** $\frac{3}{7}$ **d.** $\frac{3}{11}$

2. Write the following decimals as fractions, if possible. Change to simplest form or lowest terms.

   a. 0.625   **b.** 0.49   **c.** 91.333 . . .

   d. 1.7   **e.** $0.\overline{9}$ **f.** $0.9\overline{3}$

   g. $0.\overline{53}$ **h.** 0.1213141516171819110111112113114115 . . .

   (There is a pattern in part (h). Assume that the pattern you see continues. Is there a repeating block of digits?)

3. **a.** Are there any fractions between $\frac{7}{15}$ and $\frac{8}{15}$? If so, how many are there?

   b. Are there any decimal numbers between $\frac{7}{15}$ and $\frac{8}{15}$?

4. Find decimal numbers between each pair of numbers:

   a. 0.4 and 0.5

   b. 0.444 and 0.445

   c. 1.3567 and 1.35677777 . . .

   d. 0.00000111111 . . . and 0.000001100110011 . . .

5. Place the following in order from smallest to largest without using a calculator:

   $\frac{2}{3}$ $\frac{5}{6}$ $0.\overline{56}$ 1.23 $\frac{3}{17}$ $\frac{12}{15}$ $\frac{11}{29}$ $\frac{11}{24}$ $0.2\overline{6}$ $\frac{1}{4}$ 0.21

6. Explain how you know there is an error, without calculating:

   $\frac{\text{some whole number}}{7} = 4.29\overline{23456789}$.

7. One type of calculator can show only 8 digits. Suppose the calculator answer to a calculation is 8.1249732. Explain how the exact answer could be

   a. a terminating decimal.

   b. a repeating decimal.

   c. an irrational number.

8. Draw lines to show what value these decimal numbers and percents are close to. (Don't use a calculator.)

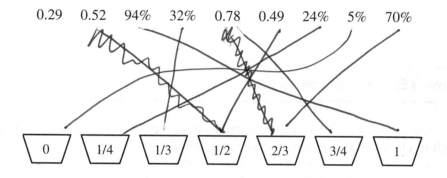

   0.29   0.52   94%   32%   0.78   0.49   24%   5%   70%

   0   1/4   1/3   1/2   2/3   3/4   1

9. Complete the following table.

Decimal form	Fraction	Percent
0.48	$\frac{48}{100}$	
	$\frac{4}{5}$	
		457%
		0.1%

10. Chris says, "0.3 is bigger than 0.65 because tenths are bigger than hundredths."

   Sam says, "0.28 is bigger than 0.3 because 28 is bigger than 3."

   Lars says, "0.72 is bigger than 0.6 because 0.72 has seven tenths and 0.6 has only six tenths and the hundredths don't matter here."

   a. Discuss these answers. Which is correct? Would you have made any of these errors?

   b. Order these from smallest to largest: 0.7   0.645   0.64

   c. Here are the ways that Chris, Sam, and Lars ordered these numbers from smallest to largest. Match the name with the order. Use the reasoning above to figure out which name goes with which ordering.

      _____ 0.7   0.64   0.645

      _____ 0.645   0.64   0.7

      _____ 0.64   0.645   0.7

11. A student says, "My calculator shows 0.0769231 for $\frac{1}{13}$ when I divide 1 by 13." Does this mean that $\frac{1}{13}$ is equivalent to a terminating decimal? Explain.

12. A student says, "My calculator shows that $\sqrt{2}$ is 1.4142136. And $1.4142136 = \frac{14,142,136}{10,0000,000}$, which is a rational number. But you said $\sqrt{2}$ is an irrational number. Which is it, rational or irrational?" How would you respond to the student?

13. Go to http://illuminations.nctm.org/, then to **Activities**. Check 3–5 and 6–8, then **Search**. Scroll down to **Fraction Model I** and click to open. Read **Instructions**. Use this applet to complete the following table:

Fractions	Decimal	Percent
	0.25	
$\frac{11}{10}$		
	3.1	
$\frac{13}{20}$		
		250%
$\frac{17}{4}$		
	1.8	
$\frac{14}{5}$		
	3.4	
		30%

14. Again go to http://illuminations.nctm.org/ and to **Fraction Model III**. Read the instructions and then complete the following table:

Fraction	Decimal	Percent
		500%
$\frac{50}{54}$		
$\frac{95}{67}$		
	1.5	
	0.04	
		73%
		2351%
$\frac{1}{3}$		

6.4 | Estimating Fractional Values

In Chapter 5 you practiced estimating with whole numbers and percents. An understanding of fractions makes estimating with fractions also quite easy. Using numerical benchmarks with fractions can simplify estimating computational results. Recognizing errors when computing with fractions is also a by-product of knowing benchmarks for fractional values.

Activity 9　　Happy Homeowner?

Consider the following situation:

◆ You have heard that housing costs should be about $\frac{1}{3}$ of your income. Your income is $1300 per month, and you currently spend $695 per month in housing payments. ◆

a. Name as many quantities as you can that are involved in this situation.

b. Which quantity in this situation has a value of $\frac{1}{3}$?

c. Which quantity in this situation has a value of $\frac{695}{1300}$? Is this fraction close to a familiar fraction?

d. Can you tell whether you are paying more or less for housing than the guidelines suggest without a calculator or lengthy computations?

Just as benchmarks can be useful in getting a feel for large values of quantities, they can also be helpful in dealing with small numbers. Whenever we have a quantity whose value is expressed as a fraction, it may be useful to compare this fractional value to a more familiar value, such as 0, $\frac{1}{3}$, $\frac{1}{2}$, $\frac{2}{3}$, or 1. In Activity 9, for example, being able to tell quickly whether the fraction is more or less than $\frac{1}{3}$ allows us to gain an understanding of the situation without extensive calculations. We were able to make this decision based on the fact that $\frac{695}{1300}$ is close to $\frac{700}{1400}$, which is equivalent to $\frac{1}{2}$. (Note that the denominator would need to be close to 2100 for the fraction to be closer to $\frac{1}{3}$.) Making these types of comparisons can give us a feel for the relative size or magnitude of less familiar fractions. Developing the ability to estimate with fractions is the focus of this section.

Discussion 4　　Formalizing "Close To"

1. Describe ways of telling (by simple inspection and without using a calculator) when a fraction has a value close to 0. Is $\frac{2}{3}$ close to 0? How about $\frac{2}{5}$? How about $\frac{2}{9}$? How about $\frac{2}{18}$?

Notes

2. Describe ways of telling when a fraction has a value close to 1. Is $\frac{7}{16}$ close to 1? How about $\frac{9}{18}$? How about $\frac{17}{18}$? How about $\frac{97}{108}$?

3. Describe ways of telling when a fraction has a value close to $\frac{1}{2}$. Is $\frac{4}{8}$ close to $\frac{1}{2}$? Is $\frac{5}{8}$ close to $\frac{1}{2}$? How about $\frac{9}{16}$? How about $\frac{7}{16}$?

4. Describe ways of telling when a fraction is close to $\frac{1}{3}$.

5. Describe ways of telling when a number is larger than 1; smaller than 1.

6. Describe ways of telling when a number is a little more than $\frac{1}{2}$; a little less than $\frac{1}{2}$.

Activity 10   Number Neighbors

For each of the following fractions, indicate whether it is closest to 0, $\frac{1}{2}$, 1, or whether it really is not close to any of these three numbers. Think of each fraction as a point on the number line.

1. $\frac{3}{8}$ 2. $\frac{5}{4}$ 3. $\frac{2}{9}$ 4. $\frac{4}{7}$ 5. $\frac{1}{3}$

6. $\frac{1}{6}$ 7. $\frac{8}{9}$ 8. $\frac{9}{8}$ 9. $\frac{4}{9}$ 10. $\frac{5}{6}$

11. $\frac{21}{45}$ 12. $\frac{13}{15}$ 13. $\frac{34}{64}$ 14. $\frac{13}{84}$ 15. $\frac{3}{7}$

In Activity 10, a fraction was close to 1 when its numerator and denominator were close. For example, 13 is close to 15, so $\frac{13}{15}$ is close to 1. This "rule" works when the numbers in the numerator and denominator are fairly large. For example, 13 and 15 are only two apart, as are 2 and 4. But to say that $\frac{2}{4}$ is close to one is not accurate because $\frac{2}{4}$ is the same as $\frac{1}{2}$.

Which number is closer to 0, $\frac{1}{8}$ or $\frac{1}{9}$? $\frac{1}{9}$ is the smaller of the two (that is, if something is cut into 9 equal pieces, one of them is smaller than one of 8 equal pieces of the same quantity). So we know that $\frac{1}{9}$ is closer to 0.

Activity 11   Reasoning with Fractions

1. You now know that $\frac{1}{8}$ is larger than $\frac{1}{9}$. How can you use this information to tell which fractional value is closer to 1:

   $\frac{7}{8}$ or $\frac{8}{9}$? Explain your reasoning (without using decimals).

Notes

2. For each given pair of numbers, tell which fractional value is closer to $\frac{1}{2}$. Explain your reasoning.

   a. $\frac{11}{25}$ or $\frac{12}{25}$

   b. $\frac{5}{8}$ or $\frac{9}{20}$

   c. $\frac{12}{25}$ or $\frac{7}{15}$

   d. $\frac{11}{24}$ or $\frac{9}{20}$

   e. $\frac{7}{15}$ or $\frac{13}{25}$

The knowledge gained in Activities 10 and 11 can be useful when estimating with fractions. For example, $\frac{15}{16} + \frac{1}{9}$ would be close to $1 + 0$, or simply 1.

> ***THINK ABOUT . . .***
>
> Find an estimate for $3\frac{4}{9} - 2\frac{15}{16}$.

TAKE-AWAY MESSAGE . . . Having rules of thumb about fractions close to, larger than, and smaller than 0, $\frac{1}{2}$, or 1 can be very useful in making estimates and checking whether an answer is reasonable. Thinking about rules of thumb for $\frac{1}{3}$, $\frac{2}{3}$, and $\frac{1}{4}$ comes up in the exercises. ♦

Learning Exercises for Section 6.4

1. A sign says that all merchandise is being sold for a fraction of its original price. Your friend cynically says, "Yeah, $\frac{5}{4}$ of the original price." Why is this a cynical remark?

2. A student worked the problem: "The sewing pattern called for $\frac{7}{12}$ yard of silk and $\frac{5}{8}$ yard of linen. How much fabric was in the blouse?" He wrote $\frac{7}{12} + \frac{5}{8} = \frac{23}{24}$. Is the result of the calculation sensible? How can you tell by simple inspection, without actually performing the computation?

3. Is it possible for a fraction to have a value less than 0? Explain.

4. Draw lines from the fractions to the baskets. Compare them with a classmate's when you have the opportunity. Discuss any differences. What did you do when a number could go in more than one basket?

$$\frac{4}{7} \qquad \frac{2}{9} \qquad \frac{11}{12} \qquad \frac{99}{152} \qquad \frac{17}{35} \qquad \frac{15}{34} \qquad \frac{11}{108} \qquad \frac{3}{12} \qquad \frac{9}{8}$$

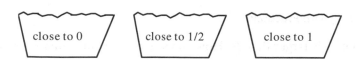

close to 0   close to 1/2   close to 1

5. When is a fraction close to $\frac{1}{3}$? When is a fraction close to $\frac{2}{3}$? After you have answered these questions, draw lines from fractions to the appropriate baskets.

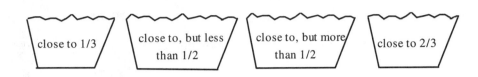

$$\frac{4}{9} \quad \frac{21}{29} \quad \frac{49}{99} \quad \frac{15}{47} \quad \frac{27}{52} \quad \frac{42}{63} \quad \frac{31}{45} \quad \frac{22}{47} \quad \frac{99}{152} \quad \frac{2}{7}$$

close to 1/3   close to, but less than 1/2   close to, but more than 1/2   close to 2/3

6. In each case, tell which quantity is larger by thinking about how close or far each fraction is from 0, 1, or $\frac{1}{2}$.

a. $\frac{3}{4}$ or $\frac{4}{9}$ of the class?

b. $\frac{1}{3}$ or $\frac{1}{4}$ of a cup?

c. $\frac{3}{4}$ or $\frac{9}{10}$ of a meter?

d. $\frac{2}{5}$ or $\frac{3}{6}$ of those voting?

e. $\frac{13}{24}$ or $\frac{11}{20}$ of the money budgeted?

f. $\frac{11}{25}$ or $\frac{17}{15}$ of the distance?

7. How can you tell when a fraction has a value close to $\frac{1}{4}$?

8. Find a fraction *between* each pair of fractional values. Assume that the two fractions refer to the same unit. Justify your reasoning. (Do not change to decimal form.)

a. $\frac{2}{5}$ and $\frac{3}{5}$

b. $\frac{8}{15}$ and $\frac{9}{12}$

c. $\frac{7}{8}$ and $\frac{9}{10}$

d. $\frac{17}{18}$ and $\frac{17}{16}$

e. $\frac{1}{4}$ and $\frac{1}{3}$

9. A child claims that $\frac{4}{5}$ and $\frac{5}{6}$ are the same because, "they are both missing one piece." What would you do to help this child come to understand these fractions better?

10. There are some commonly used fractions for which you should know the decimal equivalent without needing to divide to find it. And of course, if you know decimal equivalents it is quite easy to find percent equivalents. For each of the following, give the decimal and percent equivalents to all the ones you know. Find the others by dividing, and then memorize these too.

a. $\frac{1}{8}$

b. $\frac{1}{5}$

c. $\frac{1}{4}$

d. $\frac{1}{3}$

e. $\frac{2}{5}$

f. $\frac{3}{8}$

g. $\frac{5}{4}$

h. $\frac{1}{2}$

i. $\frac{3}{5}$

j. $\frac{5}{8}$

k. $\frac{2}{3}$

l. $\frac{3}{4}$

m. $\frac{4}{5}$

n. $\frac{7}{8}$

o. 1

p. $\frac{7}{4}$

11. Name a fraction or whole number that is *close to* being equivalent to each percent.

a. 24%

b. 95%

c. 102%

d. 35%

e. 465%

f. 12%

Notes

12. In Chapter 5 you learned ways of finding fractional equivalents for percents. For example, $10\% = \frac{1}{10}$, $25\% = \frac{1}{4}$, and $50\% = \frac{1}{2}$. Use this knowledge to *estimate* each of the following amounts.

    a. 15% of 798   **b.** 90% of 152   **c.** 128% of 56

    d. 65% of 24   **e.** 59% of 720   **f.** 9% of 59

    g. 148% of 32   **h.** 0.1% of 24   **i.** 32% of 69

13. Draw a diagram that shows why $\frac{4}{5}$ of a given amount is the same as $\frac{8}{10}$ of the same amount.

14. Draw a diagram that shows the sum $\frac{4}{5} + \frac{3}{10}$.

15. An anonymous donor has offered to pledge \$1 to a local charity for every \$3 that is pledged by the general public. Draw a picture that represents the public's donation, the matching pledge by the anonymous donor, and the total amount donated to the charity. What fractional part of the total amount donated is pledged by the general public?

16. A child claims that $\frac{1}{4}$ can be greater than $\frac{1}{2}$, and draws the following picture to support her argument:

Cake

Cookie

How would you respond to this child's claim? Can you adapt this picture to explain why $\frac{1}{2}$ is larger than $\frac{1}{4}$?

17. Estimate answers for each of the following fraction computations. Can you say whether your estimate is larger than or smaller than the exact answer would be? Remember what you learned earlier about number neighbors.

    a. $\dfrac{5}{8} + \dfrac{9}{10}$ **b.** $1\dfrac{7}{16} + 4\dfrac{3}{27} + 7$ **c.** $14\dfrac{9}{10} - 5\dfrac{1}{16}$

    d. $4\dfrac{11}{12} - 2\dfrac{15}{16}$ **e.** $\dfrac{20}{31} - \dfrac{1}{3}$ **f.** $4\dfrac{7}{16} + 5\dfrac{11}{12} - 2\dfrac{1}{8}$

18. a. *About* what *percent* of the circle at the right is each piece?

      A _____B _____ C _____ D _____E _____

      What percent is the sum of your estimates?

      Is this reasonable?

    b. *About* what *fraction* of the circle is each piece?

      A _____B _____ C _____ D _____E _____

      What should the sum of these fractional parts be?

6.5 | Issues for Learning: Understanding Fractions and Decimals

Even young children in the early grades have some understanding of parts and wholes, but they do not always relate this to the fraction symbol. There are several critical ideas[iv] that children need to understand before they can successfully operate on fractions. They include the following:

1. When a whole (in this case a continuous whole) is broken into equal parts, then the more parts there are, the smaller each part will be. Thus $\frac{1}{6}$ is smaller than $\frac{1}{5}$. Even though children might know this in a particular setting such as pieces of pizza, they still need to learn this symbolically.

2. Fractions represent specific numbers. That is, $\frac{3}{5}$ itself is the value of a quantity; $\frac{3}{5}$ is *one* number, not *two* numbers separated by a bar. When students do not understand this relationship between the numerator and the denominator they operate on them separately. They might say, for example, that $\frac{3}{5} + \frac{2}{3} = \frac{5}{8}$.

3. Equivalence is one of the most crucial ideas students must understand before operating on fractions and decimals. Children will not be able to add or subtract fractions until they can identify and generate equivalent fractions, because they often need to find an equivalent form of a fraction before they can add or subtract.

4. Children must understand why *like denominators* are necessary before one can add or subtract fractions. Only when there is a common denominator for two fractions are they adding or subtracting like pieces, because now both fractions refer to a common size for the pieces.

There are similar problems working with decimal notation. Students may not understand what the decimal point indicates. If they estimate the value of 48.85 as, for example, 50.9, then they are treating the 48 separately from the .85.

The work of Chris, Sam, and Lars shown in the Learning Exercises for Section 6.3 illustrates some common misunderstandings of decimals that have been found in a number of countries. Some children think that because hundredths are smaller than tenths, 2.34, which has hundredths, is smaller than 2.3, which has tenths. Others think that the number of digits indicates relative size, as is true for whole numbers. Thus 2.34 is considered larger than 2.4 because 234 is larger than 24.

Teachers often have students compare numbers such as 2.34 and 2.3 by "adding zeros until each number has the same number of places." Now the comparison is between 2.34 and 2.30. While this technique works, often it is not meaningful and becomes just another trick of the trade, unless children are also taught that 2.30 and 2.3 are equal; that if 2.30 and 2.3 are represented by base ten blocks, they would be represented identically. Another approach is to have students express 0.3 and 0.30 as fractions in simplest form to show that they are equivalent.

6.6 | Check Yourself

This chapter focused on understanding the meaning of the fraction symbol, particularly the part-whole meaning and the division meaning. You should be able to clearly distinguish between these two meanings by drawings that would indicate how they would be illustrated differently, but still represent the same amount. Some attention is also given to decimals and percents.

You should be able to work problems like those assigned and to meet the following objectives.

1. Distinguish between, and identify, discrete and continuous units used for a fraction representation.

2. Generate sketches that illustrate a given fraction or mixed number, and identify fractions or mixed numbers shown in any drawing, whether the number is less than 1 or greater than 1.

3. Given a part of a whole and the fraction this represents, find the whole.

4. Generate drawings that show why two equivalent fractions represent the same amount.

5. Change fractions to decimal form and percent form and change repeating and terminating decimals to fractions and to percents.

6. Define *rational number* and *irrational number* and be able to recognize each.

7. Describe the numbers that are real numbers.

8. Be able to order a set of fractions, decimal numbers, and percents from smallest to largest, without (in most cases) resorting to changing all the numbers to decimal numbers or using equivalent fractions.

9. Identify fractions that are close to 0; fractions that are close to, smaller than, or larger than $\frac{1}{2}$; and fractions that are close to, smaller than, or larger than 1. You should be able to explain your reasons for these identifications.

10. Discuss fundamental ideas about fractions that are necessary for addition and subtraction of fractions.

REFERENCES FOR CHAPTER 6

[i] Armstrong, B. E., & Larson, C. N. (1995). Students' use of part-whole and direct-comparison strategies for comparing partitioned rectangles. *Journal for Research in Mathematics Education, 26*, 2–19.

[ii] Kieren, T. Problems shared with the authors.

[iii] Sowder, J., & Markovits, Z. (1991). Students' understanding of the relationship between fractions and decimals. *Focus on Learning Problems in Mathematics, 13*, 3–11.

[iv] Mack, N. K. (1995). Critical ideas, informal knowledge, and understanding fractions. In J. T. Sowder & B. P. Schappelle (Eds.), *Providing a foundation for teaching mathematics in the middle grades,* (pp. 67–84). Albany, NY: SUNY Press.

Chapter 7

Computing with Fractions

Why do you need a common denominator to add or subtract fractions, but not for multiplying and dividing them? Why do you end up *multiplying* to divide by a fraction? If mathematics is to make sense, questions like these must have answers. This chapter reviews the step-by-step processes—the algorithms—used in computing with fractions, with a focus on making sense of these algorithms.

7.1 | Adding and Subtracting Fractions

In the last chapter you had the opportunity to develop a good understanding of the nature of fractions. In this chapter you will study the ways in which we operate with fractions and why these ways work. We begin here with addition and subtraction of fractions.

THINK ABOUT . . .

Which of these two calculations is easier:

$$\frac{79}{144} + \frac{35}{144} - \frac{13}{144} \quad \text{or} \quad \frac{3}{8} + \frac{1}{6} + \frac{2}{15}? \quad \text{Why?}$$

No doubt you recognized that the first set of calculations, despite the "ugly" fractions, is easier than the second because the denominators are all the same. Why does that make the calculations easier? Under a part-whole view of fractions, having the same denominator (or *common denominator*) means that if the unit is cut into that number of equal-sized pieces, then it is easy to add or subtract the numerators for every fraction in order to count the number of equal-sized pieces in the result. In effect the first calculation involves only 79 + 35 − 13, with the result telling the number of $\frac{1}{144}$ pieces.

In the second set of calculations, however, the different denominators mean that the pieces involved are (probably) different sizes, so it is *not* just a matter of counting pieces. In the diagram on the next page, the pieces are of different sizes, and thus they cannot just be counted to give a sum.

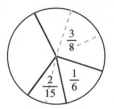

Even though it is easy to *see* the total amount for the sum in the drawing, naming that quantity is a puzzle. That is why having a common denominator is a first step in calculating sums and differences of fractions with paper and pencil. Each fraction is replaced with an equal fraction having the common denominator, which gives all underlying pieces the same size.

Finding a common denominator is not difficult: Find the product of all the given denominators (this product gives a **multiple** of each denominator). For $\frac{3}{8}+\frac{1}{6}+\frac{2}{15}$, $8 \times 6 \times 15 = 720$, so 720 could be a common denominator. We would get

$$\frac{3}{8} + \frac{1}{6} + \frac{2}{15} = \frac{270}{720} + \frac{120}{720} + \frac{96}{720} = \frac{270+120+96}{720} = \frac{486}{720} = \dots = \frac{27}{40}.$$

The drawback of this method for finding a common denominator is that you usually do more calculation than necessary because smaller denominators would also work here: 120, 240, 360, 480, 600. The smallest denominator that works here is 120.

A number is the **least common multiple (LCM)** of a set of numbers if it is a common multiple of each of the numbers (that is, each number in the set is a factor) and it is the smallest number greater than zero with this property. If the set of numbers are all denominators of fractions, then the LCM is often called the **least common denominator (LCD)**.

EXAMPLE

0, 30, 60, 90, 120… are all common multiples of 6 and 15. But the smallest nonzero multiple is 30, so 30 is the LCM.

Try computing $\frac{3}{8}+\frac{1}{6}+\frac{2}{15}$ with the least common denominator, 120, and compare the difficulty of calculation to that with the 720 denominator.

Finding the least common denominator is not a trivial task; one way is mentioned in the exercises if you do not remember any method. More attention is paid to finding the LCD in Chapter 11.

Discussion 1   Algorithms for Adding and Subtracting Fractions

Algorithms for adding and subtracting fractions are sometimes expressed symbolically as follows: $\dfrac{a}{b} + \dfrac{c}{d} = \dfrac{ad + bc}{bd}$, and $\dfrac{a}{b} - \dfrac{c}{d} = \dfrac{ad - bc}{bd}$. Do they make sense?

Apply the first rule to $\dfrac{3}{8} + \dfrac{1}{4}$. Is there an easier way to add these fractions than using the rule?

_____

Once all fractions in a set have common denominators, you can perform the operations of addition and subtraction on the numerators to find the answer. As you may recall from the previous chapter, these fractions now describe pieces of the same size, which means you are adding and subtracting like parts.

Activity 1   Can You Picture This?

1. Describe how the following drawing can be used to show $\frac{1}{2} + \frac{1}{3}$.

2. Describe how the following drawing can be used to show $\frac{1}{2} - \frac{1}{3}$.

_____

Discussion 2   Properties of Addition with Fractions

1. Does commutativity of addition hold for fractions? Explain.

2. Does associativity of addition hold for fractions? Explain.

_____

Discussion 3   Comparing Fractions Additively

Comparing fractional values additively calls for subtraction. That is, to find how much more $\frac{7}{8}$ is than $\frac{1}{2}$, you can subtract. What other situations involving fractional values would call for subtraction? Give some examples of story problems that involve fractions or mixed numbers and could be answered by subtracting.

_____

TAKE-AWAY MESSAGE . . . Addition and subtraction of fractions requires understanding that a fraction names a number, a value for a quantity; that fractions can easily be added and subtracted when they refer to a common sub-unit, which requires that they have a common denominator; and that changing the representation of a fraction to one with the common denominator requires understanding of equivalent fractions. ♦

Learning Exercises for Section 7.1

1. Explain your method for finding a common denominator for $\frac{3}{8} + \frac{1}{6} + \frac{2}{15}$.

2. Embedding calculations in contexts like story problems is often helpful in keeping track of the unit. Compare these two problems. How do you think the misunderstanding in part (a) arises?

   a. A student thinks that $\frac{3}{4} + \frac{2}{4} = \frac{5}{8}$ because of his drawing:

   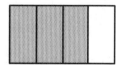 

   b. In a cake-eating contest, Ann ate $\frac{3}{4}$ of a cake and Bea ate $\frac{2}{4}$ of a cake. How much cake did they consume in all?

3. Using a rectangular region as the unit, illustrate each of the following:

   a. $\frac{2}{5} + \frac{1}{2}$ **b.** $\frac{16}{20} - \frac{2}{5}$ **c.** $\frac{2}{3} - \frac{1}{2}$

4. (Use pattern blocks for this exercise. Pattern blocks, if not available in wood, can be cut out from the Appendix: Masters for Pattern Blocks.) Choose a unit and do each of the following. Write numerical expressions for your work with the pattern blocks. Some can be done in more than one way. Record your work in sketches.

   a. Combine $\frac{1}{2}$ and $\frac{1}{6}$.

   b. Combine $2\frac{1}{2}$ and $\frac{2}{3}$.

   c. How much more is $\frac{5}{6}$ than $\frac{1}{2}$?

   d. Take $1\frac{5}{6}$ from $2\frac{2}{3}$.

   e. Take $2\frac{1}{4}$ from 4. (*Hint:* Let 2 yellow hexagons = 1 unit.)

   f. What needs to be combined with $\frac{5}{6}$ to get $2\frac{2}{3}$?

5. Eight loaves of bread are to be shared equally among 10 men. How might this be done? (This problem is from the Rhind papyrus, 1700 B.C.[i]) The diagram on the next page suggests one way:

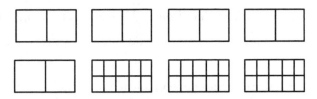

Each man gets $\frac{1}{2} + \frac{3}{10}$.

a. What part of a loaf does each man get in all?

b. How else might the loaves be shared?

c. Does each person get the same total amount in each situation? Justify that each person gets the same amount in each of your cuttings.

6. Solve this problem (written by a fifth grader):

♦ Four guys, Chico, Roberto, Bob, and Phil, eat 9 bags of corn chips. They each ate their equal shares. Later Johnny came with 11 bags and helped eat them. How many bags did Johnny eat? How many bags did Chico eat all together? ♦

7. Jim ate $\frac{1}{3}$ of a whole pizza at lunch, and $\frac{1}{6}$ of the pizza later for a snack. How much of the pizza did Jim eat? Show this with a drawing.

8. In his will Thomas gave $\frac{1}{3}$ of his estate to his daughter Jenny, $\frac{2}{5}$ of his estate to his son Will, $\frac{1}{6}$ of his estate to his granddaughter Karen, and the remaining amount to the American Heart Association. What part of Thomas's estate did the American Heart Association receive?

9. A wealthy woman's will calls for $\frac{2}{3}$ of her estate to go to her favorite charity and for each of her three great-nieces to receive $\frac{1}{16}$ of her estate. What fraction of her estate is left for other beneficiaries?

10. A cable installer working in an isolated area has 200 feet of cable left. One of his remaining jobs will take $29\frac{1}{2}$ feet of cable, a second will take $42\frac{3}{4}$ feet, and a third, 118 feet. Will he be able to do the three jobs without going to headquarters to get more cable? If he can, will he have enough cable left for a job that will take $24\frac{5}{8}$ feet? If he cannot, he will be short how many feet?

11. You have a recipe that gives $1\frac{3}{4}$ quarts of punch, and an insulated jug that holds $1\frac{1}{4}$ gallons. If you make 3 recipes of the punch, will it all fit in the jug? If not, how much punch will be left over? (1 gallon = 4 quarts)

12. A youngster mows his neighbors' yards. His lawn mower tank holds $2\frac{1}{3}$ gallons of gasoline mixture. Two of the yards take $\frac{5}{8}$ of a gallon of gasoline mixture each, a third takes $\frac{1}{2}$ gallon, and a fourth takes $\frac{2}{3}$ of a gallon. Can he mow all four yards on one tank of gasoline mixture? If he can, how much gasoline mixture will be left? If not, how much more will he need?

13. Arnie is $5\frac{1}{4}$ inches taller than Ben, Ben is $3\frac{7}{8}$ inches shorter than Carlo, and Carlo is $2\frac{1}{4}$ inches shorter than Donell. Who is taller, Arnie or Donell, and by how much?

14. Make up a story problem that might lead to each of these.

    a. $\dfrac{2}{3} - \dfrac{1}{2}$ b. $12 - 7\frac{3}{4}$ c. $2\frac{5}{8} + n = 6$

15. Describe or show a strategy you could use to compute each of these mentally.

    a. $\dfrac{3}{4} + \dfrac{5}{6} + \dfrac{1}{4}$ b. $\dfrac{3}{8} + \dfrac{1}{2}$

    c. $6\frac{3}{4} - 3\frac{1}{2} - 1\frac{1}{2}$ d. $2\frac{2}{3} + 5\frac{1}{6} + 3\frac{1}{6} - 4$

    e. $7 - 2\frac{3}{16}$ (Think: What do I need to add to $2\frac{3}{16}$ to get 7?)

    f. $\dfrac{7}{16} + \dfrac{0}{72}$ g. $\dfrac{0}{42} + \dfrac{20}{63}$

16. Here is one technique for finding the least common denominator for a given addition/subtraction calculation. Determine whether the largest denominator would work as a common denominator; if it does not, then try multiples of the largest denominator (2×, 3×, etc.). For the calculation in Exercise 1, $\dfrac{3}{8} + \dfrac{1}{6} + \dfrac{2}{15}$, try 15 (won't work because 8 is not a factor of 15), then 30 (won't), 45 (won't), 60 (won't),…, 120 (will! $120 = 8 \times 15$, and $120 = 6 \times 20$, so equal fractions to the given ones can easily be found.) Practice this technique:

    a. $\dfrac{17}{40} + \dfrac{19}{8} - \dfrac{1}{5}$ b. $\dfrac{25}{36} + \dfrac{62}{135}$ c. $\dfrac{3}{4} + 0.7 - \dfrac{17}{25}$

17. Give an example that illustrates each statement.

    a. Subtraction of fractions is not commutative.

    b. Subtraction of fractions is not associative.

7.2 | Multiplying by a Fraction

THINK ABOUT . . .

Is there a rationale for the way we multiply fractions:

$$\frac{a}{b} \times \frac{c}{d} = \frac{a \cdot c}{b \cdot d}?$$

Here is one argument for the above Think About. Suppose you want to know $\frac{2}{3}$ of $\frac{4}{5}$, or $\frac{2}{3} \times \frac{4}{5}$, perhaps to solve a story problem like:

♦ Juanita had mowed $\frac{4}{5}$ of the lawn, and her brother Jaime had raked $\frac{2}{3}$ of the mowed part. What part of the lawn had been raked? ♦

A drawing might start like this:

 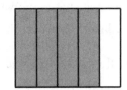

The lawn   4/5 of the lawn
                      mowed

Now comes the key step. You could take $\frac{2}{3}$ of the mowed part by first cutting each fifth in the mowed part into three equal parts, as shown below.

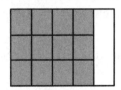

Each fifth cut into
three equal parts

Now it is a matter of taking two of the small pieces in each fifth to get $\frac{2}{3}$ of $\frac{4}{5}$. We will assume a very tidy raker:

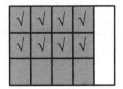   

The checked part is   The checked part is
2/3 of 4/5.   8/15 of the lawn.

The dilemma of how to describe numerically the checked part is settled by realizing that cutting the unmowed fifth into three equal parts as well will cut the whole lawn (the unit) into 15 equal pieces—fifteenths! As far as the $\frac{a}{b} \times \frac{c}{d} = \frac{a \cdot c}{b \cdot d}$ algorithm is concerned, the drawing gives a bonus: The whole lawn is cut into 3 rows of 5 identical pieces, or $3 \times 5 = 15$ identical pieces, and the mowed and raked part is made up of 2 rows of 4 of those pieces, or $2 \times 4 = 8$. Hence, $\frac{2}{3} \times \frac{4}{5}$ does equal $\frac{2 \times 4}{3 \times 5} = \frac{8}{15}$.

Notice again that in the first problem, the unit for $\frac{4}{5}$ is the entire lawn. That is, the $\frac{4}{5}$ *refers to* the whole lawn. But the $\frac{2}{3}$ *refers to* the mowed part, that is, $\frac{2}{3}$ has $\frac{4}{5}$ of the lawn as its whole (or more briefly we can say the unit for $\frac{2}{3}$ is the $\frac{4}{5}$). Thus, the

$\frac{2}{3}$ and the $\frac{4}{5}$ refer to different units. And what about the unit for $\frac{2}{3} \times \frac{4}{5}$, the $\frac{8}{15}$? This is the part of the lawn that is mowed and raked. Thus the referent unit for the $\frac{8}{15}$ is again the entire lawn. The fact that the three fractions in $\frac{2}{3} \times \frac{4}{5} = \frac{8}{15}$, or in $\frac{a}{b} \times \frac{c}{d} = \frac{a \cdot c}{b \cdot d}$ *do not* all refer to the same unit is fundamental to understanding multiplication of fractions, and a lack of understanding of this principle leads to a great deal of confusion when children are first learning to multiply fractions. One way to keep these referent units in mind is to think of $\frac{2}{3} \times \frac{4}{5} = \frac{8}{15}$ as $\frac{2}{3}$ *of* $\frac{4}{5}$ *of* 1 is $\frac{8}{15}$ *of* 1, perhaps giving a name for the unit: one whole lawn.

> ### THINK ABOUT . . .
>
> 1. Some teachers say that multiplication of fractions is easier than addition of fractions. Why might they say that? What is being overlooked by these teachers?
>
> 2. Which of these multiplications, $\frac{1}{3} \times \frac{1}{2}$ or $\frac{1}{2} \times \frac{1}{3}$, means that you begin with $\frac{1}{3}$ of a whole?

Activity 2   Juanita and Jaime Again

1. How would the drawing look if the problem had been the following:

    ◆ Juanita had mowed $\frac{2}{3}$ of the lawn, and her brother Jaime had raked $\frac{4}{5}$ of the mowed part. What part of the lawn had been raked? ◆

    Make the drawing, and name the referent unit for each of the units in the drawing.

2. Make a drawing for each of these two stories:

    ◆ Pam had $\frac{2}{3}$ of a cake. She ate half of it. How much cake did she eat? ◆

    ◆ Pam ate $\frac{2}{3}$ of a cake, and Jojo ate half of a cake. How much cake did they eat? ◆

    Tell what the referent units are for the fractions in each story.

The given argument glosses over another point that should be justified: How does the *of* in $\frac{2}{3}$ of $\frac{4}{5}$ become × in $\frac{2}{3} \times \frac{4}{5}$? One justification is to mention that the total of 3 groups *of* 6 units can be translated into 3×6 and the total of 5 amounts *of* $\frac{3}{4}$ unit can be translated into $5 \times \frac{3}{4}$. So it is plausible to translate $\frac{2}{3}$ *of* $\frac{4}{5}$ unit into $\frac{2}{3} \times \frac{4}{5}$. Another way is to link the multiplication to finding the area of a rectangular region that has dimensions $\frac{2}{3}$ unit by $\frac{4}{5}$ unit. (Try this to see whether you get $\frac{8}{15}$ of a square unit.)

Multiplying numerators to find the numerator of the product, and multiplying denominators to find the denominator of the product can sometimes be simplified. Consider the following example of the algorithm for multiplying fractions.

$$\frac{15}{32} \times \frac{8}{25} = \frac{15 \times 8}{32 \times 25}$$

By using what we know about equivalent fractions and first identifying common factors in the numerator and the denominator, we can simplify the product to be

$$\frac{15}{32} \times \frac{8}{25} = \frac{15 \times 8}{32 \times 25} = \frac{3 \times 5 \times 2 \times 2 \times 2}{2 \times 2 \times 2 \times 2 \times 2 \times 5 \times 5} = \frac{3}{2 \times 2 \times 5} = \frac{3}{20}.$$

(See Exercise 14 for a short-cut.)

TAKE-AWAY MESSAGE . . . The "rule" for multiplication of fractions—multiply the numerators to obtain the numerator of the product and multiply the denominators to find the denominator of the product—is easy to remember and do, but understanding multiplication of fractions requires knowing more than just this rule. To make multiplication of fractions meaningful, one must understand the reference units for the fractions and what the product actually stands for. ♦

Learning Exercises for Section 7.2

1. Write out an explanation, with sketches, to answer each of the following. Your explanations should make clear the referent units for each fraction.

    a. After a farmer had prepared $\frac{5}{6}$ of the field, he planted $\frac{3}{4}$ of the prepared part of the field with tomatoes. What part of the field did he plant with tomatoes?

    b. After the farmer had prepared $\frac{3}{4}$ of another field, he planted $\frac{5}{6}$ of the prepared part with potatoes. What part of the field did he plant with potatoes? (Contrast this to part a.)

    c. The worker used half of a piece of wire that was 6.4 meters long. How much wire did she use?

2. A large candy bar is sectioned off:

    If Pat gets $\frac{1}{3}$ of the gray part, then Pat gets ___1/4___ of the candy bar.

    So $\frac{1}{3} \times \frac{3}{4}$ is ___1/4___. (Notice that the algorithm involving twelfths is not needed.)

3. Shade in $\frac{5}{8}$ of four circles in at least two different ways.

How do your methods differ? What is $\frac{5}{8}$ of 4?

What is $4 \times \frac{5}{8}$? What do these questions have to do with the drawings?

4. **a.**   Shade in $\frac{3}{4}$ of 2:

b.   Using the same size rectangle as your unit, show two $\frac{3}{4}$ pieces.

Are the amounts the same or different for parts (a) and (b)?

5. Do the following problems using common sense instead of using algorithms. For part (a), think: take eight halves, that's the same as _____ wholes.

a. $8 \times \frac{1}{2} =$ **b.** $4 \times \frac{1}{2} =$

c. $2 \times \frac{1}{2} =$ **d.** $1 \times \frac{1}{2} =$

e. $12 \times \frac{1}{2} =$ **f.** $14 \times \frac{1}{2} =$

g. $\frac{98}{98} \times \frac{49}{50} =$ **h.** $\frac{17}{24} \times \frac{0}{36} =$

6. Represent these two situations with equations. Are the equations the same or different?

a.   Darryl had 12 apricots. He ate $\frac{1}{6}$ of them for lunch. How many apricots did he eat?

b.   Darryl had some pizzas, each cut into sixths. If he ate 12 pieces of the pizza, how many (whole) pizzas did he eat?

7. (Pattern Blocks) With the hexagon as the unit (or a circular region as the unit if you are not using pattern blocks), show $4 \times \frac{2}{3}$, and show $\frac{2}{3} \times 4$. Sketch, even if pattern blocks are available, for future reference.

8. Shade in $\frac{2}{3}$ of $\frac{3}{4}$ of this rectangle:

Locate the $\frac{2}{3}$. It is $\frac{2}{3}$ of what? _____

Locate the $\frac{3}{4}$. It is $\frac{3}{4}$ of what? _____

The final shaded part is *what fraction* of *what amount*? _____

9. Shade in $\frac{3}{2}$ of $\frac{1}{4}$ of this rectangle: ☐

Locate the $\frac{1}{4}$. It is $\frac{1}{4}$ of what quantity? _____

Locate the $\frac{3}{2}$. It is $\frac{3}{2}$ of what quantity? _____

The shaded part is *what fraction* of *what amount*? _____

10. a.   Shade in $\frac{3}{4}$ of $\frac{4}{3}$ of this rectangle: ☐

b.   Shade in $\frac{4}{3}$ of $\frac{3}{4}$ of this rectangle: ☐

c.   Why are $\frac{3}{4}$ and $\frac{4}{3}$ called **multiplicative inverses**? (They are also called **reciprocals**.) See part (b).

d.   Exercises 4, 6, and 7 illustrate that *computationally* $\frac{a}{b} \times \frac{c}{d} = \frac{c}{d} \times \frac{a}{b}$ even though $\frac{a}{b} \times \frac{c}{d}$ and $\frac{c}{d} \times \frac{a}{b}$ are *conceptually* different. What is this property called?

e.   Why are these calculations easy? $\frac{72}{72} \times \frac{99}{181}$ and $\frac{571}{623} \times \frac{103}{103}$?

11. (Pattern Blocks) Show each of these with pattern blocks or drawings. Make sketches of your pattern block work for later reference.

a. $\frac{2}{3} \times \frac{1}{2}$ **b.** $\frac{2}{3} \times 6$ **c.** $\frac{4}{3} \times 6$

d. $\frac{4}{3} \times 1\frac{1}{2}$ **e.** $\frac{2}{3} \times \left(\frac{3}{2} \times 4 \right)$

12. Draw a diagram that represents each of the following situations.

a.   There was $\frac{3}{4}$ of a pie left in the refrigerator. John ate $\frac{2}{3}$ of what was left. How much pie did he eat? Also tell what the whole (the unit) is for each given fraction and for the answer.

b.   Three-fourths of the class were girls. Two-thirds of the girls have dark hair. What fraction of the class is female and dark haired? (Note: What was the *whole* for each fraction?)

c.   Jackie napped for $\frac{3}{4}$ of an hour. Corrina napped $\frac{7}{6}$ as long. How long did Corrina nap? (What is the whole for each given fraction and for the answer?)

d. The following diagram and explanation is one student's solution to Exercise 12(c). Compare it to yours.

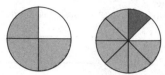

The $\frac{3}{4}$ of an hour is shaded in. I broke it into 6 parts. Now each part is $\frac{1}{8}$ of an hour. I added another sixth of the $\frac{3}{4}$ hour, which is another $\frac{1}{8}$ of a total hour. So now I know Corrina slept $\frac{7}{8}$ of an hour.

13. Make up a story problem that might lead to each calculation. (If you have trouble thinking of a situation, think about quantities of cheese.)

a. $\frac{1}{4} \times 2\frac{3}{4}$ **b.** $3 \times (\frac{1}{16} + \frac{1}{8})$ **c.** $2 \times (3 - 1\frac{1}{3})$

14. a. Students are often taught to "cancel," without justification for why it works. Explain why "canceling" works, as here, with a common factor of 3 ignored in the *first* denominator and the *second* numerator:

$$\frac{19}{\cancel{21}_{7}} \times \frac{\cancel{6}^{2}}{35} = \frac{19 \times 2}{7 \times 35} = \frac{38}{245}.$$

(*Hint for one explanation:* Here are all the steps in calculating $\frac{19}{21} \times \frac{6}{35}$, including steps that one often just thinks rather than writes:

$$\frac{19}{21} \times \frac{6}{35} = \frac{19 \times 6}{21 \times 35} = \frac{114}{735} = \frac{3 \times 38}{3 \times 245} = \frac{3}{3} \times \frac{38}{245} = 1 \times \frac{38}{245} = \frac{38}{245}.)$$

b. "Canceling" does result in less demanding calculation, so it is very attractive to students—so attractive, in fact, that they will use it on calculations like $\frac{19}{21} + \frac{6}{35}$ or in working with proportions like $\frac{19}{21} = \frac{6}{x}$. Does "canceling" work with these problems?

15. Make sketches to illustrate the following situations. Notice that the settings involve discrete things.

a. One fifth-grade class has 24 students. One-half of them are girls. Three-fourths of the boys in the class like to play football. What part of the whole class are the boys who like to play football? Would your answer change if you did not know the number of students in the class?

b. Another fifth-grade class has 32 students. One-half of them are girls. Three-fourths of the boys in the class like to play football. What part of the whole class are the boys who like to play football? Would your answer change if you did not know the number of students in the class?

c. Perhaps because there is a tendency to focus on the actual *number* of boys who like to play football, fraction multiplication seems to be difficult conceptually in settings such as the following, when the number of discrete things is unknown—One-half of a fifth-grade class is girls. Three-fourths of the boys in the class like to play football. What part of the whole class are the boys who like to play football? How do you "see" this last version?

16. a. The distributive property is very important with whole numbers: $k \times (m + n) = (k \times m) + (k \times n)$ for every choice of whole numbers k, m, and n. Is the distributive property also true if the numbers are fractions rather than whole numbers?

   b. Calculate each in *two* ways. (*Hint:* See part a.)

     i. $\frac{3}{4} \times (\frac{4}{5} + \frac{8}{15})$ **ii.** $(\frac{5}{6} \times 11\frac{7}{10}) + (\frac{5}{6} \times \frac{3}{10})$

17. Calculate each in *two* ways.

   a. $8 \times 6\frac{2}{7}$ (*Hint:* Remember that $6\frac{2}{7} = 6 + \frac{2}{7}$.)

   b. $7\frac{1}{2} \times 8\frac{4}{9}$

18. Order each set of fractions from least to greatest.

   a. $\frac{3}{4}$ $\frac{9}{19}$ $\frac{23}{25}$ $\frac{12}{78}$ **b.** $\frac{3}{9}$ $\frac{3}{2}$ $\frac{3}{14}$ $\frac{3}{7}$ $\frac{3}{4}$

7.3 | Dividing by a Fraction

Earlier you learned about the meanings of division. In this section we consider three questions: (1) Why do we invert and multiply when we divide by a fraction? (2) Do we also need to attend to the referent units for division the way we did with multiplication? (3) *When* do we divide?

We begin with the first question: *Why do we invert and multiply when we divide by a fraction?* The repeated-subtraction way of thinking about division is to ask how many of the divisors can be subtracted from the dividend, that is, for example, $12 \div 3 = 4$ because you can subtract 3 from 12 four times: $12 - 3 - 3 - 3 - 3 = 0$. Thus, $12 \div 3$ answers the question, "How many 3s are in 12?" We can use this meaning of subtraction to justify the *invert and multiply rule*.

Possibility 1: Dividing by a unit fraction, $\frac{1}{n}$.

We use the repeated-subtraction meaning of division to find $1 \div \frac{1}{4}$.

$1 \div \frac{1}{4}$ can mean, "How many one-fourths are in 1?" (*Think:* How many times can I subtract $\frac{1}{4}$ from one?) There are 4 one-fourths in 1. Therefore $1 \div \frac{1}{4} = 4 = \frac{4}{1}$.

    THINK ABOUT . . .

    Can you complete the following division in the same way?

      $1 \div \frac{1}{3}$ can mean, "How many _____ are in 1?"

      There are _____ in 1. Therefore $1 \div \frac{1}{3} = ? = \frac{?}{1}$.

We now can generalize and say that $1 \div \frac{1}{b} = b$ or $\frac{b}{1}$.

Recall that the reciprocal of a fraction $\frac{a}{b}$ is $\frac{b}{a}$. When dividing 1 by $\frac{1}{b}$, we see that the quotient is $\frac{b}{1}$, the reciprocal of $\frac{1}{b}$. And we know that $\frac{b}{1} = b$.

Return again to $1 \div \frac{1}{3} = 3$. This says that there are 3 one-thirds in 1. But $3 = \frac{3}{1}$, so to say that there are 3 one-thirds in 1 is the same as saying there are $\frac{3}{1}$ one-thirds in 1.

Then it would make sense to say there are *twice as many* one-thirds in 2 as in 1. $2 \div \frac{1}{3} = 2 \times (1 \div \frac{1}{3}) = 2 \times \frac{3}{1} = \frac{2}{1} \times \frac{3}{1} = 6.$

Similarly, $7 \div \frac{1}{3}$, telling how many one-thirds are in 7, should have 7 times as many one-thirds as 1 does, or $7 \div \frac{1}{3} = 7 \times \frac{3}{1} = 21.$

Activity 3   Dividing by Unit Fractions

Use the reasoning above to complete the following:

a. $11 \div \frac{1}{3}$ **b.** $4 \div \frac{1}{6}$ **c.** $7 \div \frac{1}{4}$ **d.** $7\frac{1}{2} \div \frac{1}{3}$

The same reasoning should apply to $2\frac{1}{2} \div \frac{1}{3}$. Two and a half should have $2\frac{1}{2}$ as many one-thirds as 1 does. $2\frac{1}{2} \div \frac{1}{3} = 2\frac{1}{2} \times \frac{3}{1} = \frac{5}{2} \times \frac{3}{1} = \frac{15}{2} = 7\frac{1}{2}$.

To test the reasoning with a diagram, consider $2\frac{1}{2} \div \frac{1}{3}$ again. If a large rectangle represents one unit, then the first row of the diagram has $2\frac{1}{2}$ units (or wholes, or ones). In the second row, each unit is cut into 3 pieces, each representing $\frac{1}{3}$. But how many one-thirds are in the $2\frac{1}{2}$? Count. There are $7\frac{1}{2}$ thirds in the $2\frac{1}{2}$ whole rectangles.

How many thirds?

$$2\frac{1}{2} \div \frac{1}{3} = 2\frac{1}{2} \times \frac{3}{1} = 7\frac{1}{2}$$

  1   2   3   4   5   6 $7\frac{1}{2}$ thirds

Thus, we can generalize and say that

$$\frac{a}{b} \div \frac{1}{c} = \frac{a}{b} \times \frac{c}{1} = \frac{ac}{b}$$

Possibility 2: Dividing by nonunit fractions.

Thus far we have considered dividing by unit fractions. (Remember that unit fractions have the form $\frac{1}{n}$.) We found that the quotient can be found by multiplying by the reciprocal of the unit fraction. Does this shortcut apply to division by fractions that are not unit fractions?

Consider $1 \div \frac{2}{3}$ in the drawing below.

$1 \div \frac{2}{3}$ can mean, "How many two-thirds are in one whole unit?"

Visually we can see that there is *one* $\frac{2}{3}$ and *half* of another $\frac{2}{3}$ in the circle. Thus $1 \div \frac{2}{3} = 1\frac{1}{2}$, which is the same as $\frac{3}{2}$. So $1 \div \frac{2}{3} = \frac{3}{2}$ $(= 1\frac{1}{2})$.

Once again, we see that dividing 1 by a fraction numerically is the same as multiplying 1 by the reciprocal of the fraction: $1 \div \frac{2}{3} = 1 \times \frac{3}{2}$. So $1 \times \frac{3}{2}$ does tell how many two-thirds are in 1. In $4 \div \frac{2}{3}$ there should be 4 times as many two-thirds as for 1, so $4 \div \frac{2}{3} = 4 \times \frac{3}{2}$.

> **THINK ABOUT…**
>
> How could you argue that $\frac{4}{5} \div \frac{2}{3} = \frac{4}{5} \times \frac{3}{2}$?

Dividing by a fraction gives the same result as multiplying by the reciprocal of the fraction. Symbolically, when the divisor is a fraction, $n \div \frac{c}{d} = n \times \frac{d}{c}$,

or, if *n* is itself a fraction,

$$\frac{a}{b} \div \frac{c}{d} = \frac{a}{b} \times \frac{d}{c} \quad (\frac{c}{d} \text{ cannot equal 0.})$$

The reciprocal of a nonzero fraction is obtained by inverting the fraction. Thus the *invert and multiply* rule is simply a different phrasing for the *multiply by the reciprocal* rule.

Activity 4   Can We Draw Pictures?

a.   Make a drawing that shows that the quotient of $\frac{4}{5} \div \frac{1}{2}$ is $1\frac{3}{5}$.

b.   Make a drawing that shows that the quotient of $\frac{1}{2} \div \frac{4}{5} = \frac{5}{8}$.

c.   Make a drawing that shows that the quotient of $1\frac{1}{2} \div \frac{4}{5} = \frac{15}{8} = 1\frac{7}{8}$.

Notes

The second question asked at the beginning of this section is: Do we also need to attend to the referent units for division the way we did with multiplication?

The answer is YES. Consider this problem:

♦ Kathleen had $\frac{3}{4}$ of a gallon of milk. She gave each of her cats $\frac{1}{12}$ of a gallon of milk. How many cats got milk? ♦

We are asking: How many one-twelfths of a gallon are there in $\frac{3}{4}$ of a gallon? $\frac{3}{4} \div \frac{1}{12} = ?$ We could subtract $\frac{1}{12}$ from $\frac{3}{4}$ nine times (there are three one-twelfths in every $\frac{1}{4}$). We can, we now know officially, write this as $\frac{3}{4} \div \frac{1}{12} = \frac{3}{4} \times 12 = 9$.

In this problem, both the $\frac{3}{4}$ and the $\frac{1}{12}$ refer to a gallon, whereas the 9 refers to the number of cats receiving milk. Actually, the $\frac{1}{12}$ can be thought of as $\frac{1}{12}$ *of a gallon per cat.* The point is that the fractions in this division have different referent units. To understand this problem, one must know the referent unit for each of the following numbers: the dividend, the divisor, and the quotient.

Discussion 4

♦ A stretch of highway is $3\frac{1}{2}$ miles long. Each day, $\frac{2}{3}$ of a mile is repaved. How many days are needed to repave the entire stretch? ♦

How can you think of this as a repeated subtraction problem? Do you get the same answer through repeated subtraction as you do by the *invert and multiply* rule?

Here the dividend and the divisor in the discussion problem both refer to miles. For repeated subtraction to fit a problem, both the dividend and the divisor must refer to the same unit. As an aside, if we look more sophisticatedly at the units, the quotient refers not to that unit (miles) but to the divisor value, the $\frac{2}{3}$ of a mile *per day.* That is, $5\frac{1}{4}$ days refers to the number of days for which $\frac{2}{3}$ of a mile is repaved per day. Continuing a closer look at the units, $3\frac{1}{2}$ *miles* at $\frac{2}{3}$ of a *mile per day* $= 5\frac{1}{4}$ *days* can also be thought of as $3\frac{1}{2}$ *miles* at $\frac{3}{2}$ *days per mile* $= 5\frac{1}{4}$ *days.*

The third question asked at the beginning is: When do we divide?

Just as with whole number problems, division is used in repeated-subtraction (measurement or quotitive) situations, as above, but also in sharing-equally (partitive) situations. Contrast the previous cats and milk problem with this problem:

♦ John had $\frac{3}{4}$ gallon of milk to feed his 9 cats. How much milk does each cat get? ♦

Here is a solution: $\frac{3}{4} \div 9$ because the $\frac{3}{4}$ of a gallon is shared by the 9 cats, presumably equally. Each cat gets $\frac{1}{12}$ of a gallon of milk.

> **THINK ABOUT . . .**
>
> How do these two problems differ in terms of the division involved? Can you make a drawing to clarify what is happening for each problem? Which one calls for a partitive view of division? Which one calls for a quotitive view of division?

Activity 5   An Alternative Approach—Draw

1. Find the answers using pictures or diagrams rather than the *multiply across* rule.

$$\frac{2}{3} \times \frac{1}{6} = \qquad \frac{3}{8} \times \frac{3}{4} = \qquad \frac{5}{6} \times \frac{3}{3} = \qquad \frac{1}{2} \times \frac{3}{8} = \qquad \frac{3}{4} \times 1\frac{1}{2} =$$

2. Find the answers using pictures or diagrams rather than the *invert and multiply* rule.

$$\frac{2}{3} \div \frac{6}{1} = \qquad \frac{3}{8} \div \frac{4}{3} = \qquad \frac{5}{6} \div \frac{3}{3} = \qquad \frac{1}{2} \div \frac{8}{3} = \qquad \frac{3}{4} \div \frac{2}{3} =$$

3. Compare your answers in Problems 1 and 2. Can you generalize what you see happening?

4. In the following, what referent unit does each fraction refer to? It may be helpful to put each calculation in a context.

$$\frac{2}{3} \times \frac{3}{4} = \frac{1}{2} \qquad\qquad \frac{1}{2} \div \frac{3}{4} = \frac{2}{3}$$

Activity 6   Illustrating

For each problem first choose an interpretation for the operation; second, act out the problem with pattern blocks (or drawings) and record the solution; and third, write a story problem for your interpretation.

1. $\frac{2}{3} \div \frac{1}{2}$

2. $\frac{2}{3} \times \frac{2}{1}$

3. $\frac{1}{2} \times \frac{2}{3}$

4. $\frac{1}{2} \div \frac{3}{2}$

5. $3 \times \frac{2}{3}$

6. $3 \div \frac{3}{2}$

Discussion 5   Can You See What I See?[ii]

1. Can you see $\frac{3}{5}$ of something in this picture?

   Where? Be explicit. ($\frac{3}{5}$ of **what**?)

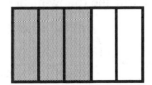

Continue on the next page.

2. Can you see $\frac{5}{3}$ of something in the given picture? Where? How did you change the way you looked at the picture in order to see $\frac{5}{3}$?

3. How can you see $\frac{6}{10}$ of something in the given picture? How did you change the way you looked at the picture in order to see $\frac{6}{10}$?

4. Can you see $\frac{5}{3}$ of $\frac{3}{5}$ in the given picture? How did you have to change the way you looked at the picture in order to see $\frac{5}{3}$ of $\frac{3}{5}$?

5. Can you see $\frac{2}{3}$ of $\frac{3}{5}$? What is the whole (the unit)? What part is $\frac{3}{5}$ of the whole? What part is $\frac{2}{3}$ of $\frac{3}{5}$ of the whole?

6. Can you see $1 \div \frac{3}{5}$?

TAKE-AWAY MESSAGE . . . Division of fractions is often associated with *invert and multiply*, but most people do not understand why this rule works and even sometimes forget which fraction to invert. By making sense of this rule, such errors should not be made. Understanding referent units for the fractions is also important when dividing so that one can make sense of the quotient. Finally, elementary school students (and adults) also need to know *when* to divide; without this knowledge knowing how cannot be of much use. ◆

Learning Exercises for Section 7.3

1. Do these problems using common sense instead of using rules. For part (a), think, "How many halves are in eight wholes?"

   a. $8 \div \frac{1}{2}$ **b.** $4 \div \frac{1}{2}$ **c.** $2 \div \frac{1}{2}$

   d. $1 \div \frac{1}{2}$ **e.** $\frac{1}{2} \div \frac{1}{2}$ **f.** $\frac{1}{4} \div \frac{1}{2}$ (Did this one surprise you?)

2. A company is promoting its pizza by giving away slices. In the first hour, they gave away 5 pizzas, each cut into sixths. How many pieces did they give away? One way to answer is to say that each of the 5 pizzas had 6 pieces, so they gave away $5 \times 6 = 30$ pieces. Another way to answer is to ask how many sixths are in 5, that is, $5 \div \frac{1}{6}$.

   Show with the following drawing that the answer is 30.

3. Use your understanding of repeated-subtraction division to complete each equation, building on the given $1 \div \frac{2}{3} = 1\frac{1}{2}$ or $\frac{3}{2}$, as in part a.

If $1 \div \frac{2}{3} = 1\frac{1}{2}$ or $\frac{3}{2}$, then . . .

a. $2 \div \frac{2}{3} = 2 \times 1\frac{1}{2}$ (or $2 \times \frac{3}{2}$) $= 3$.

b. $5 \div \frac{2}{3} =$ _____ (or _____)

c. $24 \div \frac{2}{3} =$ _____ (or _____)

d. $7\frac{1}{2} \div \frac{2}{3} =$ _____ (or _____)

e. $\frac{4}{5} \div \frac{2}{3} =$ _____ (or _____)

4. The company also gave away $\frac{1}{2}$ of a cup of soda with each slice of pizza. Use thinking rather than calculation.

How many could be served with 8 cups of soda? $8 \div \frac{1}{2} =$ _____

How many could be served with 4 cups of soda? $4 \div \frac{1}{2} =$ _____

How many could be served with 2 cups of soda? $2 \div \frac{1}{2} =$ _____

How many could be served with 1 cup of soda? $1 \div \frac{1}{2} =$ _____

How many could be served with $\frac{1}{2}$ cup of soda? $\frac{1}{2} \div \frac{1}{2} =$ _____

5. A recipe calls for $\frac{1}{2}$ of a cup of sugar. You have $\frac{3}{4}$ of a cup of sugar. How many recipes can you make (assuming that you have the other ingredients on hand)?

How many one-halves are in $\frac{3}{4}$? [OR $\frac{3}{4} \div \frac{1}{2} = ?$]

What does the $\frac{1}{2}$ refer to?

What does the $\frac{3}{4}$ refer to?

What does the solution $\frac{3}{4} \div \frac{1}{2}$ refer to? ($1\frac{1}{2}$ of *what*?)

6. How would you illustrate (with a drawing) the division $\frac{2}{3} \div \frac{1}{6}$?

Your answer to "How much is $\frac{2}{3} \div \frac{1}{6}$?" tells you *what* about $\frac{2}{3}$ and about $\frac{1}{6}$? That is, what does this answer refer to?

7. How would you illustrate (with a drawing) the division $\frac{1}{2} \div \frac{3}{4}$?

Your answer to "How much is $\frac{1}{2} \div \frac{3}{4}$?" tells you *what* about $\frac{1}{2}$ and about $\frac{3}{4}$? That is, what does this answer refer to?

8. (Pattern Blocks or drawings) "Act out" each of the following, and be able to explain your reasoning. (Be sure to specify the unit before you begin.)

    a. $\frac{5}{6} \times \frac{2}{1}$ **b.** $\frac{5}{6} \div \frac{1}{2}$ **c.** $4\frac{2}{3} \times \frac{1}{2}$

    d. $4\frac{2}{3} \div 2$ **e.** $\frac{3}{2} \times \frac{3}{1}$ **f.** $\frac{3}{2} \div \frac{1}{3}$

9. Here is a drawing for $\frac{3}{4} \div \frac{2}{3}$. How many two-thirds of a whole are in $\frac{3}{4}$ of a whole? There is obviously 1 and a little more. Describe what is represented by the light gray part and justify your answer without calculating.

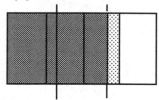

10. Make a drawing and give an explanation for this story problem: Todd can paint $\frac{3}{4}$ of a wall with one gallon of paint. How much of the wall can he cover with $\frac{3}{5}$ of a gallon?

11. Make a drawing and give an explanation for this story problem: A piece of fabric is $\frac{3}{4}$ of a yard long. Costume belts for a choir require $\frac{3}{16}$ of a yard each. How many belts can be made from the piece of fabric?

12. Sketch $\frac{7}{8} \div \frac{4}{16}$ and explain your thinking.

13. Answer the questions below for part (a) and then for part (b).

    a. $\frac{2}{3} \times \frac{3}{4} = \frac{1}{2}$ **b.** $\frac{1}{2} \div \frac{3}{4} = \frac{2}{3}$

    What does the $\frac{2}{3}$ refer to?   What does the $\frac{1}{2}$ refer to?

    What does the $\frac{3}{4}$ refer to?   What does the $\frac{3}{4}$ refer to?

    What does the $\frac{1}{2}$ refer to?   What does the $\frac{2}{3}$ refer to?

14. The following are typical word problems found in elementary school textbooks. Make a drawing for each problem, and solve.

   a. At a bake sale, one pan of brownies was $\frac{1}{3}$ full. Mr. Fuller bought $\frac{3}{4}$ of what was left. What part of the pan of brownies did Mr. Fuller buy?

   b. Latisha wanted some cake to share with her boyfriend. She bought $\frac{3}{4}$ of a carrot cake at the sale, and then gave $\frac{2}{3}$ of the cake she bought to her boyfriend. What part of the whole cake did her boyfriend receive?

   c. Bronson made cupcakes for the sale. The recipe called for $1\frac{1}{3}$ cups of sugar. He used the five cups of sugar that he had. How many recipes of cupcakes did he make if he had all the other ingredients on hand?

   d. The recipe called for $3\frac{1}{2}$ cups of flour. He could make only $3\frac{3}{4}$ recipes. How much flour did he have?

   e. Band banners each require $\frac{2}{5}$ of a yard of fabric. How many banners could be made with $5\frac{1}{2}$ yards of the fabric?

   f. Nellie is planting a flower garden. She wants $\frac{1}{2}$ of the garden to be planted with pansies, $\frac{2}{5}$ of the garden to be daisies, and the remaining part to be petunias. What part of the garden will be planted in petunias?

15. Write a story problem for each part that could lead to the calculation given.

   a. $6 \div 1\frac{2}{3}$ **b.** $7\frac{1}{2} \div 2\frac{3}{4}$ **c.** $1\frac{7}{8} \div 3$

16. Here is one popular activity that might result in some greater understanding of operations with fractions and that involves computational practice. The teacher gives a "target" number and four numbers. The student is to use each of the four numbers *once*, and whatever combination of operations it takes to get the target number.

> **EXAMPLE** Target = 24; Given 1, 2, 3, and 5.
>
> **SOLUTION** $5 + 3 = 8$, $2 + 1 = 3$, and $8 \times 3 = 24$, or at your level,
> $$24 = (5 + 3) \times (2 + 1).$$

Here are two that involve fractions and decimals.

   a. Target = 24; given $\frac{1}{2}$, $\frac{2}{3}$, 2, and 9.

   b. Target = 2.8; given 0.5, 0.8, 1, and 6.

   c. Make one up.

17. a. Is division of fractions commutative? Explain.

    b. Is division of fractions associative? Explain.

    c. Are $\frac{a}{b} \div 1 = \frac{a}{b}$, $\frac{a}{b} \div \frac{n}{n} = \frac{a}{b}$, and $1 \div \frac{a}{b} = \frac{a}{b}$ correct equations?

18. Expressions like $\dfrac{\frac{1}{4}}{\frac{2}{3}}$ or $\dfrac{7}{\frac{5}{6}}$ are called **complex fractions**, even though as parts of

an amount they are difficult to think about. But extending the $\frac{a}{b} = a \div b$ link

to include complex fractions allows a different, symbolic justification for the
invert–and–multiply algorithm for dividing fractions:

$$\tfrac{1}{4} \div \tfrac{2}{3} = \frac{\frac{1}{4}}{\frac{2}{3}} = \frac{\frac{1}{4} \times \frac{3}{2}}{\frac{2}{3} \times \frac{3}{2}} = \frac{\frac{1}{4} \times \frac{3}{2}}{1} = \tfrac{1}{4} \times \tfrac{3}{2}, \text{ showing that } \tfrac{1}{4} \div \tfrac{2}{3} = \tfrac{1}{4} \times \tfrac{3}{2}.$$

Use this complex-fractions method to confirm the following.

    a. $\frac{8}{9} \div \frac{5}{6} = \frac{8}{9} \times \frac{6}{5}$ **b.** $2\frac{1}{2} \div \frac{7}{8} = 2\frac{1}{2} \times \frac{8}{7}$

7.4   Issues for Learning: Teaching Calculation with Fractions

Calculating with fractions is something perceived to be very difficult, in part because
it is so poorly understood.

> ***THINK ABOUT . . .***
>
> Would a teacher treat these two story problems in the same way pictorially? Numerically?
>
> ◆ For a pizza party, you expect that each of the 12 attendees will eat $\frac{1}{6}$ of a pizza.
> How many pizzas should you order? ◆
>
> ◆ For a large pizza party, you plan to order 12 pizzas. One-sixth of them should be
> vegetarian. How many vegetarian pizzas should you order? ◆

Although more latitude would be allowed with children, the teacher should write
$12 \times \frac{1}{6}$ for the first story problem, but $\frac{1}{6} \times 12$ for the second one. Do you see why? Be
attentive to the order in which you write mathematical expressions, since you want
your expressions to support the concepts involved rather than just give a correct
numerical solution. The two problems in the *Think About* above deal with the commutative property of multiplication, which is not at all obvious to elementary grade
children, and teachers will need to illustrate it. Did you show 12 one-sixths, which
can be thought of in terms of repeated addition, and then $\frac{1}{6}$ of 12, or a fractional part
of a number of wholes? In the second case, we cannot use repeated addition. For
elementary-grade children who think of multiplication only in terms of repeated addition, this is a stumbling block that needs discussion.

Here are other points to be aware of, as you deal with children in the intermediate grades. Eighth graders in one fairly large-scale testing were given this story problem to solve:

♦ At one school $\frac{3}{4}$ of all the eighth graders went to one game. Two-thirds of those who went to the game traveled by car. What part of all the eighth graders traveled by car to the game? ♦

Only about 12% of the children chose to multiply, while about 55% decided to subtract and about 8% to divide! Some interviews with children suggested this thinking, "I want less than $\frac{3}{4}$. So I've got to do something to get a smaller number. . . ," and to them only subtraction and division give smaller numbers. Their idea of multiplication was that "multiplication makes bigger," so they did not consider multiplication.[iii] Research shows that many elementary students, and even some adults, think that "multiplication makes bigger and division makes smaller" is always true. This common misconception leads to a great deal of confusion when solving problems. Notice how important it is to realize that when you take only a part of a quantity (with a positive value), you will get less than the quantity. This operation on quantities is reflected in multiplying by a fraction less than 1: Multiplication *can* make smaller. Notice also that the *whole* for the two-thirds in the story above is different from the *whole* for the $\frac{3}{4}$; again, a key for understanding many problems involving fractions is to keep track of the whole for each fraction mentioned.

Learning Exercises for Section 7.4

We include here a set of problems that help you review the content of this chapter. Drawings are recommended.

1. Jerry and Joel bought a large pizza. Jerry ate $\frac{1}{3}$ of it, and Joel ate $\frac{2}{5}$ of it. Then James came over and ate $\frac{3}{4}$ of what was left. What part of the whole pizza did James eat?

2. How many germs 0.002 cm long would make a line 0.9 cm long?

3. You are preparing for a large gathering at church and are using a recipe that calls for $\frac{3}{4}$ of a cup of milk. You have 1 quart of milk (4 cups). How many full recipes can you make?

4. You are planning your vegetable garden. You plan to plant $\frac{5}{12}$ of it in corn, $\frac{1}{6}$ in different kinds of beans, and $\frac{1}{12}$ in tomatoes. You will plant the remainder equally in eggplant, onions, and squash. What part of the garden will be planted in onions and squash?

5. One medical pill uses 0.2 grams of a certain chemical and 0.6 grams of filler. You have 75 grams of the chemical and 200 grams of filler. How many of the pills can you make?

6. Your diet allows you to have $\frac{3}{4}$ of a cup of cottage cheese every day. You buy 4 containers of cottage cheese on sale, each holding 2 cups. How many full days will this cottage cheese last you?

7.   You buy a large piece of chocolate, planning to eat $\frac{1}{5}$ of it every day, Monday–Friday. But you eat $\frac{1}{3}$ of it on Monday! By what percent did your Monday consumption exceed the planned amount?

8.   A recipe calls for 2 cups of sugar.

   a.   But you used $2\frac{1}{2}$ cups instead. By what percent did you exceed the recipe amount?

   b.   Another time (diet time) you used only $1\frac{1}{4}$ cups. What percent less than the recipe amount did you use?

7.5   Check Yourself

This chapter focused on understanding how to perform arithmetic operations on fractions, and the reasons behind the rules that all of us learned long ago. With care, these operations do make sense, once you understand them. You should be able to work problems and answer questions like those assigned and that deal with the following:

1.   Fractions are numbers that can be operated on just like other numbers, but the algorithms are different from those with whole numbers.

2.   Adding and subtracting require that students understand *that* they need a common denominator to get pieces that are all the same size, *how* to find the least common denominator, and *why* it is needed. Facility with adding and subtracting fractions is expected.

3.   Multiplying fractions is easy to do, but more difficult to understand. One must understand the referent units for the multiplicand, the multiplier, and the product, and be able to interpret the product in terms of the original problem context.

4.   Dividing fractions calls for an understanding of reciprocals, the *invert and multiply* rule and the ability to describe the referent units for the divisor, dividend, and quotient. You should be able to give a rationale for the *invert and multiply* algorithm.

5.   The ability to write story problems that illustrate the different operations (and views of the operations) is essential to show your understanding, as is recognizing which view a particular problem fits.

REFERENCES FOR CHAPTER 7

[i] Streefland, L. (1991). *Fractions in realistic mathematics education.* Boston: Kluwer Academic.

[ii] Thompson, P. W. (1995). Notation, convention, and the quantity in elementary mathematics. In J. T. Sowder & B. P. Schappelle (Eds.), *Providing a foundation for teaching mathematics in the middle school* (pp. 199–221). Albany, NY: SUNY Press.

[iii] Greer, B. (1992). Multiplication and division as models of situations. In D. A. Grouws (Ed.), *Handbook of research on mathematics teaching and learning* (pp. 276–295). New York: Macmillan.

Chapter 8

Multiplicative Comparisons and Multiplicative Reasoning

In Chapter 1 you learned how to go about undertaking a quantitative analysis of a problem situation. In Chapter 3 you learned about additive comparisons: any time you want to compare two quantities to determine how much greater or less one is than another, you additively compare the quantities by finding the difference of their values. There are times, however, when you want to compare two quantities not by *how much larger* one is than another, but rather *how many times as large* one is than another. The second kind of comparison is called a *multiplicative comparison* and involves ratios. Analyzing multiplicative comparisons is the focus of this chapter.

8.1 | Quantitative Analysis of Multiplicative Situations

Suppose you plant two trees and compare their growth over a year's time. During one measuring, you find that the first tree has grown from 2 feet to 4 feet, and that the second tree has grown from 3 feet to 5 feet. Which one grew the most? There are different ways of answering this problem. One way is to look at the difference. In each case, a tree grew 2 feet. Another way to consider the growth question is to note that one tree doubled its height and the other did not. This second way of comparing two quantities is explored in this section.

> Given two quantities, whenever we want to determine *how many times as large as one of them the other one is,* we do a **multiplicative comparison** of the two quantities.

EXAMPLE 1

If length A has a value of 12 meters and length B has a value of 3 meters, the *multiplicative comparison* of A to B is 4. The multiplicative comparison of B to A is $\frac{1}{4}$.

An *additive comparison* of the two lengths might say that A is 9 meters longer than B.

Notes

Given two quantities, we can compare them either additively or multiplicatively.

EXAMPLE 2

If a city is expected to grow from 100,000 people to 130,000 people, we could claim that either the population will grow by 30,000 people (an additive comparison) or the population will become 130% of its current value (from the multiplicative comparison of the expected 130,000 persons with the 100,000 current population).

Which type of comparison we use depends on the question being asked and on the needs of the person asking the question. In Example 2, the person planning the water supply for the town will be interested in the additive comparison of the population before and the population after. But this person might also use a multiplicative comparison to estimate a new budget or to judge the adequacy of a reservoir. A government agency concerned with population growth patterns in several localities of different sizes might be more interested in multiplicative comparisons.

Discussion 1   Population Growth

Does a population growth from 1000 to 2000 people have the same implications (social, economic, etc.) for a community as a growth from 100,000 to 101,000 people? Explain.

As you may have noted in Discussion 1, the number of schools in a town that experiences a population growth of 100% will likely have to be doubled, whereas a growth of 1% (the second case) can be absorbed by the existing schools. Thus, even though "how many more people" the community has to deal with is the same in each case, what matters for planning purposes is the growth *relative* to the original size—that is, the multiplicative relation between the current and the original populations, not the difference (additive comparison) between the current and original populations.

Activity 1   Where Should I Put My Money?

A fifth-grade teacher posed this problem to his students.

♦ Jackie invested $20 in her bank, and 3 months later she received $40 back. Jolanda invested $10 in her bank, and 3 months later she received $30 back. Who got the better deal?[i] ♦

The students said it didn't matter. Why do you think they said that? What would be a good follow-up problem to pose?

Activity 2   As Time Goes By

♦ Today is Sally's birthday. She is 7 years old. At some time in the future, John will have his 39th birthday. At that time, he will be 3 times as old as Sally. How old is John now?[ii] ♦

a. Identify all the quantities in the situation, including those whose values are not known.

b. What does the 3 in the problem refer to? What quantities are being compared?

c. How would you as a teacher respond to a student who says that since John is 3 times as old as Sally, and Sally is 7 years old, John must be 21 years old now?

d. How much time will elapse between now and the time when John is 39 years old?

e. How old is John now?

f. What is the difference between Sally's and John's ages when John is 39? Twenty-five years from now? Now?

g. What can you conclude about the difference between John's and Sally's ages as time goes by?

h. As long as John is alive, will he always be 3 times as old as Sally? Explain.

Discussion 2   Analyzing Sally's and John's Ages

Consider the following diagram of the quantitative structure of the problem in Activity 2.

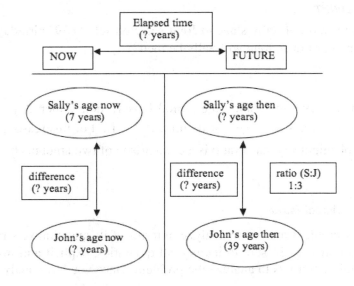

1. Based on this diagram, describe two different ways of determining John's age now.

Continue on the next page.

2. In the diagram, the quantities involved in the problem appear in rectangles and in ovals. Some of these quantities are explicitly stated in the problem, while others are not mentioned, rather they are implicit in the problem. Which quantities are explicit and which ones are implicit?

3. Sketch an alternative diagram that captures the quantities and quantitative relationships in the given problem.

The phrase "he will be 3 times as old as Sally" is a multiplicative comparison, and leads to the idea of *ratio*.

> The result of comparing two quantities multiplicatively is called a **ratio**. If x is the value of quantity A and y is the value of another quantity B, then the ratio $x : y$, or $\frac{x}{y}$, tells us how many times as large A is, as B. The ratio $x : y$ is often pronounced "x to y" or "x is to y."

The context usually makes clear whether to use the $x : y$ or $\frac{x}{y}$ notation.

EXAMPLE 3

In the problem in Activity 2, the ratio of John's age to Sally's age on John's 39th birthday is 3 to 1 (expressed as 3:1 or $\frac{3}{1}$).

> ***THINK ABOUT . . .***
> What is the ratio of Sally's age to John's age on John's 39th birthday? How many times as old as John will Sally be then?

EXAMPLE 4

If time period A is 192 hours and time period B is 12 hours, then A is 16 times as long as B. The 16 comes from $\frac{192}{12}$, or its link, 192 ÷ 12. For this reason, an elementary school book might say that a ratio is a comparison of two amounts by division.

Activity 3   Unreal Estate

Here is another problem for you to analyze in terms of its quantitative structure, perhaps making a drawing. Be sure to include all quantities, explicit and implicit ones. The intent of this activity is to analyze the problem. Once you have analyzed it, solving it is easy.

♦ A $140,000 estate was sold, and the money was split among two children and two grandchildren. The two grandchildren get the same amount of money, and each child gets two times as much as each grandchild. How much did each child get? ♦

Observe from Activity 3 that there are many ways of expressing multiplicative relationships between quantities. For example, we can say, "Each child gets twice as much as each grandchild," or "The ratio of a child's amount to a grandchild's amount is 2 to 1." Also, notice that many (although not all) questions about quantitative relationships can be answered when one simply knows the ratio of the two quantities, child's amount and grandchild's amount, even without actually knowing the values of the individual quantities.

TAKE-AWAY MESSAGE . . . This section builds on earlier work in which a quantitative analysis was required for a problem situation. This time, however, the situations were multiplicative in nature; multiplication and/or division is needed to solve at least part of the problem. Multiplicative reasoning is distinguished from additive reasoning, which calls for addition and/or subtraction. ◆

Learning Exercises for Section 8.1

Drawings will help in these exercises.

1. Four of every 5 dentists interviewed recommend Yukky Gum.

   a. Among those interviewed, what is the ratio of those who recommend Yukky Gum to those who do not?

   b. Among those interviewed, there are _____ times as many dentists who do not recommend Yukky Gum as dentists who do.

   c. What fraction of the dentists interviewed recommend Yukky Gum?

2. In Mensville for every 3 women, there are 4 men.

   a. What is the ratio of men to women in Mensville?

   b. The number of women is _____ times the number of men.

   c. The number of men is _____ times the number of women.

   d. Women make up what fraction of the total population of Mensville?

   e. What fraction of the total population of Mensville are men?

3. Two of every 3 seniors at Lewis High apply for college. Three of every 5 seniors who apply for college at Lewis High are female students.

   a. How does the number of seniors who apply for college compare to the number of seniors at Lewis High?

   b. How does the number of seniors who apply for college compare to those who don't?

   c. What fraction of the graduating seniors at Lewis High do not apply to college?

   d. What fraction of the seniors are males who apply for college? How does the number of males who apply for college compare to the number of graduating seniors?

Continue on the next page.

e. The number of females who apply for college is _____ times as large as the number of students in the senior class. What part of the senior class consists of females who apply for college?

f. How does the number of males who apply for college compare to the number of females who apply?

g. For every _____ females who apply for college, there are _____ males who apply.

h. The number of males who apply for college is _____ times as large as the number of females who apply for college.

i. The number of females who apply for college is _____ times as large as the number of males who apply.

j. What is the ratio of female seniors who do not apply for college to males who do not apply for college?

8.2 | Fractions in Multiplicative Comparisons

The problems in the preceding section, for example, Learning Exercises 2(a) and (c), illustrate the relationship between ratios and fractions. A ratio is not the same as a fraction even though the same symbol, $\frac{a}{b}$, is often used for both. Recall that a ratio is the result of a multiplicative comparison of two quantities. When we compare two quantities and know the value of the corresponding ratio, it is usually possible to deduce what fractional part one quantity is of the other quantity from that comparison. The tasks in Activity 4 will help you see the relationship between fractions and ratios more clearly.

Activity 4   Candy Bars

Below are diagrams of regions. Consider each region as a candy bar that is being shared between two people. For each candy bar, cut the bar into two pieces, A and B, so that it represents the given description of Part A and Part B.

1.
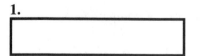

2.
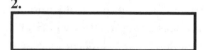

a. Part A is $\frac{1}{2}$ as large as Part B.

b. Part B is ___ times as large as Part A.

c. Part A is how much of the bar?

d. What is the ratio of Part A to Part B?

a. Part A is $\frac{1}{4}$ as large as Part B.

b. Part B is ___ times as large as Part A.

c. Part A is how much of the bar?

d. What is the ratio of Part B to Part A?

Notes

3.

4.

a. Part A is $\frac{2}{3}$ as large as Part B.   **a.** Part A is $\frac{4}{5}$ as large as Part B.

b. Part B is ___ times as large as Part A.   **b.** Part B is ___ times as large as Part A.

c. Part A is how much of the bar?   **c.** Part A is how much of the bar?

d. What is the ratio of Part A to Part B?   **d.** What is the ratio of Part B to Part A?

5.

6.

a. The ratio of Part A to Part B is 3 to 2.   **a.** The ratio of Part A to Part B is 3:4.

b. Part A is ___ times as large as Part B.   **b.** Part B is ___ times as large as Part A.

c. Part B is how much of the bar?   **c.** Part A is how much of the bar?

d. Part B is how many times as large as Part A?   **d.** Part A is how many times as large as Part B?

When using ratios to express the comparison between two quantities (for example, Part A is $\frac{1}{2}$ as large as Part B), it is extremely important to be clear about the quantities being compared (in this case, Part A to Part B, not Part A to the whole bar or Part B to the whole bar). The ratio 1:2 can also be interpreted as saying that Part A is $\frac{1}{2}$ *of* Part B, although strictly speaking this is not really the case. Part A is not *part of* Part B in the sense that we do not get Part A from Part B. However, *the measure of* Part A is $\frac{1}{2}$ the measure of Part B. In this sense, ratios and fractions are closely related.

In comparing Part A to Part B it is important to understand that a ratio of, say, 4 to 5, means that Part A consists of 4 of whatever unit Part B has 5 of. Therefore, the measure of Part A is $\frac{4}{5}$ the measure of Part B.

The same ideas used with the candy bar problems in Activity 4 can be applied to similar but more complicated situations, such as those involving more than two sharers.

EXAMPLE 5

♦ Annie, Bob, and Cass ate a whole pizza. Annie ate twice as much as Bob did, and Bob ate twice as much as Cass. What part of the pizza did each person eat? If the pizza cost $14, how much should each person pay? ♦

SOLUTION

Using ratios and natural labels for the quantities eaten, we have A:B = 2:1 and B:C = 2:1. Bob is involved in both ratios, so we can link the two. For every 2 shares Annie had, Bob had 1, or for every 4 shares Annie had, Bob had 2. Symbolically, A:B = 2:1 = 4:2 and B:C = 2:1. Although pizzas are generally circular, using rectangles to help in thinking (as in the drawing) is all right. Then, for every 4 shares Annie had, Bob had 2, and Cass had 1. Or for every 7 shares, Annie had 4, Bob 2, and Cass 1. Thus, Annie ate $\frac{2}{7}$ of the pizza, Bob ate $\frac{2}{7}$, and Cass ate $\frac{1}{7}$. From those fractions and the $14 cost for the pizza, Annie should pay $8, Bob $4, and Cass $2.

THINK ABOUT . . .

Suppose that the ratios in Example 5 had been linked this way: A:B = 2:1 and B:C = 1:$\frac{1}{2}$. Reason through to see that you would get the same answers as those in the solution given.

Activity 5   **The Orient Express**

You may wish to use diagrams like those used in Activity 4 to solve the following problem.

♦ While riding the train from Chicago to New York, Pat fell asleep after traveling half of the trip. When she woke up she still had to travel half the distance she had traveled while sleeping.[iii] ♦

1. Draw a diagram showing the entire trip with the portion that Pat slept darkened, and then compare your diagram to the diagrams on the next page. For each of the diagrams *explain* whether or not it fits the description of the situation. Assume the shaded part is the portion Pat traveled while sleeping.

2. For what part of the trip was Pat asleep?

a.

Chicago   New York

b.

Chicago   New York

c.

Chicago   New York

d.

Chicago   New York

e.

Chicago   New York

Discussion 3   Elapsed Time

At some time before the end of the day, there remains $\frac{4}{5}$ of what has elapsed since the day began at midnight.[iv]

a. Is it before noon or after noon? Explain how you can tell.

b. The number of hours that have elapsed since the day began is _____ times the number of hours that remain till the end of the day.

c. What time is it?

> TAKE-AWAY MESSAGE . . . The activities and discussions in this section have focused on distinguishing between a ratio and a fraction. For the ratio 1:2 or $\frac{1}{2}$, when comparing two quantities A and B, Quantity A need not be *part of* Quantity B in the sense that we do not necessarily get A from B. However, *the measure of* A is $\frac{1}{2}$ *the measure of* B. In the part-whole notion of a fraction, Quantity A *is part of* Quantity B. This section provided opportunities to think about the types of comparisons being made. ♦

Learning Exercises for Section 8.2

For Exercises 1 through 3, explain which questions address a multiplicative comparison and which questions address an additive comparison, in addition to finding the answers.

1. Anh uses $\frac{3}{8}$ times as many spools of thread in one month as Jack. Anh uses 2 spools of thread.

    a. How many spools does Jack use?

    b. Who uses more thread?

    c. How much more?

2. Claudia ran $9\frac{2}{7}$ laps and Juan ran 5 laps. Claudia ran how many times as many laps as Juan? How much farther did Claudia run?

3. Les is using 10 sticks of butter to make cookies. The actual recipe uses only $2\frac{3}{8}$ sticks of butter. Les is using how many times as many sticks of butter as the actual recipe? How much more butter than called for did Les use?

4. Mary used 14 meters of ribbon to make bows and strips. She used $\frac{3}{4}$ as much ribbon for bows as she did for strips. How many meters of ribbon did she use for bows and how many for strips?

5. The big dog weighs 5 times as much as the little dog. The little dog weighs $\frac{2}{3}$ as much as the medium-sized dog. The medium-sized dog weighs 12 pounds more than the little dog. How much does the big dog weigh?

6. The following problem[v] is from an SAT exam, and very few students solved it. Can you solve this problem?

   ♦ A flock of geese on a pond were being observed continuously.

   At 1:00 p.m., $\frac{1}{5}$ of the geese flew away.

   At 2:00 p.m., $\frac{1}{8}$ of the geese that remained flew away.

   At 3:00 p.m., 3 times as many geese as had flown away at 1:00 p.m. flew away, leaving 28 geese on the pond. At no other time did any geese arrive or fly away or die. How many geese were in the original flock? ♦

7. In each statement, the people named shared a large candy bar. Make a drawing and give your reasoning in finding the fraction of the bar each person ate.

   a. Al ate $\frac{4}{5}$ as much as Babs ate.

   b. Cameron ate $\frac{4}{5}$ of the bar, and Don ate the rest.

   c. Emily ate three times as much as Fran ate.

   d. Gay ate one-half as much as Haille, but three times as much as Ida.

   e. Judy ate $\frac{2}{3}$ of the bar, and Keisha ate twice as much as Lannie.

   f. Mick and Nick each ate a quarter of the bar, and Ollie ate one-half as much as Pete did.

8. If each candy bar in Exercise 7 cost $1.80, how much should each person pay?

9. A cook used all of a 2-pound chunk of cheese in making three recipes. Recipe I used one-third as much cheese as recipe II did, and recipe II used one-half as much cheese as recipe III.

   a. What part of the whole chunk of cheese, and how many pounds, did each recipe use?

   b. If the whole chunk of cheese cost $6.60, how much was the cheese in each recipe worth?

10. Arica planned to donate a total of $100 to four charities. She wanted to give twice as much to Charity A as she did to Charity B, but only one-fourth as much to Charity A as to Charity C. It worked out best if she gave $12 to Charity D. How much did she give to each of Charities A, B, and C?

11. Quinn, Rhonda, and Sue shared $\frac{3}{4}$ of a whole pizza. Quinn was hungrier than Rhonda and ate twice as much as Rhonda did. Sue ate $\frac{3}{4}$ as much as Rhonda. What part of the whole pizza did each eat?

8.3	**Issues for Learning: Standards for Learning**

Over the past several years, mathematics achievement in the United States has been shown to be lower than that of many other countries, particularly many in Asia and in Europe. This fact does not bode well for the future of the America. For this reason, the President of the United States, in 2006, created a national Mathematics Advisory Panel to make recommendations for improving students' knowledge and performance in mathematics. The Final Report[vi] of this panel was published in March, 2008.

The Panel began with evidence that algebra is the place in the curriculum where we see large failure rates because students are not properly prepared for algebra. This fact led to the primary recommendation that the mathematics curriculum in Grades Pre-K–8 should be streamlined to emphasize focused, coherent progression of mathematics learning, with an emphasis on proficiency with key topics, primarily fractions, so that students are prepared for algebra (and all future courses in mathematics). Furthermore, "proficiency with whole numbers is a necessary precursor for the study of fractions, as are aspects of measurement and geometry. These three areas—whole numbers, fractions, and particular aspects of geometry and measurement—are the Critical Foundations of Algebra" (p. xviii). Proficiency is more than computational skill—this panel members consider conceptual understanding and problem solving skills as equally important and see these capabilities as mutually supportive.

But how can district and state framework committees design curricula for these grades to assure that when students reach algebra they will have the background needed to be successful? We have never had a national curriculum in this country (most other countries do). For this reason, most textbooks are long because the publishers try to cover every topic found in every state's guidelines. But the Panel Report calls for severely limiting the number of topics taught at each grade level, and teaching those few topics so well that in future grades they will not need to be taught again. Thus the implementation of the recommendations will depend on some national consensus about the mathematics curriculum.

One way to determine at least some uniformity is to consider national guidelines such as those offered by the National Council of Teachers of Mathematics (NCTM). NCTM is an organization of approximately 100,000 mathematics teachers, and has been providing information and assistance to mathematics teachers for almost a century, primarily through conferences and publications. For example, your university library and most elementary schools have access to one or more of three NCTM journals: *Teaching Children Mathematics* (aimed at the elementary grades), *Mathematics Teaching in the Middle School* (aimed at the middle grades), and *The Mathematics Teacher* (aimed at secondary school mathematics).

NCTM has also published documents that outline standards for school mathematics. These documents are written by carefully selected groups of Pre-K–12 teachers, supervisors, and university faculty. The most recent Standards volume is called *Principles and Standards for School Mathematics* (PSSM).[vii] This book describes what students at different grade levels should learn in five content areas: Number and Operations, Algebra, Geometry, Measurement, and Data Analysis and Probability. There are also five standards discussed at each of these grade bands dealing with five processes involved in learning and doing mathematics: Problem Solving, Reasoning and Proof, Communication, Connections, and Representation. Finally, six Principles for School Mathematics are discussed. They deal with equity, curriculum, teaching, learning, assessment, and technology. For example, the equity principle states that "Excellence in mathematics education requires equity—high expectations and strong support for all students" (p. 11).

Chapters 1–11 of this course focus on the content developed in the Number and Operations standard, and present the mathematics you need to know and to do to teach this content well. The five process standards are embedded throughout the course materials. Various Issues for Learning throughout all four parts of this text contain descriptions of the content standards at each of the first three grade bands: K–2, 3–5, and 6–8. Here is a basic summary of the Pre-K-8 standards regarding Numbers and Operations.

Pre-K through Grade 2.   Students should learn to count with meaning, develop a basic understanding of our base-ten system, and be able to work comfortably with whole numbers including their composition. For example, they should recognize that 23 could be decomposed into 2 tens and 3 ones, but also into 1 ten and 13 ones. They should develop an understanding of the fractions $\frac{1}{2}$, $\frac{1}{3}$, and $\frac{1}{4}$. Various meanings of addition and subtraction of whole numbers should be understood, together with the relationship between these two operations. Situations calling for multiplication and division should be recognized, such as equal groupings and equal sharing. Students should be fluent when working with different number combinations for addition and subtraction (often called the *basic facts*) such as sums for numbers through 10. They should be able to use a variety of methods and tools for computing with numbers, including counting with objects, mental computation, estimation, paper and pencil, and calculators.

Grades 3–5.   Students' understanding of place value should expand to include large numbers and decimal numbers, and they should be able to compare these numbers and recognize equivalent ways of expressing them. A sound understanding of fractions will include the ability to compare fractions and operate on them. They should be able to recognize and generate equivalent forms of fractions, decimals, and percents. Numbers less than 0 are introduced. The various meanings of arithmetical operations and the ways that they relate to one another should be understood, as well as the effects of those operations. Properties of operations must be learned and used correctly.

Students must be fluent with operations on whole numbers, decimal numbers, and fractions. They should develop strong number sense as evidenced by their ability to mentally compute with numbers and estimate appropriately with whole numbers, fractions, and decimal numbers, and to judge the reasonableness of results of these operations. They should be able to use various types of representations and benchmarks, and they should be able to select appropriate methods and tools, including mental computation, estimation, paper and pencil, and calculators to carry out computations of various types.

Grades 6–8.   Opportunities must be provided to deepen understanding of the mathematics of the elementary school, including working flexibly with fractions, percents, and decimals, comparing and ordering these types of numbers, using properties of operations to carry out computations, and selecting appropriate ways of computing on these numbers. The students should be developing an understanding of very large numbers and using exponential, scientific, and calculator notation. Knowledge about factors, multiples, prime factorization, and relatively prime numbers can be used to solve problems. Ratios and proportions should be used to represent quantitative relationships.

The *Principles and Standards of School Mathematics* develops the standards in far more detail than is given here, and provides many examples to help readers understand how to provide instruction that will meet these standards.

As if foreseeing the National Panel report, NCTM recognized the difficulties associated with teaching mathematics with broad coverage and much repetition. Thus in 2006 NCTM released another document, *Curriculum Focal Points for Prekindergarten through Grade 8 Mathematics: A Quest for Coherence,*[viii] which was based on the PSSM. Three core focal points are addressed for each grade level. For example, the focal points at Grade 5 include developing an understanding of and fluency with division of whole numbers, understanding of and fluency with addition and subtraction of fractions and decimals, and describing three-dimensional shapes and analyzing their properties, including volume and surface area. These focal points are likely to provide guidelines for the new version of textbooks you may use when you teach.

The National Panel recognizes that teachers have a central role in mathematics education and to this end recommends that the government support initiatives for attracting and appropriately preparing, evaluating, and retraining effective teachers of mathematics. *Teaching that demands students learn, at any given grade level, a small number of topics well will require that a teacher must know these topics exceedingly well.*

> **THINK ABOUT . . .**
>
> How well do you understand the mathematics you will be teaching? In this course are you going beyond procedural learning to include conceptual understanding and problem solving skill?

8.4 | Check Yourself

This chapter returned to quantitative analyses of problems, but now the problems require multiplicative reasoning. A distinction was made between additive reasoning and multiplicative reasoning. An additive comparison requires using the difference between values of two quantities, whereas a multiplicative comparison requires using the ratio between values of two quantities. A distinction was also made between fractions and ratios, which often use the same symbols.

You should be able to work problems and answer questions like those assigned and that deal with the following:

1.   Differentiate between additive and multiplicative reasoning both by contrasting the two and by recognizing when each is used in a problem solution.

2.   Identify problems that require a multiplicative approach to solve.

3.   Undertake quantitative analyses of problems that require multiplicative reasoning. (There will be more chances to practice in Chapter 9.)

4.   Use ratios to compare quantities.

5.   Distinguish between ratios and fractions and the manner in which they are used.

6.   Identify resources for determining appropriate curricula for elementary school grades.

REFERENCES FOR CHAPTER 8

[i]Sowder, J., & Philipp, R. (1999). Promoting learning in middle-grade mathematics. In E. Fennema & T. A. Romberg (Eds.), *Mathematics classrooms that promote understanding,* (pp. 89-108). Mahwah, NJ: Erlbaum.

[ii]Adapted from Thompson, A. G., Philipp, R. A., Thompson, P. W., & Boyd, B. A. (1994). Calculational and conceptual orientations in teaching mathematics. In A. Coxford (Ed.), *Professional development for teachers of mathematics: 1994 Yearbook of the NCTM* (pp. 79-92). Reston, VA: National Council of Teachers of Mathematics.

[iii, iv]Adapted from Krutetskii, V. A. (1976). *The psychology of mathematical abilities in schoolchildren* (J. Teller, Trans.). Chicago: University of Chicago Press.

[v]Dancis, J. (no date given). *Reading instruction for arithmetic word problems: If Johnny can't read and follow directions, then he can't do math.* http://www.math.umd.edu/~jnd/subhome/Reading_Instruction.htm, June 15, 2005.

[vi]U.S. Department of Education (2008). Final Report of the National Mathematics Advisory Panel. http://www.ed.gov/about/bdscomm/list/mathpanel/index.html

[vii]National Council of Teachers of Mathematics. (2000). *Principles and Standards for School Mathematics.* Reston, VA: Author.

[viii]National Council of Teachers of Mathematics. (2006). *Curriculum focal points for prekindergarten through grade 8 mathematics: A quest for coherence.* Reston, VA: Author.

Chapter 9

Ratios, Rates, Proportions, and Percents

In this chapter we continue our work on multiplicative reasoning. We have talked in the past about how we measure certain quantities. (Recall from Section 1.1 that a quantity is any attribute of an object that can be measured or counted.) For example, we can measure length with linear units such as inches or centimeters; we can measure area in terms of square feet or square meters; and we can measure speed in terms of miles per hour or meters per second. There are, of course, many other ways to measure these quantities. Measuring via ratios and rates is the focus of this chapter, along with proportional thinking and the special case of percent.

9.1 Ratio as a Measure

Ratio was introduced in Chapter 8 as a way of comparing quantities. In this section we build on that idea in new contexts.

Discussion 1   Lot Sizes

Consider the following problem.[i]

- ◆ A new housing subdivision offers rectangular lots of three different sizes:

a. 75 feet by 114 feet

b. 455 feet by 508 feet

c. 185 feet by 245 feet

If you were able to view these lots from above, which would appear most nearly square? Which would appear least square? Explain your answers. ◆

Be sure to think about what attribute or characteristic of the lots we are interested in and in what ways this attribute can be quantified.

Notes

Notice that because we are interested in comparing the three lots in terms of their *squareness*, it would help to assign each lot a measure of its squareness to facilitate the comparison. Without a numerical value for squareness, it would be hard to decide which lot is the *most square*. How would you quantify *squareness* in this case?

Discussion 2   Downhill

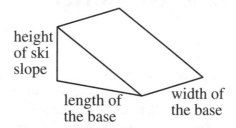

height
of ski
slope

length of
the base

width of
the base

In Japan, indoor skiing is very popular. Ski slopes are built in very large indoor arenas and covered with a plastic fiber that simulates packed snow. In one arena there are three ski slopes. Suppose you have measurements on each of the three slopes that tell you the length of the base, the width of the base, and the height of the ski slope. How could you decide which of the three slopes is the most steep or the least steep?[ii]

TAKE-AWAY MESSAGE . . . Multiplicative comparisons involve the use of ratios. Ratios can be used to indicate some measurements, such as steepness. To find out which of two slopes is steeper, for example, ratios can be compared. Recognizing when to use ratios is an indicator of the ability to reason multiplicatively. ♦

Learning Exercises for Section 9.1

1. You are running a contest to see if people can tell which of three different-sized batches of coffee (from the same type of coffee bean) is strongest. As the manager of the contest, how would *you* measure the strength of each batch?

2. These numbers are from a website.[iii] Devise a way of quantifying population growth to enable comparisons among the different countries.

Country	Population	# of Live Births Expected 2005	# of Deaths Expected 2005
China	1,305,950, 000	15,413,000	8,299,000
Mexico	106,124,450	2,024,000	482,000
South Africa	44,350,000	724,000	826,000
United Kingdom	60,438,000	603,200	548,000
United States	295,652,000	3,757,600	2,147,200

3. Discuss how each of the following attributes might be quantified.

   a. the clarity of a computer screen

   b. the shades of gray from white to black that a printer is able to make

   c. the steepness of a line on a coordinate plane

   d. the distance from one city to another

   e. population density

   f. the likelihood of drawing a red ball from a bag containing a mixture of red and blue balls

   g. quality of performance of an undergraduate in all her coursework

   h. the sweetness of a drink

   i. the strength of iced tea

4. By what process could you enlarge polygons while maintaining their shape?

5. Suppose you have two similar triangles (same shape, perhaps different sizes). Discuss the different ways the two shapes could be compared. Do any of these ways involve ratios? Do any not involve ratios?

9.2 | Comparing Ratios

Thus far we have used ratios to compare qualities such as squareness, steepness, or coffee strength. In this section we continue such comparisons and consider situations when two ratios are proportional (equal) and when they are not proportional. Unit ratios are introduced, and the $x{:}y$ and $\frac{x}{y}$ link is again illustrated.

Activity 1   Orange Juicy

The orange drink in pitcher A is made by mixing 1 can of orange concentrate with 3 cans of water. The mixture in pitcher B is made by mixing 2 cans of orange concentrate with 6 cans of water. Which will taste more *orangey*, the mixture in Pitcher A or the mixture in Pitcher B?[iv]

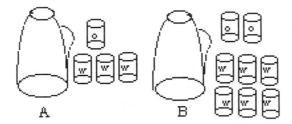

a. Give an argument to support your answer to the above question.

b. How would you, as a teacher, respond to a student who says that the mixture in Pitcher A is more orangey because less water went into making it?

c. In a fifth-grade class some students reasoned like the student in part (b). Other students in the same class argued that the mixture in Pitcher B is more orangey because it has more orange concentrate. How would you settle the argument? What is wrong with the reasoning of the students in each group?

d. There was another student who argued as follows:

> Pour 1 can of orange concentrate and 1 can of water into Pitcher A. Take 2 cans of orange concentrate and 2 cans of water and pour them into Pitcher B. The two mixtures are equally orangey because they are made with equal parts orange and water, that is, 50-50. Now there are only 2 cans of water left to go into Pitcher A and 4 cans of water left to go into Pitcher B. Because the mixtures are the same strength, when you add 4 cans of water to the mixture in Pitcher B, it will be more watery than the mixture in Pitcher A, which gets only 2 more cans of water. Therefore the mixture in Pitcher A is more orangey.

How would you deal with this student's thinking?

e. How can *oranginess* be quantified in this situation to facilitate the comparison?

Once we recognize that a ratio is, itself, a quantity, then we can compare ratios just as we compare quantities. In the problem above, we can ask questions such as these: 1 can orange concentrate and 3 cans of water, 1 to 3; 2 cans orange and 6 cans water, 2 to 6; which mixture is more orangey? Or equivalently, which is the larger ratio?

The students in Activity 1 were reasoning additively when they gave their reasons. Focusing on just one of the two quantities being combined to make the mixture, orange or water, but not both, will lead to faulty reasoning. In the *Orange Juicy* situation, one has to focus on the two quantities, amount of orange *and* amount of water. That is why a ratio of the two quantities is an appropriate measure of the strength of the mixture.

Discussion 3   Other Ratio Situations

What are some other situations in which a ratio would be needed in order to make a comparison?

When we compare two ratios, we are trying to compare the *sizes* of the ratios. If two ratios are equal (equivalent), we say that they form a *proportion*, or that the two quantities involved are *proportional*. So, the question about the orange juice mixtures could be phrased as: Are the amounts of concentrate and water proportional in the two recipes?

> A **proportion** is a statement that two ratios are equal to one another. The quantities are said to be proportional.

EXAMPLE 1

In Activity 1, the ratio of orange concentrate to water was 1:3. Any other orange juice of the same strength would have some *n* such that $1:3 = 1n : 3n$, viewing it as *n* repetitions of the 1:3 recipe. In the case where $n = 2$, we have the proportion $1:3 = 2:6$. This also can be written as $\frac{1}{3} = \frac{2}{6}$, so the earlier work on equal fractions is applicable here.

The close relationship between ratios and fractions, and the flexible use of $\frac{a}{b}$ for *a:b*, is strengthened by the important similarity in calculating equal fractions and equal ratios, shown in the following equations:

$$\frac{x}{y} = \frac{nx}{ny} \ (n \neq 0) \qquad \text{vs.} \qquad x{:}y = nx{:}ny \ (n \neq 0).$$

This similarity allows us to use the $\frac{x}{y}$ form for the *x:y* form in many calculations.

If another batch of juice is made up with 3 cans of concentrate to 7 cans of water, the ratio of concentrate to water could be expressed as 3:7. This ratio is not equal to 1:3. The new mixture is not proportional to the other mixtures. Thus, a question can be asked: Which juice is stronger, the juice with 1 can of concentrate per 3 cans of water, represented as $\frac{1}{3}$ (for the $\frac{1}{3}$:1 unit ratio), or the juice with 3 cans of concentrate to 7 cans of water, represented as $\frac{3}{7}$ (for the $\frac{3}{7}$:1 unit ratio)?

Comparing these ratios is much like comparing fractions. Which is larger? We know $\frac{1}{3} = \frac{3}{9}$, and we can reason that $\frac{3}{9} < \frac{3}{7}$ because ninths are smaller than sevenths. Thus the first juice is weaker. Alternatively, you could compare $\frac{1}{3}$ and $\frac{3}{7}$ by finding a common denominator: $\frac{7}{21}$ and $\frac{9}{21}$, but you must take care that this procedure does not simply become a rule that is not understood. The first way of comparing fractions, which depends on number sense, assures that you understand the problem. In other words, the first way is more transparent.

Another kind of comparison problem occurs when asked, *"How much water should be used with 12 cans of concentrate, given that the strength is to be equal to the 1 can of concentrate to 3 cans of water?"* This question is often called a **missing-value problem** and is represented as $\frac{1}{3} = \frac{12}{x}$. There are several ways to think about this proportion when asked to find the value of *x*. Here, for every can of concentrate you would need 3 cans of water. So for 12 cans of concentrate, you would need 12×3 cans of water, or 36 cans of water.

But suppose, instead, *I have 12 cans of water, and I want to know how much concentrate to use.* The $\frac{1}{3}$ can also be thought of as the concentrate-to-water ratio; there is $\frac{1}{3}$ can of concentrate per can of water, that is, every $\frac{1}{3}$ can of concentrate calls for 1 can of water. So for 12 cans of water, there would be $12 \times \frac{1}{3}$ cans of concentrate, or 4 cans of concentrate.

These two equivalent expressions for ratios can be written as: **1:3 is the same as $\frac{1}{3}$:1,** or $\frac{\frac{1}{3}}{1}$. Notice how these expressions were used in the previous two paragraphs. They all represent the ratio of concentrate to water. Just as the ratio 1:3 can be read as "1 can concentrate for every 3 cans water," the ratio $\frac{1}{3}$:1 can be read "$\frac{1}{3}$ can concentrate for every can of water." Having equivalent expressions for ratios often can be useful in solving ratio problems.

Both of the comparison problem solutions involving 1 can of concentrate per 3 cans of water took advantage of the unit ratio.

A **unit ratio** is a ratio for which the first quantity is represented by some nonzero number and the second quantity is represented by 1.

Discussion 4   Using Unit Ratios

Suppose the missing-value problem had asked for orange juice of the same strength as orange juice with 3 cans of concentrate per 7 cans of water. For this problem, use unit ratios to answer the following questions:

1. What is the unit ratio for concentrate to water? How much concentrate should be used to make the same strength orange juice if you have 12 cans of water?

2. What is the unit ratio for water to concentrate? How many cans of water would be needed to make orange juice of the same strength if you use 12 cans of concentrate?

Many textbooks would have the student set up a proportion to solve the first discussion problem: $\frac{3}{7} = \frac{x}{12}$, where x is called the "missing value." There are many ways of solving such missing-value proportion problems. They vary not only by efficiency but also by the transparency of the method, that is, whether the procedure makes sense. In the following three examples, consider the different ways of solving this problem in which 3 cans of concentrate and 7 cans of water make orange juice the same strength as x cans of concentrate with 12 cans of water.

EXAMPLE 2

Three cans of concentrate for 7 cans of water means that for $\frac{3}{7}$ cans of concentrate, 1 can of water is used. Thus, the unit ratio $= \frac{\frac{3}{7} \text{ cans concentrate}}{1 \text{ can water}}$. So for 12 cans of water, $12 \times \frac{3}{7} = \frac{36}{7} = 5\frac{1}{7}$ cans of concentrate are needed.

The method in Example 2 uses a unit ratio. It is commonly employed by children even if the cross-multiplication method in Example 4 has been shown to them as the "correct" way to solve proportion problems.[v]

EXAMPLE 3

In $\frac{3}{7} = \frac{x}{12}$, the ratios can be replaced by equal ratios using the same second entries (a *common denominator* in fraction terms):

$$\frac{3 \cdot 12}{7 \cdot 12} = \frac{7 \cdot x}{7 \cdot 12}.$$

Clearly the ratios will be equal when $3 \cdot 12 = 7x$ or $x = \frac{36}{7}$.

EXAMPLE 4

For $\frac{3}{7} = \frac{x}{12}$, we *"cross-multiply"* to get $7x = 36$, so $x = \frac{36}{7}$.

> *THINK ABOUT . . .*
> How are the methods in Examples 3 and 4 related?

Discussion 5   Making Sense of Proportions

Discuss each of the three solutions in Examples 2–4 in terms of whether or not they make sense of the original problem. Why might a teacher want to delay presenting the solution in Example 4?

The idea of *rate* has been used above, without actually using the term. The ideas and techniques of ratios will also apply to rates. There is not a uniform usage of the term *rate* across curricula, but we will use the term as defined below.

> A **rate** is a ratio of quantities that change without changing the value of the ratio.

EXAMPLE 5

In Activity 1, the rate is the same for the two recipes, because the ratios in the two mixtures are equal. From rate of speed expressions, such as 50 miles per hour, meaning 50 miles for every 1 hour, you know that units with *per* are describing rates. **An elementary school textbook might explain** *per* **by saying it means** *for every* **or** *for each,* **both of which are useful ways of thinking about** *per* **(and rates in general).** If we consider the two ratios in Activity 1 as rates, we say the rates are 2 cans concentrate per 6 cans water and 1 can concentrate per 3 cans water. In a common form, the rate might be given as $\frac{2}{6}$, or $\frac{1}{3}$, can of concentrate per 1 can of water, again showing the close relationship between a ratio and a fraction. Even a ratio for a fixed situation might be considered a rate: 12 boys for 4 girls (12:4) could be viewed as the rate 3 boys for every girl (3:1).

Students first learning about ratios, proportions, and rates can be assisted by setting up a table. Thus, for the problem with the ratio of $\frac{1}{3}$ representing the ratio of the orange juice concentrate to water and 12 cans of concentrate are used, a fifth-grade teacher might show a table such as the following to find the amount of water needed.

# of cans of OJ concentrate	# of cans of water
1	3
2	6
12	36

Activity 2   Cupcakes and Perfume

1. A researcher[vi] studying the ways in which students think about and solve proportion problems taught them to make tables to show their thinking. She added a third column to explain how each number in the second column was obtained. A typical problem and table is given below. (In part (b), a second problem is given without a table, and you are to make a similar table.)

    ♦ If 15 cupcakes cost $3.36, find the cost of 38 cupcakes. ♦

Cupcakes	Cost in dollars	Notes
15	3.36	given
30	6.72	× 2
5	1.12	÷ 6
3	0.672	30 ÷ 10
38	8.512	30 + 5 + 3

    The cost of 38 cupcakes was $8.51.

2. Design a three-column table such as the table in part (a) to solve this problem:

    ♦ A famous designer gave away free perfume samples in the mall, and in 15 minutes, 600 people picked up his free gifts at the cosmetic counter. If this give-away is going to be repeated at this rate, but this time for 1.5 hours, how many gift packages will be needed? ♦

Activity 3   Pepperoni to Go![vii]

Luigi's is a pizza parlor that caters to the local college crowd. The 24 members of the chess club come in to celebrate. Eighteen pizzas had been ordered in advance (all the same size). None of the tables will hold 24 persons, so they sit at two tables, each

Notes

with 9 pizzas and 12 members. We designate the change from one to two tables like this:

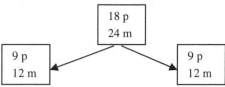

We say the distribution now is $\dfrac{9p}{12m}$ (9 pizzas for 12 members) at each of the two

new tables.

1. **a.** Construct diagrams of alternative ways the 24 members can be seated and show how they might share equitably the 18 pizzas.

    b. Here is a seating arrangement where pizzas and members were moved from one table to three different tables in such a way that everyone got a fair share of pizza:

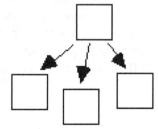

In how many different ways could 18 pizzas and 24 members have been arranged at each table so everyone got a fair share of pizza? How much pizza does each person get? Is there more than one way to distribute pizzas among members?

    c. Return to part (a). Discuss your work in terms of equivalent ratios.

2. Consider some new situations, keeping in mind that pizzas are shared fairly in each table.

    a. Would the distribution $\dfrac{10p}{14m}$ and $\dfrac{8p}{10m}$ be fair for each member?

    b. Who would get more pizza, a person sitting at a table of $\dfrac{3p}{5m}$ or a person sitting at the table of $\dfrac{7p}{9m}$?

    c. Another person has $1\dfrac{2}{3}$ pizzas. At what table might she be sitting?

    d. Can someone who is served $\dfrac{1}{2} + \dfrac{1}{3}$ pizza have sat at the table $\dfrac{2p}{5m}$?

    e. If someone is given a serving of $\dfrac{1}{2}$ pizza, at which tables might he be sitting?

    f. Someone is sitting at a table designated as $\dfrac{4p}{5m}$. At which table would she get only half as much?

Discussion 6   **When Not to Use Proportions**

Explain why proportional reasoning might not be appropriate to use in the following problems.

1.   Jake drove 72 miles during the first hour of his trip. How long will it take to drive the entire 144 miles of his trip?

2.   In a pie-eating contest, Juarez ate two pies in the first five minutes. How many pies can he eat in one hour?

3.   It took Denise 20 minutes to complete 10 out of the 20 problems that were assigned. How long will it take her to complete all 20 problems?

4.   Jim can mow the lawn in 45 minutes. Today Janyce is helping him. How long will it take for the two of them to mow the lawn?

Proportional reasoning is the major type of multiplicative thinking introduced in upper elementary and middle school. Many elementary and middle-school textbooks devote only a few pages to ratio and proportion, and simply state what a ratio is, what a proportion is, and then ask students to solve problems by setting up proportions and cross-multiplying. There is often little to no understanding of proportions developed in such lessons.

TAKE-AWAY MESSAGE . . . Proportional reasoning is sometimes referred to as the "watershed" of middle grades mathematics. This is a vitally important type of reasoning that undergirds much of the mathematics that students will encounter in secondary school and college. Teachers must have a solid understanding of this critical topic to enable their students to develop proportional reasoning. ♦

Learning Exercises for Section 9.2

Treat Exercises 1–15 as thinking exercises, rather than relying on computational procedures that you may remember. That is, your explanations should not reside solely on elaborate calculations.

1.   **a.**   Three scoops of coffee are used with 4 cups of water in a coffee machine; 4 scoops of coffee are used with 6 cups of water in another coffee machine. Which brew will be stronger? How do you know?

     b.   Which is stronger, 4 scoops for 8 cups of water or 7 scoops for 15 cups of water? How do you know?

     c.   How many scoops of coffee were there per 1 cup of water in each case? How do you know?

2.   **a.**   A certain kind of punch mix uses a 1 for 2 ratio, that is, each cup of punch concentrate is to be diluted with 2 cups of water. Sonia was mixing a large bowl of punch for a party. She miscounted and put in 8 cups of concentrate to 15 cups of water. Was the mix stronger or weaker than intended?

b. On the second batch she used 9 cups of concentrate and 19 cups of water. Was the second batch stronger or weaker than intended by the instructions? Was it stronger or weaker than the first batch?

c. List some mixes that are slightly stronger than intended.

d. List some mixes that are slightly weaker than intended.

e. List some mixes that are much stronger than intended.

f. List some mixes that are much weaker than intended.

3. Repeat Exercise 2, parts (c)–(f), with a punch that uses a 1 for 1 ratio: 1 cup of concentrate to 1 cup of water.

4. **a.** Use unit ratios on this problem:

   ◆ A manufacturer recommends 10 tablespoons of cocoa be mixed with 4 cups of milk to make hot cocoa. A school cafeteria is fixing hot cocoa for 50 first-graders. How many tablespoons of cocoa should they use if they are to mix enough to give every first-grader a cup? Given that 2 tablespoons of cocoa are equivalent to $\frac{1}{8}$ cup of cocoa, how many cups of cocoa should be used? ◆

   b. Name one rate in the problem given in part (a).

5. Adam and Matt are using different maps. On Adam's map, a line 6 inches long represents a road which is really 9 miles long. On Matt's map, a line 8 inches long represents a road which is really 12 miles long. If both boys were to measure the distance from City A to City B, who would have a longer line (in terms of inches)?

6. Car A can travel a greater distance in 3 hours than Car B can travel in 2 hours. If possible, find which car will travel a greater distance: Car A in 5 hours or Car B in 6 hours.

7. Read the following two problems.

   A) Which is stronger: 3 cups orange concentrate mixed with 4 cups water or 5 cups of orange concentrate mixed with 8 cups water?

   B) Which is stronger: 3 cups orange concentrate mixed with 5 cups water or 5 cups orange concentrate mixed with 8 cups water?

   More students answer Problem A correctly than Problem B. Explain why you think this is so.

8. Horse A can travel 40 km in 3 hours. Horse B can travel 67 km in 5 hours. If possible, find which horse can travel faster.

9. Two workers working 9 hours made 243 parts. Worker A makes 13 parts in one hour. If the workers work at a steady rate throughout the day, who is more productive, Worker A or Worker B?

10. Tuna can be bought in 12-oz cans that sell for $1.09 each or in 10.75-oz cans that sell for 98¢ each. Which is the better buy? Use unit ratios to answer this problem.

11. Jane and Scott were given identical boxes of crayons. Two weeks later, Jane had $\frac{4}{9}$ of the box left and Scott had $\frac{3}{7}$ of his box left. Who has more crayons left?

12. In Mrs. Heath's class there are 13 girls and 11 boys. In Mrs. Lauri's class 15 of 28 children are girls. In which class are the girls better represented?

13. Car A started out with a full tank of gas (12 gallons) and traveled 250 miles before it ran out of gas. Car B, whose tank capacity is 15 gallons, started out with half a tank and traveled 145 miles. Which car is more economical in terms of gasoline consumption?

14. In Boogleville, two-thirds of the men are married to three-fourths of the women. What is the ratio of men to women? (*Hint*: Draw a diagram.)

15. How can you tell whether the two ratios, 133:161 and 95:115, are equal?

16. **a.** Rewrite $a{:}b$ and $c{:}d$ as equal ratios with the same (algebraic) second entries to give a criterion for when $a{:}b$ is equal $c{:}d$. (*Hint*: First write the ratios in fraction form: $\frac{a}{b}$ and $\frac{c}{d}$, and then replace those with equal fractions having the same denominator.)

    b. (**Cross-multiplication algorithm**) The idea in part (a) can be used in solving proportions with an unknown entry—e.g., $57{:}32 = 171{:}x$. Writing the ratios as fractions ($\frac{57}{32} = \frac{171}{x}$), and then replacing the fractions with equal fractions having the same denominator ($\frac{57x}{32x} = \frac{32 \cdot 171}{32x}$) gives $57x = 32 \cdot 171$, an equation that can be solved by dividing both sides by 57, giving $x = 96$. Notice that the $57x$ and $32 \cdot 171$ could be obtained from the original $\frac{57}{32} = \frac{171}{x}$ by multiplying diagonally. This procedure illustrates a useful shortcut called *cross-multiplication*. Solve $\frac{51}{x} = \frac{17}{48}$ and $\frac{11.7}{2.16} = \frac{x}{7.2}$ using cross-multiplication. We don't focus on it here because it is often used mindlessly, without understanding.

    c. Once children learn cross-multiplication, they often use it on addition and multiplication of fractions. Does cross-multiplication give correct answers then?

17. There is a minor controversy about whether or not ratios and fractions are exactly the same. As you have seen, *computationally* they behave alike in some important situations. But consider this setting: "A good batter made 3 hits in 4 at-bats in one game, and 2 hits in 4 at-bats in the next game. How did the batter do in the two games together?" Does the natural response $\frac{3}{4} + \frac{2}{4} = n$ give the correct answer?

18. Complete the table for the following problem:[viii]

    ♦ Cheese costs $4.25/pound. Nancy selects several chunks for a large party and when they are weighed, she has 12.13 pounds of cheese. How much will it cost her? ♦

pounds	cost	notes
1	$4.25	given
10		
2		
0.1		
12.1		
0.05		
0.01		
0.03		
12.13		

19. A donut machine produces 60 donuts every 5 minutes. How many donuts does it produce in an hour?

    a. Is there a *rate* in this problem? If so, what is it and why is it a rate? If not, why not?

    b. What unit fraction is associated with this rate?

    c. Answer the question in part (a) using the unit rate.

    d. Set up a proportion and solve the problem without using the unit rate.

20. A certain car gets 23 miles to the gallon on open highway. How far can it travel on 12 gallons of gas, on open highway?

    a. Is there a *rate* in this problem? If so, what is it and why is it a rate? If not, why not?

    b. What unit fraction is associated with this rate?

    c. Answer the question in part (a) using the unit rate.

    d. Set up a proportion and solve the problem.

21. Name University tries to maintain an average of seven undergraduate students for every two graduate students. For every 100 graduate students admitted, how many undergraduate students would you expect to be admitted?

    a. Is there a *rate* in this problem? If so, what is it and why is it a rate? If not, why not?

    b. What unit fraction is associated with this rate?

    c. Answer the question in part (a) using the unit rate.

    d. Set up a proportion and solve the problem without using the unit rate.

22. In Mrs. Heath's class there are 12 girls and 11 boys.

    a. What is the ratio of girls to boys?

    b. Why is there not a rate associated with this problem?

23. Find two examples of the use of unit ratios in a grocery store.

24. "Numberless" problems like the ones below allow a focus on the quantities and their relationships rather than on computation. Explain your thinking for your answers for each.

    a. Andy drove more miles than Bob did, and Andy drove fewer hours than Bob did. Who drove faster—Andy, Bob, the same, or can't tell?

    b. Carla swam fewer laps than Donna did. Carla took more time than Donna did. Who swam faster—Carla, Donna, the same, or can't tell?

    c. Evan made more cookies than Fawn did. Evan took longer than Fawn did. Who baked cookies faster—Evan, Fawn, the same, or can't tell?

9.3 | Percents in Comparisons and Changes

You have worked on some problems involving percents in previous sections, and of course you have encountered them many times in your daily life. Percents provide us with a handy way of comparing fractions when the values are "messy." Percents also are used as a way to discuss change, but care needs to be taken that percent problems are understood. *Percent* comes from words meaning *per hundred,* so the hidden ratio or rate meaning is clear.

> A **percent** is a ratio for which the value of the second quantity is understood to be 100.

So 8.5% means 8.5 per 100. Calculating percents often uses the $x{:}y$, $\frac{x}{y}$, and $x \div y$ links.

Discussion 7   When Are Percents Handy?

Consider each of these two problems. What is the advantage of using percents in situations such as these?

1. One discussion class has 28 females and 17 males. A large lecture class has 106 females and 62 males. In which class is the female population more dominant?

2. Suppose you scored 15.5 points out of a possible total of 20 points on the first quiz and 59 points out of a total possible of 75 points on the second quiz. How would you figure out on which quiz you did better?

One can think of percent as a standardized way to express ratios or fractions in order to facilitate comparisons. For example, when we find an equivalent ratio for which the value of the second quantity is 100, we are finding a percent. If we compare test grades by finding ratios that are equivalent to $\frac{15.5}{20}$ and $\frac{59}{75}$ but with 100 as the denominator, we are finding a percent. We can write $\frac{59}{75}$ as 78.7% and $\frac{15.5}{20}$ as 77.5%. Now the two quiz performances given in Discussion 7 are easy to compare.

> ***THINK ABOUT . . .***
>
> In Activity 1 in the last section, you were asked which of two mixtures tasted more "orangey." One could (but need not) think in terms of percents. What percent of the mixture in Pitcher A (1 orange to 3 water) is orange? What percent is water? How about in Pitcher B (2 orange to 6 water)?

Solving percent problems is really no different from solving ratio and proportion problems.

Some textbooks teach percents by introducing three different types of percent problems. All have the form *a% of b = c,* and in each case, only one of *a, b,* or *c* is unknown. These three types of problems are sometimes taught as three different types, with a rule for each. The rules are usually forgotten. There is really just one rule for solving these problems.

Activity 4   Three Kinds of Percent Problems? Or Just One?

Each of these problems can easily be solved mentally. Compare your mental strategies that depend on good number sense. Then for each problem, set up a proportion for which one ratio has 100 as the value of its second quantity. Compare these methods.

1. 30 is what percent of 45?

2. What number is 50% of 60?

3. 16 is 25% of what number?

Did these seem like three different kinds of problems to you, or basically the same kind of problem? Could you solve each without thinking about which "type" it was?

Just as a fraction is a fraction *of some quantity*, a percent is a percent *of some quantity*. The next activity will help to make that clear.

Activity 5   Fair or Not?

1. The boss says, "You remember when business was bad last year, I had to cut everyone's pay by 10%? Well, business is better, so I can raise your pay by 10% now. That will put you back to where you were before the cut." Is the boss correct?

2. You buy an article on sale for 20% off in a locale where there is an 8% sales tax. You expected the clerk to figure the discount first and then the sales tax on the reduced price, but the clerk figured the sales tax first and then the discount on that price. Were you cheated? If so, by what percent? If not, explain.

Examples like those in Activity 5 show how important it is to know what a percent is a percent *of*, that is, the *base* for the percent. For Problem 2 in Activity 5, the base could be the price of the purchase, or it could be the price of the purchase plus tax. Your answers should have referred to the base (the referent) for each percent occurring in the problems.

For a problem in which there is a percent increase or a percent decrease, knowing that the base is the starting quantity helps to determine how to solve them.

EXAMPLE 6   News Item 1: *A company announced that it is increasing its work force by 15%, or 30 workers.* Can you tell how many workers will be in the work force after the increase?

Continue on the next page.

SOLUTION   The 15% refers to the starting work force, which is the base for the percent. If 15% of the starting work force is 30 workers, then 1% of the starting work force would be 2 workers, and 100% of the starting work force would be 200 workers. After the hiring, the company will have 230 workers.

EXAMPLE 7   News Item 2: *The town's budget is now $3 million. That is 25% more than it was last year.* What dollar amount was last year's budget?

SOLUTION   The *25% more* is 25% more than last year's budget, which is the base. The new budget, $3 million, is 125% of last year's budget. Dividing both by 5, $0.6 million is 25% of last year's budget, and so 100% of last year's budget is $2.4 million, that is, last year's budget was $2.4 million.

EXAMPLE 8   One school had a decline in enrollment of 12%, and now has 352 students. How many students did the school have before the decline?

SOLUTION   The *12%* is 12% of the original enrollment, so the 352 students would be 88% of the original enrollment. One percent of the original enrollment would then be 352 ÷ 88 = 4 students, so 100% of the original enrollment would have been 400 students.

Activity 6   What's the Base?

1. In a 1-hour TV slot, one week's program started with a 3-minute review of last week as a lead-in. Commercials took 30% of the total time for the slot. What percent of the total show-time was left for new developments?

2. A mayor notices these facts: The city budget last year was 25% more than the $15,000,000 budget of the previous year, and this year's budget is 12% more than last year's budget.
    a. What is this year's budget?
    b. Why is this year's budget not 37% of the budget two years ago?

3. In preparing the city budget for next year, the planners intended to keep costs the same as this year's, except for increases in the total budget of 5% for salaries, 3% for benefits, 3% for energy, and 4% for maintenance and supplies. The new budget calls for $32.2 million dollars. What is the dollar amount for this year's budget?

These examples should help to make clear how important it is to know what a given percent is a percent *of.* To repeat, in problems that involve a percent increase or decrease, the base for the percent is the original amount.

Percent can also be thought about as a way of expressing parts of wholes. Percent can be a way of introducing children to decimals and fractions, although the sequence in elementary schools is usually the reverse: fractions, then decimals, then percents. In a research study[ix] in Canada with fourth-graders, students were introduced to percents first because the researchers felt that students had a better intuitive knowledge of percents than of fractions. The students became quite adept at solving percent problems mentally (and later were able to transfer that knowledge to decimals and fractions). For example, two typical students in the study were asked for 65% of 160. Their two answers were:

"Okay, 50% of 160 is 80. Half of 80 is 40 so that is 25%. So if you add 80 and 40 you get 120. But that's too much because that's 75%. So you need to minus 10% (of 160) and that's 16. So, 120 take away 16 is 104."

"The answer is 104. First I did 50% which was 80. Then I did 10% of 160 which is 16. Then I did 5% which was 8. I added them (16 + 8) to get 24, and added that to 80 to get 104."

Activity 7   Your Turn

Use either student's procedure described above to find 45% of 180.

Discussion 8   Do You Talk the Talk?

We often misinterpret common phrases using percents. For example, 25% *larger than* $1200 is correctly interpreted to mean $1500, and 25% *as large as* 1200 is correctly interpreted to mean $300. However, 300% *larger than* 1200 and 300% *as large as* 1200 are often interpreted to mean the same thing, although 300% *larger than* $1200 is $4800 and 300% *as large as* $1200 is 3600.

Once again, drawings can help make the needed distinction.

$1200

25% larger than $1200

25% as large as $1200

You make drawings of 300% larger than $1200 and 300% as large as $1200.

TAKE-AWAY MESSAGE . . . Percent is simply a special ratio and, in fact, a very useful one that can be used in a variety of everyday situations. Percent is often used for comparisons because the denominator is always 100, so only the *numerators* have to be compared. Problems can occur when people are not paying attention to the base of the percent: Percent *of what?* With practice, one can often find percents mentally. In percent-change situations, the base for the percent is the starting value. ◆

Notes

Learning Exercises for Section 9.3

Reminder: Drawings are often very useful.

1. One coat was originally $120 but is on sale for $90; another coat was $150 but is on sale for $120. What is the percent of discount in each case? Which is the better buy? (This last question is very ambiguous. What are the different ways it could be answered?)

2. On one test you received 21 out of 28 points and on the second test you received 38 out of 50 points. On which test did you do better, in terms of percent correct? How would an instructor average these grades?

3. Consider again the problem:

   ♦ Jane and Scott were given identical boxes of crayons. Two weeks later, Jane had $\frac{4}{9}$

   of the box left and Scott had $\frac{3}{7}$ of his box left. Who has more crayons left? ♦

   Solve this problem again, but this time standardize each fraction by changing it to a percent, and then answer the question.

4. Jaqi owes Katie $60 and pays $35 towards her debt.
   a. What percent of the debt has she paid?
   b. What percent is still owed?
   c. What is her debt now?
   d. If Jaqi pays Katie another $10 towards her new debt, what percent of her new debt is paid off?
   e. What percent of her old debt is paid off?

5. If the box below represents 75% of an amount, show a box that represents 125% of the same amount. What percent of that box is the given one?

6. If the box below represents 150% of an amount, show a box that represents $33\frac{1}{3}$ % of the same amount.

7. The school budget just passed for this year is $4.2 million, which is 10% less than the budget last year. How much was the budget last year?

8. Find the percent change for each of the following cities.

   a. The population of City P increased to 125,000 from 100,000.

   b. City Q's population decreased to 100,000 from 125,000.

   c. City R's population grew to 87,450 from 72,625.

   d. City S's population went from 20,125 to 17,750.

9. City A's population is 15,000; City B's is 12,000.

   a. City A's population is what percent larger than City B's?

   b. City B's population is what percent less than City A's?

   c. City A's population is what percent of City B's?

   d. City B's population is what percent of City A's?

10. Street Scene went to 3 days instead of the usual 2 days. What percent change was that?

11. The decrease in price for notebooks was $1.60, a 40% decrease. What was the original price and what is the new price?

12. One day the Dow Jones was off by 2%. It closed at 10,567. About what was the Dow Jones the previous day?

13. Dan has a novel to read. He reads $\frac{1}{4}$ of the pages on each of Monday and Tuesday, 65 pages on Wednesday, another 20% of the pages on Thursday, and the final 61 pages on Friday. How many pages were in the novel?

14. "I'll double your pay," said the eager employer. What percent increase over your current pay would that be?

15. In changing jobs, Pat increased her hourly take-home pay by 24%, or by $3.48 an hour. What is her new hourly pay, and what was her old one?

16. "Accidents were down in our town, with about 75% as many this year as last year. This year there were about 840 accidents." If the speaker was correct, about how many accidents were there last year?

17. One department head is chatting with another. "Today, our two budgets total $1.2 million. But that's only 3% of the company's whole budget. And you spend $2 for every $1 I do." What is the company's whole budget, and what is each of the two department's budgets?

18. In one basketball game, Angie scored $\frac{1}{3}$ of her team's points, Beth scored 15% of them, and Carlita scored $\frac{1}{4}$ of the points. The rest of the team scored 16 points. The team made 60% of its points in the second half by hitting 55% of its shots.

   a. How many points did the team score in the first half?

   b. For what other quantities do you know values?

19. Dee has a part-time job and wants to buy a car. She figures that she spends about half her income on her apartment rent and utilities and about $12\frac{1}{2}$ % on food, for a total of $450 per month. She wants to allow $10 per week for entertainment and incidentals. About how many dollars are left for car payments and car expenses?

20. Review: Estimate each of the following:

   a. 35% of 121 people   **b.** 52% of 12 pounds

   c. 65% of 67 kilometers   **d.** 15% of $39.15

   e. 23% of 102 miles   **f.** 35% of 66 minutes

   g. 76% of $399   **h.** ___ % of $402 is $66

   i. 74 miles is ___ % of 298 miles   **j.** 24 pounds is 49% of what?

21. Review: Find each of the following mentally.

   a. 25% of 80 people   **b.** 40% of 160 pounds

   c. 65% of 80 kilometers   **d.** 15% of $64

   e. 12.5% of 80 miles   **f.** $33\frac{1}{3}$% of 66 minutes

   g. 75% of $700   **h.** ___ % of $350 is $70

   i. 75 miles is ___ % of 750 miles   **j.** 24 pounds is 200% of what?

22. What else can you tell from the following news clips?

   a. Four percent of the high school graduates will qualify. Nearly two-thirds of the students in the 4% group already qualify. . . About 3,600 students across the state will become newly eligible when the policy takes effect . . . A third of these newly eligible students are expected to come from urban schools; a quarter will be drawn from urban areas.

   b. The company will lay off 11% of its workforce, about 1500 workers worldwide.

9.4 | Issues for Learning: Developing Proportional Reasoning

Most adults use a cross-multiplication method to solve for a missing value in a proportion. However, research[x] shows that even when this strategy is explicitly taught to 11 and 12 year-olds, they often become confused and are unsuccessful with this method. If left on their own to solve such a problem, they commonly used the *unit method*, such as with this problem:

♦ John purchased 24 loaves of bread to sell in his grocery store last week, at a total price of $26. If he wishes to buy 30 loaves next week, how much will he have to spend? ♦

A typical answer was:

> If John is paid $26.00 for 24 loaves, this means that he must have been paying a little over $1.00 for every loaf. The exact amount is 26 divided by 24, or 1.083. If John wants to buy 30 loaves next week, that means he will have to pay 30 times 1.083, or $32.50.

Note that the student first found the price for *one* loaf of bread, then multiplied by 30. $30 \times 1.08\overline{3} = 32.5$. This can be represented as

$$\frac{26 \text{ dollars}}{24 \text{ loaves}} = \frac{1.08\overline{3} \text{ dollars}}{1 \text{ loaf}}, \text{ or } 1.08\overline{3} \text{ per loaf. So 30 loaves cost \$32.50.}$$

(Someone using a cross-multiplication approach to solving a proportion would write:

$\frac{26}{24} = \frac{x}{30}$ gives $24x = 26 \times 30 = 780$. So $x = 780 \div 24$, or 32.5, or \$32.50.)

Susan Lamon,[xi] who has been investigating proportional thinking for many years, has listed the following characteristics of proportional thinkers. Use them to evaluate whether or not you are a proportional thinker. Here are some of the characteristics she described.

1. Proportional reasoners can think both in terms of unit rates, such as 25 miles per gallon of gas, and in terms of multiple units, such as \$5.15 per 6 bottles of water.

2. Proportional reasoners are more efficient problem solvers. If water is \$5.15 for 6 bottles of water and they wanted to know the cost of 24 bottles of water they would think: 4 groups of 6 is $4 \times \$5.15$. Finding the unit price per bottle then multiplying by 24 is an earlier way of finding the price of 24 bottles, but it is less efficient and more prone to errors.

3. They can use partitioning to help them. For example, if 3 people share 5 pizzas, then each person gets $\frac{5}{3}$ pizzas. That is, each person gets $\frac{1}{3}$ of the total 5 pizzas, which is $(\frac{1}{3})5$ or $\frac{5}{3}$ pizzas.

4. They can think flexibly about quantities and find unit quantities. If cans of spinach are 3 for 99¢, then 1 can is 33¢.

5. They are not afraid of fractions and decimals and can think flexibly with these numbers.

6. They can mentally compute with fractions, decimals, and percents. For example, they know that they can find $\frac{3}{5}$ of a quantity if they know $\frac{1}{5}$ of a quantity, and 70% if they know 10%.

7. They can identify everyday situations where proportions are not useful. For example, if told that Tommy ran a mile in 5 minutes, and asked how long it would take Tommy to run 10 miles, they would not simply multiply by 5, because Tommy cannot run that fast over several miles.

8. They can solve both missing-value problems and comparison problems by reasoning about them, not just rotely using the cross-multiplication strategy.

9.5 | Check Yourself

This chapter focused on learning to understand and use ratios, proportions, and percents to solve problems. You should be able to work problems like those assigned and to meet the following objectives.

1. Identify problems where a solution can be found by comparing ratios, and explain why.

2. Compare and contrast an additive comparison with a multiplicative comparison.

3. Give examples of problems where it is convenient to use ratios as measures, and explain why.

4. Compare ratios.

5. Solve proportion problems in ways other than cross-multiplying, and explain why other ways can be more meaningful than using the cross-multiplication strategy.

6. Illustrate how tables can be used to solve proportion problems. Describe why using tables might be a better way to begin teaching proportions.

7. Solve a variety of proportion problems.

8. Solve percent problems of all types.

9. Estimate with percents.

10. Perform a quantitative analysis of a variety of types of problems in order to solve them in a meaningful way.

11. Understand all of the definitions given in this chapter.

REFERENCES FOR CHAPTER 9

[i,ii] Simon, M. A., & Blume, G. W. (1994). Mathematical modeling as a component of understanding ratio-as-measure: A study of prospective elementary teachers. *Journal of Mathematical Behavior, 13*(2), 183–197.

[iii] www.mnsu.edn/emuseum/information/population/ on June 15, 2005.

[iv] Noelting, G. (1980). The development of proportional reasoning and the ratio concept: Differentiation of stages (Part I). *Educational Studies in Mathematics, 11*(2), 217–253. (Problems are adapted from Noelting's well-known experiments with these types of ratios and proportions.)

[v] Smith, J. P. III. (2002). The development of students' knowledge of fractions and ratios. In B. Litwiller & G. Bright (Eds.), *Making sense of fractions, ratios, and proportions*, 2002 Yearbook (pp. 3–17). Reston, VA: National Council of Teachers of Mathematics. (See, in particular, page 16.)

[vi,viii,xi] Lamon, S. J. (1999). *Teaching fractions and ratios for understanding*. Mahwah, NJ: Erlbaum. In particular, see pp. 232 and 233.

[vii] Streefland, L. (1991). *Fractions in realistic mathematics education*. Boston: Kluwer Academic.

[ix] Moss, J., & Case, R. (1999). Developing children's reasoning of the rational numbers: A new model and an experimental curriculum. *Journal for Research in Mathematics Education, 30*, 122–147.

[x] Case, R. (1985). *Intellectual development: Birth to adulthood*. Orlando, FL: Academic Press. See in particular p. 398.

Chapter 10

Expanding Our Number System

Thus far we have dealt only with positive numbers, and, of course, zero. Yet we use negative numbers to describe such different phenomena as cold temperatures and debt. Negative numbers have been used for many centuries. Even though negative numbers did not come into worldwide acceptance until much later, the Chinese, in about 200 B.C., used red rods to represent positive numbers and black rods to represent negative numbers. This method is just the opposite of how we sometimes represent numbers today: we use black ink to indicate credits and red ink to indicate debits. What do you suppose "running in the red" means?

In this chapter we extend our number system to include negative numbers and how to calculate with them. We review the properties of operations on numbers and once again discuss rational numbers and real numbers. Another section introduces some curious, but mathematically useful, number systems, and the final section gives a bit more history.

10.1 | Ways of Thinking About Signed Numbers

Positive and negative numbers are sometimes called *signed* numbers because of the + sign (for a positive number) or the − sign (for a negative number) that may introduce the symbol, as in +2 or $^+2$ or −2 or $^-2$. Except for emphasis, the + sign is often omitted, suggesting that the numbers we have used thus far can be regarded as special signed numbers. It is not uncommon to place the negative sign higher so that it is not confused with subtraction, until addition and subtraction of signed numbers are well understood: −3 may be written $^-3$. Later, when there is no fear of confusion, we may use the − symbol for negative numbers and for subtraction.

One reason that signed numbers are important is that they have many applications, and so there are many ways of thinking about them. Here are some.

Discussion 1   Other Ways of Representing Signed Numbers

How could each of the following be used to think about signed numbers? Describe what positive and negative numbers, and zero, would mean.

Continue on the next page.

1. Financial matters like bank balances, profit/loss, paycheck/bill, income/debt, credit cards, etc.

2. Temperature changes

3. Sea levels

4. Sports settings like football and golf

5. Diets

6. Atomic charges (although atomic charges may not be part of the K–6 curriculum)

7. Games in which you can "go in the hole"

We will focus now on two other ways to represent signed numbers: chips of two colors and the number line. Chips of two colors are an adaptation of the ancient Chinese method of 200 B.C. We will use white for positive and black for negative. For example, three white chips can represent $^+3$ (or 3), and 4 black chips can represent $^-4$. Of course, any two colors can be used, so long as it is clear which represents positive numbers and which negative numbers.

Just as a gain of $2 can be cancelled by a loss of $2, giving a zero change in finances, a chip representation for 0 can occur in many forms.

Each of these drawings is a way of showing 0:

Notice that there is a degree of abstraction here, requiring an understanding of the representation. Two white and two black chips represent zero, even though there are four chips involved. Two white chips have, in a sense, a canceling effect on two black chips (or two black chips have the opposite effect of two white chips). It is natural to think of addition as describing putting two white chips with two black ones, and the canceling effect gives the important numerical result, $^+2 + {}^-2 = 0$. With the canceling idea in mind, chip drawings like each of the following can be interpreted as having the value $^-3$. Do you see why?

These more complicated ways of showing an integer can be handy in subtraction, as we will see.

THINK ABOUT . . .

What are several ways of showing ⁺2 with the chips, besides with two white chips? Why are these ways more abstract than showing just two white chips?

The use of the number line to illustrate signed numbers is likely familiar to you and builds on work with whole numbers and fractions. If we use the usual number line as a model for the numbers, then we can answer the question, "What's to the left of 0?" by describing the numbers to the left of zero as negative numbers. For the time being and with the usual elementary school curriculum in mind, we will first restrict ourselves to those numbers that are the opposites of the whole numbers, ⁻1 is the opposite of 1, 1 is the opposite of ⁻1, ⁻2 is the opposite of 2, and so on.

When we combine the set of whole numbers with their opposites, including zero, we obtain a set of numbers we call **integers**. That is, $I = \{\ldots {}^{-}3, {}^{-}2, {}^{-}1, 0, 1, 2, 3, \ldots\}$. These numbers can be represented on the number line as follows:

We say that 6 and ⁻6 are **opposites** or **additive inverses** of one another because their sum is 0. Generally speaking, the opposite of a is also denoted by ^{-}a, whether a is positive or negative, and $a + {}^{-}a = 0$.

THINK ABOUT . . .

What is the opposite of 2? What is the opposite of ⁻2? What is the opposite of the opposite of 2? What is the opposite of the opposite of ⁻2? What is the opposite of 0? Is ^{-}a always a negative number? What are the different meanings of the – sign in $5 - {}^{-}({}^{-}2)$?

Although ⁻6 can be read as either "negative six" or "the additive inverse of six" or "the opposite of six," ^{-}a should be read as "the additive inverse of a" or "the opposite of a," but not as "negative a," because ^{-}a can be positive.

Keep in mind that the labeling of the points for numbers on a number line comes about because of their distances from 0, a starting point. But ⁺2, say, could be thought of as any jump of length 2 units toward the right but starting anywhere (not necessarily at the 0 point), just as ⁻3 could be thought of as any jump of length 3 units, but toward the left and starting anywhere. Thinking of a signed number as a description of a jump size rather than only as a point on the number line has value in working with addition and subtraction of signed numbers.

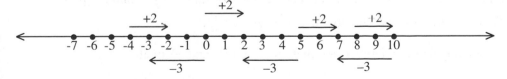

Notes

As with colored chips, 0 can be represented with a number line in a variety of ways, such as the following:

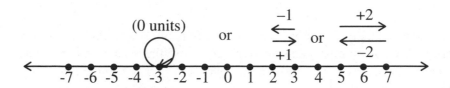

Consistent with the points for whole numbers and fractions, on the usual number line the point for a smaller number is to the left of the point for a larger number. Hence, for example, ⁻100 is less than ⁻5, or ⁻100 < ⁻5. Thinking of debts and "worse off" for < helps to make such inequalities believable.

We have focused primarily on the integers because they are the first of the signed numbers to appear in the usual elementary school curriculum. But the familiar fractions and decimal numbers can also have opposites (also called additive inverses). For example, $^-(\frac{3}{4})$ is a negative number between ⁻1 and 0 on the number line. Its additive inverse is $\frac{3}{4}$. (We have used parentheses here simply to show that the negative sign is for the entire fraction, not just the numerator.)

Signed numbers include all positive and negative integers, positive and negative fractions, and positive and negative repeating or terminating decimal numbers, that is, all *rational numbers*, extending the term introduced in Chapter 6 for nonnegative rational numbers. Similarly, as with $^-\sqrt{3}$, there are negative *irrational numbers* (numbers that have nonterminating and nonrepeating decimals). Because the rational numbers and irrational numbers together are called the *real numbers*, these show that every real number has an additive inverse. Just as every integer can be matched to a point on the number line, so can *every* real number be matched to a point on the number line. And every point on a number line corresponds to some real number. With two or more number lines arranged to give the familiar *x-y* coordinate system that you studied in algebra, this match of numbers and geometry allows many geometric shapes to be studied with algebra and many algebraic topics to be represented geometrically.

Discussion 2   Between Any Two Rational Numbers

1. Think of any two rational numbers, such as $\frac{7}{12}$ and $\frac{13}{15}$. Find another rational number between the two numbers.

2. Find another rational number between $\frac{7}{12}$ and the number you found in part a. This will give a second number between $\frac{7}{12}$ and $\frac{13}{15}$.

3. How many rational numbers are there between $\frac{7}{12}$ and $\frac{13}{15}$ in all?

Your answer to Question 3 in Discussion 2 is perhaps a surprising consequence of the line of reasoning for Question 1. The mathematical term for this phenomenon is called the *density* property of rational numbers. The rational numbers are said to be *dense*.

> A set of numbers is **dense** if, for every choice of two different numbers from the set, there is always another number from the set that is between them (the **density property**).

THINK ABOUT . . .
How does the density property assure that there are infinitely many rational numbers, not just one, between every two different rational numbers?

Hence, with the number line in mind, one might think that the points for the rational numbers completely fill up the line. But, as you know, the irrational numbers also have points on the number line. Even though the set of rational numbers is dense, there are still "empty" spaces for the irrational numbers.

TAKE-AWAY MESSAGE . . . There are many ways of thinking about integers and other signed numbers. Two of these involve chips of two colors and the number line, which can illustrate the opposing effects of a number and its additive inverse or opposite. The key feature of the additive inverse of a number a is that $a + {}^-a = 0$. All the rational and irrational numbers make up the real numbers, with every real number corresponding to a point on a number line, and vice versa. The rational numbers are dense, meaning that there is always another rational number between two given rational numbers; indeed, there are infinitely many. ◆

Learning Exercises for Section 10.1

1. Make drawings of chips to show the following. Use white for positive and black for negative, for consistency.

    a. 5   **b.** $^-6$

2. Make drawings of chips to show zero in at least four ways different from those in the text. Again, use white for positive and black for negative, for consistency.

3. Give the single integer that each of the following chip drawings can represent. Be ready to explain your thinking. (White—positive, black—negative)

    a.   **b.**   **c.**

    d.   **e.**   **f.**

4. Reorder each group of numbers from smallest to largest.

   a. $+50$, -3, -22, $\frac{3}{4}$, -75.2, $-\left(\frac{2}{3}\right)$, -1, 1

   b. 3.1, -5, $2\frac{9}{10}$, -0.9, $\frac{4}{9}$, 0.5, $\frac{13}{10}$, $-\frac{4}{9}$, -0.1, -1.2

5. a. What is $-(-8)$? Explain why you think your answer is correct.

   b. Zero is regarded as neither positive nor negative, but one occasionally runs into -0 in calculations. What is -0? Explain.

   c. Is $-a$ always negative? Explain.

6. In each part, what number is being described?

   a. the additive inverse of the additive inverse of the additive inverse of 9

   b. the additive inverse of the additive inverse of negative 9

   c. the additive inverse of the additive inverse of 6

   d. $-(-(-(-(-10.3))))$

7. A jump on a number line may be followed by another jump that starts where the first jump ends. What single integer describes the net result in each of the following?

   a.

   b.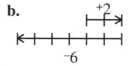

   c.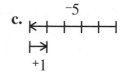

   d.

   e.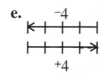

   f.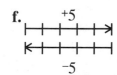

8. Give, if possible, an example of each type of number. If it is not possible, explain why.

   a. a negative real number that is not rational

   b. a negative real number that is not irrational

   c. a negative integer that is not real

   d. a negative real number that is not an integer

9. Interpret $+10$ and -4 in these settings.

   a. a financial situation of some sort

   b. a sport

   c. a temperature change

   d. a temperature

10. For $3 + 5 = n$, a child might draw a number line like the following. What might the child be thinking?

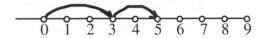

11. Sometimes the negative sign is not raised, so instead of writing $^-3$ we write -3. Why do you think this is done? What are the pros and cons of writing negative numbers this way?

12. The set of real numbers is dense. What does that mean?

13. In each part, tell whether the set of numbers is dense. Justify your answers.

   a. the set of integers

   b. the set of positive rational numbers

   c. the set of negative rational numbers

14. Give eight fractions between each pair.

   a. $\frac{7}{4}$ and $\frac{9}{5}$ **b.** $^-\left(\frac{2}{3}\right)$ and $^-\left(\frac{31}{50}\right)$

10.2 | Adding and Subtracting Signed Numbers

Just as there are several ways in which to think about signed numbers, there are several ways to think about adding and subtracting them. Here we will focus first on adding and subtracting integers via colored chips, the number line, and a money argument. Then we summarize the rules symbolically, using absolute-value language. The rules that arise with integers are applicable to all signed numbers.

We will use white chips to indicate positive integers, and black ones to indicate negative integers. We can think of the chips as positive and negative "charges" that "cancel out" one another, if there is the same number of whites as blacks. If we begin with three white chips and add three black chips, the chips cancel each other out, and we have zero: $3 + (^-3) = 0$, incorporating the important additive inverse property into this model. Again, notice that although there are 6 chips visible, the meaning attached to them allows one to say "0" for this arrangement, much like having a check for \$3 and a bill for \$3 gives, in effect, \$0.

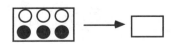

Using an optional box to surround the work is occasionally useful, especially when the sum is zero.

With the chips, adding integers with the same sign is straightforward and involves showing each addend with chips and then counting the total.

$$^{+}3 + {}^{+}2 = {}^{+}5 \qquad\qquad {}^{-}4 + {}^{-}3 = {}^{-}7$$

If the signs of the addends differ, we can use the additive inverse feature for integers. For example, for $3 + {}^{-}5 = n$, we begin with three white chips and add five black chips, but three of the black chips cancel out the three white chips, and we are left with two black chips: $3 + {}^{-}5 = {}^{-}2$

For $^{-}2 + 6 = n$, two black chips cancel two of the six white chips, leaving four white chips, so $^{-}2 + 6 = 4$.

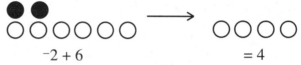

$$^{-}2 + 6 \qquad\qquad = 4$$

Notice that in effect, when the signs differ, just finding the difference in the numbers of chips for the addends and then giving that difference the sign of the larger number of chips, yields the sum. You may have learned something like that as a rule for adding numbers with different signs.

Let us turn to subtraction of integers with the chips.

Discussion 3   Subtracting with the Chip Model

How can you use the take-away interpretation for subtraction to show each of the following with chips?

1. $4 - 3$ **2.** $^{-}5 - (^{-}2)$ **3.** $4 - 7$

As you probably noticed, some subtractions are very easy and can be shown in ways similar to those used for whole numbers.

For example, for $4 - 3 = 1$, we could show the following

Or, for $^{-}5 - {}^{-}2 = {}^{-}3$,

In Discussion 3, the last problem raises the question, "What if there are not enough chips to remove, as with $4 - 7 = n$?" Two ways may have arisen, each adding equal numbers of both negative and positive chips—in effect, adding 0—and then subtracting.

OOOO ⟶ OOOO OOOOOOO ⟶ OOOO ⟶ ●●●
●●●●●●●   ●●●●●●●

4   4, so 7 whites can be taken away   after 7 whites removed $4 - 7 = {}^-3$

You may also have thought, "Why not just put in 3 more whites and 3 blacks; then you could take away 7 whites?" The answer is, "You could." The way illustrated, however, suggests at the third step, $4 - 7 = 4 + {}^-7$, and you may recognize in that equation the basic rule for subtracting signed numbers: Change the sign of the subtrahend (the number being subtracted), and add.

It may be instructive to see the symbolic form for the steps in the work for $2 - ({}^-3) = n$.

$$2 - ({}^-3) = [2 + 0] - ({}^-3) = [2 + 3 + ({}^-3)] - ({}^-3) = [5 + ({}^-3)] - ({}^-3) = 5.$$

Replace 0 with
$3 + ({}^-3)$.

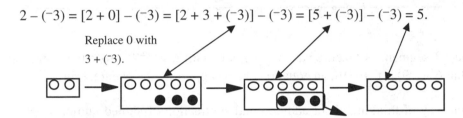

Notice that $2 - ({}^-3)$ gives the same result as $2 + 3$, supporting the usual rule for subtraction. You can even see the $2 + 3$ in the last drawing.

Let us turn to the number line. Addition and subtraction of signed numbers on a number line may already be familiar to you.

Activity 1   Hopping on the Number Line

Using the number line, find the following, in a way that makes sense.

1. $6 + 5$ 2. $3 + 4$

3. ${}^-6 + 5$ 4. $6 + {}^-9$

5. $6 + {}^-5$ 6. $6 - 5$ 7. $6 + {}^-5$

Then check your answers by reading the next paragraphs.

If you have forgotten how to use the number line for these sums, here is some help. (Draw a number line, and read the instructions slowly.) To find $3 + 4$, start at 0, move 3 units to the right, then move 4 more units to the right, to 7. (Starting at 0 allows one to read the answer from the number-line markings.) Think of a positive addend as moving to the right and a negative addend as moving to the left.

To subtract 6 – 5 using the number line, begin at 0, move to the right 6 units, and then "take away" 5 units to the left, to 1. Continuing on the number line you drew (or a copy), if you want to find 6 + (⁻5), begin at 0 and move 6 units to the right, then move 5 units to the left. Note that 6 + (⁻5) takes us to the same place on the number line as does 6 – 5, that is, 6 – 5 = 6 + (⁻5). Similarly, if you want to find 6 + (⁻9), you go from 0 to 6 and move 9 units to the left, ending at ⁻3. The 6 – 5 = 6 + (⁻5) equation suggests that 6 + (⁻9) should be 6 – 9. And from the number line, 6 – 9 = ⁻3. Again, notice that the equations 6 – 5 = 6 + ⁻5 and 6 – 9 = 6 + ⁻9 suggest the eventual rule for subtraction, even though that may seem irrelevant at this point.

How would one show 6 – (⁻9) on the number line? Rather than introduce a new interpretation of subtraction (e.g., *Do the opposite*) as is often done, we can introduce 0 in a clever way, as was done with the chips, and continue with *take-away* as the meaning for subtraction. First, show 6 as 6 + 0, in the form 6 + 9 + ⁻9, so that the ⁻9 can be "taken away."

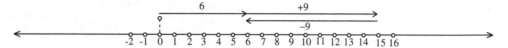

Once the ⁻9 segment is taken away, we are left with 6 + (⁺9). So our illustration means that 6 – (⁻9) = 6 + (⁺9), an equation again supporting the eventual rule.

As a final way of thinking about addition and subtraction of signed numbers, let us consider money, first looking at addition and the symbolic rules governing addition, and then similarly at subtraction. The symbolic rules use the idea of *absolute value,* so we will first review that topic.

There are times when we are interested in a number's direction—that is, whether its place on the number line is to the left or to the right of 0. At other times we are interested only in a number's distance away from 0 on the number line, and do not care in which direction we must go to arrive at the number.

> A number's distance from 0 on the number line is called the **absolute value**
> of the number, and we consider this value to be positive (or zero in the case of
> zero). We denote the absolute value of a number b as $|b|$.

EXAMPLE 1

We can say that $|6|$ is 6, and similarly, $|{-6}|$ is 6. Both 6 and ⁻6 are 6 units away from zero. Opposite numbers always have the same absolute value.

In terms of chips, absolute value can be interpreted as just how many uncanceled chips there are. For example, $|{-3}| = 3$ because there are 3 black chips (or a surplus of 3 black chips), and $|{+9}| = 9$ because there are 9 white chips (or a surplus of 9 white chips).

$|\text{-}3| = 3$ $|\text{-}3| = 3$

With absolute value in mind, we now return to the addition of signed numbers.

Activity 2   Leading to the Rules for Addition

Use examples from a money context to consider these situations.

1. Adding two signed numbers that have the same sign (for example, $^+53 + {}^+79.95$, and $^-19 + {}^-56$).

2. Adding two signed numbers with different signs (for example, $253 + {}^-79$, and $57 + {}^-84$).

Your thinking in Activity 2 could be formalized using absolute value, as is often done in algebra classes.

Addition of signed numbers when both numbers have the same sign: If both numbers are positive, then $a + b = |a + b|$. If both numbers are negative, then $a + b = {}^-(|a| + |b|)$.

Addition of signed numbers when one is positive and the other is negative:

Consider a to be positive and b to be negative.

If $|a| > |b|$ then $a + b = |a| - |b|$.

If $|a| < |b|$ then $a + b = {}^-(|b| - |a|)$.

THINK ABOUT . . .

1. How is your thinking in Activity 2 reflected in the formal addition rules using absolute value?

2. Is $|a - b| = |b - a|$ always? Is $|a| + |b| = |a + b|$ always? Is $|a - b| = |a| - |b|$ always?

Two special cases for addition, with the relevant vocabulary, should be highlighted.

Special cases:

If $a = 0$, *then* $a + b = b$ and $b + a = b$. We call 0 the **additive identity**.

If $a = {}^-b$ then $a + b = {}^-b + b = 0$ (the additive identity). We call each of b and ${}^-b$ the **additive inverse** of the other because their sum is 0.

Notice that work with chips or the number line or some other representation of signed numbers can suggest the formal statements. Having a mental image of chips or a money situation, for example, can allow you to understand where the rules come from.

Fortunately, we can use the rules for addition when we subtract, by changing from subtraction to addition according to the rule below. We noted this relationship in several of the previous calculations with the chips and the number line.

Subtraction of signed numbers:

If c and d are signed numbers, then $c - d = c + ({}^-d)$.

EXAMPLE 2

a. ${}^-5 - 2 = {}^-5 + {}^-2 = {}^-7$ **b.** $11 - {}^-5 = 11 + {}^+5 = 16$

Activity 3   Can You Add and Subtract?

Calculate, referring to the rules for addition and subtraction given on pages 209 and 210. (For each subtraction problem, first rewrite it as an addition problem.)

1. ${}^-141 + 141$ 2. ${}^-1 + {}^-1$ 3. ${}^-18.2 + {}^-4.83$

4. ${}^-75 + 413$ 5. $413 + {}^-75$ 6. ${}^-4.37 + 6.1$

7. ${}^-483 + 217$ 8. $483 + 217$ 9. ${}^-1 - 1$

10. ${}^-1 - {}^-1$ 11. ${}^-12 - {}^-41$ 12. ${}^-12 - 41$

13. $41 - {}^-12$ 14. ${}^-38 - 654$ 15. ${}^-431 - 22$ 16. $6.8 - 212$

Although we have used the take-away view of subtraction with the chips and the number line to motivate the rule for subtraction of signed numbers, the missing-addend view of subtraction could also be used. Recall that the missing-addend approach for $c - d$ would ask: What can be added to d to get c? From $c - d = x$, a symbolic line of reasoning could also result in the $c - d = c + {}^-d$ rule, as follows.

$c - d = x$ Then, thinking of missing addend for $c - d$,

$x + d = c$

$x + d + {}^-d = c + {}^-d$ (by adding ${}^-d$ to both sides)

$x + 0 = c + {}^-d$

$x = c + {}^-d$

So $c - d = x = c + {}^-d$

Activity 4   Does the Missing-Addend View Work with Chips and the Number Line?

Can the colored chips and the number line also be used with the missing-addend view of subtraction? Try them with the following.

1. ${}^-4 - {}^-2$ (Think: What can be added to ${}^-2$ to get ${}^-4$?)

2. $5 - {}^-1$

3. ${}^-6 - 2$

We have used some properties of addition without comment. The properties reviewed earlier for whole numbers and rational numbers do continue to be true when negative and irrational numbers are involved, that is, when any real numbers come up. The commutative property of addition allows us to commute the order of the addends, for example, ${}^-13 + 4 = 4 + {}^-13$. The associative property of addition allows us to change the order in which we add. For example, $(3 + {}^-7) + {}^-5 = 3 + ({}^-7 + {}^-5)$. In checking that these two sums are equal, we have ${}^-4 + {}^-5 = {}^-9$ and $3 + {}^-12 = {}^-9$ for both sides of the equation.

> *THINK ABOUT . . .*
>
> Does the associative property of addition allow you to ignore the parentheses when only addition is involved? Why or why not?

Rational numbers include all whole numbers, fractions, and repeating decimal numbers. Negative integers and negative fractions (or their decimal forms) are also rational numbers. In fact, when we add *any* two rational numbers, the sum is also a rational number. This is an example of what is called the **closure** property, a property that is not usually emphasized in grades K–6 but is useful in more advanced work.

A set of numbers is **closed** under an operation if, when operating on every two numbers in the system, the result is also in the set of numbers.

EXAMPLE 3

When we add any two positive rational numbers, such as $9\frac{3}{4}$ and 5, the sum, $14\frac{3}{4}$, is also a rational number. This property extends to include negative and positive numbers. $^{-}9\frac{3}{4} + 5 = ^{-}4\frac{3}{4}$, a rational number. In both cases, the sum of two rational numbers was another rational number, so we could say that this example illustrates that *the set of rational numbers is closed under addition.*

Even though the full set of real numbers is not commonly encountered in grades K–6, it is also true that the set of real numbers is closed under addition. For example, $\sqrt{2} + 5\sqrt{3}$ and $\sqrt{7} + ^{-}6$ are real numbers.

Finally, addition of signed numbers has two additional properties, noted earlier. The first is that 0 is the *additive identity*. The second is that every real number has an *additive inverse*.

EXAMPLE 4

a. $3 + 0 = 3$ and $^{-}3 + 0 = ^{-}3$, so 0 is the additive identity.

b. $3 + ^{-}3 = 0$, so 3 and $^{-}3$ are additive inverses of one another.

c. What is the additive inverse of $2\frac{1}{8}$? It is $^{-}2\frac{1}{8}$ because $2\frac{1}{8} + ^{-}2\frac{1}{8} = 0$. $2\frac{1}{8}$ is also the additive inverse of $^{-}2\frac{1}{8}$.

d. Similarly, $\sqrt{7}$ and $^{-}\sqrt{7}$ are additive inverses of each other because their sum equals 0.

> *THINK ABOUT . . .*
>
> Suppose you are restricted to the set of integers. Do all five of the properties for addition—closure, commutativity, associativity, additive identity, and existence of additive inverses—hold true for all integers?

The properties often (but not always) occur in mathematical situations, perhaps situations not even involving numbers. Mathematicians look for situations in which the properties do occur because the properties may lead to still other results that may be useful in the situations.

> TAKE-AWAY MESSAGE...Colored chips and the number line are just two methods of illustrating the addition of signed numbers. Their use can motivate the usual rules for adding and subtracting signed numbers. The rules apply to all the real numbers, irrational as well as rational. There are five properties for addition of rational numbers, all of which also are true for all real numbers:
>
> 1. The set of rational numbers is closed under addition. That is, for every two rational numbers a and b, $a + b$ is also a rational number.
>
> 2. Addition is commutative. That is, for every two rational numbers a and b, $a + b = b + a$.

3. Addition is associative. That is, for every three rational numbers a, b, and c, $(a + b) + c = a + (b + c)$.

4. Existence of an additive identity. It is 0. That is, for every rational number a, $a + 0 = 0 + a = a$.

5. Every rational number has an additive inverse that is rational. That is, for any rational number a, there is another rational number ^-a such that $a + {}^-a = 0$. ◆

Learning Exercises for Section 10.2

1. Using drawings of two colors of chips, find the following.
   a. $^-4 + {}^-2$ **b.** $^-4 + {}^+2$ **c.** $^-4 - {}^-2$ **d.** $^-4 - {}^+2$
   e. $(4 + {}^-3) + {}^-1$ **f.** $4 + {}^-6$ **g.** $4 - {}^-3$ **h.** $4 - {}^-6$

2. Make number-line drawings to find the following.
   a. $^+5 + {}^-7$ **b.** $^-3 + {}^-4$ **c.** $^-2 + {}^+5$ **d.** $^+2 + {}^-6$
   e. $^+6 - {}^+2$ **f.** $^+6 - {}^-2$ **g.** $^-5 - {}^-2$ **h.** $^-5 - {}^+2$

3. Add and subtract these numbers using drawings of chips, the number line, or a money situation.
   a. $^-5 + {}^-5$ **b.** $^-(^-5) + {}^-5$ **c.** $^-5 + {}^-(^-5)$
   d. $^-5 - {}^-5$ **e.** $^-5 - {}^-(^-5)$ **f.** $5 - {}^-5$

4. Calculate the following.

   a. $\frac{14}{15} + {}^-\left(\frac{3}{5}\right)$ **b.** $^-\left(\frac{4}{9}\right) - 4$

   c. $\frac{7}{13} + \left(\frac{^-7}{13}\right)$ **d.** $^-\frac{5}{9} - \left(^-\left(\frac{2}{3}\right)\right)$

   e. $2.34 - 5.612$ **f.** $^-3.4 + {}^-7$
   g. $^-5.567 - 2.33$ **h.** $3.5 - (^-8)$

5. **a.** Is the set of even integers closed under addition? Why or why not? (The even integers are ..., $^-4$, $^-2$, 0, 2, 4, ...)
   b. Is the set of multiples of 3 closed under addition? Why or why not?
   c. Is the set of odd numbers closed under addition? Why or why not? (The odd integers are ... $^-3$, $^-1$, 1, 3, 5, ...)
   d. Is the set of whole numbers closed under subtraction? Why or why not?
   e. Is the set of all integers closed under addition? Why or why not?
   f. Is the set of all integers closed under subtraction? Why or why not?
   g. Is the set of all positive rational numbers closed under subtraction? Why or why not?

6. For each of the following, say whether or not the statement is true. If it is true, state the property that makes it true.

   a. $(3 + {}^-4) + 6 = ({}^-4 + 3) + 6$ b. $(3 + {}^-4) + 6 = 3 + ({}^-4 + 6)$

   c. $2 + 0 = 2$ d. $4 + {}^-4 = 0$

   e. $17 + (4 + {}^-4) = 17 + 0$ f. $17 + (4 + {}^-4) = 21 + {}^-4$

   g. $\frac{306}{18} + {}^-4$ is a rational number. In fact, it is an integer.

   h. $(3 + {}^-4) + 6 = 6 + (3 + {}^-4)$ i. $289\frac{1}{2} + 0 = 289\frac{1}{2}$

   j. $17.638 + {}^-17.638 = 0$

7. Provide the additive inverse for each of the following:

   a. 13 b. $^-4\frac{13}{10}$ c. $-\frac{4}{9}$ d. $\sqrt{11}$

8. In Learning Exercise 5 in Section 3.2 we considered families of addition and subtraction facts such as the following:

$3 + 2 = 5$	$5 - 2 = 3$
$2 + 3 = 5$	$5 - 3 = 2$

   Complete these fact families for integers:

   a.
${}^-3 + 5 = 2$	
$5 + {}^-3 = 2$	

   b.
	${}^-2 - {}^-5 = 3$
${}^-5 + 3 = {}^-2$	${}^-2 - 3 = {}^-5$

   c.
${}^-32 + {}^-29 = {}^-61$	

9. a. $|{}^-3| = ?$ b. $-|{}^-3| = ?$ c. $|17\frac{4}{7}| = ?$ d. $|{}^-6| + |{}^-6| = ?$

   e. $|{}^-6| + |6| = ?$ f. $|{}^-6| - |6| = ?$ g. $|{}^-6| - |{}^-6| = ?$

10. Temperature change is often used as a setting for adding and subtracting integers. Design some problems that you could use to teach someone else how to add and subtract integers.

11. Is it possible to use the comparison view of subtraction with the chip model with signed numbers? With the number line? With money? (The comparison for $7 - 2$, for example, would tell how much greater 7 is than 2, or how much less 2 is than 7.)

12. For each story and with signed numbers, write an equation that describes the situation, and answer the question.

    a. An official from Company A said, "Here's how we did last year. The first quarter we earned $57,000, and the second quarter, $35,000. But during each of the third and fourth quarters, we lost $16,000." How did Company A fare, for the whole year? (Remember to use signed numbers in your equation.)

    b. Company B reports, "During the second quarter, we earned $92,000, so for the first two quarters, we have earned a total of $15,000." How did Company B do during the first quarter?

    c. Company B later reports, "We lost $125,000 in the fourth quarter, so now we have earned only $11,000 in all, for the last two quarters." How much did the company gain or lose during the third quarter?

    d. How did Company B (parts b and c) do in all, for the first and fourth quarters only?

13. Write a story problem involving financial matters for an individual (paycheck-bill, income-debt, credit cards, etc.) that could be described by each of the following. Give the answers to your questions.

    a. $105.89 + {}^{-}75 + 92.73 + 11.68 + {}^{-}99.15 = n$

    b. $87.58 + 100 - {}^{-}22.75 - 69 = n$

14. For each equation below, write a story problem involving football or golf or diets that could be described by the equation.

    a. $2 + {}^{-}5 + 14 + 2 + {}^{-}6 + 3 = n$ **b.** ${}^{-}6 + {}^{-}2 + 3 + {}^{-}1 + {}^{-}2 + 1 = n$

10.3 | Multiplying and Dividing Signed Numbers

Addition and subtraction of signed numbers usually first appear in grades 5–6, perhaps just with the integers. Multiplication and division of signed numbers are then treated in grades 6–7. You may have heard the rhyme: "Minus times minus is plus, the reason for this we need not discuss." But here we do discuss it. If you have your own doubts about why multiplying two negative numbers gives a positive number, you are in good company. Until the mid-1800s there was a great deal of resistance to that result even by many mathematicians (see Section 10.5 for some more history).

We will offer different arguments as to what the sign of a product involving negative numbers should be. The first argument will assume commutativity of multiplication and consider a pattern. The second will show that the desirable properties of multiplication necessarily lead to "negative times negative is positive." A final argument, using chips, is offered. The chips argument is given last because the usual elementary school curriculum does not include it.

Multiplications involving positive numbers or zero are already familiar. The product of two positive numbers is positive, and if zero is a factor, the product is zero. The other cases involve multiplying numbers (a) of opposite signs and (b) when both are negative. We will focus on integers, although the same results will apply to all real numbers.

Earlier we found that one way of thinking about multiplication is as repeated addition. Applying this view of multiplication to $4 \times {}^{-}2$ gives

$$4 \times {}^{-}2 = {}^{-}2 + {}^{-}2 + {}^{-}2 + {}^{-}2 = {}^{-}8,$$

suggesting that (positive) × (negative) = (negative).

But it is not so easy to think about what $^-2 \times 4$ could mean as repeated addition. *However, if multiplication of integers is to be commutative, then $^-2 \times 4$ must equal $4 \times ^-2$, which we have just shown is $^-8$.* In other words, $^-2 \times 4 = ^-8$, suggesting that (negative) × (positive) = (negative).

EXAMPLE 5

a. $3 \times ^-4 = ^-12$ **b.** $^-6 \times 14 = 14 \times ^-6 = ^-84$

The only case left is that of having two factors that are both negative. The pattern in the next activity is suggestive (and is common in the elementary school curriculum).

Activity 5   A Strange Rule?

Using the results for multiplying a negative number and a positive number, complete the patterns in these two columns. (Even if you know the answers already, look for the patterns as you go down a column.)

$$
\begin{array}{ll}
4 \times 2 = 8 & ^-4 \times 4 = ^-16 \\
3 \times 2 = 6 & ^-4 \times 3 = ^-12 \\
2 \times 2 = 4 & ^-4 \times 2 = ^-8 \\
1 \times 2 = 2 & ^-4 \times 1 = ? \\
0 \times 2 = 0 & ^-4 \times 0 = ? \\
^-1 \times 2 = ? & \mathbf{^-4 \times ^-1 = ?} \\
^-2 \times 2 = ? & \mathbf{^-4 \times ^-2 = ?} \\
^-3 \times 2 = ? & \mathbf{^-4 \times ^-3 = ?} \\
\text{etc.} & \text{etc.}
\end{array}
$$

Although the result may seem counterintuitive, the pattern suggests that the product of two negative numbers must equal a positive number. Here is a summary of all the results from this first line of reasoning. (The results actually apply to all real numbers.)

> **Multiplying two signed numbers**. If the signs of the two numbers are the same, the product will be positive. If the signs of the two numbers are different, the product will be negative.

EXAMPLE 6

a. $^-3 \times ^-4 = 12$ **b.** $^-0.2 \times ^-0.4 = 0.08$

Discussion 4   Convinced?

Did you find the pattern argument for the product of two negative numbers convincing? Do you think young students would find it convincing? (Mathematicians like patterns, but they do not trust them completely because sometimes the patterns can break down.)

The second line of reasoning for the product of two negatives rests solely on properties of multiplication that we would want to continue to be true for signed numbers, so we will look at those properties. We have already used commutativity of multiplication, but there are other important properties as well. In the following activity and discussion, notice the parallels to the corresponding properties of addition. Many will be stated in terms of rational numbers, but they are also true for real numbers.

Discussion 5   More Properties

1. Provide several examples to test whether multiplication of signed numbers is associative. That is, when three rational numbers are multiplied, does it matter which multiplication is done first: $a(bc) = (ab)c$, for every choice of rational numbers a, b, and c? For example, will $^-3 \cdot (^-2 \cdot {}^-4)$ give the same result as $(^-3 \cdot {}^-2) \cdot {}^-4$? (Recall that the multiplication symbol $\times$ is often replaced with $\cdot$. In fact, when one or both factors are represented with letters, there oftentimes is no symbol between the letters if multiplication is intended: $2 \times b = 2 \cdot b = 2b$, or $a \times b = a \cdot b = ab$.)

2. Is the set of rational numbers closed under multiplication? That is, when every choice of two rational numbers are multiplied, is the product always a rational number?

3. Is there an identity for multiplication of rational numbers? That is, for each rational number a, is there a rational number x for which $a \cdot x = x \cdot a = a$? If so, what is it?

4. Does every rational number have a multiplicative inverse? That is, if c is any rational number, then does there exist a rational number d such that $c \cdot d = d \cdot c = 1$ (where 1 is the identity for multiplication)?

5. For rational numbers, is multiplication distributive over addition? That is, if a, b, and c are any rational numbers, is it true that $a \cdot (b + c) = a \cdot b + a \cdot c$? Substitute numbers for a, b, and c and test whether or not this property appears to be true for all rational numbers. Commutativity of multiplication also gives $(x + y) \cdot z = x \cdot z + y \cdot z$ as a form of this distributivity property.

The **multiplicative identity** for the set of rational numbers is 1 because for every rational number a, $1 \cdot a = a$, and $a \cdot 1 = a$.

> If the product of two numbers is 1, each number is the **multiplicative inverse** of the other number. If a is not 0, its multiplicative inverse is often written $\frac{1}{a}$ or even a^{-1}. The multiplicative inverse of a (nonzero) fraction is sometimes called its **reciprocal**.

THINK ABOUT . . .

What is the reciprocal of $\frac{m}{n}$? How does your answer satisfy the description above? Is there a multiplicative identity for the set of integers? Do integers have multiplicative inverses? Why doesn't 0 have a multiplicative inverse?

A second way to show that defining the product of two negative numbers to be positive makes sense mathematically is illustrated in this example, which depends heavily on the distributive property.

Suppose the product of concern is $^-3 \cdot {}^-2$.

Start with $^-3 \cdot 0 = 0$. Substitute $^+2 + {}^-2$ for the first 0.

$^-3 \cdot ({}^+2 + {}^-2) = 0$ after the substitution.

$({}^-3 \cdot {}^+2) + ({}^-3 \cdot {}^-2) = 0$ using the distributive property.

$^-6 + ({}^-3 \cdot {}^-2) = 0$ using the known $^-3 \cdot {}^+2 = {}^-6$.

So $^-3 \cdot {}^-2$ must be equal to $^+6$ to make the equation true.

Basically, all this is saying is that *if* the product of two negative numbers were *not* defined to be a positive number, then at least some of the rules of numbers we so far know to be true would fail when negative numbers are included.

The rules for multiplication of integers automatically provide us ways of dividing signed numbers, both positive and negative. The missing-factor way of thinking about division is useful. Recall that for $^-16 \div 8$, say, this view of division says to think, "What times 8 gives $^-16$?" Because $^-2 \cdot 8 = {}^-16$, $^-16 \div 8 = {}^-2$. In general, **division** can be defined as follows:

> If a, b, and c are real numbers and b is not 0, then $c \div b = a$ if $a \cdot b = c$.

EXAMPLE 7

a. $12 \div 4 = 3$ because $3 \cdot 4 = 12$
b. $^-12 \div 4 = ^-3$ because $^-3 \cdot 4 = ^-12$
c. $12 \div ^-4 = ^-3$ because $^-3 \cdot ^-4 = 12$
d. $^-12 \div ^-4 = 3$ because $3 \cdot ^-4 = ^-12$

THINK ABOUT . . .

Why can't 0 be the divisor in the definition of division (". . . and b is not 0 . . .")?
How does the missing-factor view lead to (negative) $\div$ (negative) = (positive)?

> **Multiplication and division of signed numbers:** The product or quotient of two numbers with the same sign is positive. The product or quotient of two numbers with opposite signs is negative.

The equality link between $\frac{a}{b}$ and $a \div b$ extends to signed numbers. Hence, $\frac{^-17}{5}$, $\frac{17}{^-5}$, and $^-\left(\frac{17}{5}\right)$ are all equal, because $\frac{^-17}{5} = (^-17) \div 5 = ^-\left(\frac{17}{5}\right)$ and $\frac{17}{^-5} = 17 \div ^-5 = ^-\left(\frac{17}{5}\right)$. This equality between $\frac{a}{b}$ and $a \div b$ leads to a common way of defining the rational numbers in advanced work.

> A **rational number** is any number that can be expressed in the form
>
> $$\frac{\text{integer}}{\text{nonzero integer}}$$

You might wonder whether the chips of two colors can also be used to demonstrate multiplication of integers. Consider the repeated addition model of multiplication. We know that $^+2 \times ^+4 = 2 \times 4$ can be thought of as $4 + 4$. However, *repeated addition cannot serve as a model for multiplication when the first factor is negative.* Thinking about $^-2 \times 4$ as repeated addition does not make sense; how would one *add* 4 negative 2 times? Rather than appealing to commutativity of multiplication, the key is in recognizing that since repeated addition does not make sense for $^-2 \times 4$, then when the first factor is negative, we need a *new* interpretation. Since in $^+2 \times 4$ we can think of adding 4 two times, *it is not unnatural to think of $^-2 \times 4$ as subtracting 4, two times.* But how do we get started? As with repeated addition, the answer is to start with a "neutral" amount (0), but here cleverly chosen so that the subtractions are possible.

For $^-2 \times 4$, the work might proceed as follows:

Starting with 0.   Take away 2 fours; answer is $^-8$.

Notes

For $^-2 \times {}^-4$, we would take away two sets each with 4 black chips, so the answer is the 8 white chips left, or $^-2 \times {}^-4 = {}^+8$.

This process would lead us to the same rules for multiplying with signed numbers. Again, if division is considered in missing-factor terms, the rules for division of signed numbers would also continue to hold.

TAKE-AWAY MESSAGE . . . Multiplication and division of signed numbers were considered in this section. New are cases where one or both of two numbers are negative. In multiplying or dividing two positive numbers or two negative numbers, the answer is a positive number. If the two numbers have opposite signs, the answer is a negative number. These rules apply to all real numbers.

The following five properties involving multiplication are true for the rational numbers and also for all the real numbers.

1. The set of rational numbers is closed under multiplication. That is, for every two rational numbers a and b, $a \cdot b$ is also a rational number.

2. Multiplication is commutative. That is, for every two numbers a and b, $a \cdot b = b \cdot a$.

3. Multiplication is associative. That is, for every three numbers a and b and c, $(a \cdot b) \cdot c = a \cdot (b \cdot c)$.

4. Multiplication has an identity. It is 1. That is, for every number a, $a \cdot 1 = 1 \cdot a = a$.

5. Every nonzero number has a multiplicative inverse. That is, for each nonzero number a, there is another number b such that $a \cdot b = 1$. The multiplicative inverse of a is sometimes called the reciprocal of a and denoted by $\frac{1}{a}$ or a^{-1}.

Finally, there is a sixth property that relates addition and multiplication:

6. For any numbers a, b, and c, multiplication is distributive over addition. That is, for rational numbers a, b, and c, $a(b + c) = a \cdot b + a \cdot c$. [Also useful is $(x + y) \cdot z = x \cdot z + y \cdot z$.] ◆

Learning Exercises for Section 10.3

1. Use examples to test which property or properties of the five properties of addition, the five properties of multiplication, and the distributive property of multiplication over addition, do or do not hold for just the set of integers.

2. Use examples (including negative rational numbers) to illustrate that the eleven properties all hold for the set of rational numbers.

3. Does a fraction with a negative numerator and positive denominator have the same value as a similar fraction but this time with a positive numerator and

negative denominator? That is, is $\frac{-2}{5}$ equal to $\frac{2}{-5}$? Is either or both of these equal to $-\left(\frac{2}{5}\right)$? Explain in terms of a fraction representing a division.

4. Practice operations on signed numbers by completing the following computations.

   a. $^-12 \div 6$ b. $^-13 - {}^-21$ c. $^-7 \cdot (3 + {}^-5)$ d. $^-121 \div {}^-11$

   e. $\frac{14}{15} \times \left(\frac{-5}{7}\right)$ f. $\frac{-2}{5} \div 4$ g. $\frac{7}{13} \div \frac{-7}{13}$ h. $\frac{-7}{13} \times \frac{-13}{7}$

   i. $^-2 \times {}^-7 \times {}^-9$ j. $\dfrac{^-144}{16}$ k. $\dfrac{28}{^-1120}$ l. $(^-8 + {}^-2) \cdot {}^-5$ (two ways?)

   m. $(-1)^{100}$ n. $(-1)^{999}$

5. Is there an identity for multiplication of integers? If so, what is it?

6. a. Suppose you take any integer a. Can you always find another integer b such that $a \times b = 1$? (That is, does a have a multiplicative inverse in the set of integers?)

   b. Which two integers are their own multiplicative inverses?

7. Identify which of the eleven properties of addition and multiplication is exhibited in each of the following. Or, if a statement is not true, fix it so that it is, and tell which property you used.

   a. $^-7 \cdot (3 + {}^-5) = (3 + {}^-5) \cdot {}^-7$ b. $^-7 \cdot (3 + {}^-5) = {}^-7 \cdot (^-5 + 3)$

   c. $^-7 \cdot (3 + {}^-5) = {}^-7 \cdot 3 + {}^-7 \cdot {}^-5$ d. $^-7 \cdot [(3 + {}^-5) + 4] = {}^-7 \cdot [3 + (^-5 + 4)]$

   e. $^-7 \cdot [(3 + {}^-5) + 4] = {}^-7 \cdot (3 + {}^-5) + {}^-7 \cdot 4$ f. $^-7 \cdot [(3 + {}^-5) + 4] = [(3 + {}^-5) + 4] \cdot {}^-7$

   g. $\frac{-4}{5} \cdot \frac{5}{-4} \cdot {}^-7 = \frac{-4}{5} \cdot {}^-7 \cdot \frac{5}{-4}$ h. $\frac{-4}{5} \cdot \frac{5}{-4} \cdot {}^-7 = 1 \cdot {}^-7 = {}^-7$

   i. $(3 + 0) + 4 = 3 + 4$ j. $(3 + {}^-5) \cdot 6 = 3 \cdot 6 + {}^-5 \cdot 6$

8. Demonstrate, with drawings, how obtaining the following products could be demonstrated using two colors of chips.

   a. $3 \times {}^-5$ b. $^-3 \times 5$ c. $^-2 \times {}^-3$ d. $^-3 \times {}^-2$

9. Give the line of reasoning similar to the one given for $^-3 \times {}^-2 = {}^+6$ to show that $^-7 \times {}^-5$ must be $^+35$.

10. What is missing in each student's understanding?

    Ann: "I had $^-3 \times {}^-2 \times {}^-1 = {}^+6$, and you marked it wrong. But you said when you multiply negatives, you get a positive."

    Bobo: "You said two negatives make a positive, but when I did $^-2 + {}^-3 = {}^+5$, my Mom said it wasn't correct."

11. Using signed numbers, write an equation that describes each of these story problems.

♦ Little Bo-Peep loses 4 sheep every week from her very large flock, and they never come home! ♦

a. In 5 weeks, how will the number in her flock compare to the present number? (Remember to use signed numbers.)

b. Six weeks ago, how did the number in her flock compare to the present number?

♦ Godzilla has been losing 30 pounds a month by watching his diet and by exercising. ♦ (Remember to use signed numbers.)

c. If he continues at this rate, how will his weight in 6 months compare to his present weight?

d. Three months ago, how did his weight compare to his present weight?

10.4 | Some Other Number Systems

In the summaries of Sections 10.2 and 10.3, five properties were listed as being true for addition, five for multiplication, and one property that connected multiplication and addition. When all eleven of these properties hold for addition and multiplication on any set of numbers, mathematicians call this set with its two operations a **field**. (This perhaps surprising term was given by a mathematician who had a wide view of numbers.)

Discussion 6   What Makes a Mathematical Field?

1. Is the set of even integers (that is, . . . $^-6$, $^-4$, $^-2$, 0, 2, 4, 6, ...) with addition and multiplication defined as usual, a field? If not, which of the eleven properties fails?

2. Is the set of positive rational numbers a field? If not, which of the eleven properties fails?

In an earlier chapter we also talked about irrational numbers, that is, numbers that cannot be expressed as a fraction or as a repeating decimal. Numbers such as π and $\sqrt{2}$ are irrational numbers. You learned that the set of rational numbers combined with the set of irrational numbers is called the set of ***real numbers.***

Although we will not spend more time here on real numbers, it suffices to say that (1) the real numbers, with operations of addition and multiplication, form a field, and (2) every real number corresponds to a point on the number line, and every point on the number line corresponds to a real number.

Students will encounter real numbers primarily when they reach algebra, and it will be necessary for them to use the field properties to operate with real numbers in algebra and beyond.

Yet, some mathematically important number systems do not have infinitely many numbers. One such system is sometimes called *clock arithmetic*. Suppose you have a five-hour clock, that is, the numbers 0, 1, 2, 3, and 4 are evenly spaced around the clock, such as this:

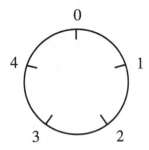

Sometimes 5 is used instead of 0, but you will soon see why 0 is used here.

When one adds in this arithmetic, it is like going around the clock the number of hours indicated by the addends, starting at 0. Thus, 2 + 4 begins at 0, goes two spaces to 2, and then goes clockwise four spaces, ending at 1. So 2 + 4 = 1, a result that looks quite strange but makes sense in this number system. Also, 4 + 2 begins at 0, moves to 4, then moves two spaces clockwise, landing on 1, so 4 + 2 = 1. Likewise 4 + 0 would mean beginning at 0, moving to 4, and then traveling 0 hours, so 4 + 0 = 4. But 0 + 4 would mean beginning at 0, going zero spaces, and then going four spaces, landing on 4, so 0 + 4 = 4.

Activity 6   Which Properties Hold?

1. Complete the following, using clock arithmetic with five numbers: 0, 1, 2, 3, and 4.

   a. 3 + 2   **b.** 4 + 4 + 4   **c.** 1 + 4   **d.** 3 + 3   **e.** 2 + (3 + 4)
   f. (2 + 3) + 4   **g.** (1 + 2) + 4   **h.** 1 + (2 + 4)   **i.** 2 + 3   **j.** 4 + 1

2. Have you illustrated, in 1, any instances of the commutative property of addition? If so, which one(s)? Try some others.

3. Have you illustrated, in 1, any instances of the associative property of addition? If so, which one(s)? Try some others.

4. Is this set of numbers closed under addition? That is, for any two clock numbers in the set, would the sum be in the set?

5. Is there an additive identity in this system? If so, what is it? (Now you see why 0 rather than 5 was chosen.)

Continue on the next page.

6. Does each number have an additive inverse? That is, for any given clock number *c*, is there a number *d* such that $c + d = 0$? (Of course, this assumes that 0 is the additive identity.)

We can also define multiplication in this system, using repeated addition. That is, $4 \times 2 = 2 + 2 + 2 + 2 = 3$ because $2 + 2$ (starting at 2 and moving clockwise 2 places) is 4. Then $4 + 2$ is 1, and finally $1 + 2 = 3$. Also, $2 \times 4 = 4 + 4 = 3$.

Activity 7   Do the Field Properties Hold in Clock Arithmetic?

1. Fill in these two tables: Some results have been entered for you:

+	0	1	2	3	4
0					
1					
2		3		0	
3					
4					

×	0	1	2	3	4
0	0				
1					
2	0			1	
3					
4					

2. Try several examples to illustrate that multiplication in the five-hour clock system is commutative and associative.

3. Is the set closed under multiplication?

4. Is there a multiplicative identity? If so, what is it?

5. Does each number in the system have a multiplicative inverse?

6. Finally, is multiplication distributive over addition? If all eleven properties hold, then clock arithmetic for 5 is a field. Is this a field?

TAKE-AWAY MESSAGE . . . The rational numbers, together with the operations of addition and multiplication, form what is called a field, as do the real numbers with addition and multiplication. A mathematical field is defined as a set of numbers with two operations for which the eleven properties we have discussed all hold. Some sets of numbers we have worked with, such as the set of whole numbers, do not form a field with addition and multiplication because one or more properties fail.

The rational numbers and real numbers are both infinite number systems. Are there any finite number systems that form a field? You have found one: clock arithmetic for a clock with numbers 0, 1, 2, 3, and 4, with operations defined as in the tables. Are there other finite fields? That's an interesting question. ♦

Learning Exercises for Section 10.4

1. What is $^-(^-3)$?

2. What is the additive inverse of $-\frac{3}{5}$?   Of 0?   Of 14?   Of 3.67?

3. **a.** What is the multiplicative inverse of $-\frac{3}{5}$?

   b. Of 14?

   c. Of 3.67?

   d. Why does 0 not have a multiplicative inverse?

4. **a.** Is the set of odd whole numbers (with addition and multiplication) a field? Why or why not?

   b. Is the set of even whole numbers (with addition and multiplication) a field? Why or why not?

   c. Is the set of integers (with addition and multiplication) a field? Why or why not? In each case, tell which properties hold, which ones do not, and provide an example in each case.

5. Consider clock arithmetic using a clock with just four numbers: 0, 1, 2, and 3, along with addition and multiplication defined similarly to the example of a clock with five numbers. Do all eleven field properties hold here? If not, which ones do not?

6. Do the same with clock arithmetic using six numbers; then do the same using seven numbers. Can you make any conjectures about when all eleven properties needed for a field will hold for a clock arithmetic? You may wish to examine other clock systems to test your conjecture further.

10.5 | Issues for Learning: A Historical Perspective

The Hindus worked with negative numbers in the seventh and eighth centuries but did not consider them as legitimate solutions to quadratic equations, such as $x^2 = 1$, which has two solutions, 1 and $^-1$. By the sixteenth century, negative numbers began to appear in algebraic expressions but were treated as fictitious or "false" numbers. Geoffrey Howson[i] tells us that "In the late 1700s and early 1800s, many in England still looked upon negative numbers with considerable misgiving. Indeed, in 1796, Frend, a Cambridge mathematician, produced an algebra text in which he avoided their use. He argued that 'multiplying a negative number into a negative number and thus producing a positive number' finds most supporters 'amongst those who love to take things upon trust and hate the labor of serious thought.' "

It is not surprising, then, that students too show some resistance to using negative numbers. Because these numbers are so commonly used for temperature and for debits, we accept their existence and usefulness in these realms. However, when we begin operating on them it becomes difficult to justify all of the operations based on

Notes

their everyday uses. Yet these numbers are of immense value in the mathematical and scientific worlds.

Mathematicians now view the use of negative numbers as obvious, but there is still a good deal of difficulty in teaching this topic. Until now, everything we've done can be found to make intuitive sense, and many models can be found to support these topics. But here we come face-to-face with a topic, multiplication and division of signed numbers, that is not at all intuitive. Thus, although negative numbers and computations with negative numbers are "inventions," they are inventions that work. "A definition free of contradictions makes formal arithmetic *logically possible*" (Hefendehl-Hebeker, p. 30).[ii]

10.6 | Check Yourself

In this chapter we have extended our number system to include all of the signed numbers. We can now add, subtract, multiply, and divide signed numbers, and in particular we considered the properties of addition and of multiplication. This number system, together with the eleven properties we found to be true of addition and multiplication, form a *mathematical field.*

You should be able to work problems like those assigned and to meet the following objectives.

1. Add, subtract, multiply, and divide rational numbers, including negative numbers, according to the rules described in this chapter.

2. Understand absolute value, apply it, and explain why it is useful in the context of working with negative and positive numbers.

3. Check whether a clearly defined set of numbers is closed with respect to a particular operation.

4. Provide examples of the closure, commutative, associative, identity, and inverse properties for addition and multiplication of rational numbers, and of the distributive property of multiplication over addition.

5. Recognize and name the properties when they are used.

6. Examine other number systems (e.g., even integer arithmetic; clock arithmetic for numbers such as 4, 5, and 6) and tell whether the eleven field properties hold in these systems.

7. Explain why operations on negative numbers, particularly multiplication, are sometimes difficult to teach.

REFERENCES FOR CHAPTER 10

[i] Howson, G. (1996, July*). Mathematics and common sense.* Paper presented at the International Conference for Mathematics Education, Seville, Spain.

[ii] Hefendehl-Hebeker, L. (1991). Negative numbers: Obstacles in their evolution from intuitive to intellectual constructs. *For the Learning of Mathematics, 11*(1), 26–32.

Chapter 11

Number Theory

Number theory is one of the oldest branches of mathematics. For many years people who studied number theory delighted in its "pure" nature because there were few practical applications of number theory. It is therefore somewhat ironic that number theory now plays important roles in keeping military and diplomatic messages secret and in making certain that people are authorized to withdraw money in electronic financial transactions.[i] (These naturally are more complicated than your secret PIN for an automatic teller machine.) Our attention will be restricted largely to the ideas from number theory that come up in the elementary school curriculum. Although number theory ideas can be applied to negative integers as well as positive ones, we will have in mind only the whole numbers, 0, 1, 2, 3, . . . , in this section. Fractions use number theory ideas, but only in a context where number theory is applied to whole-number numerators and denominators.

11.1 Factors and Multiples, Primes and Composites

Numbers are related to one another in many ways. In this section, we examine the fundamental ways that whole numbers exist when they are expressed multiplicatively.

Recall the discussion of factors in Chapter 3. Since $5 \times 6 = 30$, and $15 \times 2 = 30$, each of the numbers 5, 6, 15 and 2 is a factor of 30. (There are more.) Some numbers have many more factors. Indeed, 180 has 18 factors in all! Even a small number can have several factors: $2 \times 3 = 6$ and $1 \times 6 = 6$, so the numbers 2, 3, 1, and 6 are factors of 6. Some numbers have exactly two different factors—for example, 13 has only 1 and 13 as factors. Such numbers play an important role in number theory and are called **prime numbers**. The number 29 is another example of a number that has exactly two factors: 1 and 29, so 29 is a prime number.

It may be surprising to you that there are infinitely many prime numbers, a fact known to the ancient Greeks. There are, for example, 455,052,512 prime numbers less than 10^{10}. Indeed, with the advancing capabilities of computers (and knowledge of number theory) larger and larger primes are occasionally found. In 1978, for example, the largest known prime required 6533 digits to write. By 1985 other new primes had been found, the largest one requiring 65,050 digits to write. (How many pages would that require?) By 1992, mathematicians had found a prime number requiring 227,832 digits to write. In 1997, they found a prime requiring 895,932 digits, which would fill 450 pages of a paperback book. As of this writing, the largest known prime number has 7,816,230 digits—there is good reason for not printing it here! In fact, if you were able to write 10 digits per second (a feat in and of itself) it would take you 9 days to write this number.

> A **prime number** is a whole number that has exactly two different whole number factors. A **composite number** is a whole number greater than 1 that has more than two factors.

THINK ABOUT . . .

Does the number 1 fit the description of a prime number? Of a composite number? What about the number 0?

Discussion 1   Representing Primes and Composites

Suppose you have *n* tiles or counters as "chairs." If *n* = 6, in how many different ways can you arrange the chairs in complete rows with the same number in each row? if *n* = 13? if *n* = 14? Discuss how the possible arrangements of *n* chairs in a rectangular array are different for *n* as a prime versus *n* as a composite number.

Eratosthenes, a Greek who lived more than 2200 years ago, devised the following method of identifying primes.

Activity 1   Eratosthenes's Sieve for Finding Primes

1. Cross out 1 in the array on the following page.

   The number 2 is prime. Circle 2 in the array. Cross out all of the larger multiples of 2 in the array ($2 \times 2 = 4$, $3 \times 2 = 6$, $4 \times 2 = 8$ . . .).

   The number 3 is prime. Circle 3 in the array. Cross out all of the larger multiples of 3 in the array.

   The number 5 is prime. Circle 5 in the array. Cross out all of the larger multiples of 5 in the array.

   The number 7 is prime. Circle 7 in the array. Cross out all of the larger multiples of 7 in the array.

   What is circled next? Does this procedure ever end? Explain.

   Circle 11 in the array. Cross out all of the larger multiples of 11 in the array.

   Circle all of the numbers not yet crossed out. Are the numbers circled all primes?

1	2	3	4	5	6
7	8	9	10	11	12
13	14	15	16	17	18
19	20	21	22	23	24
25	26	27	28	29	30
31	32	33	34	35	36
37	38	39	40	41	42
43	44	45	46	47	48
49	50	51	52	53	54
55	56	57	58	59	60
61	62	63	64	65	66
67	68	69	70	71	72
73	74	75	76	77	78
79	80	81	82	83	84
85	86	87	88	89	90
91	92	93	94	95	96
97	98	99	100	101	102
103	104	105	106	107	108
109	110	111	112	113	114
115	116	117	118	119	120
121	122	123	124	125	126	etc.

2. If this array were extended, which column would 1000 be in? Which column would 1,000,000 be in?

   $2^{10} = 1024$. Which column would this number be in?

   $2^{11} = 2048$. Which column would this number be in?

Continue on the next page.

3. Find a column in the array for which the following is true: If two numbers in the column are multiplied, the product is also in that column. Each of four original columns in the array (if continued infinitely) has this property. Which four? What is the name of this property?

_____

THINK ABOUT . . .

If this array were written in four columns rather than six columns, which column would the number 1000 be in? How did you determine that?

You probably observed that all the numbers in the last column of the array are multiples of 6. You can represent each of these numbers as rectangular arrays with exactly 6 tiles in each row. Rectangular arrays can be used to illustrate some relationships between numbers. You can easily draw a rectangular array of 18 tiles with 6 in each row.

This rectangular array can illustrate the following:

$3 \times 6 = 18$.

18 is a multiple of 6.

18 is the product of 6 and 3, which are factors of 18.

THINK ABOUT . . .

Can you draw a rectangular array with 15 tiles that has 6 tiles in each row? Why or why not?

You should recall the following definitions from earlier work. Pay particular attention to these vocabulary words. They are often misused.

If $mn = p$, then m and n are called **factors** of p, and p is called a **multiple** of m (and of n). If $mn = p$ and m is not 0, then m is called a **divisor** of p. We say that p is **divisible** by m. Recall also that p is the **product** of m and of n.

EXAMPLE 1

$12 \times 15 = 180$, so 12 and the 15 are factors of 180; they are also divisors of 180. 180 is the product of 12 and 15 or, in number theory lingo, 180 is a multiple of 12 (and of 15). $0 \times 5 = 0$, so 0 and 5 are factors of 0, and 5 is a divisor of 0 but 0 is not a divisor of 0.

THINK ABOUT . . .

Why is 0 never a divisor? Think back to Chapter 3 in which dividing by 0 was discussed.

Activity 2   Vocabulary Practice

1. Use 6, 8, and 48 in sentences that involve "factor," "divisor," "product," and "multiple." Use rectangular arrays, equations, and words to describe the relationship between 6, 8, and 48.

2. Use these vocabulary words to describe the variables in $mn = p$.

3. If m is a factor of n, is n a multiple of m? If p is a multiple of q, is q a factor of p?

4. If $m = 2n$, what can you say about m?

The following activity will help us think about these relationships in different ways.

Activity 3   Which Lockers Are Open?

In a certain school there are 100 lockers lining a long hallway. All are closed. Suppose 100 students walk down the hall, in file, and the first student opens every locker. The second student comes behind the first and closes every second locker, beginning with locker #2. The third student changes the position of every third locker; if it is open this student closes it; if it is closed, this third student opens it. The fourth student changes the position of every fourth locker, and so on, until the 100th student changes only the position of the 100th locker. After this procession, which lockers are open? Why are they open? At the end of this processon, how many times did locker 9 get changed? How many times did locker 10 get changed?

TAKE-AWAY MESSAGE . . . Understanding distinctions between prime and composite numbers, and between multiples and factors (or divisors) are essential before continuing into the remaining sections of this chapter. The Sieve of Eratosthenes provides one way to find prime numbers, but is not efficient for large numbers. Prime numbers are used in cryptography and in businesses such as banking. ♦

Learning Exercises for Section 11.1

1. **a.** Give three factors of 25. Can you find more? If so, how? If not, why not?
    b. Give three multiples of 25. Can you find more? If so, how? If not, why not?

2. **a.** Write an equation that asserts that 25 is a factor of k. How could a rectangular array show this?
    b. Write an equation that asserts that m is a factor of w.
    c. Write an equation that asserts that v is a multiple of t.

3. **a.** If 216 is a factor of 2376, what equation must have a whole number solution?
    b. How does one find out whether 144 is a factor of 3456?

4. Use the notion of rectangular arrays to assert that 21 is not divisible by 5.

Notes

5. Explain why these assertions are not quite correct:

    a. "A factor of a number is always less than the number."

    b. "A multiple of a number is always greater than the number."

6. a. Give two factors of 506.

    b. Give two multiples of 506.

7. True or false? If false, correct the statement.

    a. 13 is a factor of 39.

    b. 12 is a factor of 36.

    c. 24 is a factor of 36.

    d. 36 is a multiple of 12.

    e. 36 is a multiple of 48.

    f. 16 is a factor of 512.

    g. 2 is a multiple of 1.

8. a. Write an equation that asserts that 15 is a multiple of a whole number k.

    b. Write an equation that asserts that a whole number m is a factor of a whole number x.

9. a. Suppose that k is a factor of m and m is a factor of n. Is k a factor of n? Is n a multiple of k? Justify your decisions.

    b. Suppose that k is a factor of both m and n. Is k a factor of $m + n$ also? Justify your decision.

    c. Suppose k is a factor of m but k is not a factor of n. Is k a factor of $m + n$ also? Justify your decisions. (You may want to try this with numbers first. For example, 5 is a factor of 15, but is not a factor of _____.)

10. You know that the even (whole) numbers are the elements of the set of numbers 0, 2, 4, 6, 8, . . . , and that the odd (whole) numbers are the elements of the set of numbers 1, 3, 5, 7, 9, ...

    a. Write a description of the even numbers that uses "2" and the word "factor."

    b. Write a description of the even numbers that uses "2" and the word "multiple."

    c. Write a description of odd numbers that uses "2."

11. Complete the following addition and multiplication tables for even and odd numbers. Can you then make any definite assertions about . . .

+	even	odd
even		
odd		

×	even	odd
even		
odd		

    a. the sum of any number of even numbers?

    b. the sum of any number of odd numbers?

    c. the product of any number of even numbers?

d.   the product of any number of odd numbers?

e.   whether it is possible for an odd number to have an even factor?

f.   whether it is possible for an even number to have an odd factor?

g.   Is the set of even numbers closed under addition?

h.   Is the set of odd numbers closed under addition?

i.   Is the set of even numbers closed under multiplication?

j.   Is the set of odd numbers closed under multiplication?

12. Explain why each of these is a prime number: 2, 3, 29, 97.

13. List all the primes (prime numbers) less than 100. (You can use the Sieve of Eratosthenes in the activity on the sieve.)

14. Explain why each of these is a composite number: 15, 27, 49, 119.

15. a.   Why is 0 neither a prime nor a composite number?

b.   Why is 1 neither a prime nor a composite?

c.   What is the drawback to the following "definition" of prime numbers: a whole number with only 1 and itself as factors?

16. Give two factors of each number (there may be more than two):

a.   829   b.   5771   c.   506   d. n (if $n > 1$)

17. Explain why 2 is the only even prime number. (Can you always find a third factor for larger even numbers?)

18. Conjecture: Given two whole numbers, the larger one will have more factors than the smaller one will. Gather more evidence on this conjecture by working with several (4 or 5) pairs of numbers.

19. a.   Just above a number line (at least to 50), mark each factor of 24 with a heavy dot and mark each multiple of 6 with a square.

b.   Just below the same number line, mark each factor of 18 with a triangle and mark each multiple of 18 with a circle.

c.   What are common factors of 18 and 24? What are common multiples of 6 and 18?

20. Explain without much calculation how you know that 2, 3, 5, 7, 11, 13, and 17 are not factors of $n = 2 \cdot 3 \cdot 5 \cdot 7 \cdot 11 \cdot 13 \cdot 17 + 1$.

21. 6 is called a **perfect number** because its factors (other than itself) add up to the number: $1 + 2 + 3 = 6$. What is the next perfect number?

11.2 Prime Factorization

How do you know whether a number is prime or composite? The number 6 can be written as a product of prime numbers: 2×3. The number 18 can be written as the product of three primes: $2 \times 3 \times 3$. Can other composite numbers be written as a product of primes? These questions and others are explored in the next activity.

Activity 4   I'm in My Prime

Write the numbers from 2 to 48 using only prime numbers.

			13	25	37
2	2		14	26	38
3	3		15	27	39
$2 \times 2 = 2^2$	4		16	28	40
5	5		17	29	41
2×3	6		18	30	42
7	7		19	31	43
$2 \times 2 \times 2 = 2^3$	8		20	32	44
	9		21	33	45
	10		22	34	46
	11		23	35	47
	12		24	36	48

Every whole number except 1 can be written as a prime number or as a product of prime numbers. (Why is that?)

> A number written as a product of prime numbers is in **prime factorization form**.

Continuation of Activity 4   I'm in My Prime

a. Compare your table with others.

b. Write down as many patterns as you can find in this table.

c. If the list continued, what would be the prime factorization of 1008?

d. Did you have any prime factorizations different from those of other people?

e. What can you say about numbers that are divisible by 2? By 5? By 10?

All of you should have exactly the same factorizations in Activity 4, except possibly for the order of the factors (and notational shortcuts like 3^2 for $3 \cdot 3$). This result is true in general.

> The fact that every whole number greater than 1 is either a prime or can be expressed as the product of prime numbers uniquely (except possibly for order) is called the **Unique Factorization Theorem**, or sometimes, the **Fundamental Theorem of Arithmetic**.

The Fundamental Theorem of Arithmetic means that, in some sense, the prime numbers can be regarded as the building blocks for all the whole numbers other than 0 and 1. Other whole numbers are primes or can be expressed in exactly one way as the product of primes. Thus a number theorist often finds it most useful to think of 288 as $2 \cdot 2 \cdot 2 \cdot 2 \cdot 2 \cdot 3 \cdot 3$, or $2^5 \times 3^2$.

By asking that the prime factors be given in increasing order and that exponents be used if a prime factor is repeated, one gets the standard prime factorization. For example, $180 = 2^2 \times 3^2 \times 5$ and $288 = 2^5 \times 3^2$. This form is not essential, but it makes quick comparisons of two prime factorizations easier.

Activity 5   Detective Work on Factorizations

1. Why doesn't this correct equation contradict the Unique Factorization Theorem?

    $2^8 \cdot 7^5 \cdot 892 = 2^7 \cdot 7^4 \cdot 14 \cdot 892$

2. These people are finding the prime factorization of the same number x. No one is finished. Answer (and explain) the questions below without doing any computation:

    $$\text{Aña: } x = 3^8 \cdot 7^4 \cdot 4797134197203$$
    $$\text{Ben: } x = 3^7 \cdot 7^4 \cdot \text{an odd number}$$
    $$\text{Carlos: } x = 21^2 \cdot 7^9 \cdot 3^6 \cdot \text{an even number}$$
    $$\text{Dee: } x = 3 \cdot 3 \cdot 3 \cdot 49 \cdot \text{an odd number}$$

    a. Who might agree when they finish?
    b. Who definitely will disagree?
    c. Might they all be correct, if they work forward from where they are now?

One consequence of unique factorization into primes is that any factor (except 1) of a number greater than 1 can involve only primes that appear in the number's prime factorization. For example, suppose that $n = 2100$. Then 42 is a factor of 2100 because $42 \times 50 = 2100$. If we continue to factor the 42 and 50, eventually we will get prime factors that *must* appear in the prime factorization of 2100 because the prime factorization is unique. Any prime number that does not appear in the prime factorization of 2100 cannot be "hidden" in some factor of the number.

One way to visually organize the work when finding the prime factorization of a number is to make a **factor tree**.

Thus:

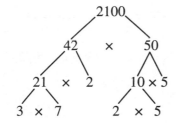

Looking at the ends of each branch of the previous factor tree, we have factors 3, 7, 2, 2, 5, 5. Thus $2100 = 2^2 \cdot 3 \cdot 5^2 \cdot 7$. Note that we could have thought of the composite numbers in other ways, for example, 42 as 6×7, or 2100 as 2×1050.

> ***THINK ABOUT . . .***
>
> If different factorizations for composite numbers in the factor tree are used, will the prime factorization be the same?

The general argument for finding the prime factorization of a number follows the same pattern. Suppose that m is a factor of n. Then there is some whole number k such that $m \cdot k = n$. This process starts a factorization of n, and the factorization *must* lead eventually to a unique set of prime factors, according to the unique factorization theorem. This result means that some of the *same* primes in the prime factorization of n must be factors of m (and of k) and that no other primes can be involved.

Activity 6   More On Primes

1. If $n = 2 \times 3^5 \times 11^2 \times 19^3$, what are four prime factors of n? What are ten composite factors of n?

2. Find the *smallest* number with factors. . .

    a. 2, 6, 8, 22, 30, and 45.   **b.** 50, 126, and 490.

How many factors does a number have? For example, consider the number 72. We could write 72 as 6×12, or 2×36, or 3×24, or 4×18 or 8×9, or as 1×72. We could organize these by listing each pair of numbers. In other words, we can find pairs of "buddy" factors. 1, 2, 3, 4, 6, 8, match with 72, 36, 24, 18, 12, and 9, respectively (i.e., 1 and 72 are buddy factors, 2 and 36 are buddy factors, etc.). So 72 has 12 factors.

We can find the prime factorization of 72 by using a factor tree or by simply factoring 72 as 6×12, and then continuing by writing 6 and 12 as a product of prime numbers. The prime factorization of 72 is $(2 \times 3) \times (2 \times 2 \times 3)$, or $2^3 \times 3^2$.

How can we use the prime factorization of a number to list all the factors of a number? We could use the knowledge of the prime factorization of $72 = 2^3 \times 3^2$ to list the factors systematically as follows:

$2^0 \cdot 3^0; \ 2^1 \cdot 3^0; \ 2^2 \cdot 3^0; \ 2^3 \cdot 3^0$ gives us factors 1, 2, 4, and 8.

$2^0 \cdot 3^1; \ 2^1 \cdot 3^1; \ 2^2 \cdot 3^1; 2^3 \cdot 3^1$ gives us factors 3, 6, 12, and 24.

$2^0 \cdot 3^2; \ 2^1 \cdot 3^2; \ 2^2 \cdot 3^2; 2^3 \cdot 3^2$ gives us factors 9, 18, 36, and 72.

THINK ABOUT . . .

What is the same about each row of factors? What is different between the rows of factors?

Counting is one of the "big ideas" of mathematics that can be found throughout mathematics. The questions "Do we have them all?" and "Are any repeats?" can usually only be answered if the counting was systematic. Be *sure* to note how the system worked to assure finding all factors.

Activity 7   Use My Rule

Systematically list all the factors of $5000 = 2^3 \cdot 5^4$. You should have 20 numbers listed.

Understanding the system will be critical in generalizing a rule that will help you effectively predict the number of factors a number has.

Discussion 2   How Many Factors?

Return to your table in Activity 4 and write each number with exponents where possible. How can you determine the number of factors of a composite number by knowing the exponents in its prime factorization? Determine a rule that will tell you the number of factors for any whole number except 0. *Hint:* for any prime number a, to the nth power, a can appear in a factor in $n + 1$ ways where the exponents are . . . (you finish; hint, see the rows of factors of 72 above). Take note of the difference between finding *all* factors and finding the *prime* factors.

TAKE-AWAY MESSAGE . . . Every whole number greater than 1 can be uniquely factored into primes (disregarding order). This fact is referred to as the Unique Factorization Theorem (sometimes as the Fundamental Theorem of Arithmetic). Another way to think about factors of a number is to list *all* factors of the number. A "buddy" system for finding all factors of a number was described, but a better way to ensure you have listed them all is to systematically list all factors using the prime factorization, and taking every possible selection from the prime factors. ♦

Learning Exercises for Section 11.2

1. State the unique factorization theorem. What does it assert about 239,417?

2. Find the prime factorization of each of the following, using a factor tree for each.

   a. 102   **b.** 1827   **c.** 1584   **d.** 1540   **e.** 121   **f.** 1485

3. Find the prime factorization of each of these numbers, using a factor tree for at least two of them.

   a. 5850   **b.** 256   **c.** 2835   **d.** 10^4 **e.** 17,280

   f. Does a complete factor tree for a number show all the factors of the number? All the prime factors of the number?

4. Name three prime factors of each of the following products.

   a. $3 \times 7^3 \times 22$ **b.** 27×22 **c.** $29^4 \times 11^6 \times 2^5$

5. What is the difference between *prime factor* and *prime factorization*?

6. Is it possible to find nonzero whole numbers m and n such that $11^m = 13^n$? Explain.

7. Which cannot be true, for whole numbers m and n? Explain why not. For the ones that can be true, give values for m and n that make the equation true.

   a. $2^9 \cdot 17^3 \cdot 67^2 = 2^7 \cdot 17^2 \cdot 34 \cdot 67 \cdot m$ **b.** $2^9 \cdot 17^3 \cdot 67^2 = 2^9 \cdot 17^4 \cdot m$

   c. $2^9 \cdot 17^3 \cdot 67^2 = 2^8 \cdot 17^2 \cdot n$ **d.** $2^9 \cdot 17^3 \cdot 67^2 = 2^9 \cdot 17^3 \cdot 134 \cdot m$

   e. $4^m = 8^n$ **f.** $6^m = 18^n$

8. Consider $m = 2^9 \cdot 17^3 \cdot 67^2$. Without elaborate calculation, tell which of the following could NOT be factors of m. Explain how you know.

   a. $2^8 \cdot 7$ **b.** $2^{10} \cdot 17^2 \cdot 67$ **c.** $2^8 \cdot 17^2 \cdot 67^2$ **d.** 34^3 **e.** 134^2

9. If 35 is a factor of n, give two other factors of n (besides 1 and n).

10. How many factors does each have?

    a. 2^5 **b.** $2^2 \cdot 3^3 = 108$ **c.** 45,000

    d. $2^7 \cdot 3^5 \cdot 11 \cdot 13^2$ **e.** 10^6 **f.** 11^6 **g.** 12^6

    Explain your reasoning for two of the parts (a)–(g).

11. Consider $19^4 \times 11^4 \times 2^5$. Which of the following products of given numbers are factors of this number for some whole number n? If so, provide a value of n that makes it true. If not, tell why not.

    a. $19^4 \times 11^3 \times 2^5 \times n$ **b.** $19^4 \times 22 \times 2^5 \times n$

    c. $19^4 \times 11^4 \times 64 \times n$ **d.** $19 \times 11 \times 2 \times n$

12. Consider $q = 19^4 \times 11^4 \times 2^5$. Which of the following are multiples of this number? If so, what would you need to multiply this q by to get the number?

    a. $19^4 \times 11^8 \times 2^5$ **b.** $19^4 \times 22^4 \times 2^5 \times 17$

    c. $19^4 \times 11^4 \times 64$ **d.** $(19 \times 11 \times 2)^5$

13. **a.** How many factors does 64 have? List them.

    b. How many factors does 48 have? List them.

    c. How many factors does $19^4 \times 11^4 \times 2^5$ have?

14. If p, q, and r are different primes, how many factors does each of the following have?

    a. p^{10} **b.** p^m **c.** q^n **d.** $p^m \cdot q^n$ **e.** $p^m \cdot q^n \cdot r^s$

15. Give two numbers that have exactly 60 factors. (The numbers do not have to be in calculated form.)

16. Give one number that has the number 121 as a factor and that also has exactly 24 factors. Is there just one possibility?

11.3	Divisibility Tests to Determine Whether a Number Is Prime

The secret military and diplomatic codes mentioned earlier usually involve knowing whether a large number is a prime, or finding the prime factors of a large number. It is a challenge to tackle a large number like 431,687 to see whether it is prime. (431,687 is not a large number for a computer, however. It was newsworthy in 1995 that it was possible to find out whether a number 129 digits long was a prime, using a network of 600 volunteers with computers. It took them eight months and about 1.5×10^{17} calculations.) Because a large number automatically has two different factors, 1 and itself, we need find only one other factor to settle the question of whether or not the number is prime. If it has a third factor, we know that the number is not a prime. If primeness is the only concern, we do not even have to look for other factors.

Activity 8   Back to Patterns in the Table

In Section 11.2 of this chapter, you were asked to find patterns in the Activity 4 table. Did you find patterns that would tell you when a number is divisible by 2? By 3? By 4? By 5? By 6? See if you can find any now.

Is 495,687,115 a prime? Is 1,298,543,316 a prime? It is likely that you saw immediately that 5 is a factor of the first number, and that 2 is a factor of the second number, so you quickly knew that each number had at least 3 factors and hence was not a prime. There are other divisibility tests beyond those for 2, 5, and 10. Perhaps you found some in the activity. Divisibility tests are useful in investigating whether a given number is a prime (and for a teacher who wishes to make up division problems that *come out even*—that is, give a remainder of 0). They can be helpful when considering whether pairs of numbers have factors in common when writing equivalent fractions and, later, in factoring algebraic expressions.

A divisibility test tells whether a number is a factor or divisor of a given number, but without having to divide the given number by the possible factor. So they could be called *factor tests* but usually are not. Nor are they called *multiples tests,* even though, for example, 112 is a multiple of 2 (but not of 5).

Here are possible statements for the divisibility tests for 2 and for 5.

> **Divisibility Test for 2:** A number is divisible by 2 if, and only if, 2 is a factor of the ones digit (i.e., the final digit is 0, 2, 4, 6, or 8).
>
> **Divisibility Test for 5:** A number is divisible by 5 if, and only if, 5 is a factor of the ones digit (i.e., the final digit is 0 or 5).

THINK ABOUT . . .

The divisibility tests for 2, 5, and 10 ignore most of the digits in a large number! Why do the tests work?

There are some easy-to-use but difficult-to-explain divisibility tests. They can be demonstrated using properties of operations and using the two conjectures that you examined in Section 11.1, Learning Exercise 9: (1) if k is a factor of both m and n, then k is also a factor of $m + n$, and (2) if k is a factor of m but k is not a factor of n, then k is not a factor of $m + n$.

THINK ABOUT . . .

Test these conjectures by putting in different numbers for each of the conjectures to be sure you understand them. (For example, suppose k is 3, m is 12, and n is 15. Does the first conjecture hold true? Does k also divide $m + n$?)

The test for divisibility by 3 is quite different from the test for divisibility by 2. The last digit of a number does not reveal whether a number is divisible by 3. For example, 26 and 36 both end in a digit which represents a number divisible by 3, but 26 is *not* divisible by 3, whereas 36 is. Furthermore, we cannot simply say that every third number in the table in Section 11.2 is divisible by 3 and have an efficient test for a large number.

Of course, if we know the prime factorization we can tell immediately whether a number is divisible by 3, but one reason we need divisibility tests is to *find* the prime factorization of a number. Thus we know that $2 \cdot 2 \cdot 2 \cdot 3 \cdot 7 = 168$, so 168 is divisible by 3 because it has 3 as a factor. How could you tell that 3 is a factor of 168, except by calculating $168 \div 3$ or knowing its prime factorization? That is, what is a divisibility test for 3?

Looking at the expanded place-value expression for 168 tells the secret. (Note which properties are used in the equations below.)

$$
\begin{aligned}
168 &= 1 \cdot 100 + 6 \cdot 10 + 8 \\
&= 1 \cdot (99 + 1) + 6 \cdot (9 + 1) + 8 \\
&= 1 \cdot 99 + 1 \cdot 1 + 6 \cdot 9 + 6 \cdot 1 + 8 \text{ (using the distributive property of} \\
&\quad \text{multiplication over addition)} \\
&= 1 \cdot 99 + 6 \cdot 9 + 1 \cdot 1 + 6 \cdot 1 + 8 \text{ (using the commutative property of addition)} \\
&= (1 \cdot 99 + 6 \cdot 9) + (1 \cdot 1 + 6 \cdot 1 + 8) \text{ (using the associative property of addition)}
\end{aligned}
$$

The numbers 99 and 9 are always divisible by 3, so $(1 \cdot 99 + 6 \cdot 9)$ is divisible by 3 by the first conjecture which you tested in the *Think About*. And by the second conjecture, 3 would need to divide the rest of the number $(1 \cdot 1 + 6 \cdot 1 + 8)$ if 3 indeed divides 168.

But $1 \cdot 1 + 6 \cdot 1 + 8$, is just $1 + 6 + 8$, which is the sum of the digits of 168. So if 3 divides $1 + 6 + 8$, then 3 divides 168. Three does divide $1 + 6 + 8 = 15$, so 168 must be divisible by 3. (If we actually did the $168 \div 3$ calculation to check whether 3 is a factor, we would find that $168 = 3 \cdot 56$, so indeed 3 is a factor of 168.)

> **THINK ABOUT . . .**
>
> Does the following approach work for 3528?
>
> $$\begin{aligned} 3528 \quad &= \quad 3 \cdot 1000 + 5 \cdot 100 + 2 \cdot 10 + 8 \\ &= \quad 3 \cdot (999 + 1) + 5 \cdot (99 + 1) + 2 \cdot (9 + 1) + 8 \\ &= \quad (3 \cdot 999 + 5 \cdot 99 + 2 \cdot 9) + (3 + 5 + 2 + 8) \end{aligned}$$
>
> You finish checking for divisibility by 3 using the process used for 168. Can you test for divisibility for 3 for any number, using this process?

However, if the number had been 3527, all would be the same except the 3+5+2+8 would now be 3+5+2+7 = 17. The number 17 is not divisible by 3, and so 3 is not a factor of 3527. (Check it out using a calculator or long division.)

Divisibility Test for 3: A whole number is divisible by 3 if, and only if, the sum of the digits of the whole number is divisible by 3.

An interesting and useful fact about dividing a number by 9 is that the remainder for the division is always the sum of the digits of the number, if the digits continue to be added until the number is less than 9. For example, $215 \div 9 = 23$ remainder 8 and $2 + 1 + 5 = 8$, the remainder. Another way of writing this is $215 = 9 \times 23 + 8$.

Why does this work? $$\begin{aligned} 215 &= 200 + 10 + 5 \\ &= 2(99 + 1) + 1(9 + 1) + 5 \\ &= (2 \times 99) + (2 \times 1) + (1 \times 9) + (1 \times 1) + 5 \\ &= [(2 \times 9 \times 11) + (1 \times 9)] + (2 + 1 + 5) \\ &= 9[2 \times 11 + 1] + (2 + 1 + 5) \\ &= 9 \times 23 + 8 \text{ and note that the } 8 = 2 + 1 + 5 \end{aligned}$$

Activity 9   What About 9?

Use the reasoning for the divisibility test for 3 and the reasoning about the remainder when dividing by 9 to devise a divisibility test for 9.

Sometimes children are taught a method for checking arithmetic calculations called *Casting Out Nines.* Perhaps you know it. This method is easy enough for an upper elementary student to use, but understanding why it works involves some of the notions we've been discussing. Here's how it works if you wish to check for errors in addition:

Notes

$$326$$
$$479$$
$$+ \ 84$$
$$889$$

Step 1: For each number, cross out ("cast out") digits that are 9 or whose sum is 9.
Step 2: Add the remaining digits until you have a number 0–8. This will be your "reduced number."
Step 3: Do the operation indicated on the reduced numbers.
Step 4: Check to see if the sum, difference, or product, as appropriate, of the reduced numbers matches the reduced number of the sum, difference, or product. If it doesn't, check further for an error.

For the above addition problem, here is an illustration of the method:

/2 /   ←2 (also, when 326 is divided by 9 the remainder is 2)
47 /   ←4+7=11; 1+1= 2 (also, when 479 is divided by 9 the remainder is 2)
+ 84   ←8+4=12; 1+2=3 (also, when 84 is divided by 9 the remainder is 3)
  88/   ←8+8=16; 1+6=7 (also when 889 is divided by 9 the remainder is 7)

If the sum is correct, then the sum of 2, 2, and 3 should equal the reduced number of the original sum. It does! $2 + 2 + 3 = 7$.

Why does this work? It is based on the fact that the sum of the digits of a number is the remainder when dividing by 9. Consider:

$326 = 9 \times 36 + 2$ (note that $3 + 2 + 6 = 11$ and that $1 + 1 = 2$)
$479 = 9 \times 53 + 2$ (note that $4 + 7 + 9 = 20$ and that $2 + 0 = 2$)
$\underline{+ \ 84 = 9 \times 9 \ + 3}$ (note that $8 + 4 = 12$ and that $1 + 2 = 3$)
889 should equal $9(36 + 53 + 9) + (2 + 3 + 3) = 9(98) + 7$, and it does.

A similar technique works for checking products.

Activity 10   Casting Out Nines

Try this technique with another sum of three large numbers using a new set of numbers. Include a number whose digits sum to 9 and a number with 9 as a digit or two digits that sum to 9. Did the sum of the reduced numbers equal the reduced number of the sum? Note that if one digit in the sum is changed (as when an error is made), the reduced number of the sum is different.

Generate a multiplication problem and use the analogous set of steps for multiplication. Now, the most important question that begs to be asked is, why does this work? Hint: What are the reduced numbers? Another important mathematical question needs to be answered: Are there circumstances when using the method would fail to catch an error?

As we have seen thus far, divisibility tests can involve looking at the last digit or summing all the digits. What about a divisibility test for 4? In the Activity 4 table in Section 11.2, numbers divisible by 4 had 2×2 as a factor. Did you notice anything about the last two digits of each of these numbers? Consider again the number 3528: $3528 = 3 \cdot 1000 + 5 \cdot 100 + 2 \cdot 10 + 8 = (3 \cdot 1000 + 5 \cdot 100) + (2 \cdot 10 + 8)$. Notice that 1000 is divisible by 4 because $1000 = 4 \cdot 250$, so $3 \cdot 1000$ must be divisible by 4. Similarly, $5 \cdot 100$ is divisible by 4 because $100 = 4 \cdot 25$. We are left with $2 \cdot 10 + 8$ or 28. If this is divisible by 4, then the entire number 2528 must be divisible by 4. With similar reasoning, 2527 is not divisible by 4.

Divisibility Test for 4: A number n is divisible by 4 if, and only if, 4 is a factor of the number formed by the final two digits of n.

Activity 11   Divisible by 8?

Use the reasoning from the divisibility test for 4 to construct a divisibility test for 8. (Consider the last three digits of the number.)

Return again to the Activity 4 table in Section 11.2 and note which numbers are divisible by 6. Note that they all have 2 and 3 as factors. Thus, applying the divisibility rules for 2 and for 3 will show whether a number is divisible by 6.

What about a divisibility test for 12? Again from the table, all of 12, 24, 36, 48 and 60 have $2 \cdot 3$ as a factor, but so do 18 and 30, which are not divisible by 12. So just testing for 2 and 3 will *not* suffice as a divisibility test for 12. All numbers divisible by 12, however, must have 4 (*two* factors that are 2s) and 3 as factors, and applying these two tests will work as a divisibility test for 12. Thus, divisibility tests that you know can help you develop new tests. We say that 4 and 3 are **relatively prime** because they have no prime factor in common, or equivalently, their only common factor is 1.

Discussion 3   Are They Relatively Prime?

Are 12 and 6 relatively prime? Are 15 and 6 relatively prime? Are 25 and 6 relatively prime? Are 7 and 11 relatively prime? Are *any* two prime numbers relatively prime?

General divisibility tests to test for composite factors $m \cdot n$: If a number p is divisible by m and also by n, and if m and n are relatively prime, then the number p is divisible by the number $m \cdot n$. This general rule can be used to construct new divisibility tests similar to what we discussed for 6 and for 12.

Divisibility tests can help us find the prime factorizations of larger numbers. Consider $n = 12{,}320$; what is its (unique) prime factorization?

We know that 2 divides the number because it ends in 0. We know 5 divides the number because it ends in 0. So we know that $2 \cdot 5 = 10$ is a factor of 12,320 (and you may have noticed that immediately). Thus we know that $12,320 = 2 \cdot 5 \cdot 1232$.

We also know that 4 divides the number 1232 because the final two digits form the number 32, which is divisible by 4. A little division then shows $1232 = 4 \cdot 308$, so we now have $12,320 = 2 \cdot 5 \cdot 4 \cdot 308$, or $2 \cdot 5 \cdot 2 \cdot 2 \cdot 308$.

But 4 is also a factor of 308 (since 8, from 08, is divisible by 4). So $12,320 = 2 \cdot 5 \cdot 2 \cdot 2 \cdot 4 \cdot 77$. Because the sum of the digits of 77 is 14, which is not divisible by 3, we know 77 and n are not divisible by 3. Nor are 2, 4, 5, or 10 factors of 77. But 77 is $7 \cdot 11$, so we finally have

$$12,320 = 2 \cdot 5 \cdot 2 \cdot 2 \cdot 4 \cdot 7 \cdot 11 = 2 \cdot 2 \cdot 2 \cdot 2 \cdot 2 \cdot 5 \cdot 7 \cdot 11,$$

which could be written more compactly using exponents as $12,320 = 2^5 \cdot 5 \cdot 7 \cdot 11$.

Activity 12   A New Way of Finding Prime Factorizations

Use the method explained here to find the prime factorizations of 1224; of 4620.

The divisibility tests for the prime numbers 2, 3, 5 are not difficult, and less simple ones for 7 and 11 exist. However, for some primes it is easier to simply divide by the prime and notice whether the quotient is a whole number, than to use complicated and hard-to-remember tests.

Suppose the divisibility test for 2 tells you that 2 is not a factor of some number n; could 4 nonetheless be a factor of n? One way to consider this is as follows: If 2 is not a factor of n, 2 cannot appear in the prime factorization of n. But if 2 cannot appear in the prime factorization, 4 could not be a factor of n, because then that 4 could give 2 as a factor (twice) in the prime factorization resulting from having 4 as a factor. (Recall that there can be only one prime factorization of n.) So if 2 is not a factor, then 4 cannot be a factor either.

> ***THINK ABOUT . . .***
>
> Give a similar argument to convince yourself that if 3 is not a factor of n, then 6 cannot be a factor of n. Give an argument that if p is not a factor of n, then $k \cdot p$ is not a factor of n.

Discussion 4   True or False?

Discuss whether each of the following is true. Explain your answers, giving counterexamples for false statements.

a. If 7 is not a factor of n, then 14 is not a factor of n.

b. If 7 is a factor of n, then 14 is a factor of n.

c. If 14 is not a factor of n, then 7 is not a factor of n.

d. If 20 is not a factor of m, then 60 is not a factor of m.

e.   If 20 is a factor of *m*, then 60 is a factor of *m*.

f.   If 60 is not a factor of *m*, then 20 is not a factor of *m*.

g.   If a number is a factor of *n*, then the number is a factor of any multiple of *n*.

h.   If a number is a factor of a multiple of *n*, then the number is a factor of *n*.

i.   If a number is not a factor of *n*, then the number is not a factor of any (nonzero) multiple of *n*.

j.   If a number is not a factor of a multiple of *n*, then the number is not a factor of *n*.

What the above means for testing for primeness is this important fact: **You need test only for divisibility by primes when deciding whether or not a number is prime**. If 7, say, is not a factor, then 14 or 21 or 28, etc., will not be factors either. You would be wasting your time in testing whether 14 or 21 or 28 were factors, once you found out that 7 was not a factor. In trying to determine whether 187 is a prime then, you would need to find out whether any one of 2, 3, 5, 7, etc., is a factor—if one is, you have found a third factor (besides 1 and 187), and so 187 would be composite. But if a prime such as 2 or 3 or 5 or 7 is not a factor, then you do not need to think about their multiples being factors.

The following discussion allows us to refine a rule in testing a number for primeness. The issue is, how many primes do you have to test in deciding whether a number like 661 is a prime? If you find that a prime like 2 or 3 or 5 or 7 is a factor of 661, you are done, of course. The number 661 would not be a prime.

Discussion 5   Testing for Primes

Check to see whether 661 is divisible by 2, by 3, by 5, by 7, by 11. To test whether or not 661 is prime, how many more primes do you think you need to test? Do you think you would need to test for divisibility by 91? Why or why not?

You may have found that you needed to test for divisibility by more primes than 2, 3, 5, 7, or 11 to find the prime factorization of 661. But as a matter of fact, you did not have to test for any prime factors greater than 23. This fact comes from the following: **When testing whether or not *n* is prime, you need test only the primes $\leq \sqrt{n}$.** This is because if both $p > \sqrt{n}$ and $q > \sqrt{n}$, then $pq > n$. Thus, either *p* or *q* must be $\leq \sqrt{n}$ if $pq = n$.

Hence, in trying to find out whether 661 is a prime, one would at worst have to try only the primes less than or equal to $\sqrt{661}$, which is about 26. Primes less than 26 are: 2, 3, 5, 7, 11, 13, 17, 19, and 23. If none of these is a factor, then 661 is a prime. Even if you have a calculator handy, it is good practice to zero in on the square root of a number with educated efforts at trial and error. For example, for $\sqrt{661}$ think 20^2 is 400 so 20 is too small, and 30^2 is 900 so 30 is too large. Check 25^2; 625 is slightly

Notes

less than 661, and 29^2 will be much larger than 661, so checking for primes less than 25 is sufficient.

THINK ABOUT . . .

What is the largest prime you need to worry about to find out whether 119 is prime? What about 247?

TAKE-AWAY MESSAGE . . . You now have divisibility tests for 2, 3, 4, 5, 6, 8, 9, 10, 12, and others that have two relatively prime factors such as 15, 18, etc. For primes other than those listed, dividing by the prime can be used to see if the prime is a factor. Using these tests can simplify the work of finding out whether or not a number is prime. You need find only one divisor for n (other than 1 and n) to show that a number is not prime. Moreover, you need not check for any primes larger than the square root of the n to determine whether or not a number is prime. ♦

Learning Exercises for Section 11.3

1. Practice the divisibility tests for 2, 3, 4, 5, 6, 8. 9, and 10 on these numbers:
   a. 43056   **b.** 700010154   **c.** 9460000000023   **d.** 71005165

2. Give a six-digit number such that
   a. 2 and 3 are factors of the number, but 4 and 9 are not.
   b. 3 and 5 are factors of the number, but 10 is not.
   c. 8 and 9 are factors of the number.

3. What could $\underline{a}$ be in $n = 4187\underline{a}432$, if 3 is a factor of n? If 9 is a factor of n? Give all the single-digit possibilities for $\underline{a}$.

4. Notice that 2 and 4 are factors of 12, but $2 \cdot 4$, or 8, is not. So a divisibility test for 8 that is NOT safe is to use the 2 test and the 4 test. Find counterexamples for these plausible-looking, but unreliable, divisibility tests.
   a. 12 is a factor of n if and only if 2 is a factor of n and 6 is a factor of n.
   b. 18 is a factor of n if and only if 3 is a factor of n and 6 is a factor of n.
   c. 24 is a factor of n if and only if 4 is a factor of n and 6 is a factor of n.

5. Try these conjectured divisibility tests with 3 or 4 examples each.
   a. 10 is a factor of n if and only if 2 is a factor of n and 5 is a factor of n.
   b. 12 is a factor of n if and only if 3 is a factor of n and 4 is a factor of n.
   c. 18 is a factor of n if and only if 2 is a factor of n and 9 is a factor of n.
   d. 24 is a factor of n if and only if 3 is a factor of n and 8 is a factor of n.

   Examine Exercises 4 and 5 to see whether you can predict when such test-two-factors approaches will work, and when they will not.

6. Using Exercise 5, determine whether
   a. 24 is a factor of 2000000000000000000000000000112.

    b. 24 is a factor of 20000000000000000000000001012.

    c. 18 is a factor of 40000000000000000000000000221.

    d. 18 is a factor of 40000000000000000000000000212.

    e. 45 is a factor of 11100000000000000000000022200.

7. Using Exercise 5, find a 15-digit number that is a multiple of 36; a 15-digit number that is not a multiple of 36.

8. The divisibility tests given here depend on the number being expressed in base ten. The tests are properties of the numeration system rather than of the numbers. Find examples with numbers written in base five to show that, say, the (base-ten) divisibility test for two does not work in base five. You will want to find a number for which two is (or is not) a factor but whose base five representation does (or does not) satisfy the divisibility test for two that you know for base ten.

9. Explain why finding only one factor of n besides 1 and n is enough to show that n is composite.

10. Suppose that $n = 2^3 \times 5^2 \times 7 \times 17^3$. Give the prime factorization of n^2 and n^3. (*Hint:* Do not work too hard.)

11. Determine whether each of these is a prime.

    a. 667   **b.** 289   **c.** 3501

    d. 47×61 **e.** 4319   **f.** 29^3

12. The numbers 2 and 3 are consecutive whole numbers, each of which is a prime. Is there another pair of consecutive whole numbers, each of which is a prime? If there is, find such a pair; if not, explain why.

13. Test each of these numbers for divisibility by 2, 3, 4, 5, 6, 8, 9, 10, 12, 15, and 18.

    a. 540   **b.** 150   **c.** 145   **d.** 369   **e.** 840

14. Which of these numbers are prime? For those not prime, give the prime factorization.

    a. 29×23 **b.** 5992   **c.** 127   **d.** 121

    e. 31^2 **f.** 1247   **g.** 3816

15. Here is an interesting conjecture that mathematicians are uncertain about even though it has been studied for more than 100 years: Every even number greater than 2 can be written as the sum of two primes (Goldbach's conjecture). Test the conjecture for the even numbers through 36.

16. Devise a way of checking to see whether or not a number is divisible by 24. Test your method on 36; on 120.

17. Are every two different primes relatively prime? Explain.

18. Which pairs of numbers are relatively prime?

    a. 2, 5   **b.** 2, 4   **c.** 2, 6   **d.** 2, 7   **e.** 2, 8   **f.** 2, 9

    g. 8, 9   **h.** 8, 12   **i.** 3, 8   **j.** 40, 42   **k.** 121, 22   **l.** 39, 169

19. Give an example of two 3-digit nonprime numbers that are relatively prime.

20. If possible, give a composite number that is relatively prime to 22.

21. a. Find $128 + 494 + 381$ and check your answer by casting out nines.

  b. Compute 23×45 and check your answer by casting out nines.

22. A result in number theory states that the product of any n consecutive positive integers is divisible by the product of the first n positive integers. For example, $5 \times 6 \times 7 \times 8 = 1680$. The theorem asserts that 1680 is divisible by $1 \times 2 \times 3 \times 4$, or 24. Verify that 1680 is divisible by 24, using divisibility rules.

Compute the product of another 4 consecutive positive integers and check to see if the product is divisible by 24.

Demonstrate this theorem for some example you choose for $n = 5$.

23. A result in number theory states that if p is a prime number and n is a positive integer, then $n^p - n$ is divisible by p. Demonstrate this for 3 cases where you choose n and p.

24. a. "I am a 3-digit number.

  I am not a multiple of 2.

  7 is not one of my factors, but 5 is.

  I am less than 125.

  Who am I?"

  b. Make up a "Who am I?" involving number theory vocabulary and ideas.

11.4 | Greatest Common Factor, Least Common Multiple

As you would suspect about an old area of mathematics like number theory, there are entire books on the subject, exploring many different and advanced areas. So the work with number theory in the elementary school curriculum touches on only a small part of number theory. Elementary school number theory usually comes up right before work with fractions. Simplifying fractions and finding common denominators for adding and subtracting fractions use number theory ideas. The same ideas carry over to algebraic fractions, so even though fraction calculators might be available, the reasoning behind the work with regular fractions will continue to be important.

Recall from Chapter 6 that a basic result about fractions is that $1 \times \frac{a}{b} = \frac{a}{b}$. The number 1 can be written as $\frac{n}{n}$, where n is any nonzero number. So, $\frac{n}{n} \cdot \frac{a}{b} = \frac{na}{nb}$. Starting with $\frac{a}{b}$, this allows one to generate any number of fractions equal to $\frac{a}{b}$ simply by making different choices for n. Read "backwards," however, $\frac{na}{nb} = \frac{a}{b}$, and the result shows that one can write a simpler fraction for a given fraction by finding a common factor of the numerator and denominator, and "canceling it out," as you might have said in earlier work.

For example, because 3 is a common factor of 84 and 162, $\frac{84}{162} = \frac{3\cdot28}{3\cdot54}$, so $\frac{84}{162} = \frac{28}{54}$, an equivalent but simpler fraction. But you should notice that $\frac{28}{54}$ can be simplified further, because 2 is a common factor of 28 and 54: $\frac{28}{54} = \frac{14}{27}$. Because 14 and 27 have only 1 as a common factor (they are "relatively prime"), $\frac{14}{27}$ is the simplest form for $\frac{84}{162}$. If you can find the greatest common factor (GCF, also called the greatest common divisor), of the numerator and denominator (which is 6), then you can get the simplest fraction in one step: $\frac{84}{162} = \frac{6\cdot14}{6\cdot27} = \frac{14}{27}$.

For reasonably small pairs of numbers, you can often "see" the greatest common factor by inspection. A systematic way would involve listing all the factors of each number and then picking out the greatest common factor.

Set of factors of 84 = {1, 2, 3, 4, 6, 7, 12, 14, 21, 28, 42, 84}

Set of factors of 162 = {1, 2, 3, 6, 9, 18, 27, 54, 81, 162}

A Venn diagram is one way of illustrating the *common* factors, 1, 2, 3, and 6.

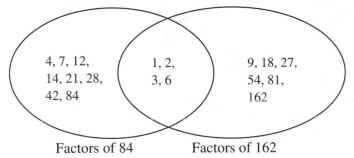

Factors of 84   Factors of 162

The region they share provides common factors; 1, 2, 3, and 6, and so 6 is the GCF of 84 and 162.

Sometimes a more efficient method would be to examine the factors of the smaller number to see which are also factors of the larger number. Usually you start with the larger factors because you are looking for the greatest common factor. For 84, you would try 84, 42, etc., working either from the complete list or hoping not to overlook a larger common factor than any you find.

Activity 13   GCFs

Find the prime factorizations of 84 and 162. What do they share in common?

Knowing how to find the least common multiple of fraction denominators can make the adding or subtracting of fractions easier. As you may recall, to find the sum of fractions like $\frac{9}{16}$ and $\frac{7}{12}$, the usual algorithm or method calls for replacing the given fractions with fractions that have the same denominators but are equal to the original fractions ("equivalent fractions with a common denominator" might be the language used). One can always multiply the numerator and denominator of each fraction by the other denominator ($\frac{9 \cdot 12}{16 \cdot 12}$ and $\frac{16 \cdot 7}{16 \cdot 12}$, or $\frac{108}{192}$ and $\frac{112}{192}$) but usually those new fractions do not lead to the simplest arithmetic. Finding the least common denominator is the usual approach, just to keep the numbers smaller. This least common denominator is just the least common positive multiple of the denominators of the fractions involved.

As with the greatest common factor, finding the least common multiple can be approached in several ways. One way, perhaps best when the idea is new, is to list all the common multiples of each number until a common one (not 0) is found. (0 is literally the least common multiple of every two whole numbers, but it is not useful in situations where least common multiples arise, as with fractions.)

Set of multiples of 16 = {0, 16, 32, 48, 64, 80, 96, 112, 128, . . .}

Set of multiples of 12 = {0, 12, 24, 36, 48, 60, 72, 84, 96, 108, . . .}

A Venn diagram can also be used to illustrate the multiples:

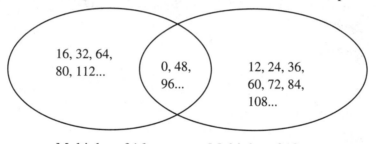

Because 48 is the least common nonzero multiple of 16 and 12, 48 would be the smallest number that could serve as a common denominator in adding, for example,

$$\frac{9}{16} + \frac{7}{12} = \frac{9 \cdot 3}{16 \cdot 3} + \frac{7 \cdot 4}{12 \cdot 4} \text{, or } \frac{27}{48} + \frac{28}{48} = \frac{55}{48} \, .$$

The sum is not always in simplest form, but if you are calculating by hand, the fractions with the least common multiple (LCM) as denominator offer the simpler arithmetic with the smaller numbers.

Activity 14   Using LCMs and GCFs

1.   What is the GCF of 68 and 102?

2.   Simplify $\frac{68}{102}$.

3.   What is the LCM of 68 and 102?

4.   What is $\frac{5}{68} + \frac{13}{102}$?

There are other methods for finding least common multiples and greatest common factors. A useful one to use with larger numbers involves their prime factorizations. Suppose that $m = 2^3 \cdot 5^2 \cdot 29 \cdot 31^2$ and $n = 2 \cdot 5^2 \cdot 31 \cdot 83$, and we need the least common multiple of m and n. First, we know this new number must be a multiple of m and of n. Any (nonzero) multiple of m will involve all of $2^3 \cdot 5^2 \cdot 29 \cdot 31^2$; similarly, any (nonzero) multiple of n will involve all of $2 \cdot 5^2 \cdot 31 \cdot 83$. Any **common** multiple of m and n, then, must involve enough 2s, 5s, 29s, 31s, and 83s to be a multiple of each of m and n. For the **least common multiple**, what is the fewest 2-factors, 5-factors, etc., so that the new number takes into account these dual needs? With $m = 2^3 \cdot 5^2 \cdot 29 \cdot 31^2$ and $n = 2 \cdot 5^2 \cdot 31 \cdot 83$, for starters the fewest possible 2-factors is 3, giving 2^3; the fewest 5-factors is 2, giving 5^2. Continuing, we get the least common multiple of m and $n = 2^3 \cdot 5^2 \cdot 29 \cdot 31^2 \cdot 83$. In finding the least common multiple this way, think "multiple" first, then "common multiple," and finally "least common multiple."

With this reasoning, the LCM of 72 and 108 is the LCM of $2^3 \times 3^2$ and $2^2 \times 3^3$. All common multiples of $2^3 \times 3^2$ and $2^2 \times 3^3$ must have *at least* three 2s and three 3s. Thus the least one is $2^3 \times 3^3$; $8 \times 27 = 216$ is the LCM.

> ***THINK ABOUT . . .***
>
> Why must all common multiples of $2^3 \times 3^2$ and $2^2 \times 3^3$ have *at least* three 2s and three 3s? Name some common multiples that satisfy this condition. Why must all common factors of $2^3 \times 3^2$ and $2^2 \times 3^3$ have *at most* three 2s and two 3s? Name some common factors that satisfy this condition.

EXAMPLE 2

Let $n = 72$ and $m = 63$. Now, $n = 2^3 \times 3^2$ and $m = 3^2 \times 7$. We could also say $n = 2^3 \times 3^2 \times 7^0$ and $m = 2^0 \times 3^2 \times 7^1$ because $7^0 = 1$ and $7 = 7^1$. Common multiples of n and m must have *at least* three 2s, two 3s, and one 7. One common multiple would be $2^3 \times 3^4 \times 7^1$, another would be $2^5 \times 7^2 \times 3^4 \times 5^2 \times 13^2$. There are an infinite number of common multiples of 72 and 63. The *least* one is the number which has each of three 2s, two 3s, one 7, and no more. That is $2^3 \times 3^2 \times 7$, or 504.

Activity 15   GCF Analysis

Do an analysis similar to the one for finding the LCM of $m = 2^3 \cdot 5^2 \cdot 29 \cdot 31^2$ and $n = 2 \cdot 5^2 \cdot 31 \cdot 83$ to find the greatest common factor of m and n. That is, what numbers are common factors of both m and n? You know that, for example, 2 is a common factor. So is 5. So is 5^2. Are there other common factors? What is the *greatest common* factor?

This analysis shows how prime factorizations can be used to find both LCMs and GCFs of two (or more) whole numbers. Consider another example, again using 72 and 63.

EXAMPLE 3

Use $72 = 2^3 \times 3^2 \times 7^0$ and $63 = 2^0 \times 3^2 \times 7^1$ again. Now some common factors would be 3, or 3^2. There are a finite number of common factors. To find the *greatest* common factor, consider the 2, the 3, and the 7, and the *least* power for which each appears: 2^0, 3^2 and 7^0 to allow the number to be a factor of both 72 and 84. So the GCF is $2^0 \times 3^2 \times 7^0$, but 2^0 and 7^0 are both just 1. Thus the GCF is $2^0 \times 3^2 \times 7^0$, or just 3^2, so 9 is the GCF.

> *THINK ABOUT . . .*
> What is the GCF of 72 and 108? Of 260 and 650?

Thus, using prime factorizations of numbers leads to easy ways of finding both the LCM and the GCF.

Activity 16   Once Again . . . Using LCMs and GCFs

1.   What is the GCF of 260 and 650; of 260 and 186; of 186 and 650?

2.   Simplify $\frac{260}{650}$, $\frac{260}{186}$, and $\frac{186}{650}$

3.   What is the LCM of 260 and 650? Of 260, 650, and 130?

4.   What is $\frac{5}{650} + \frac{13}{260}$?

The same method of finding LCM and GCF can be applied when renaming algebraic fractions. Given the factorizations of algebraic expressions, you can calculate the LCM and GCF.

Activity 17   GCF and LCM in Algebra

1.   Find the GCF and LCM of x^2y and y^2x.

2.   Find the GCF and the LCM of $(x - 2)(x + 2)$ and $(x - 2)^2$.

3.   Make up an algebraic problem of your own for others to solve.

The following problem involves many ideas from all four sections of this chapter. It is a puzzle credited to Brahmagupta (born 598 A.D.).

Activity 18   An Ancient Puzzle

♦ An old woman goes to market and a horse steps on her basket and breaks all her eggs. The rider offered to pay her for the damages and asks her how many eggs she had bought. She does not remember the exact number, but when she had taken them out two at a time, there was one egg left. The same happened when she picked out three, four, five, and six at a time, but when she took seven at a time they came out even. What is the smallest number of eggs she could have had? ◆

(*Hints:* What are common multiples of 2, 3, 4, 5, and 6? Would any of those numbers plus 1 satisfy all the conditions?)

TAKE-AWAY MESSAGE . . . In this section we returned to factors and multiples to examine ways of finding the greatest common factor (GCF) and the least common multiple (LCM) of two or more whole numbers or of two or more algebraic expressions. One way of finding the GCF was by listing common factors and taking the greatest. One way to find the LCM was to list common multiples and taking the least. Another was to use the prime factorizations of the numbers. The LCM of two (or more) numbers would be expressed by the product of each of the prime factors to the greatest power in which they exist in the original numbers. The GCF would be expressed by the product of each of the common prime factors to the least power in which they exist in the original numbers. ◆

Learning Exercises for Section 11.4

1. List four factors of each of the following numbers:
    a. 2^3 b. 27×49 c. 12   d. 15
    e. 108   f. 125   g. 72

2. List four nonzero multiples of each of the following. You may leave them in factored form.
    a. 8   b. 27×49 c. $2^2 \times 3$ d. 15
    e. 108   f. 125   g. 72

3. As you know, the Earth takes 365 "earth" days, that is, 1 year, to make one revolution around our sun. It takes Saturn about 30 earth years to make one revolution around the sun. Jupiter takes 12 earth years to do so, and Mars about 2 earth years. If Earth, Saturn, Jupiter, and Mars are aligned when they begin, in approximately how many years does it take all four planets to be aligned again?

4. You have probably noticed that when you buy hot dogs and hot dog buns, the packages do not contain the same quantities. Make up a story problem that gives quantities of hot dogs in a package and quantities of hot dog buns in a package and asks, "How many packages of each do you buy so that there are the same number of hot dogs as hot dog buns?" Would the solution involve LCM or GCF? Why?

5. For each of the following groups of numbers, find the least common (nonzero) multiple. You may leave your answers in factored form or write them out.
    a. 72 and 108   b. 144 and 150   c. 72 and 90
    d. 72 and 144   e. 144 and 567   f. 90 and 567
    g. 108 and 90   h. 150 and 350   i. 150, 35, and 270

6. For each of the following groups of numbers, find the greatest common factor. You may leave your answers in factored form or write them out.

   a. 72 and 108   **b.** 144 and 150   **c.** 72 and 90

   d. 72 and 144   **e.** 144 and 567   **f.** 90 and 567

   g. 108 and 90   **h.** 150 and 350   **i.** 150, 350, and 270

7. Give three (nonzero) multiples of each of the following (leave them in factored form).

   a. $2^3 \cdot 3$ **b.** $2^3 \cdot 7^3$ **c.** $3^2 \cdot 7^3 \cdot 11^5 \cdot 19^2$

8. In each part, find the least common (nonzero) multiple of the numbers given. Then find the greatest common factor for each part.

   a. $m = 5^2 \cdot 7^3,\ n = 5 \cdot 13^2$

   b. $m = 37^4 \cdot 47^5 \cdot 67^6,\ n = 37^6 \cdot 47^5 \cdot 71$

   c. $m = 7^2 \cdot 26,\ n = 2^2 \cdot 11 \cdot 17$

   d. $m = 10125,\ n = 26730$

   e. $m = 2^3 \cdot 7^2,\ n = 2 \cdot 5^3 \cdot 7,\ p = 3^2 \cdot 5 \cdot 7$

   f. $m = 6x^2y^5z^{12},\ n = 10xy^6z^4$

9. 0 is a common multiple of 16 and 12. Why is the least common multiple defined as the smallest nonzero value?

10. Jogger A can run laps at the rate of 90 seconds per lap. Jogger B can run laps on the same track at the rate of 2 minutes per lap. If they start at the same place and time, and run in the same direction, how long (in time) will it be before they are at the starting place again, at the same time?

11. You cut a yellow cake into 6 pieces, and a chocolate cake of the same size into 8 pieces. Then you find out that you were supposed to cut both cakes into the same (unspecified) number of pieces! As a number theory student, what do you do?

12. A machine has two meshing gears. One gear has 12 teeth and another gear has 30 teeth. After how many rotations are both gears back to their original position?

13. Paper plates are sold in packages of 25. Paper bowls are sold in packages of 40. Plastic spoons are sold in packages of 20. How many packages of each do you need to buy to have the same number of plates, bowls, and spoons?

14. A paint manufacturer produces base in 25-gallon drums and color in 10-gallon drums. A company wants to order stock for a dark blue paint mixture for which one gallon of color requires one gallon of base. How many of each should they order so that the mix comes out without any unused base or color left unmixed?

15. As in Exercise 14, a paint manufacturer produces base in 25-gallon drums and color in 10-gallon drums. A company wants to order stock for a dark blue paint mixture for which one gallon of color requires four gallons of base. How many of each should they order so that the mix comes out without any unused base or color left unmixed?

16. The principal says that the sixth graders are raising money for a field trip by selling caps with the school logo. He said that last week they raised $414 and the week before they raised $543. You were going to ask what price they were

selling for but realized you could figure out the price from what he had just told you. What was the likely selling price of the caps?

17. The principal says the seventh graders raised money for a field trip to Washington, D.C., by washing cars for a fixed price the past three weekends. He said that last weekend they raised $198 and two weekends ago they raised $252. Three weekends ago they raised $385. What was the price of the car wash?

18. You want to explore the concept of scale factor with your students in an activity in which they will create a small-scale earth and sun to show their relative sizes. The sun is approximately 1,400,000 km in diameter and the earth is approximately 12,800 km in diameter. Because you want them to initially use only whole numbers, find the GCF to know what the scale factor should be.

19. You want to explore the concept of scale factor with your students. You will work with your students to draw a scale drawing of your classroom. Your classroom has dimensions 216 inches by 282 inches. If you want them to use the smallest whole numbers possible, what should be the scale factor?

20. Find several values of m and n such that $27^m = 9^n$.

21. Write the simplest form for each fraction, using the greatest common factor:

   a. $\dfrac{135}{150}$ b. $\dfrac{36}{48}$ c. $\dfrac{84}{100}$

   d. $\dfrac{180}{160}$ e. $\dfrac{2^3 \cdot 3^5}{2^4 \cdot 3^3}$ f. $\dfrac{x^2 y^3}{x^3 y}$

22. Use the phrase "relatively prime" to describe your final answers to parts a, b, c, and d in Exercise 21.

23. Use the least common multiple in calculating these sums and differences:

   a. $\dfrac{7}{24} + \dfrac{11}{18}$ b. $\dfrac{13}{8} - \dfrac{5}{4}$ c. $\dfrac{14}{15} + \dfrac{7}{10} - \dfrac{1}{4}$

   d. $\dfrac{x}{y^2} + \dfrac{2x^2}{x^2 y}$ e. $\dfrac{6.3 \times 10^4}{2 \times 10^2} + \dfrac{7.2 \times 10^5}{3 \times 10^3}$

24. For 12 and 16, the greatest common factor is 4 and the least common multiple is 48. Compare 12×16 and 4×48. Try other pairs of numbers to see whether their greatest common factor and least common multiple are related the same way.

25. If your calculator allows you to enter and simplify fractions, use it to find simpler, and eventually the simplest, fractions for the following. (If you do not have a calculator, try them with paper and pencil.)

   a. $\dfrac{1280}{1440}$ b. $\dfrac{8530}{47,250}$ c. $\dfrac{2720}{10,000}$

26. Notice that the number 3 is a common factor of 84 and 72 and 3 is also a factor of $84 - 72 = 12$.

   a. Conjecture: If x is a common factor of m and n, then x is also a factor of ___.

   b. Test the conjecture by considering at least four examples of m and n.

   c. Find simpler names for $\frac{147}{150}$, $\frac{210}{216}$, and $\frac{111}{126}$, with help from part (a).

   d. Determine whether this conjecture is relevant to $\frac{81}{86}$, or $\frac{48}{55}$, or $\frac{112}{127}$. Explain.

27. Practice: Write the following fractions in simplest form.

   a. $\frac{15}{35}$ **b.** $\frac{28}{54}$ **c.** $\frac{150}{350}$ **d.** $\frac{12}{144}$ **e.** $\frac{150}{567}$

   f. $\frac{15}{40}$ **g.** $\frac{64}{512}$ **h.** $\frac{21}{49}$ **i.** $\frac{2223}{4536}$

28. Practice: Use the least common multiple of the denominators to calculate these sums and differences. For extra practice, also write the answer in simplified form.

   a. $\frac{39}{144} + \frac{35}{108}$ **b.** $\frac{25}{72} + \frac{81}{567}$ **c.** $\frac{36}{108} + \frac{41}{72}$

   d. $\frac{15}{39} + \frac{110}{169}$ **e.** $\frac{169}{500} + \frac{169}{650}$ **f.** $\frac{126}{504} + \frac{98}{770}$

29. As a third-grade teacher, you are designing a measurement lesson. You decide to start with a measuring lesson using nonstandard units. You create a measuring tool (a new "ruler") that will allow your students to measure classroom items and have the measure in whole units. The desks in your classroom are 27 inches wide and 36 inches long. What is the largest unit you can create that will allow this desk to be measured in whole units?

30. Go to the National Library of Virtual Manipulatives on the internet by accessing http://nlvm.usu.edu/en/nav/index.html, then clicking on **Virtual Library** at the top of the page, then click on **Numbers and Operations**, and scroll down to **Factor Tree** and open it. Click on **One** tree at the bottom of the page. Practice finding factors of numbers (chosen by the program). Then click on **Two** trees. At least five times, find the factors of two numbers provided by the program, then drag the factors into the appropriate area of the Venn diagram provided. Use this information to find the GCF and the LCM of the two numbers.

11.5 Issues for Learning: Understanding the Unique Factorization Theorem

Whole numbers can be represented in a variety of ways. Different forms of a number can provide different information about the number. For example, suppose one is asked: What are the factors of 1334? Obviously 2 is a factor, and if 1334 is divided by 2, one finds that $1334 = 2 \times 667$, so both 2 and 667 are factors. Are there more? Suppose one also knows that 23 is a divisor of 667. Can all the factors be listed now?

Suppose, again, that a number is represented as $5^2 \times 31 \times 43$. Now what are the factors? Is 11 a factor? How about 3?

Answers to these questions can tell a great deal about your understanding of prime numbers as building blocks of whole numbers. Once a number is represented as a product of prime numbers, it is quite easy to find factors and multiples of the number. You can, from this information, find all the prime factors, and in fact, all the factors of the number. This method is possible because the prime factorization of any number is unique. As you know, this is sometimes called the Fundamental Theorem of Arithmetic and other times referred to as the Unique Factorization Theorem. The theorem seems simple enough to understand, but research shows that many students (even at college level) have difficulty applying this theorem.

Consider this example [ii,iii] from one research study.

Patty was asked whether $3^3 \times 5^2 \times 7$ is divisible by 7 or 5. Patty said yes, because these factors were clearly visible. When asked whether 11 was a factor, she multiplied the given factors and obtained 4725. She said she would divide 4725 by 11 to find out whether or not 11 is a factor. But by the prime factorization theorem, 11 cannot be a factor because it is prime and does not appear in the prime factorization. The researchers concluded that Patty did not really understand or believe that the prime factorization was unique because she thought that there might be another factorization with 11 as a factor.

Why did Patty have this problem? Perhaps she saw different factorizations with composite factors and generalized that the prime factorization is just one possible factorization and in another, 11 might be a factor. For example, $3^3 \times 5^2 \times 7$ could be written as $3 \times 5^2 \times 7 \times 9$ or as $3^2 \times 5 \times 7 \times 15$. But in these cases, the factorizations are not prime factorizations.

> TAKE-AWAY MESSAGE . . . Research has shown that understanding the unique factorization theorem is more complex than it might first seem. ♦

Learning Exercises for Section 11.5

Here are some other questions that were asked of students in this study. Each of them deals with prime factorization. Try them yourself, and discuss what kinds of difficulties students might have if they do not understand that a prime factorization of a number is unique.

1. $k = 16,199 = 97 \times 167$ where 97 and 167 are both primes. Decide whether k can be divided by 5; by 11, by 17.

2. $a = 153 = 3^2 \times 17$. Is 51 a factor of a? How do you know?

3. $a = 153 = 3^2 \times 17$ and $b = 3^2 \times 19$. Which number do you think has more factors, a or b? Why?

11.6 | Check Yourself

This chapter focused on number theory, one of the oldest fields of mathematics and used today in cryptography.

Many of the ideas in this chapter center on the important result appropriately called the fundamental theorem of arithmetic—that the prime factorization of a number is unique. Factoring numbers, finding and using greatest common factors and least common multiples, and using divisibility rules, all relate to the unique factorization theorem.

You should be able to work problems like those assigned and to meet the following objectives.

1. Use the terms even, odd, factor, multiple, prime, and composite correctly, and recognize statements using these terms as true or false, with reasons for your decisions.

2. Provide a reason for why the number 1 is considered to be neither prime nor composite.

3. Use a sieve method, such as the Sieve of Eratosthenes, to find prime numbers less than a given number *n*.

4. State the unique factorization theorem, also called the fundamental theorem of arithmetic.

5. Use this theorem to determine whether or not a number is a factor of another number when both numbers are in factored form.

6. State and use divisibility rules for 2, 3, 4, 5, 6, 9, 10, 12, 15, 18.

7. Find the prime factorization of a number, perhaps using a factor tree.

8. Explain why the square root test provides a way to know which prime numbers (at most) need to be tested when determining whether or not a number is prime.

9. Determine whether a number (of a reasonable size) is prime or composite.

10. Determine the number of factors of a number from its prime factorization form.

11. Find common factors of sets of numbers; find common multiples of sets of numbers.

12. Find the greatest common factor and least common multiple of sets of numbers.

13. Discuss common errors made in using the unique factorization theorem.

REFERENCES FOR CHAPTER 11

[i] Clay Mathematics Institute: http://www.claymath.org/posters/primes/ April 12, 2005.

[ii] Zazkis, R., & Campbell, S. (1996). Prime decomposition: Understanding uniqueness. *Journal of Mathematical Behavior, 15,* 207–218.

[iii] Zazkis, R., & Liljedahl, P. (2004). Understanding primes: the role of representation. *Journal for Research in Mathematics Education, 35,* 164–186.

Part II

Reasoning About Algebra and Change

Your experience with algebra in school likely was in one or two courses devoted to the subject. So you may be surprised to learn that algebra is increasingly recognized as a continuing topic throughout the curriculum, with ideas from algebra occurring as early as the first grade and with an increased use of symbols and equations in the K–6 mathematics curriculum.

Algebra is more than manipulating numbers and letters. The work in this part of *Reconceptualizing Mathematics* first centers on a quantitative approach to algebra in Chapter 12, with considerable interplay with graphs on coordinate systems, and then in Chapter 13 focuses on describing change, most often in a context of motion and with slope as an exemplar of describing change. As one quantity changes or varies, a related quantity may also change or vary. Algebra and graphs allow you to examine some simple types of change. Algebra as a "language" is then emphasized in Chapter 14, with attention to several contexts and including some consideration to the view of algebra as a generalization of arithmetic. Mathematics is occasionally described as the science of patterns, and much work with patterns is possible in the elementary school, so algebra as a means of representing patterns gets attention particularly in Chapter 15 and throughout this text. Chapter 15 also introduces the mathematically important notion of *function* and illustrates some of its many uses. Various issues for learning aspects of algebra are treated throughout.

Chapter 12

A Quantitative Approach to Algebra and Graphing

Words like *quantity* and *value* are a part of everyday language, but in mathematics giving careful meanings to these words yields important advantages. How quantities are related is the focus of this chapter.

12.1 | Quantities and Their Relationships

Algebraic symbols, such as x, y, and n, are typically introduced in elementary schools. Rather than focusing on these symbols, this chapter embodies an alternative approach to algebra (and to the related topic of graphing) called a **quantitative approach**, which we will describe in detail in this section.

Discussion 1   When I Was Younger . . .

What do you remember about algebra from your elementary school days? From your junior high or high school days?

Traditional instruction in algebra focuses on the development of skills in manipulating algebraic symbols according to rules. For example, elementary and middle school students are instructed in techniques for evaluating expressions, solving equations, and combining like terms. These skills are extended later to include, for example, multiplying binomials, factoring trinomials, and simplifying algebraic expressions. A letter like x can be viewed as an unknown, when solving an equation like $2x + 7 = 21$, or as representing a variable quantity, as in $y = x + 15$.

We start our discussion of a quantitative approach to algebra by repeating some important terms from Chapter 1.

A **quantity** is any measurable or countable aspect of any object, event, or idea.

For example, if we take a person as the object, then measurable aspects or quantities related to that person include height, weight, shoe size, and age.

> The **value of a quantity** is the measure or count of the quantity, and the value involves a number and a unit. For example, height is a quantity, and 5 ft 6 in. is a value of that quantity.

A quantity is not the same as a number. In fact, one can think of a quantity without knowing its value. We can speak of a person's weight without knowing the actual number of pounds he or she weighs.

Two quantities are related when each value of one quantity corresponds to a value or values of another quantity. For example, the number of calories consumed while eating M&M's is related to the number of M&M's eaten. These two quantities are related predictably. As the number of M&M's eaten varies, the number of calories consumed varies in a systematic way. In contrast, a car's fuel efficiency (miles per gallon) is not related predictably to the distance traveled, because traveling 30 miles in town often gives a different fuel efficiency from that obtained when traveling 30 miles on the freeway.

A quantitative approach to algebra starts by examining how quantities are related in situations. Algebra is then used as a *language* to describe these quantitative *relationships*. Graphs are also used to represent or describe quantitative relationships in a pictorial way to examine changes in the quantities. Thus, a quantitative approach can connect the topics of graphing, algebra, and change.

Activity 1 below illustrates how it is possible to begin algebraic instruction by examining quantitative relationships *before* any symbols, such as x's, y's, or z's, are introduced. After you practice identifying quantitative relationships in this section, you will use graphs and algebra later to represent quantitative relationships. Many curricular projects in mathematics education embrace a similar quantitative approach to algebra and graphs, where the ideas use variable quantities, or *variables*, in particular contexts to lead to algebraic and graphical work and to study changes in the quantities.

Activity 1　　Identifying Quantitative Relationships

1. Determine whether the pairs of quantities below are related to each other. If so, explain whether the value of the quantity given on the right increases or decreases as the value of the corresponding quantity on the left increases.

a.	Number of minutes that have passed while driving a car at 65 mph	Amount of fuel left in the gas tank
b.	Number of minutes that have passed while driving a car at 65 mph	Amount of fuel you have used
c.	Length of one side of an equilateral triangle	Perimeter of the triangle

d.	Perimeter of a rectangle	Area of the rectangle
e.	Number of potato chips eaten	Number of calories consumed
f.	Amount of money inserted into a candy vending machine	Number of candy bars that you receive

2. For each quantity, name another quantity that is related to it.

   a. The amount of money you make from selling lemonade

   b. The amount of fuel you use on a car trip

   c. The total amount of sales tax that you have to pay for a purchase

3. The following story was written by an elementary school student to illustrate a situation in which quantities are related:

   ◆ A girl has a bag of flour. Her dog bites a hole in it. The more she walks, the more flour comes out.   ◆

   a. Name two quantities in this situation that are related. How are they related? That is, do both quantities increase, or does one quantity decrease while the other increases?

   b. Now name a different pair of related quantities in the situation. How are they related?

Some people might think that a quantitative approach to algebra differs from a traditional numerical approach primarily because the quantitative approach uses real-world situations. However, this distinction is not the major difference. Both approaches can use real-world situations, but they treat the situations differently. Consider a situation in which a car is traveling at a speed of 55 miles per hour. In a numerical approach to algebra, the formula $d = rt$ can be given (where d = distance traveled in miles; r = rate or speed in mph; and t = time traveled in hours), and students are asked to find either the distance traveled if a car travels for 2.5 hours at 55 mph or the time the car takes to travel 300 miles. A numerical approach emphasizes solving for an unknown value by substituting known values for some of the algebraic symbols.

Although solving for an unknown may be part of a quantitative approach to algebra, a quantitative approach also explores how quantities like distance and time are related. For example, changes in the amount of time that has passed can produce changes in the distance traveled. Furthermore, this relationship is systematic (that is, exhibits a pattern): If you travel 1 hour at an average speed of 55 miles per hour, you go 55 miles. If you travel 5 hours, which is 5 times as long, you will go 5 times as far, or 275 miles (assuming an average speed of 55 mph). If you travel 20 minutes, which is one-third the original time, you will travel one third the distance, or approximately 18 miles.

Teaching arithmetic or algebra with a quantitative approach means helping your students get a feeling for how quantities are related. You might explore quantitative relationships without even referring to numbers. For example, Learning Exercise 4 in this section illustrates a rich mathematical activity (one appropriate for upper elementary students) in which the challenge is to figure out which quantities are related (without determining a specific numerical relationship).

> TAKE-AWAY MESSAGE . . . Rather than focusing on letters like *x* and *y*, a quantitative approach focuses on the specific quantities involved and how they are related. An understanding of these quantities in a given situation can help students use numbers together with letters like *x* and *y* to describe and relate parts of the situation. ♦

Learning Exercises for Section 12.1

1. Elementary school students wrote the following stories. For each situation, write a sentence that shows how two quantities in the situation are related. It is possible that you can describe several relationships in each situation.

   EXAMPLE   A large block of ice is in a tub in the sun. The ice melts 3 centiliters a minute.

   SOLUTION   Here are two possible sentences: The amount of ice decreases as the number of minutes that pass increases. As the number of minutes increases, the amount of water in the tub increases.

   a. An airplane is flying miles high over Siberia, hundreds of miles from any help. Suddenly, the fuel tank ruptures and fuel starts steadily leaking out.

   b. A motor home has a water tank that holds a large amount of water. Each shower takes 5 gallons of water.

   c. You have $5 and you buy candy bars at 50¢ each.

   d. A class starts off with 16 students. Two students stop coming every week.

2. a. Write your own story similar to those that the students wrote in Learning Exercise 1.

   b. Write a sentence that shows how two quantities in the situation in part (a) are related. There may be several quantitative relationships that you can describe.

3. Determine whether the following pairs of quantities are related to one another. If they are, explain whether the value of the second quantity increases or decreases as the value of the first quantity increases. (*Problem-solving tip*: Try some examples and see what happens.)

   a. The perimeter of a square and the area of the square

   b. The base of a triangle and the area of the triangle

   c. The value of the numerator in a fraction (when the denominator stays the same) and the value of the fraction

   d. The value of the denominator in a fraction (when the numerator stays the same) and the value of the fraction

4. A pendulum gives a good place to look for relationships. You will conduct three experiments to determine what quantities affect the number of times a pendulum swings in a certain amount of time. You will need the following materials: string; several heavy objects like washers, nuts, bolts, screws, or fishing sinkers; tape; and a watch with a second hand.

   a. Make a pendulum by tying a heavy object (such as a washer) at the end of a string (Figure 1). Measure the number of swings a pendulum makes in 10 seconds. One swing is the distance the washer travels from the far right to the far left.

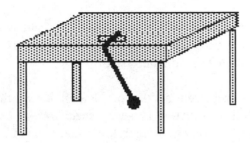

Figure 1. Making a Pendulum from String and a Weight

   b. Conduct an experiment to see if the weight of the pendulum bob (the object at the end of the string) affects the number of times the pendulum swings in 10 seconds. You will need to decide how to conduct the experiment. Then collect and record your data in a table. Finally, write a sentence expressing your conclusion.

   c. Conduct an experiment to scc if the length of the string affects the number of times the pendulum swings in 10 seconds. Decide how to conduct the experiment. Then collect and record your data in a table. Finally, write a sentence expressing your conclusion.

   d. Conduct an experiment to see if letting the pendulum go from different positions affects the number of times a pendulum swings in 10 seconds (see Figure 2). Again, decide how to conduct the experiment, collect and record data, and write a sentence expressing your conclusion.

Figure 2. Letting a Pendulum Start from Different Positions

12.2 Using Graphs and Algebraic Symbols to Show Quantitative Relationships

In the previous section, you learned about quantities that are related to one another, and you described those relationships in words. In this section you will learn to describe relationships between quantities using two additional representations: graphs and algebraic equations.

THINK ABOUT...

What do you remember about algebraic equations and graphs on coordinate systems? How are equations and graphs connected? What does the notation (4, 2) mean in a coordinate system?

First, we'll use a graph to represent a situation. Sometimes we think of a graph as a picture. However, a graph as a picture is a very specialized type of picture. Unlike paintings or even diagrams, graphs in algebra are constructed according to certain conventions. For example, if there are two variables, each is represented on a separate number line scale, called an **axis**, and labeled to make clear the quantity and the scale unit; the two number lines, or **axes**, are most often placed at a right angle with their zero points coinciding; and the scale units on each axis are uniformly spaced. Such axes give a **coordinate system**. Because of these conventions, graphs reveal particular information that a verbal description of a relationship may not. At the same time, a graph may hide or downplay other information that is highlighted by other representations, such as words or algebraic equations.

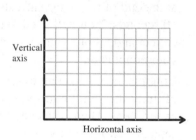

Activity 2   A Picture is Worth a Thousand Words

Consider the following situation.

♦ A block of ice sits in a tub in the sun. The block of ice consists of 16 centiliters of water that have been frozen. The block of ice melts at a rate of 3 centiliters a minute. ♦

1. Describe in words how these two quantities are related: the size of the block of ice and time.

2. Construct a set of axes and plot points to show the relationship between the amount of ice in the block of ice and the number of minutes that have passed. Be sure to label each axis with the appropriate quantity.

Discussion 2   Whose Graph, If Any, Is Best?

1. On the board, put every graph from Activity 2 that differs from others in some way. Then compare them. Are there any graphs that do not make sense? If so, why not? Are there any pairs of graphs that look different from each other but that both make sense? Does there have to be only one correct graph? Explain.

2. Does it matter which quantity is represented on the horizontal axis? (*Hint:* Try graphing the relationship twice, switching the quantities that are represented on the horizontal axis, and then comparing the two graphs. What are the advantages and disadvantages of each graph?)

3. How does each graph indicate that one quantity is increasing while the other is decreasing?

4. Why does it make sense to connect the points in this graph? (*Hint:* Does it make sense to ask how much ice is left after 2.5 minutes?)

Although different choices for what to show on each axis can generate different-looking graphs, they *literally* contain the same information. But *visually* there are advantages in following some conventions. For example, having the scales increase as one goes up or to the right is extremely common. When time is involved, placing time on the horizontal axis allows you to see whether the other variable quantity increases or decreases as time goes on.

Activity 3   Using Algebraic Symbols to Represent Quantitative Relationships

Consider this modification of the melting ice block situation:

> ◆ A block of ice sits on the sidewalk in the sun. The block of ice consists of 100 centiliters of water that have been frozen. The block of ice melts at a rate of 2.5 centiliters a minute. ◆

1. Think about the relationship between time and the amount of water that is accumulating on the sidewalk.
   a. How much water will there be after 4 minutes? 8 minutes? 20 minutes?
   b. How can you find the amount of water on the sidewalk if you know the number of minutes that have passed?
   c. If T represents the number of minutes that have passed and W represents the amount of water (in centiliters) that has accumulated on the sidewalk, write an equation that expresses the relationship between the two quantities.
   d. How can you check your equation from part (c)?

2. Now think about the relationship between time and the amount of ice that is left in the block of ice.
   a. How much ice will there be in the block after 4 minutes? 8 minutes? 20 minutes?
   b. How can you find the amount of ice in the block if you know the number of minutes that have passed?

Continue on the next page.

c. If *T* represents the number of minutes that have passed and *I* represents the amount of ice (in centiliters) that is left in the block, write an equation relating the two quantities.

d. How can you check your equation from part (c)?

e. When will the block of ice be gone? How do you know?

f. For part (c), someone wrote $I + 2.5T = 100$. What was the person thinking? Is this equation all right?

TAKE-AWAY MESSAGE . . . A graph can give a "picture" of how one quantity changes as another quantity changes. In a coordinate-system graph, graphing conventions (like uniform spacing in a scale on an axis or having the horizontal scale increase to the right and the vertical scale increase to the top) make it easier to grasp the quantitative relationship between the variables involved. Understanding how the quantities in a situation are related may enable you to write an algebraic equation for the situation. ♦

Learning Exercises for Section 12.2

1. *Help! Something's Leaking, Part 1.* Consider the following scenario, written by a student.

   ♦ An airplane is flying high over Siberia, hundreds of miles from any help. Suddenly, the fuel tank starts leaking. The tank contained 80 gallons of fuel when the tank started leaking and is leaking at a rate of 10 gallons each minute. ♦

   a. How does the amount of fuel in the tank change as time passes?

   b. Complete the following table of data that describe the relationship between the amount of fuel in the tank and the time spent flying since the rupture.

Time (in minutes)	Amount of fuel in tank (in gallons)
0	80
1	70
3	
4	

   c. How can you find the amount of fuel in the tank if you know the number of minutes that have passed?

   d. Let *T* represent the number of minutes that have passed and *G* represent the amount of fuel in the tank. Write an equation that represents the relationship between the two quantities.

   e. How can you check to see whether your equation from part (d) represents the data?

   f. When will the fuel tank be empty? How do you know?

    g. Graph the relationship between the amount of fuel in the tank and the time spent flying since the fuel leak started. (Save this graph; it will be referred to in Learning Exercise 2 in Section 12.3.)

    h. One person wrote the equation $G + 10T = 80$ for part (d). What was this person thinking? Does this equation work?

2. *Help! Something's Leaking, Part 2.* Consider the scenario in Learning Exercise 1. However, this time think about the relationship between the amount of fuel that has leaked (rather than the amount of fuel in the tank) and the time that has passed since the rupture in the tank.

    a. Describe in words how the amount of fuel that has leaked changes over time.

    b. Create a table of data to describe the relationship between the amount of fuel that has leaked and time.

    c. Use algebraic symbols to describe the relationship between the amount of fuel that has leaked and time. Be sure to label your variables.

    d. Graph the relationship between the amount of fuel that has leaked and the time spent flying. Be sure to label the quantities on each axis. (Save this graph; it is referred to in Learning Exercise 2 in Section 12.3.)

    e. How do the graphs from Learning Exercises 1(g) and 2(d) differ? What does this difference say about the quantitative relationships?

    f. At what rate is the fuel leaking? How can you tell using each graph? (See Learning Exercises 1(g) and 2(d).)

3. Geometric relationships can result in interesting graphs.

    a. Graph the relationship between the length of the side of a square and the perimeter of the square. You may first want to generate a table of data, using several squares.

    b. Graph the relationship between the length of the side of a square and the area of the square.

    c. Compare the two graphs. How are they alike? How are they different?

    d. Let s represent the number of length units in a side of a square, p the number of units in the perimeter of the square, and A the number of units in the area of the square. Write an equation to represent the relationship between the length of the side of a square and the perimeter of the square. How can you check to make sure your equation is correct? Now write an equation to represent the relationship between the length of the side of a square and the area of the square. Compare the two equations. How are they alike? How are they different? How are the differences related to differences between the two graphs?

4. *Real-World Relationships.* Describe a quantitative relationship that occurs in daily life, then apply this situation to parts (a)–(d).

    a. Identify two quantities in the situation you created and describe how the quantities are related.

    b. Represent the relationship using a table of data (make up reasonable numbers if you do not have exact ones).

    c. Represent the relationship by creating a graph. Be sure to label the quantity represented by each axis.

Notes

    d. Try to write an algebraic equation for the relationship, even though doing this might not be easy. Be sure to state the number that each algebraic symbol represents.

5. Sharing an object with others generates an interesting graph.

    a. Suppose you are sharing a pizza fairly among several people. Create a table of data that shows what fraction each person will receive for different numbers of people.

    b. Graph the relationship between the number of people sharing the pizza and the size of the piece each receives.

    c. Does it make sense to connect the points in your graph? Why or why not?

    d. Does the size of each pizza piece increase or decrease as the number of people sharing the pizza increases?

    e. Why is the shape of your graph a curve instead of a line?

    f. What, if anything, would change if the people were sharing 2 pizzas? 6 pizzas? $\frac{3}{4}$ pizza?

6. An experiment can suggest an important relationship in a circle.

    a. Locate 3 round objects of different sizes (for example, a coffee can or a tea cup) and trace around the base of each object. Alternately, use a compass to draw 3 circles of different sizes.

    b. Look at your 3 circles. As the diameters increase, what happens to the circumferences?

    c. Measure the diameter of each circle using a ruler. Measure the circumference of each circle by first placing string carefully around the rim of the circle and then measuring the string with a ruler. Record your data in a table.

    d. Graph the relationship between the diameters and the circumferences.

    e. About how many times as large is the circumference as the diameter for each circle?

    f. How can you get the information requested in part (e) above from the graph?

    g. Does it make sense to connect the points on your graph? Why or why not?

    h. Is your graph a line or a curve? Why do you think so?

    i. Let c represent the length of the circumference (in inches or cm) and d the length of the diameter (in inches or cm). Write an equation to show the relationship between the circumference and the diameter of a circle.

7. a. PharmImpact provides consulting on health plans. The company began with 30 employees but is growing rapidly. If the company hires 5 employees per month for one year, then 10 per month after the first year, how long will it take to increase the total number of personnel to 300?

    b. Draw a graph that describes this information.

12.3 | Understanding Slope: Making Connections Across Quantitative Situations, Graphs, and Algebraic Equations

When one quantity increases, another can increase, decrease, or stay the same. A new quantity that shows the relationship between such changes is very valuable and, as we will see, very useful in equations for lines. That quantity is called the **slope** of the line. We sometimes designate the slope using the letter m. The usual x-y convention is to let y represent the vertical axis and x represent the horizontal axis. You may also recall that the point where the graph of a line crosses the y-axis is called the y-intercept. Any equation of the form $y = mx + b$ has a line associated with it.

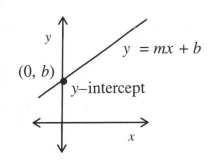

Activity 4   The Slippery Slope

The following work is one prospective elementary teacher's response to Learning Exercise 4 from Section 12.2.

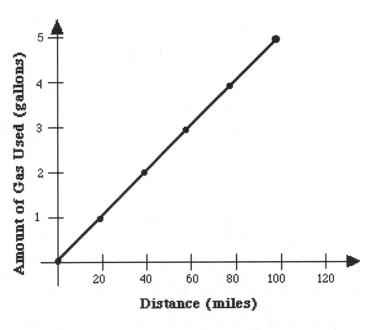

miles	gallons
20	1
40	2
60	3
80	4
100	5

The amount of fuel your car uses depends on how far you have driven.

a.   Many of you learned how to compute the slope of a line in high school. If you have forgotten, study the example given on the next page. Then compute the slope of the line in the graph given above.

Continue on the next page.

Notes   **EXAMPLE**

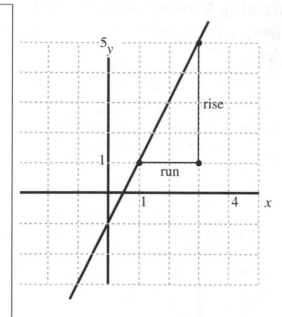

$$\text{slope} = \frac{\text{rise}}{\text{run}} = \frac{4}{2} = 2$$

or

$$\text{slope} = \frac{\text{change in the } y\text{-values}}{\text{change in the } x\text{-values}}$$

$$= \frac{5-1}{3-1} = \frac{4}{2} = 2$$

b. What does the slope that you calculated in part (a) mean in terms of the situation with the fuel?

c. Make a new graph of the same data. This time let the horizontal axis represent the amount of fuel and let the vertical axis represent the distance.

d. Calculate the slope of your graph from part (c).

e. What does the slope mean in terms of the situation with the fuel?

f. Compare the slopes from parts (a) and (c). Are they the same or different? Why?

g. Redraw the graph at the beginning of this activity, using a different scale. Let each unit on the horizontal axis equal 5 miles. Also redraw the graph from part (c), letting each unit on the vertical axis equal 5 miles. Does changing the scale change the slope? Does changing the scale alter the look of each graph? Which line is steeper and why? Is the fact that one line is steeper reflected in the slope measurement? Explain.

h. Let g represent the number of gallons of fuel used and d the number of miles traveled. From the table, it is easy to see that $d = 20g$. Is the slope of the graph represented in this equation? Explain.

Activity 4 suggests a useful interpretation of slope, as follows: If the vertical axis represents the variable y, the horizontal axis represents the variable x, and the resulting graph is a straight line, then the slope gives the change in the values of y for every one-unit change in the values of x.

THINK ABOUT . . .

What is the slope of a horizontal line? What does that slope mean?

TAKE-AWAY MESSAGE . . .With a little practice, slope is easy to calculate by finding the *rise over run*, but understanding what the resulting value means is equally important. The value of the slope can appear in some forms of an equation for a line; for example, $y = mx + b$ has m as the slope and $(0, b)$ as the point where the line crosses the *y*-axis. The visual steepness of a line can be influenced by changing the scales on one or both axes, but the slope and its meaning stay the same. For two points on the graph of a line, the slope gives the change in the values on the vertical axis for every change of one unit in the values on the horizontal axis. ♦

Learning Exercises for Section 12.3

1. **a.** The graph below shows a relationship in a bowling situation. Calculate the slope of the line.

    b. What does the slope mean in terms of the bowling situation?

    c. Draw another line on the graph that has the same slope. What does this line represent in terms of the bowling situation?

    d. What is the cost before any games are bowled? What is the *y*-intercept of the graph? What does the *y*-intercept mean in terms of the bowling situation?

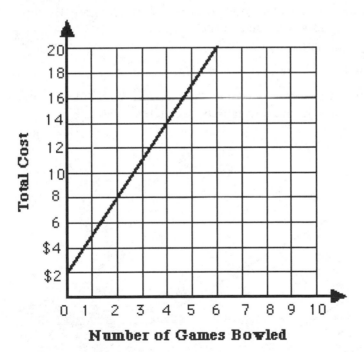

Number of Games Bowled

    e. Although such graphs are commonly used to show the linear pattern of data, why is a solid line literally not appropriate here?

2. *Help! Something's Leaking, Part 3*. Read again Learning Exercises 1 and 2 from Section 12.2. Both exercises dealt with the situation of an airplane flying over Siberia with a leaky fuel tank.

    a. The graph that you created in Learning Exercise 1(g) showed the amount of fuel in the tank over time. Calculate the slope of this graph.

b. What does this slope tell you about the situation with the airplane?

c. The graph that you created in Learning Exercise 2(d) showed the amount of fuel that had leaked over time. Calculate the slope of this graph.

d. What does the slope in part (c) tell you about the situation with the airplane?

e. Compare the two slopes in parts (a) and (c). How are they alike and why? How are they different and why? What does a *negative* slope tell you?

3. *Burning Candles, Part 1.* The following data were collected as a candle burned. The data show how the height of the candle changed over time.

Number of minutes a candle has burned	Height of the candle in centimeters
0	15
2	14
8	11
12	9
20	5

a. Graph the data. Put the height values of the candle on the vertical axis and the time values on the horizontal axis. Why is it appropriate to join the points and make a solid line in this situation?

b. Calculate the slope of the line.

c. What does the slope tell you about the candle?

4. *Burning Candles, Part 2.* Consider the following graphs for a group of three burning candles. Each line represents a different candle.

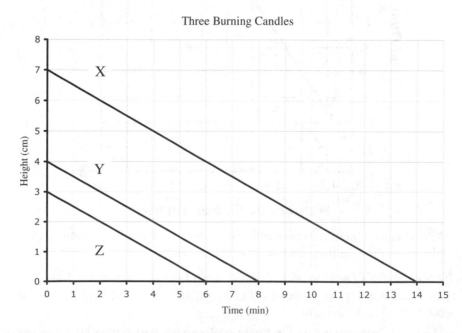

Three Burning Candles

a. What was the starting height of each candle?

b. At what rate did each candle burn? How do you know?

c. What is the slope of each line?

d. Which of the following groups of candles could be represented by the graph and why? Which candle goes with which line?

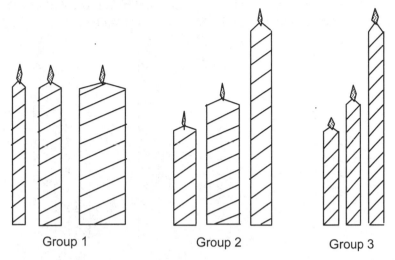

| Group 1 | Group 2 | Group 3 |

e. Write an equation to represent each candle's burning. (Make a table of data for each candle first, if it will help.)

f. How are the three equations in part (e) alike? How are they different?

g. Write an equation for a fourth candle, Candle N, whose graph is parallel to the graphs of Candles X, Y, and Z.

h. Sketch the graph of your equation for Candle N on the same grid with the graphs for Candles X, Y, and Z.

i. Describe the candle (Candle N) that you've represented by the graph and equation in parts (g) and (h).

5. *Burning Candles, Part 3.* Consider the following graphs for another group of three burning candles. Each line represents a different candle.

Three More Burning Candles

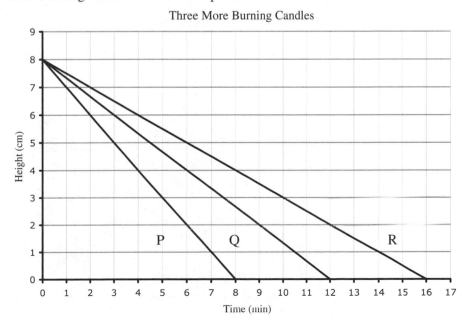

a.   What was the starting height of each candle?

b.   At what rate did each candle burn? How do you know?

c.   What is the slope of each line?

d.   Which of the following groups of candles could be represented by the graph and why? Which candle is Candle P? Candle Q? Candle R?

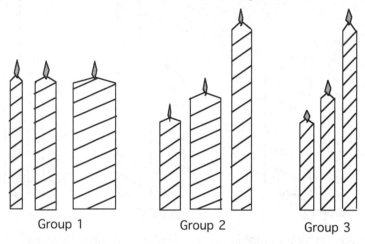

Group 1   Group 2   Group 3

e.   Write an equation to represent each candle's burning. (Make a table of data for each candle first, if it will help.)

f.   How are the three equations alike? How are they different?

g.   Write an equation for a fourth candle, Candle S, whose graph will intersect the point (0, 8) like the other three lines.

h.   Sketch the graph of your equation for Candle S on the same grid with the graphs for Candles P, Q, and R.

i.   Describe or draw the candle (Candle S) that you've represented by the graph and equation in parts (g) and (h).

6.   The following graphs show the number of quarts of strawberries picked by three people one morning.

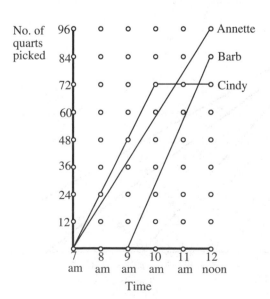

a. One of the three people was scared by a snake and quit picking. Who was that? How do you know?

b. How many quarts does Annette pick per hour?

c. At what time did Barb start picking? How many quarts does she pick per hour?

d. Which person picks strawberries fastest? How do you know?

7. The next morning Annette (see Learning Exercise 6) was ill. She started picking strawberries at 8:00 A.M. but could pick only 10 quarts of strawberries per hour. She quit picking at 11:00 A.M. Graph both days of Annette's picking on the same set of axes.

8. One Monday the manager of a drug store counted the number of shoppers at various times during the day, which are represented by the solid dots on the manager's graph below.

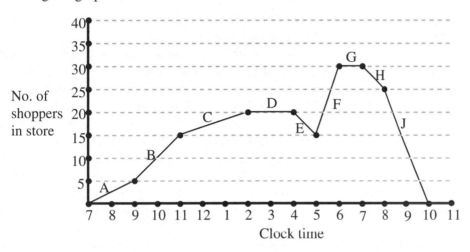

a. Why does the graph begin at 7 on the time axis rather than 0?

b. What does the manager's graph assume about what happens between the times when the manager counted the shoppers?

c. What period saw the greatest increase in customers?

d. How could segment D be interpreted?

e. How could segment B be interpreted?

f. During what hours might the manager need more cashiers?

12.4 Issues for Learning: Algebra in the Elementary Grades

Although a formal treatment of algebra is usually saved for the eighth or ninth grade, most national and state recommendations and textbooks now incorporate algebraic ideas into the elementary grades. The *Principles and Standards for School Mathematics*[i] from the National Council of Teachers of Mathematics (http://www. nctm.org) states that "By viewing algebra as a strand in the curriculum from pre-kindergarten on, teachers can help students build a solid foundation of understanding and experience as a preparation for more-sophisticated work in algebra in the middle grades and high school" (p. 370). Here are some guidelines the NCTM Standards provide as guidance in developing algebra curricula for Grades K–2, 3–5, and 6–8.

In *Grades Pre-K–2*, students should have experiences in sorting, classifying, and ordering. This work on patterns provides a way of organizing their environment. They can begin to generalize patterns such as in this table (from the NCTM Standards, p. 92):

Number of balloons	1	2	3	4	5	6	7
Cost of balloon in cents	20	40	60	80	?	?	?

Students are also expected to generalize and use symbols to represent mathematical ideas. After working with addition of two one-digit numbers for a period of time, they may come to realize that $2 + 5$ gives the same sum as does $5 + 2$ and to generalize this (commutative) property for adding any two numbers. This knowledge becomes useful when it allows them to count on from 5 (6, 7) rather than from 2 (3, 4, 5, 6, 7) when finding the sum of 2 and 5. They also learn to represent word problems with symbols. For example, "Cathy has 4 pencils. How many more are needed to have 7 pencils?" can be represented symbolically as $4 + \square = 7$. Students also should learn to model situations. For example, when given the problem "There are six chairs and stools. The chairs have four legs and the stools have three legs. Altogether there are 20 legs. How many chairs and how many stools are there?" (NCTM p. 95), students can use drawings or numbers and adjust them until they reach a total of 20 legs.

Students at this level also should learn the meaning of equality and be able to express equality in different ways. Many children at this age erroneously think of the equal sign as directional, that is, that $3 + 2 = 5$ is correct, but that $5 = 3 + 2$ is incorrect. Understanding equality means that they can write the equality in either way and they will find acceptable expressions such as $4 + 2 = 3 + 3$.

In these early grades students also begin to learn about change. They can, for example, talk about growing taller, or about the weather becoming colder.

Students in *Grades 3–5* also investigate patterns, both numerical and geometric. Page 159 of the NCTM Standards uses a pattern of "growing squares" to describe this work. Students are expected to describe the pattern, tell what the next square would look like, and say how many small squares would be needed to build it.

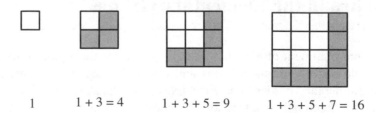

1          $1 + 3 = 4$ $1 + 3 + 5 = 9$ $1 + 3 + 5 + 7 = 16$

Modeling situations and relationships can be extended from what was presented to children in Grades Pre-K–2. For example, students might be asked to find the total surface area of consecutive towers built with cubes, placing one cube on top of another. They can use a table (and graph, at a later grade) to describe what is happening.

Cubes	Surface area
1	6
2	10
3	14
4	18
5	22

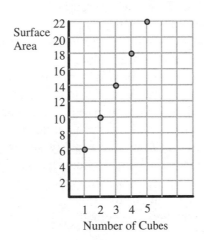

One student may describe what is happening by saying that each cube has 6 faces but when one is placed on top of another, two faces are lost, and then for n cubes write this as $6n - 2(n - 1)$, with sufficient algebra sophistication. Another might reason that each time a cube is added to the tower, there are 4 new faces. So, there are 6 faces to begin with and then 4 new ones each time: $6 + 4(n - 1)$. The students could then discuss whether these two expressions are equivalent.

Students also study change in more depth in these intermediate grades. They can study growth patterns in plants, rates of change such as the distance traveled in a certain amount of time, or the change in cost as the number of objects bought increases. These changes can be represented in tables and graphs.

In *Grades 6–8* students begin to formalize algebra. They should be able to "represent, analyze, and generalize a variety of patterns with tables, graphs, words, and, when possible, symbolic rules; relate and compare different forms of representation, and identify functions as linear or nonlinear and contrast their properties from tables, graphs, and equations" (NCTM, p. 222). In these grades students begin to develop an understanding of the different uses for variables and use symbolic algebra to represent situations and solve problems. They should be able to "model and solve contextualized [story] problems using various representations" (p. 222) and understand graphing of linear equations and the meaning of slope. The study of change becomes more formal in these grades.

A Quantitative Curriculum. Because this chapter deals with a quantitative approach to algebra, we also note here a curriculum[ii] quite different from the typical elementary curriculum that is proving to be successful. This approach adapts a Russian curriculum and is currently being tested in the United States. The major difference is the quantitative approach to mathematics that begins in the first grade. The curriculum uses letters very early, relating the letters to quantities (not their values) of length, area, volume, and mass. For example, first graders might compare the lengths of two strips of paper labeled A and B, and write $A = B$ or $A > B$ or $B > A$, as appropriate. (*To repeat:* No actual measurements

$$\begin{array}{l} C > A \\ C > B \\ A + B = C \\ C - B = A \\ C - A = B \end{array}$$

are used at this point.) Different relationships for related quantities might be expressed, perhaps as in the figure above, again without numbers. The concept of area is used as the basic meaning for multiplication: $A \times B$ means the area of a rectangle with sides of lengths A and B. Notice that this approach definitely emphasizes quantities and their relationships, with numerical work gradually entering in. Hence, the children have focused on meanings for the operations (addition and subtraction, for example) and relations like equality and inequality *before* calculation with numbers comes in. Once numbers are introduced, there is a continued emphasis on measurements. If the project (currently called *Measure Up*) is successful, you will no doubt see its influence in curricula that you may teach . . . and much longer articles about how the curriculum is designed.

12.5 | Check Yourself

After this chapter, you should be able to do problems like those assigned, and to meet the following objectives.

1. Identify increasing or decreasing quantitative relationships in a given situation.

2. Represent a given quantitative relationship with a graph (perhaps a qualitative one, without numbers) or an algebraic equation.

3. Given a graph (or perhaps an algebraic equation) for a situation, describe the quantitative relationship(s) involved.

4. Calculate the slope for a given straight-line graph, and explain the meaning of slope in a given context.

5. Relate the slope of a straight-line graph to an equation for the graph.

6. Give meaning to the equation of a line in the form $y = mx + b$.

7. Discuss how graphs portray change.

REFERENCES FOR CHAPTER 12

[i] National Council of Teachers of Mathematics. (2000). *Principles and Standards for School Mathematics.* Reston, VA: Author

[ii] Dougherty, B., & Zilliox, J. (2003). Voyaging from theory to practice in teaching and learning: A view from Hawai'i. In N. Pateman, B. Dougherty, & J. Zilliox (Eds.), *Proceedings of the 2003 Joint Meeting of PME and PMENA,* Vol. 1, pp. 17–23. Honolulu: University of Hawaii.

Chapter 13

Understanding Change: Relationships Among Time, Distance, and Rate

In Chapter 12 you were asked to draw graphs to illustrate different types of situations in which quantities change. In this chapter the focus is on a specific type of change—changes involving time, distance, and speed relationships. You are familiar with all three of these quantities. In the many contexts involving motion, these three quantities often change but in a related way. Speed is a rate and is often given in miles per hour (mi/h) or feet per second (ft/s). These units suggest that the ratio of a change in distance to a change in time is involved. In this chapter we build on these relationships graphically, algebraically, and occasionally numerically.

Notes

13.1 | Distance-Time and Position-Time Graphs

Some of you may be thinking, "This discussion will be about $d = rt$, that is, distance equals rate multiplied by time." In a way, this would be correct, but the focus here will be on understanding and interpreting situations in which the $d = rt$ formula might be relevant. In particular, you will create graphs without being concerned about the specific values of the variables, but rather by thinking about how these quantities are related.

Activity 1   Identifying Quantitative Relationships in a Motion Situation

Consider the following situation.

♦ Wile E. Coyote[i] leaves his cave, walking at a slow yet constant speed. Then he stops to build a trap for Road Runner. After several minutes, he turns around and runs back to his cave at a constant speed. ♦

(Because Wile E. and Road Runner are cartoon characters, you can assume that they can start walking or running at a constant rate instantly without first accelerating up to that rate.)

    a. Act out this situation with one volunteer, using a desk or some other object in the room as the cave.

Continue on the next page.

283

b. What quantitative relationships do you see in this situation? Identify every pair of quantities that you can.

c. For each pair of quantities that you identified in part (b), describe how one quantity is changing (increasing, decreasing, or staying the same) as the other quantity increases.

One quantitative relationship in Activity 1 is the relationship between the total distance traveled by Wile E. Coyote and the time elapsed. In Activity 2, you will graph the relationship between Wile E. Coyote's distance from his cave and time. Because no specific numerical information has been given regarding Wile E. Coyote's walking speed, his running speed, or the time he stops to build the trap, you can construct a graph without numbers. This type of graph is sometimes referred to as a **qualitative graph** or a "sketch" graph. It allows you to capture the relationship between the quantities in the situation without worrying about specific numerical relationships.

Activity 2   Creating a Distance-Time Graph

Create a graph that represents the relationship between the distance traveled by Wile E. Coyote and time given in the story in Activity 1. Be sure to think about the total distance he has traveled (that is, the number of feet he has traveled in all), not how far he is from the cave. Be sure to label the quantities on your axes. Labeling the different parts of the graph (for example, A, B, C, . . .) helps communication.

There are a number of choices to be made in creating a graph. In making a graph of the relationship between the distance traveled and time, some of you may have chosen to make a qualitative graph (without numbers), and some may have chosen to use numbers. You may have made different decisions about what quantities should be represented on each axis. Also, if different people used numbers, they probably did not all use the same range of numbers. Your decisions can affect what is conveyed about the situation. In Discussion 1, we look more specifically at what information is being conveyed.

Discussion 1   What Do the Pieces Mean?

1. Share the graphs created by different individuals or groups for Activity 2, if the graphs are different. In particular, compare a graph with no numbers to a graph with numbers. How are the graphs different or the same?

2. How did you decide which quantity should be represented by each axis?

3. What is the shape of your graph?

4. What does the part where Wile E. stops look like on your graph? How can you tell?

5. What can you say about Wile E.'s speed during each of the three segments of his journey just by looking at the graph? Explain. Can you compute the speed exactly? Why or why not?

THINK ABOUT . . .

Why does the slope in a distance-time graph tell you what the speed is? (*Hint*: What is the *meaning* of slope?)

Activity 3   Creating a Position-Time Graph

Refer to the situation with Wile E. Coyote described in Activities 1 and 2. This time, graph the relationship between Wile E. Coyote's position (that is, his distance from the cave) and time. Be sure to label each axis with a quantity. You can either make a sketch without using any numbers, or you can make up reasonable data and graph that.

Although the story was the same, the graph of the relationship between Wile E.'s distance from the cave and time looks different from the graph of the relationship between the distance traveled and time. Yet many of the same elements of the story will be conveyed. In Discussion 2, look specifically at why the graphs are different and at what information is the same.

Discussion 2   Why Is It Back to Zero?

1. Compare your position-time graph with your distance-time graph, especially for the segment in which Wile E. Coyote runs back to the cave. How are the graphs different and why?

2. What can you tell about Wile E. Coyote's speed during each segment of the journey by using the graph?

> TAKE-AWAY MESSAGE . . . Even without numbers, a qualitative graph can give information about a setting. With care, qualitative graphs about distance/position versus time can reflect information about speeds. Speed versus time graphs can provide information about distances traveled. ◆

Learning Exercises for Section 13.1

1. Consider the following situation:

> ◆ Wile E. Coyote leaves his cave walking at a slow yet constant rate. He walks to the edge of a cliff. He is planning to build a catapult that will hit Road Runner by launching a large boulder. Just as Wile E. Coyote reaches the cliff, he remembers that he left the large rubber band for the catapult back in his cave. He turns around and walks back to his cave at the same pace as before. It takes him several minutes in the cave to find the large rubber band for the catapult. He realizes that he had better hurry so he starts running (at a constant speed). About halfway to the cliff, he remembers that he left the boulder at home also. He turns around and runs home at an even faster (yet constant) speed. ◆

Continue on the next page.

a. Graph the relationship between Wile E. Coyote's *total distance* traveled and time.

b. Create a second graph, this time graphing Wile E.'s *position* (that is, his distance from the cave) and time. (Using the same scales as in part (a), and placing this second graph right under the graph from part (a), makes it easy to compare these graphs in part (c). Save this graph for later use in Learning Exercise 2 in Section 13.3.)

c. Compare the two graphs. How are they alike? How are they different?

2. The following graph shows a new journey taken by Wile E. Coyote.

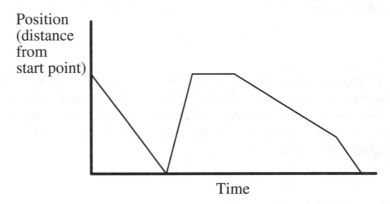

Position (distance from start point)

Time

a. Write a story that could be represented by this graph. (Remember that this graph shows Wile E.'s distance from a starting point, such as his cave. It is not a graph of the total distance traveled.)

b. Construct a new graph of the relationship represented in the given graph. This time, graph the total distance traveled over time.

3. Graphs can involve numbers, of course. Suppose Wile E. Coyote leaves his cave walking at a constant speed of 8 ft/s for 10 seconds. Then he runs at a constant speed of 12 ft/s for 5 more seconds. He realizes that he forgot something at home, turns around, and walks back to his cave at a constant speed of 5 ft/s.

a. How long does it take Wile E. Coyote to get back to the cave once he turns around and starts walking back home?

b. Graph Wile E.'s distance from the cave over time (that is, make a position-time graph). You may want to create a table of values first.

c. Sketch a second graph, this time graphing Wile E.'s total distance traveled over time. You may want to create a table of values first.

d. Compare the two graphs. How are they alike? Different?

e. How can you determine Wile E. Coyote's speed from each graph?

4. Many times, motion graphs (such as position-time graphs) can give an algebraic equation.

a. Suppose Wile E. Coyote walks at a constant speed of 4 ft/s away from his cave. Graph the relationship between his distance from the cave over time (that is, as time passes). Then write an equation representing this relationship.

b. Suppose Wile E. Coyote is at a boulder about 20 feet from his cave. He starts walking in a direction that is away from both the boulder and the cave at a constant speed of 4 ft/s. Graph the relationship between his distance from the cave and time. Then write an equation representing this relationship.

c. Suppose Wile E. Coyote walks toward his cave at a rate of 4 ft/s from a cliff that is 56 feet from the cave. Graph the relationship between his distance from the cave and time. Then write an equation representing this relationship. How are the graphs from parts (a), (b), and (c) alike and different? Why?

d. How are the equations from parts (a), (b), and (c) alike and different? Why?

e. What is the slope of the graph in part (a)? What does this slope tell you about Wile E.'s motion? Can you find the slope from your equation?

f. What is the slope of the graph in part (b)? What does this slope tell you about Wile E.'s motion? Can you find the slope from your equation?

g. What is the slope of the graph in part (c)? What does this slope tell you about Wile E.'s motion? Can you find the slope from your equation?

5. Pioneer 10 is the first man-made object to leave the solar system. Pioneer 10 will take 2 million years to get to a red star 68 light-years away. During that trip, what will Pioneer 10's average speed be, in miles per hour? (Light travels at 186,000 miles per second.)

6. Consider the following situation.[ii]

♦ An explorer went to visit a jungle village. She drove the first 25 mi of the trip along a rough road at a steady speed of 20 mi/h. She had to go the next 3 mi by canoe, at a speed of 5 mi/h. Then she had to cut her way through 12 mi of dense jungle and could manage a speed of only $\frac{3}{4}$ mi/h. Finally, she came to a path and walked the last 13 mi at a speed of 4 mi/h. How long did it take her in all to reach the village? ♦

Answer the question, explaining your reasoning. (Drawings may be useful.)

7. Rates are useful in situations other than those dealing with speed. Consider the following situations.

a. You buy 3 pounds of apples at $1.49 per pound, 0.8 pound of coffee beans at $12 per pound, and 0.8 pound of cheese at $4.80 per pound. Calculate the total spent on this shopping trip.

b. A mo-ped went 40 mi on $\frac{5}{8}$ gal of fuel. How far can the mo-ped go on a gallon of fuel?

c. A person's heart may beat at 70 beats per minute. How many beats would that give in a day? How long would it take for a billion beats, at this rate?

13.2 | Using Motion Detectors

The activities[iii] in this section involve a motion detector that is connected to a computer or a calculator. The goal of working with a motion detector is to create graphs using real motion. By creating graphs of our movement, we often become more involved in thinking about the relation between position and time than we might be if we are just imagining movement from an observer's point of view.

The motion detector is a physical device that measures how far you are from the detector over a given time interval. It works by emitting ultrasonic pulses and then recording the length of time it takes for the reflected pulses to return. Using this length of time and the known speed of sound, it calculates a distance approximately 20 times per second (although this measure can be changed using the software). The ultrasonic sounds are completely safe, so you do not have to worry about any radiation or other dangers. The range of the motion detector is between 0.45 and 6 meters.

The graph shown in the picture resulted from a student walking away from a motion detector, turning, and walking back at a steady pace in both directions. The motion detector measured the distances from itself. There is a little "noise" at the end of the graph that students were able to ignore.

Using the Motion Detector Software

The software allows you to create graphs of your distance from the motion detector over time. If your motion detector is attached correctly, you should be able to click once on the start button and begin collecting data.

Activity 4   Take a Hike

1. Create and record a graph that represents each of the following descriptions. Discuss with your group what the walker had to do to obtain the graph. Write a careful and complete explanation of what the walker did.

   a. Line with a positive slope

   b. Steeper line with a positive slope

c. Line with a negative slope

d. Less steep line with a negative slope

e. Horizontal line (that is, a line with a slope of zero)

2. Start several feet from the motion detector and then walk away from the motion detector at a constant speed. Then use the data from the graph that the computer created to find the speed at which you walked. Be sure to include the unit of measurement on the graph. (*Note:* If you click on a point, you can get the point's coordinates by looking at the bottom of the screen. This may help you determine your speed.)

3. Create a graph that is a curve. Describe what the walker did to obtain the graph. Then use the graph to determine how fast you were traveling during different parts of the trip. Why is it more difficult to find the average speed of the walker here than in Problem 2?

4. Try to recreate each of the following graphs using the motion detector. (*Note:* The vertical axis of each graph measures the walker's distance from the motion detector. The horizontal axis measures the time.) For each graph, do the following:

    •   carefully describe what the walker(s) had to do to obtain the original graph or your modified graph;

    •   describe any difficulty you may have in obtaining any part or all of the graph (some graphs may not be possible to recreate); and

    •   if the graph requires only some modifications, resketch it with your changes.

a.

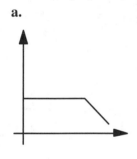

b.

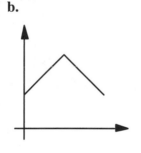

c.

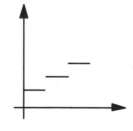

d.

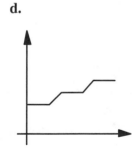

e.

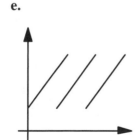

f.

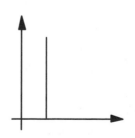

g.

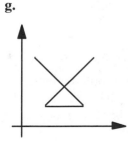

Learning Exercises for Section 13.2

Exercises 1–3 can be done without the motion detector.

1. The following graphs were obtained using the motion detector system. Describe as fully as possible the walks represented by these graphs and explain the differences between them.

    a.

    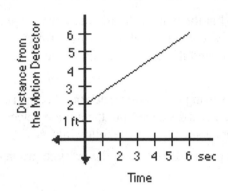

    b.

    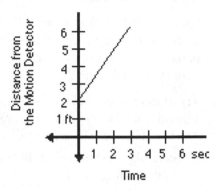

    c.

    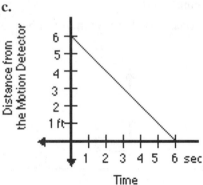

    d.

    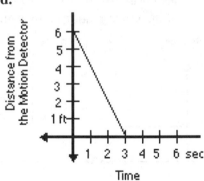

    e.

    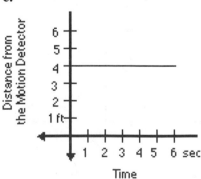

2. What was the walker's speed in each situation given in Learning Exercise 1?

3. **a.** Refer to Graph (a) in Learning Exercise 1. Create a new graph (on paper) that represents a person walking at the same rate as the person represented by Graph 1(a), but starting at a different distance from the motion detector.

b. Compare your new graph with Graph 1(a). How are they alike? How are they different?

c. Create another new graph that represents a person starting in the same position from the motion detector as in Graph 1(a), but walking at a slower rate.

d. Compare your graph created in part (c) with Graph 1(a). How are they alike? How are they different?

Exercise 4 requires using the motion detector.

4. Motion detector graphs involving curves require careful thought. Try to recreate each of the following graphs using the motion detector. (*Note*: The vertical axis of each graph measures the walker's distance from the motion detector. The horizontal axis measures the time.) For each graph, do the following:

- carefully describe what the walker(s) had to do to obtain the original graph or your modified graph;

- describe any difficulty you may have in obtaining any part or all of the graph (some graphs may not be possible to recreate); and

- if the graph requires only some modifications, resketch it with your changes.

a.

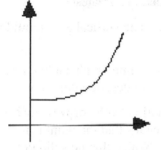

b.

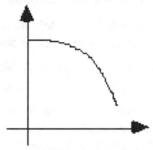

c.

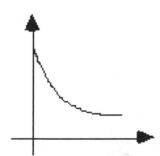

d.

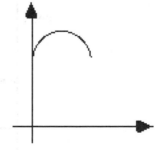

13.3 | Graphs of Speed Against Time

As we mentioned earlier, speed is a relationship between distance and time. For example, if you can travel 30 feet in 5 seconds at a steady speed, you are going at a much faster speed than someone who travels 20 feet in 5 seconds at a steady speed. Your speed is 6 ft/s, and the other person's speed is 4 ft/s. You can graph the relationship between distance and time in a situation involving motion and then ob-tain information indirectly about the speed (for example, through the slope of the graph). Alternatively, you can represent speed directly in a graph by using speed and time as the quantities represented by the axes.

> **THINK ABOUT . . .**
>
> If each of two cars is going 50 mi/h but in opposite directions, why does it make sense to think of one of the speeds as a *negative* 50 mi/h?

Activity 5   Graphing Motion

Reconsider the following situation from Section 13.1.

♦ Wile E. Coyote leaves his cave walking at a slow yet constant speed. Then he stops to build a trap for Road Runner. After several minutes, he turns around and runs back to his cave at a constant speed. ♦

1. Act out this situation. As you act it out, describe what is happening to Wile E. Coyote's speed over time. Is his speed increasing, decreasing, or not changing? During which segment of the journey is his speed the greatest?

2. Graph Wile E. Coyote's speed over time. (*Note:* The vertical axis should repre-sent speed, not distance or position.)

3. Compare your graph in Problem 2 to the distance-time graph and the position-time graphs that you constructed in Section 13.1 to describe this same situation.

4. Could the graph below represent Wile E.'s situation? Why or why not? (For clar-ity, at a particular value for time, an open dot means that the point is not in-cluded; a solid dot means the point is included. Notice that no solid dot is joined to an open dot by a vertical line segment.)

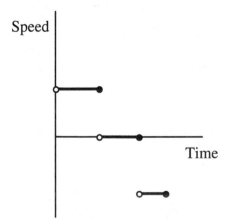

Although negative speeds can be interpreted and make sense when thinking of slopes in distance-time graphs, they may not be important in some contexts. Your instructor will let you know how alert you should be to the possibility of using negative speeds in making your speed-time graphs.

> TAKE-AWAY MESSAGE . . . Because speed is a quantity that can change over time, a graph showing speed versus time makes sense. When a speed involves a decrease in distance, it is reasonable to consider that a negative speed, but for many purposes doing so is not essential. ♦

Learning Exercises for Section 13.3

1. Graph each of the following situations, using the same speed-time graph. Then compare the graphs: How are they alike, and how are they different?
    a. Wile E. Coyote walks at a constant speed of 4 mi/h.
    b. Wile E. Coyote runs at a constant speed of 10 mi/h.
    c. Wile E. Coyote gets in a go-cart and travels at a constant speed of 15 mi/h.

2. In Exercise 1(b) from Section 13.1, you constructed a position-time graph for the following situation. Now construct a speed-time graph, and then compare the two graphs.

> ♦ Wile E. Coyote leaves his cave walking at a slow yet constant rate. He walks to the edge of a cliff. He is planning to build a catapult that will hit Road Runner by launching a large boulder. Just as Wile E. Coyote reaches the cliff, he remembers that he left the large rubber band for the catapult back in his cave. He turns around and walks back to his cave at the same pace as before. It takes him several minutes in the cave to find the large rubber band for the catapult. He realizes that he had better hurry so he starts out from his cave running (at a constant speed). About halfway to the cliff, he remembers that he left the boulder at home also. He turns around and runs home, at an even faster (yet constant) speed. ♦

3. The graph below is a distance-time graph for a cartoon object's trip. Graph the *speed* at which the object is traveling over time.

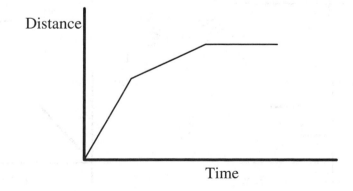

4. Consider the following situation. Since this is the cartoon world, assume it is possible to attain a constant speed without accelerating.

♦ Bart Simpson leaves his home and runs to a gas station at a constant rate. He stops suddenly for several minutes. Then he walks back home at a constant rate. ♦

Represent Bart's motion by sketching the following three different graphs:

a. a position-time graph (that is, a graph of Bart's distance from home over time)

b. a distance-time graph (that is, a graph of Bart's total distance traveled over time)

c. a speed-time graph

5. On each set of axes given below, sketch a graph to represent the following situation:

♦ A 5-inch flower is planted in a pot. It starts growing at a slow but constant rate. When it is moved into the sun, the plant starts growing at a faster (yet constant rate) until it is 3 times the original height. Then the plant is moved into a shady corner and it stops growing. ♦

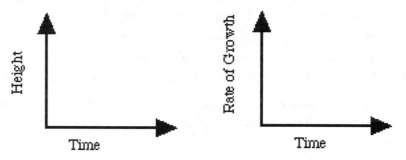

6. For each graph given, write a story about a journey that Bart Simpson took that could be described by the graph. If the graph represents an impossible situation, explain why. Add open and solid dots to the graphs (as in Activity 5, Problem 4) if your instructor wants you to.

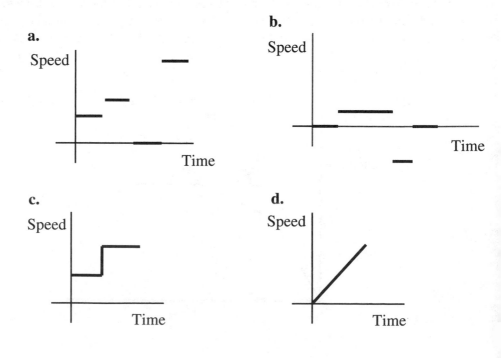

7. For each of the following situations, draw two graphs, each of which fits the situation by showing two quantities varying simultaneously. The graphs should differ from each other in the quantitative relationship that they describe. For example, you may want to draw a distance-time graph and then a speed-time graph. Be sure to label the axes. Even though these describe real situations, it is all right to assume cartoon-like changes in speeds.

   a. Felecia walked from her house to the store. About halfway to the store, she realized that she had forgotten to bring any money. So she turned around and walked back home, this time walking a little faster. It took her several minutes at home to find her money. Then she left the house and ran all the way to the store.

   b. Pat drove to work on the city streets, stopping at three red lights along the way.

   c. A long-distance truck driver has an all-day trip of highway driving. He stops for a rest or meal break every two hours.

   d. A loaded truck drives up a hill and then down the hill.

   e. A space rocket was launched. It sped up when its booster rockets were fired. Then the rocket traveled at a constant speed, in a circular orbit around Earth for several days, collecting data. It re-entered the atmosphere and eventually came down safely by parachute.

8. Each of the following containers pictured (side views) is being filled with water at a steady rate. Sketch qualitative graphs that show the height of the water in the container as time goes on. Assume that the water keeps running for a while after the container is full.

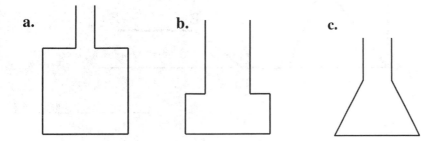

a.   b.   c.

9. Below is a side view of a roller coaster.[iv]

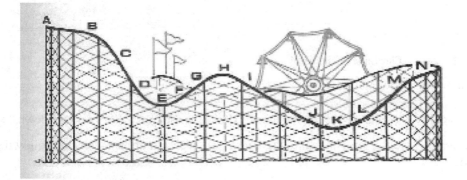

Continue on the next page.

a. Is the speed greater at B or at C? Why?

b. Is the speed greater at G or at H? Why?

c. Sketch a qualitative graph for the *speed* of the roller coaster, versus its position on the track.

13.4 Interpreting Graphs

In most of the work in this chapter so far, we have started with a situation, and you were asked to construct a graph that represents a relationship between quantities in that situation. That process will be reversed in this section. You will be given a graph and asked to create a situation that might be represented by the graph and to interpret the graph in terms of the quantities in that situation.

Activity 6   Tell Me a Story

Write a story that could be represented by the following graph. In your story, identify the quantitative relationship that is being graphed.

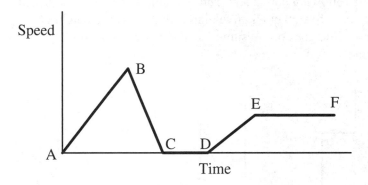

Wasn't it difficult to see that as the speed increased, it is unlikely that someone was going *up* a hill, and that as the speed decreased, it is unlikely that someone was going *down* a hill? Children have the same difficulty with distance-time graphs. (See Section 13.5.)

Activity 7   Climbing to the Top!

Consider the following situation:

♦ A child climbs up a slide at a constant speed, stops at the top, and then slides down. ♦

Examine the graphs on the next page and for each graph answer the following questions.

Continue on the next page.

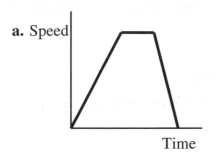

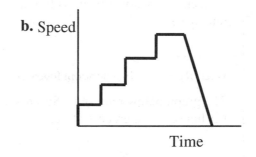

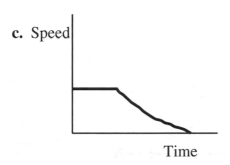

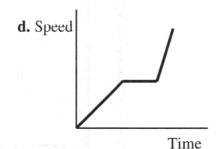

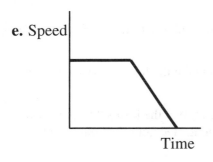

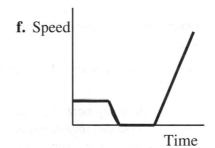

1. Which graph best models the situation? Give your reasoning.

2. Which graph looks most like a playground slide? Could this graph represent the situation? Why or why not?

3. For each of the other graphs, explain how the graph fails to model the situation.

Many questions arise naturally from the types of graphs you have constructed and analyzed so far—for example, during what part of a person's journey was he or she going the fastest? While it is possible to answer a question like this by examining visually the steepness of different parts of the speed-time graph, it will be important for you, as a teacher, to also create explanations that include a discussion of the quantities involved, quantities such as time versus distance or speed versus time. Giving explanations is what you will be doing when you teach, so giving explanations here is good practice, even though some of the ideas are more advanced than those you will be teaching. Good explanations tell *why* something might have happened and are not just reports of *what* happened. Good explanations should use technical language correctly and not mix up different ideas (for instance, using *height* when *rate* is intended).

Activity 8   Explanations Involving Time and Distance

The graph below represents Susan's distance from home, over time, for her trip from her house to the grocery store.

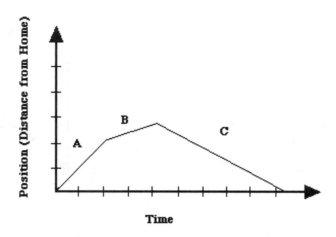

1. During which segment of her journey did Susan walk the farthest? How do you know?

2. During which segment of her journey did Susan take the longest? How do you know?

3. During which segment of her journey did Susan travel the fastest? Explain why. Be sure to use distance and time in your argument. (Do not rely simply on a visual estimation of steepness.)

TAKE-AWAY MESSAGE . . . Interpreting speed-time graphs requires careful thought, with a focus on how the speed (not the distance) is changing. Part of a teacher's job is to explain. Giving good explanations takes practice and, in part, careful attention to the language used.

Learning Exercises for Section 13.4

1. For each of the following situations, circle *one* graph on the following page that best represents the situation. Explain why you selected that graph.

   a. Tanya starts to run up Mount Soledad on Mountain Road. She begins at a stand-still and quickly gets up to a comfortable yet slow pace. She runs at this constant rate until she gets to the top of Mount Soledad. She slows to a stop and enjoys the view for about 15 minutes. Then she runs down the steep side of the mountain on Capri Road, going faster and faster until she reaches her top speed.

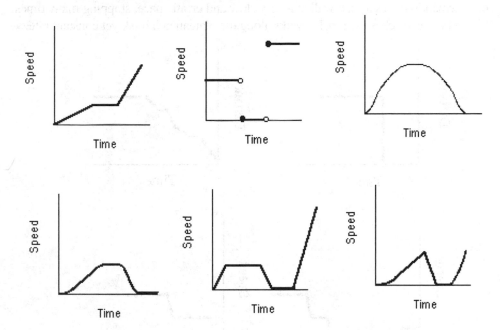

b. A train pulls into a station and then stops to let off its passengers.

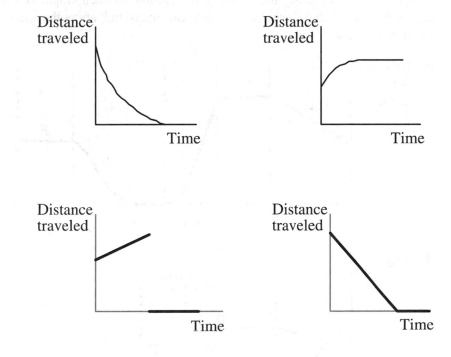

c. Armando scales a rock wall at a very slow and erratic pace, stopping many times. When he reaches the top, he walks along the plateau at a brisk yet constant rate.

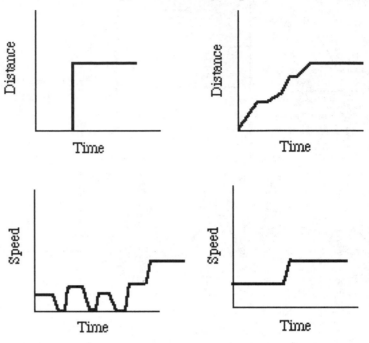

2. Tell a story about a journey that could be represented by each graph. Tell what happened in each lettered part of the graph. Be sure to talk about the speed represented by each part.

a. Distance from home

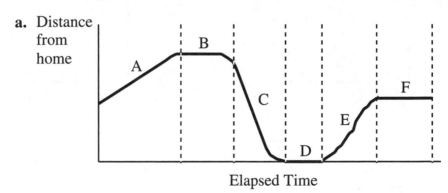

Elapsed Time

b. Speed

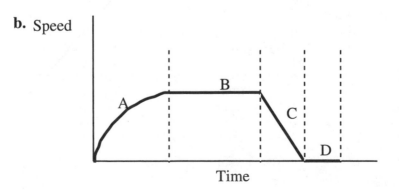

Time

3. Suppose the speed-time graph in Learning Exercise 2 represents Janet's bike ride. For part of her ride, Janet was going up a steep hill and became very tired. Which segment of the graph might reflect that part of her ride? Explain.

4. The following graphs show the motion of two different boats.

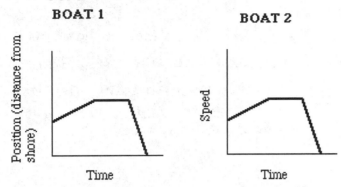

BOAT 1   **BOAT 2**

a. Tell a story about the journey of the two boats that could be described by the graphs above.

b. Notice that the graphs look identical except for the labels on the axes. Could Boat 1 and Boat 2 be the same boat—that is, could the two graphs be describing the same motion? Why or why not?

c. Is there more than one way to interpret each graph? If so, give an alternate story for each graph. If not, explain why not.

5. The work from two students follows. They were both asked to write a story for a journey that could be represented by the following graph. For each student, describe what you think the student understands mathematically and what he or she doesn't understand.

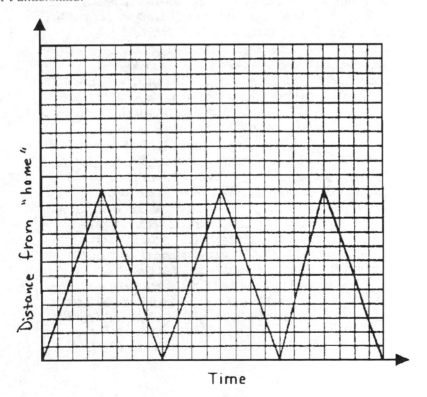

Notes

STUDENT #1:

This is a graph of my speed up a hill. It took me 4 hours to get up the hill, but I reduced the time by going down hill. I reached the bottom in half time it took me to reach the top. I continued doing this for 16 hours straight. The last few hours I got tired and didn't ride up the steep hill but a less steep hill.

STUDENT #2:

A Math Story

The Sea Hog (Militaries latest lard powered submarine) is prepared to go. The admiral who will navigate the vessel is explaining to the crew why lard is a better fuel in times of defense cuts.

The Sea Hog sets off. Buy the time it is 12 miles out to sea the admiral realizes that he had carelessly left the weapons back at the port. He sets back at the same speed he set out at. About 3 mph (lard is not a very good submarine fuel as far as speed is concerned).

The admiral had called ahead and asked for the weapons to be ready on port by the time he returned to avoid delay. When he had reached port he didn't need to stop or even slow down. They just threw the weapons in.

The Sea Hog sets out again at about 3 mph until again about 12 miles from shore. Then it was to the admirals surprise that this was not really his crew, His was back at the Dock.

When the admiral had returned the submarine wasn't even stop or slow down. The wrong crew jumped off the right crew jumped on.

3 hours later It was 12 miles out that it was discovered that there wasn't enough lard to make the trip. (I cant tell you to where the trip was. TOP SECRET you know). They head back and decided to try again tomorrow.

6. The following graph represents Jordan's bike trip.

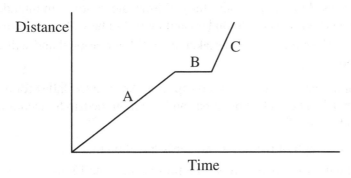

   a. Which segment of Jordan's trip took the most time? How do you know?
   b. During which segment of his trip did Jordan go the farthest? How do you know?
   c. During which segment of his trip did Jordan travel the fastest? How do you know? Use distance and time in your argument.
   d. Explain how you know that Jordan stopped during segment B. Use time and distance in your argument.

7. The following graph represents the change of the height of two candles (Candle A and Candle B) over time, as they burn.

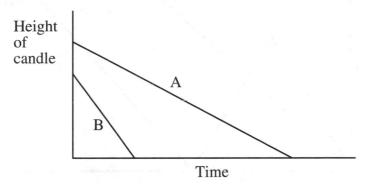

   a. Which candle was taller before they were lit (at $t = 0$)? How do you know?
   b. Which candle burned out faster? How do you know?
   c. Which candle burned at a faster rate? How do you know? Use height and time in your argument.

8. Interpret the following graph[v] that gives information about an oven. Why is the last part of the graph wiggly?

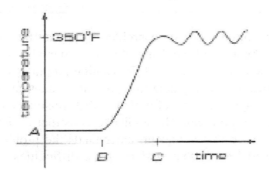

9. The following problem is from a seventh-grade unit on rate and proportionality. The unit was used in a large-scale study of SimCalc, a program intended to provide all students with access to understanding of fundamental mathematics, using technology[vi]. The study was undertaken by SRI International and will eventually be published.

"Every year a soccer team makes the trip from Abilene to Dallas for a special challenge match. They take both a bus and a van on the trip to accommodate all players and boosters."

Following is a graph of the bus's and van's travel on that trip.

a. What did the van do after traveling for one and a half hours?

b. What happened here? Tell the story of this trip."

On the Road

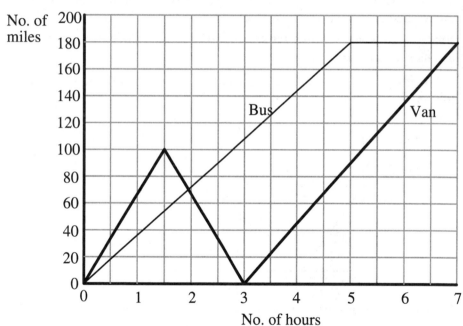

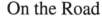

13.5 | Issues for Learning: Common Graphing Errors

In the past, algebra has often focused on problems that can be solved by symbolic representation alone.[vii] As a result, students often consider visual representations as unnecessary. Our previous work (in Part I: Reasoning About Numbers and Quantities) illustrated the efficacy of being able to represent a quantitative situation with a picture or diagram. A graph is a form of a picture that illustrates a situation and can lead to the solution of the problem. The ability to construct a visual representation such as a graph is evidence that a student understands the problem situation being presented. Yet it is well known that students have difficulties when constructing graphs.

Graphing errors result from either not knowing the *conventions* of drawing graphs or not understanding a problem well enough to represent it with a graph. Conventions of graphing have developed over time and have become agreed-upon ways of representing information graphically. Following are some of these conventions:

1. A two-dimensional graph (used when two variables are being considered) has horizontal and vertical axes perpendicular to each other, with the intersection representing 0 on each axis.

2. Numbers along an axis must be equally spaced. That is, the distance between 3 and 4 must be the same as the distance between 1 and 2; the distance between 5 and 10 must be the same as the distance between 10 and 15. (There are exceptions, such as graphing involving special scales, but those are well beyond the scope of elementary and middle school mathematics.)

3. The axes typically show 0. However, if there are great distances between 0 and the points of interest, we can indicate a break in the otherwise uniform scale within the graph, for example by a crooked line such as the following:

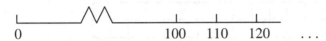

4. In analyzing relationships between quantities, we usually look at how one variable, called the dependent variable, depends on the other variable, called the independent variable. The independent variable is located along the horizontal axis, often called the *x*-axis, and the dependent variable is located along the vertical axis, often called the *y*-axis. For example, the distance traveled is dependent on time traveled, not the reverse. Thus time would be represented on the horizontal axis, distance on the vertical axis.

Some common graphing errors are demonstrated in the following student-drawn graphs based on the given table that tells the number of minutes a candle has burned.

Number of minutes a candle has burned	Height of the candle in centimeters
0	15
2	14
5	11
12	9
20	5

Notes

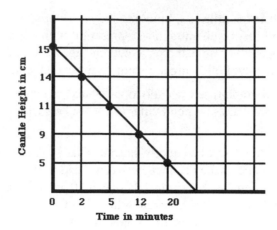

Figure 1. Student #1's Graph

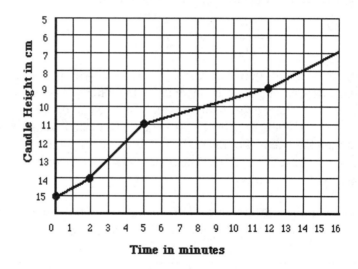

Figure 2. Student #2's Graph

Activity 9   **What Are the Graphing Errors?**

1. **a.** What error(s) did Student #1 make?

    b. What do you think this student doesn't understand?

2. **a.** What errors(s) did Student #2 make?

    b. What do you think this student doesn't understand?

3. **a.** Make a correct graph of the data.

    b. What information about the quantitative relationship is captured in your graph that was lost in the students' graphs?

Research has also shown that when students in both elementary school and high school are asked to interpret graphs, they often exhibit what is known as the *"graph as picture" misconception.*[viii] They ignore the quantities on the axes, interpreting the graph as a realistic image or picture of an object or event. For example, a group of students were shown the graph below. Then they were asked to describe a journey that they took that could be described by the graph. Two typical incorrect responses are given below.

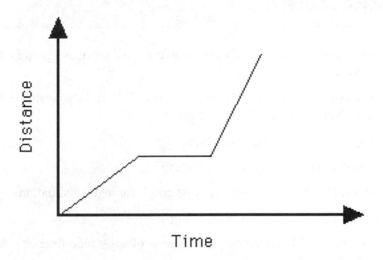

Student 1:   *"First I started walking up a hill. Then the hill flattened out. Then there was another, steeper hill that I walked up."*

Student 2:   *"I rode my bike down a street. Then I turned a little to the right and rode for a while. Then I turned left and rode a long way."*

Discussion 3   What Does the Graph Say?

1.   Explain what each student might have been thinking.

2.   Why does it make sense to say that both of these students have the "graph as picture" misconception?

3.   What is a correct interpretation of the graph?

A graph is only one way of representing a situation, but it is a powerful way that in many cases makes a problem situation easier to understand. Some situations can be represented with a table, an equation, and a graph, each showing the information given in the problem. Students should be able to move among these representations with ease, although equation representations are usually learned later than tables and graphs.

Graphing calculators are now being used in algebra classes in many institutions. These calculators offer new ways of coming to understand quantitative situations by producing graphs quickly and efficiently. They also provide, for example, the capability of considering and comparing a variety of quantitative situations, and of zooming in and out to understand better how a graph represents a situation. If used

Notes

properly, graphing calculators can also help students develop a fundamental understanding of graphs—how they are made and what they tell us.

13.6 | Check Yourself

After this chapter, you should be able to do problems like those assigned and to meet the following objectives.

1. Draw qualitative graphs for a situation (such as a Wile E. Coyote story), both a distance-time graph and a position-time graph.

2. Write a story for a given qualitative graph.

3. Relate speed to slope in a distance-time graph.

4. Sketch a speed-time graph or distance-time graph for a given situation.

5. Write a story for a given speed-time graph.

6. Interpret the changes illustrated by various parts of a distance-time or position-time or speed-time graph.

7. Explain and illustrate what is meant by the "graph as picture" misconception (Section 13.5).

REFERENCES FOR CHAPTER 13

[i] Wile E. Coyote and Road Runner are favorite cartoon characters created by animator Chuck Jones in 1949 for a cartoon series produced by Warner Brothers.

[ii] Adapted from Greer, B. (1987). Nonconservation of multiplication and division involving decimals. *Journal for Research in Mathematics Education*, 18(1), 37–45.

[iii] All activities and exercises in Section 13.2 were written by Helen Doerr and Preety Nigam from Syracuse University and revised by Janet Bowers and Joanne Lobato from San Diego State University.

[iv] The sketch and problem are from the National Council of Teachers of Mathematics, *Curriculum and Evaluation Standards for School Mathematics*, p. 83, 1989, as an example of reasoning about graphs.

[v] The graph is from the National Council of Teachers of Mathematics, *Curriculum and Evaluation Standards for School Mathematics*, p. 155, 1989.

[vi] http://math.sri.com/

[vii] Yerushalmy, M., & Schwartz, J. L. (1993). Seizing the opportunity to make algebra mathematically and pedagogically interesting. In T. A. Romberg, E. Fennema, and T. P. Carpenter (Eds.), *Integrating research on the graphical representation of functions* (pp. 42–68). Hillsdale, NJ: Erlbaum.

[viii] Kaput, J. J. (1987). Representation systems and mathematics. In C. Janvier (Ed.), *Problems of representation in the teaching and learning of mathematics* (pp. 19–26). Hillsdale, NJ: Erlbaum.

Chapter 14

Algebra as a Language and as Generalized Arithmetic

Many problems can be solved in different ways: numerically with tables of values, pictorially with graphs, and symbolically with algebraic equations. Elementary school children, of course, do not know much algebra, so you are more likely to use tables and graphs if you teach in elementary school. Algebra can also be thought of as the generalization of arithmetic. We will explore all of these ideas in this chapter.

14.1 Using Algebraic Symbols to Represent Relationships

In Chapters 12 and 13 you were asked to write related equations for some tables of values and some graphs. In this section, you will learn to work with situations that can be described by two line graphs or two equations.

Activity 1   From Graphs to Algebra

Graphs 1–4 on pages 310 and 311 show different linear relationships. For each graph, complete these two tasks:

a. Write a story that the graph could represent.

b. Write an equation that will allow you to find the distance from home for any given time. Let t represent the time that has passed in hours and d the distance from home in miles.

Graph 1

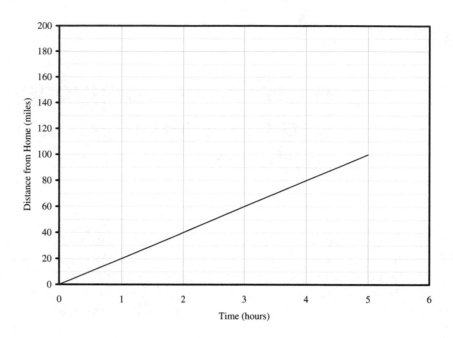

Graph 2

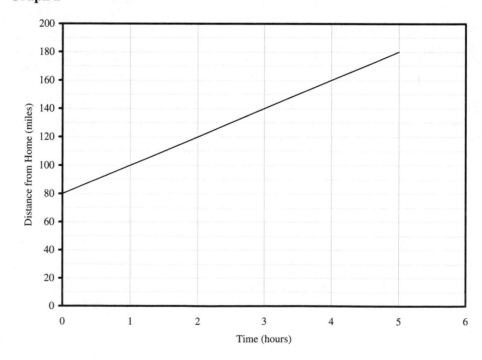

Hint: Compare Graph 1 with Graph 2. How do the *d* values in the two graphs compare, for $t = 0$ (or 1, or 2, and so on)?

Graph 3

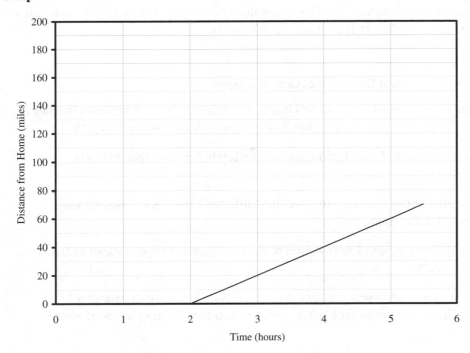

Hint: Compare the values of *d* in Graph 3 with those in Graph 1, when *t* = 2 (or 3, or 4, and so on).

Graph 4

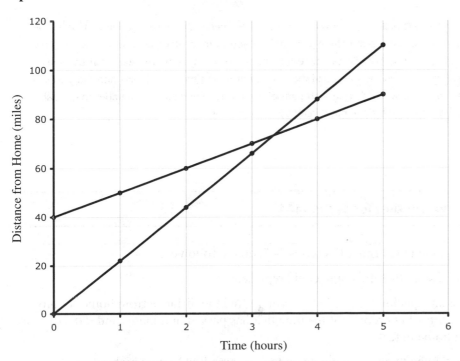

Hint: Use your ideas in writing equations for Graphs 1–3 to help get an equation for the line starting at (0, 40) and an equation for the line starting at (0, 0).

The graphs in Activity 1 did not all begin at (0, 0). But from those graphs, you may have noticed what happens if a line graph does not begin at 0 on one or both axes. Let's pursue these ideas in the following discussion.

Discussion 1   What Does All That Graphing Mean?

1. What is the slope of each line in Graphs 1–3 in Activity 1? What does the slope mean in terms of your story? How is the slope reflected in the equation?

2. Compare Graphs 1 and 2. How are they different? How is this difference reflected in the equations?

3. Compare Graphs 2 and 3. How are they different? How is this difference reflected in the equations?

4. What does the point of intersection of the two lines in Graph 4 mean in terms of your story?

5. Why might it make sense to set the expressions for the two distances d from Graph 4 equal to each other? What would that mean in terms of your story?

6. Set the two expressions for d from Graph 4 equal to one another, and then solve for time t. What does this value of t tell you?

TAKE-AWAY MESSAGE . . . Knowing where a line meets the y-axis (in other words, the y-intercept) and the slope of the line can help you write an algebraic equation for the line: $y = (\text{slope})x + (y\text{-coordinate where the line meets the } y\text{-axis})$. The axes can be labeled differently, such as the t-axis and the d-axis, but calling them the x-axis and the y-axis is most common. When dealing with parallel lines, it is important to remember that parallel lines have the same slope but different y-intercepts. ♦

Learning Exercises for Section 14.1

For each graph in Learning Exercises 1–5, do the following.

a. Write a story that the graph could represent.

b. Write an equation that will allow you to find the distance from home for any given time. Let t represent the time that has passed in minutes and d the distance from home in feet.

c. Why do you think some points on the lines are highlighted by bold dots?

1.

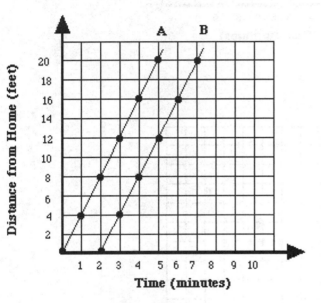

2.

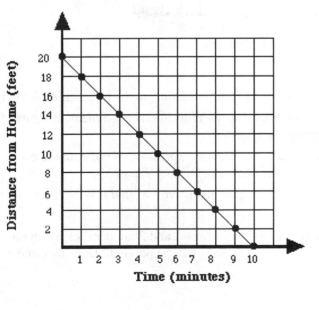

3.

Notes

4.

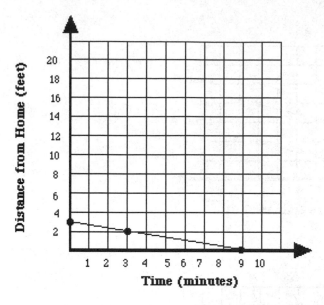

5.

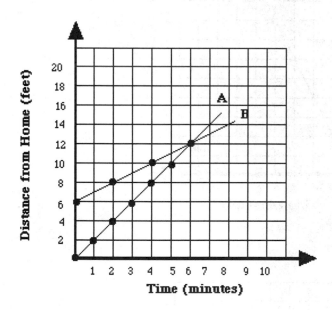

6. Answer the following questions by examining the graphs in Learning Exercise 5.

    a. For lines A and B, what does their point of intersection mean in terms of your story for Learning Exercise 5?

    b. Why might it make sense to set the two expressions for *d* equal to each other? What would that mean in terms of your story?

    c. Set the two expressions for *d* equal and solve for time *t*. What does this value of *t* tell you?

7. The lines in the graphs in Learning Exercises 1 and 2 are parallel. What about their equations could tell you that the lines will be parallel? Does that make sense?

For each story given in Learning Exercises 8–11, do the following.

    a. Draw a graph that represents the story.

    b. Write an equation (or equations) that relates the distance from home to the time traveled. Let t represent the time that has passed in minutes and d the distance from home in blocks.

8. Janel and Jamal were at home one day doing nothing, and decided to go to the mall together. At 11:00 Janel started walking from home to the mall at 5 minutes per block. She arrived at the mall 20 minutes later. Jamal got a phone call that held him up, so he started 5 minutes later, walking at the same pace as Janel.

9. Janel and Jamal decided to go to the mall again. Janel started walking from home to the mall 4 blocks away at a steady pace, and she arrived there in 20 minutes. Jamal got a phone call that held him up, so he started 5 minutes later, but he arrived at the mall at the same time Janel did.

10. Janel and Jamal's mother asked them to go to the mall to pick out a present for their dad. Janel started walking the 4 blocks to the mall and arrived 20 minutes later. Jamal left from a friend's home 2 blocks from the mall, walking at the same pace as Janel.

11. Carolyn was at the mall, which is 10 blocks from home, and she received a phone call to return home immediately. She walked home at 4 minutes per block.

For Learning Exercises 12–14, graph each pair of equations on the same set of axes, and write a description of a situation represented by the equations.

12. $d = 4t$ and $d = 6t$ **13.** $d = 4t$ and $d = 4t + 2$ **14.** $d = t + 1$ and $d = \frac{3}{2}t$

14.2 | Using Algebra to Solve Problems

This section gives you practice with three representations of a problem—numerical, graphical, and algebraic—that might be used in solving a problem. As you work with the problems in this section, judge the relative efficiency and accuracy of these methods but also keep in mind the limited algebra background that elementary school students would likely have. The first two problems may be familiar to you from Chapter 1.

EXAMPLE 1

Solve the following problem in three different ways. (As illustrations, we will give four ways, the fourth to emphasize the value of quantitative reasoning.)

◆ The last part of the triathlon is a 10K (10 kilometers, or 10,000 meters) run. When competitor Aña starts running this last part, she is 600 meters behind competitor Bea. But Aña can run faster than Bea can. Aña can run (on average) 225 meters each minute, and Bea can run (on average) 200 meters each minute. Who wins, Aña or Bea? If Aña wins, tell when she catches up with Bea. If Bea wins, tell how far behind Aña is when Bea finishes. ◆

Continue on the next page

(PARTIAL) SOLUTION 1

(*Numerical and the most basic*) Make a table that shows Aña's and Bea's positions every minute. If the positions are ever equal before the race is over, then Aña has caught up. Here are two versions of such a table:

	Version 1				Version 2	
Time (min)	Aña's position (m)	Bea's position (m)		Time (min)	Aña's position (m)	Bea's position (m)
0	0	600		0	0	600
1	225	800		5	1125	1600
2	450	1000		10	2250	2600
3	675	1200		15	3375	3600
4	900	1400		20	4500	4600
5	1125	1600		25	5625	5600
...	...	...				

Version 1, with positions recorded at each minute, might even make you think that Aña would never catch up! But if we add a fourth column that records Aña's distance behind Bea, we would see that Aña *is* catching up, but only by 25 m/min. Version 2 recognizes that Aña is going to take several minutes to catch up and records positions every 5 minutes. Again, adding a fourth column showing how far Aña is behind Bea might be helpful. The Version 2 table does show that after 25 minutes Aña is ahead, so she has caught up. A little more calculation (or a lot more, for the Version 1 table) shows that Aña catches up after 24 minutes, when both have run 5400 meters.

SOLUTION 2

(*Graphical*) The idea is to show each woman's distance-time graph. Where the graphs meet (if they do meet) indicates that the distances are the same and Aña has caught up. If Aña catches up before the 10,000 meters have been run, we have an answer. If the women have run more than 10,000 meters, then Bea wins, and the graph can show how far Aña is behind when Bea finishes.

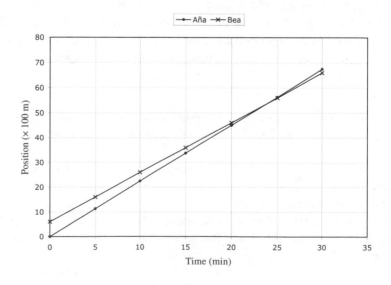

Immediately, you will notice that to make the graphs, you need at least a few rows of data in a table, and more importantly, that it may be difficult to read the exact solution from the graph. But the graphs make clear that at some time just short of 25 minutes, Aña catches up.

SOLUTION 3

(Algebraic) Either a table or a knowledge of the slopes and the starting points in the race leads to equations for the two women's distances traveled.

$$\text{Aña:} \quad d = 225t \qquad \text{Bea:} \quad d = 200t + 600$$

If Aña is to catch Bea their distances must be exactly the same. So, $225t$ must equal $200t + 600$, leading to $25t = 600$, or $t = 24$. So Aña catches Bea after 24 minutes. Is the race already over? No, because Aña's distance is $225 \times 24 = 5400$ meters, indicating that they both are a little more than halfway into the 10,000-meter race.

SOLUTION 4

(Quantitative reasoning) Aña catches up by 25 m every minute. She needs to catch up a total of 600 m, so the question becomes: How many 25's make 600? This question suggests a repeated subtraction division, so $600 \div 25 = 24$. Next, check to see whether the race is over: $24 \times 225 = 5400$, and so the race is still on.

Discussion 2   Pros and Cons (for Whom?)

What are pros and cons for each of the solution methods shown in Example 1? Which method(s) might be accessible to elementary school children? Why? Which method seems most insightful? Which method(s) require more prior experience in mathematics?

EXAMPLE 2

Solve the following problem in three ways.

♦ My brother and I walk the same route to school every day. My brother takes 40 minutes to get to school, and I take 30 minutes. Today, my brother left 8 minutes before I did. How long will it take me to catch up with him? ♦

SOLUTION 1

(Numerical) The problem resembles the triathlon problem, so a similar approach should work. But we do not have information on the actual distances traveled. Notice that the quantity, what *fraction* of the trip has been traveled, might give a breakthrough. Let's create a table, keeping in mind that we need not go minute-by-minute if that looks too cumbersome.

Continue on next page

Table 1

Part of whole trip covered

My time (min)	Bro	Me
0	$\frac{8}{40}$	0
1	$\frac{9}{40}$	$\frac{1}{30}$
2	$\frac{10}{40}$	$\frac{2}{30}$
3	$\frac{11}{40}$	$\frac{3}{30}$
...	...	...

Table 2

Part of whole trip covered

My time (min)	Bro	Me
0	$\frac{8}{40}$	0
5	$\frac{13}{40}$	$\frac{5}{30}$
10	$\frac{18}{40}$	$\frac{10}{30}$
15	$\frac{23}{40}$	$\frac{15}{30}$
20	$\frac{28}{40}$	$\frac{20}{30}$
25	$\frac{33}{40}$	$\frac{25}{30}$

As in the triathlon problem, the first table looks as though it will take too long to create, and it involves the comparison of fractions (perhaps by using a common denominator or decimals). In the second table, using common denominators or decimals shows that I catch Brother some time before 25 minutes. (*Note*: We can also use excellent number sense—$\frac{33}{40}$ is $\frac{3}{40}$ more than $\frac{3}{4}$, and $\frac{3}{40}$ is less than the $\frac{1}{12}$ difference between $\frac{3}{4}$ and $\frac{5}{6}$.) So we would have more calculations to do, working backwards, to get equality at $t = 24$ minutes.

SOLUTION 2

(*Graphical*) The idea of using parts of the whole trip makes the graph easy to draw.

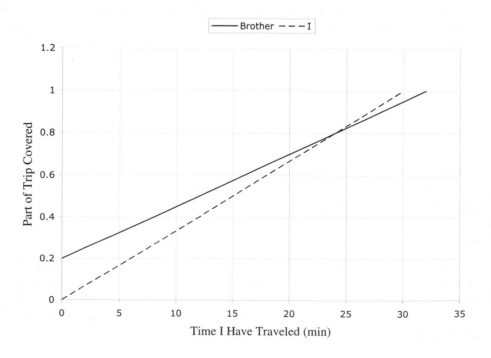

THINK ABOUT . . .

Why was the graph in Solution 2 easy to draw?

Again, it is difficult to read the exact answer from the graph drawn here, but a good guess would be about 24 minutes for the catch-up time.

SOLUTION 3

(Algebraic) In the triathlon problem, we knew the speeds. We do not know them here, except that the total distance is traveled in a certain number of minutes. Also, we do not know the total distance, but we can label it *TD*. We now have two equations.

$$\text{Brother:} \qquad d = \tfrac{TD}{40}(t+8)$$

$$\text{I:} \qquad\qquad d = \tfrac{TD}{30}t$$

So to find if I catch Brother, we equate the distances.

$$\tfrac{TD}{40}(t+8) = \tfrac{TD}{30}t$$

Fortunately the *TD*s divide out, giving

$$\tfrac{1}{40}(t+8) = \tfrac{1}{30}t.$$

Solving this equation gives $t = 24$ (min) for the time it takes me to catch up.

SOLUTION 4

(Quantitative reasoning) Brother has a head start of $\tfrac{8}{40} = \tfrac{1}{5}$ of the way to school. Each minute, I go $\tfrac{1}{30}$ of the way to school, and Brother goes $\tfrac{1}{40}$ of the way. So each minute, I catch up by $\tfrac{1}{30} - \tfrac{1}{40} = \tfrac{1}{120}$ of the way. How many $\tfrac{1}{120}$'s are there in $\tfrac{1}{5}$? Because $\tfrac{1}{5} \div \tfrac{1}{120} = 24$, I catch up with Brother in 24 minutes.

Discussion 3   Pros and Cons Again

Again, what are the pros and cons for each of the solution methods used in Example 2? Why? Which method(s) might be accessible to elementary school children? Which method seems most insightful?

Often there are multiple ways to solve a problem. Each way can provide a different insight into the problem, and different ways call on different abilities.

Activity 2   Solving a Problem Using Tables, Graphs, and Equations

Consider the following problem.

♦ A new electronic gaming company, called Pretendo, charges $180 for each gaming system and $40 for each game. The main competitor, Sega-Nemesis, charges $120 for a gaming system and $50 for each game. Sega is cheaper if a customer buys only one game. However, Pretendo eventually will be cheaper to own because each game costs less. How many games does a customer have to buy for the total expenditure for the two brands to be the same? (Remember that a customer must buy one gaming system before he or she can purchase games.) ♦

Attack the problem in the following ways.

1. *Solve using arithmetic.* You may want to use a chart or table.

2. *Solve by making a graph.* Graph the total cost of a Sega-Nemesis system for different numbers of games purchased. On the same grid, graph the total cost of a Pretendo system for different numbers of games purchased. Solve the problem by interpreting your graph.

3. *Solve using algebraic equations.* Write an equation that tells you the total cost of a Sega-Nemesis system for different numbers of games purchased. Write an equation that tells you the total cost of a Pretendo system for different numbers of games purchased. Use these two equations to find the solution.

4. Can you think of a quantitative reasoning solution? If so, describe your solution.

In Activity 2, you used different representations to answer the question posed in the problem. By solving the problem in different ways, you can focus more fully on the relationship between the different representations. The chart, or table, is created from the story narrative. The graph is a plot of the points in your chart or table. The algebraic equation is created from the relationships you identified when reading the narrative, from looking at entries in the table, or perhaps from the graph. A quantity such as the difference in price per game may enable you to see a quantitative solution.

> TAKE-AWAY MESSAGE . . . A problem can be approached by making a table of values, by drawing a graph, or by using algebra. Because these methods can be somewhat mechanical, it is easy to overlook the fact that reasoning about the quantities involved can lead to a solution based on insight into how the quantities are related. Thus, it is always a good idea to think about a problem before starting to write. Each method of approaching a problem has its advantages and disadvantages, depending on whether understandability is an aim, on who the solver is, on how quickly a solution must be obtained, or on how accurate the solution must be. ♦

> ### Learning Exercises for Section 14.2

1. Suppose Tony and Rita are racing. Tony starts 50 feet ahead of the starting line because he is slower than Rita. Tony's speed is 10 ft/s. Rita's speed is 15 ft/s.

   Let t represent the number of seconds that have elapsed since the start of the race.

   a. What does the expression $15t$ tell you in terms of the race?

   b. Write an equation to show the relationship between the time that has elapsed in the race and Tony's distance from the starting line.

   c. Write an equation to show the relationship between the time that has elapsed in the race and Rita's distance from the starting line.

   d. If you solved the equation $15t = 50 + 10t$ for t, what would you have found (in terms of the situation of the race)?

   e. Use algebra to find the time at which Rita will catch up to Tony.

   f. How far will Tony have run when Rita catches up to him? How far will Rita have traveled?

   g. How far apart are Rita and Tony after 35 seconds?

   h. Show the original situation with distance-time graphs by plotting points describing Rita's distance and Tony's distance on the same grid.

2. Going into the 10,000-m part of a triathlon, Kien is 675 meters behind Leo. But Kien can run a little faster than Leo: 265 m/min versus 250 m/min. Can Kien catch Leo before the race is over? If so, tell when. If not, how far behind is Kien when Leo crosses the finish line?

3. Sister and Brother go to the same school and by the same route. Brother takes 40 minutes for the trip, and Sister takes 50 minutes. One day, Sister gets a 15-minute head start on Brother.

   a. Can Brother catch Sister before they get to school?

   b. If so, how many minutes from school are they when he catches her? If not, where is Brother when Sister gets to school?

For Learning Exercises 4–9, solve each problem in at least three ways:

   a. First solve by generating a table of data.

   b. Use graph paper to graph each relationship in the problem on the same set of axes. Interpret your graph to solve the problem.

   c. Write an equation to describe each relationship in the problem. Use the two equations to solve the problem algebraically.

   d. Use quantitative reasoning to solve the problem.

4. Suppose Turtle runs at 55 ft/s. Rabbit runs at 80 ft/s, but gives Turtle a 5-second head start. How many seconds will Turtle have run when Rabbit catches up with him?

5. Suppose Turtle runs at 42 ft/s. Rabbit runs at 53 ft/s, but gives Turtle a 3-second head start. How far will Turtle have run when Rabbit catches up with him? (Answer exactly—do not give decimal approximations.)

6.   A fishing boat has been anchored for several hours 200 miles from shore. It pulls up its anchor and cruises away from shore at a rate of 33 mph. At the same time that the fishing boat starts moving, you leave shore in a speedboat, traveling at a speed of 50 mph. How long (in hours and minutes) will it take you to catch up to the fishing boat? (Give your answer to the nearest minute.)

7.   Suppose you are a famous musician about to sign a recording contract. You are offered two choices.

Option A: $2.25 profit for every CD sold

Option B: $300,000 up front, plus $0.75 for every CD sold

How many CDs would you have to sell for the two options to be of equal value? Which option would you select and why?

8.   You have just moved to a new city and have called the phone company to set up an account. The phone company tells you that it has two new plans, as follows.

Plan A: $15.50 per month plus $0.05 per call

Plan B: $5 per month, plus $0.40 per call

a.   What is the rate of change (or slope) of each of the lines describing the plans?

b.   When is Plan A the better deal?

c.   When is Plan B the better deal?

d.   Which plan would you select and why?

9.   You are offered two different jobs selling encyclopedias. One has an annual salary of $24,000 plus a year-end bonus of 5% of your total sales. The other has a salary of $10,000 plus a year-end bonus of 12% of your total sales. How much would you have to sell to earn the same amount in each job?

10.   Reflect on the different methods you used to solve the problems assigned from Learning Exercises 4–9. List at least one advantage *and* one disadvantage for each given method.

a.   table

b.   graph

c.   algebra

14.3 | Average Speed and Weighted Averages

The famous fable of the turtle and the rabbit involves a race between these two animals. On the one hand, we have the capricious rabbit, whose confidence in his ability to travel very fast causes him to travel erratically, at best. On the other hand, the slow but steady turtle plods along at a constant pace. As we know from the moral of the story, the turtle wins the race! In this section, we explore situations such as the rabbit-turtle race to develop a better understanding of average speed and weighted averages in general.

Activity 3   GPA

Consider the following story.

◆ Janice went to Viewpoint Community College for 3 semesters. She earned 42 credits and had a grade-point average (GPA) of 3.4. She then moved to State U for 5 semesters where she earned 80 credit hours before graduating and had a GPA of 2.8. What was her overall GPA when she graduated? She had to have an average GPA of 3 or better to enter a graduate program. Did she have that? ◆

a. What does "grade-point average" mean?

b. How many grade points did Janice earn at VCC?

c. How many grade points did Janice earn at SU?

d. What is the total number of grade points Janice accumulated?

e. What is the total number of credits Janice accumulated?

f. What can you do with the information from parts (d) and (e)?

g. Is the result in part (f) the GPA that you predicted?

Activity 4   To Angie's House and Back

Consider the following story.

◆ Wile E. Coyote decided to visit his friend Angie Coyote, who lives 400 meters away in another cave. He walked the 400 meters at a steady pace of 4 meters per second. When he arrived, he was anxious to get home, so he ran the 400 meters at 8 meters per second. What was his average speed for the entire trip? ◆

You probably answered the question by saying that the average speed for the trip was 6 m/s—that is what most people would say. But consider these questions:

1. How long did it take Wile E. to get to Angie's cave?

2. How long did it take Wile E. to get home?

3. What was the total time walking?

4. What was the total distance walked?

5. From the formula $d = rt$, what was the rate (speed) for the entire trip? (*Hint*: It is not 6 m/s.) What is going on?

The two problems in Activities 3 and 4 illustrate average rates and weighted averages. Just averaging averages is not sufficient. Why? What must be considered in each problem to get the correct answer?

The key in Activities 3 and 4 is this question: What does the phrase *grade-point average* mean and what does the phrase *average speed* actually mean? *Find the average* usually signals a computational procedure, but the resulting (and important) number can be interpreted in a useful way. For example, a GPA of 3.0 for 122 credits can be interpreted to mean the grade value that Janice would have earned for each credit, *if her total grade points were distributed equally over all of her credits*. A class average of 81.3% on a test can be thought of as the percent each student would have gotten on the test, *if the total of the percents for the class were distributed equally among all the students taking the test*. If the average number of children per family in a community is 2.6, that number can be interpreted as how many children each family would have *if the total number of children were spread equally among all the families.*

Fortunately, the average can be determined graphically, not just numerically, as suggested by Activity 5.

Activity 5   The Wile E.-Angie Situation with a Graph

Make a total distance versus elapsed time graph for Activity 4 on the following coordinate system.

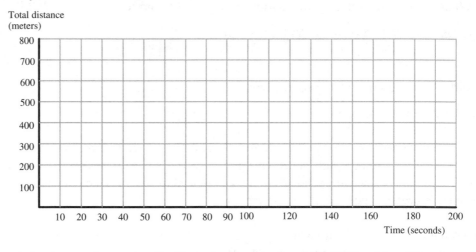

Now join the starting point (0, 0) to the final point (150, 800) with a line segment. What is the slope of this line? Why does the slope give the average speed? (*Hint:* Think of what *average* can mean.)

THINK ABOUT...

How could a graph showing total distance versus elapsed time give the average speed if Wile E.'s trip involved three segments? Why does that work?

The notion of average speed can be sharpened by considering a race situation, as in the next activity.

Activity 6   Turtle and Rabbit Go Over and Back

The software program Over & Back is available at http://sdmp-server.sdsu.edu/nickerson/ob. Briefly, the program acts out this situation: Turtle and Rabbit run a race to a certain place, and then run back to the starting point. Rabbit's speed over and speed back can be different, but Turtle's speed both ways is the same. The speeds and *total* distances can be changed by clicking on them.

Race 1: Rabbit's speed over is 4 m/s and back is 2 m/s. Turtle's speed both ways is 3 m/s. The total distance is 20 m. Who do you think will win, or do you think they will tie? If they do not tie, how could you adjust Turtle's speed so that they do tie? Should you make Turtle's speed *more than* or *less than* 3 m/s?

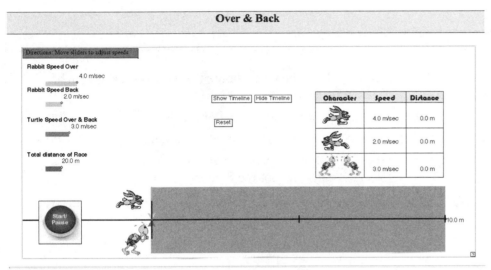

This page uses JavaSketchpad, a World-Wide-Web component of *The Geometer's Sketchpad*. Copyright © 1990-2001 by KCP Technologies, Inc. Used with permission. © Patrick Thompson, 1992; JavaSketchpad version developed by Janet Bowers, *Interactive Educators*.

Race 2: Rabbit's speed over is 8 m/s and back is 2 m/s. Total distance is still 20 m. What speed should Turtle go (the same both ways) to tie?

Race 3: What would happen in Race 1 if the total distance was 40 meters instead and speeds are set so that Rabbit and Turtle tie for the 40-meter race? In Race 2? If the total distance was 100 meters? Explain your thinking.

Race 4: Solve the problem using your own choices for a different Rabbit-Turtle race.

You may have noticed that knowing how much time is spent at each of Rabbit's speeds is important in calculating Turtle's speed to tie. That is, to calculate a tying speed, Rabbit's individual speeds must be weighted by the time spent at each of them.

Discussion 4   Thinking It Through

1. If Turtle and Rabbit tie, how does Turtle's speed compare to the (weighted) average of Rabbit's two speeds? Why?

Continue on the next page.

2. Do you think that the outcome of the race depends on the total distance they run if they run a longer race? What if they run a shorter race? Explain your answers.

TAKE-AWAY MESSAGE . . . When an average is requested, it is common just to add the values and then divide by how many values are used. But this technique does not give a correct *overall average* for averages and rates, in general. Unless each average is based on the same number of items, you must use a *weighted* average. In the case of distance, the weighted average reflects how much time each rate, or speed, was in effect. A distance-time graph can help make clear that the average rate can be thought of as the total distance spread evenly over the total time. ♦

Learning Exercises for Section 14.3

1. One day, Duke earns $8.00/h for the first 4 hours that he works, and then he earns $16.00/h for the next 4 hours.
   a. How much money has he earned at the end of the day?
   b. What hourly rate must he work at for 8 hours to earn the same daily amount?
   c. If Duke worked at $8.00/h for 2 hours and at $16.00/h for 6 hours, what would be his average hourly rate for the 8 hours?

2. In Tokyo, a taxi cab ride can commonly cost as much as $100.00 or more. The breakdown on how much you might be charged by the mile is as follows, converting from units used in Tokyo:
   $8.00/mile for the first 7 miles.
   $4.00/mile for the next 9 miles.
   $2.00/mile for every mile after that.
   a. How much would a 30-mile cab ride cost?
   b. What is the average dollar/mile rate for the 30-mile ride?

3. John is participating in the triathlon. He swims at a rate of 2 mi/h, and he can run at a rate of 6 mi/h. The course is broken down in the following manner:
   1st leg—swimming—6 miles
   2nd leg—running—15 miles
   3rd leg—bicycling—18 miles

   How fast will John have to bicycle if he wants to finish the race in 7 hours flat?

4. Make graphs to help find the following.
   a. The average cost per mile for the taxi ride in Learning Exercise 2(b).
   b. John's bicycle speed in Learning Exercise 3 to finish in 7 hours.

5. Jasmine transferred to State University from City Community College. At CCC she earned 36 credits and had a GPA of 3.2. She has been at State now for two semesters and has earned 24 credits with a GPA of 2.6. What is her overall GPA?

6. Kayla typed for two hours at 70 words/minute, then took a coffee break for 15 minutes, and then typed for another hour at 55 words/minute. Homer, on the other hand, typed at one speed for the total $3\frac{1}{4}$ hours. How fast did he type if he typed the same number of words as Kayla did over the $3\frac{1}{4}$ hours?

7. Rabbit's pride has suffered, and he wants to run more races. His friends are all betting on which race will be closest and which will not be close. Arrange in order the races below so that your race 1 is the closest (and most exciting), your 2 the next closest, and your 3 not very close at all. The total distance is 100 meters. (If Over & Back is available, you can check your answers, but make predictions first!)

R Over (m/s)	R Back (m/s)	T Both (m/s)	Predicted winner?	Rank of how close the race will be	Speed at which T would have to run to tie
8	2	5			
0.5	9.5	5			
4.5	5.5	5			

8. In an Over & Back race of 40 meters total distance, Rabbit's speeds are 5 m/s over and 10 m/s back. Turtle's speed both ways is 6 m/s.

   a. Who will be ahead 1.5 seconds after the race starts and by how much?

   b. Who will be ahead 5.5 seconds after the race starts and by how much? Can you tell when and where Rabbit catches up with Turtle?

   c. Who wins the race and by how much time? How many meters is the loser behind when the race is over?

   d. Would your answers to parts (b) and (c) change if Rabbit's speeds were reversed: 10 m/s over and 5 m/s back? (Turtle's speed stays at 6 m/s each way.)

9. Understanding average speed is often difficult because of the influence of calculating averages. But notice Xenia's reasoning below. Xenia was 7 years old when her mother shared this story!

   Mother, while driving: "If we drove for two hours on the freeway, at 60 mph, and then got off the freeway and drove for an hour through the city at 20 mph, what was our average speed?"

   Xenia thought for a while and said, "I think it would be something like 50."

   Mother had asked Xenia to explain her reasoning so often that it was a habit by now, so Xenia continued, "I think that because we went 60 a lot longer than we went 20, so the 20 will only pull the 60 down a little bit."

   a. Is Xenia's reasoning correct?

   b. What would the exact average speed be?

   c. What does the answer to part (b) mean?

10. In a race of 120 meters total distance, Rabbit gave Turtle a 4-second head start. Then Rabbit ran 2 m/s over, and ran an unknown speed back. Turtle ran 3 m/s both ways, after the head start.

    a.   What fractional part of the way over was Turtle's head start?

    b.   If Rabbit and Turtle tied, how fast did Rabbit run on the way back? (Do not overlook Turtle's head start.)

    c.   If Turtle had run 3.173 m/s (with the same head start) and Rabbit had run as given and as in part (b), who would have won the race?

11. In a race of 60 meters total distance, Rabbit ran 5 m/s over, stopped to eat a carrot for 4 seconds, and then ran back in 5 seconds. Turtle ran at the same speed, over and back.

    a.   What was Rabbit's speed back?

    b.   If Turtle and Rabbit tied, what was Turtle's speed over and back?

    c.   Twelve seconds into the race, where were Rabbit and Turtle located?

12. Suppose Tabatha rode her bike 3 miles in half an hour, then 12 miles in 1 hour.

    a.   Graph this information. What is Tabatha's average speed for each of the two legs of her journey?

    b.   Carly rode her bike 15 miles in 1.5 hours. What is her average speed for this trip? Graph this information onto the same graph as in part (a).

    c.   What was Tabatha's average speed?

    d.   What was Carly's average speed?

    e.   If your answers are the same for parts (c) and (d), why? If your answers are different for parts (c) and (d), why?

13. Jerold took a taxi from his hotel to the airport. For the first 15 minutes the taxi was slowed down by traffic and traveled just 4 miles. The taxi then entered a tunnel and drove 2 miles in 5 minutes. Once out of the tunnel the taxi drove another 7 miles in 15 minutes. The taxi then entered the freeway and drove 15 miles in 15 minutes. Finally, the taxi exited the freeway, drove 4 miles in 10 minutes, and then dropped Jerold off for his flight.

    a.   Make a graph of Jerold's trip.

    b.   What was his average speed during each of the 5 legs of his trip?

    c.   Find the average rate for Jerold's trip.

    d.   Cassie was at the same hotel as Jerold, and she took a later taxi to the airport, 32 miles away. The trip took an hour at a steady speed. Graph her journey on the same graph as Jerold's trip.

    e.   What does this new line on the graph tell you?

14.4 | Algebra as Generalized Arithmetic

Some states now consider algebra to be an eighth-grade subject. However, most teachers and curriculum organizers acknowledge that preliminary work with algebra should be a part of the curriculum before the eighth grade. First-graders, for example, may see $4 + 3 = n$ instead of just $4 + 3 = $ ___. And children may look for patterns in a variety of numerical settings (looking ahead to Chapter 15). Students in the intermediate grades may draw coordinate graphs for simple equations, as was done in Chapters 12 and 13.

This section treats one prominent view of algebra: algebra as generalized arithmetic. Consider, for example, how properties of operations can be generalized, moving from arithmetic to algebra. Here are two basic problems.

♦ A boy wants to buy chocolates. Each chocolate costs 50 cents. He wants to buy 3 chocolates. How much money does he need? ♦

♦ A boy wants to buy chocolates. Each chocolate costs 3 cents. He wants to buy 50 chocolates. How much money does he need? ♦

As you know, *without calculating*, the products involved in the problems will give the same answer. However, Brazilian street children[i] given these two problems could do the first but not the second. The total of 3 fifties is *conceptually quite different* from the total of 50 threes, even though we know each will give the same total.

This remarkable relationship always holds with multiplication of two numbers (and less surprisingly with addition), and is generalized as the commutative property of multiplication: $a \times b = b \times a$ for every choice of numbers a and b. The $\times$ sign is easily confused with the variable x, so both the raised dot (as in $a \cdot b$ or $2 \cdot b$) and juxtaposition (as in ab or $2b$) are commonly used in algebra to indicate multiplication. Commutativity is then compactly expressed by the statement $ab = ba$ for every choice of numbers or algebraic expressions a and b, the usual algebraic form. Any algebraic expressions can play the roles of a and b. For example, commutativity of multiplication assures that $(3x + 8)(2x + 5)$ and $(2x + 5)(3x + 8)$ will be equal for any choice of the variable x.

Other properties of operations, like associativity of addition or multiplication and distributivity of multiplication over addition, have roots in arithmetic.

Our place-value numeration system gives another illustration of algebra as a generalization of arithmetic. You know that one expanded form of 452 is $400 + 50 + 2$, or $4 \cdot 100 + 5 \cdot 10 + 2$. A similar expanded form uses exponents: $452 = 4 \cdot 10^2 + 5 \cdot 10^1 + 2 \cdot 10^0$, or just $4 \cdot 10^2 + 5 \cdot 10 + 2$. The last form does not require knowledge of 0 as an exponent.

If we use the variable x instead of 10 in the last expression, we get the expression $4 \cdot x^2 + 5 \cdot x^1 + 2$, or $4x^2 + 5x + 2$, which is a **polynomial in x**.

> A **polynomial in some variable** is any sum of number multiples of (nonnegative) powers of the variable. The expressions that are added (or subtracted) are called **terms** of the polynomial, so $4x^2$, $5x$, and 2 are the terms of the polynomial $4x^2 + 5x + 2$.

Arithmetic that has been learned conceptually can lead naturally to polynomial arithmetic. Here is an example of how addition of polynomials is "just like" addition of multi-digit whole numbers.

	Consider	and contrast that with
	452	$4x^2 + 5x + 2$
	$+324$	$+\ \ 3x^2 + 2x + 4$

The parallel is clearer in the expanded form:

$$4 \cdot 10^2 + 5 \cdot 10 + 2 \qquad\qquad 4x^2 + 5x + 2$$
$$+\quad 3 \cdot 10^2 + 2 \cdot 10 + 4 \qquad\qquad +\quad 3x^2 + 2x + 4$$

The usual algorithm for adding whole numbers transfers to the polynomial form:

$$4 \cdot 10^2 + 5 \cdot 10 + 2 \qquad\qquad 4x^2 + 5x + 2$$
$$+\quad 3 \cdot 10^2 + 2 \cdot 10 + 4 \qquad\qquad +\quad 3x^2 + 2x + 4$$
$$7 \cdot 10^2 + 7 \cdot 10 + 6 \qquad\qquad 7x^2 + 7x + 6$$

The usual algorithms are efficient in part because they ignore the many steps that are necessary if one had to be explicit about the properties of operations involved. The properties are clearer when the calculation is written in horizontal form. For example, $452 + 324$ is the same as $(4 \cdot 10^2 + 5 \cdot 10 + 2) + (3 \cdot 10^2 + 2 \cdot 10 + 4)$, but the usual algorithm calculates $(2 + 4) + (5 + 2) \cdot 10 + (4 + 3) \cdot 10^2$, in that order. The vertical form, however, gives the answer as $(4 + 3) \cdot 10^2 + (5 + 2) \cdot 10 + (2 + 4)$.

Discussion 5   Properties Working for Us

What properties assure that…

$$(4 \cdot 10^2 + 5 \cdot 10 + 2) + (3 \cdot 10^2 + 2 \cdot 10 + 4)$$

is indeed the same as

$$(4 + 3) \cdot 10^2 + (5 + 2) \cdot 10 + (2 + 4)?$$

(*Reminder:* Properties include not only commutativity of addition and multiplication, but also the associative properties, the additive identity (0), the multiplicative identity (1), distributivity of multiplication over addition, and so on. See Sections 10.2 and 10.3.)

Isn't it fortunate that the usual algorithm for adding multi-digit whole numbers allows us to bypass being explicit about each use of a property? The usual algorithm for multiplying multi-digit whole numbers also disguises the fact that properties can explain why the algorithm gives correct answers. The same properties apply to the multiplication of polynomials.

Discussion 6   Multiplying Polynomials Is Like Multiplying Whole Numbers

1. How does   transfer to

$$\begin{array}{r} 32 \\ \times\,4 \\ \hline \end{array}$$ $$\begin{array}{r} 3n+2 \\ \times\,4 \\ \hline \end{array}?$$ What property is involved?

2. How does   transfer to

$$\begin{array}{r} 32 \\ \times\,14 \\ \hline \end{array}$$ $$\begin{array}{r} 3n+2 \\ \times\ n+4 \\ \hline \end{array}?$$ What property is involved?

Writing the calculations in Discussion 6 in horizontal form helps you see what properties are being used.

For the numerical calculation:

$$4\times(30+2)=(4\times30)+(4\times2) \qquad \text{(distributivity)}$$

For the corresponding algebraic calculation:

$$4\times(3n+2)=(4\times3n)+(4\times2) \qquad \text{(distributivity)}$$

So, distributivity (of multiplication over addition) is involved in the numerical calculation as well as in the algebraic calculation as well. Further, $(10 + 4) \times 32 = (10 \times 32) + (4 \times 32)$ does not give all the steps in the usual algorithm until we use distributivity again:

$$(10\times32)+(4\times32)=(10\times[30+2])+(4\times[30+2])$$

This last equation gives the following, but not in the usual algorithm order because that algorithm starts at the right.

$$(10\times[30+2])+(4\times[30+2])=(10\times30)+(10\times2)+(4\times30)+(4\times2).$$

The four multiplications shown on the right-hand side are the basic ones that we compute when multiplying 14 and 32.

Similarly, $(n + 4)(3n + 2)$ involves the sum of the four multiplications, 4×2, $4 \times 3n$, $n \times 2$, and $n \times 3n$. (Compare the vertical form.) Notice that each term in the $n + 4$ expression is multiplied by each term in the $3n + 2$ expression. In either the numerical or the algebraic case, distributivity is used more than once.

Notes

Discussion 7   Algebraic and Numerical Division Algorithms

How does $12\overline{)276}$ transfer to $x+2\overline{)2x^2+7x+6}$?

TAKE-AWAY MESSAGE . . . If you understand the underlying reasons for properties and procedures with numbers, then you can generalize those reasons to corresponding situations with polynomial expressions. ♦

Learning Exercises for Section 14.4

1. Evaluate and then express each of the following as a general property, using variables. Give the name of the property.

   a. $(18 \times 93) + (18 \times 7)$ can be calculated mentally and exactly by $18 \times (93 + 7)$.

   b.   12 nickels plus 8 nickels has the same penny value as $12 + 8$, or 20, nickels.

   c. $(231 + 198) + 2$ can be calculated exactly by $231 + (198 + 2)$.

   d. $(17 \times 25) \times 4$ can be calculated mentally and exactly by $17 \times (25 \times 4)$.

   e. $\dfrac{117}{298} \times \dfrac{39}{39}$ is an easy mental calculation.

   f. $\dfrac{0}{24} + \dfrac{13}{35}$ is an easy mental calculation.

   g.   Each of 4 pockets has a dime and 7 pennies. Calculate the total value in two ways.

2. Write each of the following numbers first in an expanded form using exponents, and then give the suggested polynomial.

   EXAMPLE

   $6012 = 6 \cdot 10^3 + 0 \cdot 10^2 + 1 \cdot 10^1 + 2$, or $6 \cdot 10^3 + 1 \cdot 10 + 2$. A polynomial form for 6012 is $6x^3 + x + 2$ (with $x = 10$).

   a. 7403   **b.** 41,792   **c.** 5000

   d. 142_{five} **e.** 2897_{twelve} **f.** 101101_{two}

3. Use the numerical calculation to transfer to the algebraic calculation. Give the answer to the algebraic calculation.

   a.   8143 $8x^3 + x^2 + 4x + 3$

   $\underline{+1305}$ $\underline{+x^3 + 3x^2 + 5}$

   b.   234 $2x^2 + 3x + 4$

   $\underline{+98}$ $\underline{+9x + 8}$

   (Notice the contrast for "carries" when x is unknown. That is, with a known value for x, such as $x = 10$, $3x + 9x = 12x$ leads further to 12×10, or $100 + 2 \times 10$.)

c. $\begin{array}{r} 34 \\ \times\, 12 \\ \hline \end{array}$ $\begin{array}{r} 3n + 4 \\ \times\ n + 2 \\ \hline \end{array}$

d. $\begin{array}{r} 235 \\ \times\, 86 \\ \hline \end{array}$ $\begin{array}{r} 2x^2 + 3x + 5 \\ \times\ \ \ \ \ 8x + 6 \\ \hline \end{array}$

(As in part (b), notice the contrast when x has no specified value.)

In parts (e) and (f), give a corresponding algebraic expression and calculate the answer to the algebra version.

e. $\begin{array}{r} 1407 \\ +\, 493 \\ \hline \end{array}$

f. $\begin{array}{r} 675 \\ \times\, 12 \\ \hline \end{array}$

4. Calculate the sum and product of the polynomials in each part.

a. $3x^2 + 7x + 4$ and $4x^2 + 9x + 3$

b. $\frac{7}{8}x + \frac{1}{6}$ and $\frac{5}{3}x + \frac{3}{4}$

c. $0.8x + 0.73$ and $1.3x + 0.9$

d. $174x + 19$ and $288x + 58$

e. $7x + 6$ and $10x + {}^-3$

f. $4x + 7$ and $3 + 9x$

g. $3x + {}^-5$ and ${}^-2x + {}^-7$

h. $x + 3$ and $2x + 0.5$

i. $x + 2,\ 3x + 5,$ and $2x + {}^-9$

5. Areas and volumes can give insight into some algebraically equivalent expressions. Using sketches, find or verify equivalent expressions in the following.

a. $(x + y)^2 = \ldots$

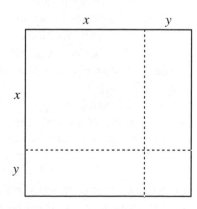

b. $(x + y)^3 = x^3 + 3x^2y + 3xy^2 + y^3$

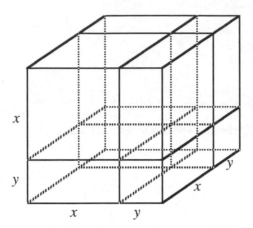

c. $x(x + y) = \ldots$ (make your own drawing)

d. $(x + 2)(x + 3) = \ldots$

14.5 | Issues for Learning: Topics in Algebra

There has been a great deal of research on the learning and teaching of algebra. Now that the elementary school curriculum is including more ideas of algebra, there is naturally more research done with elementary school children. This section will draw primarily from compilations of the research[ii, iii] and present some of the findings, with an eye toward alerting you to the expectations that now exist and to some of the obstacles that children seem to encounter in learning algebra.

In Section 13.5, we mentioned several types of common errors made by students with coordinate graphs. In this section, we consider four of the difficulties that children face in dealing with algebraic ideas and notations, according to the research. These include (a) difficulties in dealing with differences in algebraic notation, including differences in algebraic notation from arithmetic notation; (b) confusion about the meaning of variables; (c) conventions like the order of operations; and (d) dealing with elementary but conceptually more difficult equations.

Difficulties with algebraic notation. Algebraic notation can cause confusion with children who are quite comfortable with numbers. Some students believe that if the letter for a variable appears later in the alphabet, then the later letter represents a larger value. So, they believe, if $a = 5$, then n or x would have a value greater than 5.

Many students think that different variables must have different values. For example, only about three fourths of a large group of sixth graders responded correctly when asked, "Is $h + m + n = h + p + n$ always, sometimes, or never true?" To prompt students to acknowledge the possibility that two different variables, in this case m and p, could have the same value, teachers used the following problem and asked students to write an equation for the problem.

EXAMPLE 3

♦ Ricardo has 8 pet mice. He keeps them in two cages that are connected so that the mice can go back and forth between the two cages. One of the cages is blue, and the other is green. Show all the ways that 8 mice can be in two cages.[iv] ♦

> *THINK ABOUT ...*
>
> How can Example 3 lead to an acceptance that two variables can have the same value? (Use *b* for the number of mice in the blue cage and *g* for the number in the green cage.)

Children are so accustomed to replacing an indicated calculation, say $152 + 389$, with the answer, 541, that they often have trouble regarding an expression like $x + 2$ as a single value. It is as though there is a compulsion to write a single expression, without operation signs, as the answer. So, for example, children might write $7n$ for $3n + 4$, or write $5xy$ for $2x + 3y$. The children have what researchers call an "apparent lack of closure" for expressions like $3n + 4$ or $2x + 3y$, not seeing them as representing a single value.

> *THINK ABOUT ...*
>
> What equation would you write to describe the following situation?
> At one university, there are 6 times as many students as professors.

Confusion about the meaning of variables. You should have said "$6P = S$" if you used P to stand for the number of professors and S to stand for the number of students. However, if you are like about two out of every five college students going into engineering (who presumably should be very mathematically able), you wrote something like the equation $6S = P$. This phenomenon has proved resistant to change, even when students make a correct drawing, so teachers, mathematics educators, and psychologists have looked for explanations. One idea is that the phrasing, "6 times as many students as professors" invites a translation into $6S = P$. Another hypothesis notes that, just as 12 inches = 1 foot, $6S = P$ gives a sort of measurement relationship: 6 students "make" 1 professor. Some regard the mistake $6S = P$ as further evidence of students' weak understanding of the symbol =. Many feel that students are using S as a label for "students" rather than for the number of students.

Your algebra teachers may have been insistent that you be explicit in your work, as in "$x = $ the number of gallons of gasoline" and not just "$x = $ gasoline." For the letters in algebra do represent numbers. You, like your algebra teachers, will have to emphasize the number nature of a variable, not its mnemonic (memory-aiding) role.

Order of operations. Some conventions in algebra (often not emphasized in arithmetic) appear to be difficult for students. Conventions are just how we do things, like write a 5 or a letter of the alphabet, but not for any intrinsic reason. If someone had decided at one time that we should make a symbol for five that looks different from the one we use, then that could have happened without loss...so long as the convention is widely followed. Writing "$n + n + n$" instead of "nnn" is an example, important because under our conventions, nnn means $n \cdot n \cdot n$.

A useful but arbitrary convention is the order of operations, useful because it allows us to avoid a lot of parentheses: First do calculations in parentheses (or other grouping symbols), then exponents, then multiplications and divisions as you encounter them going from left to right, and finally additions and subtractions as you encounter them going from left to right. "Please excuse my dear Aunt Sally" is a mnemonic you may have used (for *p*arentheses, *e*xponents, *m*ultiplications/*d*ivisions, *a*dditions/*s*ubtractions.)

> ### THINK ABOUT…
> What is the answer to this calculation: $3 + 15 \div 3 - 4 \times 2$?
>
> **A.** $^-9$ **B.** $^-2$ **C.** 0 **D.** 4 **E.** 5

Further research and development. The increased attention to algebra in elementary school has resulted in several research projects. One group of researchers[v] has been investigating how children can arrive at some of the properties of operations, like commutativity of addition or distributivity, through careful teacher planning and questioning. For example, in connection with a "How many of each?" activity focusing on the different ways that one could have 7 peas and carrots, first-grade children noted that 5 peas and 2 carrots has an "opposite," 2 peas and 5 carrots. Second graders, in making up a list of ways to make 10, referred to "turn arounds" in noting that $7 + 3$ also gives $3 + 7$. Students were convinced that such would always be true and verified it with problems like $17 + 4$ and $4 + 17$.

Despite this apparent mastery of commutativity of addition, when the children were asked whether, say, $13 + 12 = 12 + 13$ was true, the children refused to endorse it (even after verifying that each sum was 25). The children had formed the "=" means "Write the answer" belief mentioned above, and for $12 + 13 = 13 + 12$, "There's no answer here." Another group of children expressed commutativity of addition as the "switch-around rule." But as an example of over-generalizing, many of the children thought that the switch-around rule also applied to subtraction, so that $7 - 4 = 3$ and $4 - 7 = 3$.

The point here is that the basis for algebraic ideas can be laid at quite early ages, even without being formalized with conventional language or notation. Curricular materials that you use may provide opportunities to learn important ideas such as commutativity, without focusing on the term "commutativity."

Technology can be used to help young children work with algebraic ideas. There are, of course, drill and practice computer "games" for integer arithmetic. But more importantly, there is also computer software (like Over & Back) that involves quantities that can vary, like distance and speed, thus allowing instructors to introduce graphs, numerical tables, and the associated algebra, often with activities to be discussed among a small group of students. Spreadsheets, invented for business, can also be tailored to help to introduce algebraic variation and algebraic labeling.

Thus, with the increased attention to algebra in the elementary school curriculum, there has been a corresponding increase in novel curricular approaches to help bypass some difficulties and to give meaningful bases for algebraic ideas. With various states and districts now requiring algebra at the eighth grade, the importance of preparation for algebra in the elementary grades is clear. The topics covered in *Reasoning about Algebra and Change* (Chapters 12–15) will support your ability to deal with introductions to algebra.

Learning Exercises for Section 14.5

1. Explain why, in a turtle-rabbit race, writing just "T = turtle" and "R = rabbit" is not good practice. What should be written instead?

2. Practice the order of operations conventions in evaluating these expressions.

   a. $19 - 5 \times 2 + 6 \div 3 - 2^3 + 3(^-1)^3 + (8 + {}^-8)7$

   b. $4\frac{1}{2} + 9\frac{1}{8} + \frac{7}{8} \cdot (2^2)^4 - 3 \cdot (6 - {}^-2)^2$

3. For each given value of x, find the value of $2x^2 - 7x - 5$.

   a. 3   b. $^-4$ c. $\frac{2}{3}$ d. $\frac{-1}{2}$

4. For each of the following equations, make up a story problem that could be described by the equation.

   a. $n + 7 = 13$ b. $7 + n = 13$

   c. $n - 6 = 9$ d. $14 - n = 6$

   e. $2n + 1.95 = 4.15$ f. $\frac{n}{25} = 76\%$

5. What property is suggested by viewing the following drawing in two ways, as in the curriculum adapted from Russia? (See Section 12.4.)

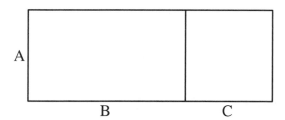

6. How does a drawing for the students-professors problem presumably make clear that the equation $6S = P$ is inappropriate?

14.6 | Check Yourself

After this chapter, you should be able to do problems like those assigned and to meet the following objectives.

1. Write or recognize an equation for a given situation or graph.

2. Use a designated method (numerical, graphical, algebraic) to solve a problem or use quantitative reasoning to solve it.

3. Give some points in favor of, and against, numerical, graphical, or algebraic methods of solving a problem.

4. Write a story for a given graph, showing alertness to changes in slopes, changes in time, or changes in distance or position.

5. Deal with weighted averages, as in finding an average speed or a grade-point average.

6. Give a (noncomputational) explanation of "average."

7. Name the properties involved in given numerical or algebraic work.

8. Give parallel numerical and algebraic calculations, and point out how they are alike.

9. Calculate the sum and product of two polynomials.

Note: The Over & Back activities and learning exercises in Section 14.3 were adapted from those written by Dr. Helen Doerr and Preety Nigam from Syracuse University, and revised by Dr. Janet Bowers and Dr. Joanne Lobato from San Diego State University. Dr. Bowers designed, programmed, and implemented the version of Over & Back used at San Diego State University, based on the original version by Dr. Patrick Thompson.

REFERENCES FOR CHAPTER 14

[i]Schliemann, A. D., Araujo, C., Cassundé, M. A., Macedo, S., & Nicéas, L. (1998). Use of multiplicative commutativity by school children and street sellers. *Journal for Research in Mathematics Education, 29*, pp. 422–435.

[ii]Kieran, C. (1992). The learning and teaching of school algebra. In D. Grouws (Ed.), *Handbook of research on mathematics teaching and learning*, pp. 390–419. New York: Macmillan. (A similar handbook, edited by Frank Lester, Jr., became available in 2007 from National Council of Teachers of Mathematics.)

[iii]National Research Council. (2001). *Adding it up: Helping children learn mathematics*. J. Kilpatrick, J. Swafford, & B. Findell (Eds.). Mathematics Learning Study Committee, Center for Education, Division of Behavioral and Social Sciences and Education. Washington, DC: National Academy Press.

[iv]Stephens, A. C. (2005). Developing students' understandings of variable. *Mathematics Teaching in Middle School, 11*(2), pp. 96–100.

[v]Schifter, D., Monk, S., Russell, S. J., Bastable, V., & Earnest, D. (2003, April). Early Algebra: What Does Understanding the Laws of Arithmetic Mean in the Elementary Grades? Paper presented at the annual meeting of the National Council of Teachers of Mathematics, San Antonio. (This work may now be described in a book by D. Carraher, J. Kaput, & M. Blanton, *Algebra in the Early Grades*.)

Chapter 15

Patterns and Functions

Mathematics is sometimes described as *the science of patterns*, because it involves the study of patterns in numbers, in shapes or objects, and even in systems. This brief description highlights the importance in mathematics of patterns, especially an important type of pattern called *functions*. Exercises in recognizing, describing, and extending patterns occur in the curriculum even in the first grade. Numerical patterns often involve some calculation practice within the larger goal of seeing what the pattern is. In this chapter, our focus is on patterns, in general, and functions. We also discuss proportion again, but this time as a linear function representable by a graph that goes through the origin.

15.1 Numerical Patterns and Functions

The primary focus of this section will be numerical patterns. However, you should be aware that repeating patterns of blocks or shapes, as in the following diagram, can appear in first-grade textbooks.

The following sequence of numbers is an example of a typical numerical pattern exercise given in the early grades.

♦ What numbers go in the blanks to continue the pattern?

7, 17, 27, 37, ___, ___. ♦

In later grades children might be asked to tell what the 51st number in the pattern is, a more challenging exercise, with the intent that the child *not* fill in all the intervening blanks.

THINK ABOUT . . .
Jan decided that the 51st number would be 507. How do you think Jan reasoned?

339

Asking about the 51st number suggests that the list can be associated with the counting numbers by referring to a number's location in the list: 7 is the 1(st) number in the pattern, 17 is the 2(nd), 27 is the 3(rd), and so on. This association leads to tables, as in the following example.

EXAMPLE 1

Make a table for this pattern of numbers: 3, 6, 9, 12, 15, ...

SOLUTION

Location in the list	1(st)	2(nd)	3(rd)	4(th)	5(th)
Actual number	3	6	9	12	15

(*Note*: The horizontal form is common in elementary school books because it fits on a textbook page a little better.)

We can rewrite this table vertically:

Location in the list	Actual number
1	3
2	6
3	9
4	12
5	15

Or, if we let x represent location and y represent the actual number in that location, then the table looks like this one:

x	y
1	3
2	6
3	9
4	12
5	15

This last table, with the column headings x and y, should help you see that work with patterns can lead to algebraic expressions, such as $y = 3x$ for the pattern in this example. The use of x and y also suggests that work with such tables is linked to coordinate graphs.

Tables like those in Example 1, in which each value of x corresponds to exactly one value of y, incorporate the basic idea of a mathematical **function**. You may be familiar with notations such as $f(x)$, which denotes the value associated with x. That is, instead of y as a column heading, one could use $f(x)$ and write $f(x) = 3x$. Letters other than f can be used, as in $g(x) = 2x + 3$; the context usually makes the notation clear, as well as what numbers are acceptable for x and for $f(x)$.

A **function** from one set to another (which may be the same set) is a correspondence in which each element of the first set is assigned to exactly one element of
the second set.

Based on what is given in Example 1, the first set (for x) consists of the whole numbers 1 through 5, and the second set (for y) would be any set containing 3, 6, 9, 12,
and 15. The equation representing the correspondence, $y = 3x$, is sometimes called
the **function rule**. So, from a more advanced mathematical viewpoint, when you
work with patterns, as you did in previous chapters with tables, graphs, and algebra,
you are also working with *functions*. Many of your previous graphs involved straight
lines, so the related functions are often called **linear functions**.

With a given table of given values and their corresponding values, you can do a
What's my rule? activity in which you look for a pattern and express its function rule.

> ***THINK ABOUT . . .***
>
> *What's My Rule?* for the following data?

When you say . . .	25	16	40	3
I say . . .	75	66	90	53

Using a table to find a function rule is a good practice, but doing so has risks. One
risk is that, even though you think that you have found the function rule, it might not
be the correct one. For example, the table in the above *Think About* "obviously" suggests the equation $y = x + 50$, but the function rule *might* actually be $y = x + 50 +
(x - 25)(x - 16)(x - 40)(x - 3)$. (Check to see that this function rule does give the
correct values in the table.) Which function rule is correct? For the given table of
numbers, either could be.

If the table were about some real situation, then you could check other values for x.
The guide we usually rely on is called *Occam's razor*, or the *principle of parsimony*:
The simplest explanation is the best one. So, if there is no way to check further, the
function rule $y = x + 50$ would naturally be the one used (but tentatively). At some
stage in their mathematics education, children should know that trusting a generalization based on a pattern is risky, but most work in schools proceeds as though the
simplest rule is the only one possible.

Some elementary school programs may include
not only work with patterns but also exposure to
functions in the guise of *function machines* like
the one pictured. The words *input* and *output*
might be used instead of x and y in tables. For
example, the function rule $y = 2x + 5$ [or $f(x) = 2x
+ 5$] might not appear, but could be expressed as
"output equals two times the input, plus 5." Children might be asked to complete a table for such a
machine and then to make a corresponding graph.

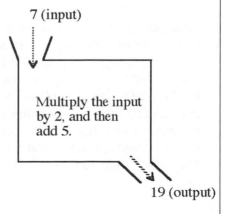

7 (input)

Multiply the input
by 2, and then
add 5.

19 (output)

Notes

Rather than trust completely a function rule or pattern based on a table of values, the mathematically sound way to proceed is to look for a justification that the rule must be correct. We will use the problem in Activity 1 to illustrate what a possible justification might look like. Note that the use of a specific large number, such as 100 in Activity 1, means that a child does not have to be algebraically sophisticated to reason about the situation.

Activity 1   Making a Row of Squares from Toothpicks

Pat made a pattern of squares from toothpicks, as in this drawing.

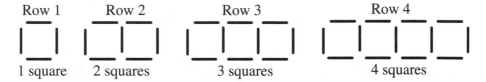

| Row 1 | Row 2 | Row 3 | Row 4 |
| 1 square | 2 squares | 3 squares | 4 squares |

How many toothpicks would Pat need to make a row with 100 squares? More generally, how many toothpicks would it take to make a row with n squares? (A good approach to solving this problem is to make a table, perhaps like the following one.)

Number of squares	Number of toothpicks
1	
2	
3	
4	
⋮	
100	
n	

THINK ABOUT . . .

Can you give a more complicated equation that also describes the entries in your table for Activity 1? (*Hint*: Remember that it is possible to use the equation $y = 3x + (x - 1)(x - 2)(x - 3)(x - 4)(x - 5)$, instead of the equation $y = 3x$ for the tables in Example 1.)

Your table in Activity 1 likely showed that the row with 1 square requires 4 toothpicks, the row with 2 squares requires 7 toothpicks, and so on. Did you see a pattern that enabled you to predict that it would take 301 toothpicks for the row with 100 squares and $3n + 1$ for the row with n squares? Perhaps you made a graph to get these results. The results for 100 and n certainly seem to fit the pattern. But is there a risk in endorsing these results enthusiastically? Some other rule might apply, perhaps as the number of squares gets much larger than 100. Is there any way, besides using *Occam's razor*, to argue that the results will always be correct for all values of n? The answer happens to be *yes*.

When dealing with patterns in mathematics, we try to justify the results in some way to show that the result *must be* true in *all* cases, not just the cases examined.

Discussion 1   Are These Justifications Convincing?

Which of these arguments, used to justify the result for the row with 100 squares, could be modified to justify the general $3n + 1$ result for a row of n squares, from Activity 1? If an argument is not strong, explain why.

1. *Mike*: "I needed 4 toothpicks for the first square, and then 3 more for each of the 99 squares after that. I got 301." In general, Mike's argument suggests the rule $f(n) = 4 + (n - 1)3$ for n squares.

2. *Nadia*: "I checked two more cases, and they worked. So it has to be all right."

3. *Oscar*: "Well, I put down 1 toothpick, and then every time I put down 3 more, I got another square. So $1 + 100 \times 3$." In general, Oscar's reasoning suggests the rule $f(n) = 1 + 3n$.

4. *Paloma*: "Across the top, there would be 100 toothpicks. In the middle, 101. And on the bottom, 100. So, 301." In general, Paloma's reasoning suggests the rule $f(n) = n + (n + 1) + n$.

5. *Quan*: "100 squares would take 400 toothpicks by themselves. But when you put them together, you don't need the extra ones inside, so subtract 99." In general, Quan's reasoning suggests the rule $f(n) = 4n - (n - 1)$.

6. *Ricky*: "Everyone I asked said the same thing, 301."

Because the toothpick problem is based in reality, there is a good chance that a mathematically sound justification can be offered, as illustrated by several of the arguments given in Discussion 1. If the table were just about numbers (with no context given), there would be no way to know whether the rule (or an algebraic equivalent) that you find is true in all cases, except with *Occam's razor*.

One type of pattern found in beginning work is so common that it has a name, and as a teacher, you should know about it even though the terms may not come up in elementary school. A pattern can be formed by adding (or subtracting) the same number, called the **common difference**, to any number in a list to get the next number. For example, consider the pattern 18, 23, 28, 33, 38, 43, ... The same number, 5 (the common difference), is added to a number to get the next number: **18 + 5 = 23, 23 + 5 = 28, 28 + 5 = 33**, and so on. Such patterns are called **arithmetic sequences**. The description of the nth term in an arithmetic sequence gives an equation whose graph is a straight line.

Activity 2   The *n*th Number in an Arithmetic Sequence

Find a function rule for the *n*th number in each of these arithmetic sequences. It may be instructive also to graph the values in the first table.

1.

Location?	Number?
1	75
2	82
3	89
4	96
⋮	⋮
n	

2.

Location?	Number?
1	a
2	$a + d$
3	$a + 2d$
4	$a + 3d$
⋮	⋮
n	

THINK ABOUT . . .

Why do Aña's and Bea's locations in the triathlon problem (from Example 1 in Section 14.2) give arithmetic sequences? What is the common difference for each sequence? Show that their locations after 20 minutes of running are 4500 m for Aña and 4600 m for Bea. (Note that $n = 21$ because time starts at 0 rather than 1.)

A pattern in which each number in a list is obtained by *multiplying* the number that precedes it by the same number is called a **geometric sequence**. For example, 4, 8, 16, 32, 64, . . . is a geometric sequence, with the multiplier being 2: **4 × 2 = 8, 8 × 2 = 16, 16 × 2 = 32**, and so on. The multiplier is often called the **common ratio**. Do you see why? Geometric sequences get less attention than arithmetic ones in the elementary school curriculum, but Learning Exercise 7 shows that in general, a function rule for the *n*th number in a geometric sequence can also be determined.

More complicated functions can involve two or more input quantities, as Activity 3 suggests.

Activity 3   The Soda Machine

PopsiCo has a machine for restaurants into which you pour containers of Secret Formula and identical containers of water. Out of the machine come cups of soda.

All the fluid that goes into the machine comes out of the machine. So, if 1 gallon of fluid (Secret Formula and water combined) goes into the machine, then 1 gallon of soda pop comes out of the machine.

Machine #3099 works this way: When you pour 3 containers of

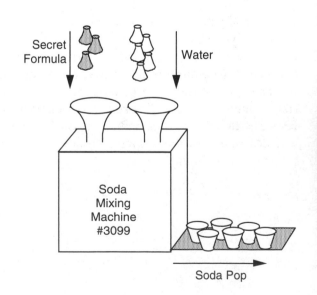

Secret Formula and 5 containers of water into the machine, you get 6 cups of soda pop out of the machine.

1. How many *cups* does one *container* of fluid hold? Explain.

2. How many *containers* of fluid does one *cup* hold? Explain.

3. What fraction of each cup is made up of Secret Formula? How do you know?

4. What fraction of each cup is made up of water? Explain.

5. Complete this table:

Number of containers of Secret Formula	Number of containers of water	Number of cups of soda pop
3	5	6
	8	
4		
		9
7		
	18	
n		
	k	
		h

Activity 3 provides an opportunity to review proportional thinking, introduced in Chapter 9 where you learned that a *rate* is a ratio of quantities that change without changing the value of the ratio. In Activity 3, Machine #3099 used 3 containers of Secret Formula for every 5 containers of water, so other mixtures would be equivalent to this mixture only when the ratio of the amounts of Secret Formula to water is $\frac{3}{5}$. That is, $f{:}w = 3{:}5$, or $\frac{f}{w} = \frac{3}{5}$, where f indicates the number of containers of Secret Formula and w the number of containers of water. Notice that $\frac{f}{w} = \frac{3}{5}$ leads to the expression $f = \frac{3}{5} w$. (Multiply both sides of $\frac{f}{w} = \frac{3}{5}$ by w.) Thus, given the number of containers of water, we could find the number of containers of the Secret Formula by multiplying the number of containers of water by $\frac{3}{5}$.

> **THINK ABOUT . . .**
>
> How many containers of Secret Formula should be used with 15 containers of water to obtain soda pop with the same taste as a mixture using 3 containers of Secret Formula to 5 containers of water? Why?

A graph of the function rule $f = \frac{3}{5} w$ would look like the following:

Notes

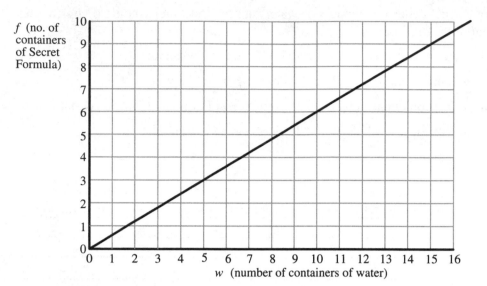

f (no. of containers of Secret Formula)

w (number of containers of water)

THINK ABOUT . . .

Use the graph to answer again the question: How many containers of Secret Formula should be used with 15 containers of water to obtain soda pop of the same taste as a mixture using 3 containers of Secret Formula to 5 containers of water?

Discussion 2   Is There More than One Rate Here?

Activity 3 involves another quantity: the number of cups of soda pop. Is this quantity related as a rate to either the number of containers of water or the number of containers of Secret Formula?

Many problems from Chapter 9 dealt with proportional relationships between quantities.

Activity 4   Donuts and Graphs

Learning Exercise 19 from Section 9.2 begins as follows:

♦ A donut machine produces 60 donuts every 5 minutes. How many donuts does it produce in an hour? ♦

a.   Identify the rate in this problem.

b.   What unit ratio is associated with this rate?

c.   Write a proportion that could be used to find the number of donuts produced in an hour.

d.   Make a graph of the number of donuts produced every minute. What is the slope of the line? (Remember to put *time* on the horizontal axis.)

The graphs in the soda pop and donut situations represent *proportional relationships*. In each case, the equation that describes the graph has the form $y = mx$, where m is some fixed value, and so the line begins at $(0, 0)$.

> If we can express a relationship in the form $y = mx$, the relationship between y and x is *proportional* because then the ratio $y : x$ always has the same value, m.

EXAMPLE 2

In the relationship $f = \frac{3}{5} w$, the number $\frac{3}{5}$ is the fixed value, and the relationship has the form $y = mx$, where f corresponds with y and w corresponds with x. This relationship is a linear function whose graph is a straight line beginning at $(0, 0)$.

EXAMPLE 3

In the donut problem in Activity 4, 12 donuts are produced every minute. This relationship can be expressed as $d = 12t$, where d is the number of donuts and t is the number of minutes. Again the equation has the form $y = mx$, with 12 as the constant m.

THINK ABOUT . . .

What is the slope of the line in Example 2? In Example 3? What does each slope mean?

Discussion 3   **Proportionally Related?**

1. Suppose that Clairisa can run 5 meters per second and Karlene can run 4 meters per second. Make a distance-time graph for each runner on the same coordinate system. How are the graphs different? How are they the same?

2. What is the equation in each case?

3. Are the distance and the time proportionally related in each case?

4. What is the slope of each line graph?

5. What is the unit rate for each runner?

6. Suppose that another runner, Tabbie, begins the race at the 4-meter marker and runs 4 meters per second. Make a graph of Tabbie's run. Will Clairisa overtake Tabbie? If so, when?

7. Write an equation to describe Tabbie's run.

8. Are Tabbie's distance and time proportionally related? Why or why not?

TAKE-AWAY MESSAGE . . . The study of patterns underlies a good part of mathematics and is the basis for the more advanced study of mathematical functions. Many numerical patterns can be described by function rules that enable us to determine the actual number at any location in the pattern. Although a pattern based on only examples might not be correct, many times it is possible to find a justification showing that the pattern will be true in general. A linear function takes the form $y = mx + b$ and gives a straight-line graph. As a special case, when $b = 0$, the equation takes the form $y = mx$, indicating that the variables are related proportionally. ◆

Learning Exercises for Section 15.1

1. For each pattern, give the next four entries and any particular entry requested, as suggested by the pattern. Assume that the patterns continue indefinitely.

    a. ABABAB __ __ __ __ ; the 100th entry is ____.

    b. ABBAABBA __ __ __ __ ; the 63rd entry is ____.

    c. 6.5, 7.3, 8.1, 8.9, ___, ___, ___, ___; the 20th entry is ____.

    d. 100, 95, 90, 85, ___, ___, ___, ___; the 30th entry is ____.

    e. 2, 6, 18, 54, ___, ___, ___, ___

    f. 5, 2.5, 1.25, 0.625, ___, ___, ___, ___

    g. $\frac{1}{1}, \frac{1}{2}, \frac{1}{3}, \frac{1}{4}, \frac{1}{5}$, ___, ___, ___, ___; the 100th entry is ____.

    h. $\frac{1}{2}, \frac{2}{3}, \frac{3}{4}, \frac{4}{5}$, ___, ___, ___, ___; the 100th entry is ____.

    i. 2, 4, 6, 8, 2, 4, 6, 8, ___, ___, ___, ___; the 30th entry is ____.

    j. 1, 4, 2, 8, 5, 7, 1, 4, 2, 8, 5, 7, 1, 4, ___, ___, ___, ___; the 40th entry is ____.

    k. Which of the sequences in parts (a)-(j) are arithmetic sequences?

    l. Are there any geometric sequences in parts (a)-(j)? If so, tell which parts.

2. **a.** Examine these (correct) calculations and look for an easy rule for multiplying by a power of 10. Write the rule.

$12.3457 \times 10 = 123.457$	$23 \times 10 = 230$
$12.3457 \times 100 = 1234.57$	$23 \times 100 = 2300$
$12.3457 \times 1000 = 12{,}345.7$	$23 \times 1000 = 23{,}000$
$12.3457 \times 10{,}000 = 123{,}457.$	$23 \times 10{,}000 = 230{,}000$
$12.3457 \times 100{,}000 = 1{,}234{,}570.$	$23 \times 100{,}000 = 2{,}300{,}000$

    b. Why does your rule work?

3. **a.** Examine these (correct) calculations and look for an easy rule for dividing by a power of 10. Write the rule.

$512.345 \div 10 = 51.2345$	$8.41 \div 10 = 0.841$
$512.345 \div 100 = 5.12345$	$8.41 \div 100 = 0.0841$
$512.345 \div 1000 = 0.512345$	$8.41 \div 1000 = 0.00841$
$512.345 \div 10{,}000 = 0.0512345$	$8.41 \div 10{,}000 = 0.000841$
$512.345 \div 100{,}000 = 0.00512345$	

    b. Why does your rule work?

Notes

c. How can this idea be used to find 1% of a known amount? 10% of a known amount?

4. Find a possible function rule for each table or graph. Then use your rule to find the numerical value for *n*, if *n* is indicated.

a.

x	y
1	9
2	30
3	51
4	72
⋮	⋮
n	1038

b.

x	f(x)
1	78
2	56
3	34
4	12
⋮	⋮
n	⁻120

c.

input	output
1	0
2	8
3	16
4	24
⋮	⋮
n	1608

d.

input	output
50	8
51	8.3
52	8.6
53	8.9
⋮	⋮
n	15.8

e.

x	g(x)
1	1
2	4
3	9
4	16
⋮	⋮
n	900

f.

x	h(x)
1	2
2	6
3	12
4	20
5	30
⋮	⋮
n	9900

g.

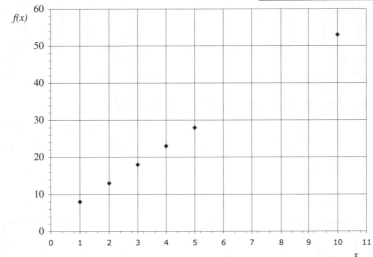

h.

x	y
3	12
1	2
4	17
2	7
⋮	⋮
n	547

i.

x	f(x)
2	35
1	19
3	51
0	3
4	67
⋮	⋮
n	403

j.

x	f(x)
0	$\frac{1}{2}$
1	$1\frac{1}{6}$
2	$1\frac{5}{6}$
3	$2\frac{1}{2}$
4	$3\frac{1}{6}$
⋮	⋮
n	$8\frac{1}{2}$

Continue on the next page.

k. Which of parts (a) through (j) are examples of arithmetic sequences?

l.

x	y
1	1
2	8
3	27
4	64
⋮	⋮
n	729

m.

x	y
1	3
2	10
3	29
4	66
⋮	⋮
n	1002

n.

x	y
0	4
3	8
4	$9\frac{1}{3}$
5	$10\frac{2}{3}$
⋮	⋮
n	84

5. Find a function rule for each of the following patterns, and justify that your rule will be true in general.

a. The number of toothpicks to make Shape n in the pattern:

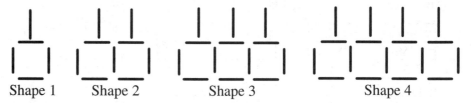

Shape 1   Shape 2   Shape 3   Shape 4

b. The number of toothpicks to make Double-decker n:

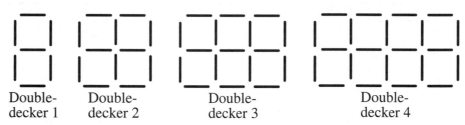

Double-   Double-   Double-   Double-
decker 1   decker 2   decker 3   decker 4

c. The number of toothpicks to make Shape n:

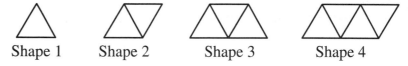

Shape 1   Shape 2   Shape 3   Shape 4

d. The number of toothpicks to make Shape n:

Shape 1   Shape 2   Shape 3

e. The number of toothpicks to make Rowhouse n:

Rowhouse 1   Rowhouse 2   Rowhouse 3

f. Make up a toothpick pattern of your own, and challenge others to find a rule for it.

6. Lee and Ronnie are discussing the patterns given in Learning Exercise 5. Lee says, "Someone told me that for part 5(e), the function rule $f(n) = 5n + 6 + 2(n-1)(n-2)$ works just fine." Ronnie says, "I don't know, I heard that $g(n) = 5n + 6 + 18(n-1)(n-2)(n-3)$ works all the time."

a. How might you convince Lee that the function rule told to her is incorrect?

b. How might you convince Ronnie that the function rule overheard is incorrect?

c. Make up a function rule for part 5(e) that works for the first 4 shapes, but does not work in general.

7. Look for a rule that gives the *n*th number in the geometric sequence given by the table.

a.

x	y
1	5
2	10
3	20
4	40
5	80
...	...
n	...

b.

x	y
1	a
2	ar
3	ar^2
4	ar^3
5	ar^4
n	....

8. The numbers 1, 1, 2, 3, 5, 8, . . . are an example of a Fibonacci (fee ba-NAH-chee) sequence, which is a pattern that appears in nature, art, and geometry.

a. What are the next four numbers in that Fibonacci sequence? (*Hint:* Look at two adjacent numbers, and then the next one.)

b. Amazingly, the *n*th number in that Fibonacci sequence is
$$\frac{(1+\sqrt{5})^n - (1-\sqrt{5})^n}{2^n\sqrt{5}}.$$ Verify that for $n = 1$ and $n = 2$, the expression does give the first two numbers in the pattern, 1 and 1.

c. Give decimals for the first ten ratios of consecutive Fibonacci numbers: $\frac{1}{1}, \frac{2}{1}, \frac{3}{2}, \frac{5}{3}, \frac{8}{5}, \ldots$ The ratios get closer and closer to a special value that is called the ***golden ratio***. The golden ratio is often used in art to make pleasing proportions.

9. Some *sums* of patterns are not difficult to predict.

a.

How many evens (starting with 2)?	Sum of those evens
1	**2**
2	$2 + 4 = $ **6**
3	$2 + 4 + 6 = $ **12**
4	$2 + 4 + 6 + 8 = $ **20**
5	$2 + 4 + 6 + 8 + 10 = $ **30**
n	$2 + 4 + \ldots + (2n) = $?

b. Use part (a) and algebra to show that

$$1 + 2 + 3 + 4 + \ldots + n = \frac{n(n + 1)}{2}.$$

c. Use part (b) and algebra to show that

$$6 + 12 + 18 + 24 + \ldots + (6n) = 3n(n + 1).$$

d. What is the sum of the first *n odd* numbers? (*Hint*: Make a table, or use your results from parts (b) and (a).)

10. Rather than just finding the *n*th number in an arithmetic sequence, many times we want to find the *sum* of the first *n* numbers. Look for a pattern in the following table to see whether the sum of the first *n* terms in an arithmetic sequence is predictable. (*Hint*: See Learning Exercise 9(b).)

How many?	Arithmetic sequence	Sum
1	a	a
2	$a + d$	$a + (a + d) = 2a + d$
3	$a + 2d$	$a + (a + d) + (a + 2d) = 3a + 3d$
4	$a + 3d$	$\ldots = 4a + 6d$
5	$a + 4d$	$\ldots = 5a + 10d$
n	$a + (n - 1)d$	$\ldots = ?$

11. How many small squares will be in an *n*-step stairway like those shown in the following diagram? (*Hint*: See Exercise 9(b).)

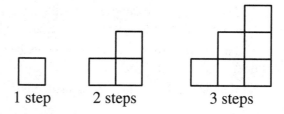

1 step   2 steps   3 steps

12. Formulas can be viewed as defining functions. For example, the formula $C = \frac{5}{9}(F - 32)$ tells what Celsius temperature, *C*, corresponds to a Fahrenheit temperature, *F*.

a. What Celsius temperatures correspond to the boiling point of water (212° F), the freezing point of water (32° F), normal body temperature (98.6° F), and a comfortable temperature of 70° F?

b. Use algebra to write the Fahrenheit temperature *F* as a function of the Celsius temperature: $F = \ldots$.

13. a. What is the *n*th fraction in the following sequence?

$$\frac{1}{2}, \ \frac{1}{4}, \ \frac{1}{8}, \ \frac{1}{16}, \ \frac{1}{32}, \ldots$$

b. What is the *sum* of the first *n* of those fractions? To what number is the sum getting closer and closer?

14. a. What digit is in the ones' place in the calculated form of 3^{250}?

b. What digit is in the ones' place in the calculated form of 7^{350}?

c. What digit is in the ones' place in the calculated form of $3^{250} \cdot 7^{350}$?

d. Write down how you would proceed to find the digit in the ones' place in the calculated form of 7^{n}.

15. *Jump-It* is a label for this puzzle. There are two colors of round markers, 3 of each color. They are arranged on a 7-square row, as below.

a. Can you switch the colors, so that each color is on the other end with an empty square in the middle, subject to these two rules?

Rule 1. A marker can be moved to an adjacent empty square.

Rule 2. A marker can "jump" a marker in the next square, if there is an empty square on the other side of the jumped marker.

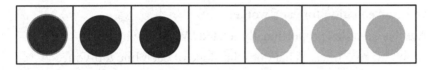

b. What is the minimum number of moves for the markers to change ends? (*Hint*: It is not 17.)

c. What is the minimum number of moves, if there are *n* markers on each end, with an empty square in the middle? (*Hint*: A good problem-solving approach is to look at simpler problems and look for a pattern. Here, there is a pattern relating the number on each end and the minimum number of jumps.)

16. (See *Activity 3* in this section.) A new PopsiCo Machine #4138 works this way: When you pour 4 containers of Secret Formula and 2 identical containers of water into the machine, you get 11 cups of soda pop out of the machine.

a. How many *cups* does one *container* of fluid hold? Explain.

b. How many *containers* of fluid does one *cup* hold? Explain.

c. What fraction of each cup is made up of Secret Formula? Explain.

d. What fraction of each cup is made up of water? Explain.

e. Show that the relationship between containers of Secret Formula and containers of water is a proportional one.

17. A particular bologna machine gives 8 packages of bologna for every 7 pounds of raw food.

a. How many packages of bologna could be produced by 1 pound of raw food?

b. How many pounds of raw food make 1 package of bologna?

c. If 10 pounds of raw food are put into the machine, how many packages of bologna would the machine give?

18. Chris and Sam biked from Childress to Navalo, a distance of 82 miles. Chris's average speed was 12 miles per hour, and Sam's average speed was 10 miles per hour.

a. Chris and Sam begin at the same time. On the same coordinate system, make distance-time graphs showing Chris's and Sam's trips from Childress to Navalo.

b. Write equations for each of the bikers.

c. What is the slope of each line?

d. Abby also biked from Childress to Navalo at 10 miles per hour, but she began an hour earlier than Chris and Sam. Graph Abby's trip on the same coordinate system as that for Chris's and Sam's trips. Write the equation for Abby's trip, as shown on the graph. What is the slope for Abby's graph?

e. Which graphs show proportional relationships? Why?

19. Learning Exercise 9 in Section 9.2 gives the following problem:

♦ Two workers working 9 hours made 243 parts. Worker A makes 13 parts in one hour. If the workers work at a steady rate throughout the day, who is more productive, Worker A or Worker B? ♦

Assume the workers begin work at the same time and both work for 9 hours.

a. Write an equation for each worker.

b. Are the variables proportionally related? Why or why not?

c. Graph the two lines. What does the slope of each line tell you?

20. Which of these five graphs show a proportional relationship?

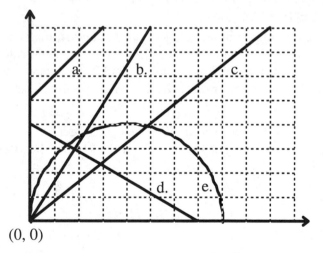

(0, 0)

21. Which of the following situations provides a proportional relationship between the two variables suggested? Make clear what the variables are.

a. The distance d traveled by a rock dropped from a tall building can be described by the equation, $d = 16t^2$, where d is in feet and t is the number of seconds after the rock is dropped.

b. The speed s of a falling body t seconds after it is released is given by $s = 32t$.

c. Every 7 crackers have 120 calories.

d. Tickets for a balcony section cost $45 each.

22. What digit is in the 99th decimal place in the decimal for $\frac{1}{7}$? Explain your reasoning.

23. Each of the three students below is arguing that his/her function rule is the correct one. What do you say to them?

Abe: $f(x) = 2(x + x)$ Beth: $f(x) = 4x$ Candra: $f(x) = x + x + x + x$

24. Many function rules that appear in elementary school will be simple, but polynomial rules like $f(n) = 2n^3 + 3n + 8$ can occur. The variable can also appear in exponents, as in geometric series. Verify for $n = 1, 2, 3, 4, 5,$ and 6, that $f(n) = (^-1)^n$ gives the nth number in this list:

$$-1, 1, -1, 1, -1, \ldots.$$

25. Figure out a shortcut for squaring a number ending in 5.

15.2 More Uses for Functions

Many patterns and functions deal with numbers, or numbers inside problems, as with the toothpick arrangements shown in Section 15.1. But there are other situations in which numbers play only a part of the role or even no role at all. For example, in tossing a coin and noting whether heads or tails comes out on top, you may have heard used the phrase "the probability of heads is $\frac{1}{2}$." In this case, each outcome of the coin toss is either heads or tails, an object rather than a number, but each outcome corresponds to a number. Hence, a notation like $P(heads) = \frac{1}{2}$ is quite reasonable and does resemble the typical $f(x)$ notation. Activity 5 gives an example of a function that does not involve numbers at all.

Activity 5   **Through the Looking-Glass**

Suppose that the vertical line in the following drawing is a mirror. If the cartoon figure looks at itself in the mirror, which point (A, B, or C) do you think is $f(P)$? Use your answer to write $f(P) = $ ____. If S is the entire head on the left of the mirror, sketch what you think $f(S)$ is.

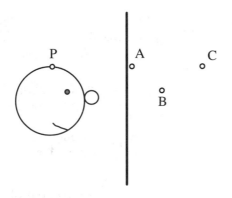

If you sketched a cartoon head of the same size looking at itself, you probably have a good feel for this sort of function, one in which points correspond to points in a particular way. Numbers need not appear at all with some functions, yet a notation like $f(P) = C$ makes sense.

But most patterns and functions do involve numbers. As with the toothpick patterns in Section 15.1, there can be a shape involved, as in Activity 6.

Activity 6   Walk the Walk

What is the perimeter (distance around the outside) of the *n*th shape in the pattern below? Measure in toothpicks (the heavy segment is a toothpick). Ignore the dashed lines that show the squares and the small empty spaces between toothpicks. Write your finding in function form:

$$p(\text{Shape } n) = \underline{\hspace{2cm}}.$$

Can you justify that your function rule is indeed trustworthy?

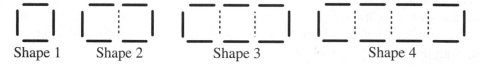

Shape 1   Shape 2   Shape 3   Shape 4

You know that two numbers can be combined in a variety of ways, for example, using addition or multiplication. You may be surprised that functions can often be *combined* as well. The function machine representation from Section 15.1 can be used to illustrate the idea behind combining functions: *The output from the first function becomes the input to the second function.* The combination of the two machines can be thought of as a function itself. Let us consider an example.

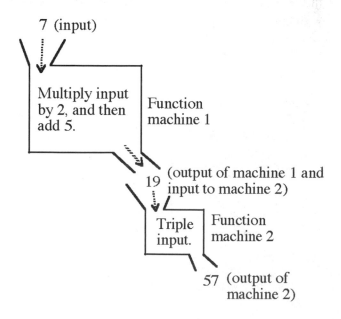

7 (input)

Multiply input by 2, and then add 5.   Function machine 1

19   (output of machine 1 and input to machine 2)

Triple input.   Function machine 2

57 (output of machine 2)

EXAMPLE 4

Refer to the previous function machine diagram. The output 19 from the first function is the input for the second function, which triples its input. The final output 57 is the result of the two-function combination. If we consider just the beginning input and the final output, we see that for an initial input of 7, the combination then gives a final output of 57. The rule for the combination can even be predicted from the two individual function rules: *output* = 2 × *input* + 5 and *output* = 3 × *input*. Notice that the input to the second machine is the 2 × *input* + 5 for the original input. That is, for the combination,

final output = 3(2 x *original input* + 5), or

output = 6 x *original input* + 15.

The usual algebraic shorthand certainly takes less space: From $y = 2x + 5$ first, and $y = 3x$ second, the combination is given by $y = 3(2x + 5) = 6x + 15$.

Activity 7   Does Order Matter?

Because this combination of functions is analogous to, say, multiplication of numbers, a natural mathematical question is whether this combination of functions is commutative or associative. Investigate commutativity with the function machines pictured on page 356. Investigate associativity by making up a third function machine to use with the given two.

The final activity in this section involves a well-known problem. The results show that a variety of function rules can describe different aspects of the same setting.

Activity 8   The Painted Cube[i]

Suppose that cubes of different sizes (such as 1 by 1 by 1, 2 by 2 by 2, 3 by 3 by 3) are made from 1 by 1 by 1 cubes and are then dipped in paint and dried. If such a cube is now taken apart, how many unit cubes will have paint on 3 squares, on 2 squares, on 1 square, and on 0 squares? What are the results for the general n by n by n cube?

The Painted Cube illustrates that function rules for real situations, not just made-up tables, can involve second and third powers of numbers. Even higher powers are possible in other problems.

> **THINK ABOUT . . .**
>
> Did you give *justifications* for your function rules for Activity 8? If not, try to think of a justification for each of your results.

Notes

Learning Exercises for Section 15.2

1. Explain how these everyday sentences make sense mathematically (if the characteristics are quantifiable).

    a. "Sales of a CD is a function of the singer's popularity."

    b. "Success is a function of how much you work."

    c. "Reaction time is a function of blood alcohol content."

2. Find a function rule that gives the perimeter of the *n*th shape in each of the following patterns. Justify that your rule will always work. (Use the shortest segment as the measuring unit.)

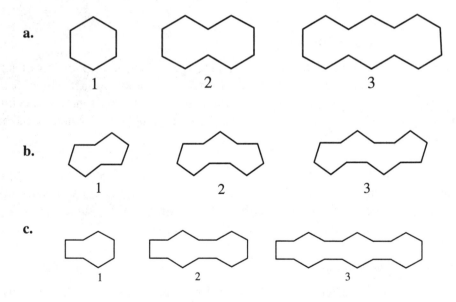

3. For each input give the output for the combination, first Machine 1, then Machine 2.

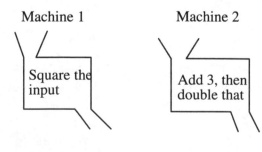

   a. Input = 5   **b.** Input = 10   **c.** Input = *x*

d-f. Now use the combination, first Machine 2, then Machine 1.

   d. Input = 5   **e.** Input = 10   **f.** Input = x

   g. In combining machines, does order matter? How do you know?

4. (*Extension of the Activity 8 problem*) Suppose a rectangular solid is made up of
1-cm cubes, dipped in paint, and then dried and taken apart into the individual
cubes. If the rectangular solid has dimensions m cm, n cm, and p cm, how many
cubes have 3 squares painted, 2 squares painted, 1 square painted, and 0 squares
painted? (*Hint*: Because there are three variables, finding a pattern is difficult. Instead, try the reasoning you may have used to justify the results for the Painted
Cube problem. Here is a drawing of a 3 cm by 4 cm by 6 cm rectangular solid on
which to practice your reasoning.)

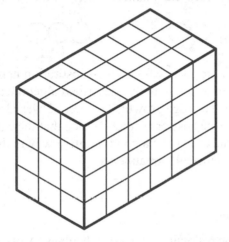

15.3 | Issues for Learning:
The National Assessment of Educational
Progress and Achievement in Algebra

The National Assessment of Educational Progress (NAEP, usually pronounced
"nape") has been recording achievement at the fourth, eighth, and twelfth grade for
several decades. Measures of mathematics achievement over the years provide a
snapshot of how well the youths of our country are performing. Only a few of the
test items are released because, once released, items cannot be used again. The released items, and performance on these items, can be seen at http://nces.ed.gov/
nationsreportcard/. All of the test items discussed in this section were used in the
2003 testing.

The following two test items were used in the Grade 4 algebra assessment. The second one was also used in the Grade 8 assessment.

Notes

Test Item 1.   M = 2, K = 6, and L = 3. What is K + L − M?

A) 1   B) 5   C) 7   D) 11

Test Item 2.

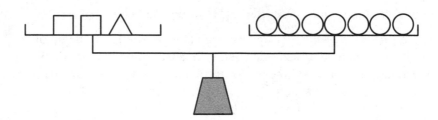

The objects on the scale above make it balance exactly. According to this scale, if △ balances ○○○, then ☐ balances which of the following?

A) ○   B) ○○   C) ○○○   D) ○○○○

At the fourth grade, 77% were successful on the substitution item, but only 39% were correct on the balance item, which might be described algebraically with two equations, $2x + y = 7$ and $y = 3$. To judge growth, Test Item 2 was also given to eighth graders, 75% of whom got the answer correct. Notice that the equal sign does not appear in the item, so balances may be a good intuitive way to think about equations, as they have been in some curricular treatments.

Activity 9   A Balancing Act

1.   Write equations for the following "balance" displays. A black dot represents 1.

a.

b.

2.   How do you solve each of these equations? Compare your algebraic work with actions on a balance representation.

a. $3x + 2 = x + 10$ b. $x + 7 = 1 + 4x$

Consider next two NAEP items dealing with patterns, given to both Grade 4 and Grade 8 students. What percent correct would you estimate for each of the following items?

Test Item 3. Peter wrote down a pattern of A's and B's that repeats in groups of 3. Here is the beginning of his pattern with some of the letters erased. Fill in the missing letters.

$\underline{A}\,\underline{B}\,\_\,\underline{A}\,\_\,\underline{B}\,\_\,\_\,\_$

Test Item 4. The table below shows how the chirping of a cricket is related to the temperature outside. For example, a cricket chirps 144 times each minute when the temperature is 76°.

Number of Chirps Per Minute	Temperature
144	76°
152	78°
160	80°
168	82°
176	84°

What would be the number of chirps per minute when the temperature outside is 90° if this pattern stays the same? Answer _____ Explain how you figured out your answer.

More than half (52%) of the Grade 4 students were successful on Test Item 3, but only 65% of the Grade 8 students successfully put B, B, A, B, B in the blanks. On Test Item 4, about half (49%) of the fourth graders scored at least minimally, but only a few (3%) gave fully correct answers (notice that the item asks for an explanation). Recognizing patterns can be either easy or difficult. Patterns that repeat, such as A, B, B, A, B, B, . . as shown in Test Item 3 are usually easier to understand than patterns that increase, as in Test Item 4.

Test items pertaining to other areas of algebra are also available. Items that deal with ordered pairs expressed in function notation are not included at Grade 4, but are included at Grade 8. The Grade 8 test covers content usually included in Grades 5, 6, and 7. The following NAEP item is one such problem. Approximately half of the eighth graders could give the correct answer for this item.

Test Item 5.

x	y
0	−3
1	−1
2	1

Which of the following equations is true for the three pairs of points of x and y values in the table above?

A) $3x + 2 = y$ B) $3x - 2 = y$ C) $2x + 3 = y$
D) $2x - 3 = y$ E) $x - 3 = y$

Not all algebra test items involve variables. A *Think About* feature in Section 14.5 used this Grade 8 NAEP item on order of operations:

Test Item 6.

$3 + 15 \div 3 - 4 \times 2 =$

A) $^-9$ B) $^-2$ C) 0   D) 4   E) 5

Because order of operations is so important in algebra, this item is a good one to test for that understanding. Only 52% successfully chose C, showing that the rather complicated order of operations convention does require careful and repeated attention.

There are, of course, many other items on the NAEP test. NAEP results have become more important in the last decade because they provide not only national results but also individual state results. Hence, they serve as a way of comparing progress at the national and state levels, from one test administration to the next. Thus it is good to be acquainted with the types of items appearing on the NAEP test and perhaps to try some of them in your own classrooms.

15.4 Check Yourself

After studying this chapter, you should be able to do problems like those assigned, and to meet the following objectives.

1. Find a specific number, or an expression for the nth number (or a function rule), in a given pattern or table. Generate your own data for some situations.

2. Explain what a function is, and why functions are important in mathematics.

3. Explain why a function rule based only on examples might not be 100% reliable.

4. For selected situations, find a general function rule and give a justification that it is 100% reliable.

5. Illustrate and identify arithmetic sequences and geometric sequences.

6. Give an example of a function that does not involve numbers.

7. Illustrate how two functions can be combined, perhaps with function machine representations. Test this combination idea for commutativity and associativity.

REFERENCE FOR CHAPTER 15

Phillips, E. (1991). *Patterns and Functions, from the Addendum Series, Grades 5–8*. Reston, VA: National Council of Teachers of Mathematics.

Part III

Reasoning About Shapes and Measurement

The real world is made up of objects that have shapes. It is no surprise then that the mathematics curriculum gives attention to geometric shapes, particularly those commonly seen in manufactured goods. Manufacturing naturally requires many sorts of measurements, including those of geometric shapes. So, it also is no surprise that measurement is treated in the elementary school mathematics curriculum.

Although Part III of *Reconceptualizing Mathematics* begins with attention to several three-dimensional shapes, Part III also treats two-dimensional ideas with a teacher-view in mind (Chapters 16, 17, 21). Symmetry and tessellations (Chapters 18 and 19) show some esthetic possibilities with geometric shapes, as well as being topics of mathematical interest. Scale models and photographic enlargements are two examples of the general topic of similarity (Chapter 20). Transformation geometry (Chapter 22) allows these three topics (symmetry, tessellation, and similarity) to be placed under one umbrella.

The important topic of measurement is the focus in the remaining chapters of Part III. Measurement in the early chapters is largely restricted to length and angle size, and length and angle size are revisited more deeply with measurement basics in Chapter 23. Chapter 24 treats the measurement of area and volume, with a focus on related formulas and their origins in Chapter 25. Chapter 26 deals with the historical and practical Pythagorean theorem, along with a look at some nongeometric measurements.

Unfortunately, in some elementary school classrooms geometry and measurement are given little attention to allow more time for work with numbers. But the measurement of geometric quantities gives many opportunities to work with numbers involved in measurements, many of which students can make themselves. Your work in Part III should help you to see many ways to make shapes and measurement an important part of the mathematics you teach. For a teacher, geometry and measurement are more than vocabulary and formulas.

Chapter 16
Polyhedra

Our physical environment, from ants to atoms to buildings to flowers to planets to zippers to zoos, is three-dimensional. In many elementary school curricula the children's first work with geometry involves three-dimensional shapes, often hands-on, in which the children work with wooden or plastic blocks of different shapes. So it is appropriate to start our work with three-dimensional (3D) shapes, introducing more sophisticated vocabulary and ideas as we go. Because polyhedra are extensions of polygons to three-dimensional shapes, our discussion will refer to different polygons and several geometric ideas that you are familiar with from earlier mathematics courses. If you need a quick review of some of these ideas, you may find Figures 1 and 2 in Section 17.1 and the Glossary helpful. We will discuss polygons in greater detail in Chapter 17.

In Section 16.1 we introduce some of the 3D vocabulary in a familiar context, and then in subsequent sections we discuss several special 3D shapes, showing how to draw them and giving some special relationships associated with them.

16.1 | Shoeboxes Have Faces and Nets!

An ordinary shoebox has a 3D shape that is commonly encountered in a variety of sizes: for example, children are familiar with a refrigerator carton, a game box, a cereal box, or a marker or crayon box, to name a few.

Activity 1   Drawing a Shoebox

You are quite familiar with the shape of a shoebox. Try to draw one.

There are different ways to draw a shoebox shape, but one way follows the steps shown in Figure 1 on the next page. (Children might even call the starting shape a box, because that is a term they commonly use for a rectangle.)

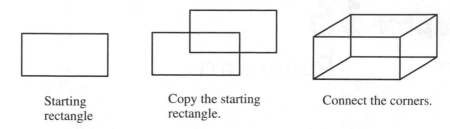

| Starting rectangle | Copy the starting rectangle. | Connect the corners. |

Figure 1

If you did not know how to make such a drawing, you should practice with different starting rectangles and with different depths at the second of the three steps.

The flat parts of a shoebox are examples of two-dimensional (2D) or **planar regions**, because they require only a flat surface. These flat parts or planar regions are called the **faces** of the shoebox (not the colloquial term *sides*, which is reserved for line segments and rays in shapes). The corner points of the shoebox are more precisely called **vertices** (singular: **vertex**), and the line segments where two faces meet are called **edges** (and the edges *are* sides of the faces). Vertices are sometimes shown with a large dot for emphasis. In a drawing of a shoebox, do you see 6 faces, 8 vertices, and 12 edges?

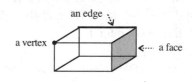

If you start the drawing with a rectangle with all of its sides the same length (a square) and adjust the depth so that all the edges have the same length, you could get a **cube**.

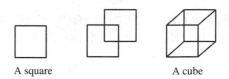

A square   A cube

> ***THINK ABOUT . . .***
>
> How many faces, vertices, and edges does a cube have?

A special dot paper, called isometric dot paper, gives an alternative way to draw shapes made of cubes. (A sample of isometric dot paper is in Appendix G. Use it to make copies for future assignments.) A shape drawn on paper does not always show the back view, so some edges of solid cubes cannot be seen and so they may not be drawn. Figure 2 shows an example of a cube and a shape made of cubes on isometric dot paper. Do you see six cubes in the second shape? Can you identify parallel lines and what would be right angles in actual 3D cubes?

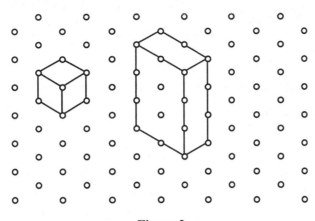

Figure 2

Activity 2   A Pile-Up

Draw a pile of cubes, 4 cubes tall, on isometric dot paper.

For manufacturing purposes, boxes may be made from patterns on flat material, and then folded up and taped. Vice versa, some edges of a box can be cut so that the box can be unfolded to lie flat but in one connected piece. Unfolded versions of a 3D shape are called **nets**.

Discussion 1   Straighten Up

Which of the nets in Figure 3 gives a shoebox shape without its lid, if it is folded up and taped?

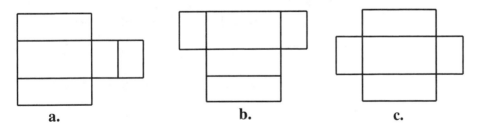

a.   b.   c.

Figure 3

You will get more practice with nets in the Learning Exercises in order to prepare for the next section.

TAKE-AWAY MESSAGE . . . An ordinary shoebox allows you to talk about its faces, vertices, and edges and to illustrate the idea of a net for a 3D shape. Drawing a shoebox is relatively easy, and the same method can be used to draw a cube. ♦

Notes

1. Draw a box that would be shaped like a box holding a large refrigerator.

2. Draw a pile of four cubes free-hand (not with isometric dot paper).

3. How many faces, vertices, and edges does each of these have?

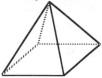 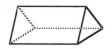

    a. An Egyptian pyramid   **b.** A prism from science class

4. How do you know that the following net will *not* give a complete cube?

5. For visualization practice, some K–8 curricula use actual 3D models of arrangements of cubes. These curricula have the students show the front view (as you look at the shape *directly* from the front), the view from the right, and the view from the top (again as you approach the shape from the front). A slightly more difficult version of this visualization would be to draw those views, but starting from a *drawing* rather than from a model. Here is an example:

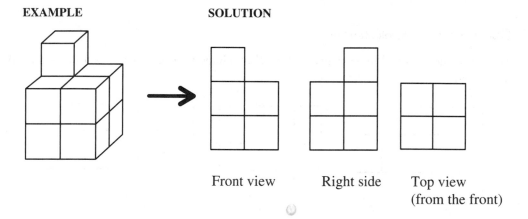

                          Front view   Right side   Top view
                                                          (from the front)

Sketch the front, right-side, and top views for each cube arrangement.

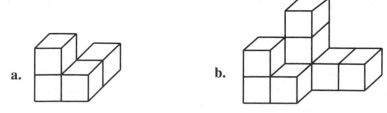

  a.   **b.**

Continue on the next page.

c. Sketch the view from the *left* of the shapes in parts (a) and (b). How are they related to the views from the right?

6. a. Draw an isometric version of the cube arrangement given in the example in Learning Exercise 5. The isometric version for the example is started for you in the following diagram.

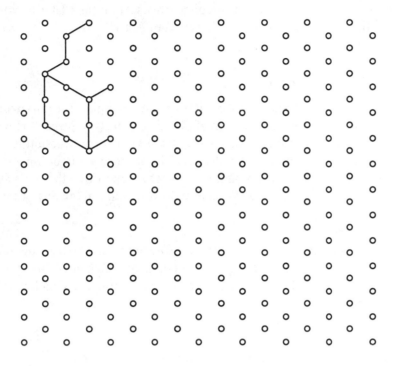

b. Draw an isometric version of the cube arrangement in Learning Exercise 5(a).

7. (*Website*) The National Council of Teachers of Mathematics' Website has several sample lessons on geometry and measurement. Go to http:// illuminations.nctm.org/Lessons.aspx and look for "Isometric Drawing Tool" under Activities. Briefly describe the software in these lessons.

16.2 | Introduction to Polyhedra

Activity 3   Fold Them Up (preliminary homework activity)

Write your name inside the outlines for shapes A–M (their nets), found in Appendix G. Before cutting out the shape, try to imagine what the final, folded-up shape will look like. Cut around the outside of each shape, fold on the other line segments (a ruler helps make sharp folds; fold so the shape letter and your name will show), and then tape the shape together. Find a small container so that you can bring the shapes to class without damaging them. We will occasionally refer to the collection as your *kit.* Add to your collection any small containers or boxes or unusual shapes that you have on hand. On separate paper, jot down the names for the shapes that you know.

This section covers some important categories of 3D shapes and illustrates that defining them precisely is not trivial. Throughout this section (and later ones) you will be asked questions about the folded-up shapes from Activity 3.

Discussion 2   Sorting Shapes

Each of the shapes you made in Activity 3 is an example of a **polyhedron** (plural: **polyhedra**), a closed surface made up of planar regions (flat pieces). How would you sort shapes A–K into different sets? Write down your word descriptions for the sets. Do you know any vocabulary for the sets? Look at any three-dimensional shapes other than A–K that students brought to class. Do they fit into the sets you have? Are any of the shapes not polyhedra? What else do you notice about any of the shapes?

The planar regions in a polyhedron are the **faces** of the polyhedron, the line segments in which faces meet are the **edges**, and the points at which edges meet are the **vertices** of the polyhedron. The word *polyhedron* comes from the Greek words for *many* (poly-) and *face* (-hedron).

Discussion 3   Defining Types of Polyhedra

1. As you may know, shapes A, D, G, and I are called **pyramids**. Come to a consensus about a definition for pyramid. (Do not look up a definition. The intent of this discussion is to have you focus on relevant and irrelevant characteristics of types of shapes.) One face is called the **base** of the pyramid. Which face do you think is the base? What is the shape of the base called?

2. Shapes B, C, E, and F are called **prisms**. Come to a consensus about a definition for prism, as you did in Problem 1. Two faces in each prism are called the **bases** of the prism. Which faces are the bases? How are the bases of a prism related to each other? What is the shape of the bases called?

Other vocabulary words—*lateral edge, right* or *oblique prism, regular pyramid*—appear in the Learning Exercises. Adding pertinent information to the entries in the Glossary toward the end of this book, or making your own glossary, either on 3x5 cards or with a word processor, is a good idea. You probably have your favorite way to practice vocabulary.

Activity 4   Quantities Associated with Polyhedra

Recall that a quantity is anything that can be measured or counted.

1. Pick one of the shapes A–K and tell what quantities you can associate with it.

2. Pick another one of the shapes A-K. Are the same quantities you selected in Problem 1 relevant to this shape as well? Explain.

Activity 5   The Quantities V, F, and E for Pyramids

1. Find all the pyramids there are in shapes A–K. Count the number F of faces, the number V of vertices, and the number E of edges for each pyramid. Organize the data in a table and look for patterns or relationships.

2. Find similar counts for a hexagonal pyramid, a 100-gonal pyramid, an n-gonal pyramid, and an $(x + y)$-gonal pyramid and add these counts to your data. Do the patterns or relationships hold for these pyramids also? Can you justify these counts without referring to the patterns?

3. One relationship that you may have overlooked relates all three quantities—V, F, and E—along with possibly a specific number. If you did not see such a relationship earlier, look for one now.

Activity 6   The Quantities V, F, and E for Prisms

1. Similarly to what you did in Activity 5, find all the prisms there are in shapes A–K. Count the number F of faces, the number V of vertices, and the number E of edges for each one. Organize the data in a table and look for patterns or relationships.

2. Find similar counts for a hexagonal prism, a 100-gonal prism, an n-gonal prism, and an $(x + y)$-gonal prism and add these counts to your data. Do the patterns or relationships hold for these prisms also? Can you justify these counts without referring to the patterns?

3. One relationship that you may have overlooked relates all three quantities, V, F, and E. If you did not see such a relationship earlier, look for one now. (*Hint*, if you want one: Insert a column or row to your data that gives the value $V + F$.)

If you are studying on your own, at this point you may be stuck finding the relationship hinted at in Problem 3 of the last two activities. Patterns are not always easy to notice. If you are stuck, look up **Euler's formula** in the glossary. (Euler is pronounced "oiler.") Euler's formula is important enough to memorize. $V + F = E + 2$

TAKE-AWAY MESSAGE . . . There are different types of polyhedra, with many vocabulary words associated with them. Two particularly important types of polyhedra are pyramids and prisms. Writing careful definitions for pyramids and prisms is not easy, as you found out. Euler's formula for polyhedra gives a result applicable to most of the polyhedra you are likely to encounter. ◆

Learning Exercises for Section 16.2

(Unfamiliar words in these exercises may be found in the Glossary.)

1. Which of the shapes A–K meet the criterion given in each statement?
   a. All the faces are parallelograms (including special parallelograms, such as rectangles and squares).
   b. A base is a pentagonal region.
   c. All the triangular faces are equilateral.
   d. None of the triangular faces is equilateral.
   e. Two faces are parallel and congruent, but the shape is not a prism.
   f. More than one face is an isosceles trapezoid.
   g. All the edges are congruent.
   h. No pair of edges are parallel.

2. a. For each prism, how do the **lateral edges** (the edges not on a base) appear to be related? What shape are all the **lateral faces** (the faces that are not bases)?
   b. How many **lateral edges** (the edges not on the base) does a 50-gonal pyramid have? How many **lateral faces** (the faces that are not the base) does this pyramid have? What shape are they?

3. a. *Who am I?* or *What am I?* exercises are common in elementary programs. Ideally, the clues are revealed one at a time, and then what is known from the revealed clues is discussed. Answer *Who am I?* for the following example.

   EXAMPLE

   I am a polyhedron.

   I have 7 faces.

   Six of my lateral edges are equal in length.

   One of my faces has 6 sides.

   Who am I?
   b. Make up a *Who am I?* exercise.

4. Is there a polyhedron that has the fewest number of vertices? The greatest number? Explain.

5. a. Test the relationship you found in Activities 5 and 6 (Euler's formula), using shapes H, J, and K, and any other polyhedron you have that is neither a pyramid nor a prism.
   b. Suppose a polyhedron has 10 vertices and 15 edges. How many faces does it have?
   c. Suppose another polyhedron has 20 faces and 30 edges. How many vertices does it have?
   d. Can the number of vertices, the number of faces, and the number of edges of a polyhedron all be odd numbers? Explain.

6. What geometric name (using adjectives, as appropriate) applies to each of these objects?

    a. a shoebox

    b. an unsharpened pencil with flat sides (and no eraser)

    c. a filing cabinet

    d. an unused eraser (the separate kind, not on a pencil)

7. React to the following scenarios.

    a. "I was thinking. A square pyramid has 4 triangular faces and a square base. Each triangular face has 3 sides, which are edges of the pyramid. So there should be 4 times 3, or 12, lateral edges, plus the 4 on the square base, 16 edges in all. But I counted and found only 8 edges. What is wrong with my reasoning?"

    b. "What is the matter with my thinking here? I know a cube has 8 vertices. But a cube has 6 square faces, and a square has 4 vertices. So it seems there should be 6 times 4, or 24, vertices, not 8."

8. For the following types of polyhedra, investigate to see whether the total number of *angles* on all the faces is predictable. For example, the cube, a special prism, has 4 angles on each of its 6 faces, so it has 24 angles.

    a. pyramids

    b. prisms

9. If the lateral edges of a prism make right angles with the edges that they meet at the bases, the prism is called a **right prism** (and an **oblique prism**, otherwise). A **regular pyramid** has as its base a polygonal region with all its sides the same length and all its angles the same size, and all its lateral edges the same length. If the lateral edges of a pyramid are not all the same length, it is an **oblique pyramid**. Sometimes the vertex that is not on the base is called the **vertex** of the pyramid, or the **apex** of the pyramid.

    a. Which, if any, of the shapes in your kit are right prisms?

    b. What shape are all the lateral faces of a right prism?

    c. Are there any regular pyramids in your kit?

10. How many of the angles on *all* the faces of a prism could be *right* angles in each case given?

    a. The prism is a triangular prism.

    b. The prism is a quadrilateral prism.

11. Geometry is all around you. Go for a ten-minute walk, with paper and pen/pencil in hand. (The walk can be inside if the weather is bad.) Sketch any shapes, two-dimensional and three-dimensional, that you recognize as being common or noteworthy. Next to the sketches, write the names for shapes that you can identify.

12. With a piece of string or a rubber band, show how a straight cut across a right rectangular prism (for example, shape E or F in your kit) could give each of the following two-dimensional figures.

    a. an equilateral triangle

    b. an isosceles triangle that is not equilateral

    c. a rectangle

    d. a parallelogram that is not a rectangle

13. Make sure that you are comfortable with these vocabulary terms: polyhedron, pyramid, prism, face, lateral face, edge, lateral edge, vertex, vertices, oblique prism, right prism, and regular pyramid. What does it mean to be *comfortable* with a word or phrase? How can you organize a lot of vocabulary to keep it straight and remember it?

16.3 | Representing and Visualizing Polyhedra

Even when a 3D shape is not present, the idea of the shape may be communicated by a word or a drawing. The conventions of 2D drawings for 3D shapes must be learned, of course, if such drawings are to be interpreted as intended. This section treats the variety of ways for communicating the ideas of particular shapes.

> ***THINK ABOUT…***
>
> What do you see when you look at this drawing?

Do you see a regular hexagon with some segments drawn to its center? Or do you see a cube? (Do you see both shapes now?) Three-dimensional shapes are often represented by two-dimensional drawings. Without a context suggesting three dimensions, these drawings are ambiguous, and children often do not interpret them in the way that was intended. *Reading* such drawings is important for understanding the ideas they represent, and being able to draw a variety of 2D and 3D shapes is a useful skill, especially for a teacher.

Representations of a Polyhedron

A drawing of a polyhedron is one *representation* of the polyhedron. Strictly speaking, like all geometric objects a polyhedron is an ideal object that exists only in one's mind—an idea to which we have assigned the verbal label *polyhedron*. Physical-world representations of polyhedra might include boxes, but boxes have rounded vertices and their faces are rarely perfectly flat, so boxes are only approximate representations of polyhedra. We usually ignore these flaws and become comfortable with approximate representations of ideal geometric objects, such as, for example, a cardboard box for a prism, a stretched piece of string or a pencil for a line segment, or a piece of paper for a rectangular region. And in the last section, you have made very good representations of several polyhedra, using paper models. Indeed, the flat patterns or nets that you cut out to make the polyhedra give another type of representation for polyhedra. Hence, we have at least three nonverbal representations for polyhedra: physical models, drawings, and nets.

Our overall task is to be able to *translate* among the different representations. You have already practiced some of these translations. For example, you started with a 3D model of a cube, and then you gave the word *cube* for this object. Another translation you possibly have done is when shown the drawing of a cube in the last Think About, you might have then given the word *cube* for the drawing.

In the diagram to the left in Figure 4, we show in general the different representations of a polyhedron. Next, in the diagram on the right, we show the different translations among these representations of a polyhedron.

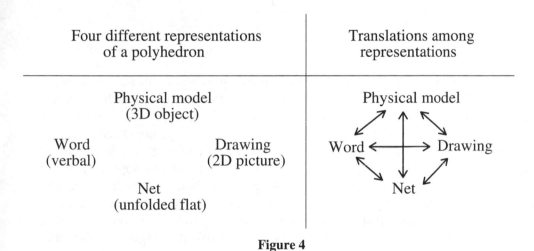

Figure 4

Some Examples of Translations

Two specific translations shown in Figure 4 are the translation going from a physical model or a word to a net. These translations are the reverse of what you did in Section 16.2: You started with a net and obtained a physical model and then eventually a word name. In Activity 7 below you will be asked to do a reverse task: You start with a physical model or a word, and then obtain a net for the shape.

Activity 7   Unfolding a Cube

Using a cube or just thinking about a cube, draw a net for it.

Starting with the physical model is the easiest way to do the type of translation in Activity 7. Place the model on a piece of paper, trace around the face touching the paper, and then in steps "roll" the model on its edges so you can trace around the other faces. It is a good idea to have some system in mind so that some faces are not repeated or omitted. Starting with just a word, like *cube*, and then trying to sketch the net involves more demanding visualization practice. This type of task forces you to visualize the shape and to do the "rolling" or unfolding mentally. Compare Activity 7 with the next one for difficulty.

Activity 8   Reading a Net

How might a person have obtained the following net for a cube, where the marked face was drawn first? (Use a cube if you have trouble visualizing what might have happened.)

A second type of translation is going from a drawing to words (that is, "reading" a drawing). There is no single standard drawing for a three-dimensional shape, unfortunately. One kind of drawing you have probably seen is a *perspective* drawing, such as the one in Figure 5, which attempts to represent how your eye might see an object. In a perspective drawing, some segments that are actually parallel in the shape itself may appear to converge in the drawing, and distant segments will appear shorter in the drawing even though they are the same length in the actual shape. For example, in Figure 5, the parallel lines AB and CD appear to converge at the point X, called the *vanishing point* by artists. Consequently many measurements on perspective drawings will not be to scale. For this reason, perspective drawings, although common in art, are not popular in drafting and mathematics.

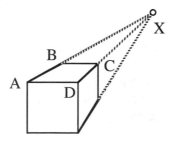

Figure 5   Perspective
drawing of a cube

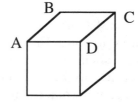

Figure 6   Drawing of a cube
in mathematics (no perspective)

The common type of drawing in mathematics does attempt to display actual parallel segments as being parallel in the drawing by pretending that the drawer's eye is slightly in front of, above, and to the right of the object (see Figure 6 above). The right angles in the face of the cube closest to the viewer do look almost like right angles. But most of the right angles in the actual cube are not right angles in the drawing, and so some faces look like parallelogram regions rather than the square regions they actually are. Hence, reading this representation requires understanding this distortion; a parallelogram in the drawing of a polyhedron *may* indeed represent a square or rectangle in the three-dimensional object. (Look at an actual cube with your eye in the position described above, and with your eyes "squinty.") As Figure 7 below illustrates, showing all the edges removes some possible ambiguity. Making the **hidden edges**—the ones you can't actually see in a paper model—lighter or dashed also helps to remove some of the visual ambiguity even when all of the edges are shown. Shading may also help the eye to "see" what is intended.

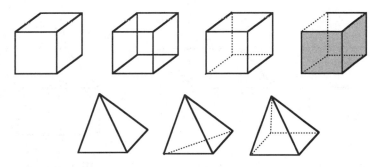

Figure 7   Alternate representations: cubes with no hidden edges shown, with all edges shown, with hidden edges dashed, and with two faces shaded; pyramid with no hidden edges shown, and pyramids with ambiguity removed by showing hidden edges

Elementary school teachers and students sometimes use everyday objects to create frameworks for different polyhedra. For example, they might use toothpicks or plastic coffee stirrers for edges, with miniature marshmallows or raisins for vertices. Using such objects can help students to see both the visible edges and those edges hidden in two-dimensional drawings.

A third type of translation is from a word or physical model to a drawing. Drawing three-dimensional shapes can be done in different ways, as the drawings in Figures 5, 6, and 7 suggest.

> Our standard drawing in this text will be the type showing parallel segments in the object as parallel in the drawing and viewing the object from slightly in front, above, and to the right. Equal lengths in the shape should be equal in the drawing, insofar as possible. To remove some ambiguity, we will show hidden edges with lighter or dashed segments and add shading as we see fit.

For drawing the face in front, it is often possible to draw some edges to be horizontal. One way to make good drawings of prisms is to concentrate on drawing the top base first (because all its edges are visible), recognizing that your viewpoint is in front of, above, and to the right of the prism. Hence, there is usually some distortion of the actual shape of the base, because you are looking at it from an angle. Because the lateral edges are all the same length and all parallel, next draw the lateral edges—first the visible ones and then the hidden edges, more lightly or dashed. Sometimes these other edges are too close to each other so you have to adjust the original base. With experience when you sketch the top base you can avoid such difficulties by *not* locating a vertex right above or right below another vertex on the same base. Finally, sketch the bottom base, first the visible edges and then the hidden ones. These edges should be parallel to ones in the top base, so you have a chance to adjust any lengths of lateral edges that might be off. An example is in order.

EXAMPLE 1

Draw a right rectangular prism.

SOLUTION

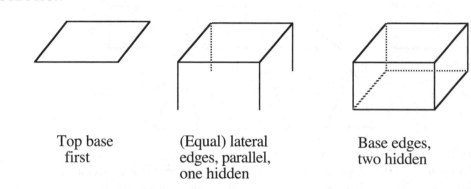

Top base
first

(Equal) lateral
edges, parallel,
one hidden

Base edges,
two hidden

Similarly, one way to draw pyramids is to start with the base, trying to anticipate which edges will be hidden. Then locate the other vertex of the pyramid and join it to each vertex of the base, keeping in mind which edges will be hidden. Figure 8 below shows an example of how to draw an oblique rectangular pyramid. Notice that from our viewing angle, the rectangular base will appear to be a parallelogram.

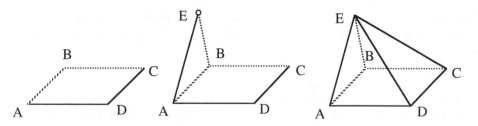

Figure 8   Drawing an oblique rectangular pyramid

TAKE-AWAY MESSAGE...There are several ways of representing the idea of a 3D shape—word, net, model, or drawing. Starting with any of these representations, you should be able to get to the other representations. The Learning Exercises invite you to practice making sketches and many of the translations among representations. ♦

Notes

Learning Exercises for Section 16.3

1. Describe where your eye might be if you are looking at a cube and see each of the following shapes.

    a. 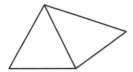   b.   c.

2. a. What is the maximum number of faces you can see when looking at a paper model of a cube from outside the cube? The minimum?

    b. What is the maximum number of vertices you can see?

    c. What is the maximum number of edges you can see?

3. Draw an enlarged copy of the following drawing and put in hidden edges to show that it is actually a drawing of a pentagonal pyramid.

    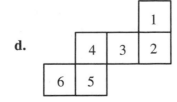

4. Make a drawing of each of the following shapes. Be sure to show the hidden edges.

    a. A right rectangular prism

    b. A triangular right prism

    c. A square pyramid

    d. A right octagonal prism

    e. A pentagonal pyramid

    f. A cube

    g. A triangular prism in which the edges make 14 right angles with each other

    h. A polyhedron with 8 edges and 5 faces

5. If the following nets were folded up to give cubes, which pairs of faces would be opposite each other?

    a.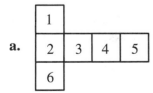

    b.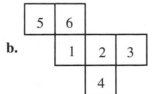

    c.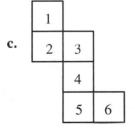

    d.

6. Using the three-dimensional shapes from the nets for shapes A-K in Appendix G, draw nets that are different from the given original nets for the shapes specified.

    a. Shape A   b. Shape C
    c. Shape F   d. a different net for Shape F

7. Which, if any, of the following nets will give a triangular pyramid?

    a.   b.   c.   d.

8. Consider the shape shown below that has been drawn on isometric dot paper. (*Note*: Observe how the dots are arranged. Where is one's eye, in viewing an isometric drawing? Do isometric drawings appear to retain parallelism for segments that are parallel in the original? Are segments of equal lengths in the original also equal in the isometric drawing? Are right angles in the original also right angles in the drawing?)

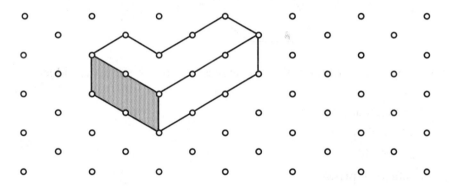

    a. Draw an isometric version of the given shape, but from a different viewpoint.
    b. Does Euler's formula apply to this polyhedron?
    c. What is the best name for the polyhedron above?
    d. Sketch a net for the polyhedron.
    e. What are the surface area and the volume for this polyhedron? (Use the natural units—the smallest squares and smallest cubes.)

9. Sketch a cube, label the bottom face B, and then check (√) the edges that could be cut to yield each given net. (The letter B in each net marks the bottom face of the cube.)

    a.   b. 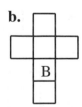   c.

10. The following cubes have been cut on the *dashed* edges. Draw the nets that would result if the cube is then unfolded. (If the cube is not cut so it will unfold, then correct the cuts.) Try this first as an exercise in visualizing; look at a cube if you are uncertain after visualizing.

Notes

a. 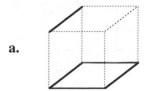 b. 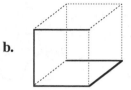 c.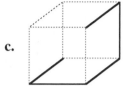

11. Make up an exercise like Learning Exercise 9 or 10 for shape A.

12. The game of dominoes has playing pieces that can be represented as two squares joined by a side. Connecting four squares similarly would give a 4-omino, or a tetromino (*tetra-* means 4).

a. Show all the differently-shaped tetrominoes. Two tetrominoes have the same shape if one can be moved so that it matches the other. The first three tetrominoes below are all the same:

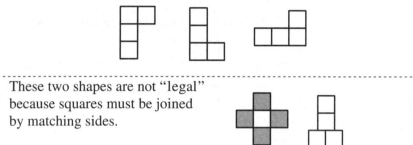

These two shapes are not "legal" because squares must be joined by matching sides.

b. How many differently-shaped pentominoes (*penta-* means 5) are there?

c. Give the area and perimeter of each pentomino.

d. Is the following statement true? *Shapes that have the same area also have the same perimeter.* Explain.

e. Is the following statement true? *Shapes that have the same perimeter also have the same area.* Explain.

13. Which pentominoes, viewed as nets, can be folded to give *open* cubes—that is, cubes with one face missing?

14. The sketch in each drawing shows a cross section of a cube. Identify the type of shape in each cross section.

a. 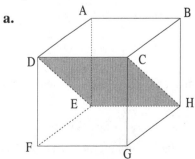 b.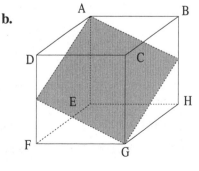

15. A teacher might wish to add tabs to a net so that the students can use glue or paste instead of tape. The strongest polyhedron will have two faces sharing an edge also sharing a tab. Copy the nets below and indicate where tabs should be put to give a strong polyhedron.

a. 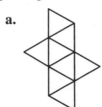   b. 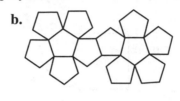   c.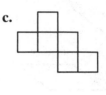

16. Give the most informative name for the polyhedron that each net would make.

a. 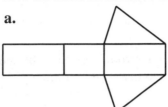   b.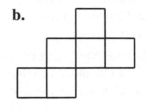

17. Draw an isometric version of 3D shapes that have the following views.

a.

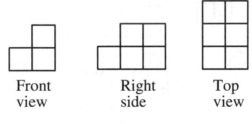

Front   Right   Top
view   side   view

b.

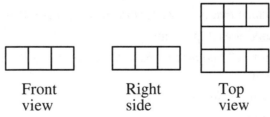

Front   Right   Top
view   side   view

18. Consider the following right rectangular prism.

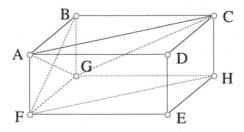

a.   Edge AF is perpendicular to (makes right angles with) which of these? (The bar notation is common for line segments.)

edge FE, or $\overline{FE}$ edge AD, or $\overline{AD}$ edge AB, or $\overline{AB}$

segment AG, or $\overline{AG}$ segment BF, or $\overline{BF}$ segment FH, or $\overline{FH}$

   b.   Name the endpoints of three edges that are parallel to edge AD.

19. Some visualization tests include tasks such as the following: Imagine a piece of
paper that is successively folded, and has a hole or holes punched into the last
folded position. The task is to identify how the holes would appear when the
paper is unfolded. Try the following tasks.

a.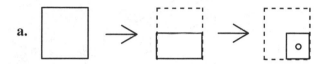

b.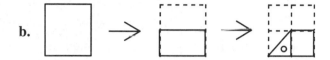

c.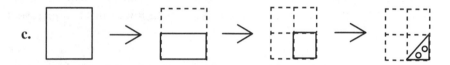

   d.   Design another task for folding a piece of paper.

16.4 | Congruent Polyhedra

Replacement parts for a car or a computer, cookies cut from a cookie cutter, or
blouses made from the same pattern—every object in one of these groups mentioned
is expected to be *exactly the same size and shape*. They can be regarded as copies of
one another. If these shapes were holograms, they could be made to coincide completely. Hence, matched, or *corresponding*, parts (such as segments, angles, curves,
or faces) have the same measurements.

Activity 9   Exactly Alike

Which of the following 3D objects are exactly the same size and shape?

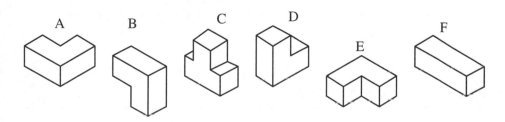

Notes

THINK ABOUT...

Are 3D objects G and H exactly the same size and shape? It may be helpful to make the shapes from cubes, if you have any. *Hint*: Think of reflecting in a mirror.

G 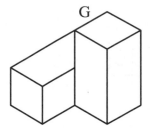   H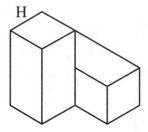

Matching shapes often is done by mentally or physically moving one shape so that it *looks exactly like* the other shape. The movement may be a turn or a slide, for example. The movement may even be a reflection in a plane, as is the case with G and H in the Think About. The movement might even be a combination of turns, slides, and reflections.

The movements involved are important mathematically, because they are fundamental to decisions about whether two shapes can be matched exactly in size and shape.

Discussion 4   How Do You Decide?

What movements might be involved in deciding whether the shapes A–F in Activity 9 are exactly the same size and shape?

As you may recall, the technical word for this "exactly the same size and shape" idea is **congruence**, and shapes related by congruence are called **congruent shapes**. Shape A in Activity 9 is *congruent* to shape B, for example, but *not congruent* to shape F: There is no way to move either shape A or shape F to match the other shape exactly, even with reflections in planes. That is, there is no way to match the points in shapes A and F so that measurements of all corresponding parts are equal. So, shapes A and F are not congruent.

TAKE-AWAY MESSAGE . . . Three-dimensional shapes may be congruent, even if they are not in the same position. You may have to turn, or slide, or reflect a shape to see that it is exactly like a congruent shape. ♦

Learning Exercises for Section 16.4

1. **a.** Sketch shapes congruent to shapes I and J shown on the next page by using a reflection in a plane for each shape.

    b. Sketch shapes congruent to shapes I and J by using a turn for each shape.

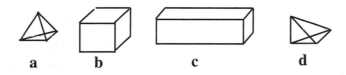

2. Are any of the polyhedra sketched below congruent? Explain how you know.

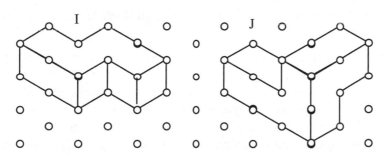

3. A hidden shape is known to be congruent to a 3 cm by 4 cm by 6 cm right rectangular prism. What is the total of the areas of all the faces of the hidden shape?

4. **a.** Is a shape congruent to itself? Explain your thinking.

   b. If shape P is congruent to shape Q, is shape Q congruent to shape P? Explain your thinking.

   c. If shape R is congruent to shape S, and shape S is congruent to shape T, is shape R congruent to shape T? Explain your thinking.

5. Sketch all possible noncongruent polyhedra in which each polyhedron is made up of four congruent cubes. When two cubes are connected, they must share a face. (*Hint*: There are more than five noncongruent ones.) Make up a name for all such polyhedra, using your knowledge of prefixes. (See **prefixes** in the Glossary.)

6. **a.** Suppose that you and a friend are going to talk by telephone, and that each of you has a prism. Prepare a list of all the questions you *might* need to ask your friend, so that you will be able to tell whether your friend's prism is congruent to your prism.

   b. Prepare another list of questions that would enable you to determine whether two pyramids are congruent.

7. **a.** On isometric paper, sketch a shape congruent to the shape having the following three views. Because shapes on isometric paper do not have a clear *front* face, interpret *front* below to be *front left*, and *right* to be *front right*.

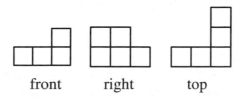

front   right   top

   b. On isometric paper, sketch a shape congruent to your shape in part (a), but from a different viewpoint.

   c. Sketch the front, right, and top views of your shape in part (b). (Call the left front the *front* view.)

Continue on the next page.

d. What movement would show that the original shape from part (a) and your shape are congruent?

8. Chemists know that molecules of some substances exist in mirror-image versions (*chiral* molecules). Drugs made with them can have quite different effects. One version of thalidomide is a sedative but the chiral version causes birth defects. One version of limonen has a lemon smell but the chiral version smells orangey. Sketch chiral versions of these "molecules." (The drawings represent molecules in either triangular pyramid or cubic arrangements, with the dots showing atoms and the dashed segments representing chemical bonds. They are not actual molecules of any substance, and X and Y are made-up elements.)

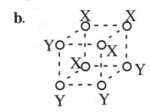

9. This section has focused on congruent *polyhedra*. How would you define congruent *polygons* in a similar way? Sketch an example of congruent quadrilaterals, and tell how you know they are congruent.

16.5 | Some Special Polyhedra

The types of polyhedra that have been highlighted in earlier sections lead to a classification that bypasses some polyhedra of historical (and aesthetic) interest: the regular polyhedra.

> A **regular polyhedron,** or **Platonic solid,** is a polyhedron all of whose faces are congruent regular polygonal regions of one particular type, with the same arrangement of polygonal regions at each vertex. *Regular polygons* have all their sides the same length and all their angles the same size.

In this section, we will focus on the *convex* regular polyhedra. By convex, we mean those shapes that are not "dented in" anywhere.

> *THINK ABOUT…*
>
> You may not realize that you already have at least three types of regular polyhedra in your kit of polyhedra. Can you find them? Recall that all of the faces must be identical, and the arrangement of the regions at each vertex must be the same.

A regular polyhedron is named on the basis of how many faces it has (face: *-hedron*, plural *-hedra*). A **regular *tetra*hedron** has four faces, each an equilateral triangular region. A **regular *hexahedron*** has six faces, each a square region. (A regular hexahedron is most often called a cube, if you were wondering.) A **regular *octahedron*** has eight faces, each an equilateral triangular region. Did you find a regular tetrahedron, a regular hexahedron, and a regular octahedron in your kit?

A natural question would be, "Is there a regular polyhedron for every number of faces, or at least for every *even* number of faces?" Perhaps surprisingly, the answer is "No." There are only five types of regular polyhedra. The other two types are the **regular dodecahedron** (*dodeca-* means 12) and the **regular icosahedron** (*icosa-* means 20). Figure 8 shows nets for these two types; verify that they have the proper number of faces (see also your shapes L and M).

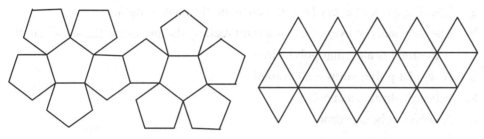

A net for a dodecahedron   A net for an icosahedron

Figure 8

The regular polyhedra were well known to the ancient Greeks, and they assumed an almost mystical air during some periods of history. For example, Kepler (1571–1630) described a model of the planets that involved (erroneously) the regular polyhedra to go along with Kepler's important laws of planetary motion. At that time, the regular polyhedra were also linked to the view that the universe was made up of four basic elements: air, fire, earth, and water. The regular octahedron represented air; the tetrahedron represented fire; the cube represented earth; and the icosahedron represented water. To complete this theory, the dodecahedron represented the universe.

You may have seen the regular polyhedra only in novelties, such as a calendar with one month per face of a dodecahedron. So it may surprise you to find that the regular polyhedra do indeed have real significance and appear in nature. Crystals of some minerals are shaped like the regular polyhedra, as are some simple organisms. For example, crystals of ordinary table salt are shaped like cubes, and many viruses are shaped like regular icosahedra.

TAKE-AWAY MESSAGE . . . Shapes that were perhaps just intellectual playthings to the ancient Greeks turn out to represent objects in the real world that were largely unknown to the Greeks. The power of mathematics to represent real-world phenomena is one reason that mathematics is so valuable and so attractive to many people. ♦

| Learning Exercises for Section 16.5 |

1. Decide whether each statement is always true, sometimes true, or never true.

   a. A cube is a polyhedron.

   b. A polyhedron is a cube.

   c. A right rectangular prism is a cube.

   d. A cube is a right rectangular prism.

   e. A regular polyhedron is a prism.

   f. A prism is a regular polyhedron.

   g. The diagonals of every face of a cube are the same length.

   h. The diagonals of every face of a right rectangular prism are the same length.

   i. A pyramid is a regular polyhedron.

   j. A regular polyhedron is a pyramid.

   k. A hexahedron is a cube.

   l. A cube is a hexahedron.

2. Wondering about the number of types of regular polyhedra is a natural question to a mathematician. Why is there an advantage in knowing how many types there are of something?

3. From their biological names, what is the general shape of these organisms?

   a. Circogonia icosahedra

   b. Circorrhegma dodecahedra

   c. Circoporus octahedrus

4. **a.** If you take two regular tetrahedra (see shape A in your kit) and put them face to face, you get a polyhedron with six faces, each of which is shaped like an equilateral triangle. Why is this polyhedron *not* counted as a regular polyhedron? (Read the description of a regular polyhedron carefully.)

   b. Sketch another hexahedron that is not a regular hexahedron.

   c. Make a net for a tetrahedron that is not a regular tetrahedron.

5. **a.** On a cube, find four vertices that give a regular tetrahedron.

   b. What shape do the remaining four vertices give?

6. Check to see whether Euler's formula applies to each type of regular polyhedron. (Record your counts in a table; do you notice anything?)

7. A polyhedron may be made up of two or more types of regular polygonal regions, with the same arrangement of regions at each vertex (like your shape J). These shapes are called **semiregular polyhedra** (or sometimes **Archimedean polyhedra**), and they were also studied extensively even in ancient times (for example, by Archimedes, 287–212 B.C.).

   a. The sketches on the next page represent two semiregular polyhedra. What regular polygons are involved in each polyhedron? (Hidden edges are not shown in the second sketch.)

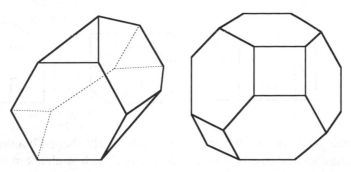

Notes

b. Check the first semiregular polyhedron in part (a) to see whether Euler's formula applies. Why is it difficult to check the second polyhedron in part (a)? Can you remedy that difficulty?

c. Make up a natural question about semiregular polyhedra. (See Learning Exercise 2.)

8. Which of the five types of regular polyhedra is your favorite? Why?

9. a. Must all the edges of a regular polyhedron be the same length? Explain.

b. Must each angle in every face of a regular polyhedron have the same size? Explain.

c. Must all the edges of a semiregular polyhedron be the same length? Explain.

d. Must each angle in every face of a semiregular polyhedron have the same size? Explain.

10. Use isometric dot paper to show two different nets for a regular octahedron.

16.6 | Issues for Learning: Dealing with 3D Shapes

The lack of an opportunity to learn about geometry can account for some of the difficulties that children (and adults) have with 3D geometric shapes, including the conventional vocabulary. For example, only about one-fourth of the 13-year-olds in one national testing program[i] could give the term *cube* when shown a model of a cube; many children used *square* for the cube, not distinguishing between the 2D nature of the square faces and the 3D nature of the shape. With most elementary school mathematics textbooks now covering the basic vocabulary for 3D shapes, children today usually have the opportunity to learn the names of the shapes…unless teachers skip those pages!

Two special aspects of dealing with drawings of 3D shapes lead to difficulties for learners: (1) Making such drawings and (2) interpreting them. You perhaps have seen children's drawings of houses, such as those shown on the next page for a house shaped like a cube, with a door in the front and windows on the right and left sides of the house. The increasing sophistication in the drawings may be due to natural development or increased exposure to, and experience with, drawings.

Notes

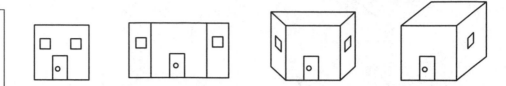

A similar development occurs for drawings of differently shaped but plain blocks, as in the following illustrations that are based on work[ii] with students in grades 1, 3, 5, 7, and 9. For other shapes, most of the children drew at different levels of sophistication, suggesting that drawing some shapes is more familiar than others. For example, the cylinder was more easily drawn than the prism, the pyramid, and the cube (drawings not shown here).

Drawings of a right rectangular prism

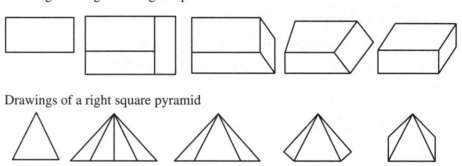

Drawings of a right square pyramid

Some elementary school textbooks include special representations, such as those with isometric dot paper or the front-side-top views in your Learning Exercises, recognizing that there is a degree of learning in interpreting and making them.

But exposure helps. For example, in one nonpublished report (by L. Jaslow), a teacher asked a mixed Grades 1-2 class to make nets for a cube. The illustrations below show how some of the initial ideas looked. But after discussing the nets and deciding that a turned version of, say, Harrison's would not be different, the children were able to find most of the different nets of a cube.

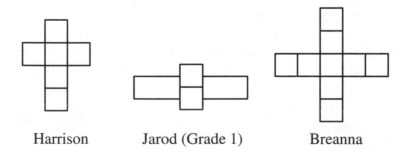

Harrison   Jarod (Grade 1)   Breanna

Textbooks, of course, rely on 2D drawings for solid shapes. But "reading" such drawings does not happen automatically for many children. For example, in one international testing[iii], given a drawing of a cube without the hidden edges indicated, only 40%

of the fourth graders and 34% of the third graders picked the correct number of edges for the cube, from the multiple choices. More importantly as a foundation for understanding volume, in a U.S. testing program only 33% of fourth graders could tell how many small cubes would make the larger cube, as in the drawing at the right, with 32% choosing 12 as the answer and 29% choosing 24. Research suggests that older children also have difficulty when attempting to give such counts from drawings of right rectangular prisms[iv], because quite often they have difficulty "seeing" all the hidden cubes or, while counting somewhat systematically, unintentionally double-counting. For example, for a 3 x 3 x 4 rectangular solid a fifth grader might count the 9 cubes in the front, say there are 9 more on the back (giving 18 so far), see the 12 cubes on the right, say there are 12 more on the left, and then say a grand total of 42 cubes. Such a student is unaware that he is double-counting several cubes and missing others completely. Other children might avoid the double counting but still miss counting all of the cubes.

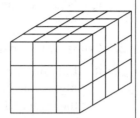

In a teaching experiment[v] with third graders, having the children build polyhedra (often pyramids) meeting certain criteria, but of their own designs, helped the children focus on important attributes of polyhedra (again, often pyramids). For example, the children's shapes below helped them focus on what makes a pyramid a pyramid. (Why are these not pyramids?)

TAKE-AWAY MESSAGE . . . Although there is some evidence of developmental constraints in making drawings or in attending to all of the dimensions involved, instruction that builds carefully from actual models seems to be helpful. But in particular, the opportunity to learn is crucial. ♦

Learning Exercises for Section 16.6

1. **a.** Why might so many third graders have chosen 12 for the number of small cubes required to make the cube shown to the right? (*Hint*: Recall that many confuse square with cube.)

    b. How might a child have decided that the correct answer was 24?

    c. Where is this child's thinking incorrect? "Four in the front and four in the back; that's 8. Four on the right and four on the left; that's 8 more. 16 in all."

2. Consider the prism shown at the right.

    a. Explain how the fifth grader was double counting in saying, "Nine in the front and 9 in the back; 18. Twelve on the right and 12 on the left; 24 more. 18 and 24 = 42."

    b. Which cubes is the fifth grader overlooking?

16.7 | Check Yourself

The *Check Yourself* section in each chapter of this book gives you a guide to many of the content expectations in the course. Your instructor may include others, of course, but the *Check Yourself* sections will give you some guidance in deciding whether you feel on firm ground in your understanding for the long term and in preparing for examinations. Writing your own "I should be able to…" list as you go through the course, and then comparing your list with the following guidelines, is a valuable way to see whether you are getting the point. As with most learning, the more actively involved you are, the better. Passively reading through this type of section can be just a reading exercise rather than a review, if you do not think about yourself vis-a-vis the items. For example, one way to review is to make up sample questions for the items in a *Check Yourself* section and then answer them. In reviewing past homework, you will likely take note of particular items that may have been difficult for you earlier, but think also about the items that were easy for you then as well (the human mind does forget!).

Chapter 16 has involved several vocabulary words for three-dimensional shapes. Some of these may have been new to you, so you will need to devote some care to remember them and keep them straight. In addition, it is likely that your instructor has brought up several vocabulary words about two-dimensional shapes, and these may or may not have been review for you. Some relationships between shapes (for example, congruence) and within a shape (for example, that the lateral edges of a prism are parallel and have the same length), as well as relationships about all polyhedra (for example, Euler's formula), deserve special attention.

Here are some more specific guidelines, with more detail than will usually be the case. You should be able to work problems like those assigned and to meet the following objectives.

1. Use the vocabulary. You should be adept at giving adjectives as well as naming the basic shape: for example, *right hexagonal prism* instead of just *prism*. There is a lot of vocabulary, and several of the words start with the letter *p* (for example, polyhedron, pyramid, prism, parallel, and so on) so the words can easily be confused. Some vocabulary words are introduced through Learning Exercises, and you do not want to overlook them. Learning Exercise 13 in Section 16.2 gives many of the words for 3D shapes that you should have mastered. The approach to congruent shapes (Section 16.4) may have been new to you, as well as the names for the regular polyhedra (Section 16.5).

    Note: Several terms about 2D shapes, as well as the measurement ideas of angle size, perimeter, area, and volume, may have come up during class or in some exercises. The degree of familiarity you should have with such terms at this time should be clear from what your instructor has said in class. Much of the 2D vocabulary is examined in the next chapter, and both area and volume receive extensive attention later in this book.

2. Give, preferably by your knowledge of the type of shape, the number of faces or vertices or edges for a given shape. For example, how many edges does a 200-gonal prism have? How many are lateral edges?

3. State and use Euler's formula for polyhedra.

4. Translate among the different representations: word, physical model, drawing, or net. For example, starting with, say, a name like *right square prism*, give the other three representations. Some of these translations involve having a good mental picture (or, if you are not a good visualizer, a good word description) of what a shape is, as in "Make a sketch of a right pentagonal prism." Your instructor may also expect you to be able to use isometric dot paper in making some drawings.

5. Show in your drawings an awareness of hidden line segments and show that you know to retain parallels and equal lengths whenever the view allows.

6. Recognize and draw congruent polyhedra.

7. Make with cubes, or sketch on isometric paper, a polyhedron that fits a given front-view, side-view, top-view information (from the Learning Exercises).

8. Tell what a *regular polyhedron* is and name the types or name the type from a given drawing.

9. Describe the difficulties that learners often have in drawing 3D shapes or interpreting drawings of 3D shapes (Section 16.6).

Notes

REFERENCES FOR CHAPTER 16

[i] Carpenter, T., Coburn, T. G., Reys, R. E., & Wilson, J. W. (1978). *Results from the first mathematics assessment of the National Assessment of Educational Progress.* Reston, VA: National Council of Teachers of Mathematics.

[ii] Mitchelmore, M. C. (1978). Developmental stages in children's representation of regular solid figures. *Journal of Genetic Psychology*, 133, 229-239.

[iii] Trends in International Mathematics and Science Study. http://nces.ed.gov/timss/

[iv] National Assessment of Educational Progress. http://www.nces.ed.gov/nationsreportcard/naepdata/

[v] Ambrose, R., & Kenehan, G. (2005). *Children's Evolving Understanding of Polyhedra in the Classroom.* Manuscript submitted for publication.

Chapter 17

Polygons

Flat, or planar, shapes made up of straight pieces are common models for many real-world items in Western societies. This chapter features a common type of shape, the polygon, and several ideas and facts associated with them, including the notion of hierarchical relationships among the various types of polygons.

17.1 | Review of Polygon Vocabulary

You may need to brush up on your 2D geometry vocabulary. Words that you may have forgotten often come back with a little review, and there may be terms that did not come up in your study of Chapter 16.

> **THINK ABOUT...**
>
> How many vertices (corner points) does a 10-sided shape have? A 100-sided shape? Does every such type of shape have the same number of vertices as sides? How many angles does a 6-sided shape have? An n-sided shape? Does every such type of shape have the same number of angles as sides?

This section quickly reviews many of the geometric terms associated with polygons (*poly-* means many; *-gon* means angle). You should be adept at two *translations*: (1) Give the best name for a given shape, and (2) draw or pick a shape, given its name.

All of the shapes in Figure 1 on the next page are polygons. As the arrangement suggests, one common way of classifying polygons is by the number of angles (or vertices or sides) that the polygon has. Each name involves a prefix indicating the number of angles, vertices, or sides, followed by either *-gon* or *-angle* or *-lateral* (sides). The Glossary has some of the prefixes; for polygons of 6 or 7 sides, the Greek prefixes are the common ones. The term n-gon allows us to be general about the number, n, of angles, vertices, or sides.

Notes

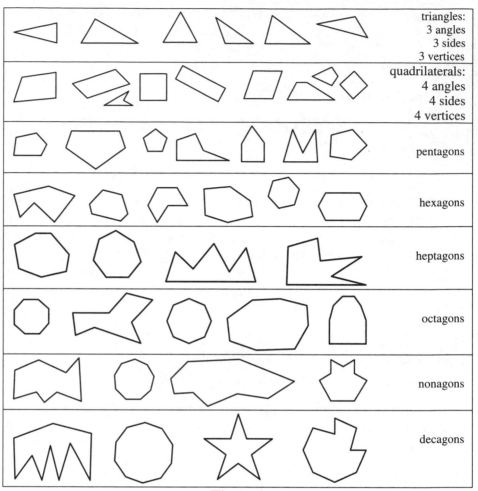

Figure 1

triangles:
3 angles
3 sides
3 vertices

quadrilaterals:
4 angles
4 sides
4 vertices

pentagons

hexagons

heptagons

octagons

nonagons

decagons

How would you define polygons? Here is a common description.

A **polygon** is a closed planar figure made up of line segments joined end to end, with no crossings or re-use of endpoints.

THINK ABOUT...

Explain why each of these shapes is not a polygon.

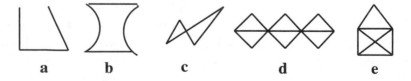

a   b   c   d   e

A polygon consists of just the points *on* its line segments. The points *inside* a polygon make up its **polygonal region** (pronounced pa LIG a nal). If the context is clear, however, even experts often describe a polygonal region by naming the polygon that bounds it. For example, a face of a cube is often called a *square* instead of the more precise *square region*.

Polygons   Polygonal regions

A few important adjectives can be applied to all types of polygons. An **equiangular** polygon is a polygon whose angles all have the same size. An **equilateral** polygon is a polygon whose sides all have the same length. Because these adjectives refer to different parts of a polygon, they represent separate ideas, in general. However, the two ideas go hand in hand for triangles. If a triangle is equiangular, it is automatically equilateral, and vice versa. Other polygons also can be both equiangular and equilateral; in this case, the polygons are called **regular** polygons. For example, because a square is both equiangular and equilateral, a square is a *regular* quadrilateral. A rectangle that is not also a square is equiangular but is not regular because it is not equilateral.

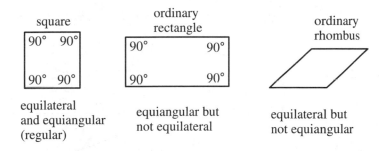

Triangles can be further classified in two ways. One way focuses on the size of the largest angle. An **acute triangle** has each angle measuring less than 90° in size; a **right triangle** has an angle that is 90° in size; and an **obtuse triangle** has an angle that is more than 90° in size. (Practice using these adjectives with the triangles in Figure 1.) The second way to classify triangles deals with the relative lengths of the sides of the triangle. The sides of a **scalene triangle** all have different lengths. If at least two sides of a triangle have the same length, the triangle is an **isosceles triangle**. If all three sides have the same length, the triangle is an **equilateral triangle**. (Practice using these adjectives with the triangles in Figure 1.)

THINK ABOUT...
Why is an equilateral triangle a special isosceles triangle?

Quadrilaterals come in a great many varieties. Several types are shown here.

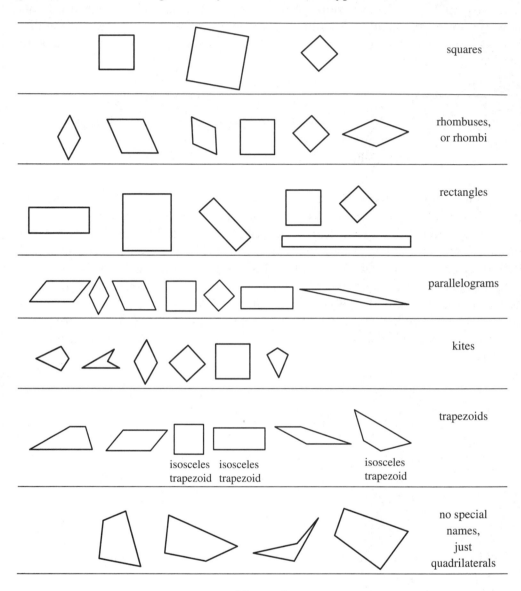

squares

rhombuses,
or rhombi

rectangles

parallelograms

kites

trapezoids

no special
names,
just
quadrilaterals

Figure 2

Activity 1   From Examples to Definitions

Without looking up definitions, write definitions for these types of quadrilaterals: square, rhombus, rectangle, parallelogram, kite, and trapezoid. Compare your definitions with those of someone else in your class. Figure 2 should help you determine the important elements for your definitions.

This book is written without extensive use of many of the notations common in advanced mathematics, partly because their use in elementary school is unpredictable. The following notations are reminders; feel free to use them (or your instructor may wish you to use them).

- Point: Capital letter (A, B, . . .)
- Line segment with endpoints at P and Q: $\overline{PQ}$
- Ray starting at C and going through D: $\overrightarrow{CD}$
- Line through D and E: $\overleftrightarrow{DE}$
- Polygon with vertices F, G, H, and I: FGHI

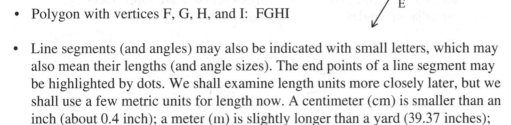

- Line segments (and angles) may also be indicated with small letters, which may also mean their lengths (and angle sizes). The end points of a line segment may be highlighted by dots. We shall examine length units more closely later, but we shall use a few metric units for length now. A centimeter (cm) is smaller than an inch (about 0.4 inch); a meter (m) is slightly longer than a yard (39.37 inches); and a kilometer (km) is about 0.62 mile.
- Angles are named either by naming just the vertex, or if needed for clarity, as for angle D in the drawing above, naming a point on one side, the vertex, and then a point on the other side: $\angle$D, or $\angle$CDE.

Vocabulary for Angles

A review some of the angle vocabulary that can arise in connection with polygons can be useful (we have already used some terms, as in classifying triangles). We will introduce other angle-related terms later. *Note*: Although we leave the main "theory" of measurement to later chapters (Chapter 23), our discussion assumes some familiarity with angle-size (and length) measurements. Angle size can be measured with the **protractor** and is usually measured in degrees (°) in elementary school. (Appendix F treats how to use the protractor if you have never used one.)

A **right angle** has size 90° (like a corner of a sheet of paper); lines that make right angles are called **perpendicular**. An **acute angle** has size less than 90°; an **obtuse angle** has size greater than 90° but less than 180°; and a **straight angle** has size 180°. Strictly speaking, the sides of an angle are rays, but line segments are often used to indicate the angle.

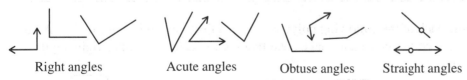

Right angles   Acute angles   Obtuse angles   Straight angles

Adjacent angles are angles with the same vertex and a common side between them. **Supplementary angles** are two angles whose sizes add up to 180°; supplementary angles do not have to be adjacent but may be. **Complementary angles** (note the spelling) are two angles whose sizes add to 90°.

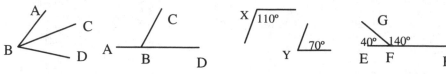

Angles ABC and CBD
are adjacent angles.

Angles X and Y are supplementary,
as are ∠EFG and ∠GFH.

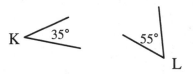

Angles K and L are complementary.

An **exterior angle** of a polygon is formed by the extension of one side of the polygon through a vertex of the polygon and the other side of the polygon through that vertex. We commonly refer to an angle inside a

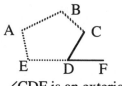

∠CDF is an exterior
angle of ABCDE.

∠KJH is an exterior
angle of GHJ.

polygon as an angle of the polygon, or an **interior angle** of the polygon, for clarity. Angles AED and EDC are interior angles in pentagon ABCDE.

TAKE-AWAY MESSAGE . . . Dealing with polygons involves a lot of nouns and adjectives, especially with quadrilaterals. The vocabulary is simplified a little by some use of prefixes and root suffixes such as *-gon*. We also use several adjectives to describe angles. ♦

Learning Exercises for Section 17.1

1. Name each of the following polygons. If an adjective applies, use it also. A little box in a corner is used to make clear that the indicated angle is a right angle (90°).

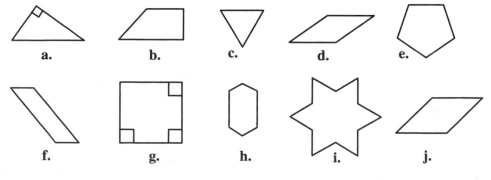

a.   b.   c.   d.   e.

f.   g.   h.   i.   j.

Notes

2. Sketch an example, if it is possible, of each shape described. If any are not possible to sketch, explain why.

   a. a trapezoid with at least one right angle

   b. a hexagon with two sides perpendicular (make right angles, or angles of 90°)

   c. a pentagon with two sides parallel

   d. a regular quadrilateral (What is this shape usually called?)

   e. an equiangular quadrilateral that is not equilateral (What is this shape usually called?)

   f. an equilateral quadrilateral that is not equiangular (What is this shape usually called?)

   g. a parallelogram that has exactly one right angle

   h. a trapezoid that has equal-sized angles next to one of the parallel sides (an **isosceles trapezoid**)

   i. an isosceles right triangle

   j. a scalene obtuse triangle

   k. an isosceles obtuse triangle

   l. an equilateral right triangle

   m. a rhombus that is also a rectangle

   n. an isosceles triangle with all sides the same length

   o. a kite with exactly one right angle

   p. an equilateral hexagon that is not a regular hexagon

   q. a regular pentagon that is not an equilateral pentagon

3. The reasonings below give incorrect conclusions. Explain why.

   a. "I don't get it. A hexagon has six sides, and each side has two endpoints, which are vertices of the hexagon. Six times two is twelve. Why doesn't a hexagon have twelve vertices?"

   b. "Hmm. An octagon has eight sides. It takes two sides to make an angle of the octagon. There are *four* twos in eight, so it seems that an octagon should have *four* angles, not eight!"

4. Give the best names for all the faces in these shapes.

   a. a regular hexagonal pyramid

   b. a right rectangular prism

   c. shape D in your kit of polyhedra

   d. shape K in your kit of polyhedra

5. Many classrooms have sets of **tangrams**, cardboard or plastic pieces that can be fit together to make a variety of shapes. The tangram pieces can be cut from a square region, as in the drawing shown at the right.

   a. What shape is each of the seven tangram pieces?

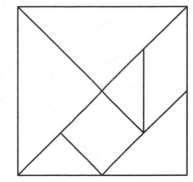

Notes

b. Using the segments in the drawing, find as many of each type of polygon as you can: isosceles right triangles; isosceles trapezoids; trapezoids that are not isosceles; parallelograms that are not rectangles. (*Hint*: Some may involve more than one tangram piece.)

c. Let the entire square region be 1. Give the fractional value for each of the seven tangram pieces.

d. Trace the tangram pieces, cut them out, and, without looking at the diagram, put them together again to form a square.

e. Tangrams are often used in classrooms to make different shapes. Can you use the pieces to make something—a cat, for example?

6. Sometimes ideas are presented to elementary school children by *concept cards*. Here is a pair of concept cards for the ideas of **convex** polygon and **concave** polygon:

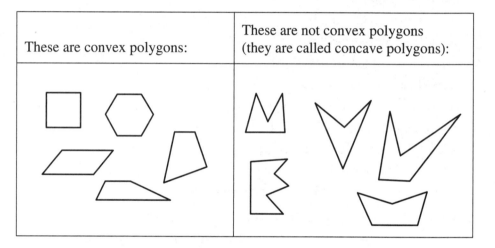

These are convex polygons:	These are not convex polygons (they are called concave polygons):

a. Draw another example of a convex polygon and of a concave polygon.

b. How would you describe convex polygons, in words? Concave polygons?

c. Make up a pair of concept cards for the idea of parallelogram.

d. Give a word description of *kite* from the information in the following concept cards.

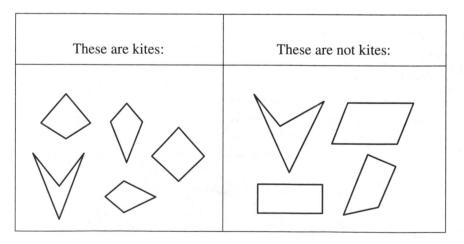

These are kites:	These are not kites:

7. For each part (a)–(f), copy the regular hexagonal region. (Answers for the first three parts are in the standard set of Pattern Blocks in Appendix G.)

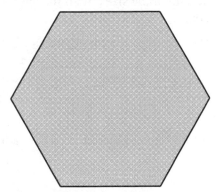

   a. Cut the hexagonal region into three identical rhombi.

   b. Cut the hexagonal region into six equilateral triangles.

   c. Cut the hexagonal region into two isosceles trapezoids.

   d. Cut the hexagonal region into 12 identical right triangles.

   e. Cut the hexagonal region into six identical kites.

   f. Cut the hexagonal region into four identical trapezoids.

8. What are some quantities associated with a polygon? With a polygonal region?

9. A **diagonal** of a polygon is a line segment joining two vertices of the polygon that are not joined by a side. The dashed segments show three of the nine diagonals in this hexagon.

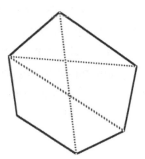

   Make and continue a table like the one indicated, and try to predict the total number of diagonals in a 12-gon, a 20-gon, and an *n*-gon.

Number of vertices	Number of diagonals
3	0
4	2
5 (etc.)	

10. You know that the sizes of all the angles in a triangle add up to 180°. Justify that the sum of the sizes of all the angles in every quadrilateral is 360°. *Hint*: Draw one diagonal. Does your justification work on quadrilaterals such as the one shown at the right?

Notes

11. Record and extend the results from Learning Exercise 10 about the sum of the degree measures of all the angles in a polygon, making a table like the one started. Predict what the sum of the sizes of all the angles of a 20-gon would be. Do the same for an *n*-gon.

Number of sides	Sum of angles
3	180°
4	
5 (etc.)	

12. Find the missing sizes of the angles marked in each quadrilateral. (*Hint*: See Learning Exercise 10.)

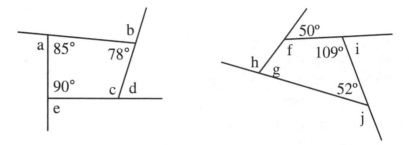

k.   Make an educated guess (a conjecture) about the sum of the sizes of all the exterior angles of every quadrilateral, using just one exterior angle at each vertex.

l.   Give a justification that your conjecture in part (k) will always be correct.

13. Use Learning Exercise 11 to help find the sizes of each of the following angles.
  a.   each (interior) angle of an equiangular pentagon
  b.   each exterior angle of an equiangular pentagon
  c.   each (interior) angle of an equiangular octagon
  d.   each exterior angle of an equiangular octagon
  e.   each (interior) angle of an equiangular *n*-gon
  f.   each exterior angle of an equiangular *n*-gon

14. Find the missing sizes of the angles marked in each pentagon.

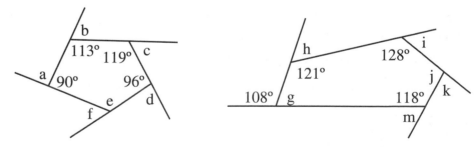

n.   Make an educated guess (a conjecture) about the sum of the sizes of the exterior angles of every pentagon, using just one exterior angle at each vertex.

o.   Give a justification that your conjecture in part (n) will always be correct.

15. Are the following statements true? Give your reasoning.

    a. The two acute angles in a right triangle are complementary.

    b. A triangle cannot have more than one right angle.

    c. The supplement of an angle of size $x°$ will have size $180° - x°$.

16. The Greeks tied much of their work with numbers to geometry. For example, they might think of the first, second, third, fourth, (and so on) square numbers by building increasingly larger squares of dots:

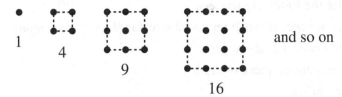

and so on

    a. Draw a square to verify that the fifth square number is indeed 25.

    b. Give an algebraic expression for the *n*th square number. Do the same for the $(x + 1)$st square number.

    c. The Greeks identified the **triangular numbers** in a similar way.

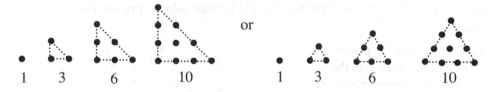

According to this pattern, the third triangular number is 6, and the fourth triangular number is 10. Make a table like the following one. Extend the results to help predict the number of dots in the 10th triangular number, the 20th triangular number, and the *n*th triangular number.

Triangular number	Number of dots involved
1st	1
2nd	3
3rd	6
4th	10

17. Some middle-grades teachers have their students illustrate particular geometric ideas by folding small pieces of paper. (The straight edges and right angles of the paper are not to be used. Pretend the paper is irregularly shaped.) For example, folding a piece of paper and creasing it gives a straight line segment, which can then be marked with a pencil. Use quarter-sheets of scrap paper to show each of the following geometric ideas.

    a. the line segment through two points marked on the paper

    b. the bisector of an angle drawn on the paper (Can you make the angle without using a ruler?)

    c. a right angle

Continue on the next page.

d. one line that is perpendicular to a line segment marked on the paper, at the midpoint of the marked line segment (the **perpendicular bisector** of the line segment)

e. the perpendicular to a marked line, at a point marked on that line

f. two parallel lines

g. a square

18. Practice making the polygon versus polygonal region distinction by giving the best names for the following models.

   a. this sheet of paper (Does it represent a rectangle, or a rectangular region?)

   b. a triangle made of coat-hanger wire

   c. a triangular-shaped piece of cloth

   d. a face of a prism

   e. a face of a pyramid

   f. a picture frame

   g. a hexagonal window frame

   h. a hexagonal window

19. Experiment to test whether this plausible-sounding conjecture (educated guess) appears to be true: In a triangle, the greater side is opposite the greater angle.

20. Trace and label the points shown to the right, and then show each geometric object on a single drawing.

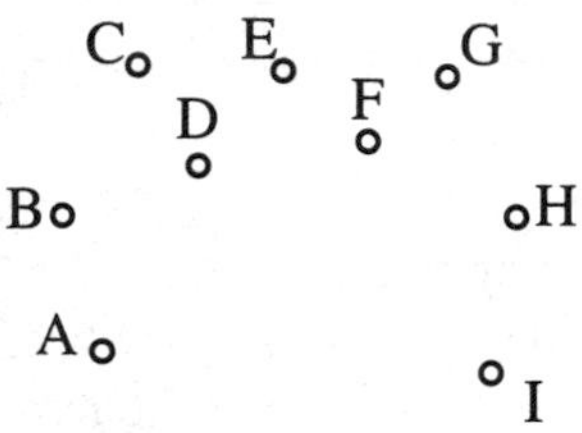

   C∘   E∘   ∘G
        D∘   F∘
   B∘   ∘H

        A∘
                ∘ I

   a. $\overrightarrow{IA}$ b. ∠IBA   c. region BCDEFGH   d. $\overline{AH}$

   e. $\overrightarrow{HI}$ f. $\overrightarrow{BA}$ g. $\overleftrightarrow{HB}$

21. Make sketches to show each geometric object.

   a. polygon PQRS   b. $\overrightarrow{NM}$ c. $\overleftrightarrow{FG}$

   d. $\overline{AB}$ e. ∠FDE   f. region TUV

17.2	**Organizing Shapes**

This section treats one way to categorize some common geometric shapes. Categorizing things and then naming the categories seem to be natural human activities.

A person not familiar with categorizing animals might focus on differences and regard all of the following as different: apes, beagles, cobras, collies, humans, sharks, rattlesnakes, salmon, and whales. Zoologists, however, might focus on *shared* characteristics rather than differences, organizing the categories as follows (with new categories in parentheses):

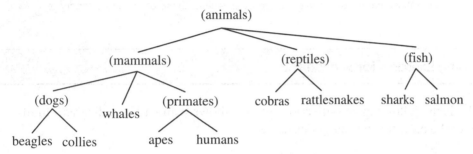

Such a **hierarchical classification** shows that lower entries can be regarded as special cases of any higher entries to which they are connected by line segments. For examples, beagles are special dogs as well as mammals and animals; apes are special mammals and special primates; salmon are special fish as well as special animals.

It is likely that at some point in your life, you were surprised to learn that humans are considered to be animals. Yet you now realize that people share many characteristics with all animals: living beings and mobility, for example. Any characteristic that is true for all animals is true for every human, even though people have many characteristics that other kinds of animals do not have. All mammals are animals with special characteristics, such as feeding their young with milk, being warm-blooded, and having hair.

Classifying Geometric Shapes

The same focus on shared characteristics, rather than differences, enables a sophisticated classification of geometric shapes. You are quite comfortable with regarding a rectangle as a quadrilateral, but you may be less comfortable with calling a rectangle a parallelogram, which is possible by focusing on particular shared characteristics of rectangles and parallelograms. In mathematics just a few (not all) of the characteristics of a class of shapes are needed to define the class, because other characteristics can be deduced logically. In future sections, you will see examples of this type of reasoning, where some facts are deduced from other established facts.

Discussion 1   A Square by Any Other Name...

Organize the following geometric shapes in a hierarchical classification diagram. Be ready to explain your method of organization.

> circles, equilateral triangles, hexagons, isosceles trapezoids, isosceles triangles, kites, octagons, parallelograms, pentagons, polygons, quadrilaterals, rectangles, rhombuses, scalene triangles, squares, trapezoids, triangles.

TAKE-AWAY MESSAGE . . . A classification into categories often lends itself to a further organization, one in which items in a sub-category have all the characteristics of the major category, as well as other characteristics. Hence, items in the sub-category can go by multiple names—those names of the major category as well as those of the sub-category. ♦

Learning Exercises for Section 17.2

---

1. Why is the following classification system (shown using a Venn diagram) limiting to the user, for the categories named?

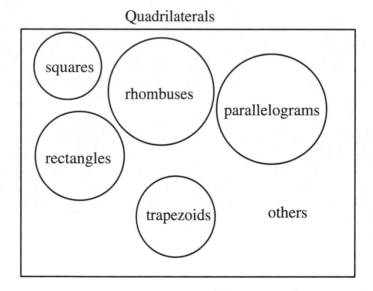

2. Decide whether each statement is always true, sometimes true, or never true. If a statement is sometimes true, sketch an example of when it is true and an example of when it is not.

   a. A square is a rectangle.

   b. A rectangle is a square.

   c. A parallelogram is a rectangle.

   d. A rectangle is a parallelogram.

   e. A trapezoid is a kite.

   f. A kite is a trapezoid.

   g. A kite is a rhombus.

   h. A rhombus is a kite.

   i. A square is a kite.

   j. A kite is a square.

   k. A right triangle is an isosceles triangle.

   l. An isosceles triangle is a right triangle.

   m. An acute triangle is a scalene triangle.

   n. A scalene triangle is an acute triangle.

3. In each given group of shapes, what characteristics are shared by the shapes? Characteristics might include lengths of sides, sizes of angles, parallelism, length of diagonals, and so on. What characteristics can be different?

   a. parallclograms, rectangles, rhombi, squares

   b. kites, rhombi, squares

   c. quadrilaterals, trapezoids

   d. trapezoids, parallelograms

   e. parallelograms, rhombi

4. Give an example of each shape, if possible. If it is not possible, explain why.

   a. a kite that is also a rhombus

   b. an obtuse triangle that is also isosceles

   c. a square that is not a parallelogram

   d. a parallelogram that is not a square

   e. a rhombus that is not a kite

   f. a rectangle that is not a parallelogram

5. Organize these terms: angles, circles, ellipses, ovals, parabolas, squiggles, zigzags.

6. If you know a four- or five-year-old, show him or her the drawing of a square in the usual orientation (vertical and horizontal sides), and ask, "What shape is this?" Many will know what it is. If the child says the shape is a square, rotate the drawing so that the sides are not horizontal and vertical, and ask, "Is this still a square?" Many will say it is not! They have focused on an irrelevant characteristic—the horizontalness or verticality of the sides—of the squares they have seen, and then have absorbed that as a requirement to be a square.

   a. What irrelevant characteristic of trapezoids is involved in the instruction, "Draw an upside-down trapezoid"?

   b. What irrelevant characteristic(s) in each scenario given might these students be assuming to be important?

      i. a student who does not regard a rectangle as also being a parallelogram

      ii. a student who does not regard a square as a special rectangle

      iii. a student who does not regard a square as a spccial rhombus

      iv. a student who does not regard a rhombus as a special kite

17.3 | Triangles and Quadrilaterals

The simplest polygons (triangles and quadrilaterals) have many properties that are not included in the statements of their definitions. For example, the opposite sides of a parallelogram are parallel by definition, but they also seem to be equal in length when you look at a drawing. However, there are risks in using drawings as proof (or in trusting patterns too much). Nonetheless, ideas have to come from somewhere. Drawings and patterns give ideas that might be justified in a general way. The basic descriptions of quadrilaterals in this section allow a sophisticated classification scheme like those given in the last section.

Activity 2   You Can't Go by Looks

In parts (a) and (b), which segment looks longer, PQ or RS? Measure each segment to check your perception. What do you notice about the object in part (c)? Is it completely safe to make conjectures based on looking at drawings?

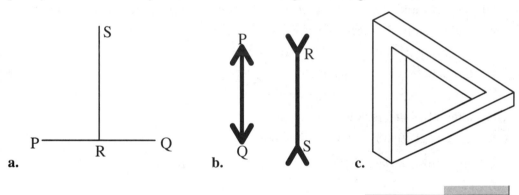

a.   b.   c.

The message from Activity 2 is, of course, that our perceptions may trick us. So, in arriving at conclusions based on drawings, we should be very cautious and tentative in asserting their truth. Drawings can be the source of ideas, however, and give us some basis for educated guesses, or **conjectures**. Activity 3 calls for making conjectures, recognizing that some conjectures may be incorrect.

Activity 3   You Can't Go by Looks, But I Think...

The aim of this activity is to form conjectures about properties of quadrilaterals or special quadrilaterals. One method of getting ideas is to examine drawings of several examples. Your conjectures might be about sides, angles, or diagonals. Your conjecture might also be about how the sides, angles, or diagonals appear to be related. Your group should consider these polygons: squares, rectangles, parallelograms, rhombi, trapezoids, isosceles trapezoids, kites, and quadrilaterals in general. Organize your conjectures for a whole-class discussion.

Your group probably found that rectangles, for example, appear to have several properties. There are two concerns: (1) Are these conjectures indeed *always* true for *every* rectangle, and (2) which of the properties should be used to define *rectangle*? We shall consider the latter concern first.

Creating a Definition

Novices often describe a shape by telling everything they know about the shape. Adopting *all* of the properties of a shape as a definition, however, would have the drawback of requiring us to verify a lot of properties unnecessarily, when checking whether a particular shape fits the definition. The unnecessary work would result because some properties are *consequences* of others, so they will happen automatically without being mentioned in the definition. Mathematicians know that there are often different ways to choose properties for an official definition. Of course, the properties chosen must indeed be adequate to identify all, and only, those shapes intended. To make clear the connections in a classification system, definitions may use properties that seem inadequate, oddly chosen, or even counterintuitive. (You should probably reread this paragraph after you have examined the definitions given below.)

As a taste of bare-bone descriptions, here are some fairly standard definitions for special triangles and quadrilaterals. A few are repeated from an earlier section for convenience. Make sketches to see that each definition does indeed describe the specific polygon. (Some drawings given in Section 17.1 may be helpful.)

An **isosceles triangle** is a triangle that has at least two sides with the same length.

An **equilateral triangle** is a triangle whose sides all have the same length.

A **kite** is a quadrilateral in which two consecutive sides have equal lengths and the other two sides also have equal lengths.

A **trapezoid** is a quadrilateral with at least one pair of opposite sides parallel.

An **isosceles trapezoid** is a trapezoid in which both the angles next to one of the parallel sides have the same size.

A **parallelogram** is a trapezoid with both pairs of opposite sides parallel.

A **rectangle** is a parallelogram with a right angle.

A **rhombus** is a kite that is also a parallelogram.

A **square** is a rectangle that is also a rhombus.

Some of these given definitions no doubt sound strange. The phrasings certainly make clear the connections between shapes. For example, the definitions explicitly say that a parallelogram is a special trapezoid and that a rectangle is a special parallelogram. Yet you know that a rectangle has *four* right angles, but the official definition says *a* right angle. Legalistically—and mathematically—a right angle does not rule out *four* right angles, in the same way as answering "Do you have a quarter?" with "Yes" does not mean you have only one quarter. Why aren't the other three right angles mentioned? You may realize that they must be a logical consequence of the parallelogram-with-right-angle requirement for a rectangle. Here the hierarchical arrangement in a classification system comes strongly into play: Each fact about every parallelogram also applies to every rectangle! Your group may have noticed that in a parallelogram the opposite angles are the same size and the pairs of consecutive angles have sizes that add to 180° (that is, they are supplementary). These two facts logically show that the other three angles of a rectangle must also be right angles. (Can you give a justification that uses *only* the second fact?)

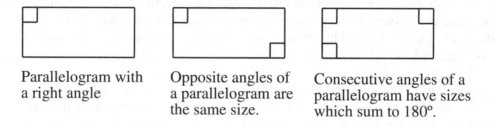

Parallelogram with a right angle

Opposite angles of a parallelogram are the same size.

Consecutive angles of a parallelogram have sizes which sum to 180°.

Hence, a hierarchical arrangement in a classification system allows us to take advantage of facts about one shape by applying them to special cases of that shape, as we just did in applying facts about parallelograms to rectangles by viewing rectangles as special parallelograms.

Discussion 2   A Rhombus Has...

The official definition of *rhombus* does not mention explicitly that a rhombus has four sides with the same length. How is that information hidden in the definition? (*Hint*: Some of your conjectures from Activity 3 may be useful.)

Hierarchical Arrangements of Polygons

The previous definitions also give the following categorization scheme, or hierarchy, for polygons. The connection between *trapezoid* and *parallelogram* would not exist if a trapezoid is defined as having exactly one pair of parallel sides, nor would the connection between isosceles trapezoids and rectangles exist.

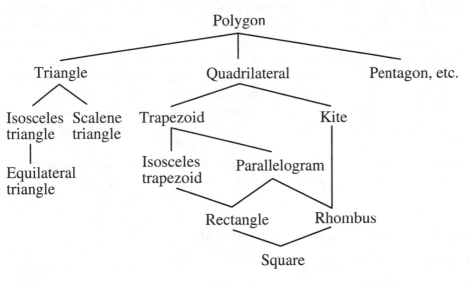

Figure 3

The hierarchy in Figure 3 shows, for example, that a rhombus is a special parallelogram and a special kite, as well as being a special trapezoid, quadrilateral, and polygon. The hierarchy of Figure 3 is the one we will use, but your instructor may prefer the hierarchy in Activity 4.

Activity 4   If the Definition of Trapezoid Changed

Many elementary school mathematics books do define a trapezoid as having exactly one pair of opposite sides parallel. In the diagram below and with that definition in mind, draw lines to show how the hierarchy for quadrilaterals would change from the previous one.

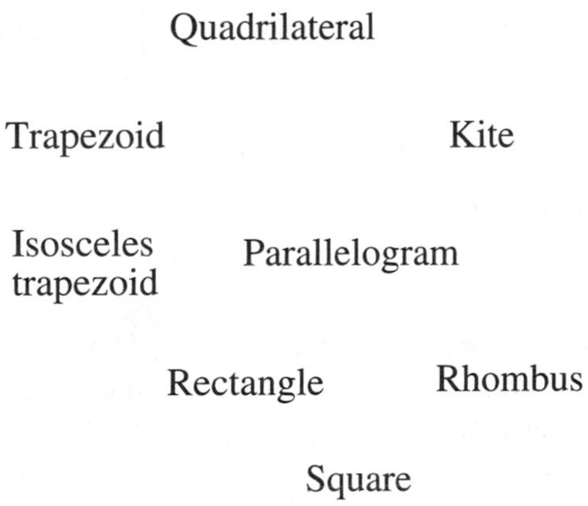

Quadrilateral

Trapezoid   Kite

Isosceles   Parallelogram
trapezoid

Rectangle   Rhombus

Square

Figure 4

In establishing that certain facts are true about a shape, sometimes we cannot take advantage of any hierarchical relationships, however. For example, your group may have conjectured (or you may remember from school geometry) that in an isosceles triangle, the angles opposite the sides of equal length have equal sizes. How could you justify that conclusion? It is not true for all triangles, so there is no help from the hierarchy. Later on, we will appeal to the concept of *symmetry* to justify some of the facts about shapes. You may remember other methods, such as the use of congruent triangles, from secondary school.

One method that we will encourage, but again with a cautionary note, is to use a pattern suggested by several examples.

Activity 5   Can Patterns Be Completely Trusted?

Look for patterns to answer the questions.

a. Notice the following pattern.

$$1^2 = 1$$
$$11^2 = 121$$
$$111^2 = 12321$$
$$etc.$$
$$1,111,111,111^2 = ?$$

b. The data in the table below are fairly accurate for humans.

Month of pregnancy	Length of fetus (cm)
2	4
3	9
4	16
5	25

How long will the baby be at birth (9 months)?

c. Can patterns be completely trusted?

Basing a conclusion solely on one or more examples is called **inductive reasoning**. Mathematicians know that conjectures from drawings and patterns cannot be completely trusted. Inductive reasoning is risky. So mathematicians look for more general arguments. For example, Euler's formula asserts that $V + F = E + 2$ for polyhedra. How can mathematicians (and you) be certain, without using just a pattern? You may have been close, in your thinking leading up to Euler's formula in Chapter 16. If you deal with a *general* n-gonal pyramid, you will have a general count: $n + 1$ vertices, $n + 1$ faces, and $2n$ edges, making it easy to check the $V + F = E + 2$ relationship. A similar kind of *general* reasoning also works for prisms. So, mathematicians seek a general argument that will apply to *all* cases at once, not just those represented by the drawing or examples examined. The surprising thing is that Euler's formula also applies to most other kinds of polyhedra, but convincing oneself of that requires a different, slightly more advanced technique that would be digressive here. In short, be happy with the conjectures you make using inductive reasoning from drawings or patterns, but be very careful in asserting that the conjectures are definitely true.

> **THINK ABOUT...**
>
> Mentally count the numbers of vertices, faces, and edges in an *n*-gonal prism, and use Euler's formula to check that your counts are correct.

TAKE-AWAY MESSAGE . . . Many facts about types of polygons are not always evident in their mathematical definitions. Inductive reasoning through careful drawings or patterns may suggest some good but tentative conjectures, but general reasoning, perhaps aided by a hierarchy, can establish that they are true. ◆

Learning Exercises for Section 17.3

1. Correct the classification system of the Venn diagram below.

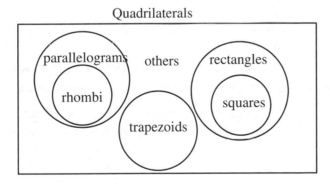

Quadrilaterals

2. Organize all the conjectures about special quadrilaterals that you have. Check the ones that have some sort of justification besides examples. Mark out any conjectures for which someone has found a **counterexample** (an example that shows that the conjecture is not true in general). You could organize your work as shown on the next page. The table on the next page includes a few conjectures as samples to help get you started.

Notes

Conjecture	Opposite sides are equal.	Opposite angles are equal.	Diagonals are equal.	Diagonals bisect the angles.	Diagonals bisect each other.
Quadrilaterals					
Trapezoids					
Isosceles trapezoids					
Parallelograms					
Rectangles					
Squares					
Kites					
Rhombuses					

3. Check your conjectures in Learning Exercise 2 with the hierarchy given in Figure 3 on page 413.

   a. Do all your conjectures about trapezoids appear to apply to parallelograms, rhombuses, rectangles, and squares?

   b. Do all your conjectures about kites appear to apply to rhombuses and squares?

   c. Do all your conjectures about parallelograms appear to apply to rectangles, rhombuses, and squares?

   d. Do all your conjectures about rhombuses appear to apply to squares?

   e. Do all your conjectures about rectangles appear to apply to squares?

4. a. Examine examples and make one or more conjectures about this situation: In a triangle, the midpoints of two sides are joined, as in Figure (a) below.

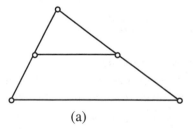

(a)

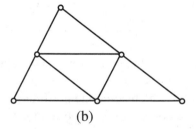

(b)

   b. Examine examples and make one or more conjectures about this situation: In a triangle, the midpoints of all three sides are joined, as in Figure (b) above.

5. Here are two informal methods of suggesting a fact you already know.

   a. Cut out a triangular region. Then, tear off the three angles of the triangle and rearrange them to show what their sum is. Try this with an unusually-shaped triangle as well.

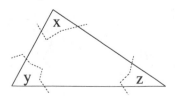

b. Use a copy of triangle PQR below and fold it to justify (experimentally) a fact you know about the sum, $x + y + z$. Does the method work on other triangles?

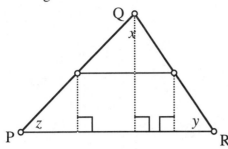
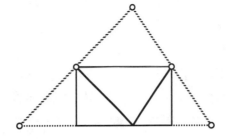

6. Find the number of degrees in each lettered angle.

a.

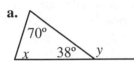

b.

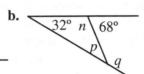

c.

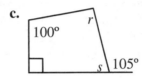

7. a. Here is a *What's My Shape?* puzzle from a research article.[i] Uncover the clues one at a time, and see what shapes are possible after each clue.

Clue 1. It is a closed figure with 4 straight sides.

Clue 2. It has 2 long sides and 2 short sides.

Clue 3. The 2 long sides are the same length.

Clue 4. The 2 short sides are the same length.

Clue 5. One of the angles is larger than one of the other angles.

Clue 6. Two of the angles are the same size.

Clue 7. The other two angles are the same size.

Clue 8. The 2 long sides are parallel.

Clue 9. The 2 short sides are parallel.

b. Make up a "What's My Shape?"

8. Pat says, "I was supposed to calculate $4 - \frac{4}{5}$, but I got mixed up and figured out $4 \times \frac{4}{5} = \frac{16}{5} = 3\frac{1}{5}$ instead. But when I did do $4 - \frac{4}{5}$, I noticed that I got the same answer, $3\frac{1}{5}$. So I think that when you subtract a fraction from a whole number, you get the same answer as you would if you did the whole number times the fraction."

a. Complete Pat's generalization in algebraic form: $a - \dots$.

b. Is Pat's reasoning correct?

9. Organize these shapes in a classification diagram: kite prisms, isosceles-trapezoid prisms, parallelogram prisms, quadrilateral prisms, rectangular prisms, rhomboidal prisms, square prisms, and trapezoid prisms.

10. Fact: The sum of the measures of all the angles in all of the faces (the *face angles*) of any trapezoidal prism is 2160°. Without calculation, give the sum of the measures of all the face angles of a rhomboidal prism. Explain your reasoning. (*Hint*: See Learning Exercise 9.)

17.4 | Issues for Learning: Some Research on 2D Shapes

The coverage of geometry in the elementary school curriculum is not so well defined as the coverage of numbers and operations. Indeed, some research found that teachers in Grades 4 and 5 in some entire school districts devoted essentially no time to geometry![ii] Of course, state guidelines usually call for attention to geometry, and most teachers do spend a fair amount of time on shapes. So it is a bit surprising to find that children can entertain such ideas as the following ones.[iii]

Why is each of these children's ideas incorrect, in general?

*   An angle must have one horizontal ray.

*   A right angle is an angle that points to the right.

*   A segment is not a diagonal if it is vertical or horizontal.

*   A square is not a square if its base is not horizontal.

*   The only way a figure can be a triangle is if it is equilateral.

*   The angle sum of a quadrilateral is the same as its area.

*   If a shape has four sides, then it is a square.

Where do such incorrect ideas come from? One possible source might be in the limited number of examples that children may see, both in their textbooks and in their teachers' drawings. Some of the ideas listed are natural, especially when the children have seen only examples incorporating the ideas, with angles always having a horizontal side, right angles always oriented toward the right, or equilateral triangles and squares being the only examples of triangles and quadrilaterals. Thus, a first message from the research is that a teacher should be sure that the students see a great variety of examples, with some omitting irrelevant attributes like horizontalness or a particular orientation. Look again at the sketches of polygons and quadrilaterals in Section 17.1 to see how we have attempted to give a variety of examples. Research also suggests that including a variety of non-examples is also a good idea. The non-examples allow a discussion to go beyond "No, it is not an example" to a focus on why the non-example is not an example. (See also the non-examples of polygons in Section 17.1.) Exercises like *What's My Shape?* (Learning Exercise 7 in Section 17.3) allow a consideration of what might be important features of a polygon.

We do not want our emphasis on hierarchies and hierarchical relationships in this book to imply that young children can learn these ideas easily. Indeed, some studies show that some children have difficulty with multiple classifications, even with familiar objects.[iv] Here are examples from another study[i] that illustrate the misconceptions and the difficulties for some children with multiple classifications. The children were presented with the drawings in Figure 5. When the children were asked to identify the squares, rectangles, and (if the child was familiar with the words) parallelograms and rhombuses in a similar collection of drawings, one third-grader chose shapes 2, 6, 7, 9, and 12 as squares. A fifth-grader chose 2, 4, 5, 7, 8, and 13 as squares, and 3, 6, 9, 10, and 12 as rectangles. The difficulty with the multiple classifications implied by a hierarchy is also illustrated by an eighth-grader who chose 2 and 7 as squares; 9 and 12 as rectangles; 3, 5, 6, and 10 as parallelograms; and 8 and 13 as rhombuses. The eighth-grader, when asked for definitions, gave definitions that made the types of quadrilaterals separate categories—for example, for parallelogram, "two parallel lines the same length are connected by two slanting lines the same length. The slanting lines are a different length than the parallel lines," thus ruling out rectangles, rhombuses, and squares as parallelograms.

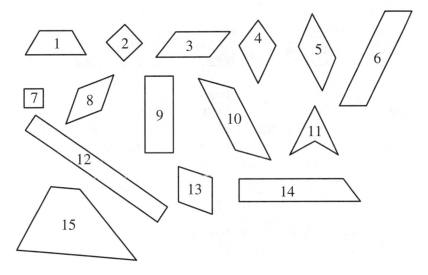

Figure 5

One viewpoint, with some research support, is that a person's understanding of a shape might develop in levels. For example, given a drawing of a rectangle, at the lowest level a child might say it is a rectangle *solely* because the shape *looks like* a rectangle (perhaps because it incorporates some irrelevant aspect such as different lengths for the two dimensions). A next level might be represented by a child's calling a shape a rectangle because of the angle sizes and the pairs of parallel sides of equal lengths. A still more advanced level might be shown by students who apply the definition of rectangle to the particular shape and find that the shape meets the conditions of the definition. The researchers think that starting at an advanced level of understanding, such as a definition, might be "over the head" of someone who is at only an earlier level, such as recognizing a shape by how it looks.

Some of the "wrong" answers can be explained by the common school practice of expecting only the most informative name for a shape. But this practice hides the hierarchical relationships that can be important in understanding shapes and in later work in geometry.

> TAKE-AWAY MESSAGE . . . Dealing with, or even avoiding, some of the misunderstandings children can have regarding conventional geometric ideas might entail (a) giving a great variety of examples that perceptually vary common but irrelevant characteristics, and (b) including non-examples to allow a focus on the important relevant features. Better learning might result when many examples and non-examples are used, along with a definition that might be appropriate at some grade level. Teachers might keep in mind that there are probably levels of understanding of any given geometric term and thus not assume that correct recognition of shape names is adequate evidence of the desired level of under-standing. Understanding that a shape can have several names may be related to children's cognitive development and hence may require careful planning for a genuine appreciation of hierarchies. ♦

Learning Exercises for Section 17.4

1. Based on the examples she has seen, a child might think that a trapezoid is "a shape with 4 sides, top and bottom are parallel, bottom longer than top, no sides the same size, fairly large, no right angles, and cut off at the top." Which of these characteristics are relevant? Draw some examples that vary the irrelevant characteristics that she associates with trapezoids.

2. A child once rejected a long, thin triangle as being a triangle because the shape was "too sharp." What might have led to the child's idea?

3. Suppose a child thinks that angle A is larger than angle B. What irrelevant characteristics for angle size does the child seem to have?

4. Give a collection of examples and non-examples that you think would be good for the idea of rhombus.

5. How might the following children have been thinking?

    a. The third-grader who chose 2, 6, 7, 9, and 12 as squares in Figure 5.

    b. The fifth-grader who chose 2, 4, 5, 7, 8, and 13 as squares, and 3, 6, 9, 10, and 12 as rectangles, in Figure 5.

17.5	**Check Yourself**

Chapter 17 has included a review of many terms about 2D shapes and also has taken them in what may be new directions for you: writing precise definitions (especially for the types of quadrilaterals) and the hierarchical arrangement of categories and sub-categories of polygons. Along the way, you should have developed and tested several conjectures about triangles and quadrilaterals, possibly with some of those conjectures being incorrect in general. Such false conjectures illustrate the dangers of expecting completely reliable conclusions from drawings or examples alone (inductive reasoning). Establishing a reliable conjecture requires a general argument that covers *all* cases.

You should be able to work problems like those assigned and to meet the following objectives.

1. Use, recognize, illustrate, spell(!), and perhaps define the various terms associated with polygons given in this chapter, including *n-gon*. Occasionally terms are mentioned first in the exercises (isosceles trapezoid, diagonal).

2. Describe the difference between *polygon* and *polygonal region*.

3. Use appropriately (and spell) the adjectives *equiangular*, *equilateral*, and *regular*.

4. Give the sum of the angles of any polygon, knowing just the number of sides or angles or the name of the polygon (Learning Exercise 11 in Section 17.1).

5. Give the accepted hierarchy for the terms involved in this chapter.

6. Appreciate the role of a hierarchy in organizing relationships and information.

7. Use hierarchical relationships to answer such questions as "Is a square a rectangle?"

8. State and use the definitions in Section 17.3, or the definitions approved by your instructor. For example, you should be able to recognize and create examples of a rhombus and to recognize non-examples of rhombuses.

9. Apply whatever conjectures turned out to be true, particularly conjectures about the types of quadrilaterals and the advantages from using hierarchical relationships.

10. Use terms such as *conjecture* and *counterexample* knowledgeably.

11. Give an argument to convince someone that the sum of the angles of a triangle is indeed 180° and the sum of the angles of a quadrilateral must be 360° (Learning Exercises 5 in Section 17.3 and 10 in Section 17.1, respectively).

12. Tell why even a good drawing or a pattern from several examples (inductive reasoning) cannot be trusted in creating conjectures.

Notes

REFERENCES FOR CHAPTER 17

[i] Burger, W. F., & Shaughnessy, J. M. (1986). Characterizing the van Hiele levels of development in geometry. *Journal for Research in Mathematics Education, 17,* 31–48.

[ii] Porter, A. (1989). A curriculum out of balance: The case of elementary school mathematics. *Educational Researcher, 18,* 9–15.

[iii] Clements, D. H., & Battista, M. T. (1992). Geometry and spatial reasoning. In D. Grouws (Ed.), *Handbook of research on mathematics teaching and learning* (pp. 420–464). New York: Macmillan.

[iv] Inhelder, B., & Piaget, J. (1964). *The early growth of logic in the child.* (Trans. by E. Lunzer & D. Papert). New York: W.W. Norton.

Chapter 18

Symmetry

Symmetry is of interest in many areas, for example, art, design in general, and even the study of molecules. This chapter begins with a look at two types of symmetry of two-dimensional shapes, and then moves on to introduce symmetry of polyhedra (and of three-dimensional objects in general).

18.1 Symmetry of Shapes in a Plane

Symmetry of plane figures can appear as early as Grade 1, where symmetry is restricted to **reflection symmetry**, or **line symmetry**, for a figure, as illustrated at the right. The **reflection line**, the dashed line in the figure, cuts the figure into two parts, each of which would fit exactly onto the other part if the figure were folded on the reflection line. Many flat shapes in nature have reflection symmetry, and many human-made designs incorporate reflection symmetry into them.

You may have made symmetric designs (for example, snowflakes or Valentine's Day hearts) by first folding a piece of paper, next cutting something from the folded edge, and then unfolding. The line of the folded edge is the reflection line for the resulting figure.

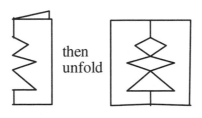

then unfold

A given shape may have more than one reflection symmetry. For example, for a square there are four reflection lines, each of which gives a reflection symmetry for the square. Hence, a square has four reflection symmetries.

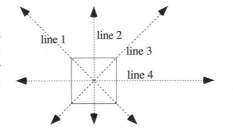

line 1　line 2　line 3　line 4

A second kind of symmetry for some shapes in a plane is **rotational symmetry**. A shape has rotational symmetry if it can be rotated around a fixed point until it fits exactly on the space it originally occupied. The fixed turning point is called the **center** of the rotational symmetry. For example, suppose square ABCD below is rotated counterclockwise about the point highlighted as the center. The dashed segment to vertex C is used here to help keep track of the number of degrees turned. A prime mark is often used as a reminder that the point is associated with the original location. For instance, we denote B' as the point to which B would move after the rotation.

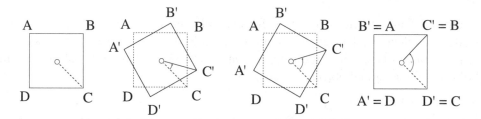

Eventually, after the square has rotated through 90°, it occupies the same set of points as it did originally. The square has a rotational symmetry of 90° with center at the highlighted point. Convince yourself that the square also has rotational symmetries of 180° and 270°. Every shape has a 360° rotational symmetry, but in counting the number of symmetries the 360° rotational symmetry is counted only if there are other rotational symmetries for a figure. Hence, a square has four rotational symmetries. Along with the four reflection symmetries, the square has eight symmetries in all.

> ***THINK ABOUT...***
>
> The rotations in the figure above were all counterclockwise. Explain why 90°, 180°, 270°, and 360° *clockwise* rotations do not give any new rotational symmetries.

The symmetries make it apparent that they involve a movement of some sort. We can give the following general definition.

> A **symmetry of a figure** is any movement that fits the figure onto the same set of points it started with.

Activity 1   Symmetries of an Equilateral Triangle

What are the reflection symmetries and the rotational symmetries of the equilateral triangle KLM? Be sure to identify the lines of reflection and the number of degrees in the rotations.

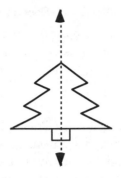

Notice that when we use the word *symmetry* with an object in geometry, we have a particular figure in mind, such as the tree shown at the right. And we must imagine some movement, such as the reflection in the dashed line, that gives the original figure as the end result. Many points have "moved," but the figure as a whole occupies the exact same set of points after the movement as it did before the movement. If you blinked during the movement, you would not realize that a motion had taken place.

Rather than just trusting how a figure looks, we can appeal to symmetries in some figures to justify some conjectures for those figures. For example, an isosceles triangle has a reflection symmetry. In an isosceles triangle, if we bisect the angle formed by the two sides of equal length, those two sides "trade places" when we use the bisecting line as the reflection line. Then the two angles opposite the sides of equal length (angles B and C in the figure) also trade places, with each angle fitting exactly where the other angle was.

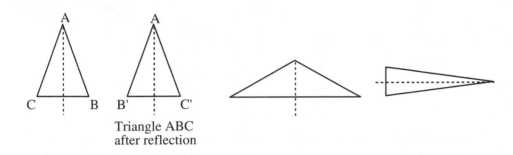

Triangle ABC
after reflection

So, **in an isosceles triangle the two angles opposite the sides of equal length must have equal sizes**. Notice that the same reasoning applies to every isosceles triangle, so there is no worry that somewhere there may be an isosceles triangle with those two angles having different sizes. Rather than looking at just one example and relying on what appears to be true in the example, this reasoning applies to all isosceles triangles and as a result, gives a strong justification for not having *equal angles* as part of a definition of isosceles triangle.

Discussion 1   Why Equilateral Triangles Have to Be Equiangular

Use the previous fact about isosceles triangles to deduce that all three angles of an equilateral triangle must be of the same size.

In Discussion 1 you used the established fact about angles in an isosceles triangle to justify in a general way the fact about angles in an equilateral triangle. Contrast this method with just looking at an equilateral triangle and trusting your eyesight.

Activity 2   Does a Parallelogram Have Any Symmetries?

Trace a general parallelogram and look for symmetries. Does a parallelogram have any reflection symmetries? Does it have any rotational symmetries besides the trivial 360° symmetry?

Here is another illustration of justifying a conjecture by using symmetry. Previously you may have made these conjectures about parallelograms: **The opposite sides of a parallelogram are equal in length, and the opposite angles are the same size.** The justification takes advantage of the 180° rotational symmetry of a parallelogram, as suggested in the following sketches. Notice that the usual way of naming a particular polygon by labeling its vertices provides a good means of talking (or writing) about the polygon, its sides, and its angles.

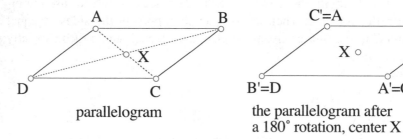

parallelogram

the parallelogram after
a 180° rotation, center X

Activity 3   Symmetries in Some Other Shapes

How many reflection symmetries and how many rotational symmetries does each of the following polygons have? In each case, describe the lines of reflection and the degrees of rotation.

a. regular pentagon PQRST

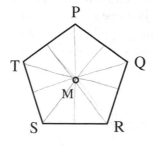

b. regular hexagon ABCDEF

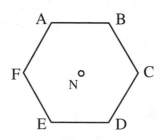

c. a regular *n*-gon

TAKE-AWAY MESSAGE . . . Symmetries of shapes is a rich topic. Not only do symmetric shapes have a visual appeal, they make the design and construction of many manufactured objects easier. Symmetry is often found in nature. Mathematically, symmetries can provide methods for justifying conjectures that might have come from drawings or examples. ♦

Learning Exercises for Section 18.1

1. Which capital letters, in a block printing style (for example, A, B, C, D, E, F, G, H, I, J, K, L, M, N, O, P, Q, R, S, T, U, V, W, X, Y, Z) have reflection symmetry(ies)? Rotational symmetry(ies)?

2. Identify some flat object in nature that has reflection symmetry, and one that has rotational symmetry.

3. Find some human-made flat object that has reflection symmetry, and one that has rotational symmetry. (One source might be company logos.)

4. What are the reflection symmetries and the rotational symmetries for each of the following polygons? Describe the lines of reflection and give the number of degrees of rotation.

   a. an isosceles triangle with only two sides the same length

   b. a rectangle that does not have all its sides equal in length (Explain why the diagonals are *not* lines of symmetry.)

   c. a parallelogram that does not have any right angles

   d. an isosceles trapezoid

   e. an ordinary, non-isosceles trapezoid

   f. a rhombus that does not have any right angles

   g. a kite

5. Shapes other than polygons can have symmetries.

   a. Find a line of symmetry for an angle.

   b. Find four lines of symmetry for two given lines that are **perpendicular** (that is, that make right angles). Find four rotational symmetries also.

   c. Find three lines of symmetry for two given parallel lines.

   d. Find several lines of symmetry for a circle. (How many lines of symmetry are there?)

   e. How many lines of symmetry does an ellipse have?

6. Explain why this statement is incorrect: "You can get a rotational symmetry for a circle by rotating it 1°, 2°, 3°, and so on, about the center of the circle. So, a circle has exactly 360 rotational symmetries."

7. Copy each design and add to it, so that the result gives the required symmetry described in parts (a)–(e).

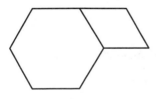
Design I

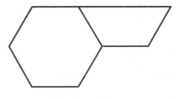
Design II

   a. Design I, rotational symmetry

Continue on the next page

    b.   Design I, reflection symmetry

    c.   Design I, reflection symmetry with a line different from the one in part (b)

    d.   Design II, rotational symmetry

    e.   Design II, reflection symmetry

8. Pictures of real-world objects and designs often have symmetries. Identify all the reflection symmetries and rotational symmetries in the following pictures.

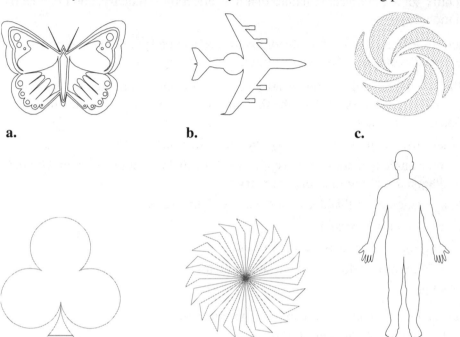

    a.   **b.**   **c.**

    d.   **e.**   **f.**

9. *(Pattern Blocks)* Make an attractive design using Pattern Blocks (or the paper ones found in Appendix G). Is reflection symmetry or rotational symmetry involved in your design?

10. Suppose triangle ABC has a line of symmetry k.

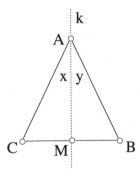

What does that tell you, if anything, about the following objects?

    a.   segments AB and AC (What sort of triangle must ABC be?)

    b.   angles B and C

    c.   point M and segment BC

    d.   angles x and y

11. Suppose that m is a line of symmetry for hexagon ABCDEF.

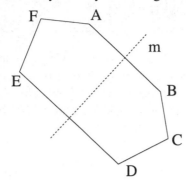

What does that tell you, if anything, about the following objects.

a.   segments BC and AF? Explain.

b.   segments CD and EF?

c.   the lengths of segments AB and ED?

d.   angles F and C? Explain.

e.   other segments or angles?

12. Suppose that hexagon GHIJKL has a rotational symmetry of 180°, with center X.

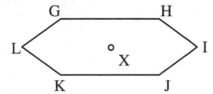

What does a 180° rotation tell you about specific relationships between segments and between angles in the hexagon?

13. a.   Using symmetry, give a justification that the diagonals of an isosceles trapezoid have the same length.

b.   Is the result stated in part (a) also true for rectangles? For parallelograms? Explain.

14. a.   Using symmetry, give a justification that the diagonals of a parallelogram bisect each other.

b.   Is the result stated in part (a) also true for special parallelograms? For kites? Explain.

15. Examine the following conjectures about some quadrilaterals to see whether you can justify any of them by using symmetry.

a.   The "long" diagonal of a kite cuts the "short" diagonal into segments that have the same length.

b.   In a kite like the one shown at the right, angles 1 and 2 have the same size.

c.   All the sides of a rhombus have the same length.

d.   The diagonals of a rectangle cut each other into four segments that have the same length.

18.2 | Symmetry of Polyhedra

In Section 16.4, we informally linked congruence of polyhedra to motions. Because we linked symmetry of 2D shapes to motions also, it is no surprise to find that symmetry of 3D shapes can also be described by motions. This section introduces symmetry of 3D shapes by looking at polyhedra and illustrating two types of 3D symmetry. Have your kit of shapes handy!

Reflection Symmetries

Clap your hands together and keep them together. Imagine a plane (or an infinite two-sided mirror) between your fingertips. If you think of each hand being reflected in that plane or mirror, the reflection of each hand would fit the other hand exactly. The left hand would reflect onto the right hand, and the right hand would reflect onto the left hand. The plane cuts the two-hands figure into two parts that are mirror images of each other; reflecting the figure—the pair of hands—in the plane yields the original figure. The figure made by your two hands has **reflection symmetry with respect to a plane**. Symmetry with respect to a plane is sometimes called **mirror-image symmetry**, or just **reflection symmetry**, if the context is clear.

Activity 4   Splitting the Cube

1. Does a cube have any reflection symmetries? Describe the cross-section for each reflection symmetry that you find.

2. Does a right rectangular prism have any reflection symmetries? Describe the cross-section for each reflection symmetry that you find.

Rotational Symmetries

A figure has **rotational symmetry with respect to a particular line** if, by rotating the figure a certain number of degrees using the line as an axis, the rotated version *coincides* with the original figure. Points may now be in different places after the rotation, but the figure *as a whole* will occupy the same set of points after the rotation as before. The line is sometimes called the **axis of the rotational symmetry**, or **axis**. A figure may have more than one axis of rotational symmetry. As with the cube pictured on the next page, it may be possible to have different rotational symmetries with the *same* axis, by rotating different numbers of degrees. Because the two rotations shown—a 90° rotation and a 180° rotation—affect at least one point differently, they are considered to be two different rotational symmetries. The cube occupies the same set of points *in toto* after either rotation as it did before the rotation, so the two rotations are indeed symmetries.

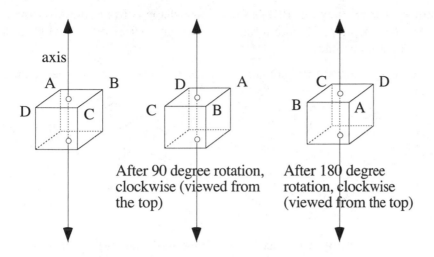

After 90 degree rotation, clockwise (viewed from the top)

After 180 degree rotation, clockwise (viewed from the top)

Similarly, a 270° and a 360° rotation with this same axis give a third and a fourth rotational symmetry. For this one axis, then, there are four different rotational symmetries: 90°, 180°, 270°, and 360° (or 0°).

Activity 5   Rounding the Cube

1. Find all the axes of rotational symmetry for a cube. (There are more than three.) For each axis, find every rotational symmetry possible, giving the number of degrees for each rotational symmetry.

2. Repeat Problem 1 for an equilateral-triangular right prism (see shape C in your kit of shapes).

> TAKE-AWAY MESSAGE . . . Some three-dimensional shapes have many symmetries, but the same ideas used with symmetries of two-dimensional shapes apply. Except for remarkably able or experienced visualizers, most people find a model of a shape helpful in counting all the symmetries of a 3D shape. ♦

Learning Exercises for Section 18.2

1. Can you hold your two hands in *any* fashion so that there is a rotational symmetry for them (besides a 360° one)? Each hand should end up exactly where the other hand started.

2. How many different planes give symmetries for these shapes from your kit? Record a few planes of symmetry in sketches, for practice.

    a. Shape A   **b.** Shape D   **c.** Shape F   **d.** Shape G

3. How many rotational symmetries does each shape in Learning Exercise 2 have? Show a few of the axes of symmetry in sketches, for practice.

Notes

4. You are a scientist studying crystals shaped like shape H from your kit. Count the symmetries of shape H, both reflection and rotational. (Count the 360° rotational symmetry just once.)

5. Describe the symmetries, if there are any, of each of the following shapes made of cubes.

a. 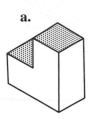   **b.** 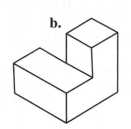   **c.** 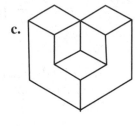   Top view for c: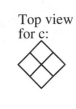

6. Copy and finish the following incomplete "buildings" so that they have reflection symmetry. Finish each one in two ways, counting the additional number of cubes each way needs. (The building in part (b) already has one plane of symmetry; do you see it? Is it still a plane of symmetry *after* your additional cubes?)

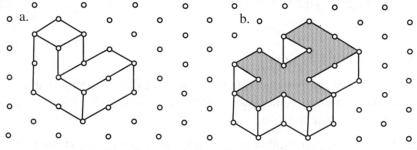

a.   b.

7. Design a net for a pyramid that has exactly four rotational symmetries (including only one involving 360°).

8. Imagine a right octagonal prism with bases like ⬣ . How many reflection symmetries will the prism have? How many rotational symmetries?

9. The cube shown below is cut by the symmetry plane indicated. For the reflection in the plane, to what point does each vertex correspond?

A -> ___   B -> ___   C -> ___   D -> ___

E -> ___   F -> ___   G -> ___   H -> ___

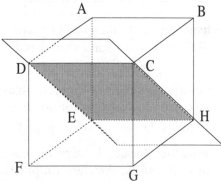

10. Explain why each pair is considered to describe only one symmetry for a figure.

    a. a 180° clockwise rotation and a 180° counterclockwise rotation (same axis)

    b. a 360° rotation with one axis and a 360° rotation with a different axis

11. (*Suggestion: Work with a classmate.*) You may have counted the reflection symmetries and rotational symmetries of the regular tetrahedron (shape A in your kit) and the cube. Pick one of the other types of regular polyhedra and count its reflection symmetries and axes of rotational symmetries.

Notes

18.3   Issues for Learning: What Geometry and Measurement Are in the Curriculum?

Unlike the work with numbers, the coverage of geometry in grades K–8 is not uniform in the United States, particularly with respect to work with three-dimensional figures. Measurement topics are certain to arise, but often the focus is on formulas rather than on the ideas involved.

The nationwide tests used by the National Assessment of Educational Progress give an indication of what attention the test writers think should be given to geometry and measurement.[i] At Grade 4, roughly 15% of the items are on geometry (and spatial sense) and 20% on measurement. At Grade 8, roughly 20% of the items are on geometry (and spatial sense) and 15% on measurement. Thus, more than a third of the examination questions involve geometry and measurement, suggesting the importance of those topics in the curriculum.

The book *Principles and Standards for School Mathematics*[ii] offers a view of what could be included in the curriculum at various grades, so we will use it as an indication of what geometry and measurement you might expect to see in grades K–8. *PSSM* notes, "Geometry is more than definitions; it is about describing relationships and reasoning" (p. 41) and "The study of measurement is important in the mathematics curriculum from prekindergarten through high school because of the practicality and pervasiveness of measurement in so many aspects of everyday life" (p. 44). In particular, measurement connects many geometric ideas with numerical ones, and it allows hands-on activities with objects that are a natural part of the children's environment.

In the following brief overviews, drawn from *PSSM*, you may encounter terms that you do not recognize; these will arise in later chapters of this book. *PSSM* includes much more detail than what is given here, of course, as well as examples to illustrate certain points. Throughout, *PSSM* encourages the use of technology that supports the acquisition of knowledge of shapes and measurement. *PSSM* organizes its recommendations by grade bands: Pre-K–2, 3–5, 6–8, and 9–12. Only the first three bands are summarized here. These brief overviews can give you an idea of the scope and relative importance of geometry and measurement in the K–8 curriculum, with much of the study beginning at the earlier grades.

Grades Pre-K–2. Children should be able to recognize, name, build, draw, and sort shapes, both two-dimensional and three-dimensional, and recognize them in their surroundings. They should be able to use language for directions, distance, and location, using terms such as *over*, *under*, *near*, *far*, and *between*. They should become conversant with ideas of symmetry and with rigid motions such as slides, flips, and turns. In measurement, the children should have experiences with length, area, and volume (as well as weight and time), measuring with both nonstandard and standard units and becoming familiar with the idea of repeating a unit. Measurement language involving words such as *deep*, *large*, and *long* should become comfortable parts of their vocabulary.

Grades 3–5. Students should focus more on the properties of two- and three-dimensional shapes, with definitions for ideas like triangles and pyramids arising. Terms like parallel, perpendicular, vertex, angle, trapezoid, and so forth, should become part of their vocabulary. Congruence, similarity, and coordinate systems should be introduced. Students should make and test conjectures, and they should give justifications for their conclusions. They should build on their earlier work with rigid motions and symmetry. They should be able to draw a two-dimensional representation of a three-dimensional shape and, vice versa, make or recognize a three-dimensional shape from a two-dimensional representation. Links to art and science should arise naturally.

Measurement ideas in Grades 3–5 should be extended to include angle size. Students should practice conversions within a system of units (for example, changing a measurement given in centimeters to one in meters, or one given in feet to one in inches). Their estimation skills for measurements, using benchmarks, should grow, as well as their understanding that most measurements are approximate. They should develop formulas for the areas of rectangles, triangles, and parallelograms, and they should have some practice at applying these to the surface areas of rectangular prisms. Students should offer ideas for determining the volume of a rectangular prism.

Grades 6–8. Earlier work should be extended so that students understand the relationships among different types of polygons (for example, squares are special rhombuses). They should know the relationships between angles, lengths, areas, and volumes of similar shapes. Their study of coordinate geometry and transformation geometry should continue, perhaps involving the composition of rigid motions. Students should work with the Pythagorean theorem. Measurement topics would include formulas dealing with the circumference of a circle and additional area formulas for trapezoids and circles. The students' sense that measurements are approximations should be sharpened. They should study surface areas and volumes of some pyramids, pyramids, and cylinders. They should also study rates such as speed and density.

A second document, *Curriculum Focal Points for Prekindergarten through Grade 8 Mathematics: A Quest for Coherence,*[iii] was published after *PSSM*. This document provides a list of three focal points for each grade. In this way, teachers can be sure that fundamental ideas are treated at each grade level when not everything in a textbook can be completed in the school year. For example, here is one Curriculum Focal Point for Grade 3:

Describing and analyzing properties of two-dimensional shapes.

Students describe, analyze, compare, and classify two-dimensional shapes by their sides and angles and connect these attributes to definitions of shapes. Students investigate, describe, and reason about decomposing, combining, and transforming polygons to make other polygons. Through building, drawing, and analyzing two-dimensional shapes, students understand attributes and properties of two-dimensional space and the use of those attributes and properties in solving problems, including applications involving congruence and symmetry (page 15).

The Grade 4 Focal Point continues this work by focusing on developing an understanding of area and determining area, and in Grade 5 continues on to three-dimensional shapes, including surface area and volume.

18.4 Check Yourself

You should be able to work problems like those assigned and to meet the following objectives.

1. Define symmetry of a figure.

2. Sketch a figure that has a given symmetry.

3. Identify all the reflection symmetries and the rotational symmetries of a given 2D figure, if there are any. Your identifications should include the line of reflection or the number of degrees of rotation.

4. Use symmetry to argue for particular conjectures. Some are given in the text and others are called for in the Learning Exercises, but an argument for some other fact might be called for.

5. Identify and enumerate all the reflection symmetries (in a plane) and the rotational symmetries (about a line) of a given 3D figure.

REFERENCES FOR CHAPTER 18

[i] Silver, E. A., & Kenney, P. A. (2000). *Results from the Seventh Mathematics Assessment of the National Assessment of Educational Progress*. Reston, VA: National Council of Teachers of Mathematics.

[ii] National Council of Teachers of Mathematics. (2000). *Principles and Standards for School Mathematics*. Reston, VA: Author.

[iii] National Council of Teachers of Mathematics. (2006). *Curriculum Focal Points for Prekindergarten through Grade 8 Mathematics: A Quest for Coherence*. Reston, VA: Author.

Chapter 19

Tessellations

Covering an endless flat surface (a plane) with a given shape or shapes is called a **tessellation**. Tessellations, a topic that appears in many elementary curricula nowadays, offer an opportunity for explorations, some surprises, connections to topics such as area, and a relation to artwork. The attention to tessellations in elementary school focuses on the plane, but the same ideas can be applied to space.

19.1 | Tessellating the Plane

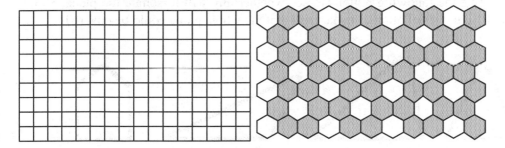

Figure 1

You have seen the two patterns shown above in tiled floors. These tilings are examples of **tessellations**, which are coverings of the plane made up of repetitions of the same region (or regions) that could completely cover the plane without overlapping or leaving any gaps. (The word *tessellation* comes from a Latin word meaning *tile*.) The first tiling in Figure 1 is a tessellation with squares (of course, it involves square *regions*), and the second tiling is a tessellation with regular hexagons. As in these two examples, enough of the covering is usually shown to make clear that it would cover the entire plane, if extended indefinitely. In the second example we show how shading can add visual interest; colors can add even more. Furthermore, a tessellation with squares can lay the foundation for children's work with area later on.

Notes

Activity 1   Regular Cover-Ups

Each tessellation pictured in Figure 1 involves one type of regular polygonal regions. A natural question is, "What other regular polygons give tessellations of the plane?" Test the following regions to see whether each type will give a tessellation of the plane.

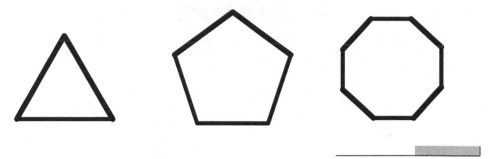

It may have been a surprise to find that some regular polygons do not tessellate the plane. Are there *any* other shapes that will tessellate?

Activity 2   Stranger Cover-Ups

Another natural question is whether regions from nonregular shapes can tessellate the plane. Test the following regions to see whether any will tessellate the plane. Show enough of any tessellation to make clear that the whole plane could be covered.

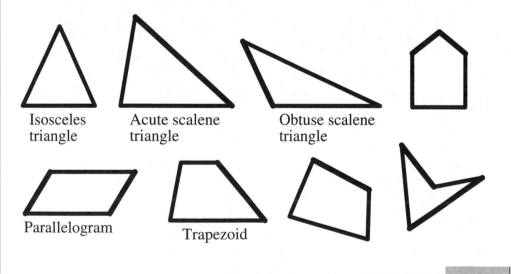

Isosceles triangle

Acute scalene triangle

Obtuse scalene triangle

Parallelogram

Trapezoid

Activity 2 may have suggested that the subject of tessellations is quite rich. If you color some of the tessellations, using a couple of colors or even just shading, you can also find a degree of aesthetic appeal in the result. Indeed, much Islamic art involves intricate tessellations (Islam forbids the use of pictures in its religious artwork). Islamic tessellations inspired the artist M. C. Escher (1898–1972) in many of his creations, some of which you may have seen. The drawing in Figure 2 shows two amateurish *Escher-type* tessellations, with additional features drawn; surprisingly, each tessellation starts with a simpler polygon than the final version might suggest. Elementary school students sometimes make these types of drawings as a part of their artwork, coloring the shapes in two or more ways.

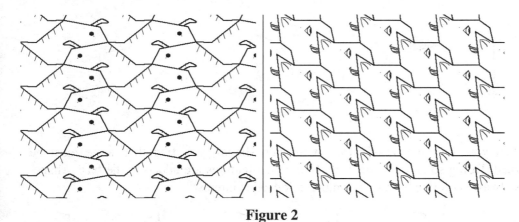

Figure 2

Creating a Tessellation

How does one get polygons that will tessellate? One way is to start with a polygon that you know will tessellate, and then modify it in one or more of several ways. For example, in the illustration below, we start with a regular hexagonal region, then cut out a piece on one side, and finally tape that piece in a corresponding place on the opposite side. The resulting shape tessellates. The final shape can then be decorated in whatever way the shape suggests to you—perhaps a piranha fish for this shape.

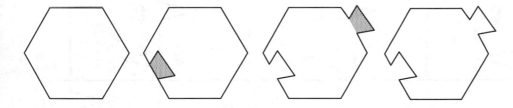

This same technique—cut out a piece and slide it to the opposite side—can be applied to another pair of parallel sides in the same region above. Again, notice that you can add extra features to the inside of any shape you know will tessellate.

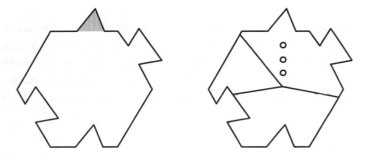

Notes

Yet another way to alter a given tessellating polygon so that the result still tessellates is to cut out a piece along one side, and then turn the cut-out piece around the midpoint of that side, as the following illustration shows.

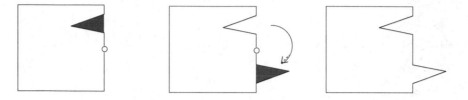

When you draw the tessellations with such shapes, you find that some must be turned. Doing so gives a different effect when features are added to the basic shape. As always, coloring with two or more colors adds interest.

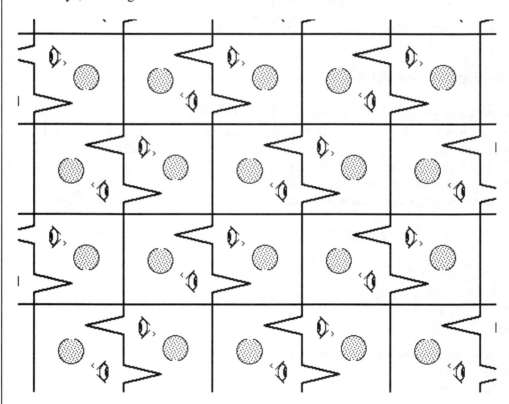

TAKE-AWAY MESSAGE . . . The fact that tessellations, or coverings, of the plane are possible with equilateral triangles, squares, or regular hexagons is probably not surprising. More surprising is the fact that these are the only regular polygons that can give tessellations. Even more surprising is the fact that every triangle or every quadrilateral can tessellate the plane. Some clever techniques allow you to design unusual shapes that will tessellate the plane, often with an artistic effect. ◆

Learning Exercises for Section 19.1

1. Test whether the regular heptagon (7-gon) or the regular dodecagon (12-gon) gives a tessellation.

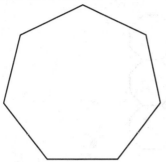 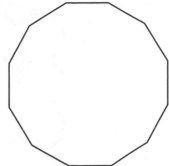

2. Verify that each of the following shapes can tessellate, by showing enough of the tessellation to be convincing. Color or "decorate" the tessellation (merely shading can add visual interest).

   a.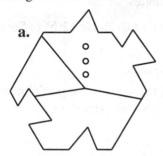

   b.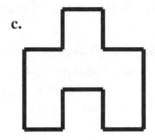

   c.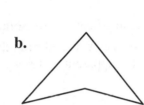

3. a. Start with a square region and modify it to create a region that will tessellate. Modify the shape in two ways; add features and shading or coloring as you see fit.

   b. Start with a regular hexagonal region and modify it to create a region that will tessellate. Modify the shape in two ways; add features and shading or coloring as you see fit.

4. Show that the following quadrilateral will tessellate. (If you can, use the grid as an aid, rather than tracing the quadrilateral and cutting the tracing out.) Add features and shading as you see fit.

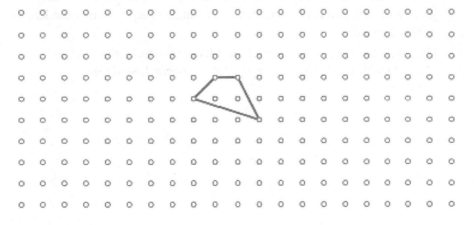

5. Which of the Pattern Blocks in Appendix G give tessellations?

6. More than one type of region can be used in a tessellation, as with the regular octagons and squares shown below. Notice that the same arrangement of polygons occurs at each vertex.

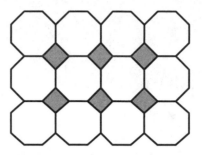

Show that the following combinations can give tessellations.

   a. regular hexagons and equilateral triangles

   b. regular hexagons, squares, and equilateral triangles

7. Will each type of pentomino tessellate? (See Learning Exercise 12(b) in Section 16.3.)

8. Tessellations can provide justifications for some results.

   a. Label the angles with sizes x, y, and z in other triangles in the partial tessellation below to see if it is apparent that $x + y + z = 180°$. (*Hint*: Look for a straight angle.)

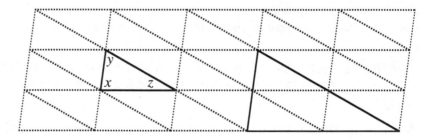

   b. Use the larger bold triangle to justify this fact: The length of the segment joining the midpoints of two sides of a triangle is equal to half the length of the third side.

   c. How does the area of the larger bold triangle compare to the area of the smaller one? (*Hint*: No formulas are needed; study the sketch.)

9. Which sorts of movements are symmetries for the tessellations given by the following? What basic shape gives each tessellation?

a.

b.

c.

d.

Notes

19.2 | Tessellating Space

The idea of tessellating the plane with a particular 2D region can be generalized to the idea of filling space with a 3D region.

> **THINK ABOUT...**
>
> Why are the following objects shaped the way they are?
>
> | | |
> |---|---|
> | most boxes | bricks |
> | honeycomb cells | commercial blocks of ice |
> | lockers | mailbox slots in a business |

When space is completely filled by copies of a shape (or shapes), without overlapping or leaving any gaps, space has been **tessellated**, and the arrangement of the shapes is called a **tessellation of space**. You can imagine either arrangement below as extending in *all* directions to fill space with regions formed by right rectangular prisms. These "walls" could easily be extended right, left, up, and down, giving an infinite layer that could be repeatedly copied behind and in front of the first infinite wall to fill space. Hence, we can say that a right rectangular prism will tessellate space and will do so in at least the two ways shown below.

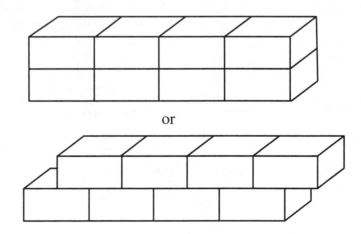

or

Although it is rarely, if ever, an explicit part of the elementary school curriculum, tessellating space with cubical regions is the essence of the standard measurement of volume.

Activity 3   Fill 'Er Up

Which of shapes A–H from your kit will tessellate space?

After your experience with designing unusual shapes that will tessellate the plane, you perhaps can imagine ways of altering a 3D shape that tessellates space and still have a shape that will tessellate.

TAKE-AWAY MESSAGE . . . The idea of covering the plane with a 2D region can be extended to the idea of filling space with a 3D region. ◆

Learning Exercises for Section 19.2

1. Are there arrangements of right rectangular prisms, other than those suggested in Section 19.2, that will give tessellations of space? (*Hint*: You may have seen decorative arrangements of bricks in sidewalks, where the bricks are twice as long as they are wide.)

2. Which of the following shapes could tessellate space (theoretically)?

    a. cola cans

    b. sets of encyclopedias

    c. round pencils, unsharpened

    d. hexagonal pencils, unsharpened and without erasers

    e. oranges

3. Which, if any, of the following could tessellate space? Explain your decisions.

    a.    **b.** 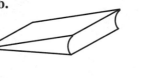   **c.**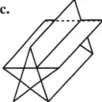

    d. each type of the (3D) Pattern Block pieces

    e. each of the base *b* pieces (units, longs, flats)

4. How are tessellation of space and volume related?

5. (*Group*) Show that shape I in your kit can tessellate space.

6. (*Group*) Will either shape J or shape K tessellate space?

19.3 | Check Yourself

This short chapter about tessellations of a plane or of space opens up an aesthetic side of mathematics, illustrating that intricate designs can be derived from basic mathematical shapes.

You should be able to work problems like those assigned and to meet the following objectives.

1. Tell in words what a tessellation of a plane is.

Notes

2. Determine whether a given shape can or cannot tessellate a plane. You should know that some particular types of shapes can tessellate, *without* having to experiment.

3. Create an "artistic" tessellation.

4. Tell in words what a tessellation of space is.

5. Determine whether a given shape can or cannot tessellate space.

Chapter 20

Size Changes and Similarity

One important feature of congruent figures is that corresponding parts of the figures have exactly the same geometric measurements. In many applications of mathematics, however, two figures may have the exact same shape but not the same size. For example, photographic enlargements or reductions should look the same, even though corresponding lengths are different. This chapter gives a precise meaning to the idea of *same shape*, first with two-dimensional shapes and then with three-dimensional shapes.

20.1 | Size Changes in Planar Figures

A moment's thought about, say, a photograph of a building and an enlargement of that photograph, makes clear that for the buildings to look alike, corresponding angles have to be the same size. Activity 1 below will help us confront the less visible aspect of *exact same shape*. That is, how are corresponding lengths related?

Activity 1   A Puzzle About a Puzzle

Special tools needed: Ruler with metric (protractor optional)

In the diagram on the following page, the pieces may be cut out and then, as a puzzle, reassembled to make the square. You are to make a puzzle shaped just like the one given, but larger, using the following rule: The segment that measures 4 cm in the original diagram should measure 7 cm in your new version.

If you work as a group, each person should make at least one piece. When your group finishes, you should be able to put the new pieces together to make a square.

Continue on the next page.

Notes

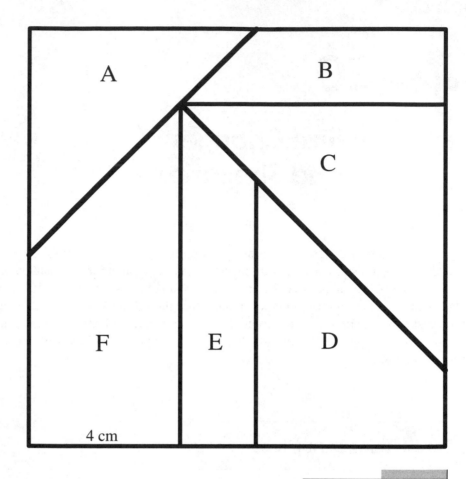

4 cm

Discussion 1   Students Discuss Their Methods

Here are some students' descriptions of their thinking for Activity 1. They have agreed that the angles have to be the same, and they plan to use the many right angles to make the larger puzzle. Discuss each student's thinking.

Lee: "7 is 3 more than 4. So you just add 3 to each length. 3 centimeters. Add 3 centimeters to 5 centimeters, and the new side should be 8 centimeters."

Maria: "7 is $1\frac{3}{4}$ times as much as 4, so a new length should be $1\frac{3}{4}$ times the old length."

Nerida: "To be the same-shaped puzzle, it's got to be proportional to look the same. But I'm not sure how to make it proportional. Do you use ratios?"

Olivia: "From 4 centimeters to 7 centimeters is 75% more, so I would add 75% to each length. For example, take a 5-centimeter length; 75% of 5 centimeters is 3.75 centimeters, so the new length would be 5 + 3.75, or 8.75, centimeters."

Pat: "If 4 centimeters grow to 7 centimeters, each centimeter must grow to $1\frac{3}{4}$ centimeters. So 5 centimeters should grow to 5 times as much, that is, 5 times $1\frac{3}{4}$ centimeters, and 6 cm should grow to 6 times $1\frac{3}{4}$ centimeters."

Activity 2   **Super-Sizing It More**

Make a sketch, share the work, and indicate all the measurements needed to get a bigger puzzle, where a 5 cm segment in the original square in Activity 1 measures 8 cm in the enlarged version. Then discuss your thinking with others.

Activity 3   **Reducing**

1. Make a sketch and indicate the measurements needed to get a smaller puzzle, where a 6 cm segment in the original square in Activity 1 should measure 4 cm on the smaller version.

2. In making an enlargement or reduction of a shape, as was done with the puzzle, how do angle sizes in the new shape compare with the corresponding ones in the original shape? How do lengths in the new shape compare with the corresponding ones in the original shape?

3. Write a set of instructions for enlarging/reducing such puzzles. Give a warning about any method that does not work, and explain why it does not work.

THINK ABOUT…

Which of the images on the next page would be acceptable as a reduced size of the given original drawing?

Original

Continue on the next page.

Notes

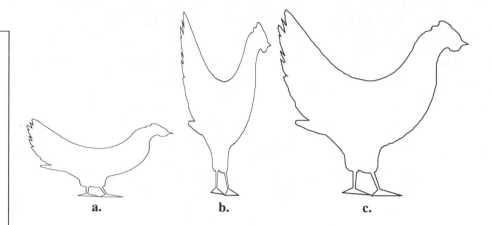

a.   b.   c.

Similarity

Enlargements or miniatures must have the exact same shape as the original. Two shapes related this way are called **similar** in mathematics, in the technical sense of the word similar and not just because they are the same general shape.

> **Two shapes are similar if the points in the two shapes can be matched so that (1) every pair of corresponding angles have the same size, and (2) the ratios from every pair of corresponding lengths all equal the same value, called the scale factor.**

The second point makes clear that it is the multiplicative comparisons of corresponding lengths, not the additive comparisons, that are crucial. This point can also be expressed in different but equivalent ways:

- (*new* length):(corresponding *original* length) = scale factor

- $\dfrac{new \text{ length}}{\text{corresponding } original \text{ length}}$ = scale factor

- (*new* length) = (scale factor) × (corresponding *original* length)

The last version makes explicit the multiplicative effect of the scale factor.

Do you see that the scale factor for the original puzzle enlargement in Activity 1 is $1\frac{3}{4}$? In most situations, which of the shapes is the new and which is the original (or *old*, if you prefer) is arbitrary. So long as the scale factor and ratios are interpreted consistently, the choice of new and original can be made either way. For example, if the lengths of the sides of a figure X are 4 times as long as those of another figure Y, then the lengths of the sides of figure Y are $\frac{1}{4}$ as long as those of figure X.

So, if you are careful about keeping corresponding angles the same size and corresponding lengths related by the same scale factor, you can make a polygon similar to a given one. Another method, called the **ruler method,** for obtaining a similar polygon is given below. Try using this method on separate paper. You will need to choose your own point for a center, your own scale factor, and your own original polygon (any triangle or quadrilateral will do). The importance of the scale factor is apparent in this method.

Steps in the Ruler Method for Size Changes

1. Pick a point (which becomes the **center** of the size change). Draw a ray from the center through a point on the original shape. Measure the segment from the center to the point on the original shape.

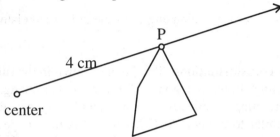

2. Multiply that measurement by your chosen scale factor (we'll use 1.7 here, so 1.7 x 4 = 6.8 cm).

3. Measure that distance (6.8 cm) from the *center* (that is important), along the ray starting at the center and going through the selected point. This distance gives what is called the **image** of the point.

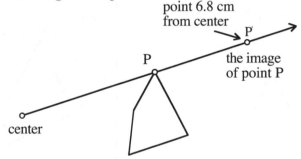

4. Repeat Steps 1–3 with the other vertices of the original polygon. Connect all the images with the ruler. The resulting polygon is the **image** of the original polygon.

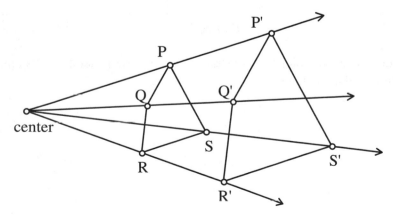

For a curved figure, the ruler method is not efficient because you have to go through the steps for too many points. But the ruler method works well for a figure made up of line segments. Starting with a more elaborate figure and then coloring the figure and its enlargement or reduction, can make an attractive display. The completed drawing often carries a three-dimensional effect.

Activity 4   Oh, I See!

a. Measure the lengths of the pairs of corresponding sides of the two quadrilaterals PQRS and P'Q'R'S' shown on the previous page to see how they are related.

b. How else do the corresponding sides appear to be related?

c. How are the pairs of corresponding angles of the polygons related in size?

Size changes, or **size transformations**, like the one shown in the ruler-method steps, are a basic way of getting similar polygons. After the size has changed, the image can be moved around by rotating or reflecting it, for example. Figure 1 gives an example. Triangle A'B'C' is similar to triangle ABC because it is the image of triangle ABC from the size change. Triangle A"B"C" is a reflection of triangle A'B'C' about the line of reflection shown, and it is still similar to the original triangle. (Note the use of the A, A' and A" to make corresponding points clear.) If a rotation or a reflection is involved, finding corresponding vertices and sides may require some attention.

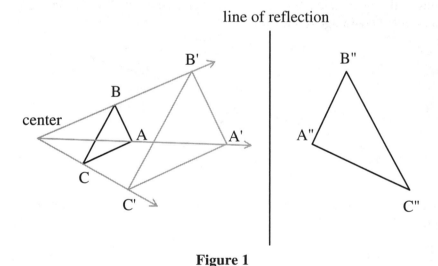

Figure 1

Let us consider some examples that illustrate how all these general results are useful in dealing with similar triangles.

EXAMPLE 1

Make a rough sketch of triangles similar to the original triangle below, (a) using a scale factor of 2.5 and (b) using a scale factor of $\frac{4}{5}$. Also, find the sizes of the angles and sides of the triangles of each new triangle.

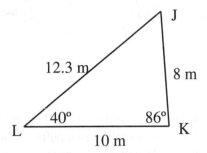

SOLUTION

The size of the angle at J can be calculated by finding $180 - (40 + 86)$, which gives $54°$. For either part (a) or (b), the angles in the similar triangles will be the same sizes as those in the original triangle: $40°$, $86°$, and $54°$.

(a) Your sketch should show a larger triangle, with sides about 2.5 times as long as those in the original. The lengths of the sides of the similar triangle will be 2.5×12.3 for the new $\overline{JL}$, 2.5×8 for the new $\overline{JK}$, and 2.5×10 for the new $\overline{LK}$, all in meters. That is, the lengths will be (about) 30.8 m, 20 m, and 25 m.

(b) In the same way, the lengths will be 9.8 m, 6.4 m, and 8 m. Your sketch of the image triangle should be smaller, because the scale factor is less than 1.

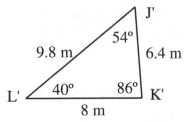

EXAMPLE 2

Suppose you are told that the following two quadrilaterals on the next page are similar. Find the missing angle sizes and lengths of sides.

Continue on the next page.

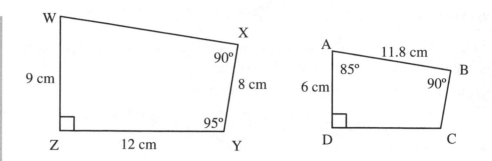

SOLUTION

We are told that the two shapes are similar, so the first thing to do is to determine the correspondence. How the shapes are drawn helps, although the given angle sizes allow just one possibility. Because corresponding angles are the same size, the angle at W has size 85°, and the angle at C has size 95°.

To determine the missing lengths, we need the scale factor. The only pair of corresponding sides for which we know measurements are $\overline{WZ}$ and $\overline{AD}$. Thinking of ABCD as the original (it is usually easier to deal with scale factors greater than 1), the scale factor is 9:6, or $\frac{9}{6} = 1.5$. So then the length of $\overline{WX}$ will be 1.5 x 11.8, or 17.7 cm. To find the missing lengths in ABCD, we can solve 8 = 1.5 x BC, and 12 = 1.5 x DC, or we can reverse the viewpoint to make WXYZ the original, and work with a revised scale factor of 6:9, or $\frac{2}{3}$. In either case, we find that $\overline{BC}$ has length about 5.3 cm, and $\overline{DC}$ is 8 cm long.

EXAMPLE 3

You are told that the two triangles below are similar, but they are deliberately not drawn to scale. Using the given measurements, find the missing lengths and angle sizes.

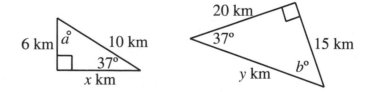

SOLUTION

The missing angle sizes present no problem because angles *a* and *b* are corresponding and the angle sum for a triangle is 180°, so *a* and *b* are both 180 − (90 + 37), or 53°.

The complication here for finding the scale factor is that the correspondence is not obvious: Does the 6 km correspond to the 20 km or to the 15 km side? Because the 6 km side is opposite the 37° angle, its correspondent in the other triangle should be opposite the 37° angle there. That would make 6 km and 15 km corresponding. (Alternatively, the 6 km side is common to the right angle and the 53° angle, so find those angles in the other triangle and use their common side.)

Similarly, the 10 km and y km sides correspond, as do the x km and 20 km sides. Using the scale factor $\frac{15}{6} = 2.5$, we find that

$$y = 2.5 \times 10 = 25 \text{ cm} \quad \text{and} \quad 20 = 2.5 \times x, \text{ or } x = \frac{20}{2.5} = 8 \text{ cm.}$$

It is slightly digressive, but let us review some language for which everyday usage is often incorrect when describing similarity and other situations. One of the segments in the illustration of the ruler method is about 2 cm, with its image about 3.4 cm. The comparison of the 2 cm and the 3.4 cm values can be correctly stated in several ways:

- "The ratio, 3.4 : 2, is 1.7." (a multiplicative comparison)

- "3.4 cm is 1.7 *times as long as* 2 cm." (a multiplicative comparison)

- "3.4 cm is 170% *as long as* 2 cm." (a multiplicative comparison)

- "3.4 cm is 1.4 cm *longer than* 2 cm." (an additive comparison and a true statement, but not the important one for similarity; note the *-er* ending on "longer")

Discussion 2   Saying It Correctly

Who is correct, Arnie or Bea? Explain. (A sketch might help, identifying the *longer than* part.)

Arnie stated, "3.4 cm is 1.7 times longer than 2 cm."

Bea argued, "3.4 cm is 1.7 times as long as 2 cm, but 3.4 cm is only 0.7 times longer than 2 cm, or 70% longer than 2 cm."

Incorrect language can be heard especially when both additive and multiplicative languages are used in the same sentence. Most people, however, do correctly fill in the blanks in statements such as "__ is 50% as big as 10" and "__ is 50% bigger than 10," so these examples might be helpful as checks in other sentences.

> TAKE-AWAY MESSAGE . . . When you want to show that two shapes are indeed similar, you need to confirm these two conditions: (1) Corresponding angles must have the same size, and (2) the lengths of every pair of corresponding segments must have the same ratio, that is, the scale factor. Vice versa, knowing that two figures are similar tells you that both these conditions have been met, which allow you to determine many missing measurements in similar figures. Using the correct language in comparing lengths in similar shapes requires some care. ◆

Learning Exercises for Section 20.1

Have your ruler and protractor handy for some of these exercises.

1. **a.** Summarize how the following are related, for a polygon and its image under a size change: corresponding lengths, corresponding angle sizes.

    b. How do the perimeters of similar polygons compare? Explain your thinking.

2. Tell whether the two shapes given in each part are similar. How do you know?

    a. A 6 cm by 7 cm rectangle, and a 12 cm by 13 cm rectangle

    b.

3. Copy and finish the incomplete second triangle to give a similar triangle, so that the 2 cm and 5 cm sides correspond. Does your triangle *look* similar to the original one?

4. With a ruler, draw a triangle and find its image for a size transformation with the scale factor 4 and with center at a point of your choice. Plan ahead so that the image will fit on the page.

5. With a ruler, draw a trapezoid and find its image for a size transformation with the scale factor 2.4 and with center at a point of your choice.

6. With a ruler, draw a triangle and find its image for a size transformation with the scale factor $\frac{3}{4}$ and with center at a point of your choice.

7. **a.** Measure the angles and sides of your polygons in Learning Exercises 4, 5, and 6. Verify the key relationships about lengths and angles in size changes that you summarized in Learning Exercise 1(a).

    b. Besides the ratio of lengths, how do a side of a polygon and its image appear to be related in the ruler method for size changes?

    c. Check the key relationships and your ideas about angles and sides from part (b) on the two similar triangles given on the next page.

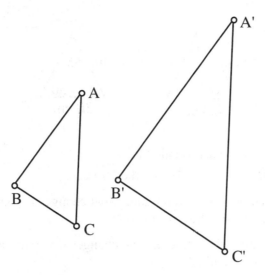

8. Find the sizes of all the angles and sides of shapes that are similar to the original parallelogram below with the scale factors:

   a. 6.1

   b. $\frac{2}{3}$

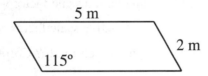

   c. What shape are the images in parts (a) and (b)?

9. Find the scale factor and the missing measurements in the similar triangles in each part. (The sketches are not drawn to scale.)

   a.

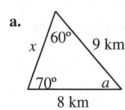

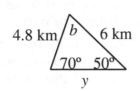

   b.

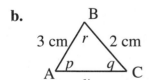

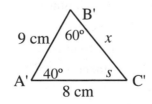

   c.

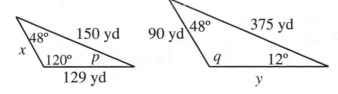

Continue on the next page.

Notes

d. (Be careful!)

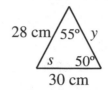

24 cm r x 50° 55°   28.3 cm

28 cm 55° y s 50°   30 cm

10. Can the center of a size transformation be

    a. inside a figure?   **b.** *on* the figure?

11. For a given scale factor and a given figure, what changes if you use a different point for the center of a size transformation?

12. For a given center and a given figure, what changes if you use a different scale factor for a size transformation?

13. Suppose the scale factor is 1 for a size transformation. What do you notice about the image?

14. Scale factors often are restricted to positive numbers.

    a. What would the image of a figure be if a scale factor were allowed to be 0?

    b. How could one make sense of a negative scale factor, say, ⁻2?

15. Is each of the following sentences phrased correctly? Correct any that is not by changing a number.

    a. 60 is 200% more than 30.

    b. 12 cm is 150% longer than 8 cm.

    c. $75 is 50% more than $50.

    d. The 10K run is 100% longer than the 5K.

16. **a.** Janeetha said, "I increased all the lengths by 60%." If Janeetha is talking about a size change, what scale factor did she use?

    b. Juan used a scale factor of 225% on a 6 cm by 18 cm rectangle. How many centimeters longer than the original dimensions are the dimensions of the image? How many percent longer are they than in the original?

17. Consider this original segment: _____

    Draw another segment that fits each description.

    a. 3 times as long as the original segment

    b. 1.5 times longer than the original segment

    c. 300% longer than the original segment

    Consider this original region:

    Draw another region that fits each description.

    d. 3 times the area of the original region

    e. 1.5 times the area of the original region

    f. 300% more than the area of the original region

18. In each part, which statements express the same relationship? Support your decisions with numerical examples or sketches.

    a. "This edge is 50% as long as that one," vs. "This edge is 50% longer than that one," vs. "This edge is half that one."

    b. "This quantity is twice as much as that one," vs. "This quantity is 200% more than that one," vs. "This quantity is 100% more than that one."

    c. "This value is 75% more than that one," vs. "This value is $\frac{3}{4}$ as big as that one," vs. "This value is $1\frac{3}{4}$ times as big as that one," vs. "This value is 75% as much as that one."

19. In each part, give a value that fits each description.

    a. $2\frac{1}{3}$ times as long as 24 cm

    b. $2\frac{1}{3}$ times longer than 24 cm

    c. 75% as long as 24 cm

    d. 75% longer than 24 cm

    e. 125% more than 24 cm

    f. 125% as much as 24 cm

    g. 250% as large as 60 cm

    h. 250% larger than 60 cm

20. How would you make a shape similar to the following parallelogram with the scale factor 4? Give two ways.

    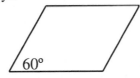
    60°

21. Explain how size transformations are involved in each of the following situations.

    a. photographs

    b. different maps of the same location

    c. model cars or architectural plans

    d. banking interest (This won't involve shapes!)

22. What is the scale of a map if two locations 3 inches apart on the map are actually 84 miles apart in reality?

23. The following diagram shows two maps with the same two cities, River City and San Carlos. Even though the second map does not have a scale, determine the straight-line distance from San Carlos to Beantown.

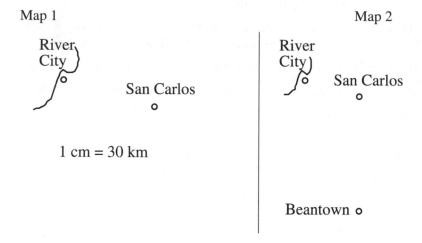

Map 1

River City

San Carlos

1 cm = 30 km

Map 2

River City

San Carlos

Beantown

24. Timelines are representations that also use scales. Make a time line 20 cm long, starting at year 0, and mark the following dates:

Magna Carta 1215
Columbus 1492
Declaration of Independence   1776
French Revolution 1789
Civil War 1861–1865

Wright brothers' flight 1903
World War II 1941–1945
First atomic bomb 1945
Commercial television 1950s
Personal computers late 1970s
Your birth

Add any other dates you wish.

25. a. Make a timeline 20 cm long to represent the following geologic times.

Cambrian, 600 million years ago (first fossils of animals with skeletons)

Carboniferous, 280 million years ago (insects appear)

Triassic, 200 million years ago (first dinosaurs)

Cretaceous, 65 million years ago (dinosaurs gone)

Oligocene, 30 million years ago (modern horses, pigs, elephants, and so on, appear)

Pleistocene (first humans, about 100,000 years ago)

b. If you were to add the Precambrian, 2 billion years ago (first recognizable fossils), and use the same scale as in part (a), how long would your time line have to be?

26. Suppose a rectangle undergoes a size change with scale factor 3, and then that image undergoes a second size change, with scale factor 4. Are the final image and the original rectangle similar? If so, what is the scale factor?

27. a. Some teachers like to use two sizes of grids and have students make a larger or smaller version of a drawing in one of the grids. Try this method, as shown.

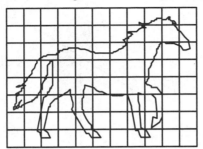

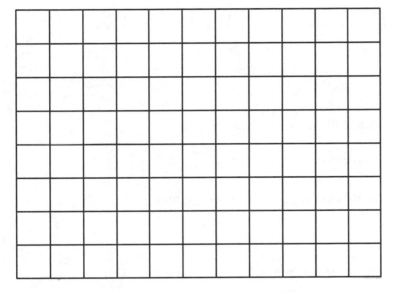

b. What scale factor is involved in part (a)? (*Hint*: Measure.)

c. Can this method be used to make a *smaller* image? Explain how or why not.

28. a. Equilateral triangle X has sides 7 cm long, and equilateral triangle Y has sides 12 cm long. Are X and Y similar? Explain.

b. Are two arbitrarily chosen equilateral triangles similar? Explain.

c. Are every two right triangles similar? Explain.

d. Are every two squares similar? Explain.

e. Are every two rectangles similar? Explain.

f. Are every two hexagons similar? Explain.

g. Are every two regular *n*-gons (with the same *n*) similar? Explain.

29. Some reference books show pictures of creatures and give the scale involved. Find the actual sizes of these creatures. (*Suggestion*: Use metric units.)

a.

Scale factor is 1:170.

b.
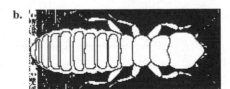
Scale factor is 7.3:1.

30. In the drawing below, x' and x'' are the images of x for size transformations with center C and the respective scale factors r and s. (These relationships are fundamental in trigonometry.)

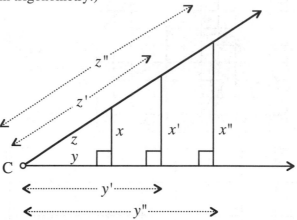

a. Find these ratios: $\dfrac{x'}{y'}$, $\dfrac{x''}{y''}$, $\dfrac{y'}{z'}$, and $\dfrac{y''}{z''}$.

b. How do these ratios compare: $\dfrac{x}{y}$, $\dfrac{x'}{y'}$, and $\dfrac{x''}{y''}$?

c. How do these ratios compare: $\dfrac{y}{z}$, $\dfrac{y'}{z'}$, and $\dfrac{y''}{z''}$?

20.2 More About Similar Figures

You know two methods for creating similar figures: (1) Apply the two criteria (make corresponding angles the same size, and use the same scale factor in changing the lengths), and (2) use the ruler method for performing a size change. This section discusses other interesting results that arise once you have similar figures and a very easy way of knowing that two triangles are similar.

Activity 5   Finding Missing Measurements

1. Suppose that original triangle PQR below is similar to triangle P'Q'R' (not shown) with scale factor 5. What are the sizes of the angles and sides of triangle P'Q'R'? The units for the lengths are kilometers (km).

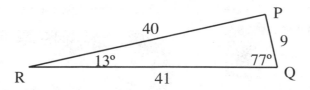

2. Find the perimeters (distance around) of triangles PQR and P'Q'R' and compare them.

THINK ABOUT...

Why are the perimeters of similar polygons also related by the scale factor?

Although the reason may be difficult to put in words, a form of the distributive property—for example, $5p + 5q + 5r = 5(p + q + r)$ —gives a mathematically pleasing justification. Do you see the two perimeters in the equation?

With lengths and perimeters of similar shapes related by the scale factor, a natural question is: How is the area of a polygon related to the area of its image, for a size change? With a size change drawing, you can conjecture the answer *without having to figure out the values of the two areas*! Examine the following figure, which uses 2 as the scale factor; you can see the relationship without finding the area of either triangle.

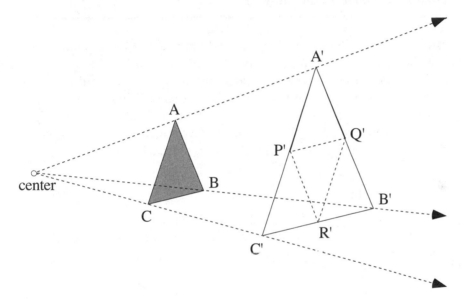

THINK ABOUT...

For a size change with scale factor 3, the area of the image of a shape is _____ times as large as the area of the original shape. (Make a rough sketch, using a triangle.) Make a conjecture for size changes with other scale factors.

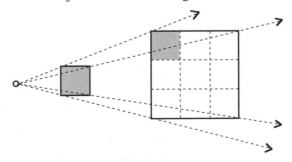

Determining Similarity of Triangles

So far we have examined creating similar shapes (Section 20.1) and the relationships that exist when two shapes are known to be similar (Section 20.1 and the previous

Notes

Think Abouts). But how would you know whether two triangles are similar, especially if both could not be in your field of vision at the same time? After thinking about it, your first response would likely be, "Measure all the angles and sides in both triangles. See whether they can be matched so that corresponding angles are the same size and the ratios of corresponding lengths are all the same (which would give the scale factor)." And you would be correct. Indeed, you would have described a method that could be applied to polygons of any number of sides, not just triangles. But for triangles we are especially lucky; we need to find only two pairs of angles that are the same size.

> **Two triangles are similar if their vertices can be matched so that two pairs of corresponding angles have the same size.**

The assertion is that the third pair of angles and the ratios of corresponding lengths take care of themselves. For example, if one triangle has angles of 65° and 38° and the other triangle does too, then even without any knowledge about the other angle and the sides, the two triangles must be similar. One triangle is the image of the other by a size change, along with possibly some sort of movement like a reflection or a rotation. But will you also know the scale factor? The answer is "No." Finding the scale factor involves knowing the lengths of at least one pair of corresponding sides.

EXAMPLE 4

Using the information given in the following triangles, (a) tell how you know that they are similar, (b) find all of the missing measurements, and (c) give the ratio of their areas. The triangles are not drawn to scale.

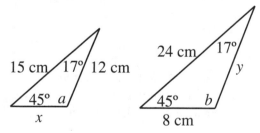

SOLUTION

(a) The 45° pair and the 17° pair assure that the triangles are similar.

(b) It is easy to find the sizes of the third angles from the angle sum in a triangle: 118°. To find the missing lengths, we need the scale factor. The drawing here makes it easy to find corresponding sides. The known lengths 15 cm and 24 cm are corresponding lengths. Using the left-hand triangle as the original, we get the scale factor = $\frac{24}{15}$ = 1.6 . Then y is 19.2 cm, and x is 5 cm (from $1.6x = 8$).

(c) The ratio of the areas is the square of the scale factor: $(1.6)^2 = 2.56$. The larger triangle has an area that is 2.56 times as large as that of the smaller triangle.

EXAMPLE 5

Given the information in the following drawings, find the missing measurements and give the ratio of the areas of the triangles. The triangles are not drawn to scale.

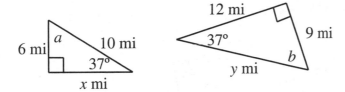

SOLUTION

Angles a and b must have 53° because the right angles have 90° and the other given angles have 37°. The right angles and either the 53° angles or the 37° angles tell us that the two triangles are similar. Finding corresponding parts takes some care, and we need to know two corresponding lengths. Perhaps after other trials, we notice that the 6 mi and 9 mi segments both are opposite the 37° angles. So, the scale factor is 1.5. Using the scale factor, we find that y is 15, x is 8, and the ratio of the areas is $(1.5)^2$, or 2.25.

TAKE-AWAY MESSAGE . . . The ratio of the perimeters of similar figures is the same as the scale factor, but the ratio of their areas is the square of the scale factor. Justifying that two triangles are similar is easy because you need to find only two pairs of angles that are the same size. Finding the correspondence in two similar figures can require some care. ♦

Learning Exercises for Section 20.2

1. Summarize how the following items are related for a polygon and its image under a size change: corresponding lengths, corresponding angle sizes, perimeters, and areas.

2. How would you convince someone that the ratio of the areas of two similar triangles is the *square* of the scale factor?

3. In each part, are the triangles similar? Explain how you know.

    a.

    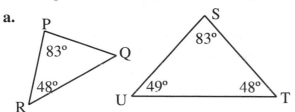

    b.   Triangle 1: angles 50°, 25° and triangle 2: angles 25°, 105°

Continue on the next page.

Notes

    c. Triangle 1: angles 70°, 42° and triangle 2: angles 48°, 70°

    d. Right triangle 1: angle 37° and right triangle 2: angle 53°

4. In parts (a)–(d), find the missing lengths. Explain how you know the figures are similar and how you know which segments correspond to each other. (The sketches are not to scale.)

a.

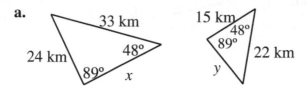

b.

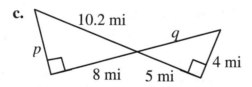

c.

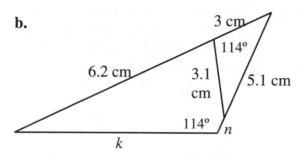

d.

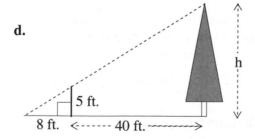

    e. Give the ratio of the areas of the triangles in parts (a) and (c).

    f. Devise a method for determining the width of a pond. (*Suggestion*: See part (d).)

5. A rectangle 9 cm wide and 15 cm long is the image for some size change of an original shape having width 4 cm.

   a. What is the scale factor of the size transformation?

   b. What type of figure is the original shape?

   c. What are the dimensions of the original shape?

   d. What are the areas of the original shape and the image? How are they related?

   e. If the description, *width* 4 cm, in the original description was replaced by *one dimension* 4 cm, which of parts (a)–(d) could be answered differently? (*Hint*: What are the names for the dimensions of a rectangle?)

6. If the two triangles in the diagram below are related by a size transformation, find the scale factor. How many centimeters is x? (This sort of diagram is common in the study of light and lenses.)

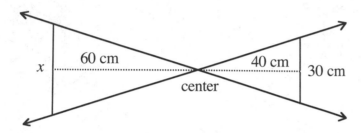

7. **a.** Your archaeological exploration has found a huge stone monument with the largest face being a triangular region. It appears to have the same proportions as a monument at another location. You telephone someone at the other location. What questions would you ask, at minimum, to determine whether the two triangles are similar?

   b. Suppose the situation in part (a) involves quadrilaterals. What questions would you ask, at minimum, to determine whether the two quadrilaterals are similar?

20.3 | Size Changes in Space Figures

A size change for a three-dimensional shape figure is much like a size change for a two-dimensional shape. This section deals with the ideas and terminology as though they were new topics and should strengthen your understandings from earlier work.

Discussion 3   Related Shapes

Which of the shapes in the following figure would you say are related in some way? Is there another collection of the shapes that are related in some way?

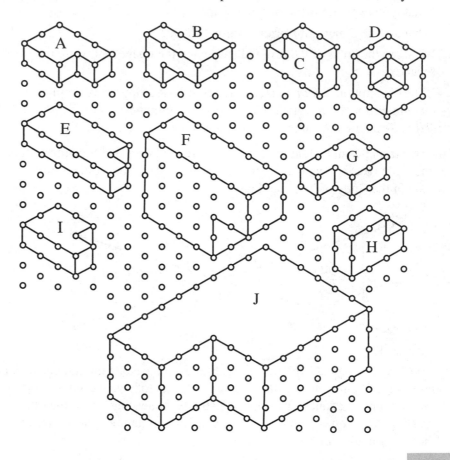

Activity 6   Here's Mine

Make or sketch other shapes that you think would be related to shape B and to shape F above. Explain how they are related.

The rest of this section focuses on one of these relationships, **similarity**.

Discussion 4   Larger and Smaller

An eccentric 10^9-aire owns an L-shaped building like the one below.

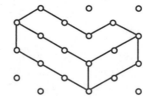

a. She wants another building designed, "shaped exactly like the old one, but twice as large in all dimensions." Make or draw a model shaped like this second building that she wants.

b. Below are some diagrams. Which, if any, of the following drawings will meet the criterion? Explain.

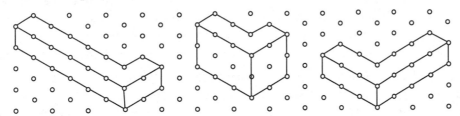

c. On isometric dot paper, show your version of a building (call it Building 2) that will meet the 10^9-aire's criterion, and compare your drawing with those of others. Discuss any differences you notice.

d. Now the 10^9-aire wants a third building (call it Building 3) designed to be shaped like the original, but "three-fourths as large in all dimensions." Make a drawing or describe this Building 3.

Buildings acceptable to the billionaire in Discussion 4 are examples of **similar polyhedra**. The word *similar* has a technical meaning and is used when one shape is an exact enlargement (or reduction) of another. What *exact* means will come out of the next Think About.

> **THINK ABOUT...**
>
> Identify some quantities in the billionaire's original building. How are the values of these quantities related to the values of the corresponding quantities in Building 2?
>
> **a.** In particular, how are *new* and *original* lengths related?
>
> **b.** How are *new* and *original* angles related?
>
> **c.** How are *new* and *original* surface areas (the number of square regions required to cover the building, including the bottom) related?
>
> **d.** How are *new* and *original* volumes (the number of cubical regions required to fill the building) related?

For a given pair of buildings, you may have noticed that the angles at the faces are all the same size. You also may have noticed that the ratio of a *new* length to the corresponding *original* length was the same, for every choice of lengths. That is,

$$\frac{\text{length in one shape}}{\text{corresponding length in other shape}}$$ is the same ratio for all corresponding segments

(assuming the ratios are formed in a consistent fashion, each ratio starting with the same building). This ratio is called the **scale factor** for the enlargement (or reduction). In a short form, we can write

$$\frac{\textbf{new length}}{\textbf{original length}} = \textbf{scale factor}.$$

An algebraically equivalent and useful form for similar figures is

(new length) = (scale factor) × (original length).

With either form, if you know two of the values, you can find the third one. Notice that if the scale factor is k, the last equation says that a new length is k times as long as the corresponding original length. The wealthy woman could have used the term *scale factor* in her requests: "Building 2 should be built with scale factor 2, and Building 3 should be built with scale factor $\frac{3}{4}$." When two polyhedra are similar, every ratio of corresponding lengths must have the same value, and every pair of corresponding angles must be the same size. Because lengths are affected by the scale factor, it is perhaps surprising that angle sizes do *not* change; that is, corresponding angles in similar shapes will have the same sizes.

> **Two 3D shapes are similar if the points in the two shapes can be matched so that (1) every pair of corresponding angles have the same size, and (2) the ratios from every pair of corresponding lengths all equal the same value, called the scale factor.**

So, corresponding lengths and angle sizes in similar figures are related. The relationships between surface areas and between volumes for similar 3D shapes are important as well. From your results in the Think About, what conjectures are reasonable?

(new surface area) = _____ × (original surface area)

(new volume) = _____ × (original volume)

We end this section with this important point: For any scale factor, say, $\frac{\text{new}}{\text{original}} = \frac{6}{7}$, the ratio $\frac{6}{7}$ does *not* necessarily mean that new = 6 and original = 7. For example, *new* could be 60 and *original* could be 70, but the ratio $\frac{\text{new}}{\text{original}}$ would still = $\frac{6}{7}$.

TAKE-AWAY MESSAGE . . . The following descriptions are all important relationships to know.

Quantities	How 2D similar shapes are related.	How 3D similar shapes are related.
Sizes of corresponding angles	equal	equal
Lengths of corresponding segments	ratios = scale factor	ratios = scale factor
Areas/surface areas	ratio = (scale factor)^2	ratio = (scale factor)^2
Volumes	(not applicable)	ratio = (scale factor)^3

> **Learning Exercises for Section 20.3**

1. Summarize the relationships among length and angle measurements in similar polyhedra. In particular, how is the scale factor involved? How are the areas of similar polyhedra related? The volumes?

2. **a.** Now the billionaire from Discussion 4 wants two more buildings sketched, each similar to the original one. Building 4 should have scale factor $1\frac{2}{3}$, and Building 5 should have scale factor 2.5. Make sketches to show the dimensions of Buildings 4 and 5.

   b. What is the scale factor between Building 4 and Building 5?

3. Are any of the following shapes similar? Explain your decisions, and if two shapes are similar, give the scale factor. (Make sure that it checks for every dimension.)

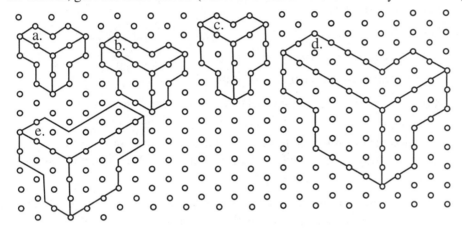

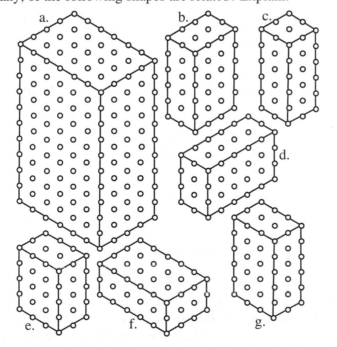

4. Which, if any, of the following shapes are related? Explain.

   h. How many shapes like shape (b) would it take to make shape (a)?

5. Are any of the following right rectangular prisms similar to a right rectangular prism with dimensions 3 cm, 7 cm, and 8 cm (in other words, a 3 cm by 7 cm by 8 cm or a 3 cm × 7 cm × 8 cm one)? If they are similar, what scale factor is involved (that is, is *every* ratio of corresponding lengths the same)? Explain your decisions, including a reference to corresponding angles of the two prisms.

    a. 5 cm × 9 cm × 10 cm

    b. 96 cm by 36 cm by 84 cm

    c. 8.7 cm × 20.3 cm × 23.2 cm

    d. 6 cm by 14 cm by 14 cm

    e. 3 inch × 7 inch × 8 inch

    f. 5 cm by 11.67 cm by 13.33 cm

    g. 9 cm × 49 cm × 64 cm

    h. 7 cm × 14 cm × 15 cm

    i. 15 mm × 35 mm × 4 cm

    j. Are the prisms in parts (b) and (c) similar?

6. **a.** A detailed model of a car is 8 inches long. The car is actually 12 feet long. If the model and the car are similar, what is the scale factor?

    b. A natural history museum has prepared a 12-foot long model of one kind of locust. They say the model is 70 times life size. What is the life size of this locust?

7. **a.** What other measurements of lengths and angles do you know about the following right rectangular prisms P and Q, if they are similar?

    b. What scale factor is involved if P is the original shape and Q is the new one?

    c. What scale factor is involved if shape Q is the original and shape P the new one?

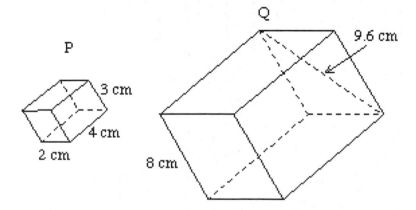

8. Olaf lives in a dorm in a tiny room that he shares with three others. He wants to live off campus next year with his friends, but he needs more money from his parents to finance the move. He decides to build a scale model of his dorm room so that when he goes home for break, he can show his parents the cramped conditions he lives in. He decides to let one inch represent 30 inches of the actual

lengths in the room. His desk is a right rectangular prism 40 inches high, 36 inches long, and 20 inches wide. He decides that his scaled desk should be $1\frac{1}{3}$ inches high, but a roommate says it should be 10 inches high. Who is right and why? What are the other dimensions of the scaled desk?

9. Make sketches to guide your thinking in answering the following questions.

   a. How many centimeter cubes does it take to make a 2 cm by 2 cm by 2 cm cube?

   b. How many centimeter cubes does it take to make a 3 cm by 3 cm by 3 cm cube?

   c. Are the two large cubes in parts (a) and (b) similar? Explain.

   d. How do the surface areas of the two cubes compare? There are two ways to answer: (1) Direct counting of squares to cover, and (2) the theory of how the scale factor is involved.

   e. How do the volumes of the two cubes compare?

10. a. Is a polyhedron similar to itself (or to a copy of itself)? If not, explain why. If so, give the scale factor.

    b. If polyhedron X is similar to polyhedron Y, is Y similar to X? If not, explain why. If so, how are the scale factors related?

    c. Suppose polyhedron X is similar to polyhedron Y and polyhedron Y is similar to polyhedron Z. Are polyhedra X and Z similar? If not, explain why. If so, how are the scale factors related?

11. a. Give the dimensions of a right square prism that would be similar to one with dimensions 20 cm, 20 cm, and 25 cm.

    b. What scale factor did you use?

    c. How does the total area of all the faces of the original prism compare with that of your prism? A rough sketch may be useful.

    d. How do the volumes of the two prisms compare?

12. Repeat Learning Exercise 11, letting the scale factor be *r*.

13. Why is it ambiguous to say, "This polyhedron is twice as large as that one"?

14. Give the dimensions of a right rectangular prism that would be similar to one that is 4 cm by 6 cm by 10 cm with

    a. scale factor 2.2.   b. scale factor 75%.

    c. scale factor $\frac{4}{7}$.   d. scale factor $3\frac{2}{3}$.

    e. scale factor 100%.   f. scale factor 220%.

15. Suppose a 2 cm by 3 cm by 5 cm right rectangular prism undergoes a size transformation with scale factor 360%. What are the surface area and volume of the image of the prism? What are its dimensions?

16. You have made an unusual three-dimensional shape from 8 cubic centimeters and want to make another one *five times as big* for a classroom demonstration. If *five times as big* refers to lengths, how many cubic centimeters will you need for the bigger shape? Explain your reasoning.

17. Can a scale factor be 0? Explain.

18. Are the following shapes similar? If not, explain why. If so, tell how you would find the scale factor.

   a. a cube with 5 cm edges and a cube with 8 cm edges

   b. every two cubes, with their respective edges m cm and n cm long

   c. every two triangular pyramids

   d. every two right rectangular prisms

   e. a rhomboidal prism with all edges x cm long and a cube with edges $3x$ cm long

19. Why can't a cube be similar to any pyramid?

20. Given a net for a polyhedron, how would you make a net that will give a larger (or smaller) version of that polyhedron?

21. One student explained the relationship between the volumes of two shapes this way: "Think of each cubic centimeter in the original shape. It grows to a k by k by k cube in the enlargement. So, each original cubic centimeter is now k^3 cubic centimeters." Retrace her thinking for two similar shapes related by the scale factor 4, using a drawing to verify that her thinking is correct.

22. Suppose the scale factor relating two similar polyhedra is 8.

   a. If the surface area of the smaller polyhedron is 400 cm^2, what is the surface area of the larger polyhedron?

   b. If the volume of the smaller polyhedron is 400 cm^3, what is the volume of the larger polyhedron?

23. Polyhedron 1, which is made up of 810 identical cubes, is similar to Polyhedron 2, which is made up of 30 cubes of that same size.

   a. What is the scale factor relating the two polyhedra?

   b. What is the ratio of the surface areas of the two polyhedra?

24. Legend: Once upon a time there was a powerful but crabby magician who was feared by her people. One year she demanded a cube of gold, 1 meter on an edge, and the people gave it to her. The next year she demanded, "Give me twice as much gold as last year." When they gave her a cube of gold, 2 meters on an edge, she was furious—"You disobedient people!"—and she cast a spell over all of the people. Why? And why should she have been pleased?

25. Make two nets for a cube so that the nets are similar as 2D shapes but also so that one net will have an area four times as large as that of the first net. When the nets are folded to give cubes, how will the surface areas of the two cubes compare? (*Hint*: How will the lengths of the edges compare, in the two nets?)

26. The index finger of the Statue of Liberty is 8 ft long. Measure the length of your index finger, the length of your nose, and the width of your mouth. Use the information to predict the length of the Statue of Liberty's nose and the width of her mouth. What are you assuming?

20.4 | Issues for Learning: Similarity

Similarity often comes up in the intermediate grades in the elementary school mathematics curriculum, but perhaps just as a visual exercise. Students are asked "Which have exactly the same shape?" for a collection of drawings. Occasionally there is a little numerical work, usually with scale drawings and maps (and the latter may not be associated with similarity in the children's minds). Although the overall situation may be changing, there is much less research on children's thinking in geometry than on number work, with only a scattering of studies dealing with similar figures. Here is a task that has been used in interviews of children of various ages.[i]

(A drawing like the one to the right is given to the student, along with a chain of paper clips.) Mr. Short is 4 large buttons in height. Mr. Tall (deliberately not shown to the student) is similar to Mr. Short but is 6 large buttons in height. Measure Mr. Short's height in paper clips (he is 6 paper clips tall in the drawing actually used in the interviews) and predict the height of Mr. Tall if you could measure him in paper clips. Explain your prediction.

Mr. SHORT: 4 Buttons

Mr. TALL (not shown): 6 Buttons

Would you be surprised to learn that more than half the fourth graders (and nearly 30% of the eighth graders) would respond something like this? "Mr. Tall is 8 paper clips high. He is 2 buttons higher than Mr. Short, so I figured he is two paper clips higher." Plainly, the students noticed the *additive* comparison of 6 buttons with 4 buttons, but did not realize that it is the *multiplicative* comparison, the ratio, that is important for similar shapes. The younger children, of course, may not have dealt with similarity, and there may be developmental reasons why numerical work with similarity does not come up earlier in the curriculum. But the older students most likely *had* experienced instruction on proportions, yet they had not fully understood the idea of similar figures and/or the relevance of the ratio relationship in the Mr. Short-Mr. Tall task.

You, or someone else in your class, may have focused on the additive comparison in working with Activity 1 (*A Puzzle About a Puzzle*) so the lack of recognition of the importance of multiplicative comparisons for similar shapes clearly can continue beyond grade eight.

TAKE-AWAY MESSAGE . . . Additive comparisons seem to be natural, perhaps from many occurrences outside of school, but multiplicative relationships, even beyond those in similarity of shapes, may require schooling. ♦

20.5 | Check Yourself

You should be able to work problems like those assigned and to meet the following objectives.

1. Appreciate that creating an enlargement or reduction (a size change) of a shape involves a particular relationship among any pair of corresponding lengths.

2. More completely, know the criteria for two figures to be similar (the two angles in every pair of corresponding angles have the same size, the lengths of every pair of corresponding segments are related by the same scale factor).

3. Use the two criteria for similarity in determining missing angle sizes and lengths in similar shapes. Applications involving similarity (for example, photographs, maps, scale drawings, and time lines) might come up.

4. Create similar polygons with the ruler method (Section 20.1).

5. Distinguish between, and use correctly, such phrases as "times as long as" versus "times longer than," or "85% as big as" versus "85% bigger than."

6. State and use the relationships between the perimeters and the areas of two similar figures.

7. Use the work-saving way of telling whether two triangles are similar.

8. Extend the ideas of similarity with 2D figures to 3D shapes. That is, be able to tell whether two given 3D shapes are similar, and for 3D shapes that are known to be similar, find missing angle sizes, lengths, surface areas, and volumes. State the relationships between the surface areas and volumes of similar 3D shapes.

9. Illustrate a difficulty that children may have with multiplicative thinking (Section 20.4).

REFERENCE FOR CHAPTER 20

Karplus, R., & Peterson, R. W. (1970). Intellectual development beyond elementary school II: Ratio, a survey. *School Science and Mathematics, 70*(9), 813-820.

Chapter 21

Curves, Constructions, and Curved Surfaces

Our attention up to this point has been on shapes made with line segments, rays, or planar regions. But, as you know, straightness and flatness do not model many real-life objects well. In this chapter we first treat curves that do lie in the same flat surface, with the most attention given to circle-related vocabulary (including some angles) and constructions. Then we deal with several ideas associated with curved 3D shapes.

21.1 | Planar Curves and Constructions

Springs and the Slinky toy are examples of familiar curves in space, but our attention will first be on **planar curves**, curves that lie in a single flat surface. Draw almost any squiggly mark on a piece of paper, and you will have drawn a curve. (As you may know, in advanced mathematics it is sometimes convenient to regard line segments and polygons as curves also.) Here are some important curves in mathematics; do you know names for them? (Notice that two are shown on coordinate systems, which are not part of the curves.)

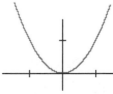 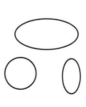 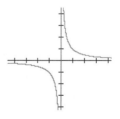

Our focus will be on the circle, a shape you know well. Most of the associated vocabulary is familiar to you, but the following drawings on the next page may suggest one or two new ideas.

477

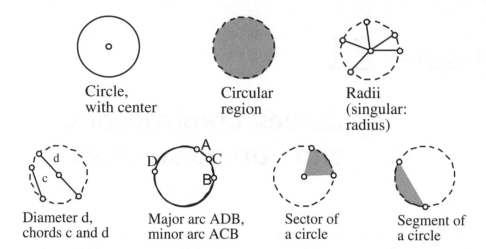

Circle, with center   Circular region   Radii (singular: radius)

Diameter d, chords c and d   Major arc ADB, minor arc ACB   Sector of a circle   Segment of a circle

THINK ABOUT...

How are a chord and a diameter alike? How is a sector of a circle different from a segment of the circle?

Discussion 1   Properties of Circles

1. What are some quantities associated with a circle?

2. What are some properties associated with a circle? The properties might involve radii, diameters, arcs, symmetries, and so on.

An angle with its vertex at the center of a circle cuts off (intercepts) a piece of the circle, called an **arc** of the circle. Sometimes an arc is measured by the size of that angle, rather than by its actual length. For example, the two arcs cut off by the 54° angle below might each be described as arcs of 54°, even though they have different lengths. The actual *length* of a 54° arc will depend on the circle it is a part of. A common notation for the arc with endpoints A and B is $\overset{\frown}{AB}$. If the major arc is intended, a third point should be used: $\overset{\frown}{ADB}$.

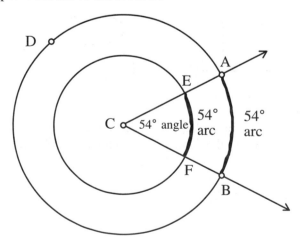

Notice that the number of degrees in major arc $\overset{\frown}{ADB}$ is 360° − 54°, or 306°.

An angle with its vertex at the center of a circle is a **central angle** of the circle, so a central angle and the arc it cuts off have the same number of degrees. Angle ACB has size 54°.

Activity 1   A Conjecture About Inscribed Angles

An angle with its vertex on a circle and its sides along chords of the circle is called an **inscribed angle.** An inscribed angle intercepts an arc, which is the arc inside the opening of the angle.

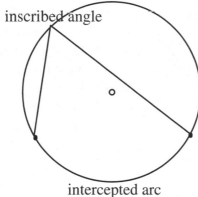

1. Measure the inscribed angle and the central angle for the intercepted arc. What relationship between the two measurements might apply? (You may have to extend the sides of the angles.)

2. In other circles, draw inscribed and central angles that intercept the same arc. Does the size of an inscribed angle always appear to be related to the number of degrees in its intercepted arc? (Recall that an arc can be measured by the number of degrees in its related central angle.)

The Greeks considered the circle to be a "perfect" shape. Part of their admiration may have grown out of their knowledge of what can be accomplished with circles (drawn by a compass) and with lines (drawn with an unmarked ruler, or a straight-edge). But other cultures have attached importance to the circle as well. For example, from the Navajo Indian viewpoint, ". . . everything an Indian does is in a circle, and that is because the Power of the World always works in circles, and everything tries to be round . . ." [i]

On the following page are some examples of how straight lines and circles, drawn with a straightedge and a compass, can be used to undertake many geometric tasks without any need for measuring tools like a protractor or a marked ruler.

Notes

The challenge:

Bisect ∠ A below (that is, "cut" it into two angles of the same size). You want to find the angle bisector of ∠ A.

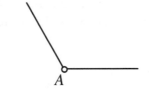

A

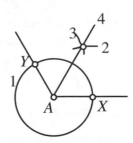

Step 1. Use *A* as a center and any radius to draw a circle.
Step 2. Draw arc with center *X* and a long enough radius.
Step 3. Draw arc with center Y and same radius used in Step 2.
Step 4. Draw a ray through *A* and the point where the arcs intersect. That ray will be the bisector of the angle.

The challenge:
Copy angle *B* at point *V* on a straight piece.

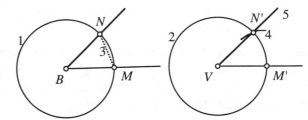

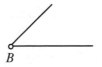

B

V

Step 1. Use *B* as center and any radius to draw a circle.
Step 2. Use *V* as center and the same radius as in Step 1 to draw a circle.
Step 3. Spread the compass to match segment *MN*.
Step 4. Use that as radius and *M'* as center to draw an arc.
Step 5. Draw a ray through *V* and where the arc and the circle intersect. The resulting angle is a copy of ∠*B*.

Notes

The challenge:

Locate the midpoint of line
segment *AB* below. (The
construction also gives a
line making right angles
at the midpoint; hence,
it is the **perpendicular
bisector** of segment *AB*.)

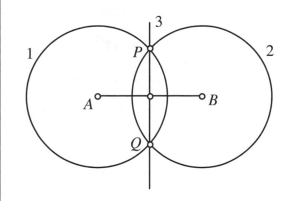

Step 1. Use *A* as center and any radius longer
than half the length of segment *AB* to
draw a circle.
Step 2. Use *B* as center and the same radius to
draw a circle.
Step 3. Join the points where the circles intersect. That line intersects *AB* at its midpoint (and makes right angles with it).

The challenge:

Locate the line that makes
right angles with (**is perpendicular to**) line *CD* and goes
through point *P*.

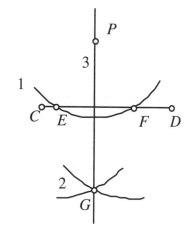

(The same steps work if point
P is *on CD*.)

Step 1. Use *P* as center and any radius
long enough to give a circle cutting *CD* in two points *E* and *F*
(you may have to extend *CD*).
Step 2. Using *E* and *F* as centers and the
same radius for each new circle, draw
arcs meeting at point *G*.
Step 3. Draw the line through *P* and *G*. It is
perpendicular to *CD*.

Notes

THINK ABOUT...

Study the finished constructions for the angle bisector, the perpendicular bisector, and the perpendicular to a line. Do you see that they build in reflection symmetry in some way?

The final basic construction allows you to draw parallel lines.

The challenge:

Locate the line that passes through point *P* and is parallel to line *GH*.

P
○

G _____ H

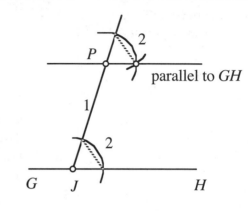

Step 1. From any point *J* on *GH*, draw ray *JP*.
Step 2. Copy an angle at *J*, at *P*, so that one side is along the ray and in a corresponding position. The second side of this angle is the desired parallel.

When you glance at the above construction of the parallel lines, it looks as though the work at *J* has been slid up to *P* in the direction and distance going from *J* to *P*.

TAKE-AWAY MESSAGE . . . Circles, one type of planar curve, are surprisingly rich in related ideas and in the constructions they allow us to do. ♦

Learning Exercises for Section 21.1

1. Tell whether each statement is always true, sometimes true, or never true. Support your decisions.

    a.   A radius of a circle can have both endpoints on the circle.

    b.   A diameter of a circle is a chord of the circle.

    c.   A chord of a circle is a diameter of the circle.

d. A radius of a circle has length that is half the length of a diameter of the circle.

e. Two circles with the same length for radius are exactly the same size.

f. The distance between the center of a circle and a point on the circle is the same as the length of the radius.

g. The bisector of an angle is a line of symmetry for the angle.

h. The perpendicular bisector of a line segment is a line of symmetry for the line segment.

2. Draw a circle. Show in your drawing and label the following items: a chord that is not a diameter; perpendicular radii; a minor arc with endpoints Q and R; and a major arc with endpoints Q and R.

3. Show that each of these shapes will tessellate the plane.

a.    **b.**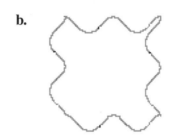

4. Describe the reflection symmetries and the rotational symmetries of each shape.

  a. a circle

  b. the curve below (it continues indefinitely in each direction)

5. For each angle size, sketch a circular region and a central angle of the given size, and tell what part of the whole circular region the sector of the angle is.
  a. 90°   **b.** 270°   **c.** 120°   **d.** 80°
  e. 180°   **f.** 45°   **g.** 135°   **h.** 60°

6. For each given circle and without measuring, find the number of degrees in each labeled angle. Arc *PQ* has 84°.

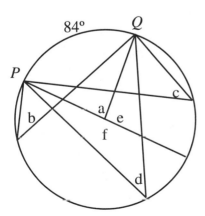
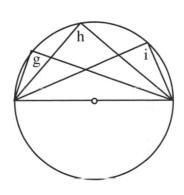

7. Give a partial justification for the conjecture about inscribed angles in Activity 1, using the special case shown below. (*Hints*: Angles in an isosceles triangle; exterior angle of triangle ABC)

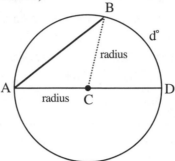

8. Using a compass and straightedge only, copy angle *X* and bisect it. Do the same for angle *Y* and angle *Z*.

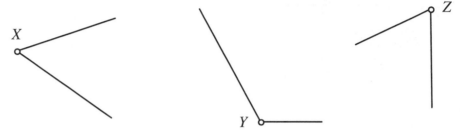

9. With a straightedge, sketch a scalene triangle. Then do the following.
   a. Using compass and straightedge only, find the midpoint of each side of the triangle.
   b. Draw segments joining each of the vertices with the midpoint of the opposite side. Does anything appear to be true?

10. In each diagram, copy the drawing and construct a line perpendicular to the given line and passing through the given point. Do not erase any key construction marks.

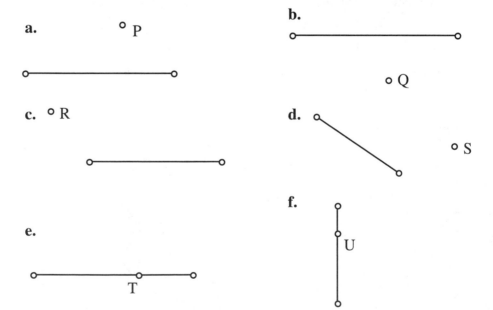

11. In each diagram, copy the drawing and construct a line that passes through the given point and is parallel to the given line. Do not erase any key construction marks.

a.   P o

b.   Q o

c.

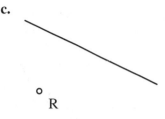

R

12. With a straightedge, draw a line segment *AB*. Using the same radius, draw circles with centers at *A* and at *B*. Label the point at which the circles intersect *C*. (If they do not intersect, use a larger radius.)

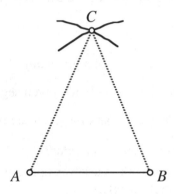

a.   How does the distance from *C* to *A* compare to the distance from *C* to *B*?

b.   Use different radii to find six other points the same distance from *A* and from *B*, like *C*. Describe where all such points seem to lie.

c.   *Finding the missing center.* A pulley broke into several pieces. To order a replacement via the Web, you need to know the radius. Copy the drawing below, and with straightedge and compass constructions, find the center and radius of the pulley. Then draw the full circle. (*Hint:* Do you see perpendicular bisectors of chords?) Notice that you have found the center of the circle using just three known points of the circle.

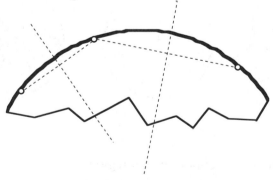

d.   Points *A* and *B* are on one circle, and points *M* and *N* are on another circle. The two circles have the same center (they are called **concentric circles**), although the location of the center is not known. Find the center with compass and straightedge constructions, and then draw the full circles.

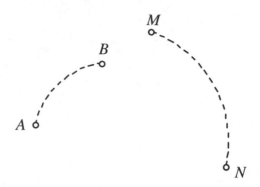

13. Using just a compass and a straightedge, draw each given angle or segment.

   a. an angle of 45°

   b. an angle of 135°

   c. an angle having size $\frac{3}{4}$ the size of a given angle

   d. a line segment having $\frac{3}{4}$ the length of a given segment

   e. a line segment with length $\frac{5}{8}$ that of a given segment

14. **a.** Why are most sewer-hole covers circular?

   b. Would the shape below work as a sewer-hole cover? (The dashed-segment triangle is an equilateral triangle.)

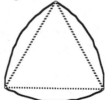

15. Can you make the following designs, using just a compass and straightedge? Make your own designs, if you prefer.

   a. 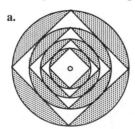   **b.** 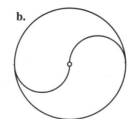   **c.**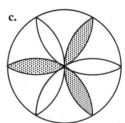

16. Sketch each described sector of a circular region.

   a. $\frac{1}{4}$ of the whole region   **b.** $\frac{1}{3}$ of the whole region

   c. $\frac{4}{5}$ of the whole region   **d.** $\frac{1}{12}$ of the whole region

17. Consider the statement that claimed to describe the Navajo Indian outlook: "... everything an Indian does is in a circle, and that is because the Power of the World always works in circles, and everything tries to be round" (from Ascher, 1991, p. 125). Identify things in the world that support this viewpoint of the Navajo.

18. **a.** Use straightedge and compass to copy angles to draw a triangle that is similar to the given triangle. You decide what size the new triangle should be.

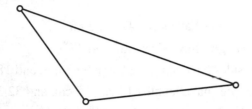

   b. Measure to find the scale factor of the size transformation relating the given triangle and your triangle.

19. With straightedge and compass, construct an equilateral triangle *ABC* that has one side the length of segment *AB*.

   A ⟳——————————————⟳ B

20. In each drawing, use a straightedge and a compass to "put triangle *PQR* back together." The letters in parentheses tell which vertices are involved.

a.

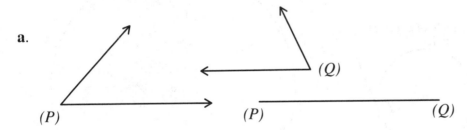

b.

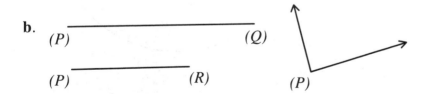

c.

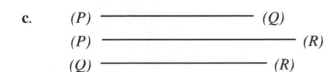

Continue on the next page.

d. Compare your triangles for parts (a), (b), and (c) with someone else's. Are they congruent? What can you conjecture about triangles using the same angle-side-angle information (as in part (a)), the same side-angle-side data (as in part (b)), or the same side-side-side segments (as in part (c))?

21. *Continuation of Exercise 20:* Are the following pairs of triangles congruent?

a. Triangle 1: Sides 12 cm and 20 cm make an angle of 33°.

Triangle 2: Angle ACB has size 33°, side AC is 20 cm, and side BC is 12 cm.

b. Triangle 3: Two angles have sizes 47° and 86°.

Triangle 4: Two angles have sizes 86° and 47°.

c. Triangle 5: The sides have lengths 25 cm, 32.3 cm, and 18 cm.

Triangle 6: The sides have lengths 18 cm, 25 cm, and 32.3 cm.

d. Triangle 7: Angles D and E have sizes 47° and 62°, respectively, and side DE is 19.7 cm long.

Triangle GHI: Angles G and H have sizes 62° and 71°, respectively, and side GI is 19.7 cm long.

22. A line that touches a circle at exactly one point is called a **tangent** to the circle. A tangent is perpendicular to the radius drawn to that point. With compass and straightedge, construct the tangents to circle C at points A and B.

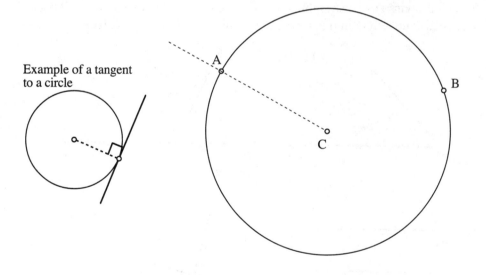

Example of a tangent to a circle

21.2 Curved Surfaces

Just as there are many planar curves, there also are many curved surfaces. Our focus will be on only three types: spheres, cylinders, and cones.

Discussion 2   Perfectly Round

You are familiar with **spheres** (the surfaces of perfectly round balls, for example). What do you know about spheres? What do terms like center, radius, diameter, and great circle mean, for a sphere?

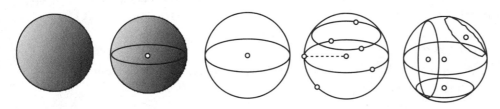

A cylinder may be thought of this way (see the sketches in Figure 1). Trace around a given planar curve with a line, always keeping the line parallel to its earlier positions; then cut the resulting infinite surface with two parallel planes. The surface formed by the two planar regions and the part of the infinite surface between the two planes is a **cylinder**.

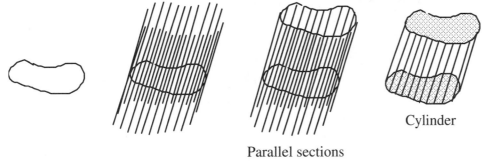

Cylinder

Parallel sections

Figure 1

The starting curve can be a circle, of course, and the tracing lines can make right angles with lines in the plane of the given curve. When both these conditions occur, we have the shape called the common **right circular cylinder**. For example, soda or soup cans are right circular cylinders. The distortion in two-dimensional sketches usually shows the circles as ellipses. Additional cross-sections sometimes help show the curvature, as in Figure 2 shown on the next page.

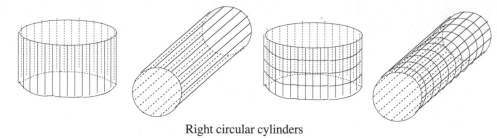

Right circular cylinders

Figure 2

As with prisms, the planar regions are called the **bases of the cylinder**, and the parallel bases are identical in size and shape (congruent). As with prisms, the line segments joining corresponding points on the two bases are not only parallel, but they also have the same length.

THINK ABOUT...

Do you see that if the original "curve" were a polygon, the resulting "cylinder" would be a prism?

Cones can be described in a somewhat similar fashion. Again start with a curve and trace around the curve with lines, but this time have all the lines go through a fixed point. Cut through all the resulting surface with a plane. The surface between the fixed point and the cutting plane, along with the planar region, give a **cone**. The fixed point is called the **vertex of the cone,** and the planar region is the **base of the cone**. If the original curve traced is a circle and all the segments joining the vertex to points on the base are the same length, then the cone is a **right circular cone**.

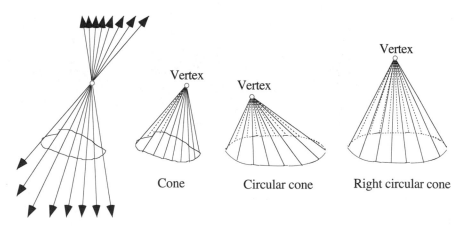

Cone   Circular cone   Right circular cone

THINK ABOUT...

In the description of a cone, what shape would you get if the original "curve" were a polygon?

Notes

Discussion 3   **Shapes of Housing**

How houses are shaped is an interesting aspect of culture and of history. What shapes are houses in Western countries? What shapes are tepees, hogans, igloos, and yurts? Why are houses shaped as they are?

TAKE-AWAY MESSAGE . . . Spheres, cylinders, and cones are the basic 3D curved surfaces and lead to other vocabulary useful in describing features of such curved surfaces. ◆

Learning Exercises for Section 21.2

1. Tell whether each statement is always true, sometimes true, or never true. Support your decisions.
   a. A radius of a sphere can have both endpoints on the sphere.
   b. A radius of a sphere has length that is half the length of a diameter of the sphere.
   c. A circular cone has reflection symmetry.
   d. A circular cylinder has rotational symmetry.
   e. Two spheres with the same length for radius are congruent.
   f. Two great circles of the same sphere have exactly the same size.
   g. Any two spheres are similar.

2. Give the most informative technical description (for example, right circular cone) for each description or drawing.
   a. a mailing tube
   b. (the most common) lipstick containers
   c. a dunce cap
   d. the sharpened end of a pencil
   e. the end of a sharp-pointed carrot, cut at an angle
   f. (Assume circular ends.)

3. Describe the reflection symmetries and the rotational symmetries of each shape.
   a. a right circular cylinder
   b. a right circular cone
   c. a sphere

4. a. Sketch a net for a right circular cylinder.
   b. Sketch a net for a right circular cone.
   c. Why do most flat maps of the world involve distortions of some regions of the world?

5. Where in the world can you find an example of the following objects?
   a. cylinder
   b. cone
   c. sphere
   d. great circle of a sphere

6. Sketch an example of each shape, if it is possible. If it is not possible, explain why.

   a. a circular cylinder that is not a right cylinder

   b. a cone that is not a circular cone

   c. a right circular cone

   d. a cylinder that has ovals as bases

   e. two non-intersecting great circles of a sphere

   f. half a sphere (a **hemisphere**), with a right circular cone having its vertex on the hemisphere and its base a great circular region

7. Prism is to pyramid as cylinder is to _____. Explain.

8. a. If the bottom layer of the cylinder shown holds $5\frac{2}{3}$ cups, how many cups would the whole cylinder hold? (What assumption did you make?)

   b. If 82.5 ml of water fills $\frac{3}{4}$ of another cylinder shaped like the one shown, how many milliliters of water will $\frac{3}{5}$ of the cylinder hold?

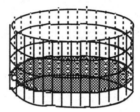

9. Sketch two spheres, one sphere with radius twice as long as that of the other.

   a. How do the diameters of the two spheres compare?

   b. In your opinion, how do their volumes compare? Their surface areas? Explain.

10. a. Roll up a sheet of paper into a cylinder shape. If a plane cut through all the curved part, what shape(s) could the cross-section be?

   b. Roll a sheet of paper into a conical shape. If a plane cut through all the curved part, what shape(s) could the cross-section be?

21.3 | Check Yourself

You should be able to work exercises like those assigned and to meet the following objectives.

1. Use the vocabulary associated with circles, spheres, cylinders, and cones. Some words should have already been familiar (center, radius, diameter, arc), but others may be less familiar to you (chord, major/minor arc, sector of a circle, segment of a circle, central angle, inscribed angle, hemisphere).

2. Use the relationship between the sizes of a central angle and an inscribed angle that intercept the same arc in the same circle.

3. Construct with compass and straightedge: the bisector of a given angle, a copy of a given angle, the perpendicular bisector of a given line segment, the perpendicular to a given line through a given point, and the parallel to a given line through a given point.

4. Draw and recognize drawings of cylinders and cones, especially right ones.

5. Use whatever relationships have arisen during class and in the assigned exercises.

REFERENCE FOR CHAPTER 21

[i]Ascher, M. (1991). Ethnomathematics: A multicultural view of mathematical ideas. Pacific Grove, CA: Brooks-Cole. p. 125.

Chapter 22

Transformation Geometry

Our earlier work with symmetry in Chapter 18 used movements such as reflections and rotations, with a focus on a given figure. These movements do not change the size or shape of the figure and are often called **rigid motions**. In this chapter we first introduce a third type of rigid motion, the *translation*, and then we look more carefully at the different rigid motions. Finally, we present the idea of combining rigid motions, and in doing so, we introduce a fourth type of rigid motion, the *glide-reflection*. In the last section of this chapter, we extend some of the earlier work with tessellations, symmetry, and similarity.

22.1 | Some Types of Rigid Motions

Activity 1[i]   (Preliminary Homework)   Let's Be Pick-y

Find all the different shapes that can be made from four toothpicks, subject to these two rules: (1) Toothpicks can touch only at endpoints, and (2) after the first toothpick, each toothpick either is perpendicular to the toothpick it touches or continues in the same straight line as the toothpick it touches. Record the different shapes you find, one shape to a box. Shapes are not different if they can be made to match. To get you started, two different shapes are shown.

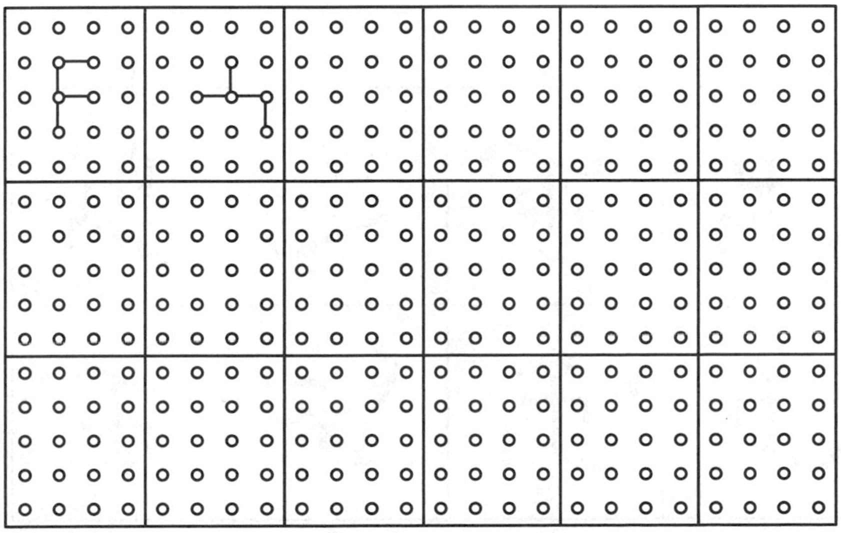

Notes

It is likely that you mentally or physically "moved" a four-toothpick shape to test whether it was different from one you already had. These mental or physical movements, leading to a type of mathematics called **transformation geometry,** are called **rigid motions** (or isometries—*iso-* means *same* and *metron* means *measure*).

> A **rigid motion**, or **isometry**, is a movement that does not change lengths and angle sizes.

THINK ABOUT...

What are some different types of rigid motions? What language would you use to describe how the shape shown in the starting box below could end up at each of the other positions?

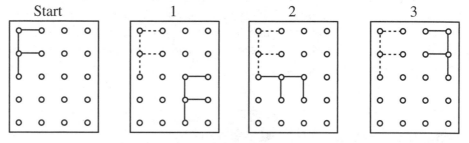

Although you may have used the informal terms *slide, turn,* and *flip* or *mirror image* (terms that are sometimes used initially with elementary school children), the technical terms for the rigid motions involved in the Think About are **translation** (see Box 1), **rotation about a point** (see Box 2), and **reflection in a line** (see Box 3).

Activity 2   A Moving Experience

Pretend that the two-dimensional shapes below are on transparencies for an overhead projector. What shapes are the same? Which rigid motions, or isometries, help you decide?

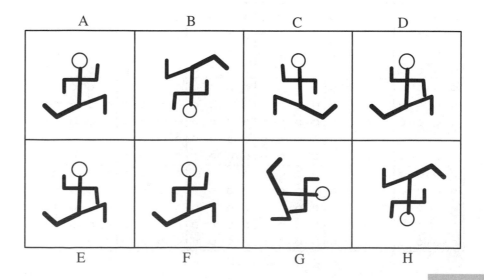

So far, we have seen these types of isometries of the plane: *reflections* (shown in Activity 2, going from A to C), *rotations* (going from A to B), and *translations* (going from A to F). If you started with shape A and imagined shape A being moved to shape F, you could call shape F the **image** of shape A under a translation: original → image. Because the shapes are identical, the words *original* and *image* help communicate which shape is the starting shape and which is the ending shape. Although we often focus on a particular shape, each rigid motion affects *every* point in the plane, not just the points in that shape.

original shape

image of the original shape for some reflection

image of the original shape for a particular translation

image of the original shape for a particular rotation

What does the phrase *congruent figures* mean to you? Transformations allow a very general view of congruence for all figures, not just for triangles.

> Two figures are **congruent figures** if one is the image of the other for some rigid motion.

This description allows shapes of any sort—segments, angles, polygons, curved regions, even 3D figures—to be congruent. It also corresponds to a physical or a mental manipulation of one shape to see whether it matches the other shape exactly. A consequence of two figures being congruent is that any original part and its image part (referred to as *corresponding parts*, or *matching parts*, in high school) will always have the same measurements, if there is an appropriate measurement.

TAKE-AWAY MESSAGE . . . Rigid motions and transformation geometry may be new to you. Their dynamic, motion-based nature clearly can involve much visualization. Because of its importance, visualization is a topic that is receiving increased, explicit attention in the elementary school mathematics curriculum, rather than just being overlooked or left to chance. Furthermore, from the mathematical point of view, transformation geometry is closer to the mainstream of modern mathematics than geometry is *a la* Euclid. Transformations of the plane are special cases of mathematical *functions*, an idea that appears in some form in every area of mathematics. ♦

Learning Exercises for Section 22.1

1. Curricula in the middle grades can use these informal terms—*mirror image, slide, flip,* and *turn*—for the isometries. Which technical term goes with each informal term?

2. **a.** Try mental manipulation to tell which *single* type of rigid motion transforms shape A to each of the other shapes. It may help to draw a face or some mark on shape A. You may wish to check by tracing a copy of shape A and moving it to another shape.

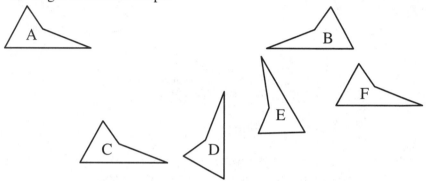

    b. Which of the shapes in part (a) are congruent? Explain.

3. What rigid motion is involved in each of the following situations? To retain the two-dimensional nature of the work in this section, assume that you are looking at a movie.
    a. A train moving along a straight track
    b. The motion of a fan blade
    c. A child sliding down a playground slide
    d. A clock-hand moving
    e. A skateboarder skating in a circular bowl
    f. A doorknob moving

4. In parts (a)–(d) make a freehand sketch to show the image of the given triangle-rectangle shape for the isometry.
    a. a reflection in line *m*
    b. a reflection in line *n*
    c. a translation 6 cm to the right
    d. a rotation of 90° clockwise with center C
    e. Which of your shapes is congruent to the original shape? Explain.

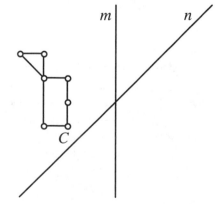

5. The term **orientation** has a technical meaning that differs from everyday usage of the term. One can assign an orientation to a figure in this way: Pick any three noncollinear points on the figure—call them *P, Q, R*. Then the order *P-Q-R* assigns a clockwise or counterclockwise **orientation** to the figure (it may be helpful to think "*clock* orientation"). Different people, or different choices for the points, can assign a different orientation to the same figure. What is of value is knowing how the orientation of a figure is affected by each type of rigid motion. The orientation of the original and the orientation of its image might be the same, or they might be reversed. Make rough sketches or examine earlier ones to tell how the orientations of an original figure and its image are related for each type of rigid motion.

    a. translation   **b.** rotation   **c.** reflection

6. Which of the isometries make sense for "moving" a three-dimensional shape?

7. Given four congruent isosceles right triangles, how many different shapes can you make, using all four triangles each time? Work mentally as much as possible, before you record and name the shapes you find. Which rigid motions did you use?

Notes

22.2 | Finding Images for Rigid Motions

Earlier, your main task was to decide what rigid motion or isometry was involved when you were given a shape and its image. In this section, your task is to find the image when you are given a shape and the type of rigid motion. With practice, drawing the image freehand can work out satisfactorily, or the structure provided by using grid paper can help in drawing images. In classrooms you may come across either computer software for finding the images of given figures for rigid motions or plastic devices, called MIRAs, for finding the images for reflections.

However, the paper-tracing methods of this section offer a low-tech (and therefore slower) means of finding images quite accurately and in a way that shows the motion involved. For making neater and more accurate drawings, use a ruler or the edge of a 3" by 5" card to draw line segments. Each paper-tracing method that follows uses two pieces of translucent paper. The thinnest paper you have can also work all right if you use a felt-tip pen.

First we illustrate a paper-tracing method for finding the image of a given figure for a particular translation. One way to describe a particular translation is to tell how far to move and in what direction. These two pieces of information can be communicated by a translation arrow, commonly called a **vector**. The length of the vector tells how far to translate, and the direction the vector is pointing tells the direction in which to translate.

TRANSLATION

Step 1. Draw the translation arrow, or vector, on Paper 1. Put a heavy dot where the vector starts.

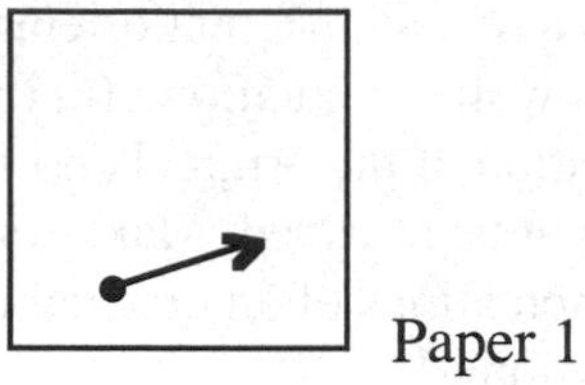

Paper 1

Step 2. Draw an original shape on Paper 1. (Plan the shape so its image will fit on the paper. It does not have to be a polygon; a face, a heart, an animal, or anything else works fine.)

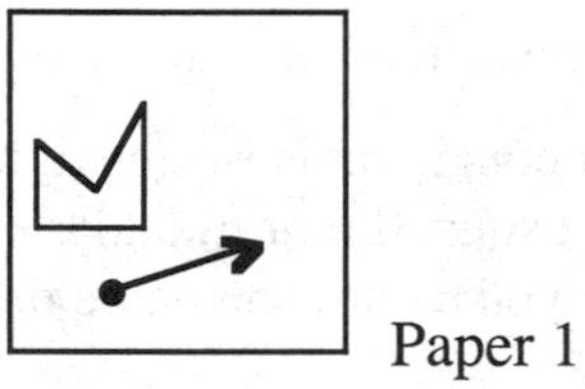

Paper 1

Step 3. Put Paper 2 on top, trace the starting dot of the vector, draw the line through the vector, and trace the original figure.

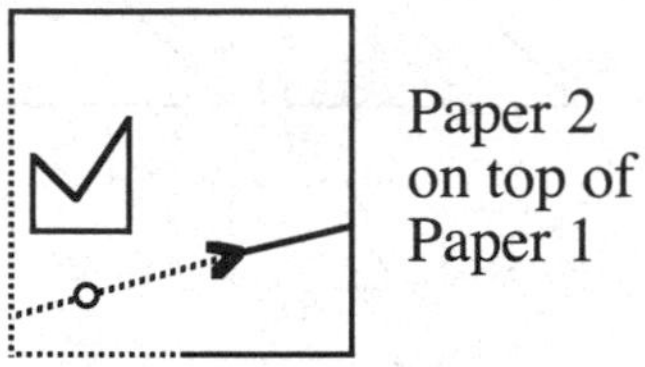

Paper 2 on top of Paper 1

Step 4. Put Paper 2 under the other paper. Keeping the line and the vector aligned, translate Paper 2 until the dot is at the vector head.

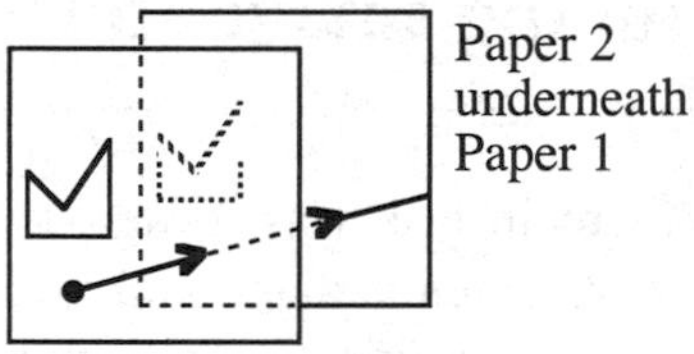

Paper 2 underneath Paper 1

Step 5. Trace the image onto Paper 1. (It is a good idea to label the original shape and the image as such.)

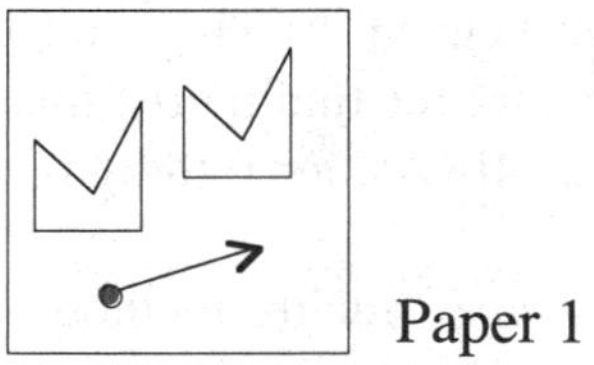

Paper 1

To find the image of a given shape for a reflection, you must know the line of reflection. Next, we illustrate a paper-tracing method for finding the reflection image of a shape.

REFLECTION

Step 1. Draw an original shape and the line of reflection on Paper 1. Put a heavy dot on the line of reflection for a reference point. (Plan so that the image will fit on the paper.)

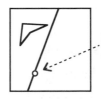

Paper 1
reference point on
line of reflection

Step 2. Put Paper 2 on top, and trace the figure, the line of reflection, and the reference point.

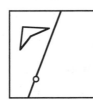

Paper 2
on top of
Paper 1

Step 3. Flipping Paper 2 over and putting it underneath, align the lines of reflection and the reference points.

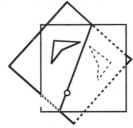

Paper 2
flipped
over and
underneath

Step 4. Trace the image onto Paper 1. Again, it is a good idea to label the original and its image.

Paper 1

Finally, to find the image of a given shape for a rotation, you must know (1) where the rotation is centered (the **center** of the rotation) and (2) an **angle** that shows the size and direction, clockwise or counterclockwise, of the rotation. We illustrate a paper-tracing method for accurately finding the rotation image of a given shape.

ROTATION

Step 1. Draw an original shape on Paper 1. Pick a point for the center of the rotation, and draw the angle of the rotation so that its vertex is at this center. Plan ahead so the image will fit on Paper 1.

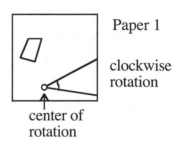

Paper 1

clockwise rotation

center of rotation

Step 2. With Paper 2 on top of Paper 1, trace the shape, the center of rotation, and the starting ray—the ray of the angle that would be rotated to give the second ray of the angle.

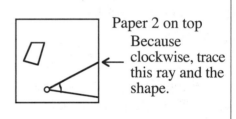

Paper 2 on top Because clockwise, trace this ray and the shape.

Step 3. Put Paper 2 underneath and align everything. With your pencil tip at the center of the rotation, turn the underneath paper in the proper clock direction until the starting ray is aligned with the second ray of the angle of rotation.

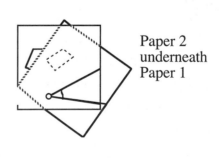

Paper 2 underneath Paper 1

Step 4. Trace the image onto Paper 1. (Again, it is a good idea to label the original and the image.)

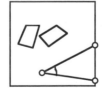

Paper 1

Activity 3   Let's Move It   Notes

The aim of this activity is to make certain you can find images accurately using the illustrated methods (or perhaps some other methods your instructor may prefer). Each person in your group should choose one of the figures below, and then find its images for a translation, a reflection, and a rotation. (Do them separately because drawings can get cluttered quickly.) Choose your own vector (translation arrow), line of reflection, and center and angle of rotation.

  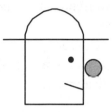

You will practice the paper-tracing methods more in the Learning Exercises or on your own, as well as practice drawing images freehand and with dot paper.

TAKE-AWAY MESSAGE . . . Paper-tracing methods can help to find accurate images for the different types of rigid motions—translations, reflections, and rotations. ♦

Learning Exercises for Section 22.2

1.   Find the image for each indicated rigid motion using paper-tracing.

   a.   The image of a shape of your choice, for a translation with the vector shown at the right.

   b.   The image of a shape of your choice for a rotation with a center of your choice and with a 90° clockwise angle.

   c.   The image of the following shape for a reflection in the heavy line segment *k*.

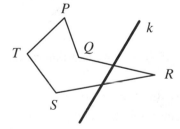

   d.   The image of a shape of your choice for a rotation with center on the shape and with a 90° counterclockwise angle.

2. Copy and sketch *freehand*, as accurately as you can, the image of shape G for the rigid motion given in parts (a)–(c).

   a. A translation 5 cm east (label the image *H*)

   b. A 90° rotation clockwise, center at *X* (label the image *I*)

   c. A reflection in line *m* (label the image *J*)

   d. Check your freehand drawings.

   e. Which type of rigid motion is most difficult for you to visualize images?

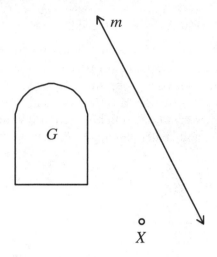

3. Choose another figure from Activity 3 and use tracing paper to find its images for a translation, a reflection, and a rotation. You can choose your own vector, line of reflection, and center and degrees of rotation.

4. Grid paper is commonly used in elementary school to help locate images for rigid motions.

   a. Find the image S′ of the given pentagon for a translation 4 units west.

   b. Find the image S″ of the pentagon for a rotation of 180 degrees, center *P*.

   c. Find the image S‴ of the pentagon for a reflection in line *m*.

   d. Find the image S‴′ of the pentagon for a reflection in line *n*.

   e. Find the image S‴″ of the pentagon for a translation with vector *v*.

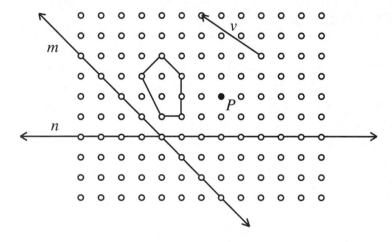

5. Find and label the image of the given quadrilateral on the next page for each rigid motion described.

   a. image A′ for a translation with vector *v*

   b. image A″ for a translation with vector *w*

   c. image A‴ for a reflection in line *j*

   d. image A‴′ for a reflection in line *k* (shade it lightly)

   e. image A‴″ for a rotation of 90° counterclockwise, center *Q*

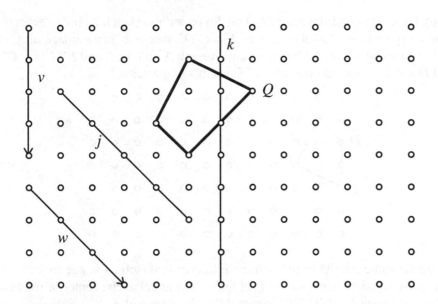

6. The regularity of isometric dot paper is also helpful in finding images. Find the image of the flag shape *CAT* for each rigid motion described.

    a. Translation with vector *v*

    b. Reflection in line *m*

    c. Rotation, 120° clockwise, center *C* (label it part (c))

    d. Rotation, 90° counterclockwise, center *T* (label it part (d))

    e. Rotation, 60° counterclockwise, center *A* (label it part (e))

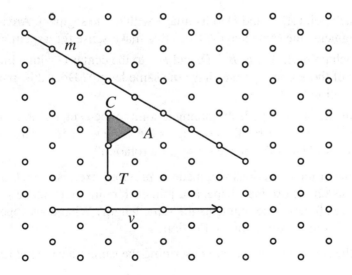

7. Copy the given quadrilateral *ABCD* on dot paper and sketch its image for a translation 6 spaces east. Label the image *A′B′C′D′*, where *A′* is the image of *A*, *B′* of *B*, and so on. Draw the line segments joining *A* and *A′*, *B* and *B′*, *C* and *C′*, and *D* and *D′*. What do you notice? Does this make sense?

8. Using the same ABCD from Learning Exercise 7, sketch its image for a 90° clockwise rotation, using vertex *C* of the quadrilateral as the center of rotation. Label the image *A″B″C″D″*, where *A″* is the image of *A*, *B″* of *B*, and so on.

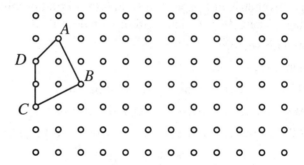

a. Join each point *A*, *B*, and *D* to its image with a line segment. Are all these line segments the same length? Does this make sense for a rotation?

b. Join each point *A*, *A″*, *B*, *B″*, *D*, and *D″* to the center *C* with a line segment. Which of these line segments have the same length? Does this make sense for a rotation?

c. Examine the angles made by joining a point to the center *C* and then to the image of the point. Are all these angles the same size? How large is each of these angles? Does this make sense for a rotation?

9. Examine one of the reflections you made in previous exercises. Pick out three or four points on the original shape, and join each point to its image with a line segment. Are all these line segments the same length? What does appear to be true? Does this make sense for a reflection?

10. Which of the following vectors are describing the same translation? Explain.

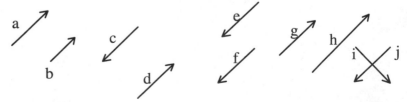

11. A rotation actually affects every point of the plane (imagine a sheet of stiff plastic). Which of the following rotations will have the same effect on every point of the plane? The center in each case is the same. Explain your decision.

    a.   rotation of 90° clockwise

    b.   rotation of 90° counterclockwise

    c.   rotation of 180° clockwise

    d.   rotation of 180° counterclockwise

12. Dot paper has some limitations when you wish to involve only points at the dots as vertices.

    a.   Experiment with square-dot paper to see which reflection lines allow the use of only points at the dots (being able to use the dots makes finding the images easier).

    b.   Experiment with square-dot paper to see which rotations allow the use of only points at the dots (which, again, makes finding the images easier).

    c.   Experiment with isometric paper in ways similar to those in parts (a) and (b).

13. You and a friend are looking at a two-dimensional shape in a plane. Your friend is visualizing where the image of the shape would be for different rigid motions. For the questions that follow, what information would you need so that you could draw the image in the very same place your friend is visualizing it?

    a.   Suppose that your friend is visualizing the image of the given shape for some translation. If you want to draw the image in exactly the spot your friend imagined it, what information about the translation would be essential?

    b.   Suppose that your friend is visualizing the image of a given shape for some reflection. If you want to draw that image in exactly the spot your friend imagined it, what information about the reflection would be essential?

    c.   Suppose that your friend is visualizing the image of a given shape for some rotation. If you want to find that image in exactly the spot your friend imagined it, what information about the rotation would be essential?

22.3 | A Closer Look at Rigid Motions

Some previous exercises should have suggested the following key relationships for the rigid motions we have seen. They are key relationships because, mathematically, knowing how a rigid motion affects each point is the most basic knowledge. In addition, these key relationships give a means of checking the results of rigid motions and of guiding the sketching of images. For someone who has difficulty with visualization, the key relationships give an alternative to strictly visual approaches. These key relationships also help in describing a rigid motion when only a shape and its image are given.

A common notation is to let P' represent the image of point P.

Type of rigid motion	Need to know	Key relationships
Reflection in line m	Line m	Line m is the perpendicular bisector of the line segment joining P and P'.
Rotation of $x°$ with center C	Center C, x, and the clock direction	1. For each point P, the distance from the center C to P is the same as the distance from C to P'. 2. Every $\angle PCP'$ has $x°$.
Translation	Distance and direction, or vector	All segments $\overline{PP'}$ have the same length and are parallel (the length and direction are summarized by the vector).

Activity 4   Practicing the Key Relationships

Using the original shape and its images shown below, illustrate each of the key relationships given in the table above using one or more points. A sample point P and its image P' are shown.

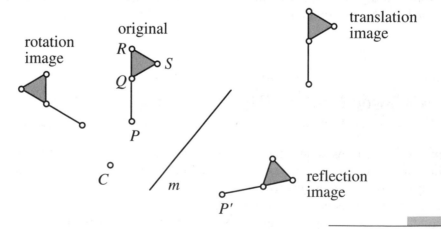

Activity 5   Constructing Images

With a compass and straightedge or tracing paper, construct the images of the given triangle below for the rigid motion described. (*Hint:* It may be a good idea to copy the pertinent parts for each on separate paper, because the drawing will get messy.)

a. a reflection in line *m*

b. a clockwise rotation of $x°$ with center C

c. a translation with vector *v*.

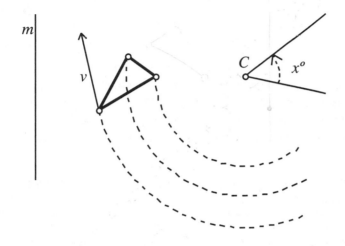

So far, the bulk of the work with rigid motions has involved finding the image given a figure and information about a rigid motion. An important variation is this situation: Given a figure and its image, determine the information needed about the rigid motion involved. The key relationships help in describing a rigid motion *fully*: If the motion is a reflection, the key relationships help to find the line of reflection; if a rotation, the key relationships help to find the center and the angle; and if a translation, they help to find the vector.

THINK ABOUT...

Which rigid motions give image 1 and image 2 below? (Describe the rigid motion fully. For example, if it is a reflection, indicate the line of reflection.)

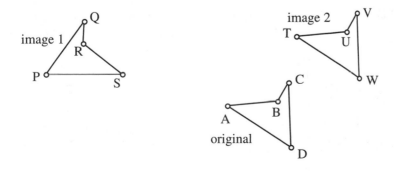

Activity 6   **Another Lost Rigid Motion**

Which rigid motion gives the result shown below? Describe the rigid motion fully. For example, if it is a reflection, indicate the line of reflection.

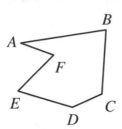

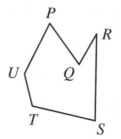

TAKE-AWAY MESSAGE . . . Key relationships for the rigid motions give the underlying mathematical relationships for points and their images. The key relationships also can help in making freehand sketches or constructions of images of shapes. Furthermore, the key relationships can help to locate the full information about an unknown rigid motion. ♦

Learning Exercises for Section 22.3

1. Draw a triangle with a ruler (and not too close to the edge of your paper). Then do the following.

    a. Use the key relationships to draw accurately the image of the triangle, for a translation 3.5 cm east. Write down how you used the key relationships. (*Hint*: Where are the images of the vertices of the triangle?)

    b. Use the key relationships to draw accurately the image of the triangle for a rotation of 90° counterclockwise, with center at your choice of point. Write down how you used the key relationships.

    c. With a new triangle and your choice for line *m*, use the key relationships to draw accurately the image of the triangle for the reflection in line *m*. Write down how you used the key relationships.

2. Trace the given shapes in each part. Then draw accurately the information needed for the motion described. (You may find it helpful to label points and their images.) Tell how you used the key relationships.

    a. The vector for the translation giving the following shape and its image. (Does it matter which shape is the original and which one is the image?)

image

b. The line of reflection for the reflection giving the following shape and its image. (Does it matter which shape is the original and which one is the image?)

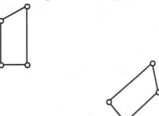

c. The angle and its clock direction for the rotation giving the following shape and its image; measure the angle also. (Does it matter which shape is the original and which one is the image?)

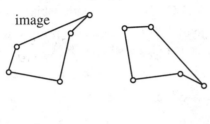

image

o
center

d. The line of reflection for the reflection of hexagon RSTUVW giving the image indicated.

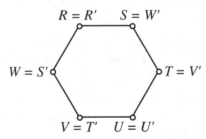

$R = R'$ $S = W'$

$W = S'$ $T = V'$

$V = T'$ $U = U'$

3. The shapes in parts (a)–(e) are different images of the given original shape. Trace the original and the image separately for each part to allow room for work. Identify the rigid motion involved, and then describe the rigid motion fully.

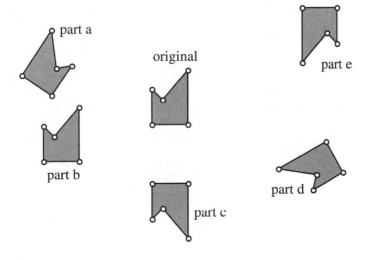

part a

original

part e

part b

part d

part c

4. Notice that in Learning Exercise 2(d), point *R* is its own image. If the image of a point is the point itself, that point is called a **fixed point**. Tell where *all* of the fixed points in the plane are, if there are any, for the following rigid motions.

   a. the reflection in some line *k*

   b. the translation 4 cm north

   c. the rotation with center *C* and angle 55° clockwise (*Hint*: There are more than 0 fixed points.)

   d. the rotation with center *Q* and angle 180°

   e. the rotation with center *M* and angle 360°

5. Copy the given figure and grid.

   a. Show the image of triangular region ABC for a 90° clockwise rotation with center P. Label it A´B´C´. (The key relationships may be helpful.)

   b. Now find the image of A´B´C´ (notice the primes) for a 90° *counter*clockwise rotation with center Q. Label it A´´B´´C´´.

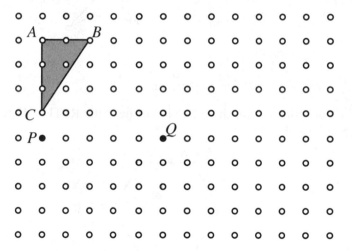

   c. What single rigid motion will give A´´B´´C´´ as the image of the original ABC? Describe it as completely as possible. (For example, if it is a reflection, what would be the line of reflection?)

6. a. If lines *m* and *n* are perpendicular, what is the image of line *n* for a reflection in line *m*?

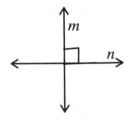

   b. If *k* is the bisector of ∠ABC, what is the image of $\overrightarrow{BA}$ for a reflection in line *k*? The image of $\overrightarrow{BC}$?

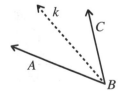

22.4 | Composition of Rigid Motions

Just as 8 and 2 can be *combined* to give another number—possibly 10, 6, 16, or 4, depending on whether the *combining* is done by adding, subtracting, multiplying, or dividing—rigid motions can be *combined* to give another rigid motion. The resulting isometry is called the **composition** of the two rigid motions (just as 16 is called the *product* of 8 and 2, for example).

The diagram in Figure 1 is an example of the composition of these two rigid motions: the translation, move 3 cm east and the reflection in line *k*.

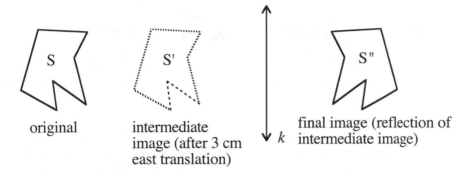

original · intermediate image (after 3 cm east translation) · *k* · final image (reflection of intermediate image)

Figure 1

Although each of these two motions affects every point in the plane, let us focus on shape S. To arrive at the composition of these two rigid motions, first do the translation to get S'. The second motion, the reflection, then *starts* with S' as its original and gives S" as the image of S'.

> The **composition** of two rigid motions is the *single* rigid motion that takes the original S to the final S'.

In this case, it looks as though a reflection in some new line *m*—a different line from line *k*—would give S" as the image of S—that is, the composition of the two given motions would be this single reflection. See Figure 2. (Notice that we use the original line *k* for the reflection and not its translation image, which is not even pictured here.)

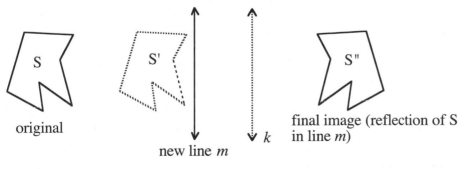

original · new line *m* · *k* · final image (reflection of S in line *m*)

Figure 2

Now let us look at how to express the composition of two rigid motions. Just as we write $8 + 2 = 10$ (or $8 - 2 = 6$, and so on), we could write:

(reflection in line *k*) ° (translation 3 cm east) = (reflection in line *m*).

Notice the order in which the motions are written; this convention is important to observe when working with compositions.

In summary, the composition of two rigid motions is achieved by doing one rigid motion first, and then using the image from that motion as the *original* for the second rigid motion. Whatever motion would be the net effect of that combination on the original is a single motion, the composition of the two rigid motions. Using the symbol ° to represent this way of combining two rigid motions, we can write

(second motion) ° (first motion) = (the composition of the motions).

One helpful way of reading the symbol ° is to pronounce it as *after*. The order of recording the first and second motions may seem backwards, but it is the conventional order in advanced mathematics.

Just as $287 + 95$ can be determined to be 382, a major question is how— or even whether—the composition of two rigid motions can be predicted from only information about the rigid motions. One composition that is of particular value occurs with the composition of a translation and a reflection. For theoretical reasons, the line of reflection must be *parallel* to the line of the vector of the translation, but the distance of the translation, or the length of the vector, can be any length. Suppose the translation is given by vector *v* in Figure 3, and the line of reflection is line *n* (notice that line *n* is parallel to the line the vector is on).

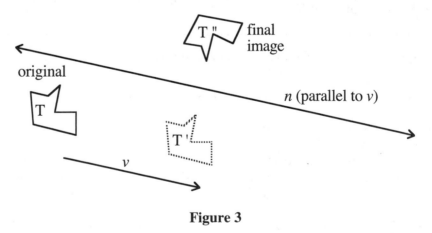

Figure 3

This type of composition has a name: a **glide-reflection.** Notice that the final image T″ is not the image of T for any single reflection, rotation, or translation.

> Whenever a translation and a reflection in a line parallel to the vector of the translation are combined, the resulting composition is a **glide-reflection**.

Glide-reflections are regarded as *single* rigid motions, even though they are defined in terms of two motions. This usage may seem strange, and it opens up the question of which other compositions will have special names. But there is a good reason for identifying glide-reflections. Adding just glide-reflections to the list of types of rigid motions makes the list *complete*. It will not be necessary to add any more types of rigid motions to the list.

Any composition of rigid motions can be described by a *single* reflection, rotation, translation, or glide-reflection.

This last statement takes some time to sink in. It asserts, for example, that the composition of 100 reflections in 100 different lines is the same as a *single* one of the rigid motions. It also assures us that, given any two copies of the same planar figure, one copy can be transformed into the other by a *single* motion.

Activity 7   Composition of Reflections in Two Parallel Lines

Carry out the composition (reflection in *n*) ∘ (reflection in *m*) and form a conjecture as to what type of rigid motion the composition of two reflections in parallel lines might always be.

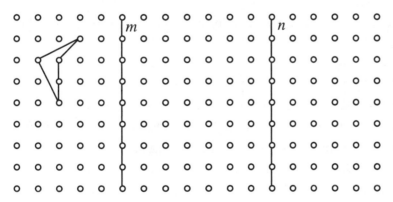

TAKE-AWAY MESSAGE . . . Composition of rigid motions, which is performed by following one motion by another, gives a sort of arithmetic for motions. One type of composition in particular, the glide-reflection, completes the list of rigid motions necessary to describe every composition of rigid motions of the plane. Certain compositions have predictable descriptions as single rigid motions. ♦

Learning Exercises for Section 22.4

1. Make measurements on the example of composition given in Figure 2 to see if there is some relationship between line *k*, line *m*, and the 3 cm east translation.

2. Using your choice of original shape, find the composition of the two rigid motions described in each part. What single rigid motion does the composition seem to be?

   a. (translation, 4 cm east) ° (translation, 2.8 cm west)

   b. (translation, 3 cm northeast) ° (translation, 6 cm southwest)

   c. (reflection in line n) ° (reflection in line m), when lines n and m are parallel

   d. (reflection in line n) ° (reflection in line m), when lines n and m are not parallel

   e. (rotation, center P, $x°$ clockwise) ° (rotation, center P, $y°$ clockwise)

   f. (rotation, center Q, $a°$ clockwise) ° (rotation, center Q, $b°$ counterclockwise)

   g. (rotation, center R, 50° clockwise) ° (rotation, center S, 60° clockwise), where R and S are different points

   h. (rotation, center T, 40° clockwise) ° (reflection in line p), where line p goes through point T

   i. (rotation, center T, 40° clockwise) ° (reflection in line q), where line q does not go through point T

3. **a.** How does a glide-reflection affect the (clockwise or counterclockwise) orientation of a figure?

   b. Summarize how the different types of rigid motions affect the orientation of a figure.

   c. Does a glide-reflection give an image that is congruent to the original shape? Explain your thinking.

4. Using only orientation as a guide, what two types of rigid motions might each of the following possibly be? (*Hint*: See Learning Exercise 3(b).)

   a. The composition of a translation followed by a rotation

   b. The composition of a translation followed by two different reflections

   c. The composition of 4 different reflections in different lines

   d. The composition of 17 different reflections

   e. The composition of an even number of reflections; An odd number of reflections

   f. The composition of 3 different rotations, followed by 7 different translations, followed by 9 different glide-reflections

5. **a.** Copy and find the image of shape U for the glide-reflection given by the translation with vector w and the reflection in line m. Use paper—tracing if you wish.

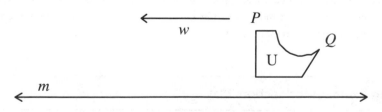

   b. Label the (final) image of P as $P´$ and of Q as $Q´$. With a ruler draw the line segments joining P and $P´$ and joining Q and $Q´$. How does the line of reflection seem to be related to these line segments? Check with other points and their images. This result is a key relationship for a point and its image for a glide-reflection.

6. **a.** In finding the composition of two rigid motions, does it matter in which order the rigid motions are done, in general? Explain.

    b. With the translation and reflection that define a glide-reflection, does it matter in which order the motions are done? Your finding is the reason why glide-reflections are defined in such a particular way.

7. What single type of rigid motion gives each lettered shape as the image of the given one? Describe each of the rigid motions as fully as you can (for example, if it is a reflection, what line is the line of reflection?). Explain how you decided.

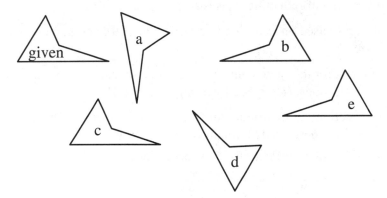

8. For each image of QRST, describe the rigid motion that gives the given image as indicated.

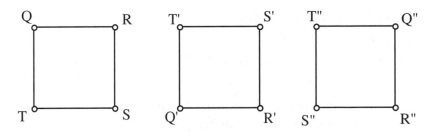

9. Trace the drawing and find two reflections so that their composition will give the same image as the original rigid motion.

    a. This translation

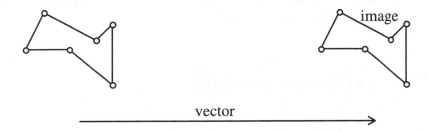

Continue on the next page.

b. This rotation

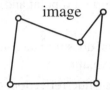

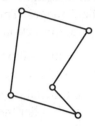

center

c. Find *other* pairs of reflecting lines for parts (a) and (b).

10. Make conjectures based on Learning Exercises 2(c), 2(d), and 9, and then gather more evidence.

11. Give an argument for this statement: Any rigid motion can be accomplished with at most three reflections. (*Hint*: See Learning Exercise 10.)

12. How many reflections, at minimum, might be needed to achieve the same effect as each composition described? Explain your reasoning.
a. A composition of 17 reflections in different lines
b. A composition of 24 reflections in different lines

13. Which rigid motion(s) could be used in describing each situation?
a. footprints in the sand
b. one's right hand in climbing a ladder
c. one's two hands in climbing a ladder
d. turning a microwave dish
e. tuning in a different radio station
f. adjusting a thermostat

14. Does a glide-reflection have any fixed points? That is, is there any point whose image under a glide-reflection is the original point?

15. a. What rigid motion is (reflection in line *k*) ∘ (reflection in line *k*)?
b. What rigid motion is (translate 10 cm north) ∘ (translate 10 cm south)?

16. Experiment to find the single rigid motion equal to the composition of three reflections in parallel lines. Then describe that rigid motion in terms of the original lines (make some measurements on the original lines).

22.5 | Transformations and Earlier Topics

Now that we have all the categories of rigid motions of the plane, we can review congruence, symmetry, tessellations, and similarity, discussing their relation to the types of transformations. Although many of the relationships carry over to three-dimensional geometry, we will work only with two dimensions here because most of our transformation geometry has been in two dimensions, with rigid motions (translations, rotations, reflections, glide-reflections) and with size transformations (size changes).

Congruence of two shapes, defined earlier as some rigid motion that gives one of the shapes as the image of the other, continues to hold, even when glide-reflections are involved. Do you see why?

Discussion 1   Each Part...

Without looking at an example, explain why a shape and its glide-reflection image must be congruent. (*Hint:* What is a glide-reflection?)

The symmetries we studied earlier were either reflection symmetries or rotational symmetries, so a natural question is: *Are there figures that have translation or glide-reflection symmetries?*

Discussion 2   A Long, Long Trail

Describe the reflections and rotations that are symmetries of each of the following figures. (Both patterns continue indefinitely.) Look for translations and/or glide-reflections that are also symmetries of the figures.

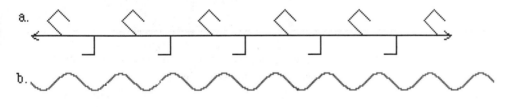

From Discussion 2 we see that each type of rigid motion is a candidate for being a symmetry of a figure. Symmetries of figures are special cases of transformations.

Tessellations too can be viewed with transformations (and congruence and symmetry) in mind.

Discussion 3   What Isometries?

Keeping in mind that tessellations continue indefinitely, describe some rigid motions that give the same pattern for each of the tessellations suggested in the following two figures. Look for translations and glide-reflections as well as reflections and rotations.

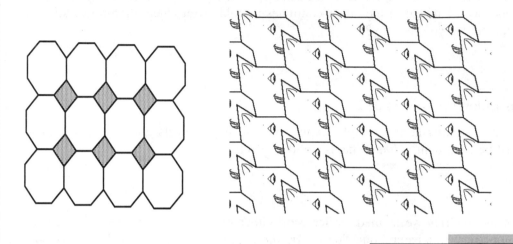

Rigid motions cannot themselves account for enlargements or reductions, of course. Size transformations must be involved if there is a change in size. The terms *similarity* and *similar figures* allow the composition of a size transformation and any rigid motion.

> Two figures are **similar figures** if one is the image of the other under (1) a
>
> size transformation or (2) the composition of a size transformation and a rigid
>
> motion.

Rigidly moving an image after a size change does not negate the similarity; it just makes it more difficult to find the center of the size change. Fortunately, in most work with similar figures, the facts that all the ratios of pairs of corresponding lengths equal the scale factor and corresponding angles are the same size, are of greater importance than the location of the center of the size change.

Recall that for triangles there is a simple test for similarity: Two triangles are similar if *two* angles in one have the same sizes as two angles in the other. How can that be? A moment's thought makes clear that the third pair of angles must also have the same size because the sizes of the three angles in every triangle add to 180°. But how does having two pairs of angles the same size make certain that there is a size transformation? The following sketches give one way to convince yourself that there will be a size transformation relating two similar triangles that are not congruent. (Do you remember how to find the scale factor before you have the center?)

Notes

Two triangles with two pairs of angles having the same size.

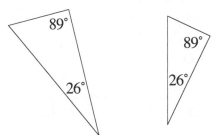

Rotate one triangle so the two sides of one angle are parallel to the sides of the corresponding angle in the other triangle.

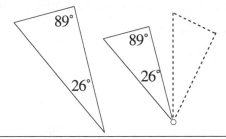

Join corresponding vertices to locate the center of the size transformation. (Can you find the scale factor another way now?)

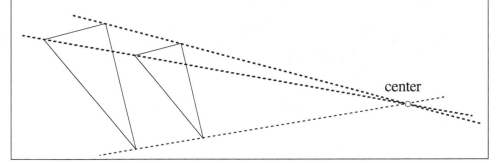

Other situations might involve a reflection rather than a rotation.

Discussion 4   And in Space?

Can three-dimensional congruence, similarity, symmetry, and tessellations also be treated by a study of three-dimensional transformations?

TAKE-AWAY MESSAGE . . . The usual secondary school topics of two-dimensional similarity and congruence, as well as symmetry and tessellations, can be treated in a very general fashion with transformations. ◆

Notes

Learning Exercises for Section 22.5

1. Describe all the symmetries possible in each diagram. (An arrow means the pattern continues.)

   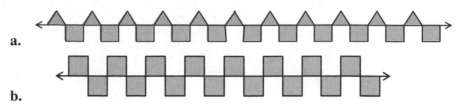

   a.

   b.

2. Examine both statements given in each part. Is each statement true? Explain your decisions.

   a. If a shape has translation symmetry, then the shape is infinite.

   If a shape is infinite, then the shape has translation symmetry.

   b. If a shape has glide-reflection symmetry, then the shape is infinite.

   If a shape is infinite, then the shape has glide-reflection symmetry.

3. Which types of symmetry does each 2D shape have?

   a. a line segment   **b.** a ray   **c.** a line   **d.** an angle

4. Design a figure that has translation symmetry. Does your figure also have glide-reflection symmetry?

5. Which transformations are symmetries for the tessellations given by the following (infinite) patterns?

   a.

   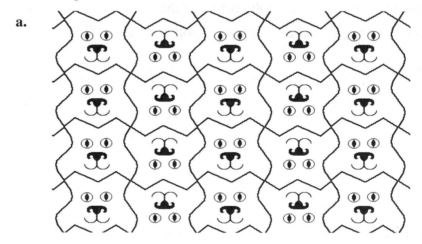

   b. 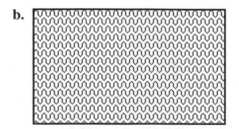   **c.**

Notes

d.

6. Information is given about angle sizes in the following four triangles. Which of the triangles, if any, are similar? Explain how you know.

   Triangle a: 65° and 32°   Triangle b: 65° and 35°

   Triangle c: 35° and 80°   Triangle d: 65° and 83°

7. Describe the image of a shape under the composition of a size transformation with scale factor 1 and a rotation of $x°$, both with the same center.

8. Use the meaning of congruence from the transformation view to answer these.

   a. If Shape 1 is congruent to Shape 2, then is Shape 2 congruent to Shape 1? Explain.

   b. Is every shape congruent to itself? Explain.

   c. If Shape 1 is congruent to Shape 2 and Shape 2 is congruent to Shape 3, is Shape 1 congruent to Shape 3? Explain.

9. Use the meaning of similarity from the transformation view to answer these.

   a. If Shape 1 is Similar to Shape 2, is Shape 2 similar to Shape 1? Explain.

   b. Is every shape similar to itself? Explain.

   c. If Shape 1 is similar to Shape 2 and Shape 2 is similar to Shape 3, is Shape 1 similar to Shape 3? Explain.

10. If it is possible, give an example of two triangles such that each pair of matching angles is the same size, but the triangles are not congruent. Must the two triangles be similar? Explain.

11. Discuss each diagram or description with transformations, symmetries, and tessellations in mind.

    a.

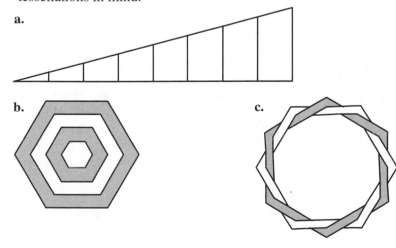

    b.   **c.**

Notes

d. any wallpaper design that is handy

12. Draw two quadrilaterals to show that having all four pairs of corresponding angles the same size is not enough to ensure that the quadrilaterals are similar.

13. (*Pattern Blocks*—See Appendix G if you do not have access to Pattern Blocks themselves.) Show patterns that would have different kinds of symmetry. (Don't forget translational and glide-reflection symmetries.)

22.6 Check Yourself

You should be able to work problems like those assigned and to meet the following objectives.

1.   Name the four types of isometries in the plane and, given a figure and its image, identify which isometry is involved.

2.   Locate the image of a point or figure for given isometry(ies), by using rough but accurate sketches (using key relationships as well as visualization). You may be directed by your instructor to use tracing paper, dot paper, a MIRA, or compass-straightedge constructions.

3.   State and apply key facts about each type of isometry.

4.   Given a figure and its image, identify the type of isometry involved, perhaps using orientation as an aid. In some cases, you may then be asked to give a full description for the transformation. (For example, if a translation is involved, what is its vector?)

5.   Tell what a glide-reflection is.

6.   Illustrate what *the composition of two motions* means, and find the (final) image of a given figure for a composition of given transformations.

7.   Recognize symmetries, including translation symmetries and glide-reflection symmetries, of given figures, and draw a figure that has translation and/or glide-reflection symmetry.

8.   Illustrate and give essential features of *similar figures*.

REFERENCE FOR CHAPTER 22

From Burns, M., & Tank, B. (1988). *A collection of math lessons: From Grade 1 through 3*. Math Solutions Publications.

Chapter 23

Measurement Basics

Of all the occurrences of numbers in daily life, most of them will involve measurements, particularly if you include monetary values. If counts are also included as measurements (as they are in advanced mathematics), virtually all uses of numbers involve measurements. Many types of measurements share certain characteristics or key ideas. We identify these key ideas of measurement in Section 23.1. Although we have regarded length and angle size as familiar concepts in earlier chapters, we will also look at them from the key-ideas-of-measurement viewpoint in Section 23.2.

23.1 | Key Ideas of Measurement

A given object has several characteristics, many of which we can quantify. For example, a particular woman has an age, a height, a shoe size, a blood pressure, a hair color, a certain amount of self-discipline, some degree of athleticism or degree of friendliness, and many other characteristics. Some characteristics are relatively easy to quantify, whereas others are not.

Finding the values of quantities associated with characteristics of objects or events often involves measurement. The term *measurement* may refer to the *process* of finding the value of a quantity, or it may refer to the *result* of that process. For instance, the measurement of the weight of an object might refer to how we measured the weight (for example, with a pan balance) or to the resulting value (for example, 18 pounds). This section covers four key features of the usual kinds of measurement, which are summarized in the Take-Away Message at the end of the section.

First our focus is on the process of measurement, particularly *direct measurement*. The **process of direct measurement** of a characteristic involves matching that characteristic of the object by using (often repeatedly) a **unit**, which is a different object having the same characteristic. The unknown weight of an object, for example, might be determined on a pan balance by directly matching it with copies or partial copies of a known unit weight. The measurement (the result) is the number of units needed to match the measured object with respect to the characteristic being measured. The measurement is the value of the quantity.

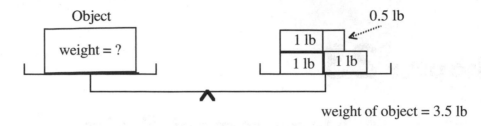

weight of object = 3.5 lb

Measuring devices like the pan balance are often used for measuring weight, although one could roughly measure the unknown weight even more directly by hefting the object in one hand and then adding copies of the unit weight in the other hand until the weight in each hand felt the same. **Indirect measurements** of quantities involve mathematical or scientific principles, such as in determining a weight with the usual bathroom scale or a scale with a spring that compresses or stretches predictably according to Hooke's law.

Discussion 1   Why Standard Units?

1. We usually use **standard units** when giving values of quantities. For example, the English system includes the ounce, pound, ton, inch, yard, mile, and so forth, and the metric system uses the gram, kilogram, metric ton, centimeter, meter, kilometer, and so forth. Why are standard units used?

2. Why are there so many different units for the same characteristic, even within one system of measurement? For example, the English system has the units ounce, pound, and ton for measuring weight.

3. Elementary school curricula often start measuring work with nonstandard units. For example, lengths might be measured with crayons or markers. Why? (Keep in mind the process of measurement.)

Most of the world uses the **metric system**, or **SI** (from *Le Système International d'Unités*). Thus it is surprising that the United States, as a large industrial nation, has clung to the English system. Although the general public has not always responded favorably to governmental efforts to mandate the metric system, international trade is forcing us to be knowledgeable about, and to use, the metric system. Some of the largest U.S. industries have been the first to convert to the metric system from the English system.

Discussion 2   Influences on the Choice of Standard Units

Why has the U.S. public resisted adopting wholeheartedly the metric system? Why do international trade and alliances influence our measurements?

Scientists have long worked almost exclusively in metric units. Part of the reason is that virtually the entire world uses the metric system, but the main reason is how sensible and systematic the metric system is. A basic metric unit is carefully defined (for the sake of permanence and later reproducibility), and larger units and smaller sub-units are related to each other in a consistent fashion (making the system easy to work in). In contrast, the English system's units are neither well defined (historically) nor consistently related. For example, the length unit *foot* possibly evolved from the lengths of human feet and is related to other length units in an inconsistent manner: 1 foot = 12 inches; 1 yard = 3 feet; 1 rod = 16.5 feet; 1 mile = 5280 feet; 1 furlong = $\frac{1}{8}$ mile; 1 fathom = 6 feet. Quick!—how many rods are in a mile? A comparable question in the metric system is just a matter of adjusting a decimal point.

The basic SI unit for length (or its synonyms) is the **meter**. (The official SI spelling is **metre**. You occasionally see *metre* in U.S. books.) The meter is too long to show with a line segment here, but two subunits fit easily and illustrate a key feature of the metric system: units smaller and larger than the basic unit are multiples or submultiples of powers of 10.

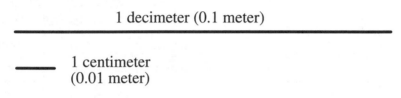

Furthermore, these subunits have names, such as *decimeter* and *centimeter*, and are consistently formed by putting a prefix on the word for the basic unit. The prefix *deci-* means 0.1, so *decimeter* means 0.1 meter. Similarly, *centi-* means 0.01, so *centimeter* means 0.01 meter. You have probably heard the word *kilometer*. The prefix *kilo-* means 1000, so *kilometer* means 1000 meters. Reversing your thinking, you can see that 10 decimeters are in 1 meter, 100 centimeters are in 1 meter, and 1 meter is 0.001 kilometer.

Two asides are in order. First, the small cubes in base ten materials often have edges of length 1 centimeter, and the longs are often 1 decimeter long. A meter stick is, of course, 1 meter long, which is slightly more than 1 yard. Second, for pronunciation of units in SI, the United States Metric Association advocates, for consistency, that the accent be on the first syllable: KILL-a-meter, not ki-LOM-ater. (Does anyone pronounce *kilogram* as ki-LOG-ram?) Common usage and some dictionaries, how-ever, do use the non-preferred pronunciation.

An important advantage of SI is the consistent combination of the symbols for the basic units and the prefixes. In the case of the characteric length, the use of the sym-bol m (for meter) along with a symbol for a prefix (such as d for deci-, c for centi-, and so on) allows us to report a length measurement quite concisely: for example, 18 cm or 1.8 dm. Many of the SI prefixes are given in Table 1 on the next page; more are given in the Glossary. You should note that the symbols for the metric units do not end with periods (a convention which is also true for most of the unit abbre-viations in the English system), and the same symbols are used for singular and plural. For example, m stands for meter and meters, and yd stands for yard and yards. In the English system the exception for not using a period is the abbreviation for inch (in.).

Metric Prefix	Metric Symbol	Meaning of Prefix		Applied to Length
tera-	T	1 000 000 000 000	or 10^{12}	Tm
giga-	G	1 000 000 000	or 10^{9}	Gm
mega-	M	1 000 000	or 10^{6}	Mm
kilo-	k	1 000	or 10^{3}	km
hecto-	h	100	or 10^{2}	hm
deka-	da	10	or 10^{1}	dam
(no prefix)		(basic unit) 1	or 10^{0}	m
deci-	d	0.1	or 10^{-1}	dm
centi-	c	0.01	or 10^{-2}	cm
milli-	m	0.001	or 10^{-3}	mm
micro-	μ	0.000001	or 10^{-6}	μm
nano-	n	0.000000001	or 10^{-9}	nm

Table 1. Metric prefixes

If you are new to the metric system, your first job will be to master the prefixes so you can apply them to the basic units for other characteristics. You may know a mnemonic for several of the metric prefixes. For example, the phrase "<u>k</u>ing <u>h</u>enry <u>da</u>nced, <u>d</u>rinking <u>c</u>hocolate <u>m</u>ilk" (although not using good capitalization) does give the most common metric prefixes. The table above shows some of the other metric prefixes. For example, *kilo-* means 1000, so 1 kilometer means 1000 meters; the symbol k for *kilo-* combined with the symbol m for *meter* give the symbol km for *kilometer*.

Here is one final note on SI: Commas are not used in writing numbers. Where we write commas in multidigit numbers, SI would have us put spaces. So 13,438 m would be written as 13 438 m, and 0.84297 km would be written as 0.842 97 km. Some countries use the comma where we use the decimal point, so some agreement is necessary to avoid potential confusions in international trade and other communication. This SI recommendation is not observed in all U.S. elementary school textbooks, however.

Activity 1   It's All in the Unit

1. Measure the width of your desk or table in decimeters. Express that length in centimeters, millimeters, meters, and kilometers.

2. Measure the width of your desk or table in feet. Express that length in inches, yards, and miles.

3. In which system are conversions easier? Explain why.

The next discussion introduces another key idea of measurement.

Discussion 3   Are Measurements Exact?

Only one of these statements can be true. Determine which one is true, and explain why is it the only one.

a. "She weighed exactly 148 pounds."

b. "She is exactly 165 centimeters tall."

c. "It is exactly 93,000,000 miles to the sun."

d. "There were exactly 5 people at the meeting."

Because actual measurements (except for counts) are only approximations, a given value should not be read to imply that it is more nearly exact than is reasonable. For example, the value 38 pounds implies that the measuring was done only *to the nearest pound*. Thus a reported "38 pounds" might describe a weight that is actually greater than or equal to $37\frac{1}{2}$ pounds and

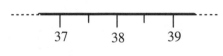

less than $38\frac{1}{2}$ pounds. Deducing that the value 38 pounds is exactly $38 \times 16 = 608$ ounces would be risky. In actuality, the object could be as light as 600 ounces ($37\frac{1}{2} \times 16$) or as heavy as just under 616 ounces ($38\frac{1}{2} \times 16$).

Discussion 4   Interpreting a Measurement Given "to the Nearest"

Suppose a length is reported as $2\frac{3}{4}$ inches, to the nearest $\frac{1}{4}$ inch.

Make a drawing of part of a ruler and argue that the length could be as short as $2\frac{5}{8}$ inches or as long as just under $2\frac{7}{8}$ inches.

Unfortunately, much school work with measurement treats the values as exact, so students can easily form the erroneous impression that the values *are* exact. But just as the ideal constructs of *line segment* and *angle* can be discussed, theoretically perfect measurements can also be discussed. For example, we can *imagine* a square with sides exactly 2 centimeters long, although drawing one even with a finely sharpened pencil is not possible. Likewise, we can *imagine* a line segment with length exactly 2 cm although we cannot actually produce one.

Which of these two ways would give a better measurement for the length of a board: measuring to the nearest inch or measuring to the nearest foot? In a direct measurement, choosing the smaller unit naturally allows the matching to be done more closely. So, usually a measurement with a smaller unit narrows the range of possible values for the measurement and lessens the error.

The numerical part of the value, however, can also imply something about the precision of the measurement. Suppose you have these measurements, all reported for the length of the same object: 2.75 feet, 2 feet 9 inches, and 33.0 inches. Which measurement is most precise, or are all three the same? At first glance, they seem to be exactly the same. But a measurement given as, say, 2.75 feet is implying that the measurement was carried out to the nearest one-hundredth of a foot, so it would be more precise than a measurement reported as 2 feet, 9 inches, which implies that the measurement was carried out only to the nearest inch (or one-twelfth of a foot). On the other hand, 33.0 inches would imply that the measurement was accurate to the nearest one-tenth of an inch (or $\frac{1}{120}$ of a foot). So, 33.0 inches would be the best approximation of the measurements 2.75 feet, 2 feet 9 inches, and 33.0 inches.

Discussion 5   Measuring Piecemeal

How can you find the distance from Anyburg to Dayville and the area of the z-shaped region?

Your method in Discussion 5 likely involved another key idea of measurement: You can measure an object by thinking of the object as cut into pieces, measuring each piece, and then adding those measurements.

TAKE-AWAY MESSAGE . . . Here is a summary of four key ideas of measurement.

1. (Direct) measurement of a characteristic of an object involves matching the object with a unit, or copies of a unit, having that characteristic. The matching should be based on the characteristic. The number of units, along with the unit, give the measurement, or the value, of the quantity associated with the characteristic.

2. Standard units are used because they are relatively permanent and enable communication over time and distance. Nonstandard units may be used in schools to allow a focus on the process of measurement.

3. Measurements are approximate. Smaller units give better approximations, although the numerical part of a reported value can have a bearing on the implied accuracy as well. (If we include counts as measurements, however, they can be exact.)

4. A quantity can be measured by thinking of the object being measured as "cut" into a (finite) number of pieces, measuring the quantity in each piece, and then adding up those measurements or values. ♦

Notes

Learning Exercises for Section 23.1

1. Some quantities that are commonly measured include length, area, volume, weight, speed, time, temperature, intelligence, student achievement, force.

   Which of the above quantities are you measuring when you measure the following quantities?

   a. how far two people are apart

   b. how much soda is in a glass

   c. how warm is the lake water

   d. how heavy is a football

   e. how much room is left to draw on, on a piece of paper

   f. how fast you can run

   g. how long it takes to walk to school

   h. how large is a football field

   i. how much carpet is needed for a room

   j. how effective is a teacher

2. What are some possible units for the quantities listed in Learning Exercise 1?

3. What characteristics of a child could be measured with the given device?

   a. a thermometer

   b. the child's math book

   c. a stop-watch

4. For which quantities could each term or phrase be a unit? (A dictionary can be useful for some items.)

   a. mm of mercury   **b.** number per square mile   **c.** acre

   d. quire   **e.** hectare   **f.** cubit

   g. candela   **h.** stone   **i.** coulomb

   j. rating point (TV)   **k.** decibel   **l.** Scoville

   m. body mass index (BMI)   **n.** section

5. Why would each of the following items *not* be satisfactory as a unit for the given quantity?

   a. a rubber band, for length   **b.** an ice cube, for weight

   c. a garage-sale item, for monetary value   **d.** a person's judgment, for temperature

   e. a pinch of salt, for saltiness   **f.** a sip, for amount of drink

6. Answer the following items about reports of measurements.

   a. Explain why this claim cannot be accurate: "The fish I caught was exactly 18 inches long!"

   b. "The fish weighed 123 pounds." What weights for the fish are possible and still have the claim be a true statement?

7. **a.** Show the shortest and longest lengths that could be reported as 7 units using the ruler.

| 1 | 2 | 3 | 4 | 5 | 6 | 7 | 8 | 9 | 10 | 11 | 12 | 13 | 14 |

b. Show the shortest and longest lengths that could be reported as 7.5 units using this ruler.

| 1 | 2 | 3 | 4 | 5 | 6 | 7 | 8 | 9 | 10 | 11 | 12 | 13 | 14 |

8. One kind of bathroom scale shows weights to the nearest half-pound.

   a. On consecutive days, a person's readings were 151.0 and 151.0 on the scale. Did the person weigh exactly the same amount each day? Explain.

   b. What weights would all give a reading of 162.0 on the scale?

   c. What weights would all give a reading of 128.5 on the scale?

   d. How much "off" could a reading of 116.0 be, on the scale? A reading of 223.5?

9. In parts (a)–(h) tell without calculating whether x is greater than 2000, equal to 2000, or less than 2000. Explain your thinking.

   a. x raisins weigh 2000 pounds   **b.** 2000 raisins weigh x pounds

   c. x yards = 2000 miles   **d.** 2000 yards = x miles

   e. x kilometers = 2000 meters   **f.** 2000 kilometers = x meters

   g. x tons = 2000 pounds   **h.** 2000 tons = x pounds

10. In parts (a)–(c), tell which of the made-up units is larger. Tell how you know.

   a. 150 ags = 100 aps   **b.** 260 bas = 1.31×10^3 bos

   c. 0.19 cons = 0.095 cins

11. Tell how one of the four key ideas of measurement could be used in determining the weight of a wiggly puppy.

12. Give the number of unit square regions there are in each figure. Explain your reasoning, especially how you used key ideas of measurement.

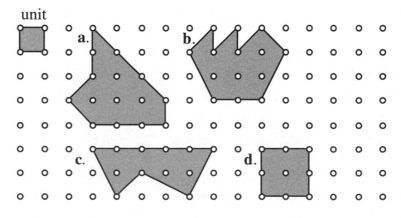

e. Let the unit region be the region shown in Figure (d). What would be the values for the number of units in Figures (a), (b), and (c)? Explain your reasoning.

13. Sections of low picket fence come ready-made and cost $2.89 for a section 27
inches long. How much would it cost to put a fence along the borders of a flower
patch shaped like the drawing below? (What key idea or ideas of measurement
did you use?)

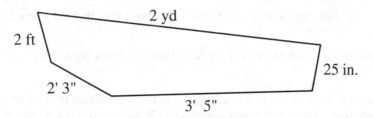

2 yd

2 ft

2' 3"

25 in.

3' 5"

14. a. Add these lengths: $5\frac{3}{4}$ inches, $7\frac{7}{8}$ inches, and $3\frac{1}{2}$ inches.

b. Make pieces of rulers (like the one below for $5\frac{3}{4}$ inches) for each measurement given in part (a). Then show where the shortest and the longest lengths
that could be described as $5\frac{3}{4}$ inches (or $7\frac{7}{8}$ inches or $3\frac{1}{2}$ inches) would end.

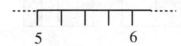

5   6

c. Add the *least* lengths that each of the measurements in part (a) could be
describing.

d. Add the *greatest* lengths that each of the measurements in part (a) could be
describing.

e. What is the range of values possible for the sum of the measurements in
part (a)?

15. One teacher's gradebook computer program shows scores to the nearest whole
point but keeps several decimal places in its memory. Use that information to
explain why the gradebook program might give a sum of 241 for scores of 82,
73, and 87.

16. Think of the sizes of the units (think metric) to help you complete the following
equalities of measurements.

a. 76.3 cm = _____ m   **b.** 2.7 m = _____ cm

c. 19 mm = _____ cm   **d.** 4.62 cm = _____ mm

e. 0.62 km = _____ m   **f.** 108 m = _____ km

g. 8.7 dm = _____ cm   **h.** 29 cm = _____ dm

i. A person 155 cm tall is _____ meters tall.

17. For some purposes, 1 second (1 s) of time is too large a unit. Fast computers, for
example, need nanoseconds to describe times. Review the metric prefixes and
complete the following.

a. ____ ms = 1.3 s   **b.** 143 ns = ____ s

c. 500 ms = ____ s   **d.** 2500 μs = ____ s

18. For historical reasons, the kilogram, rather than the gram, is the metric system's basic unit for mass. A raisin has a mass of about 1 gram (1 g). Complete the following conversions.

   a. 153.2 g = ___ kg   **b.** 3.4 g = ____ mg

   c. 2.17 kg = ____ g   **d.** 56 mg = ____ g

19. A map has the scale 1 000 000 : 1.

   a. In reality, how far apart in kilometers are two cities that are 8 cm apart on the map?

   b. Two locations that are actually 150 kilometers apart should be how far apart on the map?

20. Sometimes one can measure something by cutting it into an *infinite* number of pieces and then adding the measurements of all the pieces. What will the following infinite sum equal?

$$\frac{1}{2} + \frac{1}{4} + \frac{1}{8} + \frac{1}{16} + \ldots = ?$$ (*Hint*: Use the diagrams for an idea.)

             and so on

21. When the French were designing the metric system in the late 1700s, they invited other countries to participate. England said that "reform of weights and measures was considered 'almost impracticable'."[i] Why would anyone think that?

22. Decide whether each calculation is correct. Correct any calculation that is not correct. (*Recall*: 1 pound (lb) = 16 ounces (oz) and 1 gallon = 4 quarts.)

   a. $\overset{4}{\cancel{5}}.^{1}05$ m
        − 3 . 52 m
        ————
        1 . 53 m

   b. $\overset{4}{\cancel{5}} : ^{1}05$ p.m.
        − 3 : 5 2 p.m.
        ————
        1 : 5 3 p.m.

   c. $\overset{5}{\cancel{6}}$ lbs $^{1}3$ oz
        − 2 lbs 8 oz
        ————
        3 lbs 5 oz

   d. $\overset{5}{\cancel{6}}.^{1}3$ kg
        − 2 . 8 kg
        ————
        3 . 5 kg

   e. $\overset{3}{\cancel{4}}$ gal $^{1}1$ qt
        −   9 qt
        ————
        3 gal 2 qt

   f. $\overset{1}{2}$ hr $\overset{1}{35}$ min
        +   75 min
        ————
        3 hr 10 min

23. The following lists examples of nonmetric length units used in England at different times or in different settings:

   cubit, rod, ell, fathom, foot, furlong, hand, inch, knot, mile, pace, yard

   With those units in mind, describe one advantage of using the metric system approach to length units over the English system.

24. In earlier times in England, the following were units for measuring volume:[i]

2 mouthfuls	=	1 jigger
2 jiggers	=	1 jackpot
2 jackpots	=	1 gill
2 gills	=	1 cup
2 cups	=	1 pint
2 pints	=	1 quart
2 quarts	=	1 pottle
2 pottles	=	1 gallon
2 gallons	=	1 peck
2 pecks	=	1 half-bushel
2 half-bushels	=	1 bushel
2 bushels	=	1 cask
2 casks	=	1 barrel
2 barrels	=	1 hogshead
2 hogsheads	=	1 pipe
2 pipes	=	1 tun

   a. How many cups are in a gallon?

   b. Express each unit in terms of quarts.

   c. What feature of this system of volume units is somewhat like those of the metric system? What feature is different?

25. In 1893 the U.S. yard unit was defined to be equal to $\frac{3600}{3937}$ meter. Then in 1959 it was defined as 0.9144 meter. By how much did the new foot differ from the old foot?

26. (*Computer*) Two Websites that focus on measurement are given. Browse the sites to see what they offer.

   a. U. S. Metric Association—http://lamar.ColoState.edu/~hillger/

   b. National Institute of Standards and Technology (until 1988, the National Bureau of Standards)—http://nist.gov. You might settle on http://physics.nist.gov/GenInt/contents.html.

23.2 Length and Angle Size

Although we have treated length and angle size as familiar, they can also be looked at from the viewpoint of the key ideas of measurement. The basic classroom tools for measuring length and angle size are the ruler and the protractor. Children often use (simple) rulers as early as the first grade; they learn about protractors later, perhaps in Grade 5.

Length

We speak of the length of a piece of wire or a rectangle in two ways. The term *length* might refer to the quality or attribute we are focusing on, or it might refer to the measurement of that quality. The context usually makes clear which reference is intended.

However, what might be puzzling to elementary school students is that there are several terms, all of which refer to the *length* attribute of different objects.

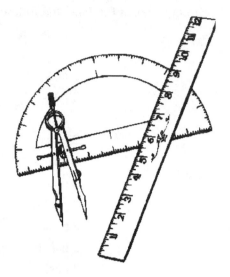

Discussion 6   Aliases for Length

Height and *width* are words that refer to lengths. What other terms refer to the same attribute as *length* does?

All the key ideas of measurement from Section 23.1 are useful in working with length. For example, early work in elementary grades often involves nonstandard units—paper clips, chains of plastic links, or pencils.

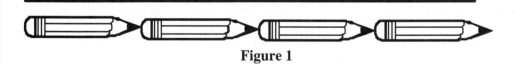

Figure 1

You should keep the approximate nature of measurements in mind. The heavy line segment shown in Figure 1 is about 4 "pencils" long, because four copies of the (same) pencil unit just about match the length of the line segment. If we measured to the nearest *half*-pencil, the measurement here would still be 4 pencils, and so we could say "4 pencils, to the nearest half-pencil" to communicate the greater precision.

The meter and the metric prefixes from the metric system give a variety of length units. If you have never established personal comparisons, or benchmarks, for some of the metric units, you should begin to do so. What does approximately 1 millimeter, 1 centimeter, 1 decimeter, 1 meter, and 1 kilometer mean to you? For many people, the width of a particular fingernail is a good benchmark for 1 cm.

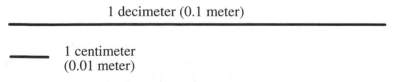

1 decimeter (0.1 meter)

1 centimeter
(0.01 meter)

Estimating measurements is a very practical skill that is often neglected in school. Having benchmarks for units can help in estimating, say, the width of a room in meters or the perimeter of a piece of paper in decimeters.

The length of a polygon is usually called its **perimeter** (*peri-* means around; *metron* means measure). (Recall that a polygon is made up of just the line segments.)

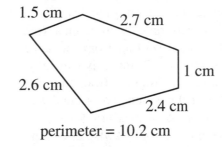

1.5 cm   2.7 cm   1 cm   2.6 cm   2.4 cm

perimeter = 10.2 cm

THINK ABOUT...

What key idea of measurement is often involved in finding the perimeter of a polygon?

The length of a circle is usually called its **circumference** (*circum-* means around; *ferre* means to carry). In everyday language, both *perimeter* and *circumference* may be used to refer to the sets of points, as well as the length measurement.

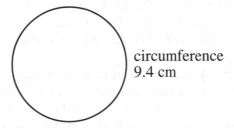

circumference 9.4 cm

Measuring the lengths of crooked curves presents difficulties. With short curves we can do the practical thing: Place a flexible measuring tape or a piece of string closely on the curve and then straighten out the tape or string and measure it. There are also small, wheeled devices that can be used to trace over a route on a map to find measurements of lengths. You may have seen an auto accident scene where a trundle wheel (a device made of a wheel) was used to measure distances.

One way to find lengths of curves that pays off is to approximate the curve by line segments and then observe what happens each time as smaller and smaller line segments are used. As all the segments get smaller and smaller, getting as close to zero length as you arbitrarily want, the sum of the lengths of all the line segments will get closer and closer to the (ideal) exact length of the curve. (Not only is this process plausible, it is also applied in the study of calculus.)

Figure 2

In Figure 2, the shorter segments in the drawing on the right should give a better approximation of the length of the curve than the segments in the drawing on the left.

Angles and Angle Size

Let us turn our attention to angles and their measurement. As you may know, angles can be viewed in two different ways—(1) statically, as two rays or segments (the **sides** of the angle) starting from the same point (the **vertex**) or (2) more dynamically, as the result of a ray rotating from an initial position to a final position. The second way allows you to speak of measuring angles in a clockwise or counter-clockwise direction.

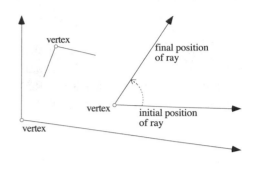

Which of the two angles shown to the right is larger? The size of an angle is determined by the opening, or the amount of rotation, or turn, involved in the angle. So the first angle has greater size. The visible length of the sides of the angle is irrelevant.

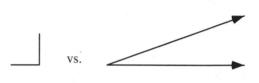

The key ideas of measurement also apply to the measurement of angle size, of course. The standard unit used in the K–8 curriculum is the **degree** (°). Across the world, societies that were advanced enough to study astronomy, such as the Mesopotamians (in what is now Iraq) and the Mayans (in what is now Mexico and Central America), knew that there were about 365 days in a solar year, and they settled on 360 as a good number with which to define a unit for angle size. Hence, a full turn of a ray about its vertex goes through 360° (a circle has 360°). Choosing 360° for a full turn means that the degree is a fairly small unit. However, for angles used in ocean navigation or astronomy, even a degree is too large a unit. To obtain smaller units, each degree can be divided into 60 equal pieces, with each piece called a **minute** ('). Each minute can then be further divided into 60 **seconds** ("). (Notice that *minute* and *second* are the same words and relationships used with time, but here are about angle size.) The metric system recognizes the degree as a unit, but the more official SI unit is called the **radian** (about 57.3°). Radians do not usually appear until high school trigonometry, where assigning positive and negative signs to angle measurements to indicate counter-clockwise and clockwise turns, respectively, also appears.

Because the degree is a relatively small unit, you could use a nonstandard unit larger than a degree, as illustrated in Figure 3, for introductory classroom work with angle-size measurement. In the drawing the size of angle X is approximately $4\frac{1}{2}$ units, and we could write $m(\angle X) = 4\frac{1}{2}$ *units,* where the letter m stands for the measurement of the angle. Indeed, rather than saying *size of the angle*, we could say *measure of the angle*.

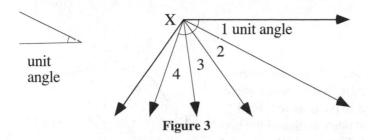

Figure 3

As you know, the usual classroom protractor shows 180°, the size of a half-turn. If you wish to measure an angle whose size is greater than 180°—for example, the counterclockwise angle shown in the following sketch—you might think of the given angle as divided into two angles: the 180° angle and a smaller angle. Measuring the smaller angle with the protractor then enables you to tell the size of the whole angle, which is 209°.

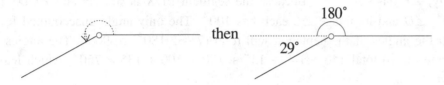

THINK ABOUT...

Do you see another way to use the protractor to get the size of the counter-clockwise angle?

You already know some important results about angle measurements. For example, the sizes of two supplementary angles add to 180°. And the sum of the sizes of the angles in any triangle is 180°. This last result leads to the more general result for n-gons: The sum of the sizes of the angles of an n-gon is $(n-2)180°$. So, for example, the sizes of the 8 angles in any octagon add up to $(8-2)180°$, or 1080°.

THINK ABOUT...

How could you show that each angle in an *equiangular* octagon has 135°?

Several ideas about lengths or angle sizes can be involved in a single problem. For example, recall how corresponding lengths and angle sizes are related in congruent polygons and polyhedra or in similar polygons and polyhedra. With congruent polygons and polyhedra, corresponding lengths are equal, as are the sizes of corresponding angles. For similar polygons and polyhedra, corresponding angles are the same size, but every two corresponding sides give the same ratio (the scale factor) for their lengths.

EXAMPLE 1

The dashed line is a line of symmetry for heptagon ABCDEFG. Some angle sizes are given in the drawing. Find the sizes of the other angles of the heptagon. (*Recall*: The sum of the sizes of the angles of an *n*-gon is $(n-2)180°$.)

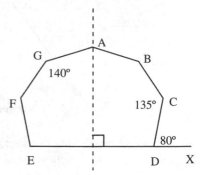

SOLUTION

Because the dashed line is a line of symmetry, $\angle B$ is the same size as $\angle G$, or $140°$. Similarly, $\angle F$ has size $135°$. Because the segment EDX is straight and $\angle CDX$ has size $80°$, $\angle D$ and its image $\angle E$ each has $100°$. The only angle unaccounted for is $\angle A$. All the angles of the heptagon will total $(7-2)180°$, or $900°$. The angles already determined total $140 + 140 + 135 + 100 + 100 + 135 = 750°$, which leaves $150°$ for $\angle A$.

As with length, some ability at estimating angle size is often useful. Most people have a good mental picture of 90°, 180°, and 270° (if they have thought about the fact that $90° + 180° = 270°$). Thinking of a half or a third of 90° (a right angle) can help in estimating angle size.

> **Take-Away Message** . . . The four key ideas of measurement from Section 23.1 all apply to length and angle size. There are many words that refer to the same characteristic as does length, including perimeter and circumference. Angle sizes are usually given in degrees, with 360° in a full turn and 180° in a half-turn. Several results about angle sizes enable us to find unknown measurements from known ones.

Learning Exercises for Section 23.2

1. Find the perimeter of each figure. (*Suggestion*: Use metric units.)

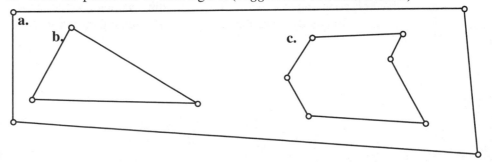

    d. Find the perimeter of each face of Shape A and Shape B from your kit of polyhedra.

2. Explain why the statement, "My brand-new pencil is exactly $7\frac{1}{2}$ inches long," is not completely true.

3. Show a segment that would measure 6 cm to the nearest centimeter but 6.5 cm to the nearest half-centimeter. How many possibilities are there?

4. A person has a broken ruler with the first 3 inches missing. However, she has measured several segments by noting where on the ruler the two end points of each segment were. Find the lengths as she did, using the following information about where the two endpoints were. Can you determine them mentally?

   a. 4 inches and $7\frac{3}{4}$ inches

   b. $5\frac{7}{8}$ inches and $9\frac{1}{4}$ inches

   c. $6\frac{7}{16}$ inches and 10 inches

5. What is your personal benchmark for each length?

   a. 1 millimeter   **b.** 1 centimeter   **c.** 1 decimeter

   d. 1 meter   **e.** 1 kilometer

6. Estimate the length of each segment in metric units, and then measure each to check your estimating powers. (Notice that you can make up your own examples for further practice.)

   a. _____

   b. _____

   c. ____

   d. _____

   e. the perimeter of the room you are in

   f. the height of the ceiling in the room you are in

   g. the length of a car you know

   h. the diameter of a quarter

   i. the height of this piece of paper

   j. the perimeter of this piece of paper

7. An imagined polygon has perimeter 24 cm with each side having a length that is a whole number of centimeters. For each given polygon, what are all the possibilities for the lengths of its sides?

   a. a quadrilateral   **b.** a rectangle   **c.** a pentagon

8. If *n* identical square regions are placed so that touching regions share a whole side, what is an expression for the *maximum* perimeter possible? Use the side of the square as the unit of length.

   Sample trials

   $n = 5$
   perimeter = 10

   $n = 5$, perimeter = 12

   $n = 1$
   perimeter = 4

9. a. How does one find the shortest distance from a point to a line, as in the drawing to the left below? How does one find the distance between two parallel lines, as in the right below?

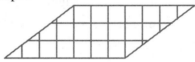

P
○

k _____

b. For parallel lines, does it matter *where* you measure the distance between them?

10. What *length* can you measure to find out how many (horizontal) rows of squares are in the following shape?

11. For the five figures below, the same size circle is shown with an inside polygon and an outside polygon. Check that the perimeters of the outside polygons are getting smaller and the perimeters of the inside polygons are getting larger as you go from Figure A to Figure E.

(A)   **(B)**   **(C)**

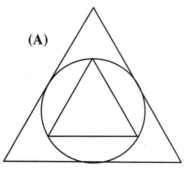
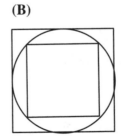
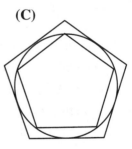

(D)   **(E)**

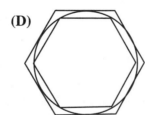
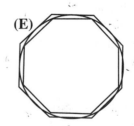

12. Complete each of the following measurement equalities.
   a.   1.2 km = ___ m   **b.**   5.3 m = ___ cm
   c.   62 mm = ___ cm   **d.**   3.25 dm = ___ cm
   e.   We write "3.4 cm + 4.3 cm = 7.7 cm," but the sum could be
            as small as ___ cm.

13. Approximate the length of the curve first with segments 2 cm long, then with segments 1 cm long, and finally with segments 0.5 cm long. What would you estimate the length of the curve to be?

14. Estimate the size of each given angle. Then copy and measure to check your estimates. (*Note*: With some protractors, you may need to extend the sides of the angles. Also, as with line segments, you can make up your own angles for more estimation practice.)

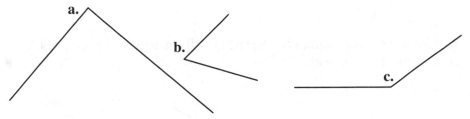

    d. Classify each of the angles in parts (a), (b), and (c) as being acute, right, obtuse, or straight.

15. a. How many degrees must you turn a doorknob to open a door? Estimate and then check.

    b. A hippopotamus can open its mouth about 130°. Sketch an angle to show your estimate of such an angle, and then check by measuring.

16. How many degrees does the minute hand of a clock go through for each given time span?

    a. from 4:00 to 4:45   **b.** from noon to 12:35

    c. from 1:00 to 1:05   **d.** from 8:48 to 9:17

    e. from 2:00 to 3:00   **f.** from 2:00 to 3:30

    g. from 6:36 to 8:19   **h.** in a whole day

17. How many seconds are in a full 360° turn? One second is what part of a full turn?

18. How many degrees of longitude separate locations with the following degrees of longitude?

    a. Location 1: 42° 16' 23" west longitude; location 2: 60° west longitude

    b. Location 3: 115° 43" west longitude; location 4: 68° 32' west longitude

    c. Location 5: 34° 52' west longitude; location 6: 19° 48' *east* longitude

19. Why are time zones roughly 15° of longitude wide?

20. The equatorial circle is about 25,000 miles long. What is the approximate length, in miles, of a 1° arc on the equatorial circle? A 1 minute arc? A 1 second arc?

21. Sketch angles with the following sizes by estimating: 30°, 45°, and 150°. Check your estimates by measuring your angles.

22. a. When two lines cross, they form pairs of angles that always have the same size. These angles are called **vertical angles** or **opposite angles**. Give a justification that a pair of vertical angles will always be the same size (without relying on checking a particular example or examples); that is, why must the ? angle in the drawing below have *x*°? (*Hint*: How is *y* related to the ? and *x*?)

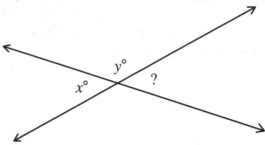

b. Without using a protractor, give the sizes of all the angles with sizes not given in the drawing below.

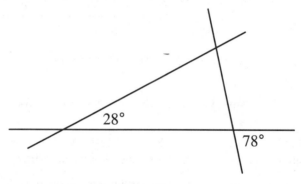

23. a. If two lines cross, four angles are formed. If a third line crosses two other lines, eight new angles are formed and can be grouped into four pairs of **corresponding angles**, which are angles located in corresponding positions, such as *b* and *w* in the following diagram. Give the other three pairs of corresponding angles here.

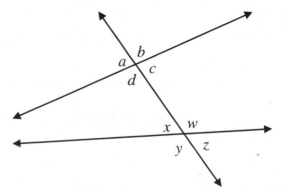

b. Are the two angles in a corresponding pair always the same size?

c. Suppose that the third line cuts two *parallel* lines. Experiment to see whether there is any relationship between the sizes of the two angles in a corresponding pair in this case. (It is easy to get parallel lines by using the lines on notebook paper.)

d. Angles such as *d* and *w* shown in the previous drawing are called **alternate interior angles.** Give another pair of alternate interior angles. How do they compare in size if the lines are parallel?

24. In the diagrams below, lines *m* and *n* are parallel. Give the sizes of the lettered angles.

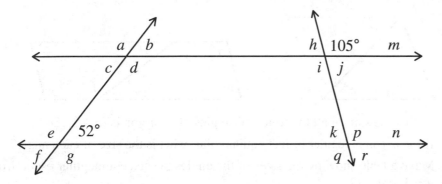

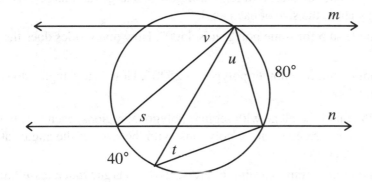

25. You know that the sizes of the angles of a triangle sum to 180°. Yet, direct measurements of the angles of a triangle may be "off," even when carefully measured.

a. Give an argument for the sum being 180° based on using angles in parallel lines rather than direct measurement. Use the following diagram in stating your argument.

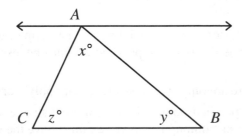

In parts (b)–(e), give the missing angle size(s) in the triangles described.

b. Two angles have sizes 72° and 39°.

c. A right triangle has an angle of 41°.

d. A triangle has angles of 56° 39' and 62° 43'.

Continue on the next page.

Notes

e.   An isosceles triangle has an angle of 20°. (There are two possibilities.)

f.   In every right triangle, what is the sum of the sizes of the acute angles?

26. In the following drawing, the triangle and the trapezoid are rotated 180° with the marked midpoints of sides as centers of the rotations. Give the measurements of angles (*a*)–(*g*), in terms of *w*, *x*, *y*, *z*.

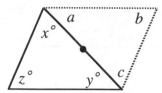   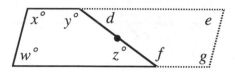

27. Recall that the sum of all the (interior) angles of an *n*-gon is $(n - 2)180°$.

a.   If the *n*-gon is regular or just equiangular, what is the size of each angle?

b.   Make a table showing the sizes of the angles in each equiangular *n*-gon from *n* = 3 to *n* = 12.

c.   As the number of sides of a regular *n*-gon gets larger and larger, what can you say about the size of each angle?

d.   The angle sum for some polygon is 4500°. How many sides does the polygon have?

e.   The angle sum for another polygon is 2520°. How many angles does the polygon have?

28. In a tessellation of the plane with regular polygonal regions, each vertex will involve the same arrangement of polygons, with the sizes of the angles at each vertex totaling 360°.

a.   Use the results from Learning Exercise 27(b) to argue that a tessellation involving exactly one kind of regular polygon is possible for only equilateral triangles, squares, and regular hexagons.

b.   A tessellation of the plane can involve more than one kind of regular polygon. Give some possibilities for such a tessellation, considering only the angles at a vertex. For example, because $90° + 135° + 135° = 360°$, one square and two octagons could give a tessellation.

29. Recall from Section 16.5 that there are only five different kinds of convex regular polyhedra.

a.   Consider a vertex of a regular polyhedron. The sum of the angles with their vertices all at one vertex of the polyhedron must be less than 360°. Explain why.

b.   Argue that there are only five possible regular polyhedra.

c.   A semiregular polyhedron may involve more than one kind of regular polygon at each vertex, although each vertex must have the same arrangement. Give some possibilities for a semiregular polyhedron, considering only the angles at a vertex.

30. Skateboarders, skiers, or snow-boarders may talk about "doing a 1080." What does that mean?

31. Three angles of quadrilateral STAR have sizes $63°\ 45'$, $110°\ 25'$, and $120.25°$. Another quadrilateral is similar to STAR, with a scale factor 2.5. What are the sizes of the angles in the second quadrilateral?

32. Tell whether the following statement is true or false, and explain your thinking: For all circles, arcs with the same number of degrees always have the same length.

33. Some teachers like to use tessellations to suggest some important geometric results. For example, fill in the measurements of the other angles that have the highlighted point as the vertex to get a justification that the sum of the angles of a triangle is $180°$, that is, $x + y + z = 180$.

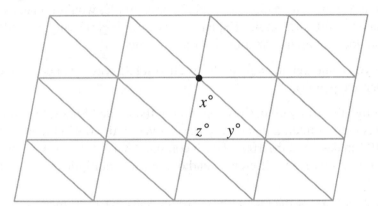

34. **a.** Any regular polygon can be fit "inside" some circle so that all the vertices of the polygon are on that circle. The center of the circle is the center of the regular polygon. Because the sides of a regular polygon are all equal, the arcs and the central angles they give must be equal. How large is each central angle for an equilateral triangle? A square? A regular pentagon? A regular hexagon? A regular n-gon?

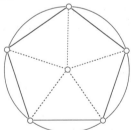

    b. How could a teacher draw a regular heptagon with the help of a compass and a protractor?

35. In parts (a)–(c), find the number of degrees x in the exterior angle.

a.
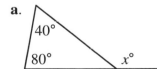

b.
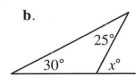

c.
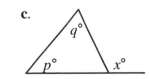

36. Just as angles in a plane are made when lines intersect, **dihedral angles** in space are made when two planes intersect:

a dihedral angle

How might one measure a dihedral angle? For example, would it make sense to talk about a 90° dihedral angle? Explain your reasoning. (Giving your ideas, rather than looking up information, is of interest here.)

37. Tell how you could get an angle of 94° if all you had was a wooden angle of 19° (and paper and pencil).

38. a. Although the 100-yard dash is common in the United States, the 100-meter dash is used in international track meets. One yard = 0.9144 meter. How do the 100-m dash and the 100-yd dash compare? Give two answers, one for the additive comparison (difference) and one for the multiplicative comparison (ratio).

  b. Repeat part (a) for the mile (1760 yards) versus the 1500-meter run.

39. Complete each of the following measurement equalities. (Conversions for some English system length units are given in the Glossary, under **English system**.)

  a.   4 miles = _____ yd   **b.**   1320 yd = _____ mi

  c.   1320 ft = _____ mi   **d.**   1.5 mi = _____ ft

  e.   12 yd = _____ in.   **f.**   84 in. = _____ yd

40. Technical words with everyday meanings or connotations can naturally be confusing to children (and others). Give different meanings or connotations for these.

  a. degree   **b.** yard   **c.** meter

  d. regular   **e.** right angle (vs. _____ angle)

41. a. A hidden shape is congruent to quadrilateral ABCD shown in the following diagram. What do you know about specific measurements on the hidden shape?

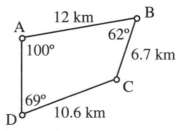

  b. Another hidden shape is similar to the given quadrilateral. What can you say about specific measurements on this hidden shape?

42. In the late 1700s, a Frenchman involved in the creation of the metric system thought the *grade*, a unit for angle size equal to one-hundredth of a right angle, would be useful.

   a. How many grades would be in a full circle?

   b. How many degrees would be in a centigrade?

43. You want to wrap the package below with fancy ribbon as pictured. How many centimeters of ribbon do you need? Allow 25 cm for the bow.

8 cm   6 cm

24 cm

44. a. With a compass and straightedge, construct a circle and a pair of perpendicular diameters for the circle. Join the endpoints of the diameters. What special quadrilateral do the endpoints appear to give? Can you justify that it *is* that shape?

   b. With a compass, draw a circle. Then, starting at some marked point, mark off points 1 radius apart around the circle. Join the points in order. What shape do these points appear to give?

   c. How might you construct a regular octagon and a regular 12-gon? (*Hint*: Use parts (a) and (b).)

45. Here is how to construct with compass and straightedge the two tangents to a circle from a point *outside* the circle: Use the segment joining the outside point *P* to the center *C* of the circle as the diameter of another circle. Where the two circles meet indicates how to draw the two tangents to the first circle. (The details of the construction are omitted in the drawing below.) Why does this method work?

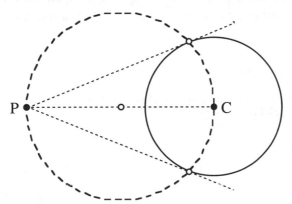

23.3 | Check Yourself

You should be able to work exercises like those assigned and to meet the following objectives.

1. Describe in general terms what the process of measurement involves.

2. State and apply the four key ideas of measurement, and recognize when they have been used.

3. State the range of values that a given measurement covers. (For example, a length reported as 15.6 cm could be as short as 15.55 cm or as long as up to 15.65 cm.)

4. Recognize the "inverse" relationship between the size of the unit and the numerical part of the measurement.

5. Apply the four key ideas of measurement to length (or its special synonyms such as perimeter, height, circumference, and so on) and to angle size.

6. Use your personal benchmarks to estimate given lengths or given segments or lengths of named objects.

7. Estimate angle sizes and lengths, and use a protractor to measure given angles and a ruler marked in English or metric units to measure given segments.

8. Use adjectives with angles correctly (for example, right angle, acute angle, obtuse angle, straight angle, supplementary angle, central angle, vertical angles, alternate interior angles, corresponding angles, exterior angle, inscribed angle, and so on), and deal with the relationships covered (for example, angles with parallel lines, angles of a triangle, and so on).

9. Convert among metric units for length, convert among English units for length, and deal with angle sizes in degrees, minutes, and seconds.

10. Determine the total of the sizes of the angles in a polygon having a given number of sides, and the size of each angle in an equiangular or regular polygon having a given number of sides.

REFERENCE FOR CHAPTER 23

[1]Klein, H. A. (1974). *The world of measurements*. New York: Simon and Schuster. (The quote in Learning Exercise 21 in Section 23.1 is from page 112.)

Chapter 24

Area, Surface Area, and Volume

If you have bought carpet or painted walls in a room, you have likely been concerned about area and surface area. But is area related to the size or weight of the rolled-up carpet, the number of gallons of paint needed, or some other quantity such as volume? This chapter deals with the ideas of area and volume and how the key ideas of measurement apply to them. Area formulas are not the focus here, but they will be covered in Chapter 25.

24.1 Area and Surface Area

The meaning of the term *area* is central to understanding what the area formulas tell us. For many children, the term just means the number generated by an area formula. However, understanding the *concept* of area is just as important.

Discussion 1   What Are *Area* and *Surface Area*?

1. What is *area*? Is area the same as, or different from, perimeter and volume? Explain.

2. What shapes would give the surface area of a square pyramid? Of a right circular cylinder?

We speak of the area of a field, a lake, a country, a geometric shape, a wall, or your body, all of which are examples of surfaces or regions— *area* is a characteristic of surfaces or regions. As with length, the term *area* is used to refer both to the attribute ("The wolf wandered over a wide area.") and to the measurement ("The area of the field is 15 acres.").

Like all direct measuring, the direct measurement of an area involves matching the surface or region with units that themselves have the attribute of area. You already know some standard units for area, such as the square inch and the square centimeter. What could serve as nonstandard units?

Discussion 2   Unusual Units for Area?

Which of the following regions could *theoretically* be used as units for measuring area? Are there advantages or disadvantages to any of them? Why is each of them shaded?

Standard units are square regions with sides whose lengths are all 1 length unit—for example, square regions with sides 1 centimeter, 1 inch, or 1 mile. These units are called *square centimeter*, *square inch*, *square mile,* and so on. The units can be denoted by the symbols cm^2, in^2, or mi^2, for example. The English system also uses the acre. (One acre = 43,560 square feet, and we do not say *square acre*.) The metric system's basic unit is the square meter, but it also recognizes the unit **are** (pronounced "air" and having the symbol a), which equals 100 m^2. From this unit we get the unit **hectare** (ha), which equals 100 a, as the prefix *hect-* suggests. The hectare is often used to measure land areas in metric-using countries.

Activity 1   Relating Metric Units for Area

Consider the following diagram.

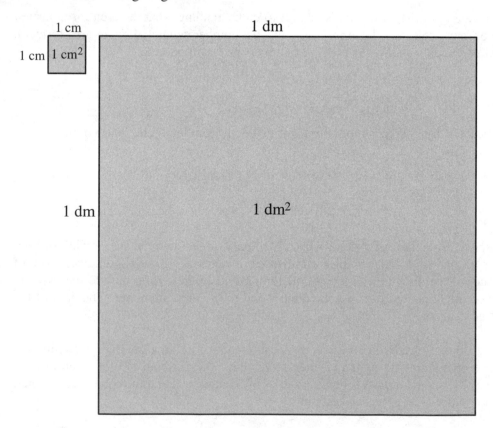

a. How many square centimeters are in a square decimeter? How many square centimeters are in a square meter? How many square decimeters are in a square meter?

b. How much of a square decimeter is a square centimeter? How much of a square meter is a square centimeter? How much of a square meter is a square decimeter?

Notes

The key idea of "cutting" a region or a surface into parts that are more easily measured is often applied at the basic level by covering a region with unit square regions, and then counting the number of square regions involved, perhaps including parts of square regions to get a better approximation. What would you say are the areas of the regions inside the curves below? (Many times, even experts say "the curved area" or "the area of the polygon" instead of the more accurate "the area of the region inside the curve" or "the area of the polygonal region.")

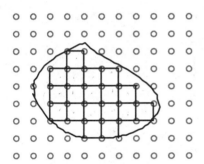   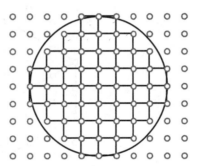

Activity 2   Thinking INSIDE the Box

Using the smallest square region defined by the dots as the unit, find the area of the region enclosed by each of the following shaded polygons. (The dashed segments with the triangular regions are a hint that helps to avoid lots of estimating. Think about pieces of rectangular regions.)

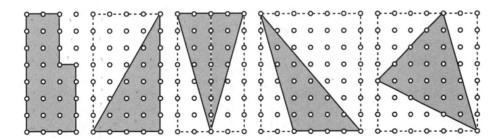

If regions are congruent, the regions have equal areas. The "reverse" statement (called the **converse** of the original statement) is this statement: If regions have equal areas, then the regions are congruent. Examine the results for Activity 2 to show that the converse is not always true.

Notes

Three-dimensional shapes such as polyhedra have surfaces, so we can speak of the **surface area** of such shapes. For example, the six faces of a cube are square regions, so the surface area of the cube would be the sum of the areas of these six square regions.

Discussion 3   Finding Surface Areas

How would one find the surface area of three-dimensional shapes, such as polyhedra from your kit of shapes? What key idea of measurement is involved?

EXAMPLE 1

Find the surface area of the given right rectangular prism.

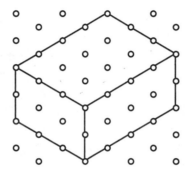

SOLUTION

Right rectangular prisms are easy to work with, because the square regions (the units) that cover the faces are easily seen by drawing in the dashed lines, as shown below. The areas of the top and bottom faces are each 12 units; the areas of the two side faces are each 8 units; and the areas of the front and back faces are each 6 units. The surface area of the prism is then 52 units, that is, 52 square regions.

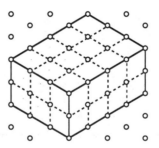

Figures that are similar also have areas that are related. One way to think about how they are related is to focus on each square region in the area of the original shape and to examine the area of that square region in the enlarged (or shrunken) version having the scale factor k.

Discussion 4   Relating Areas of Similar Shapes

The following diagram shows a square centimeter and its images for two different size changes. How are the areas of the original square centimeter and each image related? How can that relationship be predicted from knowing the scale factor?

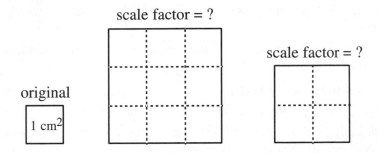

scale factor = ?

scale factor = ?

original

1 cm²

Because *every* square centimeter in an original shape gives k^2 square centimeters in a similar shape, the area of the new shape is always k^2 times the area of the original shape. If k is the scale factor, the relationship is expressed in equation form as follows.

$$\textit{new area} = k^2 \times \textit{original area}$$

EXAMPLE 2

A larger shape with scale factor 4 is similar to the octagon shown to the right.
What are the area and perimeter of the
larger shape?

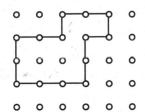

SOLUTION

From a direct counting of the units, the given shape has area 8 square units and perimeter 14 length units. With the scale factor 4, the new area is $4^2 = 16$ times as large, or $16 \times 8 = 128$ square units, and the perimeter is 4 times as large, or 56 length units. (A drawing of the larger shape makes these results clear.)

> TAKE-AWAY MESSAGE . . . Understanding area includes recognizing that *area of a region* means the number of area units required to cover the region. The key ideas of measurement all apply to area. Congruent shapes have the same areas, but not conversely: Shapes having the same area are not necessarily congruent. The surface area of a 3D shape is the number of area units required to cover the shape, and it is often obtained by finding the areas of the individual surfaces that make up the shape and adding those results. The areas of similar shapes are related by the *square* of the scale factor: The area of the image is equal to the square of the scale factor times the area of the original. ♦

Learning Exercises for Section 24.1

1. Find the areas of the shapes on page 562 by using Pattern Blocks (or Pattern Block cut-outs) as described below.

   Shape A in hexagonal regions, in trapezoidal regions, and in (wide) rhombus regions

   Shape B in hexagonal regions, in trapezoidal regions, and in (wide) rhombus regions

2. **a.** (*Pattern Blocks*) Invisible shape X has area 16 trapezoidal regions. What is its area in (wide) rhombus regions? Explain your reasoning.

   b. Invisible shape Y has area 21 trapezoidal regions. What is its area in (wide) rhombus regions? Explain your reasoning.

3. Some people use the size of a piece of toast as a benchmark for a square decimeter. Choose a benchmark for a square centimeter, a square meter, and an are.

4. Estimate each given area using an appropriate metric unit (think metric by using your benchmarks). Check your estimates when you can.

   a. the area of this page of this textbook

   b. the area of a postage stamp

   c. the area of the floor of the room you are in

   d. the area of a wall of the room you are in

   e. the area of a window in the room you are in

   f. the surface area of your body

5. Someone has been using the following nonstandard units in finding the areas of regions. For each given equality statement, tell whether *x* or 20 is greater, and explain.

Unit *P*   Unit *Q*   Unit *R*

   a. $20\ Ps = x\ Qs$ **b.** $20\ Qs = x\ Rs$

   c. $20\ Ps = x\ Rs$ **d.** $20\ Rs = x\ Ps$

   In parts (e)–(f), tell which of *y* or *x* is greater, and explain.

   e. $y\ Qs = x\ Rs$

   f. $x\ Ps = y\ Qs$

   g. If $24\ Ps = 7\ Qs$, how many *P*s make 1 *Q*? How many *Q*s make 1 *P*?

   h. If $8\ Qs = 3\ Rs$, how many *Q*s make 1 *R*? How many *R*s make 1 *Q*?

   i. If 3.7 blobs = 2.4 globs, then how many blobs make 1 glob? How many globs make 1 blob?

6. Al, Beth, and Cai are measuring the same regions, but they are using different units. (The squares indicated are all the same size.)

        Al's unit   Beth's unit   Cai's unit

For each person's measurements, give the measurements that the other two people will find for the regions.

   a. Al's measurement of a region is 16 of his units.

   b. Beth's measurement of a different region is $9\frac{1}{2}$ of her units.

   c. Cai's measurement of a third region is $6\frac{1}{3}$ of his units.

7. Make sketches to show how you could explain each of the following relationships.

   a. How many square inches are in a square foot and what part of a square foot a square inch is

   b. How many square feet are in a square yard and how many square yards make a square foot

   c. How many square yards are in a square mile

8. How many acres are in a square mile?

9. Complete, using your "metric sense" (your mental pictures) for the following units.

   a. $2.3 \text{ dm}^2 = \underline{\hspace{1cm}} \text{ cm}^2$

   b. $45 \text{ dm}^2 = \underline{\hspace{1cm}} \text{ m}^2$

   c. $19.6 \text{ cm}^2 = \underline{\hspace{1cm}} \text{ dm}^2$

   d. $0.04 \text{ m}^2 = \underline{\hspace{1cm}} \text{ cm}^2$

10. How long are the sides of a square region that has area 1 are (1 a)?

11. What is the approximate area enclosed by each shape?

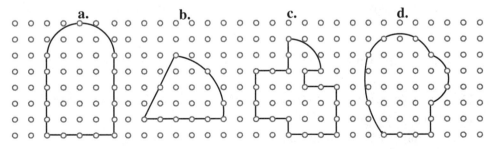

12. Determine the area enclosed by each polygon. Use the natural unit.

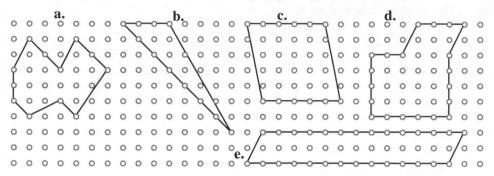

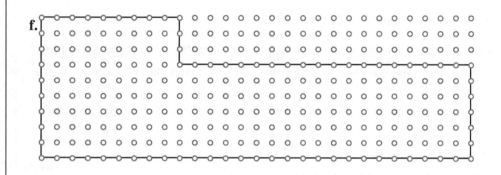

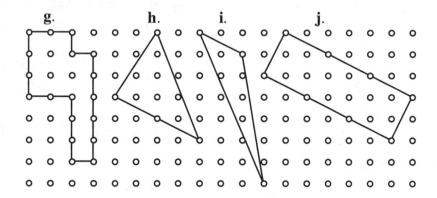

13. a.   Describe an efficient way to find the surface area of a right regular octagonal prism.

  b.   Describe an efficient way to find the surface area of a regular hexagonal pyramid.

  c.   Describe an efficient way to find the surface area of a regular octahedron (see shape H in the kit of shapes).

14. Give the surface area of each polyhedron. Use the natural unit.　　　　

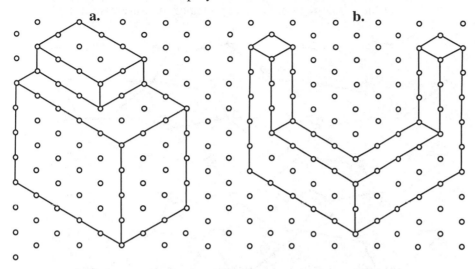

15. Draw a net for each shape to show the regions involved in finding the surface area.

    a.　a right circular cylinder　　　　　　　**b.**　a right circular cone

16. Is 4 square meters the same as a 4-meter square?

17. Many people confuse area and perimeter. How would you advise them, so that they do not mix the ideas up?

18. Rulers measure length, and protractors measure angle size. Is there a comparable school tool for measuring area? Mark a square centimeter grid on a transparent piece of plastic or on thin paper, and find the area of each given region.

    a.　　　　　　　　　　　　　　　　**b.**

19. Give the area of each tangram piece for the situation described.

    a.　The area of the whole square region is 1 area unit.

    b.　The area of the whole square region is 47 area units.

    c.　The area of the whole square region is $4\frac{2}{3}$ area units.

Notes

20. In the following diagram, suppose the shaded tessellation piece is 1 area unit. Give the area of the whole region. What key idea of measurement did you use?

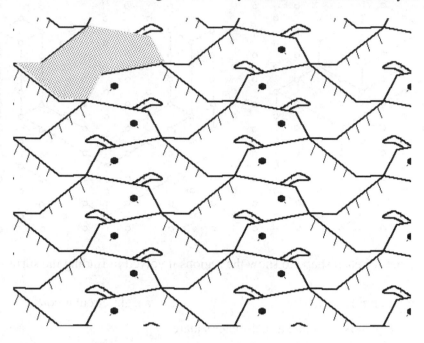

21. a. Ollie and Olivia plan to buy carpet to cover their basement floor. After measuring, they determine that the basement floor has an area of 15 square yards. When they get to the carpet store, the salesperson asks for the area of the basement floor in square feet. Ollie reasons that because 1 yard is equal to 3 feet, 15 square yards will equal 45 square feet. Is Ollie's reasoning correct? Explain, using a diagram to help in your explanation.

   b. Ollie and Olivia decide to tile their bathroom floor with ceramic tile from Italy. They know that the Italians use the metric system, so they cleverly measure the length and width of the floor in decimeters. The floor is 18 dm long and 15 dm wide. They want to be prepared for the salesperson's questions this time! What is the area of the bathroom floor in square decimeters? Square centimeters? Square meters? Explain your reasoning, using diagrams to help in your explanations.

22. Trace the following 8 by 8 square, and then cut on the solid line segments. Rearrange the four pieces to make a nonsquare rectangle. What are the length and width of the rectangle and its area? What was the area of the original square? What key idea appears to be violated here?

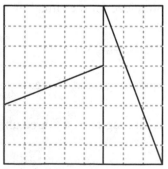

23. Two irregular shapes are similar with scale factor 5 involved. With sketches, show how the image of a square centimeter in the original shape looks in the larger shape.

24. **a.** Two polyhedra are similar with scale factor 7 involved. The surface area of the smaller polyhedron is 490 cm². What is the surface area of the larger polyhedron? Explain.

    b. Two polyhedra are similar with scale factor 8 involved. The surface area of the *larger* polyhedron is 640 cm². What is the surface area of the smaller polyhedron? Explain.

    c. Why is the ratio of the surface areas of these two pyramids likely *not* either 2.25 or $\frac{16}{9}$?

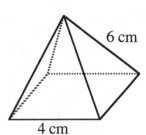
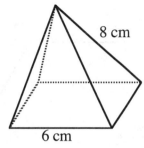

25. Two curved regions are similar, and they have areas 500 cm² and 125 cm². What scale factor is involved? How do you know? (There are two possibilities.)

26. Without actually finding the measurements, describe how you might determine each given measurement of the shaded part of the figure at the right.

    a. the perimeter

    b. the area

27. Use square-grid paper or squares to help you answer this question about shapes made with squares: For a given perimeter, will the area enclosed always be the same?

28. Is each statement correct? Correct any statement that needs correction.

    a. "The field was 6 square acres in area."

    b. "The area of a circle is 360 degrees."

    c. "It took 12 tattoo stickers to cover my whole face, so the perimeter of my face is 12 tattoo stickers."

    d. "The area of the rectangle is 20 decimeters."

    e. "One meter is 100 centimeters, so one square meter is 100 square centimeters."

Notes

For Learning Ex. 1
page 556

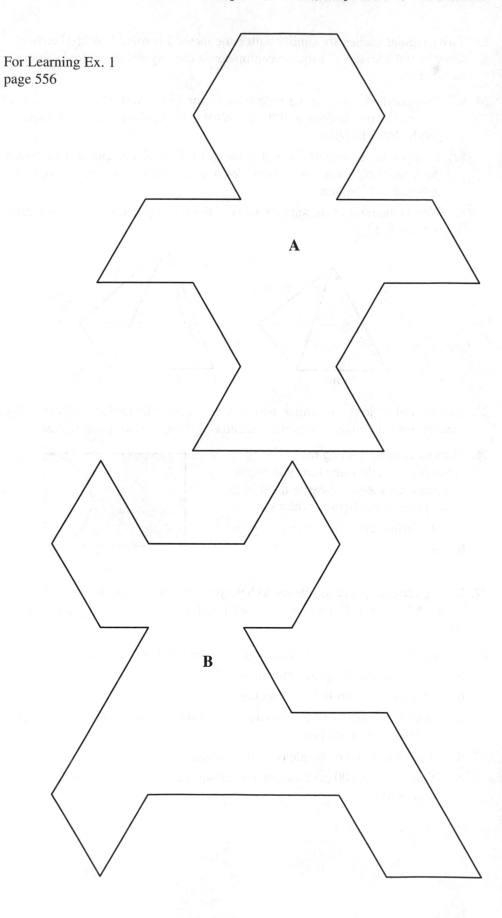

| 24.2 | **Volume** |

Any real object takes up space. Even a scrap of paper, a speck of dust, or a strand of cobweb takes up some space. The quantity of space occupied is called the **volume**. As with the terms length and area, *volume* is sometimes used for the attribute as well as the measurement or value of the attribute.

The topic of volume can appear in the curriculum as early as Grade 3, culminating in at least a few volume formulas in later grades. In this section, we treat only the main ideas of volume; we discuss the volume formulas in Chapter 25.

Boxes, cans, and other containers enclose an amount of space; we often refer to their **capacities** or to the volumes they enclose. The *material* actually making up a box involves a certain amount of space, so *literally* the volume of the box would be the volume that the box would occupy if flattened out. Usually *volume of the container*, however, refers to the capacity of the container rather than to the volume of the material that makes up the container.

The direct measurement of the volume of an object involves a matching of the object with a unit, an object having the volume attribute. Because every real object has volume, one could theoretically use any physical object as a unit for volume. The standard units, however, are cubic regions with the length of each edge of the cube having 1 length unit. For example, a cubic region with each edge 1 inch long is a standard unit called a **cubic inch** (abbreviated cu. in. although in^3 is increasingly common). Hence, volume basically involves counting the number of cubes required to match or fill a given shape.

Our attention will focus largely on those standard units in the metric system—for example, cubic centimeters, cubic decimeters, and cubic meters. Because the cubes will have sides 1 centimeter, 1 decimeter, or 1 meter, you should mentally review your benchmarks for those length units.

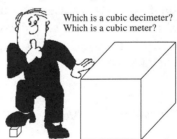

Which is a cubic decimeter?
Which is a cubic meter?

Discussion 5   Converting Metric Volume Units

Answer the following questions by thinking about the sizes of the units (and without using a formula). Explain your thinking in each case.

a. How many cubic centimeters does it take to fill a cubic decimeter box?
That is, 1000 cm^3 = 1 dm^3.   Vice versa, 1 cm^3 = .001 dm^3.

b. How many cubic decimeters does it take to fill a cubic meter box?
That is, 1000 dm^3 = 1 m^3.   Vice versa, 1 dm^3 = .001 m^3.

c. How many cubic centimeters does it take to fill a cubic meter box?
That is, 1000000 cm^3 = 1 m^3.   Vice versa, 1 cm^3 = .000001 m^3.

Notes

The cubic meter is too large a unit for many everyday purposes, so the metric system also recognizes a smaller unit, the **liter** (sometimes spelled litre), which is about 1.06 quarts, to measure volumes of liquids. You have likely seen bottles of water or soda that hold 1 or 2 liters, so you have some benchmark for the size of 1 liter. The symbol for liter is ℓ or L. Because the lower-case printed letter l looks so much like the numeral 1, the value 1 l could be misread as eleven instead of 1 liter. We can apply all the metric prefixes to liter: for example, 1 milliliter is 0.001 liter, or 1 mL = 0.001 L. Notice that although the liter and milliliter are units for volume, we do not say *cubic liter* or *cubic milliliter* because the words *liter* and *milliliter* already refer to units for volume.

The liter is related to the official cubic metric units for volume. Fortunately, the relationship is a nice one: **1 liter = 1 cubic decimeter**.

> ### *THINK ABOUT...*
>
> At one time a gallon of gasoline cost about $3 in the United States. A European visitor said to you, "That's interesting! I pay the equivalent of $1.30 per liter." Who (the visitor or you) pays more for gasoline?

Discussion 6   In the Hospital

Many medicines are measured in metric units. How are a milliliter and a cubic centimeter related in size?

Because the units cm^3 and mL are the same size, containers marked for measuring liquid volumes can use either unit. (As an aside, you may know that medical personnel most often write cc and say "see-see" rather than write cm^3 and say "cubic centimeter." They do so from long tradition rather than from any antipathy toward the official SI conventions.)

Discussion 7   Volumes by Counting

What is the volume of each polyhedron? What key idea of measurement did you use? (Use the natural cubic region as the unit.)

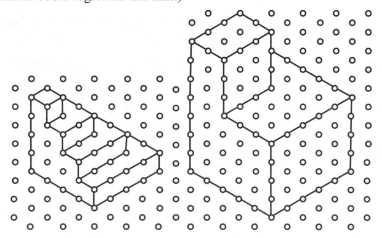

If two 3D shapes happen to be congruent, then their volumes are equal, as are their surface areas. Recall that if two 3D shapes are similar with scale factor k, then their volumes are also related in a predictable fashion although the two shapes may not be the same size:

$$new\ volume = k^3 \times original\ volume.$$

In other words, the ratio, new volume to original volume, is the cube of the scale factor. One way to see this relationship is to think of each cubic region making up the original shape, and then think about what happens to each such cube under a size change. The length of each side of the original cube is now k times as long, so the image of the original cube will be a k by k by k cube. The following diagram shows examples with scale factor 2 and scale factor 3. Check to confirm that the images have 8 (= 2^3) and 27 (= 3^3) cubes, respectively. Hence each cube in the original will give 2^3 and 3^3 cubes in the respective images. That is, the new volume will be 2^3 and 3^3 times as large as the original volume.

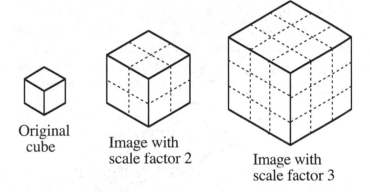

Original cube

Image with scale factor 2

Image with scale factor 3

EXAMPLE 3

Hidden shape X is congruent to the first polyhedron given in Discussion 7. Hidden shape Y is similar to that same polyhedron but larger with scale factor 6. What are the volumes of shapes X and Y?

SOLUTION

Congruent shapes have the same volumes, so shape X has volume 30 cubic units. Volumes of similar shapes are related by the third power (cube) of the scale factor. Thus, the volume of shape Y is $6^3 \cdot 30$, or $216 \cdot 30 = 6480$ cubic units.

EXAMPLE 4

A larger prism is similar to a $2 \times 3 \times 2$ right rectangular prism with scale factor 2. Sketch both prisms and compare their surface areas and volumes.

SOLUTION

In the following sketch of the smaller prism, counting gives a surface area of 32 area units (square regions) and a volume of 12 volume units (cubical regions). Hence, the

Continue on the next page.

surface area of the larger prism should be $2^2 \cdot 32 = 128$ area units, and its volume should be $2^3 \cdot 12 = 96$ volume units. You should confirm the results for the larger prism by counting in the given sketch.

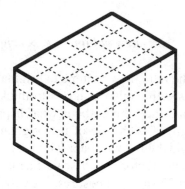

TAKE-AWAY MESSAGE . . . Volume can be measured in the metric system using two types of units. One type is based on cubic regions with basic metric length units for edges. The other type is based on the liter, which is defined as 1 cubic decimeter. Here is a summary of all the relationships for similar space figures: Given a scale factor k, corresponding angles will have the same size, but new lengths will be k times as long as the corresponding original lengths, new areas will be k^2 times as large as corresponding areas in the original objects, and new volumes will be k^3 times as large as corresponding volumes in the original objects. ◆

Learning Exercises for Section 24.2

1. Which attribute—length, angle size, area, or volume—could each of the following quantities involve? Give an appropriate metric unit in parts (a)–(m).

    a. the amount of water in a lake

    b. the amount of room on the lake for sailing

    c. the average depth of the lake

    d. the coastline of the lake

    e. the size of an oil slick on the lake

    f. the amount of water displaced by a ship

    g. the difference between sightings of two landmarks from a sailboat

    h. the amount of debris on the lake

    i. the amount of rope needed to moor a boat

    j. the amount of water that falls on the lake during a rain storm

    k. the amount of water that evaporates from a lake

    l. the part of the lake where swimming is allowed

    m. the amount of temporary fencing needed to isolate the volleyball courts

    n. how many identical advertising patches it would take to cover a sail

2. Find personal benchmarks for each given unit.

   a. 1 cm^3 **b.** 1 mL **c.** 1 dm^3 **d.** 1 L **e.** 1 m^3

3. What would be an appropriate metric unit for measuring the volume of each object?

   a. a ream of paper   **b.** a dose of medicine

   c. a gold nugget   **d.** a water tank

   e. a loaf of bread   **f.** an amount of liquid drunk daily

4. Estimate the volume of each object using metric units. (Check your estimates if it is feasible to do so. For example, some measuring cups have metric calibrations, and the labels for some objects give metric units.)

   a. a cup of water   **b.** a quart of milk

   c. a can of soda   **d.** the space of the room you're in

5. Design a net for a cube having 1 dm as the length of each edge. Will your net fit on the usual piece of paper?

6. For each equality, tell how x and y would be related ($x = y$, $x > y$, or $x < y$). Explain your reasoning.

   a. x spoonfuls = y bathtubfuls   **b.** x truckloads = y wheelbarrowfuls

7. Complete the following relationships and describe how you could derive the results (without using formulas).

   a. $1 \text{ dm}^3 =$ _____ cm^3 **b.** $1 \text{ m}^3 =$ _____ dm^3

   c. $1 \text{ L} =$ _____ cm^3 **d.** $1 \text{ m}^3 =$ _____ cm^3

8. Complete each equality.

   a. $1 \text{ cm}^3 =$ _____ dm^3 **b.** $1 \text{ cm}^3 =$ _____ m^3 **c.** $1 \text{ dm}^3 =$ ____m^3

9. Complete each statement.

   a. A decimeter is _____ as long as a centimeter, but a square decimeter is _____ as big as a square centimeter, and a cubic decimeter is _____ as large as a cubic centimeter.

   b. A meter is _____ as long as a centimeter, but a square meter is _____ as big as a square centimeter, and a cubic meter is _____ as large as a cubic centimeter.

10. Use your metric sense to complete each equality.

    a. $3.28 \text{ dm}^3 =$ _____ cm^3 **b.** $3.28 \text{ dm} =$ _____ cm

    c. $225.7 \text{ cm}^3 =$ _____ dm^3 **d.** $225.7 \text{ cm}^2 =$ _____ dm^2

11. **a.** Without using formulas, derive the relationship between a cubic inch and a cubic foot and the relationship between a cubic foot and a cubic yard. (*Hint*: Make a drawing.)

    b. One gallon is 231 cubic inches (a gallon is also 3.785 L). How many gallons are in a cubic foot?

    c. Water supplies for cities are often measured in *acre-feet*, the volume of an acre of water to a depth of 1 foot. How many gallons are in 1 acre-foot? (*Recall*: 1 acre = 43,560 ft^2.)

Notes

12. A large measuring cup has $3\frac{2}{3}$ cups of water in it. A solid piece of metal is submerged in the cup, raising the water level to the $4\frac{1}{4}$ cup mark. What is the volume of the piece of metal? Which of the four key ideas of measurement (Section 23.1) is involved here?

13. How is area different from volume? Can anything have area without having volume? Can anything have volume without having area?

14. In parts (a)–(c), give the surface area and volume of the polyhedron. Use the natural units.

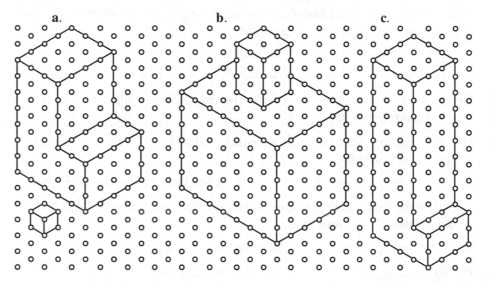

d. If the small cube above were 1 centimeter on each edge, what is the volume of each polyhedron in parts (a)–(c), in milliliters?

e. Do any of the polyhedra in parts (a)–(c) have a volume greater than 1 liter?

15. Conveniently, one liter (or one cubic decimeter) of water has a mass equal to 1 kilogram, at 4° C and at standard air pressure. At that temperature and air pressure, what is the mass of 1 milliliter of water? One cubic centimeter of water? (Some plastic cubic centimeters used in classrooms are designed to preserve this relationship.)

16. Find a way of putting 4 cubes together face to face so that the volume is 4 cubic regions, but the surface area is 16 square regions. What is the surface area of most shapes made from 4 cubes?

17. Each of the sketches on the following page represents the bottom story of a skyscraper and gives how many stories the skyscraper has. In each skyscraper, every story is just like its bottom story.

a. What is the volume of the bottom story of each skyscraper?

b. What is the area of the floor in the bottom story of each skyscraper?

c. Which skyscraper has the greater volume? Explain your reasoning.

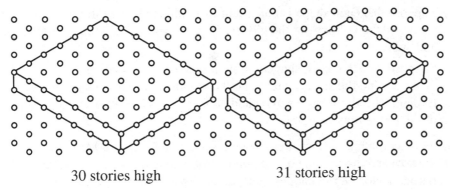

30 stories high   31 stories high

18. How many cubic regions would it take to fill the cylinder in the following sketch? What key idea(s) of measurement is(are) involved here?

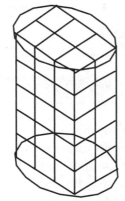

19. Cooking involves many volume units—for example, teaspoon (tsp), tablespoon (Tbsp), cup (c), pint (pt), quart (qt), and gallon (gal). Using the relationships

1 Tbsp = 3 tsp, 1 c = 16 Tbsp, 1 pt = 2 c, 1 qt = 2 pt, 1 gal = 4 qt,

complete the following conversions.

a. $4\frac{1}{2}$ Tbsp = _____ tsp   **b.** 5 tsp = _____ Tbsp

c. 8 Tbsp = _____ c   **d.** $\frac{2}{3}$ c = _____ Tbsp

e. 3 pt = _____ c   **f.** 1 gal = _____ pt or _____ c

g. $3\frac{1}{2}$ qt = _____ gal   **h.** $2\frac{1}{3}$ gal = _____ qt

i. $1\frac{1}{2}$ pt = _____ qt   **j.** $\frac{1}{3}$ qt = _____ pt

k. 1 c = _____ tsp   **l.** 3 Tbsp = _____ c

20. Consider the following diagram.

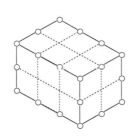

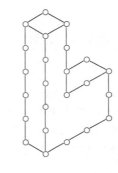

Continue on the next page.

a. Suppose that each shape is congruent to a hidden shape. Find the surface areas and the volumes of the hidden shapes. Explain. Use the natural square and cubic regions as units.

b. Suppose now that each shape is similar to another hidden shape with scale factor 5. Find the surface areas and the volumes of the two hidden shapes. Explain. Use the natural square and cubic regions as units. (A rough sketch of the image may be helpful.)

21. One polyhedron has surface area 5200 cm^2 and volume 24 000 cm^3. Give the surface area and the volume of the polyhedron's image for a size change with the given scale factor. Write enough steps to make your thinking clear.

   a. scale factor = 2   **b.** scale factor = $\frac{3}{4}$

   c. scale factor = $3\frac{1}{5}$ **d.** scale factor = 110%

24.3 | Issues for Learning: Measurement

As with geometry, the learning of measurement is not as satisfactory as one would hope, for such a practical topic. Results on items from national and international tests give some indication of possible weak spots in the learning of measurement (though it is helpful to recognize that such broad results may well disguise the excellent performance of students in some individual classrooms). In one testing[i], given drawings of a clock, a ruler, a thermometer, and a bathroom scale, 28% of the fourth graders could not identify which instruments could best be used to measure length, weight, and temperature. It is difficult to see how these students could have much understanding of measurement or how their schooling on measurement bore any relevance to life outside of school.

Some of the poor performance on tests is perhaps due to how measurement is taught. Common concerns are that measurement is little more than vocabulary and filling in blanks in such conversion exercises as *4 feet = ___ inches*, that measurement is taught without any actual measuring, and that the focus on measurement is on formulas, without any emphasis on the foundations and meanings for the formulas.

Discussion 8   When I Was Younger...

What are your memories of how you learned measurement in school? Did you have out-of-school experiences with measurement?

Neglect and limited foci may account for some of the poor test performance, but there are trouble spots in learning measurement that have become apparent through classroom research. For example,[ii] having children in a Grade 1–2 class develop their own measuring tools by repeating a unit and then measuring with the tool, revealed that for measuring a segment like the one shown below, children had difficulty deciding whether the segment was $4\frac{1}{2}$ or $5\frac{1}{2}$ units long.

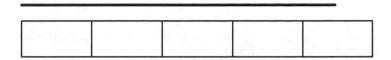

The research also made clear that counting units is not quite the same as thinking of ruler values in terms of a movement across a distance. Calling the line segments to be measured "Stuart Little trips" led to the latter understanding and even the insertion of the 0 on the home-made ruler.

1	2	3	4	5

Counting units.

0	1	2	3	4	5

Thinking of movements across a distance.

Children's early use of rulers can also be complicated by the many marks for fractions of units on the usual ruler, as performance on national test items shows. For example,[iii] 29% of 9-year-olds in one national testing identified a ruler marking of $3\frac{3}{8}$ inches as $3\frac{1}{2}$ inches, as did 13% of the 13-year-olds. Only 2% of the younger group and 25% of the older group gave the correct reading of $3\frac{3}{8}$ inches. Items that involve a slight change from the standard use of a ruler often reveal a poor grasp of what the markings on a ruler mean. For example, in 2003 a fourth-grade item[i] shown below gave these results: 42% thought the answer was 8 inches, 23% wrote $3\frac{1}{2}$, 14% wrote $10\frac{1}{2}$, and only 20% gave the correct answer.

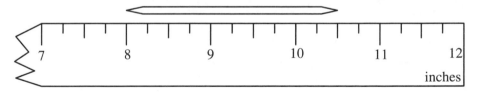

What is the length of the toothpick in the figure above?

Discussion 9   They Counted . . .

How do you think the children who thought the answer was $3\frac{1}{2}$ inches were thinking?

Even older students have difficulty with measurement when a problem involves more than one step, as in the problem shown below,[iv] with only about a third of U.S.

eighth-graders being successful. (Because the question was a multiple-choice item with four options, you could expect 25% to be successful just from guessing.) Perhaps attention to only straightforward, one-step problems leads students to expect a quick answer.

A rectangular garden that is next to a building has a path around the other three sides, as shown.

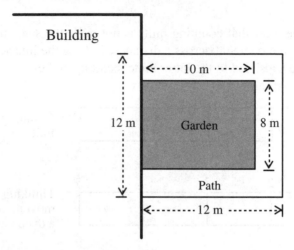

What is the area of the path?
A. 144 m²   B. 64 m²   C. 44 m²   D. 16 m²

However, items do not need to be complex to reveal conceptual gaps. Consider the following two problems, again from a national testing,^v with the percent of the seventh graders being correct given. Notice that not having the shape shown led to a somewhat greater difficulty, even when less technical vocabulary is involved.

A. What is the perimeter of
    this rectangle? (46% correct)

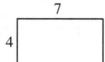

B. What is the distance
    around a 4 by 7 rectangle?
    (37% correct)

The following pair of items,^v again with the performances by seventh graders given, show a disappointing ability to give the areas of rectangular regions. Only about half of the seventh graders could answer each item correctly, even though the formula for the area of a rectangular region is usually encountered no later than Grade 4 and is routinely reviewed.

C. What is the area of this
   rectangle? (56% correct)

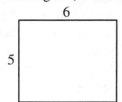

D. What is the area of this
   rectangle? (46% correct)

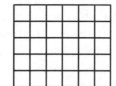

As is not unusual, the item closest to the concept of area, item D, is actually somewhat more difficult than item C (applying the formula). The most common error in
determining the areas was to give the perimeters (and vice versa, giving areas for
items seeking perimeters), illustrating confusion about the ideas of area and perimeter or about how they are calculated.

Moreover, there are developmental considerations[vi] in teaching ideas of measurement
of just about any geometric quantity. For example, and perhaps surprisingly, a 5- or
even 6-year-old often decides, "They would be the same," for the following item involving lengths:

E.   On which path, the dashed one or the zigzag one, would an ant walk
     farther, or would it be the same, in going from A to B?

Similarly, in item F below, after agreeing that the two "sticks" in the drawing on the
left are the same length, young children may say, after one stick is moved to the
right, as in the second drawing, that the moved stick is longer. This *non-conservation
of length* is common with young children.

F.

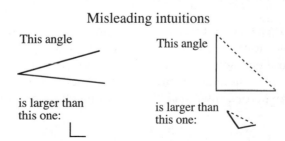

                then   (bottom stick
                                                  moved)

Children often have misleading intuitions about how angle size is measured.

Misleading intuitions

They often focus not on the
amount of turn from one side
of the angle to the other, but
on the relative lengths shown
for the sides or the distance
between the endpoints of the
segments shown for the sides.

This angle

is larger than
this one:

This angle

is larger than
this one:

Notes

Research has also shown that developmental issues are apparent with area ideas. Young children instructed to draw in squares of a given size to cover a rectangular region may draw several (rough) squares in the region but leave considerable gaps in the coverage. Later, they may proceed somewhat systematically, first drawing squares along the edges but then filling in the remaining region in a helter-skelter, often inaccurate, fashion. At some stage, they realize that a row or a column of squares can be repeated to cover a rectangular region, giving an efficient way of determining the total number of square regions required to cover the rectangular region.[vii] (The researchers also noted that grasping this row or column structure is very important for understanding the area model for multiplication.)

Another central idea of measurement is that (rigidly) moving a shape does not change its measurements. For example, it is likely that in justifying the area formula for a parallelogram region, you cut off a triangular region from one part of the parallelogram region and moved it to another part of the parallelogram, to give a rectangular region. If you were not aware that the area of the triangular region stays the same as you move it—and hence that the area of the final figure is the same as the area of the original parallelogram—this justification would not make sense. Related to this *conservation of area* is the idea of leftover, or complementary, area when a region is embedded in a larger region. For example, consider the following task.

> ◆ The drawings below show a top view of the *same* farm, with two different arrangements of the *same* barns (the dark regions). Which arrangement of barns gives more room for cows to roam over? ◆

 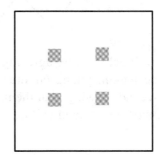

Until a certain age, people react perceptually and judge that there is more free room in the first drawing, not realizing that because the areas of the barns stay the same, the left-over or complementary area will be the same.[vi] If you have the opportunity to talk with a child 7–9 years old, you might try the task with him or her, using a sheet of paper for the farm and various numbers of blocks for the buildings.

Here is a variation of this task, in which children may give different answers to the two questions posed. Two identical grass fields have identically sized strawberry plots in them (shown in the first drawings in the following diagram). One strawberry plot is split and re-arranged, as shown. The questions are, "Is there as much room for the strawberries now," and "Is there as much room for the grass now?"

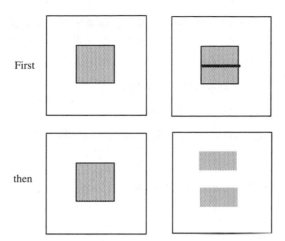

First

then

Again, if you have the opportunity to talk with children of ages 7 to 9, their answers to these questions may prove interesting.

As you might suspect, children's concepts of volume also could be improved. Already touched on (Section 16.6) is the difficulty of "reading" a 2D drawing of a 3D shape, coupled with the necessity of keeping surface area and volume ideas separate because either (or both) might be sought for a given drawing. More fundamental are ideas that parallel those for area. Consider the following tasks.[vi]

♦ Suppose that you have two identical, brand-new bars of modeling clay.

a. Pretend that you roll one of the bars into a long, sausage shape, and that you roll up the other bar into a ball shape. Which shape—the sausage or the ball—will have more clay, or will they have the same?

b. Now pretend that you have a container of water and you are going to put a shape into the container so it is completely under water. Which shape—the sausage or the ball—would cause the water to rise higher, or would they have the same effect? ♦

These ideas (*conservation of matter* for part (a), and *conservation of volume* for part (b)) take time to develop with children. For part (a), they might focus on the longer length for the sausage shape and regard the sausage as having more clay (or some might focus on the thinner aspect of the sausage and think that the ball has more clay). If you have drinking glasses of quite different dimensions, here is another conservation of volume task to try: Fill one container with liquid, pour the liquid into a different container, and ask whether there is the same amount now. If the containers have quite different shapes, many children will focus on the height, say, of the liquid and judge that there is more liquid wherever it goes higher in the container. Clearly, a grasp of conservation of volume would be a prerequisite for understanding any argument involving moving parts of a 3D region around. Try any of the preceding tasks with a primary school child if you have the opportunity.

Estimation of measurements is a practical skill that often receives little attention in the curriculum beyond looking for benchmarks for units of length. Estimation of measurements may involve computational estimation as well, as in estimating the area of a rectangular floor by estimating the product of its estimated dimensions. Estimations involving measurement can take many forms, as the following tasks suggest.[viii]

1. Estimate the length of this pencil in centimeters.

2. About how long is a pick-up truck in meters?

3. Get a meter stick and estimate the height of this building.

4. Which of those boards is about 4 feet long?

5. Think of something that is about 3 decimeters long.

Notice these characteristics in the examples:

The object is present (tasks 1, 3, and 4) or not (task 2) or perhaps not named (task 5);

the unit is present (task 3) or not (tasks 1, 2, 4, and 5); and

the estimated measurement is given (tasks 4 and 5) or not (tasks 1, 2, and 3).

Making different choices for each characteristic can lead to different sorts of estimation tasks. Having the object and unit present and the estimated measurement given is, however, just a statement and not a task. (And not having any object, unit, or estimate is not a reasonable task.)

Activity 3   Different Estimation Tasks

Using different selections of the characteristics, make up three different estimation tasks. (Try to have at least one involve some quantity besides length.)

Studies[ix] have shown that practice with estimation of measurements does improve estimation performance, and so adults do estimate better than children do although neither group does well. One study with sixth graders showed that estimating angle sizes before measuring them did give a better estimation performance than merely measuring the angles, and estimation transferred to other areas as well.

> TAKE-AWAY MESSAGE . . . Performance on wide-scale tests suggests that children's ability to deal with measurement ideas is limited for a variety of possible reasons. Some of the reasons may lie in the lack of a firm foundation with ideas that may take time, further maturation, or additional experiences to develop. Without a good foundation for the *ideas* of the quantities being measured, children may resort to a rote memorization of the many formulas, with the likelihood of confusing the formulas and applying them inappropriately. Estimation of measurements can take many forms that should be a part of the measurement curriculum. ◆

24.4	**Check Yourself**

You should be able to work exercises like those assigned and to meet the following objectives.

1. Explain what *area* means, and describe surface area.

2. Apply the four key ideas of measurement to area and surface area.

3. Describe common area units (especially metric units), and convert among them, preferably by using your metric sense for area units and perhaps with the aid of a sketch.

4. Use the relationship between the areas or surface areas of two similar shapes.

5. Explain what *volume* means.

6. Apply the key ideas of measurement to volume.

7. Describe common volume units (especially metric units), and convert among them, preferably by using your metric sense and perhaps with the aid of a sketch.

8. Use the relationship between the volumes of two similar shapes.

REFERENCES FOR CHAPTER 24

[i] http://nces.ed.gov/nationsreportcard/ National Center for Education Statistics. NAEP 1999.

[ii] Jaslow, L., & Vik, T. (2006). Using Children's Understanding of Linear Measurement to Inform Instruction. In S. Z. Smith & M. E. Smith (Eds.), *Teachers engaged in research: Inquiry into mathematics practice grades preK-2* (D. S. Mewborn, series ed.). Reston, VA: National Council of Teachers of Mathematics.

[iii] Carpenter, T., Coburn, T. G., Reys, R. E., and Wilson, J. W. (1978). Results from the first mathematics assessment of the National Assessment of Educational Progress. Reston, VA: National Council of Teachers of Mathematics. (pp. 95-96)

[iv] http://nces.ed.gov/timss/ *Trends in International Mathematics and Science Study.*

[v] Kouba, V. L., Brown, C. A., Carpenter, T. P., Lindquist, M. M., Silver, E. A., & Swafford, J. O. (1988). Results of the fourth NAEP assessment of mathematics: Measurement, geometry, data interpretation, attitudes, and other topics. *Arithmetic Teacher, 35*(9), 10-16.

[vi] Piaget, J., Inhelder, B., & Szeminska, A. (1960). The child's conception of geometry. New York: Harper & Row.

[vii] Battista, M. T., Clements, D. H., Arnoff, J. A., Battista, K., & Borrow, C. V. A. (1998). Students' spatial structuring of 2D arrays of squares. *Journal for Research in Mathematics Education, 29*(5), 503-532.

[viii] Bright, G. W. (1976). Estimation as part of learning to measure. In D. Nelson & R. E. Reys (Eds.), *Measurement in school mathematics, 1976 Yearbook*, (pp. 87-104). Reston, VA: National Council of Teachers of Mathematics.

[ix] Sowder, J. (1992). Estimation and number sense. In D. Grouws (Ed.), *Handbook of research on mathematics teaching and learning*, pp. 371-389. New York: Macmillan.

Chapter 25

Counting Units Fast: Measurement Formulas

In our discussion of measurement, the emphasis so far has been on several key ideas of measurement and their application to the measurements of length, angle size, area, and volume. You may remember formulas for some of these measurements, but we have brought up formulas only in connection with angle size to allow a clear focus on the concepts of length, area, and volume and how we measure them. Formulas are efficient, but too much emphasis on them can hide their purpose: They allow us to count units fast. In this chapter, we *do* feature formulas, emphasizing where they come from and what the formulas tell us, as well as applying them.

25.1 | Circumference, Area, and Surface Area Formulas

The basic idea of measurement is counting repetitions of a unit until an object is matched on some characteristic. This idea underlies every measurement formula. We are fortunate that for many shapes the counting can be accomplished rapidly and hence, efficiently, by using formulas. Our first formula involves a special kind of length.

Circumference

Activity 1   It's Easy as Pi

Draw several circles (or use several circular objects) and measure the circumference C and the diameter d of each circle with a tape measure or with a piece of string. Record the measurements in a table like the following one and look for a relationship (a formula) connecting C and d.

diameter

Which circle	C	d	$C + d$	$C - d$	$C \times d$	$C \div d$

In Activity 1, you found that the values in one of the columns were always a little more than 3. Ideally, the values would have been the number we call π. The number π is an interesting number. You probably know that although π is certainly a real number, it cannot be written exactly as either a finite or a repeating decimal. Hence, π is an irrational number, and values such as 3.14 and $\frac{22}{7}$ only approximate π. The special symbol π is used to communicate the exact number it represents. You may not know that π has other uses besides being involved with circles—π comes up frequently in probability and statistics, for example.

Activity 1 gives some *experimental* evidence that the ratio $C{:}d$ might always have the same value. Mathematicians would give an argument similar to this line of reasoning for circles in general: Any two circles are similar, so $C{:}C'$ will equal $d{:}d'$, or $\frac{C}{C'} = \frac{d}{d'}$. A little algebra then shows that $\frac{C}{d} = \frac{C'}{d'}$. That is, the ratio of the circumference of a circle to its diameter will always be the same and that ratio is labeled π.

For any circle with circumference C and diameter d,

$$\frac{C}{d} = \pi, \text{ or } C = \pi d.$$

We will not give special attention to other formulas dealing with length. The reason is that the idea of perimeter for polygons, for example, is better served by thinking of what perimeter means rather than learning formulas for particular polygons, such as rectangles or squares.

Area and Surface Area

Many of the formulas you may remember have to do with area. The emphasis here will be on how to *justify* the formulas, not just what the formulas are or how to use them. Rather than working through experiments that can lead to the formulas, as in Activity 1, most of the development of the formulas can be done deductively, as in the mathematician's argument stated above. But where should you start? In elementary school, the most common starting point is with the area of rectangular regions. For finding the areas of rectangles, you probably remember the formula *area* of a rectangular region equals *length* times *width*, or

$A(\textbf{rectangular region}) = lw$ for rectangles with length l and width w.

But how is it that *length* units give us a count of the square units needed for *area*? That needs explanation.

Discussion 1   Multiplying Lengths Gives Area?

Give the dimensions of the following three rectangles. Find their areas. Why *does* multiplying the two dimensions of a rectangular region give its area? (Assume for each rectangle that the small interior squares have sides with lengths 1 length unit. Fractions may be involved.)

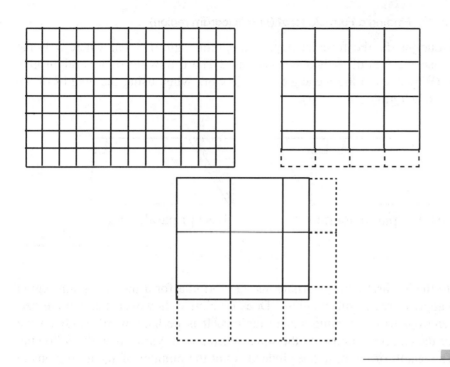

You are familiar with the hierarchical organization of quadrilaterals from Section 17.3, so it should be clear that the formula for the area of a rectangular region can be applied to a square region, where it takes the familiar form, $A(\text{\textbf{square region}}) = s^2$. (*Note*: This formula explains why s^2 is most often pronounced "s squared.") What else do we know from the following hierarchy (in which we have highlighted the relationship of squares to rectangles)?

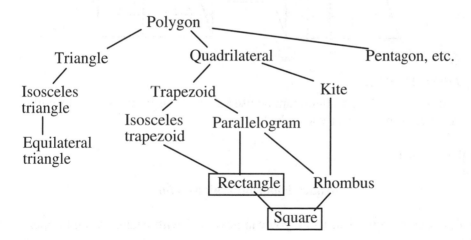

Nothing, it seems. If we could deal with polygons in general, then every special polygon would be covered. Unfortunately, there is no easy formula that does so. Even dealing with only general quadrilaterals is too ambitious. The development here follows a path common in elementary school curricula. (There are other possible sequences in making sense of the area formulas; one sequence is mentioned in the Learning Exercises.) Now that rectangular regions can be handled by a formula, you can deal with parallelogram regions.

Notes

Discussion 2   Finding a Formula for *A* (parallelogram region)

How might one justify the formula A(parallelogram region) = *bh,* where *b* is the length of a base and *h* is the height for that base? The following figures might give you an idea. (Why doesn't the rectangle formula work when using the lengths of the sides of the parallelogram?)

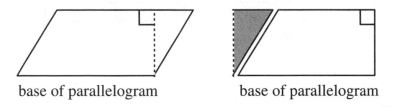

base of parallelogram   base of parallelogram

According to the hierarchy of quadrilaterals, the formula for a parallelogram region should also apply to rectangular regions. Does it? Notice, however, that we are getting quite removed from counting square regions. It is perhaps worth studying the argument for the parallelogram with the squares directly in view, as in the following drawings. The length of the base does indeed count the number of square regions in one row. The drawings also make clear why it is the *height* of the parallelogram that is important rather than the length of the other side; the height tells the number of rows of square regions there will be, whereas the length of the other side of the parallelogram does *not* tell the number of rows.

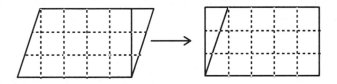

THINK ABOUT…

Can *any* side of a parallelogram be used as the base in the *A* = *bh* formula? What adjustment must you make?

With the formula

$$A\textbf{(parallelogram region)} = \textbf{\textit{bh}}$$

for parallelogram regions in hand, you can next deal with triangular and trapezoidal regions.

Activity 2   Justifying the Area Formulas for Triangles and Trapezoids

1.   Start with a triangle, as shown in the following drawing. The complete figure in the diagram suggests a way of deriving a formula for the area of the triangular region, using the formula for the area of a parallelogram region. (The highlighted

point is the midpoint of the side of the triangle.) Your justification should show that

$$A(\textbf{triangular region}) = \tfrac{1}{2}bh,$$

where b represents the length of the base of the triangle and h the height to that base.

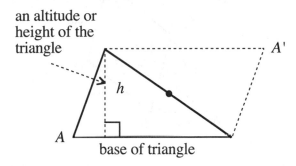

an altitude or height of the triangle

A'

h

A

base of triangle

(A height of a triangle is often called an **altitude**.)

2. Try the same method with a trapezoidal region to justify

$$A(\textbf{trapezoidal region}) = \tfrac{1}{2}h(a + b).$$

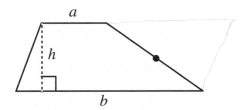

a

h

b

3. Check that the formula for trapezoidal regions also works for parallelogram, rectangular, rhombus, and square regions, as the hierarchy suggests it should.

Which polygons in the hierarchy still need attention? Although we could give attention to other polygons, there is no absolute need to do so because of this key idea of measurement: *Every polygonal region can be cut into triangular regions.* Hence, in a pinch you can find the area of any polygonal region by cutting it into triangular regions, making several measurements of lengths, applying the A(triangular region) formula several times, and then adding the areas of all the triangular regions. Of course, if the region could be cut to give some parallelogram or rectangular regions, you could save some work by having fewer regions.

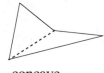

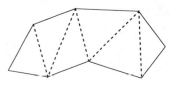

pentagon

concave quadrilateral

octagon

It should be clear that the area formulas can be very useful in finding the surface areas of polyhedra because many of their faces will be regions for which you already have formulas.

EXAMPLE 1

Find the surface area of the triangular right prism shown below.

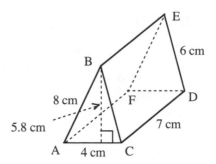

SOLUTION

Each of the two triangular bases has area $A = \frac{1}{2} \cdot 4 \cdot 5.8 = 11.6$ cm^2. Because the prism is a right prism, the other faces are rectangular regions. The surface area is, then, $11.6 + 11.6 + 42 + 28 + 56$, or 149.2 cm^2.

The final area formula we will justify is that for a circle:

$$A(\text{circular region}) = \pi r^2,$$

where r is the length of the radius of the circle. (After your experience with the circumference of a circle in Activity 1, the appearance of π again should not be a complete surprise.) Because a diameter of a circle is equal in length to two radii, the formula for the circumference $C = \pi d$ could be written $C = \pi(2r)$, or $C = 2\pi r$. This latter form is useful in deriving the formula for the area. The idea in finding the area formula for a circular region is to approximate the circular region with thinner and thinner, but congruent, isosceles triangular regions, and then to appeal to a basic idea from calculus. Notice that as more and more such triangles are fit inside the circle, the total of all their regions is getting closer and closer to filling the whole circular region. By the time the regular 17-gon is used, one's eye can scarcely see the part of the circular region that is uncovered by all the isosceles triangular regions.

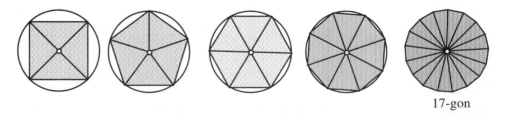

17-gon

Hence, it is very plausible that we can get arbitrarily close to the area of the circular region by taking enough of these identical, very thin isosceles triangles—that is, by using a regular n-gon with n quite large. The other key is that if we use the unequal side of the isosceles triangle as base, then the height of the triangle for that base gets arbitrarily close to the radius of the circle, as the *n*-gon gets arbitrarily close to the circle itself (check the altitudes with the triangles in the circles above). The area enclosed by each of the *n* thin triangles will be

$$\frac{1}{2}(\text{length of side of } n\text{-gon}) \times (\text{some length close to the radius}).$$

For the following reasoning, let *some length close to the radius* be denoted by ≈ radius. To get close to the area of the circular region, we can add up the areas of all the *n* triangles,

$A(\text{circular region}) \approx A(\text{all the } n \text{ triangles})$

or $A(\text{circular region}) \approx n \cdot \frac{1}{2} \cdot (\text{length of side of } n\text{-gon}) \times (\approx \text{radius})$

or $A(\text{circular region}) \approx \frac{1}{2} \cdot (n \cdot \text{length of side of } n\text{-gon}) \times (\approx \text{radius})$

or $A(\text{circular region}) \approx \frac{1}{2}(\text{perimeter of } n\text{-gon}) \times (\approx \text{radius}).$

Then, plausibly (or using the idea of *limit* from calculus), as the number of sides of the *n*-gon gets infinitely large, the perimeter of the *n*-gon "becomes" the circumference of the circle, or $2\pi r$, and the "≈ radius" becomes the radius *r*. In symbols, $A(\text{circular region}) = \frac{1}{2}(2\pi r)r$, or $\pi r r$, or

$$A(\textbf{circular region}) = \pi r^2.$$

The more complicated nature of our derivation of the area formula for a circle may make clear why you have seen very few formulas for areas of regions involving curves or curved surfaces. We will cite one more area formula, without justifying it:

$$A(\textbf{surface of a sphere}) = 4\pi r^2,$$

where *r* is the radius of the sphere. This formula is surprising because of the nonintuitive relationship that the surface area of the sphere is precisely 4 times the area of a circle having the same radius (which could be obtained on the sphere by a plane slicing through the center of the sphere).

You can find the surface area of a polyhedron by applying a key idea of measurement: Measure the area of each face, and then add those measurements.

The following table gives a summary of the area formulas and the one special formula for the length of a circle. Also useful for finding area is the idea of cutting a complicated region into pieces, and then adding the areas of the pieces to find the area of the whole region.

A(rectangular region) $= lw$ A(square region) $= s^2$	
A(parallelogram region) $= bh$	
A(triangular region) $= \frac{1}{2}bh$	
A(trapezoidal region) $=$ $\frac{1}{2}h(a+b)$	
A(circular region) $= \pi r^2$ A(surface of sphere) $= 4\pi r^2$ C(circle) $= 2\pi r = \pi d$	
Surface area of a polyhedron = sum of areas of its faces	(See Example 1 on page 584.)

If you examine the area formulas, you will notice that each formula involves multiplying two length measurements. Why such a multiplication of lengths gives a count of area units is clearest with the rectangular regions, and then gets increasingly obscure with other regions. But because we have good tools for measuring lengths, the formulas are convenient. It is noteworthy that the units behave like algebraic variables: cm × cm = cm², for example. Scientists often check the units involved to see whether a particular formula is plausible.

> TAKE-AWAY MESSAGE . . . With so many formulas, it should be clear why the *concepts* of perimeter and area (and volume) get jumbled and even lost for many students, particularly if the formulas are presented without justification. Writing the entire formula in words helps in remembering it. It is important to remember what each formula gives: a count of the number of measurement units needed to match, cover, or fill an object. ♦

Learning Exercises for Section 25.1

You will need a metric ruler for some of the Learning Exercises.

1. Organize all the formulas for geometric measurements, perhaps using index cards. Make clear what is being counted (length, angle size, area, or volume units). Include a sketch and highlight the parts that must be measured. Memorize any formulas you do not already know.

2. What is the perimeter each given figure in centimeters? (*Suggestion*: Use metric for parts (c) and (d).)

    a.   a circle with diameter 5 cm   **b.**   a circle with radius 160 km

    c.
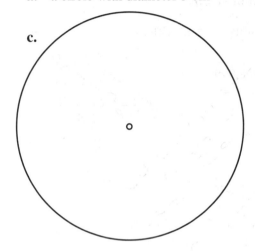
    d.
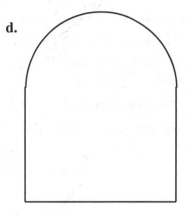

3. The equator is about 25,000 miles long. Assuming that the equator is a circle, find the radius and diameter of our Earth. Use 3.14 for π.

4. The number π is approximately 3.1415926. (A mnemonic for the digits in π is using the number of letters in each word: May I have a large container of coffee?) Computers are sometimes tested by having them calculate many decimal places for π. (More than a billion decimal places have been calculated!)

    a.   Sometimes $\frac{22}{7}$ is used as an approximation for π. About how far off is that value?

    b.   Suppose one person uses 3.14 for π and another person uses 3.1415926 to calculate the circumference of a circle with radius 12 cm. By how much do their results differ?

    c.   Suppose the two people in part (b) find the circumference of a 200-mile circular orbit for a satellite. By how much do their results differ? (The phrase "200-mile orbit" means 200 miles above our Earth. *Hint*: See Learning Exercise 3, or use as a rough approximation 8000 miles for the diameter of Earth.)

5. Which one of the following measurements is the *exact* circumference of a circle with diameter 5 cm? Explain.

    a.   15.7 cm   **b.**   15.708 cm

    c. 5π cm   **d.**   15.7079630 cm

6. You would like to make a trundle wheel to use with grade-school students. You want a wheel that will roll 1 meter in one full revolution. What should the diameter of the wheel be?

7. Suppose that a rope fits exactly around the equator. Then 40 feet more are added to the rope, and this longer rope is raised uniformly all around the equator. Which of the following could "walk" under the rope: a bacterium, an ant, a mouse, a 3-year-old child, and an adult human?

8. Answer each student whose question is given.

    a. Student: "It would be easier to just multiply the two sides of a parallelogram to get its area. Why do we have to find the height?"

    b. Student: "Where does the $\frac{1}{2}$ come from in $\frac{1}{2}bh$?"

9. Find the areas of the given regions. All units are centimeters.

    a. parallelogram *PQRS* (at the right)

    b. parallelogram: sides 9 and 16, with the 9 cm sides 8.5 cm apart

    c. rhombus: sides 12, height $4\frac{1}{2}$

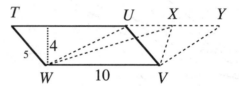

    d. parallelogram *TUVW* (shown below)

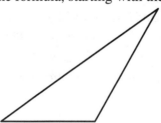

    e. triangles *WUV*, *WXV*, and *WYV*.

10. Review how the formula for the area of a triangular region was derived. Rehearse how you would explain the formula, starting with the triangle below.

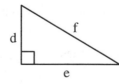

11. The base of a triangle can be any side. For each side of the given triangles, draw the segments that show the height that corresponds to that side of that triangle. With compass and straightedge, *construct* one altitude for the first and third triangles.

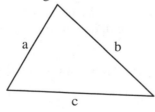
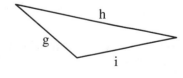

12. In finding the area of a triangle, does it matter which side you use for the base? Check your decision with the first triangle in Learning Exercise 11. (*Suggestion*: Use metric units.)

13. Count the unit squares in the following diagram to verify that the formula for the area of a triangle does give the correct number of units for the area.

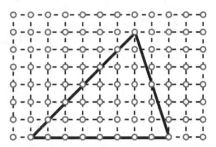

14. For the different choices of point *A*, which, if any, of the different triangles *ABC* below has the greatest area? The line that the *A*'s are on and the line that *B* and *C* are on are parallel. Explain. (*Hint*: Do *not* count squares.)

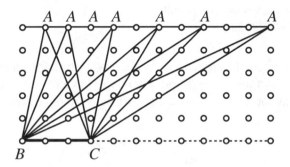

15. Does it matter where you measure the height of a trapezoid or a parallelogram in finding their areas? Explain.

16. Find the area of each trapezoidal region. (*Suggestion*: Use metric units.)

a.

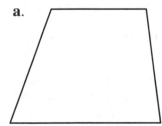

b.

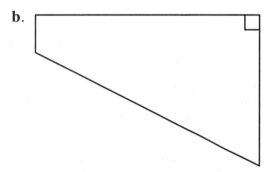

c. How can a trapezoidal region like the one in part (a) be cut into fourths with straight cuts?

17. a. What is the area of a trapezoid with height $7\frac{3}{4}$ inches and parallel sides with lengths $6\frac{1}{2}$ inches and $9\frac{1}{2}$ inches? (No decimals!)

   b. What is the area of the trapezoid in part (a) if each of its dimensions is tripled?

Notes

18. i. Find the areas of the following shapes (a)-(h). Assume that lengths are in centimeters and that angles that look like right angles are right angles.

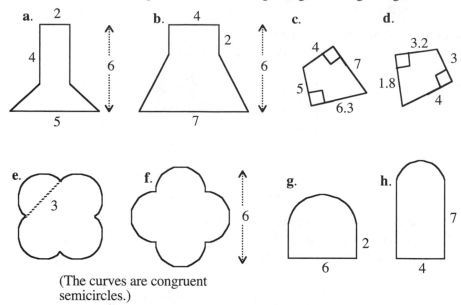

(The curves are congruent semicircles.)

ii. Suppose a company has to deal so frequently with shapes like the following shapes (i)–(l) that they would find it handy to have formulas for their areas. Find formulas for the company using just the variable measurements indicated.

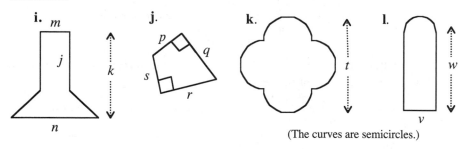

(The curves are semicircles.)

iii. Find the perimeters for shapes (c), (d), (e), (f), (g), (h), (j), (k), and (l). (Why are you not asked for the perimeters for shapes (a), (b), and (i)?)

19. a. A pizza shop charges $10.95 for a deluxe pizza with a 10-inch diameter. Is their price of $18.95 for a 14-inch diameter deluxe pizza a better buy? (Assume that no pizza is wasted if you buy the larger size.)

b. Another pizza shop uses rectangular pans, either 8 inches by 10 inches or 8 inches by 14 inches. The smaller size costs $10.95. Is their price of $16.95 for the larger size a better buy? (Again, assume that no pizza is wasted.)

20. Each circle shown on the next page has radius 2 cm.

a. What is the area of each circular region based on the formula? (Use 3.14 for π.)

b. What is the area of each grid square on both grids?

c. Using the grids in the circles on the next page, estimate the area of each circle in cm^2. Which grid gives a better estimate?

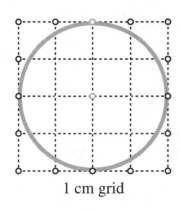

1 cm grid

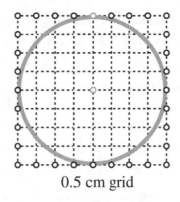

0.5 cm grid

21. Sketch and find the areas of the sectors of each circle described below.

   a. sector angle $120°$ and radius 12 cm

   b. sector angle $54°$ and radius 9.6 cm

   c. sector angle $288°$ and diameter 20 cm

   d. In general, how could you find the area of a sector of a circle, knowing the radius and size of the central angle? Explain as though you were writing a book, describing your method.

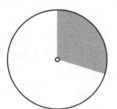 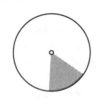

   e. How could you find the area of a sector of a circle, knowing the radius and the actual *length* of its arc?

   f. What is the perimeter of the sector in part (a), in centimeters? (Include the radii as part of the perimeter.)

   g. What is the perimeter of the sector in part (c), in centimeters?

22. If *n* rows of *n* congruent circular regions are fit into a square, as shown in the drawings below, what percent of each square region is *not* covered by the circular regions?

96 cm   96 cm   96 cm

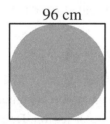 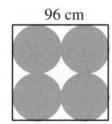 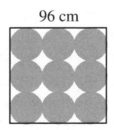

and so on

23. **a.** What is the surface area of Earth in square miles? Use 8000 miles as the diameter of Earth.

   b. Oceans cover about 70% of Earth's surface. How many square miles of *land* area are there?

   c. What is the area of the Northern Hemisphere?

24. A store has two sizes of globes, 12" and 16" in diameter.

    a. How do their surface areas compare?

    b. What is the surface area of each globe?

25. Give the surface area of each right rectangular prism described below. (*Suggestion*: Making a rough sketch may help.)

    a. length 12 cm, width 8 cm, and height 10 cm

    b. height 1.2 m, depth 40 cm, and width 80 cm

    c. length $2\frac{1}{2}$ ft, width 3 ft, and height 8 in.

    d. length x cm, width y cm, and height z cm

26. A right prism is 24 cm high and has bases like the parallelogram shown below. What is the surface area of the prism?

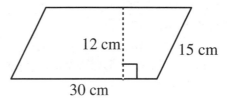

27. Find an approximate area in cm^2 for the following region, using rectangular regions 0.5 cm wide (one rectangular region is sketched). How could you improve the approximation?

28. Explain how you know that each of the following area formulas, where w, x, y, and z are the lengths of the sides, cannot possibly be correct. (*Hint*: Think units.)

    a. A(quadrilateral region) $= w \cdot x \cdot y \cdot z$

    b. A(quadrilateral region) $= w + x + y + z$

29. A region with area 14.4 cm^2 undergoes a size change with scale factor 125%.

    a. What is the new area?

    b. The new area is how many percent as large as the original area?

    c. The new area is how many percent larger than the original area?

30. Explain why a size change with scale factor k gives an image of a rectangular region that has area k^2 times as much as the original rectangular region. Does the size change affect the area of a triangular region by a factor of k^2 as well? Explain why or why not.

31. a. Justify this formula for the area of a kite: $A(\textbf{kite region}) = \frac{1}{2}dd'$, where d and d' are the lengths of the two diagonals of the kite. (Recall that the diagonals of a kite are perpendicular.)

Notes

b. To which of these polygons does the formula in part (a) automatically apply: parallelogram, trapezoid, rectangle, rhombus, square? Explain your reasoning.

32. Drawing a polygon on square-grid dot paper so that every vertex of the polygon is at a dot is easy. Perhaps surprisingly, there is a way to predict the area of the polygon from just these two numbers: the number of dots on the polygon and the number of dots inside the polygon. Use figures on dot paper and organize your work, perhaps as suggested below, in order to look for the relationship. Two examples are shown.

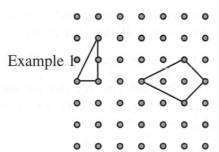

Example 1   Example 2

Number of points on the polygon	Number of points inside	Area of polygon
3	0	
4	0	1 (see Example 1)
5	0	
4	1	
5	1	
6	1	
4	2	3 (see Example 2)
(and so on)		

33. Our justification of the formula for the area of a triangular region involved creating a parallelogram region that was twice as large in area as the original triangular region. This led naturally to the formula $A = \frac{1}{2}(bh)$. (Note the use of parentheses to communicate that we took half the parallelogram's area.) It is interesting that algebraic variations of $\frac{1}{2}bh$ suggest other justifications. Explain how different approaches could have led to the following formulas. Note that the highlighted points shown are the midpoints of the line segments.

a. A(triangular region) $= \left(\frac{1}{2}b\right) \cdot h$

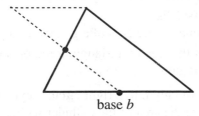

base b

b. A(triangular region) = $(\frac{1}{2}h) \cdot b$

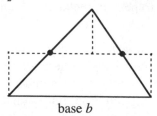

base *b*

34. a. Review how the formula for the area of a trapezoidal region was derived.

When finding a formula for the area of a trapezoidal region, you may have created a large parallelogram and taken half the area of its region, leading to $\frac{1}{2}[(a + b)h]$, or $\dfrac{(a + b)h}{2}$ for the area of the trapezoidal region. Algebraic variations of this expression suggest other possible derivations. For parts (b) and (c), explain how different approaches could have led to each expression by using the given diagram.

b. A(trapezoidal region) = $[\frac{1}{2}h] \cdot (a + b)$

c. A(trapezoidal region) = $[\frac{1}{2}(a + b)] \cdot h$

Hint: How long is the *midline*? How do you know? [The reasoning involved to answer this question may not be brief.]

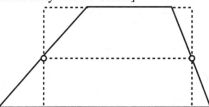

35. Sketch a trapezoid *ABCD*, with $\overline{AB}$ and $\overline{CD}$ as the parallel sides. Imagine now that points *A* and *B* move closer and closer to each other.

a. What figure is *ABCD* getting closer and closer to?

b. Use the thinking in part (a) to show that the formula for the area of a trapezoid can give the formula for the area of a triangle.

36. An alternative development of the area formulas follows the sequence of steps in parts (a)–(c), starting from the familiar A(rectangular region) = *lw*, where *l* and *w* are the two dimensions of the rectangle.

a. Derive the formula for the area of a right triangle (start with a right triangle, and relate it to some rectangle).

b. Then derive the formula for the area of a general triangle, using part (a).

c. Using the formula for the area of a triangular region, derive a formula for the area of a trapezoidal region.

37. Suppose that a sphere fits snugly into a right circular cylinder. How does the area of the sphere compare with the area of the cylinder without its two bases?

25.2 | Volume Formulas

Deriving formulas to find a volume through calculations instead of counting the cubic regions needed to match or to fill a three-dimensional object might seem like an impossible task. But, as you will see, we need only two formulas for the volumes of *all* prisms, cylinders, pyramids, and cones. Discussion 3 leads to one of those formulas.

Discussion 3   Layer by Layer

Answer the following leading questions for each prism or cylinder shown in Figure 1.

1. How many cubes are in the top layer of cubes?

2. How many layers, *h,* are in the shape? Are the layers identical in volume?

3. How can your answers to Questions 1 and 2 be used to find the volume of the prism or cylinder?

4. What is the area, *B,* of the base? Numerically, how does the area of the base compare with the number of cubes in the top layer?

5. How can *h* and *B* give the volume of the prism or cylinder?

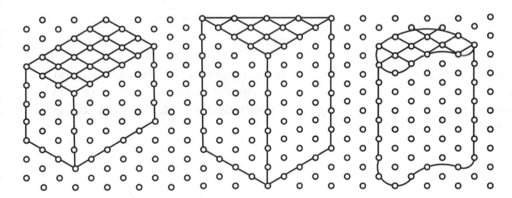

Figure 1

Discussion 3 should make apparent the formula *V*(**prism or cylinder**) = *Bh*, where *B* is the *area* of the base and *h* is the *height* of the prism or cylinder. (Notice the use of a capital *B* to remind us that the base involved here represents an area, not a length.) The type of base can lead to some other expression for *B*. For example, if the base is a rectangle with dimensions *l* and *w*, then *B* = *lw*, and so *V* = *Bh* = *(lw)h* =*lwh*. (You probably recognize this volume formula now if you had forgotten it.) Because the area of the base can be easily handled as it is encountered, using *V* = *Bh* is good for *any* prism or cylinder. For example, if the shape is a circular cylinder with *r* as the radius for the base, then the *V* = *Bh* formula could become $V = \pi r^2 h$. Most boxes in everyday living are shaped like prisms or cylinders, so this $V = Bh$ formula has wide applicability.

Or does it? Did you notice that all the shapes in Discussion 3 were *right* prisms or cylinders? Would the argument still apply to *oblique* prisms or cylinders? If you think of a tall stack of index cards, or crackers, or thin slices of bread, it should be apparent that changing the stack from a right prism/cylinder position to an oblique position does not change the volume of the stack (and leaves the height the same). The changed stack still involves the same cards, crackers, or bread as at the start, so the volume will be the same.

Another way to see that $V = Bh$ also applies to oblique prisms is to imitate the method you used for changing a parallelogram region into a rectangular region without changing the area. See the diagram in Figure 2. Can you imagine how to cut off part of an oblique pile of index cards, and move it to make a right prism shape? (Look at a pile of index cards arranged as an oblique prism.) You might have to cut twice, as with shape B from your kit of polyhedra.

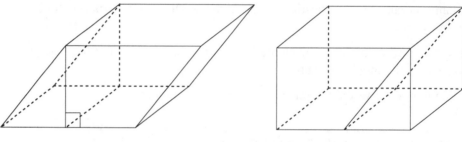

Figure 2

For any prism or cylinder, because each layer of cubes would be the same and numerically equal to the area B of the base and with the height h of the prism or cylinder telling the number of layers, the $V = Bh$ formula does indeed apply to any prism or cylinder, whether right or oblique.

EXAMPLE 2

In Example 1 in Section 25.1, we found the surface area of the triangular prism shown here. Now find its volume.

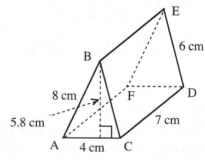

SOLUTION

$V = Bh$ applies. In the earlier example, we found that the area of the base is $B = 11.6$ cm^2. The height for the triangular prism is $h = 7$ cm. So, $V = 11.6 \times 7 = 81.2$ cm^3.

Activity 3   "Three Coins in the Fountain," or . . .

Get everyone's shape I from the polyhedra kits, and choose one person to be the assembler. (Others in the group can be advisers and assistant holders.) The task is to take two shape I's (or three, four, or however many it takes) to form a prism of some type. This activity will show how the volume of shape I is related to the volume of the prism you made:

$$V(\text{pyramid I}) = \underline{\quad} \cdot V(\text{related prism}).$$

Shape I is a special case, of course, and certainly the prism it gives is special. But the relationship holds for any pyramid, even though three copies of an arbitrary pyramid cannot be fit together to make a prism. As you might suspect, the same 1:3 relationship holds for the volume of a cone and the volume of the cylinder into which the cone would just fit.

Thus, the picture for prisms and cylinders (**V = Bh**) and for pyramids and cones (**V = $\frac{1}{3}$Bh**) is complete. The formulas could be applied to any appropriate shape—prism, cylinder, pyramid, or cone—with B perhaps being replaced by a suitable area formula for the base of the particular shape.

Here is one final formula for volume:

$$V(\textbf{sphere}) = \frac{4}{3}\pi r^3.$$

One possible justification is similar to that for the area of a circle in that it involves approximating the spherical region with pyramid regions. Imagine this reasoning: Each pyramid has its base vertices on the sphere, and its other vertex at the center of the sphere, as in this figure.

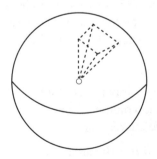

There are many, many such pyramids, all identical and filling all of the spherical region except for small spaces close to the sphere. As the bases of the pyramids get smaller and smaller, the pyramids get closer and closer to filling the sphere completely. The volume of the sphere is approximately the total of the volumes of all of the pyramids. Each pyramid has volume $\frac{1}{3}Bh$, with h being very close to the radius r of the sphere as the number of pyramids increases greatly. In adding all of these volumes, we can factor out the $\frac{1}{3}h$, leaving the sum of all the bases of the pyramids as the other factor. But by *taking the limit* (as they say in calculus) that sum becomes the surface area of the sphere, and the height h of each pyramid becomes the radius r of the sphere. So the volume is $\frac{1}{3} r \cdot (4\pi r^2) = \frac{1}{3}(4\pi r^2) \cdot r$, or V(spherical region) = $\frac{4}{3}\pi r^3$.

Just as with the area formulas, the volume formulas give the correct units. For example, if the unit for B is cm^2 and the unit for h is cm, then it makes sense that the volume formula gives cubic units: cm$^2 \cdot$ cm = cm^3. This fact again illustrates the value of paying attention to the units involved.

A summary of the volume formulas follows. In addition, sometimes the key idea of imagining a complicated 3D shape being cut into pieces that are easier to deal with, finding the volumes of the pieces, and then adding those results, is useful.

For any prism or cylinder, $V = Bh$, where B is the area of the base and h is the height of the prism or cylinder.

For any pyramid or cone, $V = \frac{1}{3} Bh$, where B is the area of the base and h is the height of the pyramid or cone.

For a sphere with radius r, $V = \frac{4}{3}\pi r^3$.

Problems can involve more than one formula, as the next example illustrates.

EXAMPLE 3

A custom-made solid iron support for an odd-shaped corner of a room is a right cylinder, 8 ft long with bases that are 135° sectors of circles with 4-in. radii. Only the curved part is to be coated with protective material. The iron weighs 490 pounds per cubic foot. (a) How much will the support weigh? (b) What is the area that is to be coated in square feet?

SOLUTION Making even a rough drawing is often helpful. This situation calls for the volume of the support, as well as the area of the curved part.

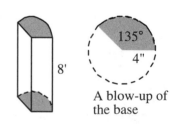

A blow-up of the base

(a) $V = Bh$ applies; h is 8 feet, and B is the area of a 135° sector. That area will be $\frac{135}{360}$ or $\frac{3}{8}$ of the whole circle area: $B = \frac{3}{8}\pi 4^2 \approx 18.85$ square inches. The height h is given in feet, but 8' = 96". So $V \approx 18.85 \times 96 \approx 1810$ cubic inches. Because $12^3 = 1728$, we know that the support has volume $1810 \div 1728$ cubic feet, or about 1.05 cubic feet. The support weighs $1.05 \times 490 \approx 515$ pounds.

(b) In a net for the support, the curved part would look like a rectangular region ($A = lw$) with length 96" and width being $\frac{3}{8}$ of the circumference of a 4-in. radius circle (use $C = 2\pi r$). So, this gives for the width $\frac{3}{8} \times 2\pi 4 \approx 9.42$", and then the part to be coated has area 96 × 9.42, or about 904 square inches. The area to be coated would be 904 ÷ 144, or about 6.3 square feet.

> TAKE-AWAY MESSAGE . . . Three volume formulas and the key idea of cutting up a complicated shape allow us to determine easily the number of cubic units it would take to fill or match a great variety of shapes.
>
> (1) $V = Bh$ for any prism or cylinder with base B and height h.
>
> (2) $V = \frac{1}{3}Bh$ for any pyramid or cone with base B and height h.
>
> (3) $V = \frac{4}{3}\pi r^3$ for any sphere with radius r. ◆

Learning Exercises for Section 25.2

1. Would $V = Bh$ for each of the following figures? (B = area of the base, h = height of shape.) Explain.

    a.  **b.** 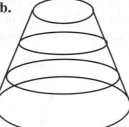 **c.**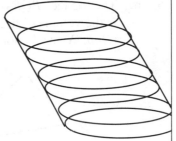

2. **a.** How many cubes, 1 cm on each edge, would fit into a right rectangular prism 7 cm by 10 cm by 12 cm?

    b. How many cubes, 2 cm on each edge, would fit into that same prism?

    c. What is the surface area of the prism in part (a)?

3. A plastics company makes many shapes with holes in them. One particular order calls for pieces 0.6 cm thick and shaped like the following shapes (a)–(c). For each shape, find the volume of plastic needed for an order calling for 1000 of each shape. Use metric units to make any measurements you need. (The shaded parts show the holes.)

    a. 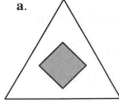 **b.** 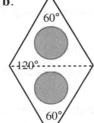 **c.**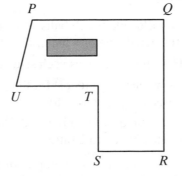

    d. What key ideas of measurement did you use in parts (a)–(c)?

4. We can make two circular cylinders without bases as follows: (1) an $8\frac{1}{2}$ inch by 11 inch piece of paper can be curved from top to bottom to give the circular cylinder without bases, and (2) the same size paper can be curved from side to side to make the cylinder.

    a. How would the lateral areas of the two cylinders compare?

    b. How would the volumes of the two cylinders compare?

    c. If two shapes have equal surface areas, will they always have equal volumes? Give an example using three-dimensional shapes made from cubes.

5. a. A prism has bases that are 6 cm by 8 cm rectangular regions. The prism is 7 cm high. Sketch the prism. What is its volume?

    b. A rectangular pyramid fits exactly into the prism in part (a), with the base of the pyramid exactly on the base of the prism and with the other vertex of the pyramid on the other base of the prism. Sketch the pyramid inside the prism. What is the volume of the pyramid?

    c. What is the surface area of the prism in part (a), if it is a *right* prism? (*Hint*: Make a drawing to help keep track.)

6. a. The top face *PQR* of the first prism drawn below is shown actual size. What is the volume of the polyhedron? Measure in triangle *PQR* with metric units. (*Hint*: What additional measurement will you need to make for triangle *PQR*?)

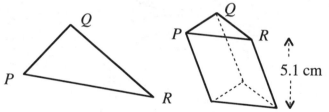

    b. Point *S* in the top face of that same prism is joined to the vertices of the opposite face to give another polyhedron. What is its volume?

    b.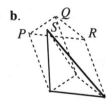

7. The Great Pyramid of Cheops, built around 4600 years ago, is a regular square pyramid 146.5 m tall and 230.4 m along each side of its base. What is its volume in cubic meters?

8. Plastic inflatable beach balls come in two sizes: 8-inch diameter when inflated, and 16-inch diameter when inflated.

    a. How much air does each size beach ball hold when inflated?

    b. How much will it cost for the plastic to make each beach ball, if the plastic costs 28¢ per square foot?

    c. The ratio of 8 to 16 is 1 to 2. Why are the answers in parts (a) and (b) not related by a 1 to 2 ratio?

9. Food for farm animals might be stored in a silo. Silos are often shaped like right circular cylinders with a right circular cone on top. Suppose that one such silo

Notes

has a diameter of 16 feet, a height of 12 feet for the cylinder, and an overall height of 15 feet.

   a. Find the volume of the whole silo in ft^3.

   b. How many bushels does the cylindrical part of the silo hold? (A bushel is 2150.42 cubic inches.)

10. a. What are the surface area and volume of a sphere with radius 1 meter?

   b. What is the volume of Earth in cubic miles? Use 8000 miles as the diameter of Earth.

   c. What is the volume of our sun in cubic miles? Use 870,000 miles as the diameter of the sun.

   d. How many Earths would make the volume of our sun?

11. Half a sphere (called a **hemisphere**) can fit exactly into a cylinder, as can a cone with its base at one base of the cylinder and its vertex on the other base.

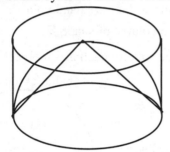

   a. Find the ratio of the volume of the hemisphere to that of the cone. (Archimedes, an ancient Greek, knew these ratios.)

   b. What is the ratio of the volume of the hemisphere to that of the cylinder?

12. There are two bars of new clay, each shaped like a right rectangular prism with dimensions $\frac{1}{2}$", 2", and 8". One of the clay bars is rolled into a sphere, whereas the other bar stays its original shape.

   a. Are the two final shapes congruent?

   b. How do the volumes of the bar and the sphere compare?

   c. What is the radius of the sphere?

13. a. A can of tennis balls often holds three tennis balls. What part of the can do the balls fill? (*Hint*: Let the radius of the can be *r*. What is then the height of the can?)

   b. A sphere fits snugly inside a cube. What percent of the cube's volume is outside the sphere?

14. A cube and a sphere each enclose 1000 cm^3. Which shape is taller, and by how much?

15. Many types of explosions depend on very fast burning, which in turn depends on the surface area exposed. Suppose a ball of gunpowder material is in the shape of a sphere with volume 36π cm^3. Now suppose that this ball is broken into small spheres with diameters all equal to 0.1 mm. What is the ratio of the original surface area to the total surface area of all the smaller spheres?

16. In the 1990s an asteroid came quite close to Earth, and it will return in the future. At first the asteroid was believed to be $\frac{1}{3}$ mile in diameter, but later measurements indicated its diameter was $\frac{1}{10}$ mile.

   a. Assuming that the asteroid was spherical, find the volume of the $\frac{1}{3}$ mile in diameter version.

   b. What percent of the $\frac{1}{3}$ mile in diameter version is the $\frac{1}{10}$ mile version?

17. a. Consider shapes A, F, G, and I from your polyhedra kit. What would you measure to determine the surface area and volume of each shape?

   b. How might you find the volume of shape K?

18. Find the volume and surface area for each given object.

   a.

8 cm tall (cylinder)

Diameter 6 cm

   b. radius of top = 5 cm

height of cylinder 3 cm

Give formulas for the volumes of the following, using only the measurements indicated by variables.

   c.

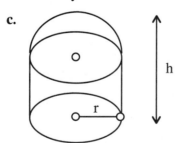

h

r

hemisphere on top of right circular cylinder

   d.

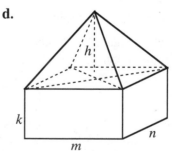

h

k

m

n

The base is a rectangular region.

   e. Give formulas for the volume and surface area of a right circular cylinder that has height h and whose base has radius r.

19. The expression x^3 is most often pronounced "x cubed," instead of the more generic "x to the third power." Where does the "x cubed" come from?

20. a. Find the surface area of a cube with edges 8 cm long.

   b. Give a formula for the surface area of a cube with edge length equal to *s* cm.
SA(cube) = _____

   c. Find the volume of a cube with edges 8 cm long.

   d. Give a formula for the volume of a cube with edge length equal to *s* cm.
V(cube) = _____

   e. Can the surface area and the volume of a cube ever be the same? Can they ever be *numerically* the same?

21. Explain why a size change with scale factor *k* gives an image of a right rectangular prism that has volume k^3 times as much as the volume of the original prism. Does the size change affect the volume of a pyramid by a factor of k^3 as well? Explain why or why not.

22. a. Give a formula for the volume of a sphere in terms of the diameter *d*.

   b. Give a formula for the volume of a hemisphere (half a sphere) in terms of the radius *r*.

   c. Give a formula for the area of a sphere in terms of the diameter *d*.

   d. Give a formula for the area of a hemisphere in terms of the diameter *d*.

23. You want to make a dog house from a piece of plywood 4 feet by 8 feet. Design the largest dog house you can. (The plywood must cover the sides and the roof.)

24. Areas of rectangular regions and volumes of right rectangular prisms can give insight into some algebraically equivalent expressions. Using sketches and labeling subregions, find or verify equivalent expressions in the following.

   a. $(x + y)^2 = $ _____

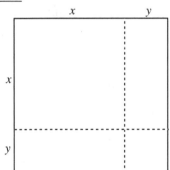

   b. $(x + y)^3 = x^3 + 3x^2y + 3xy^2 + y^3$

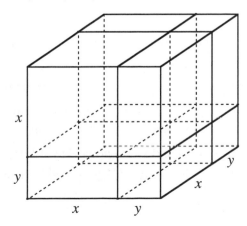

Continue on the next page.

c. $x(x + y) =$ _____ (make your own drawing)

d. $(x + 2)(x + 3) =$ _____

25. Here are examples of *Fermi problems*, named after Enrico Fermi, a physicist who was involved in early experiments with splitting the atom. In a Fermi problem, the idea is not to calculate carefully and extensively, but to use thoughtful estimates and minimal arithmetic (and probably scientific notation) as much as possible to arrive at an idea of the size of the answer.

a. How many kernels of popped popcorn would fit into your mathematics classroom?

b. What if the popcorn were not popped?

c. How many toilet flushes could be made with all the water from a 2-cm rainfall on your city?

d. How many dollar bills would it take to cover the surface of Earth?

e. How many oranges would it take to fill Earth?

f. If all the people in the world lay head-to-foot in a line, how many times would the line go around the equator (or what part of an equator if the line wouldn't go around once)?

25.3 | Check Yourself

Formulas will offer an opportunity for your students to practice calculation (and estimation) in real contexts, particularly if they have to make length or angle measurements themselves.

You should be able to do exercises like those assigned and to meet the following objectives.

1. Use the circumference, area, and volume formulas from this chapter. It is probably a good idea to list them all so that you can see whether any are similar and hence need special attention to keep straight. Knowing where the formulas come from and what the formulas tell you when they are used is essential.

2. Justify the area formulas using either the basic idea of area or formulas already established.

3. Take advantage of the hierarchy of quadrilaterals in applying the formulas for their areas.

4. Show some appreciation of the strange but perfectly good number π.

5. Use a "layer" argument to justify the formula for the volume of any prism or cylinder, and know that the argument does not always apply.

6. Use a key idea of measurement and your knowledge of formulas to give formulas for the perimeter, area, or volume of different sorts of shapes.

Chapter 26

Special Topics in Measurement

It could be argued that the first special topic in this chapter, the Pythagorean theorem, is a measurement topic. If so, is it about lengths or about areas? The Pythagorean theorem is so important that it deserves its own section. The final section in this chapter, Section 26.2, serves as a reminder that measurement is a pervasive process in life. That fact supports the view that measurement deserves a significant role in the school curriculum.

26.1 | The Pythagorean Theorem

Relatively few results in elementary mathematics are associated with a name, perhaps because the original discoverer is not known. But in mathematics one result is always associated with Pythagoras: the Pythagorean theorem.

Right angles are common in many shapes encountered in the western world, and the heights of triangles, trapezoids, parallelograms, prisms, pyramids, cylinders, and cones involve right angles. These right angles can often be associated with some right triangle.

Right triangles come in all sizes and shapes. The sides of the triangle that give the right angle are sometimes called the **legs** of the right triangle, and the other side, the longest, is called the **hypotenuse**. It would seem that all we could rely on for *all* right triangles would be the one right angle and the fact that the hypotenuse is longer than either leg.

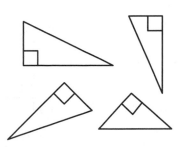

Fortunately, the lengths of the legs and the hypotenuse of a right triangle are related, although in a nonintuitive way. Perhaps that is the reason, along with its multitude of uses, why the relationship is so famous. The relationship is associated with Pythagoras (ca. 570 B.C.), although the ancient Babylonians, Indians, and Chinese knew it long before him. The relationship is called the Pythagorean theorem.

> The **Pythagorean theorem**: In a right triangle having legs of lengths
> a and b and hypotenuse of length c,
> $$a^2 + b^2 = c^2.$$

Interestingly, no well-developed algebraic notation existed at the time of Pythagoras for the square of a number. Where we write s^2 and think $s \cdot s$, the Greeks, not having that notation, thought of a geometric square! Hence, they interpreted the Pythagorean theorem geometrically, as follows.

Pythagoras' version: For a right triangle, the sum of the areas of the square regions drawn on each leg is equal to the area of the square drawn on the hypotenuse. That is, area of region I + area of region II = area of region III. The algebraic symbolism that we use for the square of a number, x^2, was not invented until the 1600s. We wonder what symbols people will use in the 2400s!

The complete history of how the relationship was discovered and justified for *all* right triangles is lost, but since Pythagoras's time there have been more than 350 different mathematical justifications of it, including ones by Euclid, Leonardo da Vinci, and President James Garfield. Activity 1 shows an experimental way of verifying the relationship with the area interpretation, in a way that elementary students can understand.

Activity 1   Illustrating the Pythagorean Theorem with Areas

Trace the lettered regions in the following diagram, cut them out, and reassemble them to match the square region drawn on the hypotenuse.

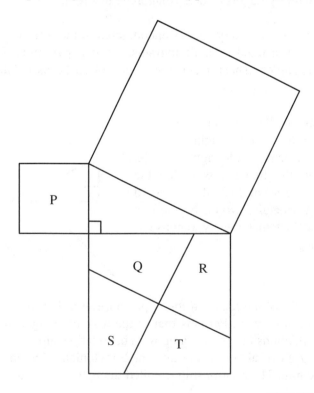

Following are some examples to give just a glimpse of the usefulness of the Pythagorean theorem. Knowing any two of the three lengths of the sides of a right triangle allows you to calculate the length of the third side.

EXAMPLE 1

Suppose a right triangle has one leg with length 5 cm and hypotenuse with length 13 cm. How long is the other leg?

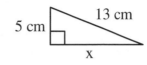

SOLUTION

Letting x represent the length of the other leg, the Pythagorean theorem asserts that $5^2 + x^2 = 13^2$. That is, $25 + x^2 = 169$, or $x^2 = 169 - 25 = 144$. So $x = \pm\sqrt{144} = {}^+12$ or ${}^-12$ (${}^\pm12$ or ±12 for short). The other leg is 12 cm long. (The negative square root, ${}^-12$, does not make sense because a negative length is not possible here.)

As you know, square roots of most whole numbers are not themselves whole numbers. For example, if the legs had lengths 3 cm and 8 cm, then $3^2 + 8^2 = h^2$ would give $9 + 64 = h^2$, or $h^2 = 73$, with $h = \pm\sqrt{73} \approx 8.5440037$. So the length of the hypotenuse would be about 8.5 cm. (If the 3 cm and 8 cm were ideal measurements of ideal segments, the exact $\sqrt{73}$ cm would be appropriate.)

Although most calculators have a square-root key, finding a square root by trial and error can be fairly efficient (and emphasizes the meaning of square root). For example, suppose you want a decimal value for $\sqrt{119}$. Because $10^2 = 100$ and $20^2 = 400$, you immediately know that $\sqrt{119}$ is between 10 and 20. Because $11^2 = 121$, $\sqrt{119}$ must be slightly less than 11. Checking the value 10.9, we get $10.9^2 = 118.81$, so $\sqrt{119}$ is about 10.9.

> ***THINK ABOUT...***
>
> How do you know that $\sqrt{784}$ is between 20 and 30? Between 25 and 30?

EXAMPLE 2

How is the height of an equilateral triangle related to its side?

SOLUTION

In many situations, we might know s and want to find h (see the drawing above), rather than vice versa. The symmetry of the equilateral triangle gives two right triangles with legs h and $\frac{s}{2}$. By focusing on one of the right triangles, the Pythagorean theorem gives

$$h^2 + (\tfrac{s}{2})^2 = s^2, \text{ or } h^2 + \tfrac{s^2}{4} = s^2$$

$$h^2 = s^2 - \tfrac{s^2}{4} = \tfrac{4s^2}{4} - \tfrac{s^2}{4} = \tfrac{3s^2}{4}. \text{ Finally, } h = \pm\sqrt{\frac{3s^2}{4}} = \pm\frac{s\sqrt{3}}{2}.$$

Thus, given just the length of a side of an equilateral triangle, we can find its height. ($\sqrt{3} \approx 1.732$)

EXAMPLE 3

A tower on level ground is to be supported by two wires of lengths 30 m and 40 m (after being fastened). The wires will be attached 24 m up the tower. How far from the foot of the tower will the wires hit the ground? (The planners are not sure there is enough room.)

SOLUTION

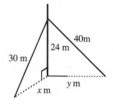

Towers should meet level ground to make right angles, so the Pythagorean theorem is useful, as is a drawing. We get $x^2 + 24^2 = 30^2$, or $x^2 = 900 - 576$. So $x^2 = 324$, and $x = 18$ (trial and error or calculator). Similarly, $y^2 + 24^2 = 40^2$, leading to $y = \pm\sqrt{1024}$, so $y = 32$.

Because right angles are needed in finding heights for many area and volume problems, the Pythagorean theorem is often useful in such settings.

Activity 2   The Pythagorean Theorem Goes to Egypt

A regular square pyramid has a base with edges 10 cm long and with its other edges 12 cm long. Show that its volume and surface area are, respectively, 323.3 cm^3 and 318 cm^2. (*Hint:* Find y first, then x.)

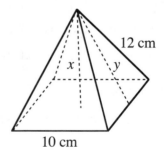

The Pythagorean theorem *begins* knowing that you have a right triangle and makes an assertion about the sides. The vice versa situation, called the **converse** in logic, also turns out to be true in this case. If you *begin* by knowing that $a^2 + b^2 = c^2$ for the sides a, b, and c of a triangle, then the triangle is a right triangle (the converse of the Pythagorean theorem). The ancient Egyptians knew this fact, and they used it to make right angles, as do carpenters and fence builders nowadays. For example, because $3^2 + 4^2 = 5^2$, finding points 3 feet and 4 feet from a corner so that the points are 5 feet apart will assure a right angle at the corner.

> ### THINK ABOUT...
>
> Consider an isosceles right triangle with legs 1 unit long. Confirm that the hypotenuse has length $\sqrt{2}$ units.

You may know that $\sqrt{2}$ is irrational and thus cannot be written as the ratio of two integers: $\frac{\text{integer}}{\text{integer}}$. One legend says that the Pythagoreans had built a sort of "religion" around rational numbers, so when they found out that $\sqrt{2}$ was irrational even though it described a perfectly reasonable line segment, they were shocked and decided to keep it a secret. One of the group, however, told others. The legend says that the Pythagoreans took this person on a boat trip ... and he did not come back.

> TAKE-AWAY MESSAGE . . . The Pythagorean theorem is one of the very useful results for geometry. In a society where so many right angles occur, the theorem allows the calculation of many measurements. The theorem's converse, also true, allows one to create a right angle using only lengths. ♦

Learning Exercises for Section 26.1

1. What does the Pythagorean theorem assert about each triangle?

a. 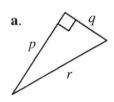   b. 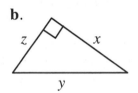   c.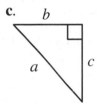

2. A common mistake with square roots is to think that $\sqrt{a^2 + b^2}$ is equal to $a + b$. Find a numerical example that shows this equality is incorrect.

3. Find the perimeter and area for each triangle pictured or described. Give an exact length and also an approximation.

a. 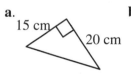   b. 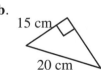   c.   d.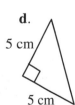

   e. right triangle with legs 1.6 m and 6.3 m
   f. right triangle with one leg 2.1 cm and hypotenuse 2.9 cm
   g. right triangle with legs 15 in. and 36 in.
   h. right triangle with one leg 4 m and hypotenuse 8.5 m

4. Find the length of a diagonal for each shape described.
   a. a square, 10 cm on each side

Continue on the next page.

b.   a square, *s* cm on each side

c.   a rectangle, 10 cm by 24 cm

d.   a rectangle, *m* cm by *n* cm

5.   Draw and find the length of each diagonal of each face of the following right rectangular prism and the *inside* diagonal of the prism, as shown. How long are the other *inside* diagonals?

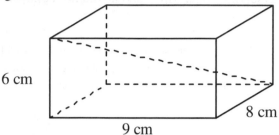

6.   **a.**   Give an expression for the length of an *inside* diagonal of a right rectangular prism that is *x* cm by *y* cm by *z* cm.

b.   Will a 5-foot fishing rod fit inside a box that is 24 inches by 30 inches by 30 inches?

c.   How long is an *inside* diagonal of a cube with edges of length *e*?

d.   A 10-cm cube has all of its vertices on a sphere. What is the radius of the sphere?

7.   The fire department needs to buy a ladder that will reach to the top of a two-story building—say, 22 feet. For safety's sake, when the full ladder is used, the distance the bottom of the ladder is from the building should be about $\frac{1}{4}$ the length of the ladder. The department can choose ladders that are 24', 28', and 32'. What size ladder should they buy? (*Hint:* If the ladder is *x* feet long, its bottom should be $\frac{x}{4}$ feet from the building.)

8.   A plan calls for running a pipe from *P* to *Q* to *R*. The pipe costs \$5.89/m. If it is feasible to run the pipe directly from *P* to *R*, how much money would you save?

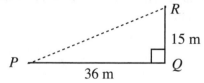

9.   The following pyramid has a rectangular base, with several measurements and its other vertex given. What are the surface area and volume of the pyramid?

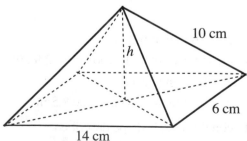

Notes

10. a. Find the areas of the semicircular regions drawn on the sides of the following right triangle, with $a = 6$ cm and $b = 8$ cm. How are the areas of the three regions related?

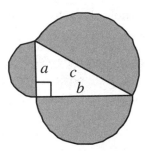

b. Use the variables a, b, and c to see in general whether the three areas are always related for a right triangle.

11. a. Show that the area enclosed by an equilateral triangle is given by $\dfrac{s^2\sqrt{3}}{4}$, where s is the length of a side of the triangle.

b. Find the areas enclosed by the equilateral triangles drawn on the sides of the following right triangle, with $a = 5$ cm and $b = 13$ cm. How are the areas of the three regions related?

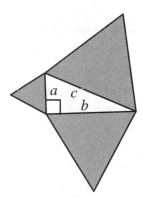

c. Use the variables a, b, and c to see in general whether the three areas are always related for a right triangle.

12. President Garfield's reasoning to justify that the Pythagorean theorem was based on the following drawing.

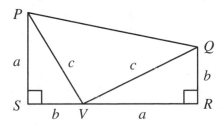

Confirm that $a^2 + b^2 = c^2$ for the right triangle by doing the following steps.

a. Find the area of the whole shape by treating it as made up of three right triangular regions.

b. Then find the area of the whole shape by treating it as a trapezoid.

c. Compare the results from parts (a) and (b).

13. Triples of whole numbers such as the earlier 3–4–5 and 5–12–13 are called **Pythagorean triples** because they are positive integers that fit an $x^2 + y^2 = z^2$ relationship. Which of the following are Pythagorean triples?

a. 5, 6, and 7

b. 6, 8, and 10

c. 9, 12, and 15

d. 12, 16, and 20

e. If x, y, and z give a Pythagorean triple, will kx, ky, and kz also be a Pythagorean triple?

f. Use the idea in part (e) to generate 12 more Pythagorean triples.

14. **a.** Find the length of segment PQ on the given coordinate system.

b. Find the lengths of the other marked segments.

c. Point P has coordinate (3, 5) and Q has coordinates (1, 1). Give the coordinates of the other lettered points in the diagram. How can they be used to help find the lengths of the segments? For example, suppose you wanted to find the length of the segment joining the points with coordinates (50, 30) and (43, 6). Can it be done without extending the graph?

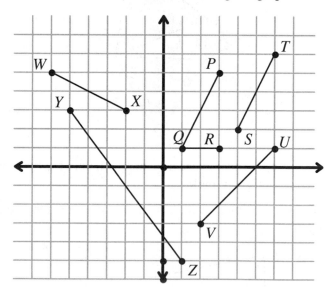

15. There are examples of situations in which an if-then statement is true, but its converse is not always true. In each of the following parts, decide whether both if-then statements are always true. If one is not, identify it and explain why it is not true.

a. If two rectangles are congruent, then they have equal areas.

   If two rectangles have equal areas, then they are congruent.

b. If n^2 is a positive whole number, then n is a positive whole number.

If n is a positive whole number, then n^2 is a positive whole number.

c. If $x^2 = 4$, then $x = 2$.

If $x = 2$, then $x^2 = 4$.

d. If p is a factor of the product qr, then p is a factor of q or of r.

If p is a factor of q or of r, then p is a factor of the product qr.

16. Here is another ancient Greek result, called Hero's formula (or Heron's formula):

The area of a triangle is given by $\sqrt{s(s-a)(s-b)(s-c)}$, where a, b, and c are the lengths of the sides of the triangle, and s is half the perimeter of the triangle.

  a. Apply the formula to a triangle with sides 15, 36, and 39.

  b. Verify using the converse of the Pythagorean theorem that the 15–36–39 triangle is a right triangle, and find its area using the triangle-area formula. Does the result agree with that of part (a)?

17. How many different lengths are possible on dot paper with 6 rows of dots and 6 dots in a row? The following examples show that there are 2 different lengths possible with 2 by 2 dots, and 5 different lengths possible with 3 by 3 dots. (In the drawing, two new ones overlap two of the old ones.)

18. Give the perimeter and area of each polygon. Use the natural units.

a.   **b.**   **c.**   **d.**

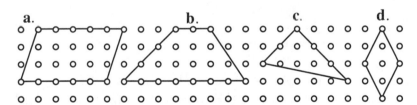

19. The following drawings are nets for polyhedra. Find the surface area and volume for each polyhedron. (*Hint*: Draw the polyhedron and label it with what you know.)

a.   2.5 cm

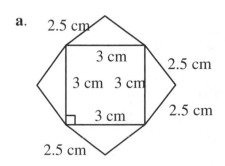

3 cm
2.5 cm
3 cm 3 cm
2.5 cm
3 cm
2.5 cm

b. (rectangular pyramid)

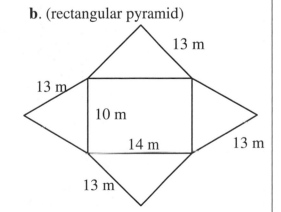

13 m
13 m
10 m
14 m
13 m
13 m

20. A large pile of sand has dimensions as in the figure at the right.

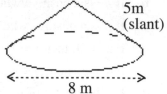

5m
(slant)

8 m

   a. Approximately what shape is the pile of sand?

   b. What is the volume of the pile of sand?

   c. How many children's sandboxes shaped like right square prisms 30 cm high with sides 1.5 m long will the sand fill?

21. a. A right circular cone has height 12 cm and 4 cm radius on the base. How far is it from the vertex to a point on the circle at the base?

   b. A piece of paper cut from an 8-inch circle and shaped like the sector below is cut out and rolled up to give a circular cone shape. What is the volume of the cone?

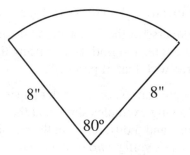

8"   8"

80°

22. A new and larger triangle X is similar to the triangle shown below with the size transformation having scale factor 4. What is the area enclosed by triangle X?

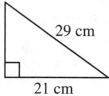

29 cm

21 cm

23. An antenna on top of a building will be held steady by wires from *P* to *A*, *B*, *C*, and *D*, as pictured in the following diagram. How many feet of wire are needed? Assume that consecutive dots shown are 10 feet apart and allow 1 extra foot for each wire for tying the ends with a slight sag in the wires.

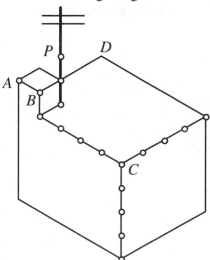

24. A **segment of a circle** is the region formed by a chord of a circle and the circle. The area of a segment can be found for some angles, such as the 60° angle shown in the drawing, without trigonometry. Find the area of the sector shown for a circle with radius 10 cm. (*Hint*: Use a key idea of measurement.)

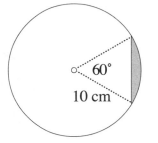

25. Give a geometric interpretation of the algebraic equation, $a^3 + b^3 = c^3$. Mathematicians conjectured for many years that there are no positive whole numbers a, b, and c that make the equation true, unlike the situation when the exponents all equal 2 (the Pythagorean triples).

26. A canal 4 meters wide makes a 90° turn. Is it possible to make a bridge across the canal if you have only two boards, each 3.9 meters long (and no nails)?[i]

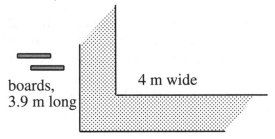

boards,
3.9 m long

4 m wide

27. There are several congruent right triangles in the following squares. How can the drawings be used to justify the Pythagorean theorem?

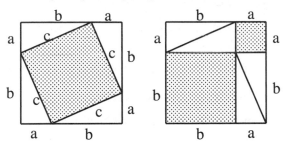

28. Find the missing angle sizes and lengths using the information in each sketch and your knowledge of triangles.

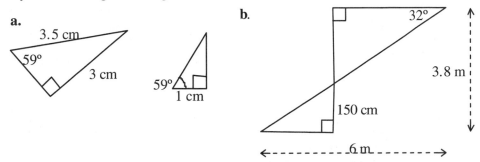

a.
3.5 cm
59°
3 cm
59°
1 cm

b.
32°
3.8 m
150 cm
6 m

29. Starting with an isosceles right triangle with each leg 1 unit long, and building onto the hypotenuse continually as shown in the diagrams on the next page, gives a sequence like the one started. Find the lengths of the hypotenuses of the right triangles.

Notes

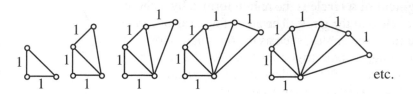

etc.

26.2 | Some Other Kinds of Measurements

Working exclusively with measurements of geometric quantities can obscure the fact that all sorts of other quantities also are measured. Indeed, it is difficult to think of an everyday occurrence of a number that does not arise from a measurement, especially when counts and monetary cost are considered to be measurements.

Technical fields, of course, have many specialized measurements. But everyday life also uses a surprising number of measurements, even outside geometric quantities. You will recognize some of them in Discussion 1.

___

Discussion 1   From Rings to a Lottery

What are units for values for the following quantities? (*Hint:* Look up carat and karat.)

a. the size of a diamond in a ring   **b.** the purity of the gold in a ring

c. the purity of the water you drink   **d.** the popularity of television shows

e. the amount of nutrition in a food   **f.** the healthiness of your gums

g. the chances of winning a lottery

In the elementary curriculum, working with actual measurements not only can teach something about quantitative aspects of many kinds of nonmath situations but also can enable children to attach meanings to numbers. As a reminder, we repeat the key ideas about geometric measurements from Section 23.1. It will be of interest to find that they do not apply to all kinds of measurements.

Key Idea 1:   The direct measurement of some characteristic in an object involves matching the object with a unit, or copies of a unit, having that characteristic. Many measurements are made indirectly using mechanical or scientific principles instead of direct comparisons.

Key Idea 2:   Standard units are used because they ease communication and are relatively permanent in that they can be reproduced. The main system of standard units in the world is the metric system (SI).

Key Idea 3: Counts can be exact, but other measurements are approximate. Smaller units can give better approximations.

Key Idea 4: A quantity can sometimes be measured by thinking of the object as "cut" into a finite number of pieces, measuring the quantity in each piece, and then adding those measurements. (This one is the key idea that does not always apply.)

Discussion 2   Key-ing on Cereal

How might the key ideas of measurement be used with the quantity of calories in a particular kind of breakfast cereal?

Discussion 3 deals with standard units.

Discussion 3   Another Argument for One Simple System

You may have heard the following questions, which are given as "trick" questions.

a. Which is heavier, a pound of feathers or a pound of iron?

b. Which is heavier, a pound of feathers or a pound of gold?

If you were tricked by part (a) in Discussion 3 (the two are equally heavy), you are not alone. Many people, especially children, think about the *densities* of iron and feathers. You may also have been tricked in part (b): A pound of feathers is heavier than a pound of gold! Feathers (and iron) are measured with the *avoirdupois* ounce (28.34952 grams), with 16 avoirdupois ounces in 1 avoirdupois pound (453.5924 g), whereas precious metals like gold are measured with the *troy* or *apothecaries'* ounce (31.10348 g), with 12 troy ounces in 1 troy pound (373.2417 g). The word *gallon* could also give trick questions. A *U.S. gallon* means something different than what a *Canadian gallon* does: 1 U.S. gallon = 231 cubic inches, but 1 Canadian (or Imperial) gallon = 277.42 cubic inches. Such complications are another good reason for having ONE standard system of units.

Angle size, length, area, and volume are, of course, part of every elementary school curriculum, as are time, temperature, and mass (or weight, although technically mass and weight are not the same idea). You know the basic standard SI units for length (the meter, m), time (the second, s), and mass (the kilogram, kg), and the basic units for area (the square meter, m^2) and volume (the cubic meter, m^3; also the liter, L). No doubt you are also somewhat familiar with the degree Celsius for temperature, which is a unit that is the same size as the official SI degree Kelvin unit.

As you know, the basic units can lead to units for other quantities, such as meters per second (m/s) for speed or the number of people per square kilometer for population density. Only a few such *per* units, use for quantities called **rates**, appear in the typical elementary school curriculum, perhaps because rates and ratios sometimes receive just computational attention in a few story problems or perhaps because they are conceptually more difficult. (Isn't that a reason why they should receive *more* attention?) For example, researchers and teachers have found that some children interpret a given speed like 50 miles per hour too narrowly. The children might think that asking how many miles one can go in a *half* hour at that speed does not make sense, because the speed is 50 miles per *hour*. Or, when asked to express the speed in terms of miles per century for a car that goes 50 miles per hour, one child said that would be impossible because the car would wear out before a century could pass. Many children (and adults) have trouble viewing a rate as the *relationship between* the two quantities involved, much like the difficulty some children have in regarding a fraction as one number instead of the two numbers in the numerator and the denominator. Furthermore, measurements of rates do not follow all of the key ideas given earlier.

Discussion 4   Per-fection, Not Per-fiction

What might each of the following rates be measuring? What does each phrase or sentence mean?

a. 65 miles per hour

b. $16.50 per child

c. 7.2 grams of medicine X per liter

d. There was a return of 75 percent on the questionnaires we sent out.

A rate like $19.99 per square yard means $19.99 for every *one* square yard, or that the cost for each whole square yard is $19.99. One of the benefits of expressing rates in terms of 1 of the "per" units is that different rates can then be compared easily.

Discussion 5   Who Went Fastest?

Who had the highest average speed?

Al went 102 miles in 2 hours.

Beth took 20 minutes to go 18 miles.

Carla traveled 36 miles in $\frac{3}{4}$ hour.

Dong went 180 miles in $4\frac{1}{2}$ hours.

Discussion 6   Caution with Rates

a. A student has 112 honor points for her first 36 units, giving a grade point average (GPA) of 3.1. She then takes 6 units in summer school and gets a 3.5 GPA for the summer. Is her GPA on all her work now 3.3? Explain.

b. You go 100 miles in 2 hours, and then go 120 more miles in 3 more hours. What was your average speed for the whole trip? (*Hint:* It is not 45 mph.)

c. In summer school, a student earned a C in a 3-unit course and an A in a 1-unit course. She thought her average grade was B, or a GPA of 3.0, but a friend said that her GPA for the summer was 2.5. Who is correct? (The school operates on a system in which A is 4 honor points per unit, B is 3, and so on.)

As the examples suggest, the *per* (meaning *for each* or *for every*) nature of rates means that finding a total rate based on unequal pieces of the *per* quantity, as the numbers of units in part (a) of Discussion 6 or the times in part (b) of Discussion 6, does not usually follow Key Idea 4. You must find the totals for both quantities involved in the *per* expression, rather than find the rate for each piece and then add them. Similarly, finding an average rate requires finding the totals for each quantity over the whole situation, not part by part. In contrast, if a rate is steady or the same all the time, then it can be measured or applied using any value of the *per* quantity. Or if, for example, the numbers of hours spent for each distance had been the same in part (b) of Discussion 6 (say each part of the trip took 2 hours), then the usual average of 50 mph and 60 mph, $(50 + 60) \div 2 = 55$, is correct. Another way to find the average speed is to look at 220 miles in 4 hours, which gives an average speed of 55 mph.

TAKE-AWAY MESSAGE . . . It is not difficult to find reasons for the usefulness of a single set of standard units like the metric system, because people from so many different occupations or locations can measure quantities. Working with *per* quantities or rates requires some care, because they do not behave entirely like the geometric measurements studied. ◆

Learning Exercises for Section 26.2

1. If you know someone from a culture quite different from that of the United States, ask her/him whether she/he used measurements units in the other culture that are not used in the United States (and, if so, tell what the units are used for).

2. Skim a newspaper for examples of different measurements. Tell what quantities are being measured.

3. Talk to someone with a major different from yours. What different sorts of measurements are made in that field?

4. Give the least and the greatest measurement possible for each reported measurement.

   a. 98 ms   **b.** 150 m, to the nearest m   **c.** 1.42 L

5. Explain how Key Idea 4 might be applied in measuring the volume of a large amount of liquid.

6. Give a new example to show that Key Idea 4 is not reliable in rate situations.

7. (*Dictionary*) Many dictionaries include a table of weights and measures. Check such a table to see whether there are units with which you are not familiar.

8. These are all examples of nonmetric length units used in England at different times or in different settings: cubit, rod, ell, fathom, foot, furlong, hand, inch, knot, mile, nail, pace, and yard. Use these units to illustrate one advantage of the metric system approach to length units.

9. **a.** In your opinion, why has the United States been slow to embrace the metric system?

   b. Are there advantages/disadvantages in children's having to learn two sets of units—metric and English?

10. Answer each of the following questions.

   a. "I have taken 72 units, and my GPA is 3.1. If I take 15 units next term and get a 4.0, what will my GPA be then?"

   b. Nerita's record: For her first 30 units, 96 honor points; for her next 24 units, her GPA was 3.5; and last term her GPA for 12 units was 2.5. What is her overall GPA for those 66 units?

   c. Kien drove 175 miles in $3\frac{1}{2}$ hours, and then he ran into slow traffic and averaged only 25 mi/h for the next 75 miles. The final part of his trip took 2 hours for 100 miles. What was his average speed for the whole trip?

   d. A softball player batted .364 for her first 88 at-bats. Then she was slightly injured and hit only .250 for her next 40 at-bats. What was her overall batting average?

11. The Body Mass Index (*BMI*) is one rough rate measurement of whether one is overweight. The *BMI* is defined by $BMI = \frac{\text{weight}}{\text{height}^2}$, where the weight is measured in kilograms and the height in meters. What are the *BMI*s of Alicia, Beth, and Carlita? *Approximations*: 1 kg = 2.2 lb, 1 m = 39.37 in.

   a. Alicia is 1.73 m tall and weighs 78 kg.

   b. Beth is 163 cm tall and weighs 145 pounds.

   c. Carlita is 5' 2" tall and weighs 121 pounds.

   d. Donna is 5' 7" tall. Her *BMI* is 28. How much does she weigh in kilograms? In pounds?

   e. Donna (see part (d)) wants her *BMI* to be under 25. How much weight does she have to lose?

12. Some curricula recommend using linked number lines to represent rate relationships. For example, questions about a medicine that uses 12 mL of water for every $\frac{3}{4}$ g of drug could involve the following drawing as an aid.

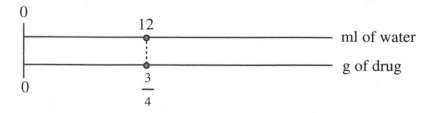

Use the drawing to help answer the following questions.

a. How much water should be used with $\frac{1}{4}$ g of drug?

b. How much water should be used with 1 g of drug?

c. How much drug would be used with 24 mL of water?

d. How much drug would be used with 20 mL of water?

e. How much drug would be used with 6 mL of water?

13. Celsius temperatures (°C) and the common Fahrenheit (°F) temperatures are related as in the diagram.

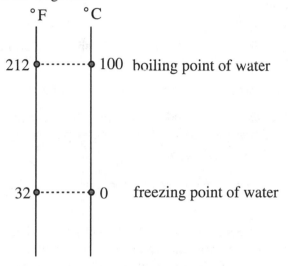

a. From the diagram, which unit is larger, the Fahrenheit degree or the Celsius degree? How are the units related numerically? How do you know?

b. From the diagram, 20° C is about what Fahrenheit temperature? How do you know?

c. Use the diagram to determine the Fahrenheit temperature when it is ⁻40° C.

14. In each part, tell which of the speed units is larger. Explain your thinking.

a. 1 km per s, or 1 m per s

b. 1 km per s, or 1 km per h (h is the metric symbol for hour)

c. 1 m per s, or 1 km per h

d. 1 yd per s, or 1 mile per h

15. In the United States, the gasoline-miles relationship (*mileage*) is most often given in miles per gallon (fuel efficiency). Other countries might use something like gallons per mile (fuel consumption) if they used English units for volume and length.

a. How are the two related? That is, how would 25 miles per gallon be expressed in terms of gallons per mile? Explain your thinking.

b. Suppose you are visiting a metric country. How would 11 liters per 100 kilometers be expressed in terms of kilometers per liter? Explain your thinking.

16. An outstanding runner can run 100 meters in 10 seconds. What is the runner's speed in the given speed unit?

    a. in meters per second

    b. in kilometers per hour

    c. What does your answer for part (a) mean?

    d. What does your answer for part (b) mean?

17. An outstanding runner can run 100 yards in 10 seconds. What is the runner's speed in the given speed unit?

    a. in yards per second

    b. in miles per hour

    c. Contrast your work for Learning Exercise 16(b) and for Learning Exercise 17(b). Which work was easier? Why?

18. a. Whose fudge was most expensive? Explain your thinking.

        ◆Amy spent $13.98 for 2 pounds of fudge. Bea's 3.6 pounds of fudge cost $24.44. Conchita paid $1.60 for a quarter-pound of fudge. Danyell got $\frac{3}{8}$ pound of fudge for $2.70.◆

    b. What was the average price per pound for the four kinds of fudge combined?

19. Answer the following questions.

    a. A teenager complains about not having enough clothes, so her parents say that she can buy 4 blouses, with an average cost of $25/blouse. The teenager sees $40 blouses and a $10 blouse on sale and calculates the average of $40 and $10. She buys 3 of the $40 blouses and a $10 blouse. Why were her parents unhappy?

    b. At a lunch with four friends, you order a salad and drink for $9.99, but each friend orders a more elaborate meal costing $14.99. What is a fair way to split the bill?

    c. For a large picnic, you buy 10 packages of chips for $2.59/bag and 2 bags of pretzels for $1.99/bag. Why is the average price per bag for the items *not* $2.29?

20. Here are two problems from a professional journal for teachers of mathematics in the middle grades.[ii] What rates are involved? Solve the problems.

    a. ◆Marlin's company sells a mineral supplement (for livestock) at $18.20 per 50-pound bag. If each cow is fed 10 ounces of this supplement per day, find the daily cost per cow.◆

    b. ◆A competing product sells for $16 per 50-pound bag but must be fed at the rate of 12 ounces per cow per day. Find the daily cost per cow.◆

21. The smallest angle measured would cut off an arc 20 kilometers long if its vertex were placed at the center of a circle of radius 1500 light-years. What part of a degree is that angle? One report said that measuring this angle is comparable to seeing a single virus on Earth from the moon. (The speed of light is 3×10^8 m/s; a light-year is the distance light travels in a year.)

22. Water covers about 71% of Earth's surface (including lakes and rivers). How many people per square mile would there be if all Earth's population were spread out evenly over the land surface on Earth? Pretend that Earth is a perfect sphere.

23. Here are the nutrition facts from one kind of snack cracker:

    Serving size 1 oz (28 g)
    Servings per container 4.5
    Calories 110   Calories from fat 30
                        % daily value

Total fat 3 g	5%
Saturated fat 0 g	0%
Cholesterol 0 mg	0%
Sodium 300 mg	3%
Total carbohydrate 19 g	6%
Dietary fiber 3 g	10%
Sugars 2 g	
Protein 4 g	
Vitamin A	0%
Vitamin C	0%
Calcium	16%
Iron	5%

    a. Find some rates that are included in the analysis.

    b. How many calories are in the whole box of snack crackers?

    c. How many milligrams of sodium are in the whole *daily value*, according to the analysis?

    d. Is it accurate to say that the crackers contain twice as much fiber as they contain fat? Explain.

    e. How many boxes of crackers would you have to eat to get your complete daily requirement of calcium?

24. One recipe for molasses squares calls for $\frac{1}{3}$ cup powdered sugar, $\frac{1}{3}$ cup molasses, $\frac{1}{8}$ teaspoon each of salt and soda, $\frac{7}{8}$ cup flour, and some other ingredients. This recipe gives 16 two-inch square bars.

    a. If a bakery used this recipe and wanted to make 300 molasses bars, what amounts of the given ingredients would be needed? How many square feet would the bars cover?

    b. A dieter decides that making 12 molasses bars would be acceptable. What amounts of the ingredients are needed for making 12 molasses bars?

    c. How are rates involved here?

25. A motorist traveled for 5 hours at an average speed of 55 miles per hour, and then went another 200 miles in $3\frac{1}{2}$ hours. What was the motorist's average speed for the whole trip?

26. What does this statement mean: "In our community the average family has 2.6 children"?

27. a. If a hen and a half lay an egg and a half in a day and a half, how long will it take a dozen hens to lay a dozen eggs? (This is an old puzzler.)

  b. If 10 painters can paint 15 houses in 9 days, how many days will it take 20 painters to paint 20 houses?

  c. If 5 painters can paint 3 houses in 7 days, how many days will it take 8 painters to paint 10 houses?

26.3 | Check Yourself

You should be able to work exercises like those assigned and to meet the following objectives.

1. State the Pythagorean theorem and apply it to problems involving length, area, and volume (and right triangles, perhaps even ones not shown). The multitude of problems to which the Pythagorean theorem can be applied is one reason the theorem is so important.

2. Interpret the Pythagorean theorem and expressions such as x^2 and x^3 geometrically.

3. Deal with square roots.

4. Use the converse of the Pythagorean theorem to decide whether a triangle is a right triangle.

5. Tell why the metric system avoids certain difficulties that are involved in other sets of units.

6. Explain what a given rate means (for example, 45 g/L).

7. Illustrate that Key Idea 4 does not always apply in certain rate situations, but show that you can deal with those situations.

REFERENCES FOR CHAPTER 26

[i] Fomin, D., Genkin, S, & Itenberg, I. (1996). *Mathematical circles* (*Russian experience*) (M. Saul, Trans.). Providence, RI: American Mathematical Society. (Problem 22, page 3)

[ii] Hilgart, F. (1996). Livestock production by the numbers: Taking the measure of things. *Mathematics Teaching in the Middle School, 1,* 712-717.

Glossary

A number such as [1.] at the end of an entry refers to Section 1.1, the section in which the entry first appears. Terms that are related to some noun or are adjectives may often be found with the associated noun. Some terms first appear in exercise lists, but are nonetheless important. The Web site, http://nw. pima.edu/dmeeks/spandict/, currently gives English-to-Spanish translations of many mathematical terms.

abacus—a mechanical calculating device, still used in parts of the world. [2.2]

absolute value of a number—on a number line, the distance of the number from 0; operationally, the number without a positive or negative sign. Denoted |x|. [10.2]

addends—numbers that are added; in $3 + 5 = 8$, 3 and 5 are addends. [3.2]

additive combination of quantities—the quantities are put together, either literally or conceptually, to form a new quantity. [3.1]

additive comparison of two quantities—the quantities are compared in a how-much-more or how-much-less sense. [3.1]

additive identity—the number (0) that, when added to any other number, gives a sum = the other number: $0 + a = a$ for all choices of a. [10.2]

additive inverse of a number—the number that, when added to the given number, gives a sum = 0. The numbers ⁻2 and 2 are additive inverses of each other, because ⁻2 + 2 = 0. [10.1]

algorithm—a systematic method for carrying out some process; for example, the way you usually multiply 28 and 35 is an algorithm for multiplying whole numbers. [3.3]

altitude—see **height**. [25.1]

angle—(1) two rays from the same point; (2) a ray along with the result of its turning on its endpoint to a final position. The common point is its **vertex**, and the rays are its **sides**. [17.1], [23.2]

    acute angle—an angle smaller than a right angle (that is, has size less than 90°). [17.1]

    adjacent angles—angles with a common side between them. [17.1]

    alternate interior angles—angles like those marked x and x' and also marked y and y' in the following drawing. [23.2 Learning Exercises]

    central angle—an angle with its vertex at the center of a circle. [21.1]

    complementary angles—two angles having sizes that sum to 90°. [17.1]

    corresponding angles—(1) a pair of angles like those marked a in the drawing following (also those marked b, those marked c, or those marked d in the drawing below); (2) in congruent or similar shapes, angles that match. [23.2 Learning Exercises]

    dihedral angle—two half-planes from the same line. [23.2 Learning Exercises]

    exterior angle of a polygon—an angle formed by one side of a polygon with the extension of another side that passes through an endpoint. [17.1]

G-1

inscribed angle—an angle with its vertex on a circle, and its sides chords of the circle. [21.1]

obtuse angle—an angle having size between $90°$ and $180°$. [17.1]

right angle—an angle of $90°$. [17.1]

straight angle—an angle with its sides along a straight line (that is, has size $180°$). [17.1]

supplementary angles—two angles with sizes that sum to $180°$ (for example, x and y in the following diagram). [17.1]

vertical angles—the non-adjacent angles formed when two lines cross (for example, a and d, also b and c, in the following diagram). [23.2 Learning Exercises]

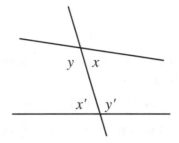
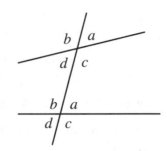

arc of a circle—see **circle**. [21.1]

are—a metric system unit for **area** (100 square meters). [24.1]

area of a region—the number of square units that would be required to cover the region. The region could be a 2D region, or it could refer to all the surfaces of a 3D figure, in which case it is called the **surface area**. [24.1]; formulas for determining areas. [25.1]

arithmetic sequence—a pattern of numbers in which the same number, called the **common difference,** is added to (or subtracted from) any number in a list to get the next number in the list. [15.1]

array—a rectangular arrangement of objects; useful in illustrating multiplication. [3.4]

associative property

    of addition—$(a + b) + c = a + (b + c)$ for every choice of numbers a, b, and c;

    of multiplication—$(a \times b) \times c = a \times (b \times c)$ for every choice of numbers a, b, and c. Noun form: associativity of … [3.4]

axis (plural: **axes**)—one of the number lines used in a **coordinate system.** [12.2]

axis of a rotational symmetry of a 3D shape—the line about which the shape is rotated. [18.2]

base of a prism or pyramid—see **prism** or **pyramid**. [16.2]

benchmark for a number—a number that is close to the given number and is useful for the purpose at hand. [5]

benchmark for an amount—a familiar amount that gives a standard of comparison. [5.3]

bisector

    of an angle—a ray that cuts a given angle into two angles of the same size. [construction of, 21.1]

    of a line segment—a line that goes through the midpoint of the segment. [construction of, 21.1]

capacity of a 3D container—the **volume** that the container can hold. [24.2]

center of a rotational symmetry of a shape—the point about which the shape is rotated. [18.1]

circle—the 2D shape formed by all points at a given distance from a given point, called the **center** of the circle. Any segment from the center to a point of the circle is a **radius** (plural, *radii*) or the length of such a segment. An **arc** of a circle is the piece of the circle between two points of the circle; the shorter piece is a **minor arc** and the longer one, a **major arc**. A **chord** of a circle is any line segment with endpoints on the circle. A **diameter** of a circle is any chord through the center of the circle, or the length of such a chord. A **circular region** is the set of points inside a circle. A **sector** of a circle is the region formed by two radii and the circle (a pie shape). A **segment** of a circle is the region formed by a chord of the circle and the circle. [21.1] **Concentric circles** are circles with the same center. [21.1] The **circumference** of a circle is its length. [23.2]

common factors of two (or more) numbers—each of the numbers will have its own factors. Common factors are those that are factors of both (or all the) numbers. [6.2]

common multiples of two (or more) numbers—each of the numbers will have its own multiples. Common multiples are those that are multiples of both (or all the) numbers. [7.1]

commutative property

of addition—$a + b = b + a$ for every choice of numbers a and b;

of multiplication—$a \times b = b \times a$ for every choice of numbers a and b. Noun form: commutativity of ... [3.4]

comparison language—language that communicates (1) additive comparisons, as in *more/bigger/longer than* or *less than*, or (2) multiplicative comparisons, as in *times as much as*, or (3) both additive and multiplicative comparisons, as in *times bigger than* or *percent less than*. [20.1]

comparison subtraction situation—a situation in which an **additive comparison** is involved. [3.2]

compatible numbers—a phrase sometimes used to describe numbers that give easy approximations or exact answers—e.g., in $62.1 + 24.3 + 40.9$, 62 and 41 are "compatible" because their sum is about 100; with multiplication, 4 and 25, or 5 and 20, for example, are compatible because their product is 100. [3.7] Learning Exercises

composite (number)—a whole number greater than 1 that is not a prime number. [11.1]

composition of rigid motions—the rigid motion that describes the net effect, from original shape to final shape, when one rigid motion is followed by another. [22.4]

cone—the 3D surface resulting when a fixed point is joined to every point of a 2D curve, along with the region of the curve. The fixed point is the **vertex** (or apex) of the cone, and the 2D region is the **base** of the cone. In a **right circular** cone, the base is a circular region and the line through the vertex and the center of the circular base is perpendicular to every diameter of the base. In **oblique circular** cones, such a line is not perpendicular to every diameter. [21.2]

congruent shapes—shapes for which some rigid motion gives one shape as the image of the other; this rigid motion assures that the shapes are exactly the same shape and the same size. [22.1], [16.4, for 3D]

conjecture—a tentative result, usually based on one or more examples or drawings; an educated guess. [17.3]

coordinate system—in algebra, a means of showing relationships between variables. With two variables, two number lines, called **axes,** are usually placed at right angles with their zero points coinciding. Points in the system are located by using their positions relative to the axes. Each point is associated with an ordered pair of numbers, (x, y), called the **coordinates** of the point. [12.2]

counterexample—an example that shows that a given statement is not always true. For example, 9 is a counterexample to "Every odd number is a prime number." [11.3]

cross-multiplication algorithm—a shortcut algorithm for solving proportions with a missing value. [9.2] (and Learning Exercise 16 in [9.2])

cube—a **polyhedron** made up of 6 square regions, also called a **regular hexahedron**. [16.1], [16.5]

cylinder—the 3D surface formed by tracing around a 2D curve with a segment of a fixed length, so that the segment stays parallel to all its positions, plus the region of the 2D curve and the (parallel) 2D region defined by the other endpoint of the segment. The two regions are the **bases** of the cylinder. A **circular** cylinder results if the 2D curve is a circle, and is a **right circular** cylinder if the segment joining the centers of the two bases is perpendicular to every diameter of the bases, and an **oblique circular** cylinder otherwise. [21.2]

decagon—a **polygon** having 10 sides. [17.1]

degree ($^\circ$)—for angle measurement, the size of an angle formed by a ray $\frac{1}{360}$ of a full turn from the other ray of the angle. Hence, there are 360 degrees in a full turn. A **minute** (') for angle size is $\frac{1}{60}$ of a degree, and a **second** (") is $\frac{1}{60}$ of a minute. [23.2]

denominator—the "bottom" number in a **fraction**. [6.1]

density of a set of numbers—given two numbers from the set, there is always a third number in the set that is between the given numbers. The set is said to be dense. [10.1]

diagonal of a polygon or **prism**—a line segment that joins two vertices of the **polygon** or **prism** but is not a side of the polygon or is not completely in a face of the prism. [16.4 Learning Exercises], [26.1 Learning Exercises]

difference—in an **additive comparison**, the term applied to the quantity that tells how much more or less one is than the other. [3.1]

digit—any of the simple symbols 0, 1, 2, 3, 4, 5, 6, 7, 8, 9. In base b, there would have to be symbols for 0, 1, 2, . . . , $b - 1$. [2.1]

distributive property—usually refers to the valuable distributive properties of multiplication over addition: $a \times (b + c) = (a \times b) + (a \times c)$, or sometimes $(b + c) \times a = (b \times a) + (c \times a)$, for every choice of numbers $a, b,$ and c. Noun form: distributivity. The latter form, with division replacing multiplication, is also a correct property ("right" distributivity of division over addition). Subtractions can replace the additions. [3.4]

dividend—in a division expression like $364 \div 15$, the 364 is the dividend. [3.5]

divisibility test—a short way of determining whether one number is a **divisor** (or a **factor**) of another. [11.3]

divisor—in a division expression like $5.64 \div 3$, the 3 is the divisor; in number theory, used as a synonym for factor. Cannot be 0. [3.5]

dodecahedron—a polyhedron having 12 faces; in a **regular dodecahedron** the faces are congruent regular pentagonal regions. [16.5]

edge

of a polyhedron—see **polyhedron**. [16.2]

lateral edge—see **prism** and **pyramid**. [16.2]

hidden edge—an edge in a drawing of a 3D shape that cannot be seen from the viewpoint of the drawer; it is often indicated by dashed or lighter marks. [16.3]

English system of measurement units—a commonly used system in the United States, also called the **British** or **customary system**. A few of the units and their relationships follow.

Length units	*Area units*
1 mile (mi) = 5280 feet (ft) = 1760 yards (yd)	Square inch (in^2), square foot (ft^2), and so on
[1 nautical mile = 6076 feet]	1 acre (A) = 43,560 square feet
1 yard = 3 feet	
1 foot = 12 inches (in.)	*Volume units*
1 fathom (fath) = 6 feet	Cubic inch (in^3), cubic foot (ft^3), and so on
1 rod (rd) = 16.5 feet	1 gallon (gal) = 4 quarts (qt) = 8 pints (p or pt)
	1 (U. S.) gallon (gal) = 231 in^3

equal additions algorithm—a nonstandard algorithm for subtraction; taught in many other countries as their **standard algorithm** but not in the United States. [3.3]

equal fractions—fractions that name the same value. Also called **equivalent fractions**. [6.2]

equal ratios—ratios that express the same **multiplicative comparison**. [9.2]

equiangular polygon—a polygon whose angles are all the same size. [17.1]

equilateral polygon—a polygon whose sides are all the same length. [17.1]

equivalent fractions—fractions that name the same numerical value. Also called **equal fractions**. [6.2]

Euler's formula for polyhedra—$V + F = E + 2$ (or any algebraic equivalent), where V is the number of vertices of a given polyhedron, F is the number of faces, and E is the number of edges. [16.2]

even number—a whole number that can be expressed as 2 times some whole number. The number 0 is an even number, as are 2, 4, 6, 8, … [10.2] Learning Exercises

face of a polyhedron—see **polyhedron**; **lateral face**—see **prism** and **pyramid**. [16.2]

factor, factor of—in multiplication, any of the numbers being multiplied—for example, in 3.2×2.4, each of 3.2 and 2.4 is a factor; in number theory, a whole number that can appear as a factor in an expression yielding some whole number—e.g., 6 is a factor of 24 (because $6 \times 4 = 24$). [3.4]

factor tree—a diagram to arrive systematically at the **prime factorization of a number.** Contrast the different **tree diagram**. [11.2]

family of facts—for addition and subtraction, the set of four addition/subtraction equations that are related—e.g., $2 + 4 = 6$, $4 + 2 = 6$; $6 - 2 = 4$, and $6 - 4 = 2$ is a family of facts. For multiplication and division, it is the same idea: e.g., $3 \times 5 = 15$, $5 \times 3 = 15$, $15 \div 5 = 3$, and $15 \div 3 = 5$ is a family of facts. [3.2]

Fibonacci sequence—a pattern of numbers (for example, 1, 1, 2, 3, 5, 8, . . .) in which two consecutive numbers in a list are added to get the next number; named after the Italian mathematician Leonardo Fibonacci (ca. 1175–1250). Learning Exercises [15.1]

fixed point—see **rigid motion**. [22.3 Learning Exercises]

flip—an informal name for a **reflection**. [22.1]

fraction—a **numeral** of the form $\frac{\text{number}}{\text{nonzero number}}$. A fraction could be signaling a part-whole relationship, a division, or a **ratio**. [6.1]

function—a correspondence that assigns each element of a first set to exactly one element of a second set. Both sets can be identical. The correspondence is often specified by a **function rule** (for example, an equation). [15.1]

fundamental counting principle—a principle that applies to multiplication settings involving two or more choices. [3.4]

Fundamental Theorem of Arithmetic—a statement asserting that a number (> 1) is either a prime or has a unique prime factorization. Also called the **Unique Factorization Theorem**. Contrast the quite different **fundamental counting principle**. [11.2]

gcf or GCF—shorthand for **greatest common factor**. Also **gcd** or **GCD**. [6.2]

geometric sequence—a pattern of numbers obtained by multiplying a number in a list by the same number, called the **common ratio,** to get the next number in the list. [15.1]

glide-reflection—a type of rigid motion, the composition of a translation and a reflection in a line parallel to the vector of the translation. [22.4]

golden ratio—the value, approximately 1.618, that is approached by the ratios of consecutive numbers in a **Fibonacci sequence.** (Some texts give the reciprocal, 0.618, as the golden ratio.) Learning Exercises [15.1]

great circle of a sphere—the largest circle possible on the surface of a sphere. Its radius and center are the same as those of the sphere. [21.2]

height

of a triangle—a line segment from a vertex of the triangle that makes a right angle with the opposite side; also, the length of that segment. Sometimes called the **altitude**. [25.1]

of a trapezoid or parallelogram—a line segment making right angles with each of two parallel sides; also, the length of that segment. [25.1]

of a prism or cylinder—a line segment from the plane of one base to the other base so that it is perpendicular to every line in the other base that it meets; also, the length of that segment. [25.2]

of a pyramid or cone—the line segment from the vertex of the pyramid or cone that makes a right angle with every line in the base that it meets; also, the length of that segment. [25.2]

heptagon—a polygon having 7 sides. [17.1]

hexagon—a polygon having 6 sides. [17.1]

hexahedron—a **polyhedron** having 6 faces; a **regular hexahedron** is a cube. [16.5]

hierarchy—in the context of this book, a classification system in which shapes in a subcategory have the properties of the category (as well as other properties not shared with all shapes in the category). [17.2]

hypotenuse of a right triangle—the side opposite the right angle. [26.1]

icosahedron—a **polyhedron** having 20 faces; in a **regular icosahedron** the faces are equilateral-triangular regions. [16.5]

image of a point or shape—the corresponding point or shape that a transformation gives for the point or shape. [22.1] Finding images for a size change [20.1]; finding images for rigid motions [22.2]

inductive reasoning—using one or more examples as the basis for a **conjecture**. [17.2]

integer—any of the numbers ..., $^-3$, $^-2$, $^-1$. 0, 1, 2, 3, 4,... [10.1]

irrational number—a number that cannot be written in the form $\frac{\text{integer}}{\text{nonzero integer}}$; that is, a number that is not a **rational number**. Decimals of irrational numbers are **nonterminating** and do not **repeat**. [6.3]

isometric dot paper—paper with dots arranged in an equilateral triangle pattern, which is useful for one type of drawing of 3D polyhedra. [16.1]

isometry—another name for a **rigid motion**. [22.1]

key words—individual words that sometimes, but not always, signal a particular operation—e.g., "left" often occurs in story problems in which subtraction gives the answer. Not recommended without paying attention to the whole context of the problem. [3.2] Learning Exercises

kilometer—a metric system unit for measuring length or distance; equals 1000 **meters**; about 0.621 miles. [1.3]

kite—a quadrilateral with two consecutive sides having the same length and the other two sides also having the same length. [17.1], [17.2], [17.3]

lattice method for multiplication—a nonstandard **algorithm** for multiplication; occasionally appears in an elementary school textbook series. [4.1] Learning Exercises

lcm or LCM (or lcd or LCD)—shorthand for **least common multiple;** the number that is the least of all the (nonzero) multiples of the given numbers (denominators). [7.1]

leg of a right triangle—either of the two sides making the right angle. [26.1]

length—the characteristic of one-dimensional shapes that is measured with a ruler; for example, width, height, depth, thickness, perimeter, and circumference refer to the same characteristic. [23.2]

line—short for *straight line*, a straight path that continues forever in two directions. A **line segment** is the piece of a line between two points called endpoints. A **ray** is the piece of a line that starts at a point and continues forever in one direction.

measurement division—see **repeated subtraction division settings**. [3.5]

measurement of a characteristic—(1) the process of direct measurement, in which the given object is compared to a unit with respect the characteristic; or (2) the resulting number and unit (for example, 3 inches). Standard units are most common, for purposes of communication and permanence (see, for example, **metric system** and **SI**); key ideas of [23.1]

mental computation—calculation carried out mentally, most often in a nonstandard way. Useful in estimation but may also give exact answers. [5.1]

meter—the basic **metric system** unit of measurement of length or distance; about 39.37 inches or 1.09 yards. [1.3]

metric system—the most common international system of standard units for measurement; see **SI**. The basic unit for length is the meter (metre); see **metric prefixes** [23.1]; area units [24.1]; volume units [24.2]

minuend—the number from which another number is subtracted; in 18 – 6, the minuend is the 18; the 6 is the **subtrahend**. [3.2]

missing-addend situation—a situation that involves quantities that are related additively, but the addend for one of the quantities is missing; in $31 + n = 58$, n is a missing addend. Sometimes called a **missing-part** situation. [3.2]

missing-factor view of division—divisions that are based on multiplication settings where a factor is missing but the product is known. In $13 \times n = 182$, n is a missing factor and can be found by $182 \div 13$. [3.5]

multibase blocks—blocks of different sizes that reflect the different **place values** for some numeration system. [2.3]

multiple of a number—any **product** involving the given number as a **factor**—e.g., 36 is a multiple of 12 (because $3 \times 12 = 36$). [3.4]

multiplicand—occasionally used in the United States to refer to the second **factor** in a multiplication expression. In 5×36, 36 is the multiplicand. [3.4]

multiplicative comparison of two quantities—the comparison of the two **quantities** by seeing how many times as large one of them is, compared to the other. See **ratio**. [8.1]

multiplicative inverse of a number—that number which, when multiplied by the given number, gives a product = 1. For example, $\frac{11}{16}$ and $\frac{16}{11}$ are multiplicative inverses of each other, because $\frac{11}{16} \times \frac{16}{11} = 1$. Also called the **reciprocal**. 0 does not have a multiplicative inverse. [7.2] Learning Exercises

multiplier—occasionally used in the United States to refer to the first **factor** in a multiplication expression. In 5×36, 5 is the multiplier. [3.4]

negative integer—any of the numbers $\ldots, ^{-}3, ^{-}2, ^{-}1$. [10.1]

net for a 3D shape—a 2D pattern that gives the 3D shape when folded up. [16.1]

***n*-gon**—a polygon having n sides, where n is a whole number greater than 2. [17.1]

nonagon—a polygon having 9 sides. [17.1]

nonterminating decimal—a decimal that has infinitely many place values. [6.3]

notations—symbols that represent geometric objects and are common and may even appear in elementary school mathematics textbooks. [17.1], [21.1]

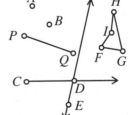

point: capital letters, *A, B,* and so on

line segment with endpoints at P and Q: $\overline{PQ}$

ray starting at C and going through D: $\overrightarrow{CD}$

line through D and E: $\overleftrightarrow{DE}$

polygon with vertices *F, G, H,* and *I*: $FGHI$

line segments (and angles): can also be indicated with small letters, which may also mean their lengths (and angle sizes). A book may also use a darkened-in dot for an endpoint to show it is definitely included (and then the open dot would mean the endpoint is not included).

angles: named either by naming just the vertex, or if needed for clarity, as for angle D in the drawing above, naming a point on one side, the vertex, and then a point on the other side: $\angle D$ or $\angle CDE$

arcs of circles: $\overarc{ST}$, with S and T the endpoints of the arc; $\overarc{SUT}$ for clarity

numeral—a word or symbol to communicate a number idea. [2.1]

numeration system—a system for naming or symbolizing numbers; two examples: our base-ten place-value system, Roman numerals. [2.1]

numerator—the "top" number in a **fraction**. [6.1]

Occam's razor—a philosophical principle stating that when given competing explanations, the simplest one is best. [15.1]

octagon—a polygon having 8 sides. [17.1]

odd number—a whole number that can be expressed as 1 more than an even number. [10.2] Learning Exercises

operator view of multiplication—a view that involves a fractional part of a quantity; also called **part-whole multiplication.** [3.4]

order of operations—an agreement specifying which operation(s) should be done first when simplifying expressions involving addition, subtraction, multiplication, and/or division. The convention helps to avoid a lot of parentheses. [14.5]

orientation of a figure—a clock direction (clockwise or counterclockwise) assigned to a 2D shape. [22.1 Learning Exercises]

parallel lines or **parallel planes**—Lines in the same plane that never meet or planes that never meet. Notation: $x \parallel y$. Compare with **skew lines**.

parallelogram—a quadrilateral with both pairs of opposite sides parallel. To emphasize hierarchical concerns, *quadrilateral* can be replaced by *trapezoid*. [17.1, 17.3]

partitive division settings—see **sharing division settings**. [3.5]

part-whole multiplication setting—a setting that involves a fractional part of a quantity; also called **operator view.** [3.4]

pentagon—a polygon having 5 sides. [17.1]

pentomino—a connected 2D shape made of 5 square regions with each square sharing at least one side with another square. [16.3 Learning Exercises]

percent—the number of hundredths in a ratio or a fraction when expressed as a decimal. Roughly, "out of one hundred" or "per hundred." [9.3]

perimeter of a polygon or closed curve—the distance along the polygon or closed curve. It is a type of length and must be kept distinct from the idea of area. [23.2]

perpendicular bisector of a segment—a line that passes through the midpoint of the segment and makes right angles with the segment; construction of [21.1]

perpendicular lines—lines that make right angles. [17.1], [18.2 Learning Exercises] Perpendicular to a line, construction of [21.1]. Notation: $x \perp y$ means lines x and y are perpendicular.

pi (π) —the number that expresses the ratio of the circumference of any circle to its diameter. Pi does not have an exact terminating or repeating decimal, so the small Greek letter π is used when the exact value is meant. Approximate values for π often used are $\frac{22}{7}$ and 3.14, or more exactly but still approximately, 3.1415926536. [25.1]

place value—the numerical value associated with a particular position in a symbol—e.g., the place values in the base ten numeral 234 are 100 (for the position of the 2), 10 (for the position of the 3), and 1 (for the position of the 4). [2.2]

plane—a perfectly flat, endless surface. A **planar region** is a region in a flat surface. [16, 17]

polygon—a closed plane figure made up of line segments joined end to end without crossing over. The line segments are called the **sides** of the polygon, and the endpoints are the **vertices** of the polygon (singular—**vertex**). A **diagonal** is a line segment joining two vertices that are not consecutive. [17.1] There are many special polygons. One way of classifying some of them is given in a **hierarchy** (as in the following diagram). [17.3] Shapes lower in the diagram are special versions of any shape that they are connected to higher in the diagram—for example, a rectangle is a special parallelogram or a special quadrilateral. A hierarchy recognizes that any fact known about all parallelograms, say, applies to any special parallelogram like a rhombus or rectangle or square.

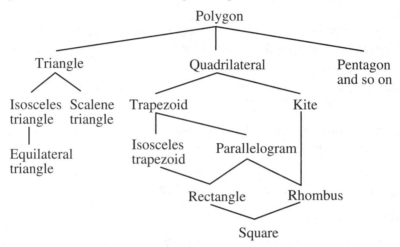

A **convex** polygon is a polygon for which every line segment joining points of the polygon lies entirely on or within the **polygonal region**; it is **concave** otherwise. [17.1 Learning Exercises]

polygonal region—all of the points inside a polygon. The polygon is just the line segments. The distinction is possibly important because teachers often use a cardboard cutout to illustrate a polygon. The edges of the cutout show the polygon, but the cardboard itself actually shows a polygonal region. [17.1]

A triangle   A triangular region

polyhedron (plural, **polyhedra** or **polyhedrons**)—A closed 3D surface made up of planar regions (flat pieces). [16.2] The planar regions are the **faces** of the polyhedron. The line segments where faces meet are called the **edges** of the polyhedron. The points at which edges meet are called the **vertices** (singular—**vertex**) of the polyhedron. A **diagonal** of a polyhedron is any line segment that is not a side or a diagonal of a face but joins two vertices. [26.1 Learning Exercises] **Pyramids** and **prisms** are special polyhedra. If all the faces of a polyhedron are **regular** polygons that are exactly alike and not arranged in some odd way, the polyhedron is called a **regular polyhedron**. [16.5]

polynomial in x—a sum of number multiples of (nonnegative) powers of x. The addends are called **terms** of the polynomial. [14.4]

positive integer—any of the numbers 1, 2, 3, . . . , viewed as integers. [10.1]

prefixes—descriptive terms preceding a main term; prefixes can be of two types, general and metric.

General Prefixes (with some license)

	Latin	*Greek*			*Latin*	*Greek*
1	uni-	mono-	7		sept-	hept-
2	bi-	di-	8		oct-	oct-
3	tri-	tri-	9		non-	enne-
4	quad-, quadr-	tetr-	10		dec-	dek-
5	quint-	pent-	100		cent-	hect-
6	sex-	hex-	1000		mill-	kilo-
			many		mult-	poly-

The Greek prefixes for 10, 100, 1000, and so forth are used in the metric system for larger multiples of the base unit (for example, dekameter, hectometer, kilometer), whereas the Latin prefixes for 10, 100, 1000, and so forth are used for the fractional subunits (for example, decimeter, centimeter, millimeter). See the following table.

Metric Prefixes

Prefix	*Symbol*	*Meaning of Prefix*	*Applied to Length*
yotta-	Y	10^{24}	Ym
exa-	E	10^{18}	Em
peta-	P	10^{15}	Pm
tera-	T	10^{12}	Tm
giga-	G	1 000 000 000 or 10^9	Gm
mega-	M	1 000 000 or 10^6	Mm
kilo-	k	1000 or 10^3	km
hecto-	h	100 or 10^2	hm
deka-	da	10 or 10^1	dam
no prefix		1 or 10^0	m
deci-	d	0.1 or 10^{-1}	dm
centi-	c	0.01 or 10^{-2}	cm
milli-	m	0.001 or 10^{-3}	mm
micro-	µ	0.000001 or 10^{-6}	µm
nano-	n	0.000000001 or 10^{-9}	nm
pico-	p	10^{-12}	pm
femto-	f	10^{-15}	fm
atto-	a	10^{-18}	am
zepto-	z	10^{-21}	zm
yocto-	y	10^{-24}	ym

prime (number)—a whole number that has exactly two factors. The numbers 0 and 1 are not prime numbers. [11.1]

prime factorization of a number—the expression of the number as the product of prime numbers. [11.2]

prism—a polyhedron having two faces (called **bases**) that are parallel and congruent (informally, *exactly alike in size and shape*) and whose other faces (called **lateral faces**) are parallelogram regions (or special parallelogram regions such as rectangular ones) formed by joining corresponding vertices of the bases. Some edges of a prism are on the two bases; the other edges are called **lateral edges**. [16.2] A prism is a **right prism** if the lateral edges (the ones not on the bases) are perpendicular to the edges at the bases, and is **oblique** otherwise. [16.2 Learning Exercises]

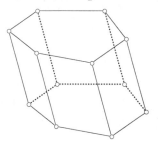   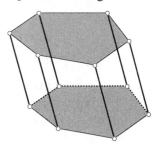   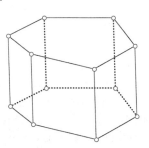

An oblique hexagonal prism   The two bases and the lateral   A right hexagonal prism
                              edges highlighted

product—the result of a multiplication calculation. [3.4]

proportion—an equality between two ratios. [9.2]

protractor—a tool for measuring angles. [17.1, Appendix F]

pyramid—a polyhedron with one face being any sort of polygonal region (often called the **base** of the pyramid) and with all the other faces being triangular regions with one vertex in common. [16.2] The edges not on the base are called **lateral edges**, and the nonbase faces are called **lateral faces**. If the base is shaped like a regular polygon and the lateral faces are all congruent, the pyramid is called a **regular pyramid** (see shapes A and G in Appendix G). [16.2 Learning Exercises]

pyramid—a polyhedron with one face being any sort of polygonal region (often called the **base** of the pyramid) and with all the other faces being triangular regions with one vertex in common. [16.2] The edges not on the base are called **lateral edges**, and the nonbase faces are called **lateral faces**. If the base is shaped like a regular polygon and the lateral faces are all congruent, the pyramid is called a **regular pyramid** (see shapes A and G in Appendix G). [16.2 Learning Exercises]

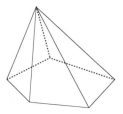   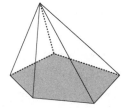   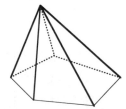

An oblique pentagonal   The base of the pyramid   The lateral edges of the
pyramid   (shaded)   pyramid highlighted

Pythagorean theorem—the important relationship among the lengths of the three sides of a right triangle: The sum of the squares of the lengths of the **legs** equals the square of the length of the **hypotenuse**. [26.1]

Pythagorean triple—three nonzero whole numbers, *a*, *b*, and *c*, whose squares are related as expressed in the Pythagorean theorem: $a^2 + b^2 = c^2$. [26.1 Learning Exercises]

quadrilateral—a polygon having 4 sides. [17.1]

quantitative analysis—determining the quantities in a situation and how they are related. Crucial for solving many story problems. [1.2]

quantitative structure—how the **quantities** in a situation are related. [1.2]

quantity—any measurable or countable aspect of any object, event, or idea. The **value of a quantity** is the measure or count of the quantity. The value of a variable quantity, or **variable,** is often represented by a letter (for example, $x, y, h, d, \ldots$). [1.1], [12.1]

quotient—the answer to a division calculation. [3.5]

quotitive division—see **repeated-subtraction division settings**. [3.5]

rate—a ratio of quantities that vary, but the ratio stays the same. [9.2]

ratio of two quantities—the result of comparing the quantities multiplicatively (see **multiplicative comparison of two quantities**). Written $a{:}b$ or $\frac{a}{b}$. [8.1]

rational number—a number that can be written in the form $\frac{integer}{nonzero\ integer}$. In early work the integers are whole numbers. The decimal for a rational number is either terminating, or nonterminating but repeating. [6.3]

ray—see **line**.

real number—any **rational** or **irrational** number. [6.3]

reciprocal of a number—a synonym for **multiplicative inverse of a number.** [7.2] Learning Exercises

rectangle—a parallelogram with a right angle. (*Note*: This definition necessarily leads to all four angles being right angles.) [17.1], [17.3]

reflection in a line—a 2D **rigid motion** in which a point on either side of the line has its image as though the line were a mirror. See also **symmetry**. [22.1], [22.2]

reflection symmetry with respect to a plane (for a 3D shape)—a reflection in a plane that gives the original shape as the image. [18.2]

regrouping algorithm for subtraction—the standard algorithm for subtraction in the United States; "borrowing" is sometimes used but not recommended. [3.3]

regular polygon—a polygon that is both **equiangular** and **equilateral**. [17.1]

regular polyhedron—a polyhedron whose faces are all the same regular polygonal regions and have the same arrangement at each vertex. Also called **Platonic solids**. [16.5]

relatively prime numbers—numbers that have only 1 as a common factor. [11.3]

remainder—in a **take-away subtraction setting,** the amount left over; in a division calculation like $17 \div 3$, the amount left over when no more 3s can be subtracted: $17 \div 3 = 5$ R 2. [3.2], [3.5]

repeated addition multiplication settings—settings in which quantities with the same values are combined additively; abstractly, a short way to describe calculations in which the same addend is repeated—e.g., $5 + 5 + 5 + 5 + 5 + 5$ can be described by 6×5 (U.S. convention on order of the 6 and 5). [3.4]

repeated-subtraction division settings—settings in which same-valued quantities are taken away from a quantity. Sometimes called the **measurement** or the **quotitive** view of division. [3.5]

repeating decimal—a **nonterminating** decimal that has a block of digits that repeat endlessly, as in $4.13535353535\ldots$(forever). That number may be abbreviated as $4.1\overline{35}$. [6.3]

representation—a way of communicating or thinking about something; in geometry, a drawing, a model, a net, a word, or even an equation can be a representation. [16.3]

rhombus—a **kite** that is also a **parallelogram**. (*Note*: This definition necessarily leads to all four sides having the same length.) [17.1], [17.3]

rigid motion—a matching of the points in the plane (or space) with points, so that original lengths are the same as lengths in the **images**. [22]   A **fixed point** for a rigid motion is a point that is its own image. [22.3 Learning Exercises]

rotation about a point—a 2D rigid motion in which the plane is turned about a point, called the **center** of the rotation. See also **symmetry**. [22.1]

rotational symmetry with respect to a point (for a 2D shape) or **with respect to a line** (for a 3D shape)—a rotation about the point, called the **center**, or about a line, called the **axis**, such that the image is the same as the original shape. [18.1], [18.2]

Russian peasant algorithm—a nonstandard algorithm for multiplying whole numbers. [4.1] Learning Exercises

scaffolding algorithm—a nonstandard algorithm for division that may be used as a lead-in to the **standard algorithm.** [3.6]

scale factor—the common ratio of the image length to the original length for a **size change**. [20.1, for 2D], [20.3, for 3D]

sector of a circle—see **circle**. [21.1]

segment of a circle—see **circle**. [21.1]

sharing division settings—settings in which a quantity is put into a designated number of equal-valued amounts. Sometimes called **partitive division.** [3.5]

SI—The metric system of standard units. SI is short for *Système International d'Unités*, the International System of Units. The strengths of the system are that subunits and larger units are related to a basic unit by a power of 10 and that the basic units are carefully defined for reproducibility (in most cases). The table for metric prefixes (under **prefixes**) gives the subunits and larger units and applies them to the meter (symbol: m), the basic unit for length. [23.1]

signed numbers—positive and negative numbers. Called signed numbers because of the + or – sign, as in $^+4$ or $^-12$. [10.1]

similar shapes—shapes that are related by a size change, possibly along with a rigid motion of some sort. Noun—**similarity**. [20.1, for 2D], [20.3, for 3D]

simplest form (fractions)—a **fraction** in which the **numerator** and **denominator** have no common factors other than 1. Preferred to the common "reduced" form. [6.2]

size change or **size transformation**—a matching of the points of a plane (or space) such that the size of every angle is the same as in its image and such that the ratio of an image length to the original length is always the same value, called the **scale factor**. The **center** of a size change is the point with which the matching is done. [20.1]

skew lines—lines in space that never meet but are not parallel (for example, the bottom edge of the front wall, and the top edge of the side wall). Contrast with **parallel lines**, which are in the same plane.

slide—an informal name for a **translation**. [22.1]

slope of a line—the rate of change for the two variables involved; the slope is calculated by $\frac{\text{change in } y\text{-values}}{\text{change in } x\text{-values}}$ for two points on the line and is commonly denoted as $\frac{\text{rise}}{\text{run}}$. [12.3]

speed—the ratio of the distance traveled to the time elapsed. Speed is a **rate** often given as miles per hour or feet per second, for example. [13]

sphere—the 3D set of points at a fixed distance from a fixed point, called the **center** of the sphere. [21.2] A **hemisphere** is half a sphere. [21.2 Learning Exercises]

square—a rectangle that is also a rhombus. (*Note*: This definition necessarily leads to all four angles being right angles and all four sides having the same length.) [17.1], [17.3]

standard algorithm—one of the usual methods for adding, subtracting, multiplying, or dividing numbers; may vary from country to country. [3.3]

standard units—in measurement, an accepted system of units, such as the **metric system**. [23.1]

subtraction of integers—a formal definition is $a - b = a + {}^-b$, for every choice of integers a and b. More basic meanings for subtraction often apply. [10.2]

subtrahend—the number being subtracted in an expression like $18 - 6$; 6 is the subtrahend; 18 is the **minuend**. [3.2]

sum—the result of an addition. [3.1]

surface area—see **area**. [24.1]

symmetry of a 2D or 3D shape—a rigid motion that gives an image that is the same shape as the original shape. The type of rigid motion can be suggested by an adjective: reflection symmetry, line symmetry or mirror-image symmetry, or rotational symmetry. [18.1], [18.2]

take-away subtraction situation—a situation in which a part of an amount is removed from the whole amount. (The whole amount can also be removed.) [3.2]

tangent to a circle—a line that has exactly one point in common with the circle. A tangent is perpendicular to the radius to that point. [21.1 Learning Exercises]

tangram—a type of puzzle, typically made up of pieces cut in a certain way from a square region. [17.1 Learning Exercises]

tessellation of a plane (or space)—a covering of a plane (or space) with a limited number of types of regions. In a **regular** tessellation of the plane, all the regions are one type of regular polygonal region. [19.1, for 2D], [19.2, for 3D]

tetrahedron—a polyhedron having 4 faces; a **regular tetrahedron** has faces that are equilateral-triangular regions. [16.5]

tetromino—a connected 2D shape made of 4 square regions with each square sharing at least one side with another square. [16.3 Learning Exercises]

transformation geometry—a term for a school geometry topic that features **rigid motions** and **size changes**. [22]

translation—a type of rigid motion in which the image of a point is the point that is a fixed distance in a fixed direction from the original point. [22.1]

trapezoid—a quadrilateral with at least one pair of opposite sides parallel. Many books use *exactly one pair*, but the definition here allows the trapezoid family to relate to other special quadrilaterals. To retain that value without causing other difficulties, the **isosceles trapezoid** is defined awkwardly, as a trapezoid in which both angles adjacent to one of the parallel sides are the same size. Under either definition, the two sides of an isosceles trapezoid that may not be parallel have the same length. [17.1 Learning Exercises], [17.3]

tree diagram—a diagram for systematically showing settings that fall under the **fundamental counting principle**. Contrast **factor tree**. [3.4]

triangle—a polygon having 3 sides. In an **acute triangle**, all three angles are acute; a **right triangle** has a right angle, and an **obtuse triangle** has an obtuse angle. The lengths of the sides of a **scalene triangle** are all different, but an **isosceles triangle** has at least two sides with the same length, and an **equilateral triangle** has the same length for all three sides. See also **polygon**. [17.1]

triangular numbers—the numbers 1, 3, 6, 10, 15,…, $\frac{n(n+1)}{2}$,…, so called because they give counts of dots that can be arranged in a triangle. The arrangement of 10 bowling pins gives the fourth triangular number ($n = 4$). [17.1 Learning Exercises]

turn—an informal name for **rotation**. [22.1]

Unique Factorization Theorem—a statement asserting that a number (> 1) is either a prime or has a unique prime factorization. Also called the **Fundamental Theorem of Arithmetic**. [11.2]

unit ratio—a **ratio** in which the second entry is 1, as in 7 to 1. [9.2]

unit—with **quantities:** the unit of measurement; with **fractions:** the whole in the part-whole relationship (what = 1); with **measurement:** the size of the comparison object, for example, mile. [1.1], [6.1], [23.1]

value of a quantity—the measure of the **quantity** or the number of items counted; a value of a quantity involves a number and a unit—e.g., 3 pints (for the quantity, the amount of milk in the jug). [1.1]

variable—see **quantity.**

vector—the direction and distance associated with a given **translation**, often shown by an arrow of the correct length and pointed in the correct direction; in general, a quantity that may have two or more subquantities. [22.2]

vertex of a polygon—see **polygon**; of a polyhedron—see **polyhedron**; of an angle—see **angle**.

volume of a closed 3D region—The number of 3D units that could fit inside the region, or that could be used to make an exact model of the region. The units are usually cubic regions (for example, cm^3). The metric system also uses the liter (litre). [24.2]; formulas for determining volumes [25]

weighted average—an average that is used when the total amount is not spread evenly over the number of items being considered. [14.3]

whole number—any of the numbers 0, 1, 2, 3, 4, and so on.

Summary of Formulas

Formula	Reasoning
Sum of angle sizes for n-gon = $(n-2)180°$	Split polygon with n sides into $(n-2)$ triangles.
A(rectangular region) = lw Special case: A(square region) = s^2	w rows l square regions in each row
A(parallelogram region) = bh	
A(triangular region) = $\frac{1}{2}bh$	
A(trapezoid region) = $\frac{1}{2}h(a+b)$	
A(circular region) = πr^2 C(circle) = $2\pi r = \pi d$	Area: Based on the total area of infinitely many triangles (Section 25.1) Circumference: Similarity (Section 25.1)
Surface area of a polyhedron = sum of the areas of its faces	Key idea: Measure an object by cutting it into pieces, measuring each piece, and adding.
$V = Bh$ for any prism or cylinder with base B and height h	Base B numerically gives the number of cubes in one layer; h gives the number of layers.
$V = \frac{1}{3}Bh$ for any pyramid or cone with base B and height h	Suggested by experiment; no general justification given in this book
A(surface of sphere) = $4\pi r^2$	Area formula: No justification given in this book
$V = \frac{4}{3}\pi r^3$ for any sphere	Volume formula: Based on the total volume of infinitely many pyramids (Section 25.2)

Answers and Hints for Learning Exercises

Note to students: The selected answers below give you some indication about whether you are on the right track. They are NOT intended to be the type of answers you would turn in to an instructor. **Your complete answers should contain all the work towards obtaining an answer**, as described in the Message to Prospective and Practicing Teachers.

Here are a few examples of complete answers:

Learning Exercise 2a in Section 1.2

The quantities and their values are:

Regular price of CDs	$9.95
Regular price of tapes	$6.95
Discount this month	10%
Discounted price of CDs	90% of $9.95 = $8.96
Discounted price of tapes	90% of $6.95 = $6.26
New discount on 3 items	20%
Number of CDs bought	1
Number of tapes bought	1
Amount spent on CDs	$8.96
Amount spent on tapes	$6.26
Sales tax	6%
Amount spent	?

This drawing represents the problem

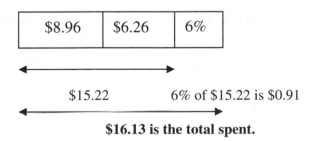

$15.22   6% of $15.22 is $0.91

$16.13 is the total spent.

Learning Exercise 10 in Section 2.3

This counting system begins repeating words on the fourth number, obi na. Because obi is one, and na does not thus far have a meaning, na is probably 0. Thus the system repeats on the fourth number. It appears that obi is 1, fin is 2, mus is 3, obi na is 10, obi obi is 11, and so forth. This would be a base-four system. Continuing to 20: obi (1), fin (2), mus (3), obi na (10), obi obi (11), obi fin (12), obi mus (13), fin na (20), fin obi (21), fin fin (22), fin mus (23), mus na (30), mus obi (31), mus fin (32), mus mus (33), obi na na (100), obi na obi (101), obi na fin (102), obi na mus (103), obi obi na (110). (Note that in obi na na, the obi is in the sixteens place. Obi na na would mean $16 + 0 + 0$. The 20th place is obi obi na, or $16 + 4 + 0$.)

Learning Exercise 9 in Section 3.1

We need to find the weight of the sum of the medicine available from companies A, B, and C. A diagram will help. Here is one possible diagram.

Company A's medicine is represented by a line marked 1.3 mg. Company C's medicine is represented next because it is easier to find—it is 0.9 mg less than A's medicine. Thus Company C has 0.4 mg of medicine. The difference between Company B's medicine and Company C's medicine is half of 1.3 mg, so it is 0.65 mg over and above Company C's medicine, which is 0.4 mg. Thus Company B has 0.4 mg + 0.65 mg which is 1.05 mg. The total medicine furnished by the companies is $(1.3 + 0.4 + 1.05)$ mg, or 2.75 mg.

Learning Exercise 2 in Section 5.4

$3 \times 10^4 \times 4 \times 10^6 = 12 \times 10^{10}$. This expression is not in scientific notation because $12 > 10$. In scientific notation this product would be expressed as 1.2×10^{11}.

Answers for Chapter 1

1.2 Quantitative Analysis

1b.

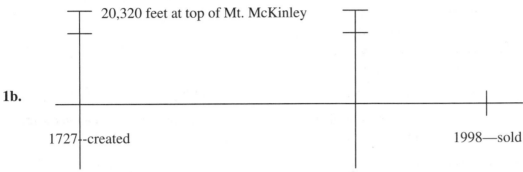

20,320 feet at top of Mt. McKinley

1727—created   1998—sold

Time period is 1998 – 1727 = 271 years

1c.

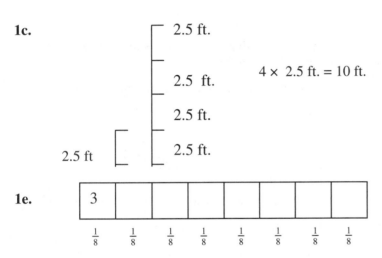

2.5 ft.

2.5 ft.   4 × 2.5 ft. = 10 ft.

2.5 ft.

2.5 ft

2.5 ft.

1e.

3							
$\frac{1}{8}$	$\frac{1}{8}$	$\frac{1}{8}$	$\frac{1}{8}$	$\frac{1}{8}$	$\frac{1}{8}$	$\frac{1}{8}$	$\frac{1}{8}$

Each box represents 3 students. There are 8 boxes. Thus there are 24 students.

1f.

15 yrs	10 yrs	3	3	3	3

Each box represents one dog year. Thus the dog is 37 years old in human years.

2a. Quantities and Values

Regular price of CDs	$9.95
Regular price of tapes	$6.95
Discount this month	10%
Discounted price of CDs	90% of $9.95 = $8.96
Discounted price of tapes	90% of $6.95 = $6.26
New discount on 3 items	20% (Notice that this is not needed.)
Number of CDs bought	1
Number of tapes bought	1
Amount spent on CDs	$8.96

Amount spent on tapes $6.26
Sales tax   6%
Amount spent   ?

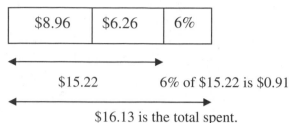

$15.22   6% of $15.22 is $0.91

$16.13 is the total spent.

4. (Advice: Work through each step of this problem slowly and thoughtfully.)

An important issue involves the assumptions that one must make when analyzing a situation quantitatively. In Brother and I, for example, we must assume things like

- both brother and I walk at a constant speed,

- brother and I go to the same school, and

- brother and I take the same route to school.

It is important to be aware of the assumptions that you make when analyzing a situation, because thinking about these assumptions helps you understand the situation better.

Consider the following diagram depicting the situation at, say, 8 minutes after my brother takes off for school.

What other distances besides the distance from home to school are made evident by this diagram?

Consider these quantities and their values. (You may list more than what is here.)

Distance from home to school : unknown

Time taken for brother to go from home to school: 40 minutes

Time taken for me to go from home to school: 30 minutes

Difference between the time my brother left for school and I left for school: 8 minutes

Distance traveled by brother in 1 minute: $\dfrac{1}{40}$ of total distance

Distance traveled by me in 1 minute: $\dfrac{1}{30}$ of total distance

Distance I gain on brother each minute: $\dfrac{1}{30} - \dfrac{1}{40} = \dfrac{1}{120}$ of total distance

Distance between brother and me at time zero: $\dfrac{8}{40} = \dfrac{1}{5}$ of total distance

If brother has covered $\frac{1}{5}$ of the distance when I begin, and I catch up to him at the rate of $\frac{1}{120}$ of the

total distance each minute, it will take me $\frac{1}{5}$ distance $\div \frac{1}{120}$ distance/minute or 24 minutes to catch

up. I will be $\frac{24}{30}$ of the way to school, or $\frac{4}{5}$ of the way. Brother will be $\frac{8}{40} + \frac{24}{40} = \frac{32}{40} = \frac{4}{5}$ of the

distance to school.

6. First, each quantity is listed, and then the value of each quantity is determined, if possible.

   1. Distance (length) of the last part of the triathlon: 10,000 m

   2. Distance between Aña and Bea at the start of the last part: 600 m

   3. Distance between Aña and Bea during the last part: varies

   4. Distance between Aña and Bea at the time they meet: 0 m

   5. Distance between Aña and Bea at the end of the 10,000 m race: not known

   6. Average speed (rate) at which Aña runs: 225 m/minute

   7. Average speed (rate) at which Bea runs: 200 m/minute

   8. Distance Aña runs in 1 minute: 225 m

   9. Distance Bea runs in 1 minute: 200 m

   10. Difference between the average speeds: Aña runs 25 m/minute faster than Bea

   11. Difference between the distance Aña runs in 1 minute and the distance Bea runs in 1 minute: 25 meters

   12. Time it takes Aña to run the last part of the triathlon: 10,000 m ÷ 225 m/minute = 44.44 minutes

   13. Time in takes Bea to run the last part of the triathlon: 10,000 m ÷ 200 m/minute = 50 minutes

   14. Time from when Aña begins the last running part to the time she passes Bea: not known

   15. Time from when Bea begins the last running part to the time when Aña catches up: not known

   Make a drawing (or drawings) to represent the problem and the relationships among the quantities.

   Consider the following diagram depicting the situation at the start of the running part of the triathlon. Aña and Bea are 600 m apart.

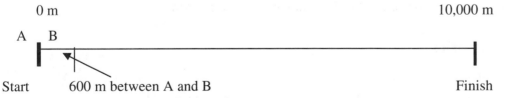

   Now, consider the situation 1 minute later. Aña has run 225 m, Bea has run 200 m, + 600 m headstart, is 800 m, so after 1 minute they are 575 m apart.

Using this process, I know they would be 550 m apart after 2 minutes, 525 m after 3 minutes, etc. Notice that the value of that distance between Aña and Bea *varies,* that is, it is not 600 m except at the beginning. A critical value of the distance between Aña and Bea will occur when Aña overtakes Bea (if she does). At this time the distance would be 0.

Finally, solve the problem using the drawings.

One way is to think: In each minute of the race, Aña gains 25 m on Bea. Because Aña begin the race 600 meters behind Bea, it will take Aña 600 m divided by 25 m/minute, or 24 minutes, to catch up to Bea.

7. A quantitative analysis would produce the following quantities, values, and relationships:

Length of board: 200 inches

Width of board: 12 inches (Note that we do not need this information.)

Length of each shelf: unknown

Number of shelves: 4

Total length of shelves placed end to end: not given, but can be found by the relationship of length of each shelf and total number of shelves: 4 times length of one shelf.

Length of the part of the board left over: 16 inches

Length of the part of the board used for shelves: Total − left over = 200 − 36 = 164

Length of one shelf is length of board used divided by the number of shelves: 164 ÷ 4 = 41. Each shelf is 41 inches.

9. Speed of train leaving Moscow: 48 km/h
Speed of train leaving Sverdlovsk: 54 km/h
Time of travel: 12 hours
Distance traveled by first train: 48 km/h × 12 h = 576 km
Distance traveled by second train: 54 km/h × 12 h = 648 km
Distance between cities: 1822 km

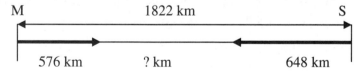

Distance apart after 12 hours is 1822 km − (576 km + 648 km) = 598 km.

1.3 Values of Quantities

2. b. miles per gallon

5. a. width of a fingernail   **b.** a paperclip   **c.** a quart   **d.** width of a door

    e. a little more than half a mile   **f.** three cans of mushroom soup

Of course, you may have others. You might want to compare your answer with the answers of others.

6. An inch is approximately 2.5 cm, a mile is approximately 0.6 m, a quart is approximately 1 liter.

1.4 Issues for Learning: Ways of Thinking About Solving Story Problems

1.  $17 weekly allowance

2. Sara

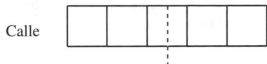

Calle

Juniper   25 stickers   Calle: 50 stickers, Sara 10 stickers
In all, 85 stickers

3.  $32 $128 weekly earnings

4. Hat

Sweater

Coat   Hat $19 (Sweater $38)

<------- $114 ------->

9.   139 in all

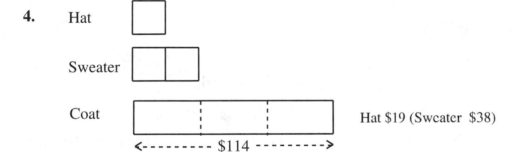

36 jazz   R & B 36 ¦ 36   classical

31 are classical.
$(36 + 36 + 36 + c = 139,$
or $108 + c = 139,$ and $c = 139 - 108,$
missing addend).

Answers for Chapter 2

2.1 Ways of Expressing Values of Quantities

4. a. 2113   **b.** 185

5. a. MMLXVI   **b.** LXXVIII

6. a. 903   **b.** 49

7. Twins, couple, dyad, brace, duet, duo, double, twosome, twice, bicompounds like bicycle, both, and dicompounds like dipolar are others.

2.2 Place Value

1. **a.** 35.7; 35   **c.** 436.2; 436   **d.** 456.654; 456

   e. 4566.54; 4566   **g.** 234.7; 234   **h.** 23,470; 23,470   **i.** 23.47; 23

2. No. The ones place, not the decimal point, divides the number into two parts with similar names on both sides.

3. **b.** It depends on the placement of the decimal point.

4. Three thousand two hundred; Thirty-two hundred. They have the same value because they have the same number of hundreds: three thousand is thirty hundreds.

6. **a.** and **b.** No regrouping into tens.

   c. Regrouping (in this case "borrowing" is not understood.)

   d. Digits are misplaced in quotient.

   e. No regrouping into tens. In all cases, the work indicates a lack of understanding of place value.

7. 1635 is exactly 1635 ones, is 163.5 tens, is 16.35 hundreds, is 1.635 thousands, . . . , 16,350 tenths, 163,500 hundredths.

9. To the right, yes. To the left, no. (For whole numbers.)

2.3 Bases Other Than Ten

2. **a.** 22_{four} **b.** 20_{five}

3. **a.** 10_{four} **b.** 10_{eight} **c.** 10_{twenty} **d.** 10_b **e.** 100_b

   f. 1100_b **g.** 1002_{three} **h.** 430_{five} **i.** 1000101_{two} **j.** 1000_{twelve}

4. 1, 10, 11, 100, 101, 110, 111, 1000, 1001, 1010, 1011, 1100, 1101, 1110, 1111, 10000, 10001, 10010, 10011, 10100

5. **a.** There cannot be a "4" with base three.   **b.** There cannot be a "7" with base seven.

6. **a.** forty-three $= 43_{ten}$ **b.** thirty-four

   c. two hundred seven and twenty-four ten-thousandths

9. **a.** $<$ **b.** $=$ **c.** $>$

11. **a.** twenty   **b.** twenty   **c.** twelve   **d.** sixty

12. 3 fives $+ 4$ ones $+ \dfrac{2}{5}$; 19.4_{ten}

13. **a.** $9\dfrac{11}{16}$

14. **a.** $\dfrac{1}{4}$ in base twelve is the same amount as in base ten. $\dfrac{1}{4}$ is $\dfrac{3}{12}$ in base 10. $\dfrac{3}{12}$ in base 12 would be $\dfrac{3}{10}$, or 0.3_{twelve}

   c. 0.2_{eight}

15. a. 42_{ten} or just 42. The place values in the base two numeral given are, starting at the right, 1s, 2s, 4s, 8s, 16s, 32s. Taking into account the digits, $101010_{two} = 1 \times 32 + 1 \times 8 + 1 \times 1 = 32 + 8 + 1 = 41$.

   b. 1310

16. a. 13_{nine} **b.** 14_{eight} **c.** 15_{seven} **d.** 20_{six} **e.** 22_{five}

17. a. 202_{seven} **b.** 400_{five} **c.** 91_{eleven} **d.** 1100100_{two}

18. a. 212   **b.** 78

19. Three longs and 4 small blocks; 3 flats and 4 longs

20. a. You should have 2 flats, 3 longs, and 4 small cubes where the flat is five units by five units.

   b. You should have 2 flats, 3 longs, and 4 small cubes where the flat is six units by six units.

22. You should have 2 flats, 3 longs, and 4 small cubes.

23. a. If the small cube is the unit, then 3542 could be represented with 3 large cubes, 5 flats, 4 longs, and 2 small cubes.

   b. 0.741 could only be represented if the large block is the unit. Then 0.741 would be represented with 7 flats, 4 longs, and 1 small cube.

   c. If the flat represents one unit, then 11.11 would be represented with one large cube, one flat, one long, and one small cube.

24. Let the unit be the same in both cases: say, a flat. Then 5.21 would be represented as 5 flats, 2 longs, and 1 small unit; 5.4 would be represented as 5 flats and 4 longs. More units would be needed to make 5 flats and 4 longs. (Some children actually say: "5.4 is bigger because it's got more wood.")

25. A number could be written in different numeration systems. (The idea of several different ways of writing a number is extremely important with fractions.)

2.4 Operations in Different Bases

1. Answer, either way: 10220_{three}

2. Block answers should yield:

   a. 1111_{five} **b.** 1011_{two} **c.** 132_{four} **d.** 268_{ten}

3. (Assigns work on internet)

4. a. 3204_{five} **b.** 611_{nine}

5. a. 101_{nine} **b.** 506_{seven} **c.** 2203_{five} **d.** 524_{eleven}

6. More difficult because we don't know our basic multiplication and division facts in bases other than ten.

7. a. 1030_{four} **b.** 413_{five} **d.** 1111_{two}

8. Block or cutout answers should yield:

   a. 121_{four} **b.** 132_{five} **c.** 165_{eight}

9. Cutouts for base 6 would consist of small squares, longs the length of 6 small squares, flats the size of 6 longs side-by-side.

Answers for Chapter 3

3.1 Additive Combinations and Comparisons

3. 50 students

4. C and D are combined, A and B are combined, A and D are compared, B and C are compared.

5. a. The point is that here there will be many answers. Any scores giving a difference between B's and B's opponents' scores = 34, with B's score greater, will solve the problem (but not uniquely).

   c. See the important points in parts (a) and (b). Both types of answers give potentially valuable information in mathematics. If there are many answers, perhaps one will be cheaper, say. If there are no answers, then that gives potentially valuable information about an endeavor.

6. Connie bought 13 Tootsie Rolls. (Answer only; no complete solution provided.)

7. a. Annie weighed $1\frac{3}{4}$ pounds less than Carmen on that day.

   b. Many values can lead to the same differences.

8. A drawing of the two pieces, one under the other, shows that once the difference of $\frac{1}{4}$ lb is "removed," the remaining two pieces are equal in weight (and total $\frac{3}{4}$ lb), so the smaller piece weighs $\frac{3}{8}$ lb and the larger weighs $\frac{5}{8}$ lb. Notice that algebra is not necessary, especially with the help of a drawing.

9. Here is an example of an expected complete answer:

   We need to find the weight of the sum of the medicine available from companies A, B, and C. A diagram will help. Here is one possible diagram. Company A's medicine is represented by a line marked 1.3 mg. Company C's medicine is represented next because it is easier to find. It is 0.9 mg less than A's medicine. Thus Company C has 0.4 mg of medicine. The difference between Company B's medicine and Company C's medicine is half of 1.3 mg, so it is 0.65 mg over and above Company C's medicine, which is 0.4 mg. Thus Company B has 0.4 mg + 0.65 mg which is 1.05 mg. The total medicine furnished by the companies is (1.3 + 0.4 + 1.05) mg, or 2.75 mg.

   A ——————————————— 1.3 mg ———————————

   (1.3 − 0.9) mg = 0.4 m   9 mg

   C ————————————┼ ···

   B   0.4 mg   (0.5 × 1.3) mg = .65 mg
   ————————————— ·······································

10. $\frac{1}{8}$ (answer only)

11. Example: For # 6, one additive combination is, the number of Tootsie Rolls combined with the number of Milky Ways. One additive comparison is, the number of Reese's Cups is 4 less than the number of Hershey Bars.

3.2 Understanding for Teaching About Addition and Subtraction

1. **a.** take-away

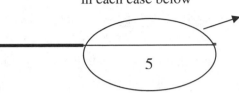

b. comparison

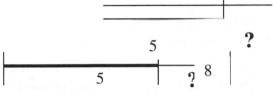

c. missing-addend $(5 + ? = 8)$

2. **b.** Colleen had pennies in her piggy bank. She took out 17 and gave them to her brother. She counted the ones she had left and found she had 24 pennies left. How many pennies did she have in her piggy bank before she gave some to her brother?

4. **a.** The baseball team has 12 players and 9 were wearing gloves. How many players were not wearing gloves?

5. **c.** $m - p = x; m - x = p; p + x = m; x + p = m$

8. **a.** missing-addend   **b.** missing-addend   **c.** take-away

   d. comparison   **e.** comparison

10. Mr. Lewis's students did not recognize the comparison problem as a problem calling for subtraction because they had only worked with take-away problems in class.

11. The drawings are quite easy to make.

   a. 8.25 ft.   **b.** $\frac{6}{15}$ students   **c.** 6 cm

   d. $\frac{1}{6}$ part   **e.** 25 beads   **f.** 15.36 pints

3.3 Children's Ways of Adding and Subtracting

2. Case A: 40 and 50 is 90, 8 more is 98, then 9 more is 99, 100, 101, 102, 103, 104, 105, 106, 107.

Case B: 50 and 60 is 110. Then take 2 away to get 108, then 1, and get 107.

Case C: 50 and 59 is, 50 and 50 is 100, and 9 more is 109, but take 2 away, so it's 107.

Case D: 264 + 357: 2 plus 3 is 5 so its 200 + 300, so its somewhere in the 500s. Now add tens. They are 6 and 5. Start at 60; 70, 80, 90, 100, you are in the 500s because of the 200 + 300 but now you're in the 600s because of the 60 and 50. But you've got one more ten. So 500 + 60 + 50, you'd have 610. Now add 4 more onto 10 which is 14. And add 7 more: 15, 16, 17, 18, 19, 20, 21. And that is 621.

Case E. 58 – 9. 58 – 8 is 50, and take away 1 more to 49.

> Also: 9 + 7 is 18, then 10 is 28 and 10 more is 38 and 10 more is 48 and 10 more is 58. Four tens is 40, and 9 more is 49.

Case F. 368 – 132. 3 take away 1 is 2 and you make it into hundreds so 200. Then you add 60 and get 260, – 30 is 230, + 8 is 238, – 2 is 236.

Case G. 800 – 452. 8 to get to 460, then 40 to get to 500, then 300 more, so 348.

3. & 4. Case A (3) The student is first adding the tens (30 + 30) then each of the ones: 60 + 9 then 69 + 7. The 7 is added by counting on. (4) This will not be difficult to remember, and is a form of mental computation that is quite natural. Children should be able to continue using this procedure.

Case B (3) The student is rounding up on both addends, then subtracting the appropriate number of ones. (4) This is also a common way of mental adding and should not be forgotten.

Case C (3) The student rounded the first number up to 40, then added the tens and the ones, and compensated for the rounding. (4) This method might be slightly more difficult because it would be easy to forget the need for compensating at the end.

Case D (3) The student is adding from left to right; hundreds, then tens; then ones. So many steps and intermediate sums are hard to remember mentally, and so the student does make one error, then corrects it. (4) The method itself will not be difficult to remember because the direction from left to right is the way we read. However, the difficulty is remembering all the partial addends, so this might be easier if the solver could jot down partial sums along the way.

Case E (3) The student is using a variation of adding on to the second number to reach the first number. The student adds an 8 to get to 15, then adds tens to get to 65. Another example of this method might be 43 – 9: Add 4 to get 13, then 10 more to 23, 10 more to 33, ten more to 43, so I've added 3 tens and a 4; 34. (This is sometimes called shopkeepers' math, because if you gave a shopkeeper $10 for something that cost $6.25, she might count out money saying, "$6.25, $7.00, $8.00, $9.00, $10.00" while giving you 3 quarters and 3 one dollar bills.) In some curricula, the "empty" number line might be used (see below). (4) This is not too difficult to remember, but it might, for some people, be easier to add to ten, then tens, then whatever more is need: 43 – 9 would be 1 to get to 10, then 30 to get to 40, then 3 more: 1 + 30 + 3 is 34.

Case F (3) The student is working from left to right, first getting 300 from the hundreds, then adds in the 50 from 354 to get 350, and then subtracts the 30 from 350, for 320. He/she then adds the 4 from 354, and has the subtraction of 9 from 339 remaining, which he/she does by seeing 9 as 4 + 5, and subtracting each part. (4) Despite the jumping back and forth between the numbers and the operations, this child shows good number sense. Children for whom the jumping might be difficult to keep track of might have trouble with understanding this student's explanation.

Case G (3) The student is using a missing-addend approach: What must you add to 268 to get 500. (4) This approach also shows good number sense and an awareness of different ways of thinking about subtraction. There is a memory load (without paper), so some children might have difficulty with keeping track of how much has been added. An "empty" number line might help keep track of the numbers added. See the next exercise.

3.4 Ways of Thinking About Multiplication

1. a.   6 × 2: XX XX XX XX XX XX

   2 × 6: XXXXXX   XXXXXX

b.   Possibly…

   $5 \times \frac{1}{2}$ and

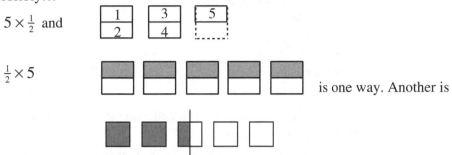

   $\frac{1}{2} \times 5$

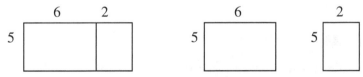   is one way. Another is

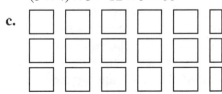

c.   Did you get 25 different possibilities?

3.   Not any fraction, but multiplying by a fraction less than 1. If the multiplier is a whole number or a fraction is greater than 1, then "multiplication makes bigger" is all right.

5.   6 twelves, plus $\frac{1}{2}$ twelve—a repeated addition multiplication as well as a part-of-an-amount multiplication.

6. a.   Just a sample: How much will 32 pencils cost at 29¢ each?

d.   Make sure that the situation would involve twelve $\frac{3}{8}$ s.

e.   Make sure that $\frac{2}{3}$ of 6 (pizzas?) is featured.

7. a.   8 chicken breasts, $1\frac{1}{3}$ cups onion, $1\frac{1}{3}$ Tbsp olive oil, $2\frac{2}{3}$ cups apples, $1\frac{1}{3}$ Tbsp margarine, 2 cups apple juice, $3\frac{1}{3}$ Tbsp honey, $\frac{2}{3}$ tsp salt

b.   4 chicken breasts, $\frac{2}{3}$ cup onion, $\frac{2}{3}$ Tbsp olive oil, $1\frac{1}{3}$ cups apples, $\frac{2}{3}$ Tbsp margarine, 1 cup apple juice, $1\frac{2}{3}$ Tbsp honey, $\frac{1}{3}$ tsp salt

9. a.   Property: Multiplication is distributive over addition.

b.   Note that no drawing is called for. A demonstration might be as follows:

   $3 \times (4 \times 5) = 3 \times 20 = 60$

   $(3 \times 4) \times 5 = 12 \times 5 = 60$

c.

If turned 90 degrees, this would show 6.5 × 3. The area is the same for both.

10. a. R1, R2, R3, R4, R5, R6

W1, W2, W3, W4, W5, W6

B1, B2, B3, B4, B5, B6

G1, G2, G3, G4, G5, G6

Thus the answer is 24. The rest are not listed: only the final number is provided.

b. 12

11. $2^8 = 256$ so there must be 8 ways to choose between two things to arrive at 256 different kinds of hamburgers.

13. $(3 \times 4 \times 3) \times 12{,}486$ with the first multiplications from the fundamental counting principle, and the last from repeated addition. $449,496

15. a. 77.1   **b.** 0.76 (or just .76)   **c.** 17.85   **d.** 1.46   **e.** 0.14924   **f.** 0.09022

3.5 Ways of Thinking About Division

1. Repeated subtraction: Show 12, with groups of 3 circled with arrows indicating they are removed. Sharing: Show 12, then "put" them into two equal amounts, perhaps with an arrow drawn from each to one of the amounts, keeping them equal ("deal" out the 12 into two equal piles).

5. b. (sample) Abe went up the long trail and came down by the 3.5 km one. Bert went up and down the 2.4 km trail. Who walked farther, and by how much?

e. (sample) A runner prepares for a 10K run by running on Mt. Azteca. How many times would it take her to run the 2.4 km trail to make 10 km?

6. a. In the testing, eighth graders would give the results of the division calculation, $1500 \div 36$ ($41\frac{2}{3}$ or 41 R 24), as though those were the number of buses needed. But the company should actually supply 42 buses.

b1. 38

b2. 4. Did you get your answer from the division calculation?

9. 8. 8. 8, 8, 8. $10^n a \div 10^n b = a \div b$.

3.6 Children Find Products and Quotients

1. The first student's method is related to estimating because she first estimated the quotient to be between 2080 and 2240, then found the remainder to obtain the exact answer.

4. The method used here is taught by some teachers, because the steps are more easily understood than the traditional algorithm most of us learned. The major advantage of this method is that it can be easily understood, based on the subtraction notion of division. We ask: How many 27s are in 3247? We know there are at least 100 because $27 \times 100 = 2700$ is less than 3247, so we first subtract 100 27s. We could next take away ten 27s, or we could take away twenty 27s; the choice depends on one's number facility. This is another advantage. The disadvantage is that it takes longer than the standard algorithm (but perhaps not if one counts all the additional time needed to learn the standard algorithm for division).

5. This procedure was invented by a very precocious child. Most first graders would not have been able to do this. However, prospective teachers should recognize that they will sometimes have very bright students whose thinking is not always easily followed.

> To find $63 \div 9$:
> $60 \div 10 = 6$
> $6 + 3 = 9$
> $9 \div 9 = 1$
> $6 + 1 = 7$, so $63 \div 9 = 7$

3.7 Issues for Learning: Developing Number Sense

1. **b.** $46 - 17$, because more is taken away in $46 - 19$

3.

This way removes 32×3, about 90.   This way removes 2×83, about 160.

Thus, more is lost the second way, so the first way gives a closer estimate.

Or, if 32 is rounded to 30, and the 83 is not rounded, the answer is off by 2×83 or about 160. If 83 is rounded to 80 and the 32 is not rounded, the answer is off by 3×32 or about 90, so rounding the 83 yields a closer estimate. (The temptation is to say "round the 32 because only 2 is being dropped, but if 83 is rounded to 80, 3 is being dropped.")

4. **a.** None of the addends have 1 in the ones place, so the sum can't.

6. **a.** 47 and 52 are "compatible," adding about to 100, and 36 and 69 are somewhat compatible, with sum about 100. Sum about $200 + 20$ or 30: 220 or 230.

    b. About 40×40, or 1600   **c.** $1200 - 900$ is easy to calculate.   **d.** $35,000 \div 50 = 700$

7. **a.** Repeated subtraction: There will be more 9.35s in 56 than there are 10s.

    Sharing: "Splitting" 56 into 10 amounts will give less than splitting it into fewer than 10 amounts.

8. 0.68×5 is trivial compared to 0.34×150, which is about a third of 150.

Answers for Chapter 4

4.1 Operating on Whole Numbers and Decimal Numbers

1. **a.** Let the flat be the unit, because a unit that can be cut into hundredths is needed. Then large cubes represent tens, longs represent tenths, and small cubes represent hundredths.

    Step 1. Lay out two rows: the first has 5 large cubes, 6 flats, and 2 longs. Directly below are 3 large cubes, 4 flats, 5 longs, and 2 small cubes.

Step 2.   Begin filling a third row. First bring down (directly below) the small cubes; there are 2 thousandths.

Step 3.   Bring down (to the third row) the longs. There are 7, representing 7 tenths.

Step 4.   Bring down the flats. There are 10. Trade for a large cube and place the cube in the next left column with the other cubes. The flats column is now empty, representing 0 ones.

Step 5.   Bring down all the large cubes. There are 8 plus the one from Step 4, for a total of 9, representing 9 tens.

Step 6.   Write down the number represented, from left to right:

   9 cubes, 0 flats, 7 longs, and 2 small cubes, representing 90.62.

c.   45.6 –21.21

   a.   Using the flat as the unit, place 4 large cubes, 5 flats, and 6 longs on the table.

   b.   Trade 1 long for 10 small cubes, and remove 1 small cube, leaving 4 large cubes, 5 flats, 5 longs, and 9 small cubes. (0.01 has been removed.)

   c.   Remove 2 longs, leaving 4 large cubes, 5 flats, 3 longs, and 9 small cubes. (0.2 has been removed.)

   d.   Remove 1 flat, leaving 4 large cubes, 4 flats, 3 longs, and 9 small cubes. (1 has been removed.)

   e.   Remove 2 large cubes, leaving 2 large cubes, 4 flats, 3 longs, and 9 small cubes. (1 has been removed.) The remaining blocks represent 24.39.

d. $2912 \div 8$

Here is one way this could be acted and written, using the sharing notion of division. The small block is used to represent 1.

Place or draw 2 blocks, 9 flats, 1 long, and 2 small blocks. Write:

$$8\overline{)2912}$$

Think of how to place the blocks in 8 piles with the same amount in each pile. Change the 2 blocks to 20 flats; there are now 29 flats; place 3 in each of 8 piles.

$$
\begin{array}{r}
3 \\
8\overline{)2912} \\
\underline{24} \\
5
\end{array}
$$

There are 5 remaining flats. Change them to longs; there are now 51 longs.

Distribute the longs; there will be 6 longs in each pile, with 3 longs remaining.

$$
\begin{array}{r}
36 \\
8\overline{)2912} \\
\underline{24} \\
51 \\
\underline{48} \\
3
\end{array}
$$

Change the 3 longs to 30 units. There are now 32 units. Distribute them to the piles, 4 per pile.

$$\begin{array}{r} 364 \\ 8\overline{)2912} \\ \underline{24} \\ 51 \\ \underline{48} \\ 32 \\ \underline{32} \end{array}$$

In each pile there are 3 flats, 6 longs, and 4 units per pile. The quotient is therefore 364.

2. These involve just whole numbers, so the small cube can be the unit. It is instructive to act them out with base materials or toothpicks, noticing the trades.

   a. 1123_{five}

4. Samples, with 57×623.

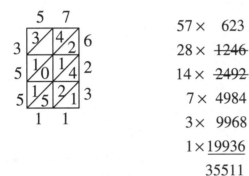

$$\begin{array}{r} 57 \times 623 \\ 28 \times \cancel{1246} \\ 14 \times \cancel{2492} \\ 7 \times 4984 \\ 3 \times 9968 \\ 1 \times \underline{19936} \\ 35511 \end{array}$$

5. **a.** 500 (twice as many as for $4000 \div 16$)   **b.** 1000 (e.g., four times as many as for $4000 \div 16$)

   c. 125 (half as many as for $4000 \div 16$)   **d.** 125 (half as many as for $4000 \div 16$, since 32 is twice 16)

   e. $62\frac{1}{2}$ (half as many as for $4000 \div 32$)   **f.** 500 (twice as many as for $4000 \div 16$)

   g. 1000   **h.** 10,000

Answers for Chapter 5

5.1 Mental Computation

1. **b.** $23(98 + 2)$ (using the distributive property) $= 23 \times 100 = 2300$ is one possibility.

2. These are some possible ways:

   a. $365 + 35 + 40 = 400 + 40 = 440$ **d.** $500 - 50 = 450$

   g. $44 \times \frac{100}{4} = 11 \times 100 = 1100$ **h.** $(0.75 \times 100) \times 88 = 100 \times 0.75 \times 88 = 100 \times 66 = 6600$

   i. $8 \times (30 + 2) = 240 + 16 = 256$ (Some might use $2^3 \times 2^5 = 2^8 = 256$.)

3. **a.** $\frac{1}{4}$ of $60 = 15$

   d. $8 \times 10\%$ of $710 = 8 \times 71 = 8 \times 70 + 8 \times 1 = 560 + 8 = 568$
     (or $4 \times 20\%$ of $710 = 4 \times 142 = 400 + 160 + 8 = 568$)

   g. $1\frac{1}{4} \times 40 = 50$ **h.** 100   **i.** 3.2

4. **a.** 120   **c.** 89

5.2 Computational Estimation

1. 0.76 is about $\frac{3}{4}$ and 62 is about 60. $\frac{3}{4}$ of 60 is 45.

2. Now I want to be sure I have enough money, so I must be careful not to underestimate. I could say 80¢ × 60 or $48 would be close, and $50 (accounting for 2 more tablets) is more than enough.

3. The second. The first would be less than 84.63, the second would be more than 84.63.

6. Only SOME ways of estimating the answers are shown here.

   b. A few ways: $\frac{100}{4} \times 80 = 2000$ (so the estimate should be less than 2000)

      $25 \times 76 \approx 25 \times 75 = 25 \times 25 \times 3 = 625 \times 3 = \underline{1875}$

      or $25 \times 75 = 20 \times 75 + 5 \times 75 = 1500 + 375 = \underline{1875}$

      or $25 \times 80 = 80 \times 25 = 8 \times 25 \times 10 = 2000$ so 25×76 is <u>a little less than 2000</u>

      or $25 \times 80 = 5 \times 5 \times 80 = 5 \times 400 = 2000$ so 25×76 is <u>a little less</u> than 2000

      or $20 \times 70 = 1400$ and $30 \times 80 = 2400$, so 25×76 is about in the middle of 1400 and 2400 which would be <u>about 1900</u>.

     (There are more ways than what are shown here.)

7. **a.** The price is about $\frac{1}{4}$ off $50, or $12.50 off. About $37.50.

5.3 Estimating Values of Quantities

(Students do not have answers to any of these exercises.)

5.4 Using Scientific Notation for Estimating Values of Very Large and Very Small Quantities

1. **b.** 2.04×10^2 **c.** 2.04×10^{-2}

2. Twelve is not between 1 and 10.

3. **a.** 9.9×10^{18} **b.** 3×10^{-4} **c.** 8×10^{-17} **d.** 2.1×10^2

5. $314 \times 10^4 + 2.315 \times 10^4 = 316.315 \times 10^4 = 3.16 \times 10^6$. Numbers must have the same power of ten to be added.

7. Suppose n is 5. Then $2n$ is 10; $2^n = 32$; $n^2 = 25$; $10^n = 100{,}000$.

10. A gigabyte. 2^{30} is 1,073,741,824. See http://encyclopedia.thefreedictionary.com/gigabyte.

Answers for Chapter 6

6.1 Understanding the Meanings of $\frac{a}{b}$

1. Infinitely many ways, even with straight cuts! Cuts through the point where the diagonals intersect will give two congruent and therefore same-sized pieces. Curved or zigzag cuts through that point can also give halves.

2. **d.** One possibility: A rectangular region could be marked into 4 equal pieces, with none shaded.

   e. One possibility: 3 rectangular regions are shaded (showing that $3 = \frac{3}{1}$).

3. Be sure to contrast parts (a) and (b). In part (a), the unit is the whole piece of licorice whip. In part (b), the unit is the segment between any two consecutive whole numbers, and the labeling convention would have the $\frac{3}{4}$ in only one place. Mark halfway between 0 and 1, then halfway between $\frac{1}{2}$ and 1. The second mark is at $\frac{3}{4}$

5. **a.** Two square regions of the same size, each marked into 2 equal pieces, with 3 of the pieces shaded.

   b. Start with 3 square regions; how you show the division can vary. Think of how 3 brownies could be shared by 2 people. One way would be to cut one brownie in half: $3 \div 2$. Each person gets $\frac{3}{2}$, or $1\frac{1}{2}$ brownies. Another way would be to cut each brownie in half, then each person would receive three halves.

6. **c.** Hexagon $= \frac{1}{2}$; trapezoid $= \frac{1}{4}$; blue rhombus $= \frac{1}{6}$; triangle $= \frac{1}{12}$

10. **a.** A is fair, B is fair (each piece is a quarter of the total rectangle), C is not fair, D is fair. (Can you see why? Recall the formula for the area of a triangle and apply here.) E is fair. F is not. (Try tracing and matching parts.) G and H are not fair, I is fair, J is not fair, K and L are both fair in that in each case the pieces are the same. However, in K, if $1.25 is charged for each of 2 pieces, then $5.00 is the cost of 8 pieces. Thus 7 pieces would be less than $5.00; a good deal for the buyer but not for the Student Education Association. In L, the total number of pieces is more than 8, so the Student Association would make more money selling pieces of 2 rather than selling the whole cake.

    c. None

    d. That the pieces a fraction brings to mind should be the same size but not necessarily the same shape. Those considered not fair are those with pieces that are not the same size.

11. The shaded part of the second region shows $\frac{1}{4}$ (compare it to the equal-sized first region). How the other markings are made is irrelevant with the first region as a guide. Without the first region as a guide, it would be just an "eyeball" estimate to say $\frac{1}{4}$.

15. a.

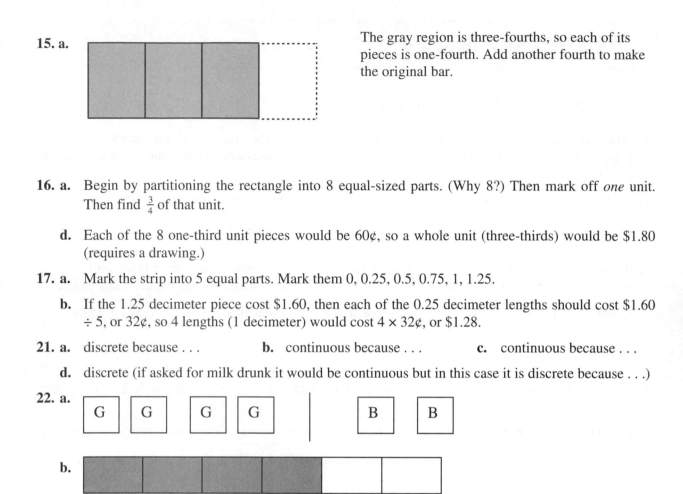

The gray region is three-fourths, so each of its pieces is one-fourth. Add another fourth to make the original bar.

16. a. Begin by partitioning the rectangle into 8 equal-sized parts. (Why 8?) Then mark off *one* unit. Then find $\frac{3}{4}$ of that unit.

d. Each of the 8 one-third unit pieces would be 60¢, so a whole unit (three-thirds) would be $1.80 (requires a drawing.)

17. a. Mark the strip into 5 equal parts. Mark them 0, 0.25, 0.5, 0.75, 1, 1.25.

b. If the 1.25 decimeter piece cost $1.60, then each of the 0.25 decimeter lengths should cost $1.60 ÷ 5, or 32¢, so 4 lengths (1 decimeter) would cost 4 × 32¢, or $1.28.

21. a. discrete because . . .   **b.** continuous because . . .   **c.** continuous because . . .

d. discrete (if asked for milk drunk it would be continuous but in this case it is discrete because . . .)

22. a.

b.

e.

f.

6.2 Equivalent (Equal) Fractions

1. c. Common denominators are useful when adding and subtracting fractions.

2.   **a.** One way

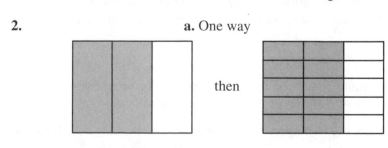

then

b. Can be similarly drawn.

4. $\dfrac{6}{10}$

5. a. $\dfrac{5}{8}$ **d.** $\dfrac{xz^3}{y}$ **e.** $\approx 1.3 \times 10^{11}$

6. a. $\dfrac{3}{4} > \dfrac{3}{5}$ because fourths are larger than fifths.

    b. $\dfrac{102}{101} > \dfrac{75}{76}$ because $\dfrac{102}{101} > 1$ and $\dfrac{75}{76} < 1$.

    d. $\dfrac{8}{9} < \dfrac{9}{10}$ because $\dfrac{8}{9}$ is $\dfrac{1}{9}$ away from 1, but $\dfrac{9}{10}$ is $\dfrac{1}{10}$ away from 1.

    e. $\dfrac{13}{18} > \dfrac{34}{62}$ because $\dfrac{13}{18} > \dfrac{12}{18} = \dfrac{2}{3}$ but $\dfrac{34}{51} < \dfrac{34}{62} = \dfrac{2}{3}$ so $\dfrac{13}{18} > \dfrac{2}{3} > \dfrac{34}{62}$.

7. b. 18 marbles

8. Reducing usually refers to making something smaller, but equivalent fractions are equal to one another.

9. a. C   **b.** D

10. b. $\dfrac{1}{10} = 0.1 < 0.2 = \dfrac{1}{5} = \dfrac{3}{15} < 0.4$

11. (Internet exercise)

12. a. $\dfrac{2}{3} > \dfrac{1}{2}$ **b.** $\dfrac{3}{5} < \dfrac{7}{11}$ **c.** $\dfrac{3}{10} < \dfrac{5}{12}$

    d. $\dfrac{2}{5} > \dfrac{5}{16}$ **e.** $\dfrac{3}{4} > \dfrac{7}{11}$ **f.** $\dfrac{5}{14} > \dfrac{5}{16}$

6.3 Relating Fractions, Decimals, and Percents

1. a. 0.375   **b.** 2.3   **c.** $0.428571428571428571\ldots = .\overline{428571}$

2. a. $\dfrac{5}{8}$ **c.** $\dfrac{274}{3}$ **d.** $\dfrac{17}{10}$ **e.** $\dfrac{1}{1}$ **g.** $\dfrac{53}{99}$

    h. No, so this number is irrational and cannot be written as a fraction.

3. a. Yes, infinitely many—can you find ten? How do you know $\frac{1}{2}$ works? Here are two others: $\frac{29}{60}, \frac{31}{60}$.

    b. Yes, infinitely many—can you find ten?

4. a. One possibility is 0.45.   c. One possibility is 1.3572.

5. $\frac{3}{17}, 0.21, \frac{1}{4}, 0.\overline{26}, \frac{11}{29}, \frac{11}{24}, 0.\overline{56}, \frac{2}{3}, \frac{12}{15}, \frac{5}{6}, 1.23$. Many can be ordered by using number sense. For example, $\frac{3}{17} < \frac{3}{15} = \frac{1}{5} = 0.2 < 0.21$. One more difficult ordering is $\frac{2}{3}, \frac{12}{15}, \frac{5}{6}$, but $\frac{12}{15} = \frac{4}{5}$, and ordering $\frac{2}{3}, \frac{4}{5}, \frac{5}{6}$ yields to number sense (compare to 1).

7. a. It could be $8.124973200000\ldots$, that is, there are only 0s after the 2.

b. It could be 8.1249732732732. . . that is, the 732 repeats.

c. It could be 8.124973212112111211112 . . . (There is a pattern but it does not repeat.).

9. Complete the following table:

Decimal form	Fraction	Percent
0.48	$\frac{48}{100}$	48%
0.8	$\frac{4}{5}$	80%
4.57	$\frac{457}{100}$	457%
0.001	$\frac{1}{1000}$	0.1%

11. Your response could point out that calculator answers are cut off (truncated) or rounded, and may or may not be exact. If you divide 1 by 13 and continue indefinitely, you will find that the decimal number continues beyond 0.0769231.

13. (Table is filled by using an internet site.)

Fractions	Decimal	Percent
$\frac{1}{2}$	0.25	25%
$\frac{11}{10}$	1.1	110%
$\frac{31}{10}$	3.1	310%
$\frac{13}{20}$	0.65	65%
$\frac{9}{4}$	2.25	250%
$\frac{17}{4}$	4.25	425%
$\frac{9}{5}$	1.8	180%
$\frac{14}{5}$	2.8	280%
$\frac{17}{5}$	3.4	340%
$\frac{3}{10}$	0.3	30%

6.4 Estimating Fractional Values

3. Yes, fractions can have negative values. For example $-\frac{1}{2} < 0$ but $\frac{1}{2} > 0$.

4. $\frac{2}{9}, \frac{11}{108}$ are close to 0; $\frac{4}{7}, \frac{99}{152}, \frac{17}{35}, \frac{15}{34}$ are close to $\frac{1}{2}$; $\frac{11}{12}, \frac{9}{8}$ are close to 1; and $\frac{3}{12}$ could be considered as close to 0, or to $\frac{1}{2}$, or both because it is halfway between 0 and $\frac{1}{2}$. Also, $\frac{99}{152}$ is about $\frac{2}{3}$ so not really close to $\frac{1}{2}$ but closer than it is to 1.

5. A fraction is close to $\frac{1}{3}$ when the denominator is about three times as large as the numerator. A fraction is close to $\frac{2}{3}$ when the numerator multiplied by 3 is about the size of the denominator multiplied by 2. (For some there could be more than one answer.)

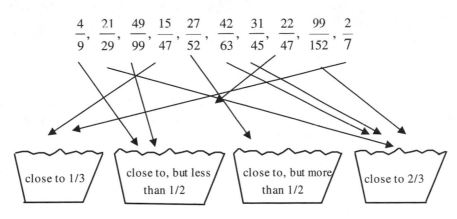

$$\frac{4}{9}, \frac{21}{29}, \frac{49}{99}, \frac{15}{47}, \frac{27}{52}, \frac{42}{63}, \frac{31}{45}, \frac{22}{47}, \frac{99}{152}, \frac{2}{7}$$

7. The denominator is about 4 times the numerator (or the numerator is about one-fourth the denominator).

8. **a.** $\frac{2}{5}$ is less than $\frac{1}{2}$ and $\frac{3}{5}$ is greater than $\frac{1}{2}$, so $\frac{1}{2}$ is in between.

   e. One way: Use equivalent fractions with 12 as the denominator.

10. **a.** $\frac{1}{8} = 0.125 = 12.5\%$ **b.** $\frac{1}{5} = 0.2 = 20\%$ **c.** $\frac{1}{4} = 0.25 = 25\%$

   d. $\frac{1}{3} = 0.3333.... = 33.3\%$ **e.** $\frac{2}{5} = 0.4 = 40\%$

   f. $\frac{3}{8} = 3 \times \frac{1}{8} = 3 \times 0.125 = 0.375 = 37.5\%$ **g.** $\frac{5}{4} = 1.25 = 125\%$

11. **a.** Slightly less than $\frac{1}{4}$ **b.** Slightly less than 1   **c.** Slightly more than 1

   d. Slightly more than $\frac{1}{3}$ **e.** About $4\frac{2}{3}$ **f.** About $\frac{1}{8}$

12. Here is just ONE possible way to estimate each.

   a. 10% of 800 + 5% of 800 is 80 + 40 = 120.

   b. 10% of 150 is 15. 90% is about 150 − 15 which is 135.

13. Sketch $\frac{4}{5}$, and then cut each fifth into two equal pieces.

17. **a.** About $\frac{1}{2} + 1 = 1\frac{1}{2}$ **b.** About $1\frac{1}{2} + 4 + 7 = 12\frac{1}{2}$

   c. About 15 − 5 = 10   **d.** About 5 − 3 = 2

   e. About $\frac{2}{3} - \frac{1}{3} = \frac{1}{3}$ **f.** About $4\frac{1}{2} + 6 - 2 = 8\frac{1}{2}$

Answers for Chapter 7

7.1 Adding and Subtracting Fractions

1. One way: $8 = 2^3$, $6 = 2 \times 3$, and $15 = 3 \times 5$. The denominator must have all of these factors, that is, it must have at least 2^3, 3, and 5 as factors. $2^3 \times 3 \times 5 = 120$ is the smallest common denominator. Any other denominator must be a multiple of 120.

   (For another way, see Exercise 16 below.)

3. Parts a and b will require more than one unit, and some extra markings to get pieces of the same size.

   c. $\dfrac{2}{3} - \dfrac{1}{2}$

   $\dfrac{2}{3}$ is first shaded; $\dfrac{1}{2}$ is double shaded. The portion of light shading is the difference: $\dfrac{1}{6}$ of the whole rectangle.

4. a. Let the yellow hexagon be the unit. Then $\dfrac{1}{2}$ is represented by 1 red trapezoid, and $\dfrac{1}{6}$ by a green triangle. Placed together, they can be replaced by 2 blue rhombuses, which represent $\dfrac{2}{3}$.

   e. Let 2 hexagons represent the unit. Now the trapezoid represent $\dfrac{1}{4}$. The number 4 would be presented by 8 hexagons. I need to take away $2\dfrac{1}{4}$. How much needs to be removed from 4 to reach $2\dfrac{1}{4}$? Replace 1 of the 8 hexagons with 2 trapezoids. Remove $2\dfrac{1}{4}$ (4 hexagons and a trapezoid), leaving 3 hexagons and a trapezoid, or 2 hexagons and 3 trapezoids, which represents $1\dfrac{3}{4}$.

   f. This is essentially the problem $2\dfrac{2}{3} - \dfrac{5}{6}$. Let the hexagon represent the unit. $2\dfrac{2}{3}$ would be represented by 2 hexagons and 2 rhombuses. Replace 1 hexagon by 6 triangles. Remove 5 triangles. There is 1 hexagon (1), 2 rhombuses (or $\dfrac{2}{3}$) and a triangle ($\dfrac{1}{6}$). Each rhombus can be exchanged for 2 triangles. There is now 1 hexagon (1), and 5 triangles ($\dfrac{1}{6}$), that is $1\dfrac{5}{6}$.

5. a. $\dfrac{8}{10}$ b. Each loaf may have been cut into 10 parts.

   c. Yes. (Place a dark line over each $\dfrac{3}{10}$ to show that there are exactly ten $\dfrac{3}{10}$s.)

6. Each of the original four gets $9 \div 4 = 2\dfrac{1}{4}$ bags. After Johnny comes, each of the five gets $11 \div 5 = 2\dfrac{1}{5}$ bags. So Johnny gets $2\dfrac{1}{5}$ bags. Chico had $2\dfrac{1}{4} + 2\dfrac{1}{5} = 4\dfrac{9}{20}$ (about $4\dfrac{1}{2}$ bags).

7. He ate $\frac{1}{3} + \frac{1}{6} = \frac{1}{2}$ of a pizza. (Note: not $\frac{1}{6}$ of what was left, but $\frac{1}{6}$ of the whole pizza.)

9. One way: $\frac{2}{3} + \frac{1}{16} + \frac{1}{16} + \frac{1}{16}$, or $\frac{2}{3} + \frac{3}{16} = \frac{41}{48}$, so there will be $\frac{7}{48}$ of her estate left.

11. $4 \times 1\frac{1}{4} = 5$, so the jug holds 5 quarts. $1\frac{3}{4} + 1\frac{3}{4} + 1\frac{3}{4} = 5\frac{1}{4}$, so $\frac{1}{4}$ quart of drink will be left over.

12. $\frac{5}{8} + \frac{5}{8} + \frac{1}{2} + \frac{2}{3} = 2\frac{5}{12}$ gallons, so he cannot mow all four yards on one tank. He will be $2\frac{5}{12} - 2\frac{1}{3} = \frac{1}{12}$ of a gallon short.

14. a. Caution: A common error is to lose track of the unit, which should be the same for the two fractions. Why is "Pam had half of a cake. She ate a third of it. How much cake did she eat?" incorrect (even though it does give the correct numerical answer)?

   b and c. The mixed numbers encourage you to think of a measurement situation, using English system units.

15. a. $\dfrac{3}{4} + \dfrac{1}{4} = 1$, and $1 + \dfrac{5}{6} = 1\dfrac{5}{6}$

   c. $3\dfrac{1}{2} + 1\dfrac{1}{2} = 5$, so the total of the two fractions being subtracted total 5. $1\dfrac{3}{4}$

   e. $4\frac{13}{16}$ **f.** $\frac{7}{16}$ ($\frac{0}{72}$ is just 0!)

16. a. $\frac{17+95-8}{40} = \frac{104}{40} = \frac{13}{5} = 2\frac{3}{5}$

   b. LCD = 540. $\frac{375+248}{540} = \frac{623}{540} = 1\frac{83}{540}$. (Compare doing this with 36×135 as the common denominator!)

17. a. Almost any example you try will show that subtraction is not commutative. Avoid subtracting a fraction that is equal to the other fraction, however, such as $\frac{12}{18} - \frac{18}{27}$, and $\frac{18}{27} - \frac{12}{18}$.

   b. So long as you avoid 0 as the third fraction, you should find a counterexample to $\left(\frac{a}{b} - \frac{c}{d}\right) - \frac{e}{f}$ being equal to $\frac{a}{b} - \left(\frac{c}{d} - \frac{e}{f}\right)$.

7.2 Multiplying by a Fraction

2. $\frac{1}{4}$ of the candy bar. $\frac{1}{4}$

3. One way: Cut each circular region into two equal pieces, giving 8 in all; then $\frac{5}{8}$ of the 4 circles would be 5 of the pieces. This is $\frac{5}{8}$ of 4 which is $2\frac{1}{2}$.

   A second way: Cut each circular region into 8 equal pieces; shade 5 pieces in each circle to get $\frac{5}{8}$ of the 4 circles. $\frac{5}{8}$ of 4 is $2\frac{1}{2}$ (or $\frac{20}{8}$ with the second method). To represent $4 \times \frac{5}{8}$ draw a region with 8 equal parts, shading 5 of them. Do this four times: $\frac{5}{8} + \frac{5}{8} + \frac{5}{8} + \frac{5}{8} = \frac{20}{8} = 2\frac{1}{2}$

5. a. 4   **b.** 2   **c.** 1   **d.** $\frac{1}{2}$

6. a. $\frac{1}{6} \times 12 = 2$ **b.** $12 \times \frac{1}{6} = 2$

7. $4 \times \frac{2}{3}$ 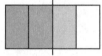 $\frac{8}{3}$

Alternatively, $2\frac{2}{3}$

$\frac{2}{3} \times 4$

$\frac{2}{3} \times 4$ $2\frac{2}{3}$

$\frac{2}{3}$ of the first 3 + $\frac{2}{3}$ of the last one

Alternatively, take $\frac{2}{3}$ of each hexagon and get the first row.

8. $\frac{3}{4}$ of the rectangle is shaded. $\frac{2}{3}$ of that amount is $\frac{1}{2}$.

12. a. Make certain your drawing shows $\frac{2}{3}$ of the $\frac{3}{4}$ pie. The unit for the $\frac{2}{3}$ is the $\frac{3}{4}$ pie. The answer is $\frac{1}{2}$ of the pie, although your work may show $\frac{2}{4}$ of the pie or $\frac{6}{12}$ of the pie.

b. You probably used a rectangular region here, rather than the circular regions from part (a). "Pies" suggest circles, but "class" doesn't, so it is natural <u>not</u> to use circular regions for part (b).

The whole for the $\frac{3}{4}$ is the number of students in the class; the whole for the $\frac{2}{3}$ is just the part of the class that are girls. The size of the class does not matter, a fact that is surprising to some students, who are not aware that $\frac{2}{3} \times (\frac{3}{4}$ of the number of students in the class) is equal to $(\frac{2}{3} \times \frac{3}{4})$ of the number of students in the class. See Exercise 15.

c. $\frac{7}{6}$ of $\frac{3}{4} = \frac{7}{8}$ **d.**   The drawing is correct.

13. a. Example: A recipe calls for $2\frac{3}{4}$ cups of sugar. Anh is making only $\frac{1}{4}$ of the recipe. How much sugar will she use?

14. b. No, "canceling" should be used only with multiplication or as a label for simplifying when using the $\frac{an}{bn} = \frac{a}{b}$ principle for equality of fractions and ratios.

15. a. $\frac{3}{8}$. Here is a drawing to help you. The number of students in the class is irrelevant.

girls	boys
	F
	F
	F

Add
lines to
make
equal
pieces.

girls	boys
	F
	F
	F

b.   The same answer as in part (a). Again, the number of students in the class is irrelevant.

18. b. $\frac{3}{14}$ $\frac{3}{9}$ $\frac{3}{7}$ $\frac{3}{4}$ $\frac{3}{2}$ because the denominators are descending, or $\frac{3}{14}$ is close to 0, $\frac{3}{9}$ is $\frac{1}{3}$, $\frac{3}{7}$ is slightly less than $\frac{1}{2}$, $\frac{3}{4}$ is between $\frac{1}{2}$ and 1, $\frac{3}{2} > 1$.

7.3 Dividing by a Fraction

1. a. 16 **b.** 8 **c.** 4 **d.** 2 **e.** 1 **f.** $\frac{1}{2}$

3. b. $5 \times 1\frac{1}{2}$ (or $5 \times \frac{3}{2}$) $= 7\frac{1}{2}$ **c.** $24 \times 1\frac{1}{2}$ (or $24 \times \frac{3}{2}$) $= 36$

d. $7\frac{1}{2} \times 1\frac{1}{2}$ (or $7\frac{1}{2} \times \frac{3}{2}$) $= 11\frac{1}{4}$ **e.** $\frac{4}{5} \times 1\frac{1}{2}$ (or $\frac{4}{5} \times \frac{3}{2}$) $= 1\frac{1}{5}$

4. 16, 8, 4, 2, 1

6. There are four $\frac{1}{6}$ units in $\frac{2}{3}$ unit.

7.

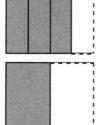

How many of these

are in this?

What part of the $\frac{3}{4}$ is the same as $\frac{1}{2}$? $\frac{2}{3}$?

$\frac{2}{3}$ refers back to the whole square.

How many halves are in $\frac{3}{4}$ of a whole?

There are $\frac{2}{3}$ halves in $\frac{3}{4}$ of a whole.

8. a. Using the hexagon as the unit, find $\frac{5}{6}$ of 2 hexagons. To do so, replace the 2 hexagons with 6 rhombuses. $\frac{5}{6}$ would be 5 rhombuses, which can be replaced with 1 hexagon and 2 rhombuses: $1\frac{2}{3}$.

b. Let the hexagon be the unit. Replace it with 6 triangles. How many halves (how many trapezoids) can be used to replace the 6 triangles. 4 of the triangles would be one $\frac{1}{2}$. The other 2 triangles would be $\frac{2}{3}$ of a half, for a total of $1\frac{2}{3}$.

Notice that (a) and (b) have the same answer. You do (c), (d), (e), and (f) in a similar fashion, noting equivalent answers.

10. With 1 gallon, $\frac{3}{4}$ of the wall can be painted. So $\frac{3}{5}$ of a gallon of paint will cover $\frac{3}{5}$ of $\frac{3}{4}$ of the wall. $\frac{3}{5} \times \frac{3}{4} = \frac{9}{20}$

12. You are explaining why $3\frac{1}{2}$ is the answer, referring to your sketch. (Where is the $3\frac{1}{2}$ in your sketch?)

13. a. The $\frac{2}{3}$ refers to the $\frac{3}{4}$ of the unit. The $\frac{3}{4}$ refers to the unit. The $\frac{1}{2}$ refers to the unit.

b. The $\frac{1}{2}$ refers to the unit. The $\frac{3}{4}$ refers to the unit. The $\frac{2}{3}$ refers to the $\frac{3}{4}$ of the unit. (Note that the answers to (a) and (b) are the same. We are emphasizing repeated subtraction here.)

14. a. $\frac{1}{4}$ pan **b.** $\frac{1}{2}$ cake **c.** $3\frac{3}{4}$ recipe **d.** $7\frac{1}{4}$ cups You make the drawings.

15. Possible answer: **a.** Cherie has 6 yards of fabric and wants to make as many identical skirts as possible. Each requires $1\frac{2}{3}$ yards of fabric. How many skirts can she make? (What happens to the remainder here?) Another: Val has 6 cups of flour and wants to make cookies. One batch calls for $1\frac{2}{3}$ cups of sugar. How many batches can he make? (What happens to the remainder in this situation? Can it be used for part of another batch? Can the fabric be used for another skirt?)

You do (b) and (c).

16. a. $(\frac{2}{3} \times (2 \times 9)) \div \frac{1}{2}$

17. a.   No—try almost any example.   **b.** No   **c.** Yes, yes ($\frac{n}{n} = 1$), no

7.4 Issues for Learning: Teaching Calculation with Fractions

1. $\frac{1}{5}$, from $\frac{3}{4} \times \left[1 - (\frac{1}{3} + \frac{2}{5})\right] = \frac{3}{4} \times \left[1 - \frac{11}{15}\right] = \frac{3}{4} \times \frac{4}{15}$

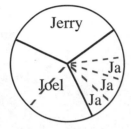

2. $0.9 \div 0.002 = 450$

3.   5 full recipes, since $4 \div \frac{3}{4} = 5\frac{1}{3}$

4. $1 - (\frac{5}{12} + \frac{1}{6} + \frac{1}{12}) = 1 - \frac{8}{12} = \frac{1}{3}$ and the $\frac{1}{3}$ is shared by 3. $\frac{2}{3}$ *of* $\frac{1}{3} = \frac{2}{9}$

5.   333, because $75 \div 0.2 = 375$, but $200 \div 0.6$ is only $333\frac{1}{3}$.

6.   10 full days, because $(4 \times 2) \div \frac{3}{4} = ... = 10\frac{2}{3}$.

7. $66\frac{2}{3}\%$ The excess amount was $\frac{1}{3} - \frac{1}{5} = \frac{2}{15}$. Comparing the $\frac{2}{15}$ to the planned $\frac{1}{5}$ gives $\frac{2}{15} \div \frac{1}{5} = \frac{10}{15} \approx 66\frac{2}{3}\%$.

8.   a.   25% The excess was $\frac{1}{2}$ cup, and $\frac{1}{2}$ cup compares to 2 cups is $\frac{1}{4}$ or 25%.

   b.   37.5% You used $\frac{3}{4}$ cup less than the designated 2 cups. $\frac{3}{4} : 2 = 3 : 8 = \frac{3}{8} = 37.5\%$

Answers for Chapter 8

8.1 Quantitative Analysis of Multiplicative Situations

2.   a.   4:3 or $\frac{4}{3}$ **b.** $\frac{3}{4}$ **c.** $\frac{4}{3}$ **d.** $\frac{3}{7}$ **e.** $\frac{4}{7}$

   Assume that #5 and #6 of **Activity 1 Candy Bars** are homework. Making a drawing for part (a) is an important idea.

5.   b. $\frac{3}{2}$, or $1\frac{1}{2}$ **c.** $\frac{2}{5}$ **d.** $\frac{2}{3}$ (compare b)

6.   b. $\frac{4}{3}$, or $1\frac{1}{3}$ **c.** $\frac{3}{7}$ **d.** $\frac{3}{4}$

8.2 Fractions in Multiplicative Comparisons

2. The first question, involving a multiplicative comparison, is answered by turning the ratio $9\frac{2}{7}:5$ into the fraction form, and simplifying. $9\frac{2}{7}:5 = \frac{9\frac{2}{7}}{5} = \frac{65}{35} = 1\frac{6}{7}$. Claudia ran $\frac{9\frac{2}{7}}{5} = \frac{65}{35} = 1\frac{6}{7}$ times as many laps as Juan. The second question involves another additive comparison and leads to Claudia's running $9\frac{2}{7} - 5 = 4\frac{2}{7}$ laps farther than Juan.

4. This is like a Candy Bar problem with an addition—the value (14 meters) for the whole amount. The given sentence translates into a R:S = 3:4 ratio, which gives $\frac{3}{7}$ as the R part of the whole ribbon. So the ribbon part is $\frac{3}{7} \times 14 = 6$ meters, and the strips part is 8 meters.

5. a. The quantitative analysis should include the dogs' weights, the two multiplicative comparisons, the additive comparison, and the parts-whole relationships.

    b. A drawing is definitely helpful here, because there are two multiplicative comparisons and an additive comparison involved.

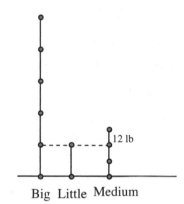

Big Little Medium

The other thirds of the medium dog's weight must also be 12 lb each, so the medium dog weighs 36 pounds. The little dog's weight matches 2 of the 12-lb pieces, so the little dog weighs 24 lb. Finally, the big dog weighs 120 lb.

7. b. Cameron, $\frac{4}{5}$ of the bar; Don, $\frac{1}{5}$. Notice that there is no multiplicative comparison in part (b).

    c. Emily, $\frac{3}{4}$ of the bar; Fran, $\frac{1}{4}$.

    d. Gay, $\frac{3}{10}$ of the bar; Haille, $\frac{6}{10}$ or $\frac{3}{5}$; Ida, $\frac{1}{10}$.

    f. Mick and Nick, each $\frac{1}{4}$ of the bar; Ollie, $\frac{1}{6}$; Pete, $\frac{2}{6}$ or $\frac{1}{3}$.

8. a. Al, 80¢ (Note: not $0.80¢); Babs, $1   **b.** Cameron, $1.44; Don, 36¢

    c. Emily, $1.35; Fran, 45¢   **d.** Gay, 54¢; Haille, $1.08; Ida, 18¢

    e. Judy, $1.20; Keisha, 40¢; Lannie, 20¢   **f.** Mick, 45¢; Nick, 45¢; Ollie, 30¢; Pete, 60¢

9. b. I, 66¢; II, $1.98; III, $3.96

10. Charity A, $16; charity B, $8; charity C, $64

11. Quinn ate $\frac{8}{15} \times \frac{3}{4} = \frac{2}{5}$ of the whole pizza; Rhonda, $\frac{4}{15} \times \frac{3}{4} = \frac{1}{5}$ of the pizza; and Sue, $\frac{3}{15} \times \frac{3}{4} = \frac{1}{5} \times \frac{3}{4} = \frac{3}{20}$ of the pizza. The fifteenths come from thinking of Q:R as 8:4, so that S:R's 3:4 can be used in the same drawing. Note the different uses of $\frac{3}{4}$.

Answers for Chapter 9

9.1 Ratio as a Measure

2. One way: Determine the change in population from the numbers of live births and deaths. Then divide that difference by the number of 1000s in the population. (What does this accomplish?) If you do the calculations, are you surprised at the answers, from country to country?

3. a. The usual way for most computers: the size of the tiny dots that make up the display (pixels)

    b. The number of dots of black per square inch

    c. The slope, just as you did with the ski slopes

    d. The number of miles or kilometers between them

    e. The number of people per square mile (or square kilometer)

    f. The fraction, $\frac{\text{number of red balls}}{\text{total number of balls}}$ (this is how the "probability" would be assigned)

    g. A common way: the grade point average (the number of honor points per unit of credit)

    h. The ratio of the number of teaspoons of sugar used to the volume of liquid involved

    i. The ratio of the number of tea bags used to the amount of water used

4. Keep the angles the same, but multiply the length of each side by the same number to keep the ratio of *new length* : *old length* the same for every side. (The polygons are then said to be "similar," in the technical sense of geometry.)

9.2 Comparing Ratios

1. a. Sample explanation: Using scoops of coffee to cups of water ratios, the two brews give 3:4 or $\frac{3}{4}$:1, versus 4:6 or $\frac{4}{6}$:1 $= \frac{2}{3}$:1. Comparing $\frac{3}{4}(= \frac{9}{12})$ and $\frac{2}{3}(= \frac{8}{12})$ gives that the 3 scoops for 4 cups is stronger.

    b. In the same way (but using number sense to compare the fractions per 1 cup), the 4 scoops for 8 cups is stronger.

    c. These are illustrated in the solutions given above, in case you immediately rewrote the ratios as fractions (4:6 = $\frac{4}{6}$, for example) and reasoned with those forms alone.

3. Answer similarly to the answers in #2c, d, e, and f. To get a ratio slightly greater than 1:1, you might have to "jump" to something like 11:10 rather than just 2:1, which would be quite strong.

4. The first question translates into 10:4 = x:50 (or $\frac{10}{4} = \frac{x}{50}$ or $\frac{5}{2} = \frac{x}{50}$), giving x = 125 Tbsp. Notice that another, less "mechanical," line of reasoning also makes sense: the cocoa requires 10 ÷ 4 = $2\frac{1}{2}$ Tbsp of cocoa per cup of milk. So for 50 cups, they need 50 × $2\frac{1}{2}$, or 125, Tbsps. Then the ratio, 2:$\frac{1}{8}$, for the number of Tbsp:the number of cups of cocoa, might lead either to $\frac{2}{\frac{1}{8}} = \frac{125}{x}$, or to the rate, 16 Tbsp per cup and 125 ÷ 16. Either gives an answer of $7\frac{13}{16}$ cups of cocoa.

6. Try different values for the distances A and B can travel. Suppose B travels 10 miles in 2 hours, and A travels 12 miles in 3 hours; or 18 miles in 3 hours; or 24 miles in 3 hours. Would all of the numbers fit the situation? Now can you answer the question?

8. A's rate is $\frac{40}{3} = 13\frac{1}{3}$ km per hour; B's rate is $\frac{67}{5} = 13\frac{2}{5}$ km per hour. So B travels slightly faster (has a slightly greater speed).

9. We need to determine B's rate of working. Using A's rate, A will make $9 \times 13 = 117$ parts in 9 hours, so B must have made $243 - 117 = 126$ parts in the 9 hours. B's rate, then, is $\frac{126}{9} = 14$ parts per hour, slightly faster than A's. So B would be more productive.

10. Finding the price per ounce (the "unit price") gives $\frac{109}{12} = 9\frac{1}{12}$ cents per ounce for the larger can, and $\frac{98}{10.75} = 9\frac{5}{43}$ cents per ounce for the smaller can. So the larger can is a slightly better buy. If you used an ounces:cents approach, you would get the same end result but your rates, and your reasoning about the final values, would be different from those here.

11. Compare $\frac{4}{9}$ and $\frac{3}{7}$, either by finding equal fractions with a common denominator ($\frac{3}{7} = \frac{27}{63}$ and $\frac{4}{9} = \frac{28}{63}$) or by changing the fractions to decimals. Jane has slightly more crayons left.

12. One approach is to compare the *number of girls* : *number of boys* ratios, another is to see what fractions of the whole class are involved: $\frac{13}{24}$ versus $\frac{15}{28}$. Mrs. Heath's class has a slightly greater representation of girls.

13. Comparing the two rates from $\frac{250}{12} = 20\frac{5}{6}$ miles per gallon and $\frac{145}{7.5} = 19\frac{1}{3}$ miles per gallon shows that Car A is more economical.

14. Assume no bigamy! Rather than the algebraic $\frac{2}{3}$M = $\frac{3}{4}$W approach, try making a diagram. Start with a rectangle for all the men, and mark the married men. Then, keeping in mind that the number of married men = the number of married women, add to the diagram to show all the women. Adding a few more line segments enables you to see the M:W ratio of 9:8.

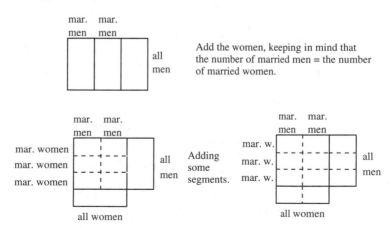

15. There are different ways. (1) Replace the ratios with equal ratios having the same second entries: $(133 \times 115):(161 \times 115)$ and $(95 \times 161):(115 \times 161)$; and then compare 133×115 and 95×161. (2) Change the ratios to fraction form and then use methods that you earlier learned to determine whether or not two fractions are equal. Or (3) Change the ratios to fractions and then to decimals (this way is probably easiest with a calculator). The fact that the ratios are equal may make one suspect that there might be an easier way. Simplify each ratio: $\frac{133}{161} = \frac{7 \times 19}{7 \times 23} = \frac{19}{23}$ and $\frac{95}{115} = \frac{5 \times 19}{5 \times 23} = \frac{19}{23}$! See Exercise 16 for a shortcut way.

16. **a.** $a{:}b = (ad){:}(bd)$ (or $\frac{a}{b} = \frac{ad}{bd}$) and $c{:}d = (bc){:}(bd)$ (or $\frac{c}{d} = \frac{bc}{bd}$). Then the ratios (or fractions) are equal if $ad = bc$.

    b. $x = 144$; $x = 39$

    c. Not in general. Try it on, say, $\frac{1}{4} + \frac{1}{8}$ and $\frac{1}{2} \times \frac{1}{2}$.

17. Because $\frac{3}{4} + \frac{2}{4} = \frac{5}{4}$, which apparently would mean 5 hits in 4 at-bats, this way cannot be correct. Indeed, 3:4 "+" 2:4 here should equal 5:8, 5 hits in 8 at-bats. (The " " marks are a reminder that this is not the usual addition of numbers.) Critics say that ratios should be added this way: $a{:}b$ "+" $c{:}d = (a+c){:}(b+d)$.

19. **a.** The rate is 12 donuts:1 minute, or $\frac{12 \text{ donuts}}{1 \text{ minute}}$. This is a rate because it remains the same when quantities change, that is, this same rate applies whether one is determining number of donuts for any particular time period.

    b. $\frac{12 \text{ donuts}}{1 \text{ minute}}$

    c. $\frac{12 \text{ donuts}}{1 \text{ minute}}$ so 60×12 donuts in 60 minutes, or 720 donuts in an hour.

    d. $\frac{12}{1} = \frac{x}{60}$. Multiply both sides of the equation by 60. $x = 720$ donuts.

21. **a.** The desired rate is $\frac{7 \text{ ugrads}}{2 \text{ grads}}$, because as the numbers of undergraduates and graduate students change, the ratio should stay the same.

    b. $\frac{7 \text{ ugrads}}{2 \text{ grads}} = \frac{3.5 \text{ ugrads}}{1 \text{ grad}}$, or 3.5 undergrads per graduate student.

    c. 3.5 undergrads for each graduate student, so if there are 100 graduate students there should be 350 undergrads.

    d. $\frac{7}{2} = \frac{x}{100}$. Multiplying both sides by 100 gives $x = 350$.

22. The ratio of girls to boys is 12:13. The number of girls and the number of boys does not vary.

23. (Problem to be done in grocery store.)

24. **a.** Andy drove faster, because he covered more miles in less time, so his mph would be greater. (You may be helped by making up values for the quantities.)

    b. Donna swam faster, because Carla swam fewer laps in more time, so her laps per minute would be less than Donna's.

    c. Can't tell. Make up numbers to show that any of the first three possibilities could happen.

9.3 Percents in Comparisons and Changes

2. Test 1: 75%; Test 2: 76%. The instructor would probably weight the tests the same, and give the average as $\frac{75\% + 76\%}{2} = 75.5\%$. But combining the points, you received 59 out of the 78 possible, or about 75.6%. If the scores were quite different, the two methods give noticeably different results (try the two methods on 10 out of 20 and 80 out of 100).

3. $\frac{4}{9} = 44.\overline{4}\%$ and $\frac{3}{7} = 42.\overline{857142}\%$ So Jane has more left.

7. $4.2 million is 90% of $4.67 million.

8. a. 25%

9. a. 25% (Notice the "larger than.")

10. 50% increase

11. $4.00; $2.40

14. 100%

15. Pat's new salary will be $17.98 an hour, and her old salary was $14.50 an hour.

16. About 1120

18. 24 points in the first half. Angie, Beth, and Carlita accounted for $\frac{1}{3} + \frac{3}{20} + \frac{1}{4} = \frac{11}{15}$ of the points (using fractions to avoid inaccuracies with the $\frac{1}{3}$). That means that the other 16 points represent $\frac{4}{15}$ of the total points, so $\frac{1}{15}$ of the total points would be 4 points, giving 60 for the total points scored. 40% of those points, or 24 points, were scored in the first half.

19. About $230. The sketch below may help, with a focus on the $\frac{5}{8}$ of her income being $450.

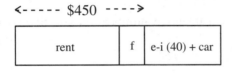

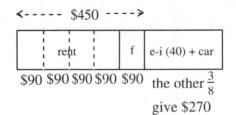

20. a. $\approx \frac{1}{3}$ of 120, or 40 people (Why is $\frac{1}{3}$ better than 0.3 of 120?)

   b. $\approx \frac{1}{2}$ of 12, or 6 pounds

   c. $\approx \frac{2}{3}$ of 66, or 44 kilometers

   d. $\approx$ 15% of 40, or $6 (10% of 40, plus half of that)

   e. $\approx \frac{1}{4}$ of 100, or 25 miles (Why is $\frac{1}{4}$ better than 0.2 or $\frac{1}{5}$?)

   f. $\approx \frac{1}{3}$ of 66, or 22 minutes

   g. $\approx \frac{3}{4}$ of 400, or $300

   h. 66 is $\approx \frac{2}{3}$ of 100, so $\approx \frac{1}{3}$ of 200, so $\approx \frac{1}{6}$ of 400. $\frac{1}{6}$ is half of $\frac{1}{3}$ so about 16%.

   i. 74 miles is $\approx \frac{3}{4}$ of 100 miles, so $\approx \frac{1}{4}$ or 25% of 300 miles.

   j. 24 pounds is $\approx$ 50% of 48 pounds

21. a. 20 people   **b.** 64 pounds   **c.** 52 kilometers   **d.** $9.60   **e.** 10 miles

22. a. $2\frac{2}{3}\%$ of all the students already qualify; $1\frac{1}{3}\%$ of all are newly eligible = 3600 students, so 1% of all = 2700 students and 100% of all = 270,000 students; 1200 students are newly eligible from urban schools, 900 from urban areas.

    b. $11\% \approx \frac{1}{9}$, so about $9 \times 1500 = 13{,}500$ workers

Answers for Chapter 10

10.1 Ways of Thinking About Signed Numbers

1. a. 5 white chips (or 5 more white chips than black)

3. a. $^{+}2$, or 2   **b.** $^{-}1$ **c.** $^{-}3$

4. a. $^{-}75.2, ^{-}22, ^{-}3, ^{-}1, ^{-}(\frac{2}{3}), \frac{3}{4}, 1, ^{+}50$

5. a. 8   The additive inverse, or opposite, of $^{-}8$ is 8.

    b. $^{-}0 = 0$ The "oppositing" across 0 would leave 0 where it is. More exactly, $0 + x = 0$ has $x = 0$ as the solution, so 0 behaves as its own additive inverse.

    c. ^{-}a is not always negative. For example, if a is a negative number, its additive inverse, ^{-}a, is positive.

6. a. $^{-}9$ **b.** $^{-}9$

7. a. $^{+}1$, or 1   **b.** $^{-}4$ **c.** $^{-}4$

    d. 0   **e.** 0   **f.** 0

8. a. Any negative number that does not have a terminating or repeating decimal. Examples include $^{-}\sqrt{2}, ^{-}\sqrt{3}, ^{-}\sqrt{5}, ^{-}\sqrt{6}, \ldots$, as well as special numbers like $^{-}\pi$.

    b. Any negative number that can be written in the form $^{-}\dfrac{\text{whole number}}{\text{nonzero whole number}}$.

12. Between every two real numbers, there is another real number. (Their average is one example.)

13. a. Not dense. There is not another integer between consecutive integers, like 1 and 2.

    b. Yes, dense. There is always a positive rational number between every two given positive rational numbers. For example, the average of two rational numbers is a rational number and is between the two.

    c. Yes, dense. There is always a negative rational number between every two given negative rational numbers.

14. Rewrite the given numbers with a large common denominator. For example, for part (a), use $\frac{3500}{2000}$ and $\frac{3600}{2000}$, and for part (b), $^{-}(\frac{2000}{3000})$ and $^{-}(\frac{1860}{3000})$. You can then find several rational numbers between the pairs.

10.2 Adding and Subtracting Signed Numbers

Note: Common here is the –6 form rather than the ⁻6 form, because of software limitations.

1. a. ●●●●   ●●   **b.** ●●●●   **c.** ●● ✕✕

         –4 + ⁻2 = –6   ○○   ⁻4 – ⁻2 = –2

                       ⁻4 + 2 = –2

d. ●●●●   ●● ✕✕

        ⁻4 – 2 = –6

2. a. (sample)

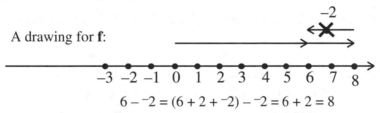

               +5 + –7 = –2

b. ⁻7   **c.** ⁺3   **d.** ⁻4

A drawing for **f**:

$$6 - {}^-2 = (6 + 2 + {}^-2) - {}^-2 = 6 + 2 = 8$$

4. a. $\frac{1}{3}$ **b.** $^-4\frac{4}{9}$

5. a. Yes: the sum of any two even integers is an even integer. $2m + 2n = 2(m + n)$, and if m and n are integers, so is $(m + n)$.

    b. Yes: the sum of any two multiples of 3 is another multiple of 3.

    c. No: Example: $3 + 5 = 8$ is not odd.

6. a. Yes, because addition is commutative.   **b.** Yes, because addition is associative.

    c. Yes, because 0 is the additive identity.   **i.** Yes, because 0 is the additive identity.

    j. Yes, because the numbers are additive inverses of each other.

7. a. ⁻13   **b.** $4\frac{13}{10}$ **c.** $\frac{4}{9}$ **d.** $^-\sqrt{11}$

8. a. ⁻3 + 5 = 2   2 – 5 = ⁻3
      5 + ⁻3 = 2   2 – ⁻3 = 5

    b. 3 + ⁻5 = ⁻2   ⁻2 – ⁻5 = 3
       ⁻5 + 3 = ⁻2   ⁻2 – 3 = ⁻5

    c. ⁻32 + ⁻29 = ⁻61   ⁻61 – ⁻29 = ⁻32
       ⁻29 + ⁻32 = ⁻61   ⁻61 – ⁻32 = ⁻29

12. a. 57000 + 35000 + ⁻16000 + ⁻16000 = n. Company A earned $60,000 for the year.

    d. From (b) and (c), ⁻77000 + ⁻125000 = n, and the company lost $202,000 during those two quarters.

10.3 Multiplying and Dividing Signed Numbers

3. $\dfrac{^-2}{5}$ is the same as $^-2 \div 5$, which is negative, and can be written $^-\left(\dfrac{2}{5}\right)$.

$\dfrac{2}{^-5}$ is the same as $2 \div {}^-5$, which is negative and can be written $^-\left(\dfrac{2}{5}\right)$.

Thus, all three expressions are naming the same number.

4.   l.   50   **m.** 1   **n.** $^-1$

6.   a.   No. The multiplicative inverse of most integers a is is not an integer.

   b.   1 is its own multiplicative inverse, as is $^-1$. ($1 \cdot 1 = 1$, and $^-1 \cdot {}^-1 = 1$.)

7.   a.   Multiplication is commutative.   **b.**   Addition is commutative.

   i.   Zero is the additive identity.   **j.**   Multiplication is distributive over addition.

8.   a. $3 \times {}^-5 = {}^-5 + {}^-5 + {}^-5 = {}^-15$, so draw 3 groups, each with 5 black chips.

   b.   Start with 0 in the form of 15 whites and 15 blacks. To find $^-3 \times 5$, subtract 5 whites three times, leaving 15 blacks, or $^-15$.

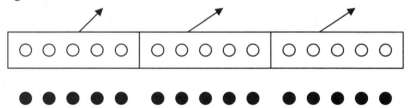

11.   a. $^+5 \times {}^-4 = n$ ($n = {}^-20$) She will have 20 fewer sheep than at present.

   c. $^+6 \times {}^-30 = n$ ($n = {}^-180$) He will weigh 180 pounds less than at present.

   d. $^-3 \times {}^-30 = n$ ($n = {}^+90$) He weighed 90 more pounds than at present.

10.4 Some Other Number Systems

5.   Be sure to set up addition and multiplication tables before doing this problem.

When working with clock arithmetic on a 4-hour clock, the multiplicative inverse of 1 is 1, and of 3 is 3. But 2 does not have a multiplicative inverse.

Answers for Chapter 11

11.1 Factors and Multiples, Primes and Composites

1.   a.   1, 5, and 25. There are no more because 25 is a perfect square of a prime number.

   b.   25, 50, 75, ... Any whole number multiplied by 25 will be a multiple of 25.

2. a. $k = 25 \times$ some whole number, or $k = 25m$, for some whole number m. A rectangular array would need 25 on one side and m on another side.

3. a. $216x = 2376$, or $x = 2376 \div 216$.

4. 21 squares could be in rectangular arrays only as 1 by 21, 21 by 1, 7 by 3, and 3 by 7. An array with 5 squares on one side would require 4.25 squares on the other side, but rectangular arrays allow only whole numbers on each side.

5. a. A number is a factor of itself.   **b.** A number is a multiple of itself.

6. a. 2 and 253 (Others are 1, 11, 22, 23, 46, and 506.)

   b. 506, 1012, 1518 (There are an infinite number of multiples of 506.)

7. True or false? If false, correct the statement.

   a. 13 is a factor of 39. True because there exists a whole number, namely 3, such that $13 \times 3 = 39$.

   b. 12 is a factor of 36. True because there exists a whole number, namely 3, such that $12 \times 3 = 36$.

   d. 36 is a multiple of 12. True because there exists a whole number, namely 3, such that $12 \times 3 = 36$.

   e. 36 is a multiple of 48. False because there is no whole number n such that $48n = 36$.

   f. 16 is a factor of 512. True because there exists a whole number, namely 32, such that $16 \times 32 = 512$.

9. a. Yes, because for some whole numbers x and y, $m = kx$ and $n = my$, substituting the first into the second, $n = (kx)y = k(xy)$. The latter also shows that n is a multiple of k.

   b. Yes, because $m = kx$ and $n = ky$ for some whole numbers x and y, $m + n = kx + ky = k(x + y)$. So k is a factor of $m + n$.

   c. Suppose $k = 6$, $m = 12$, and $n = 15$. Now k is a factor of m but not of n. $m + n = 27$, and 6 is not a factor of 27. (This is a counterexample.)

10. a. An even number is a number that has 2 as a factor.

   b. An even number is a number that is a multiple of 2.

   c. An odd number is a number that can be expressed as $2n + 1$ for any whole number n.

11.

+	even	odd
even	even	odd
odd	odd	even

×	even	odd
even	even	even
odd	even	odd

   a. The sum of any number of even numbers is even.

   b. The sum of an even number of odd numbers is even (put them in pairs), so the sum of an odd number of odd numbers is odd.

   d. The product of any number of odd numbers is odd.

   e. No, an odd number cannot have an even factor.

   g. Yes

   h. No, e.g., $3 + 5 = 8$

13. Each of them has only 1 and itself as factors.

2, 3, 5, 7, 11, 13, 17, 19, 23, 29, 31, 37, 41, 43, 47, 53, 59, 61, 67, 71, 73, 79, 83, 89, 97

14. 3 is a factor of 15, so 15 has at least these three factors: 1, 15, and 3. Hence it is not prime. Similarly, each of the other numbers has at least three factors. $119 = 7 \times 17$.

16. a. 1 and 829   **d.** n and 1

19. c. Common factors of 18 and 24 are 1, 2, 3, 6. Common multiples of 6 and 18 are 18, 36, 54, etc. All multiples of 18 are also multiples of 6.

11.2 Prime Factorization

2. a. 102   102 (Note: The remaining parts should also have a factor tree.)

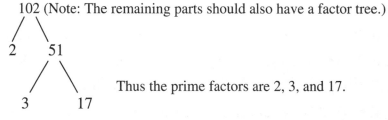

Thus the prime factors are 2, 3, and 17.

(Note: Factor trees should also be used to find the following prime factorizations.)

b. $1827 = 3^2 \cdot 7 \cdot 29$ **c.** $1584 = 2^4 \cdot 3^2 \cdot 11$ **d.** $1540 = 2^2 \cdot 5 \cdot 7 \cdot 11$

e. $121 = 11^2$ **f.** $1485 = 3^3 \cdot 5 \cdot 11$

3. Different factor trees are possible, but these prime factorizations should be the same for the different factor trees (except possibly for the order of the factors):

a. $5850 = 2 \cdot 3^2 \cdot 5^2 \cdot 13$ **b.** $256 = 2^8$ **c.** $2835 = 3^4 \cdot 5 \cdot 7$

d. $10^4 = 2^4 \cdot 5^4$ **e.** $17280 = 2^7 \cdot 3^3 \cdot 5$

4. a. 2, 3, 7, and 11 are prime factors of $3 \times 7^3 \times 22$. (There are only these 4 prime factors. Any three of these is a correct answer.)

5. The prime factorization of a number gives all of the prime factors of the number. A prime factor of the number would be just one of those primes.

6. Think about 11^m. This number, in prime factorization, has only 11 and powers of 11 as factors. Now think about 13^n. This number, in prime factorization, has only 13 and powers of 13 as factors. The fundamental theorem of arithmetic says that prime factorizations are unique. 13 does not appear in the list of factors of 11^m. So 13 cannot be a factor of 11^m for any value of m. This says that 13^n cannot equal 11^m for any values of m and n.

7. a. $m = 2 \cdot 67$ **c.** $n = 2 \cdot 17 \cdot 67^2$ would make the equation true.

e. $4^m = (2^2)^m = 2^{2m}$ and $8^n = (2^3)^n = 2^{3n}$ so the given equation will be true if it is possible to find m and n so that $2m = 3n$. There are many such pairs of values for m and n that will work, for example, $m = 3$ and $n = 2$, or $m = 6$ and $n = 4$.

8. a. $2^8 \cdot 7$ could not be a factor of m, because m does not have 7 in its prime factorization (which is unique, and hence could not have another factorization with a 7 in it).

b. Similarly, the part (b) number already has too many 2s to be a factor of m.

c. The part (c) number is a factor of m, because all of its factors appear in the prime factorization of m.

10. a. 6   **b.** $3 \times 4 = 12$ **c.** $45,000 = 2^3 \cdot 3^2 \cdot 5^4$ has 60 factors

     e. $2^6 \cdot 5^6$ has 49 factors   **f.** 7 factors

11. a. $19^4 \times 11^3 \times 2^5 \times n$ is a factor of $19^4 \times 11^4 \times 2^5$ if $n = 11$.

     b. $19^4 \times 22 \times 2^5 \times n$ cannot be a factor of $19^4 \times 11^4 \times 2^5$ because $19^4 \times 22 \times 2^5 \times n = 19^4 \times 11 \times 2^6$ $\times n$. There is one too many 2s in $19^4 \times 11 \times 2^6 \times n$ to be a factor of $19^4 \times 22 \times 2^5 \times n$.

12. a. $19^4 \times 11^8 \times 2^5$ Yes, multiply q by 11^4.

     b. $19^4 \times 22^4 \times 2^5 \times 17 = 19^4 \times 11^4 \times 2^9 \times 17$ Yes, multiply q by $2^4 \times 17$.

14. a. 11   **e.** $(m + 1)(n + 1)(s + 1)$

15. $2^5 \cdot 5^9$ is one possibility.

16. $2^7 \cdot 11^2$ is one possibility. 2 can be replaced by other primes for other possibilities.

11.3 Divisibility Tests to Determine Whether a Number Is Prime

1. a. 2, 3, 4, 6, 8, 9 are (some of the) factors of 43,056 (5 and 10 are not factors).

     c. 3 is one factor of the number (but 2, 4, 5, 6, 8, 9, and 10 are not).

2. a. The solution is not solely trial and error. If 2 and 3 but not 9 are factors, then the ones digit must be even and the sum of the digits must be a multiple of 3 but not of 9. If 4 is not a factor, then 4 is not a factor of the right-most two digits. By starting with the ones place, here is one result: 200,022. There are many others.

3. 3 must be a factor of the sum of the digits. The known digits give a sum of 29. So if $a = 1$ or 4 or 7, then 3 will be a factor of the number. Similarly, if 9 is to be a factor, then 9 must divide the sum of the digits. With a current sum of 29, the only digit value that works for a is 7. (Why not 16?)

5. In each case, (a) through (d), the two factors are relatively prime, so examples can be found. If the two factors are not relatively prime, then one cannot make such statements. For example, is it true to say, in (b), 12 is a factor of n if and only if 2 is a factor of n and 6 is a factor of n? No, 18 has both 2 and 6 as factors, but 12 is not a factor of 18. But one could say: 12 is a factor of n if and only if 3 is a factor of n and 4 is a factor of n, because 3 and 4 are relatively prime.

6. a. 8 and 3 are factors of 24, and are relatively prime. Thus, a number is divisible by 24 if and only if it is divisible by 8. 8 is a factor because it divides 112. 3 is a factor because the sum of the digits is 6. Therefore 24 is a factor.

     b. 012 is not divisible by 8, so the number is not divisible by 8 or by 24.

     c. Use the 2-test and the 9-test. No, the number is not divisible by 2.

7. To be a multiple of 36, the number must be divisible by 4 and by 9. Thus choose a 2-digit number divisible by 4, say 24, for the final two digits. To be divisible by 9, the sum of the digits must be divisible by 9, so add a number to 24 to obtain the number divisible by 9, say 3. So 300,000,000,000,024 would be such a number. To obtain a number NOT divisible by 36, change the first digit to 2. Now the sum of the digits is not divisible by 9. Or, change the last two digits to form a number NOT divisible by 4, such as 23.

8. One example: eight $= 13_{\text{five}}$. Two is certainly a factor of eight, but not of the 3 in 13_{five}, so the usual 2-test does not work. Or, nine $= 14_{\text{five}}$, and two is not a factor of nine, but 14_{five} ends in an even number.

9. If n is prime, it has *exactly* two factors, 1 and n. Finding a third factor means n is not prime, which means it is composite. For example, 169 has 1 and 169 as factors. But 169 also has 13 as a factor, and so is a composite number.

12. No, because in any two pairs of consecutive numbers, one is even so has 2 as a factor.

13. Which of these numbers is divisible by 2? By 3? By 4? By 5? By 6? By 8? By 9? By 10? By 12? By 15? By 18?

   a. 540 is divisible by 2, by 3, by 4, by 5, by 6, by 9, by 10, by 12, by 15, and by 18. It is not divisible by 8.

   b. 150 is divisible by 2, 3, 5, 6, 10, and 15, but not by 4, 8, 9, 12, or 18.

   d. 369 is divisible by 3 and 9 but not by 2, 4, 5, 6, 8, 10, 12, 15, or 18.

14. a. 29×23 is not prime. 29 and 23 are factors.

   b. 5992 is not prime because it obviously has a factor of 2.

   $5992 = 2^3 \times 7 \times 107$.

   d. $121 = 11^2$, so 121 is not prime.

   f. $1247 = 29 \times 43$, so 1247 is not prime. (Remember, all primes less than $\sqrt{1247}$ must be tested, that is, for all primes equal to or less than 31 because $\sqrt{1247} \approx 35.3$.

   g. 3816 is divisible by 2, so is not prime. (In fact, $3816 = 2^3 \times 3^2 \times 53$.)

15. $4 = 2 + 2; 6 = 3 + 3; 8 = 3 + 5; 10 = 5 + 5; 12 = 5 + 7$ (you finish).

17. Yes, because they have only 1 as a common prime factor.

18. a, d, f, i. (k—121 and 22 have 11 as a factor in common)

19. 125 and 243. (Note that $125 = 5^3$ and 243 is 3^5. There are many others.)

21. a. $128 + 494 + 381 = 1003$----4.

   128---11---$2;$ 494---17---$8;$ 381---12---$3;$ $2 + 8 + 3 = 13$---$4.$

22. a. Consider $8 \times 9 \times 10 \times 11$, which is 7920. This number is divisible by 3 because the sum of the digits is 18, which is divisible by 3. Also, 920 is divisible by 8: $920 = 8 \times 115$. Thus 97,920 must be divisible by 24.

   b. Suppose these 5 consecutive numbers are chosen: 4, 5, 6, 7, and 8. $4 \times 5 \times 6 \times 7 \times 8 = 6720$. The theorem claims that this number must be divisible by $1 + 2 + 3 + 4 + 5$, which is 15. Because 6720 ends in 0, it is divisible by 5. Because the sum of the digits is 15 which is divisible by 3, 6720 is divisible by 3. Because 3 and 5 are relatively prime, 6720 must be divisible by 15.

23. Here is one case. Let $p = 5$, and $n = 4$. Then by this theorem, $4^5 - 4$ should be divisible by 5. $4^5 = 4 \times 4 \times 4 \times 4 \times 4 = 1024$. When 4 is subtracted the result is 1020, which is divisible by 5. You choose more to try.

24. Three-digit numbers less than 125 that are multiples of 5 are 100, 105, 110, 115, and 120. But 100, 110, and 120 are divisible by 2, so they can't work, leaving 105 and 115. But 7 is a factor of 105, so that too must be discarded, leaving only 115.

11.4 Greatest Common Factor, Least Common Multiple

1. a. 2^3 {1, 2, 4, 8} (there are no more)   **b.** 27×49 {1, 27, 49, 27 × 49} (there are more)

c. 12 {1, 2, 3, 4} (there are more)   **e.** 108 {1, 2, 3, 4} (there are more)

f. 125 {1, 5, 25, 125} (there are no more)

2. Notice that there are an infinite number of multiples for each case. Here we list just 4.

a. 2^3 { $2^4, 2^5, 2^6, 2^7 \ldots$}   **b.** 27×49 {$2 \times 27 \times 49, 27^2 \times 49, 27 \times 49^2, 27^2 \times 49^2 \ldots$}

c. 12 {24, 36, 48, 60 . . .}   **e.** 108 {108, 216, 324, 431 . . .}

f. 125 {250, 375, 500, 625 . . .}

3. 60 years

5 and **6.** One can begin by factoring each of the numbers below.

$72 = 2^3 \cdot 3^2$ $108 = 2^2 \cdot 3^3$ $144 = 2^4 \cdot 3^2$ $150 = 2 \cdot 3 \cdot 5^2$

$350 = 2 \cdot 5^2 \cdot 7$ $567 = 3^4 \cdot 7$ $90 = 2 \cdot 3^2 \cdot 5$ $270 = 2 \cdot 3^3 \cdot 5$

a. The LCM of 72, 108 is $2^3 \cdot 3^3 = 216$.   The GCF of 72 and 108 is $2^2 \cdot 3^2 = 36$.

b. The LCM of 144 and 150 is $2^4 \cdot 3^2 \cdot 5^2 = 3600$.   The GCF of 144 and 150 is $2 \cdot 3 = 6$.

c. The LCM of 72 and 90 is $2^3 \cdot 3^2 \cdot 5 = 360$.   The GCF of 72 and 90 is $2 \cdot 3^2 = 18$.

7. a. Three possibilities of many: $2^3 \cdot 3^2$ and $2^3 \cdot 3 \cdot 23$ and $2^6 \cdot 3^7 \cdot 7^2$.

8. a. LCM is $5^2 \cdot 7^3 \cdot 13^2$ and the GCD is 5.

b. LCM is $37^6 \cdot 47^5 \cdot 67^6 \cdot 71$ and the GCD is $37^4 \cdot 47^5$.

e. LCM is $= 2^3 \cdot 3^2 \cdot 5^3 \cdot 7^2$ and the GCD is 7.

f. LCM is $30 \, x^2 y^6 z^{12}$ and the GCD is $2 \, xy^5 z^4$.

9. 0 is always a common multiple of two numbers, but it is not useful as a denominator in work with adding or subtracting fractions, for example.

10. Jogger A is at the start at 0 sec, 90 sec, 180 sec....

Jogger B is at the start at 0 sec, 120 sec, 240 sec, etc.

The LCM of 90 and 120 is 360. So after 360 sec, or 6 minutes, they are again both at the start. Jogger A has gone around 4 times, Jogger B has gone around 3 times.

12. The gear with 12 teeth will rotate 5 times and the large one twice to get back to the original positions. Note that 60 is the LCM of 12 and 30: $12 \times 5 = 30 \times 2 = 60$.

14. Order 2 drums of base and 5 drums of color.

15. One gallon of color takes care of 4 gallons of base, so 1 drum of color takes care of 40 gallons of base. LCM(40, 25) = 200. Use 8 drums of base and 5 drums of color.

16. GCF(414,543) = 3, so $3.

18. GCF is 1600. So if 1 cm represents 1600 km, the sun would have a diameter of 875 cm and the earth 8 cm.

20. For example, $m = 2, n = 3$; $m = 4, n = 6$; $m = 6, n = 9$; . . .

21. Hint: Think of "greatest common factor" in this order; First "factor," then "common factor" and finally "greatest common factor."

    a. $\dfrac{9}{10}$ **b.** $\dfrac{3}{4}$ **c.** $\dfrac{21}{25}$

22. a. The answer is in simplest form because 9 and 10 are relatively prime.

    b. The answer is in simplest form because 3 and 4 are relatively prime.

    c. The answer is in simplest form because 21 and 25 are relatively prime.

    d. The answer is in simplest form because 9 and 8 are relatively prime.

23. a. $\dfrac{65}{72}$ **b.** $\dfrac{3}{8}$

24. Another pair: For 24 and 36 the GCF is 12, and the LCM is 72. $12 \times 72 = 864$, and $24 \times 36 = 864$.

25. a. $\dfrac{8}{9}$ **b.** $\dfrac{853}{4725}$

26. a. If x is a common factor of m and n, then x is also a factor of $m - n$.

    b. One example: If $m = 48$ and $n = 36$, then 6 is a factor of both. 6 is also a factor of $48 - 36 = 12$.

    c. $\dfrac{49}{50}$ $\dfrac{35}{36}$ $\dfrac{37}{42}$

    d. Yes, for $\dfrac{81}{86}$, a common factor of 81 and 86 would have to be a common factor of 5. That is, a common factor would have to be 1 or 5. 5 is not a common factor, so there are no common factors of 81 and 86 besides 1, so they are relatively prime.

27. a. $\dfrac{15}{35} = \dfrac{3}{7}$ **b.** $\dfrac{28}{54} = \dfrac{2^2 \cdot 7}{2 \cdot 3^3} = \dfrac{14}{27}$ **c.** $\dfrac{150}{350} = \dfrac{3}{7}$

    d. $\dfrac{12}{144} = \dfrac{1}{12}$ **e.** $\dfrac{150}{567} = \dfrac{2 \cdot 3 \cdot 5^2}{3^4 \cdot 7} = \dfrac{50}{189}$

28. a. $\dfrac{39}{144} + \dfrac{35}{108} = \dfrac{39}{2^4 \cdot 3^2} + \dfrac{35}{2^2 \cdot 3^3} = \dfrac{39 \cdot 3}{2^4 \cdot 3^2 \cdot 3} + \dfrac{35 \cdot 2^2}{2^2 \cdot 3^3 \cdot 2^2} = \dfrac{117 + 140}{2^4 \cdot 3^3} = \dfrac{257}{432}$

    b. $\dfrac{25}{72} + \dfrac{81}{567} = \dfrac{25}{2^3 \cdot 3^2} + \dfrac{81}{3^4 \cdot 7} = \dfrac{25 \cdot 3^2 \cdot 7}{2^3 \cdot 3^2 \cdot 3^2 \cdot 7} + \dfrac{81 \cdot 2^3}{3^4 \cdot 7 \cdot 2^3} = \dfrac{1575 + 648}{2^3 \cdot 3^4 \cdot 7} = \dfrac{2223}{4536}$

    Or

    $\dfrac{25}{72} + \dfrac{81}{567} = \dfrac{25}{2^3 \cdot 3^2} + \dfrac{3^4}{3^4 \cdot 7} = \dfrac{25 \cdot 7}{2^3 \cdot 3^2 \cdot 7} + \dfrac{1 \cdot 2^3 \cdot 3^2}{7 \cdot 2^3 \cdot 3^2} = \dfrac{175}{2^3 \cdot 3^2 \cdot 7} + \dfrac{72}{2^3 \cdot 3^2 \cdot 7} = \dfrac{175 + 72}{2^3 \cdot 3^2 \cdot 7} = \dfrac{247}{504}$

    Note that $\dfrac{2223}{4536} = \dfrac{3^2 \cdot 13 \cdot 19}{3^4 \cdot 2^3 \cdot 7} = \dfrac{13 \cdot 19}{3^2 \cdot 2^3 \cdot 7} = \dfrac{247}{504}$

On the remaining parts we will simplify fractions before adding or subtracting.

c. $\dfrac{36}{108} + \dfrac{41}{72} = \dfrac{2^2 \cdot 3^2}{2^2 \cdot 3^3} + \dfrac{41}{2^3 \cdot 3^2} = \dfrac{1}{3} + \dfrac{41}{2^3 \cdot 3^2} = \dfrac{1 \cdot 2^3 \cdot 3}{2^3 \cdot 3^2} + \dfrac{41}{2^3 \cdot 3^2} = \dfrac{24 + 41}{2^3 \cdot 3^2} = \dfrac{65}{72}$

e. $\dfrac{169}{500} - \dfrac{169}{650} = \dfrac{169}{2^2 \cdot 5^3} - \dfrac{13^2}{2 \cdot 5^2 13} = \dfrac{169}{2^2 \cdot 5^3} - \dfrac{13 \cdot 2 \cdot 5}{2 \cdot 5^2 \cdot 2 \cdot 5} = \dfrac{169 - 130}{2^2 \cdot 5^3} = \dfrac{39}{500}$

29. The GCF of 27 and 36 is 9. A new "ruler" with unit 9 inches gives whole-number answers for the width and length of the desks (3 units by 4 units).

30. (Assignment using Virtual Library.)

11.5 Issues for Learning: Understanding the Unique Factorization Theorem

1. k cannot be divided by 5, 11, or 17. Some students try to use divisibility rules to check for divisibility when this is not necessary.

2. 51 is a factor of a because $51 = 3 \times 17$, and both 3 and 17 are factors. Some student would divide 153 by 51 to obtain an answer, but this is not necessary.

3. a and b both have the same number of factors: $6 = (2 + 1)(1 + 1)$. A common error is to think that the larger number has more factors.

Answers for Chapter 12

12.1 Quantities and Their Relationships

1. a. Samples: The amount of fuel in the tank decreases as the number of minutes increases. The amount of fuel leaked out increases as the number of minutes increases.

3. b. It could happen that the height of the triangle is decreasing in such a way that the product of the base and height (which is twice the area) remains constant. Or, it might happen that the height is constant, in which case the area increases as the base increases. Or, it might be the case that the height is decreasing in such a manner that the product of the base and height is decreasing, in which case the area decreases.

12.2 Using Graphs and Algebraic Symbols to Show Quantitative Relationships

1. d. $G = 80 - 10T$

   f. $T = 8$ minutes. When the tank is empty, $G = 0$, so $0 = 80 - 10T$, and $T = 8$.

   h. The total of the fuel in the tank and the fuel leaked should equal 80 gallons. That equation is algebraically equivalent to the one in part (d).

2. a. As time increases, the amount of fuel that has leaked out increases.

   b.

time (min)	0	1	2	3	4	...
fuel leaked (gal)	0	10	20	30	40	...

c. $g = 10t$, where g represents the number of gallons leaked out and t represents the number of minutes that have elapsed.

d.

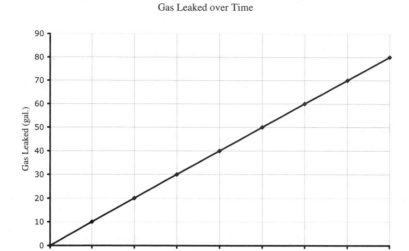

e. The graph in Learning Exercise 1(g) is decreasing, whereas the graph in 2(g) is increasing. Both graphs are straight lines, but the graph in 1(g) has a negative slope (goes down from left to right), and the graph in 2(d) has a positive slope (goes up from left to right). These slopes mean that in 1(g), the amount of fuel is decreasing over time, whereas the opposite is true in 2(d) for the amount of fuel leaked.

12.3 Understanding Slope: Making Connections Across Quantitative Situations, Graphs, and Algebraic Equations

2. a. The slope is $^{-}\frac{10}{1}$, or $^{-}10$.

b. This slope tells us the amount of fuel the airplane is losing per minute.

c. The slope is $\frac{10}{1}$, or 10.

d. This slope tells us the amount of fuel that is leaking out, per minute. (We could think of this as fuel being gained into the atmosphere.)

e. The slopes are alike except for the sign. That is, the first slope is negative, and the second is positive. The negative slope indicates the amount of fuel being lost by the plane per minute, whereas the positive slope indicates the amount of fuel being leaked (gained) into the atmosphere per minute. In conventional graphs, a negative slope indicates that values from the vertical axis *decrease* as values from the horizontal axis increase.

4. d. Group 3 because . . . (*Hint:* The heights tell only part of the story.)

5. d. Group 1 because . . . The order of the candles is . . .

6. a. Cindy. She did not pick any more strawberries after 10 AM.

b. $19\frac{1}{5}$ quarts per hour

c. 9 AM; 28 quarts per hour

d. Barb. The slope of her line is greatest of the three. Alternatively, Barb picks 28 quarts per hour, Annette picks $19\frac{1}{5}$ quarts per hour [part (b)], and Cindy picked 24 quarts per hour while she was picking.

Answers for Chapter 13

13.1 Distance-Time and Position-Time Graphs

3. a. He has to travel 140 ft, at the rate of 5 ft/s, so it takes him 28 s to return home.

b.

t	0	5	10	15	20	25	30	35	40	43
d (from cave)	0	40	80	140	115	90	65	40	15	0

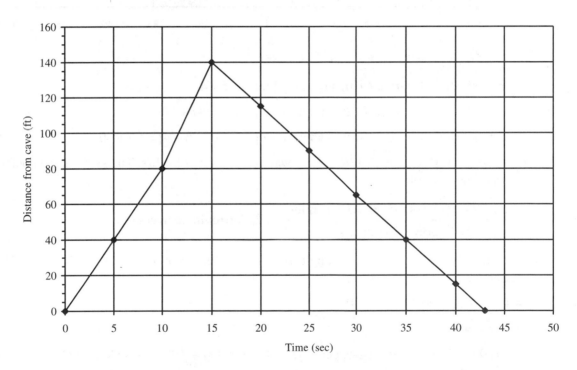

c.

t	0	5	10	15	20	25	30	35	40	43
total distance	0	40	80	140	165	190	215	240	265	280

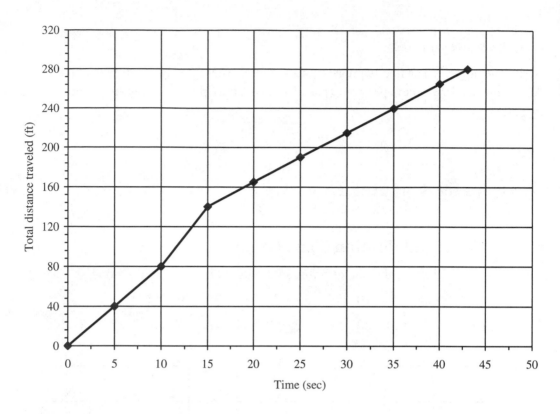

4. **a.** Your graph should start at (0, 0) and have slope 4. $d = 4t$

    b. Your graph should start at (0, 20) and have slope 4. $d = 4t + 20$

    c. Your graph should start at (0, 56) and have slope ⁻4. $d = 56 - 4t = 56 + {}^-4t$

    f. The slope is 4. It tells us that Wile E. is walking at a rate of 4 ft/s. The slope is the coefficient of the time (the multiplier of t).

5. $\dfrac{68 \times (365 \times 24 \times 60 \times 60 \times 1.86 \times 10^5) \text{ miles}}{(2 \times 10^6)(365 \times 24) \text{ hours}} \approx 22{,}766 \text{ mi/h}$, on average.

6. Road 1 h, 15 min + canoe 36 min + jungle 16 h + path 3 h, 15 min = (in all) 21 h, 6 min. Was your explanation the same for each part?

7. **a.** $4.47 + $9.60 + $3.84 = $17.91

    b. 64 miles

    c. 24 × (60 × 70) = 100,800 beats per day; 1,000,000,000 ÷ 100,800 is about 9920.6 days, or more than 27 years.

13.2 Using Motion Detectors

1&2. **a.** The walker started 2 ft away from the motion detector, and then walked away from the motion detector at a constant speed for 6 s. (The speed was $\frac{2}{3}$ ft/s.)

  b. The walker started 2 ft away from the motion detector, and then walked away from the motion detector at a constant speed for 3 s. The walker in part (b) walked faster than did the walker in part (a). (Walker (b)'s speed was $\frac{4}{3}$ ft/s.)

  c. The walker started 6 ft away from the motion detector. The walker walked to the motion detector in 6 s at a constant speed. (The speed was 1 ft/s.)

  d. The walker started 6 ft away from the motion detector. The walker walked to the motion detector in 3 s at a constant speed. The walker in part 1(d) walked at a faster constant speed than the walker in part 1(c). (The speed in part (d) was 2 ft/s.)

  e. The walker was 4 ft away from the motion detector, and stood there for 6 s. (The speed was 0 ft/s.)

4. a. (Sample) The walker started a short distance from the motion detector. He/she started walking away from the motion detector very slowly, and then gradually increased speed until (s)he was walking very quickly.

13.3 Graphs of Speed Against Time

3.

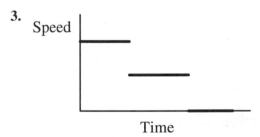

All three parts of the graph are straight horizontal line segments, each indicating constant speed. They differ by their positions on the vertical axis; the height signifies the speed in each of the cases. If you made this graph as a companion to that of the given graph, the times for the different pieces should match.

6. a. (sample) Bart trotted evenly to the corner. There he saw some friends stopped ahead, so he sped up at a steady pace to catch them. When he did, they chatted a little while. But then they realized they might be late to the game so they decided to run as fast as they could.

9. a. C. The change in height per unit of horizontal distance is greater during C than in B.

  b. G. During H, the speed of the roller coaster is about 0, but during H, the speed is positive although decreasing.

  c. Very roughly...

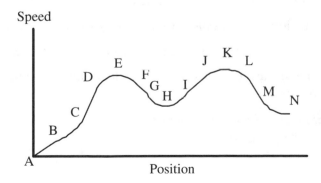

13.4 Interpreting Graphs

1. **a.** The fifth graph is most reasonable. The first part shows her speed increasing until she gets to the comfortable pace, at which she runs until she slows to a stop (the decrease of speed to 0). Then the increasing speed as she runs downhill fits the last part of the fifth graph.

   b. Notice that the graph involves *distance traveled*.

   c. Notice that some graphs are for distance-time and others speed-time.

3. C, because her speed is decreasing to 0.

8. The oven is turned on at B, and heats up to 350°. It cools and warms up to keep the temperature about 350°.

9. **a.** "No. of miles" must be the number of miles from Abilene, rather than the total number of miles traveled. The van, then, turned back toward Abilene after traveling 100 miles in the one and a half hours.

   b. Your story should give some reason for the van's returning to Abilene. It could also mention that the bus arrived in Dallas two hours before the van did.

Answers for Chapter 14

14.1 Using Algebraic Symbols to Represent Relationships

1. **b.** Line A: $d = \frac{1}{2}t$ Line B: $d = \frac{1}{2}t + 4$

   c. Bold points may come from data actually observed.

2. **b.** A: $d = 4t$ B: $d = 4t - 8$
   (Notice that each d value in B is 8 less than the corresponding value in A.)

3. **b.** $d = {}^-2t + 20$ (notice the negative), or $d = 20 - 2t = 20 + {}^-2t$

4. **b.** $d = {}^-\frac{1}{3}t + 3$ (or an algebraic equivalent, as in Learning Exercise 3)

5. **b.** A: $d = 2t$ B: $d = t + 6$

1-5.**c.** Bold points may come from data points actually observed.

6. **a.** If your stories involved the same theme, but different people, starting distances, and speeds, then the point of intersection would give the time when the distances were the same.

   b. Setting the two expressions equal would give the time when the distances are equal.

   c. $t = 6$, which is reflected in the graph as the time when the two distances are equal.

7. The slopes are equal. This makes sense because if the slopes are the same, then for a given run, the graphs will have the same rise.

8. Note that 5 minutes per block = $\frac{1}{5}$ block per minute.

a. Distance from home (blocks)

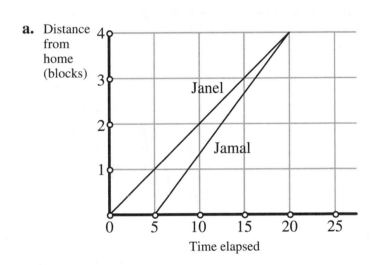

b. Janel: $d = \frac{1}{5}t$

   Jamal: Same slope as Janel's but 5 minutes or 1 block behind her.

$d = \frac{1}{5}t - 1$

9.

a. Distance from home (blocks)

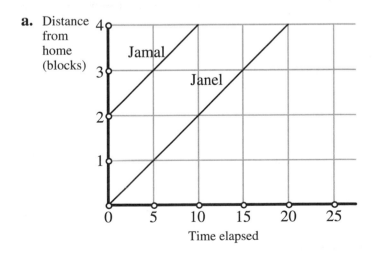

b. Janel: $d = \frac{1}{5}t$

   Jamal: Slope = $\frac{4}{15}$, time delayed by 5 minutes.

$d = \frac{4}{15}(t - 5) = \frac{4}{15}t - \frac{4}{3}$

10.

a. Distance from home (blocks)

b. Janel: Slope = $\frac{4}{20} = \frac{1}{5}$.

$d = \frac{1}{5}t$

   Jamal: Same slope as Janel's, but Jamal was ahead in distance by 2 blocks.

$d = \frac{1}{5}t + 2$

11.

a.

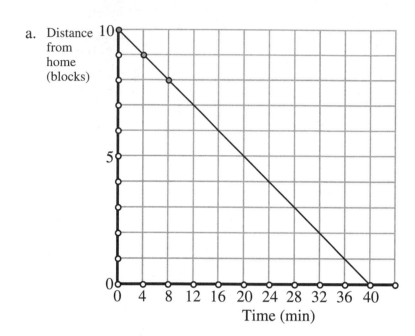

Distance from home (blocks)

Time (min)

b. 4 min/block = $\frac{1}{4}$ block/min. (Since she is walking toward home, the slope should be negative.)

$d = 10 - \frac{1}{4}t = {}^{-}\frac{1}{4}t + 10$

12.

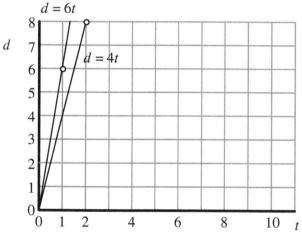

$d = 6t$

$d = 4t$

13.

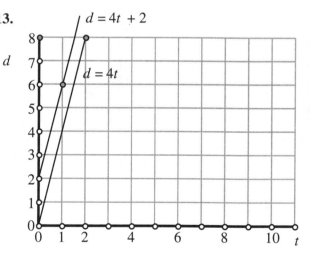

$d = 4t + 2$

$d = 4t$

14.

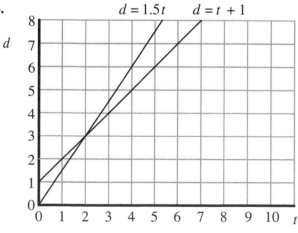

$d = 1.5t$ $d = t + 1$

14.2 Using Algebra to Solve Problems

1. **g.** 125 ft

    h. Tony's graph: Through (0, 50), with slope 10; Rita's graph: Through (0, 0), slope 15.

2. Kien cannot catch Leo before the race is over. When Leo finishes the 10K run (after 37.3 minutes), Kien will be 115.5 meters behind.

3. **a.** No (it takes Brother 40 minutes to get to school, so with her 15-minute head start, Sister would already be at school).

    b. Sister will have traveled 35 more minutes after Brother starts, so Brother will be $\frac{35}{40}$ or $\frac{7}{8}$ of the way to school.

4. 16 seconds, counting the headstart time

5. $607\frac{1}{11}$ ft (including the 126 ft headstart)

6. 11 hours, 46 minutes

7. The plans give the same profit at sales of 200,000 CDs. Before that point, Option B gives more profit. After 200,000 CDs are sold, Option A gives more profit.

8. **a.** A: 0.05   B: 0.4

    b. Plan A costs less if you make more than 30 calls per month.

    c. Plan B costs less if you make fewer than 30 calls per month.

9. $200,000 in sales

14.3 Average Speed and Weighted Averages

3. 12 mi/h (He has to cover the 18 miles in $1\frac{1}{2}$ h.)

5. Be careful—the number of credits at each place matters!

6. 60 words per minute

8. It is almost essential to draw a picture of the race track.

    a. Turtle will be ahead by 1.5 m.

    b. Rabbit will have forged ahead by 2 m. At the 20 m mark, when they head back, R will have traveled for 4 s, and T for $3\frac{1}{3}$ s. So on the way back, R will travel for 1.5 s, and thus go 15 m. T, on the other hand, will travel $5\frac{1}{2} - 3\frac{1}{3}$ s on the way back, or $2\frac{1}{6}$ s, and thus go 13 m. So R is ahead by 2 m after 5.5 s. When R heads back (after 4 s), T has a $\frac{2}{3}$ s lead, or 4 m. Because R catches up by 4 m each second (on the way back), it will take 1 more second for R to catch T, at the 10-m mark from either end, when both have traveled 5 s.

    c. It takes R 4 + 2 = 6 seconds to finish. After 6 s, T has gone 36 m, 20 m over and 16 back. So T is 4 m behind when the race is over.

    d. The part (b) answers will change (R will be 4.5 m ahead, and after the start was always ahead of T), but the part (c) answers will stay the same because it will take R the same amount of time to win.

9. c. If traffic had allowed, they would have covered the same distance if they had traveled at $46\frac{2}{3}$ mi/h all the way.

10. a. $\frac{12}{60} = \frac{1}{5}$ of the way over.

   b. 10 m/s (Rabbit ran for 36 s, total.)

   c. Turtle, because 3.173 m/s is a faster speed than the speed giving a tie.

11. a. 6 m/s

   b. 4 m/s

   c. Rabbit was 12 m from the turn-around point, or 18 m from the finish line. Turtle was 18 m from the turn-around point, or 12 m from the finish line.

   Notice how important it is to have the quantities involved clearly in mind.

12. a. The graph coordinates are (0, 0), (0.5, 3), (1.5, 15).

   6 m/h and 12 m/h

   b. 10 mi/h If Carly's speed did not vary, the graph would be a line from (0, 0) to (1.5, 15).

   c. 10 mi/h

   d. 10 mi/h

   e. Their averages are the same because they traveled the same distance in the same amount of time.

14.4 Algebra as Generalized Arithmetic

2. a. $(7 \times 10^3) + (4 \times 10^2) + (0 \times 10^1) + 3$; $7x^3 + 4x^2 + 3$, with $x = 10$

   b. $(4 \times 10^4) + (1 \times 10^3) + (7 \times 10^2) + (9 \times 10^1) + 2$; $4x^4 + x^3 + 7x^2 + 9x + 2$, with $x = 10$

   c. 5×10^3; $5x^3$ with $x = 10$

   d. Writing the fives in base ten, $(1 \times 5^2) + (4 \times 5) + 2$; $x^2 + 4x + 2$, with $x = 5$

   e. Writing the twelves in base ten, $(2 \times 12^3) + (8 \times 12^2) + (9 \times 12^1) + 7$; $2x^3 + 8x^2 + 9x + 7$, with $x = 12$

   f. Writing the twos in base ten, $(1 \times 2^5) + (0 \times 2^4) + (1 \times 2^3) + (1 \times 2^2) + (0 \times 2^1) + 1$;

   $x^5 + x^3 + x^2 + 1$, with $x = 2$

3. a. $9x^3 + 4x^2 + 4x + 8$

   b. $2x^2 + 12x + 12$

   c. $8 + 6n + 4n + 3n^2$, or $3n^2 + 10n + 8$

   d. $30 + 18x + 12x^2 + 40x + 24x^2 + 16x^3$, or $16x^3 + 36x^2 + 58x + 30$

   e. $\begin{array}{r} x^3 + 4x^2 + 0x + 7 \\ +\ \underline{\quad 4x^2 + 9x + 3} \\ x^3 + 8x^2 + 9x + 10 \end{array}$

   f. $\begin{array}{r} 6x^2 + 7x + 5 \\ \times\ \underline{\qquad x + 2} \end{array}$
   $(10 + 14x + 12x^2) + (5x + 7x^2 + 6x^3)$, or $6x^3 + 19x^2 + 19x + 10$

4. a. Sum: $7x^2 + 16x + 7$; product: $12x^4 + 55x^3 + 88x^2 + 57x + 12$

   b. Sum: $\frac{61}{24}x + \frac{11}{12}$; product: $\frac{35}{24}x^2 + \frac{269}{288}x + \frac{1}{8}$

   d. Sum: $462x + 77$; product: $50112x^2 + 15564x + 1102$

   f. Sum: $13x + 10$; product: $36x^2 + 75x + 21$

   h. Sum: $3\pi x + 3.5$; product: $2\pi^2 x^2 + 6.5\pi x + 1.5$

   i. Sum: $6x + {}^-2$; product: $6x^3 + {}^-5x^2 + {}^-79x + {}^-90$

5. a. $\ldots = x^2 + 2xy + y^2$

   b. Describe the 8 pieces in the cube, and add them.

   c. $\ldots = x^2 + xy$

   d. $\ldots = x^2 + 2x + 3x + 6 = x^2 + 5x + 6$, with a drawing similar to that of part (a).

14.5 Issues for Learning: Topics in Algebra

1. Not only could different quantities be associated with each animal (time traveled, speed, distance traveled, distance from other animal, . . .), but "T = turtle" suggests that the T is a label for the animal rather than some quantity associated with the animal.

2. a. 0 (*Joke*: "All that work for nothing.")

   b. $45\frac{5}{8}$

3. a. $^-8$ **b.** 55   **c.** $^-8\frac{7}{9}$ **d.** $^-1$

4. Samples:

   a. After Peter Rabbit nibbled 7 carrots more, Farmer Jones said, "You have nibbled 13 carrots!" How many carrots had Peter nibbled earlier?

   b. Peter nibbled 7 carrots for lunch, and then nibbled some more for dinner. In all, Peter nibbled 13 carrots. How many carrots did Peter nibble for dinner?

   c. Junior had $9 left after he spent $6 on food. How much did he have before he bought food?

   d. Junior had $14 and spent some on food. Then he had $6. How much did he spend on food?

   e. Donita bought two tablets and a mechanical pencil. The pencil cost $1.95. How much did each tablet cost, if she paid $4.15 for all the items?

   f. Lee got 76% on a 25-item T-F quiz. How many did Lee get correct?

5. The distributive property (of multiplication over addition):

   $A \times (B + C)$ initially, then splitting the two rectangular regions apart gives $A \times B$ and

   $A \times C$. Since the same area quantity is involved each time, $A \times (B + C) = A \times B + A \times C$.

6. A drawing would no doubt show a larger share for the number of students than for the number of professors. But then 6 times the number of students would clearly not equal the number of professors.

Answers for Chapter 15

15.1 Numerical Patterns and Functions

1. **i.** 4 (with 2, 4, 6, 8 as repeating numbers)

   j. 2, 8, 5, 7; 8 (with 1, 4, 2, 8, 5, 7 as repeating numbers)

   k. Parts (c) and (d) are arithmetic sequences (not parts (g) and (h), although their numerators are arithmetic sequences, as are their denominators).

   l. Parts (e) and (f) are geometric sequences.

2. **a.** Count how many zeros are in the power of 10 (or look at the exponent), and move the decimal place that many places to make a larger number. If the original number is a whole number, just annex that many zeros.

   b. Each place value is made that many times as large as it was originally, so each digit moves to the left that many places.

3. **a.** Count how many zeros are in the power of 10 (or look at the exponent), and move the decimal place that many places to make a smaller number. If the original number is a whole number, put in a decimal point first.

   b. Each place value is reduced by that power, so each digit moves to the right that many places.

4. **b.** $f(x) = 100 - 22x$; $n = 10$

   c. $output = 8 \times input - 8$; $n = 202$

   d. $output = 0.3 \times input - 7$; $n = 76$

   e. $g(x) = x^2$; $n = 30$

   h. $y = 5x - 3$; $n = 110$

   i. $f(x) = 16x + 3$; $n = 25$

   j. $f(x) = \frac{2}{3}x + \frac{1}{2}$; $n = 12$

   l. $y = x^3$; $n = 9$

   m. $y = x^3 + 2$; $n = 10$

   n. $y = \frac{4}{3}x + 4$; $n = 60$

5. **a.** $f(n) = 4n + 1$

   b. $f(n) = 5n + 2$

   c. $f(n) = 2n + 1$

   d. $f(n) = 3n + 4$

   e. $f(n) = 5n + 6$

7. **a.** $y = 5 \cdot 2^{n-1}$ **b.** $y = a \cdot r^{n-1}$

8. **a.** 13, 21, 34, 55   **c.** The values get closer and closer to 1.61 ($\frac{1+\sqrt{5}}{2}$, exactly).

9. **a.** $n(n + 1)$, or you may have seen $n^2 + n$

   d. $1 + 3 + 5 + 7 + \ldots + (2n - 1) = n^2$.

10. Sum of first n numbers in the arithmetic sequence $= na + \frac{(n-1)n}{2}d$. Notice the adjustment needed in Learning Exercise 9(b) here, because the sequence 1, 3, 6, and so on, starts with $n = 2$ rather than $n = 1$. So you have to subtract 1 from how many numbers are being added, to use Learning Exercise 9(b).

11. Since the n-step stairway involves $1 + 2 + \ldots + n$ small squares, it will have $\frac{n(n+1)}{2}$ small squares, from Learning Exercise 9(b).

12. **a.** $100°$ C, $0°$ C, $37°$ C, and about $19°$ C. (These values are worth memorizing.)

    b. $F = \frac{9}{5}C + 32$

13. **a.** $\frac{1}{2^n}$

    b. $\frac{1}{2} + \frac{1}{4} = \frac{3}{4}$, $\frac{1}{2} + \frac{1}{4} + \frac{1}{8} = \frac{7}{8}$, $\frac{1}{2} + \frac{1}{4} + \frac{1}{8} + \frac{1}{16} = \frac{15}{16}$ suggest tentatively that the sum of the first n such fractions would be $\frac{2^n-1}{2^n}$.

14. **a.** 9   **b.** 9   **c.** 1

    d. The *ones* digits follow a repeating cycle of four digits: 7, 9, 3, 1. Find out how many full cycles there are in n, and look at the remainder, by calculating $n \div 4$. The remainder tells you which number to go to in the next cycle. For example, 7^{778} will end in 9 because $778 \div 4 = 194$ R 2, and the second number in the (next) cycle is 9.

15. **a.** Yes, the switch can be made.

    b. 15 (If you keep getting 17, there is one crucial point at which you can avoid any moves in the wrong direction.)

16. **a.** $1\frac{5}{6}$ cups per container. Because 11 cups come from 6 containers, each container must contain $\frac{1}{6}$ of the 11 cups.

    b. $\frac{6}{11}$ container per cup. Similarly, because 11 cups come from 6 containers, 1 cup must contain $\frac{1}{11}$ of the 6 cups.

    c. $\frac{2}{3}$ is Special Formula. Four containers of Special Formula are mixed with 2 containers of water, giving 6 containers in all, so $\frac{4}{6}$ of the mixture must be Special Formula.

    d. $\frac{1}{3}$ is water, reasoning as in part (c).

    e. The ratio 4:2 for formula to water will apply to other mixtures. Alternately, the equation $f = 2w$ relating the number of containers of formula, f, and the number of containers of water, w, shows a proportional relationship.

17. **a.** $\frac{8}{7}$, or $1\frac{1}{7}$, packages per pound

    b. $\frac{7}{8}$ pounds in one package

    c. $10 \times \frac{8}{7} = 11\frac{3}{7}$ packages

19. a. For A: $p = 13h$ (where p is the number of parts and h is the number of hours).
   For B: $p = 14h$ (Note that $\frac{243-(9\times13)}{9}$ is 14. Or, $243 \div 9 = 27$, and $27 - 13 = 14$.)

   b. Both expressions have the form $y = mx$ and so both are proportional relationships.

   c. Both graphs start at (0, 0); the graph for A has slope 13, and the graph for B has slope 14. The slopes tell you how fast each worker works, 13 parts/h for A, 14 parts/h for B.

20. Only graphs b and c. They are linear and go through (0, 0).

21. Only b, c, and d. In part (a), the equation is not of the correct form. In part (c), the variables are the number of crackers and the number of calories. In part (d), the variables are the number of tickets and the total dollar cost.

22. 2. The decimal has a repeating block, 1-4-2-8-5-7, six digits long. So from $99 \div 6 = 16$ R 3, there would be 16 full blocks, with 3 entries into the next block: 1-4-**2**.

15.2 More Uses for Functions

1. a. If a singer's popularity could be assigned a value, then there would be a correspondence between that value and the number of CD's sold.

   b. If success could be assigned a value, then knowing the number of hours worked could predict the success value.

   c. For a given person, knowing his/her blood alcohol content could enable one to predict his/her reaction time.

3. c. $2(x^2 + 3)$, or $2x^2 + 6$ **d.** 256   **e.** 676

Answers for Chapter 16

16.1 Shoeboxes Have Faces and Nets!

1. Your "box" should be taller than it is wide or deep.

2. Did you start at the top and take advantage of the last cube drawn when adding later cubes?

3. a. 5 faces, 5 vertices, 8 edges   **b.** 5 faces, 6 vertices, 9 edges

4. The net shows only 5 faces, and a cube has 6 faces.

5. a.

Front view   Right side   Top view (from front)

   b. Do you see *two* possible answers for the top view, depending on what might or might not be hidden in the back left corner?

   c. They are like views from the reverse (or mirror images).

6.

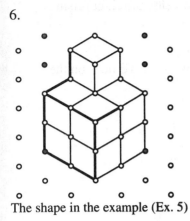

The shape in the example (Ex. 5)

5. a (one possibility)

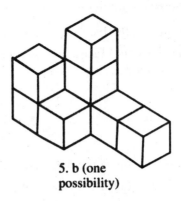

5. b (one possibility)

16.2 Introduction to Polyhedra

1. a. B, E (squares are special parallelograms), F
    b. G
    c. A, C, H (and M, if used)
    d. D, G, I, J
    e. H, J, K (and L and M, if used)
    f. K (What about C, E, F, and J? Some people regard a rectangle as a special isosceles trapezoid, as we will see later.)
    g. A, E, H (and L and M, if used)
    h. A, G

2. a. Lateral edges of a prism are equal in length and parallel to each other. The lateral faces of a prism are parallelogram regions (or special parallelogram regions, such as rectangular regions).
    b. 50 edges, one edge from each vertex of the base to the vertex not on the base; 50 faces, one face for each side of the base.

3. a. A hexagonal pyramid

4. There is a polyhedron with the fewest number of vertices: a triangular pyramid (4 vertices); if there were only 3 vertices, they would all lie in the same flat surface (plane) and not give a polyhedron. But a polyhedron may have any large number of edges; consider a prism or pyramid with a base with a large number of vertices. So there is not a polyhedron with the greatest number of vertices.

5. a. Unless you have a weird polyhedron of some sort that is not in the kit, the relationship will hold.
    b. 7
    c. 12
    d. No, because...

6. a. right rectangular prism
    b. right hexagonal prism (the common kind of pencil)
    c. right rectangular prism

   d. There are different possibilities, including right rectangular prism and parallelogram right prism for the most common ones.

7. **a.** The 4 edges on the base were counted twice, as were the 4 lateral edges.
   b. Each vertex is on 3 faces, so it is counted 3 times in the argument that looks at the vertices on the 6 faces separately.

9. **a.** C, E, F
   b. rectangular regions
   c. A and G

10. **a.** 14 (12 usually, but if the bases are....)
    b. 24 (16 usually, but if the bases are....)

11. Be sure to think about measurements, not just counts.

16.3 Representing and Visualizing Polyhedra

1. **a.** Looking straight at the midpoint of an edge with the cube turned so the same amount seems to be above the edge as below the edge.
   b. Looking from above and in front of an upper-right vertex from the right.
   c. Looking straight on at one face of the cube.

2. **a.** Maximum number of faces: 3; minimum: 1
   b. Maximum number of vertices: 7
   c. Maximum number of edges: 9

3. *Hint*: Add three hidden edges to the base.

4. **a.** *Hint*: See Figure 1.
   b. *Hint*: Be sure that your lateral edges appear to be parallel and perpendicular to the edges of the base that they meet.
   c. *Hint*: Adjust the quadrilateral pyramid in Figure 8.
   d. *Hint*: Sketch the top base first, remembering that you are to look at the prism obliquely. Then sketch the lateral edges, keeping them parallel and of the same length. Finally, put in the edges of the bottom base, keeping in mind which edges are hidden.
   e. *Hint*: See Learning Exercise 3.
   f. See Figure 7.
   g. *Hint*: Learning Exercise 10 in Section 16.2.
   h. One possibility is a quadrilateral pyramid. Why isn't it possible with a prism?

5. **a.** 1-6, 2-4, 3-5   **b.** 1-3, 4-6, 2-5
   c. 3-5, 1-4, 2-6   **d.** 2-4, 3-6, 1-5

7. Nets a and c only (Did you notice that b and d are really the same net?)

8. The view is from above and in front of but to the right. Although equal or parallel lengths in the actual polyhedron will also be equal or parallel in the isometric sketch, right angles in the actual polyhedron are not right angles in the isometric drawing (they only appear to be, because our minds can process the drawing).

    b. yes

    c. right hexagonal prism

    e. Volume: 4 cube regions; surface area: 18 square regions.

9. **a.** 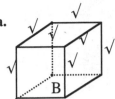   **b.** 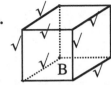   **c.**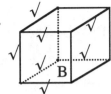

There might be other possibilities; compare yours with someone else's. This task is often difficult—what strategies did you use (for example, (1) focusing on edges that are *not* cut, (2) holding a cube as you imagined the cuts, (3) turning the net to make it easier to visualize where the base is, and/or (4) working backwards from a cut-out net to the cube)?

10.   **b.**   **c.** Same as part (b). (Do you see why?)

a.

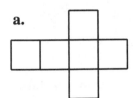   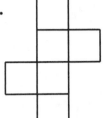

In each case, your version might be turned or even flipped from the answer here.

12. a.   *Hint*: There are 5 differently shaped tetrominoes.

    b.   There are 12 pentominoes. Did you find them all? How can you be sure?

Each has area = 5 square regions, but the perimeters…

    d.   No, for example…

    e.   No, for example… (Try some rectangular regions with the same perimeters.)

14. a.   a rectangular region, not square

    b.   a rhombus region

15. There are different possibilities for each part. One somewhat laborious way to check is to cut out your net and fold it. Another (recommended) way is to have a classmate or two look at yours.

16. a.   triangular right prism   **b.**   cube

17. a.   **b.**

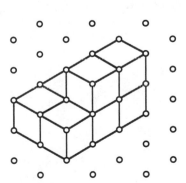   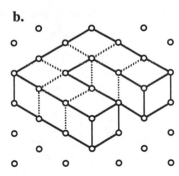

18. a. FE, AD, AB, FH   **b.** BC, GH, and FE

19. b.

16.4 Congruent Polyhedra

2. No—none can be moved to match another exactly.

3. The hidden shape will have the same sized faces and (as a result) the same areas as the given shape, so 108 cm^2.

4. a. Yes. A rotation of 360° (or 0°) will make it match itself.

b. Yes. Just reverse the motions that showed that P was congruent to Q.

c. Yes. Do all the motions that show that R is congruent to S and then continue with the motions that show S is congruent to T.

7. a.

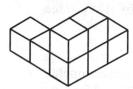

9. Possibility: Two polygons are congruent if one polygon can be moved (by rotating, reflecting, or sliding, or a combination of such motions) so that it would fit on the other polygon exactly.

16.5 Some Special Polyhedra

1. a. AT   **b.** ST   **c.** ST   **d.** AT

  e. ST   **f.** ST   **g.** AT   **h.** ST

  i. ST   **j.** ST   **k.** ST   **l.** AT

2. Knowing how many types (and what the types are) can enable you to ask, "Why are these the only ones?" and perhaps reveal something important about them. If only regular polyhedra can appear in some context for some theoretical reason, then you will know ahead of time what the possibilities are.

3. a. A 20-faced polyhedron (icosahedron), perhaps regular, made up of 20 triangular regions

  b. A 12-faced polyhedron (dodecahedron), perhaps regular, made up of 12 pentagonal regions

  c. An 8-faced polyhedron (octahedron), perhaps regular, made up of 8 triangular regions

4. a. Check to see whether there is the same arrangement of faces at every vertex.

  b. Try any quadrilateral prism that is not a cube.

  c. Some of the triangles in your net should *not* be equilateral triangles.

5. a. The tetrahedron may be more easily seen with an actual cube, especially if the cube is transparent.

   b. The other four vertices also give a regular tetrahedron.

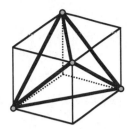

6. Euler's formula, $V + F = E + 2$, does hold. It is curious that some of the same numbers occur with the cube-octahedron and the dodecahedron-icosahedron.

7. a. First polyhedron: Equilateral triangles, regular hexagons; second polyhedron: Squares, regular hexagons

   b. Euler's formula (see answer to Exercise 6) does hold, as it does for both polyhedra, although without the hidden edges in the second one, it is likely impossible to count V, F, and E.

9. a. Yes, because adjacent faces share edges, and all the edges of a given face are the same length.

   b. Yes, because each face is the same type of regular polygonal region.

   c. Yes, for the same reason as for part (a).

   d. No. The regular polygons may be different types, as a square and a hexagon.

16.6 Issues for Learning: Dealing with 3D Shapes

1. a. They might have counted the visible square regions.

   b. One possibility: Double the count as in part (a), for the hidden parts. Or, count the 4 in front, double for the back, giving 8. Do the same for the right and left sides, for another 8. Finally, get another 8 for the top 4, plus 4 for the bottom.

   c. The counts for the right and left are counting cubes that have been counted already.

2. a. For example, the 9 in the front and the 12 on the right both count the 3 cubes at the front right corner.

   b. The student is overlooking the cubes in the inner, middle columns.

Answers for Chapter 17

17.1 Review of Polygon Vocabulary

1. a. scalene right triangle

   b. trapezoid

   c. equilateral triangle (or regular triangle)

   d. rhomboidal region

   e. regular pentagon

   f. parallelogram

   g. square

h. (equiangular) hexagon

i. equilateral 12-gon, or concave equilateral 12-gon (see Learning Exercise 6 in this section). Using less-well known prefixes, it is also an equilateral dodecagon.

j. rhombus

4. a. a regular hexagonal region and isosceles triangular regions

b. rectangular regions

c. a rectangular region and triangular regions, probably isosceles

d. rectangular regions and isosceles trapezoidal regions

5. a. Most of them are isosceles right triangles, but there are also a square and a parallelogram.

b. There are 7 isosceles right triangles, 2 (overlapping) isosceles trapezoids (not counting special ones), 3 non-isosceles trapezoids (not counting special ones), and 1 parallelogram region (not counting special ones).

8. Polygon: Number of sides, number of angles, length of each side, size of each angle, total of the lengths of the sides (the perimeter), total of the sizes of the angles, and so on. (See Learning Exercise 9.) Polygonal region: Same as polygon plus the area of the region.

9. A table helps to see a pattern that may be less obvious if the results are just written, as with 5 vertices, 5 diagonals; 6 vertices, 9 diagonals; and so on. The pattern can often then be extended from one line to the next (for a 12-gon, 54 diagonals; for a 20-gon, 170 diagonals), but without seeing the general result for n vertices. Possible (and mysterious) *Hint* 1: Add a column for twice the number of diagonals—can you relate that column to the column for the number of vertices? A pattern suggests an educated guess, but, as you will see, patterns cannot always be trusted! Hence, now that you have a conjecture, try to reason why it must be true. Better *Hint*, because it gives a general argument: Each vertex in an n-gon is joined to all but 3 of the vertices to give n - 3 diagonals at each vertex, but doing this at each of the n vertices will count each diagonal twice.

10. The sum of the sizes of the angles in each of the triangles is $180°$. When you add all of those up, you are also adding the sizes the angles of the quadrilateral.

12. a. $95°$ **b.** $102°$ **c.** $360 - (85 + 78 + 90) = 107°$ **d.** $73°$ **e.** $90°$
   f. $130°$ **g.** $360 - (130 + 109 + 52) = 69°$ **h.** $111°$ **i.** $71°$ **j.** $128°$

13. a. $\frac{(5-2)180}{5} = 108°$ **b.** $72°$ **c.** $135°$ **d.** $45°$ **e.** $\frac{(n-2)180}{n}$

14. a. $90°$ **b.** $67°$ **c.** $61°$ **d.** $84°$ **e.** All five angle sizes should add to $(5 - 2)180 = 540$, so $540 = 90 + 113 + 119 + 96 + e$, or $e = 122°$ **f.** $58°$ **g.** $72°$ **h.** $59°$ **i.** $52°$
   j. $101°$ **k.** $79°$ **m.** $62°$

15. Each is true. Your reasoning?

16. b. n^2, $(x+1)^2$

c. *Hint*: It may be helpful to add a new column, $2 \times$ # dots, and see how the entries in that column are related to the number in the first column, or to consider the differences between successive numbers of dots. Once you have a conjecture based on a pattern, see whether you can give an argument that justifies the conjecture.

19. Your trials should support the conjecture, because it is true in general.

20.

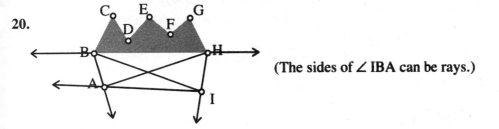

(The sides of ∠ IBA can be rays.)

21. There are many possibilities. Check to make sure the rays start at the correct points, and that D is the vertex of angle FDE. TUV should be shaded in, but not PQRS.

17.2 Organizing Shapes

1. The classification has each type of quadrilateral in a separate category, even though they share many characteristics besides having four sides. (The circles are a common way of showing the categories, and are not to be viewed as quadrilaterals themselves.)

2. a. AT   **b.** ST (Sketch a nonsquare rectangle.)

   c. ST (Sketch a parallelogram that has no right angles.)

   d. AT   **e.** ST   **f.** ST   **g.** ST

3. Samples:

   a. Shared: opposite sides parallel and equal in length; opposite angles the same size, and so on (there might be others that you notice). Different: Possible for angle sizes to differ, lengths of diagonal can differ, and so on.

   b. Shared: Have pairs of adjacent sides the same length, diagonals make right angles, pairs of opposite angles have the same size, and so on. Different: Possible for angle sizes to differ, possible for some sides to be different lengths, and so on.

   c. Shared: have 4 sides, 4 angles, 2 diagonals, angle sum is 360°, and so on. Different: Trapezoids have parallel sides, quadrilaterals may not; and so on.

   d. Shared: Two sides parallel, four sides. Different: Other pair of sides may not be parallel, sides (or angles) may all be different sizes, and so on.

   e. Shared: Both pairs of opposite sides parallel and equal in length, opposite angles are the same size, diagonals bisect each other, and so on. Different: Sides may not all have the same length, diagonals may not be perpendicular, and so on.

4. Three are not possible.

5. One possibility, using two new categories . . .

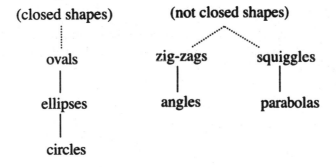

6. **a.** That the parallel sides are horizontal, with one shorter than the other and above it.

   b(i). Perhaps the student thinks a parallelogram's angles cannot be right angles—that a parallelogram's sides must be "tilted."

   b(ii). Perhaps the student thinks a rectangle must have unequal dimensions.

17.3 Triangles and Quadrilaterals

1. Kites and isosceles trapezoids do not fit easily into this Venn diagram.

Quadrilaterals

4. Stuck? Measure segments and angles—are there any possible relationships?

5. **a.** The angles can be placed next to each other so that the two outside sides appear to lie along a straight line, and their sum is therefore $180°$.

   b. The new "placements" of the three angles again appear to lie along a straight line. The method does work with obtuse and right triangles, by folding down the vertex with the largest angle size.

7. **a.** After the last clue, the shape must be a parallelogram.

8. **a.** Pat could have been thinking $a - \frac{b}{c} = a \times \frac{b}{c}$ or perhaps $a - \frac{a}{a+1} = a \times \frac{a}{a+1}$ (or perhaps something else).

   b. The first conjecture is not true in general; find a counterexample. But the second one is correct; try different values for a, and they will strengthen your belief in it. Use your algebra knowledge to show that $a - \frac{a}{a+1}$ is indeed always equal to $a \times \frac{a}{a+1}$.

9. The diagram will look like the one for quadrilaterals, but with the word "prisms" attached to each type of quadrilateral.

10. Think hierarchically (every rhombus is a special trapezoid, so the result should be the same). Or, each of the faces in each case is a quadrilateral, so the sum of all the angles in all the faces will be the same for any quadrilateral prism, $2160°$.

17.4 Issues for Learning: Some Research on 2D Shapes

1. Relevant: 4 sides, 2 sides parallel but not necessarily the "top" and "bottom." Your drawings should include the parallel sides not at the top and bottom, top longer than bottom, 2 or 3 sides equal in length, a very small one, one with 2 right angles, and one not "cut off" (perhaps like the one with 2 right angles, but with the right angles at the top).

2. It is likely that the examples that the child had seen did not have any angles small in size.

3. The child likely is focusing on the lengths of the visible parts of the sides of the angle.

4. Does your collection include rhombuses with 1, or 2, or 4 right angles and with different orientations of the parallel sides?

5. **a.** Except for the choice of 6, the child seems to be looking for right angles at all the vertices.

   b. Perhaps the child is looking for four sides of about the same length, for square, and shapes evenly "stretched out" for rectangle.

Answers for Chapter 18

18.1 Symmetry of Shapes in a Plane

1. Having reflection symmetry: ABCDEH(2)I(2)MO(2)TUVWX(2)Y
   Having (nontrivial) rotational symmetry: HINOSXZ

4. **a.** 1 reflection symmetry only (Don't count a 360° rotation unless there are other rotational symmetries.)

   b. 2 reflection symmetries; 2 rotational symmetries

   c. 2 rotational symmetries (180° and 360°)

   d. 1 reflection symmetry

   e. 0 symmetries

   f. 2 reflection symmetries; 2 rotational symmetries

   g. 1 reflection symmetry

5. **a.** The bisector of the angle.

   b. Don't overlook the lines themselves.

   c. There are actually infinitely many—do you see that?

   d. Any line through the center of the circle is a line of symmetry for the circle, so there are infinitely many lines of symmetry for a circle.

   e. 2 reflection symmetries (Do you also see 2 rotational symmetries?)

6. A rotation of *any* number of degrees, say 3.6° or $4\frac{2}{3}°$, will be a rotational symmetry.

10. **a.** The segments must have the same length, so the triangle must be isosceles.

   b. The two angles must have the same size.

   c. M must be the midpoint of segment BC.

   d. The two angles must have the same size.

12. Segment GH will have the same size as segment KJ, as will segments LG and JI, as well as segments LK and HI. Angles G and J will have the same size, as will angles K and H, and angles L and I.

14. **a.** Stuck? Try *rotational* symmetry.

   b. The result should apply to special parallelograms, but it is not true for all kites.

15. **a-b.** Use the "long" diagonal as a line of symmetry.

   c. Use the 180° rotational symmetry of a rhombus (or a possible fact about parallelograms and the hierarchy), and a reflection symmetry.

   d. Use two reflection symmetries.

18.2 Symmetry of Polyhedra

1. No, it is not possible. This right- versus left-handedness requires a reflection.

4. There are 3 through pairs of opposite edges, plus 6 planes (through vertex, perpendicular to edge) for reflection symmetries, and 3 axes of rotational symmetry, each allowing 90°, 180°, and 270° rotations (plus the 360° one), plus 4 axes allowing 120° and 240° rotations (plus the 360° one), plus 6 axes allowing only 180° (and 360°) rotations. Amazing!

5. **a.** There are 2 planes giving reflection symmetries; they are.... [There is 1 (nontrivial) rotational symmetry of 180° (what is the axis?).]

   b. No symmetries exist.

   c. There are 2 planes giving reflection symmetries and 2 rotational symmetries, counting the 360° rotational symmetry.

6. There are different possibilities. Compare with others. Do any require fewer than twice the original number of cubes?

7. *Hint*: The base must be a square.

8. 9 reflection symmetries and 16 rotational symmetries (8 from one axis, and 2 for 8 other axes, but each of the latter counts the 360° rotational symmetry counted with the first axis)

10. Does each have the same final effect, regardless of any difference in motion along the way?

11. Regular octahedron (shape H): 9 planes of reflection symmetry; 13 axes of rotational symmetry (giving 36 different rotational symmetries!)

   Regular dodecahedron (shape L) and regular icosahedron (shape M): 15 planes of reflection symmetry; 31 axes of rotational symmetry (giving 90 rotational symmetries!).

Answers for Chapter 19

19.1 Tessellating the Plane

1. What causes the difficulty?

4. If you have trouble, rotate the shape 180° about the midpoint of each side.

5. Each type of Pattern Block will tessellate the plane.

6. Examples

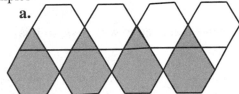 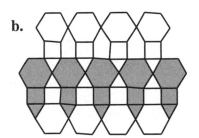

7. After experimenting a bit, you will believe, *Yes*.

8. c. The area of the larger triangle is 4 times the area of the smaller one. (Note that the *lengths* of the sides of the larger one are only twice the lengths of the sides of the smaller.)

19.2 Tessellating Space

1. Yes, there are many....

2. b, d

3. a, d, e; in (a), the curved spine could fill in the curved-in space, but in (b) the shape could not fill in the curved space. In (c), the piece(s) will not fit the inward-going spaces.

4. Volume is most often based on the number of cubical regions that fill a space; this space-filling by cubical regions is a tessellation.

Answers for Chapter 20

20.1 Size Changes in Planar Figures

2. a. Not similar. Even though the corresponding angles are all the same size, the given sides would involve different scale factors, 2 and $1\frac{6}{7}$: $12 = 2 \times 6$, but $13 = 1\frac{6}{7} \times 7$.

   b. Not similar. Even though all the sides are related by the same scale factor ($\frac{2}{3}$ or $1\frac{1}{2}$, depending on your view), the corresponding angles are not the same size.

3–6. Usually you can tell by looking at your result whether you have carried out the size transformation correctly; sides should be parallel to their images.

7. b. A side and its image appear to be parallel. (This gives a visual check for accuracy.)

   c. The lengths of the sides of the smaller triangle are about 2 cm, 3 cm, and 3.5 cm, and of the larger triangle, about 3.5 cm, 5.2 or 5.3 cm, and about 6.1 cm. These suggest a scale factor of about 1.75. The angle sizes are about 88°, 34°, and 58° in each triangle. Again, a side and its image appear to be parallel.

8. a. One pair of parallel sides has lengths 30.5 m; the other pair 12.2 m. The angle sizes are 115° and 65°.

9. a. $a = 50°$, $b = 60°$, $x = 7.2$ km, $y = 5\frac{1}{3}$ or $5.\overline{3}$ km if measurements are perfect.

    d. $r = 75°$, $s = 75°$. So x and 28 correspond, as do y and 28.3, and 24 and 30. The 24 and 30 give the scale factor. $x = 22\frac{2}{5} = 22.4$ cm, $y = 35\frac{3}{8} = 35.375$ cm

10. Yes, in both cases. If the center is on the figure, there are segments that overlap with rays, so it is visually different from the other cases.

11. The image is the same size but in a different place.

12. A change in only the scale factor will result in a change in the size and location of the image.

13. The image will be just like the original (although it may have moved if a rotation, and so on, is involved). The two will be congruent.

14. a. Just one point!

    b. After multiplying by ⁻2, measure in the opposite direction through the center.

15. Two are incorrect.

16. a. 1.6, or 160%

    b. 7.5 cm and 22.5 cm; 125% (the original is the other 100%)

17. a. The new segment should be 3 copies of the original.

    b. The new segment should be 2.5 copies of the original.

    c. The new segment should be 4 copies of the original.

18. a. The first and third express the same relationship. (Your example?)

    b. The first and third express the same relationship. (Your example?)

19. a. 56 cm   **b.** 80 cm

    c. 18 cm   **d.** 42 cm

20. One way would be to use the ruler method. Another way would be to draw a 60° angle, mark off on its sides length 4 times the lengths of the given 60° angle, and then draw parallels to finish the shape.

21. In (a)-(c), angle sizes are the same as in the original, and each length in the original is multiplied by the scale factor to get the length in the image.

    d. Say P dollars are invested at an interest rate of 5% per year. After one year, the original P dollars would become $1.05P$ dollars, as though the original is scaled up by a factor of 1.05.

22. Map scales are usually expressed as ratios or equations, so this one might be written 28 mi:1 in. or 1 in.:28 mi or 1 inch = 28 miles. Many times the units are the same, so the scale here could be written 1,774,080:1 without any need to mention units. (There are 5280 feet in a mile, and 12 inches in a foot.)

23. 150 km. *Hint*: You will have to measure the distances on the maps.

24. A scale of 1 cm = 100 years allows all of the likely dates to be shown, up to 2000. With that scale and starting with year 0 at 0 cm, the Magna Carta would be 12.1 cm from the start, Columbus, 14.9 cm; Declaration of Independence, 17.8 cm; French Revolution, 17.9 cm; Civil War, 18.6 cm; Wright brothers, 19.0 cm; Depression, 19.3 cm; WW II, 19.4 cm; atomic bomb, 19.5 cm; TV, 19.5+ cm; computers, 19.7 cm; and so on.

25. a. Here it is reasonable to have 1 cm = 30 million years. Then, starting with the Cambrian at 0 cm, Carboniferous would be at about 10.7 cm, Triassic at about 13.3 cm, Cretaceous at about 17.8 cm, Oligocene at 19 cm, Pleistocene at essentially the 20 cm mark.

  b. About 66.7 cm!

26. The original and the final image are similar; the scale factor is not 7, however.

27. b. About 2, because the dimensions of the smaller squares are roughly doubled to get the larger squares.

  c. Yes, by….

28. a. Yes. All the angles in each triangle have 60°, so corresponding angles are the same size. And, even though for these triangles we need not check, every ratio of the lengths of corresponding sides is 7:12 (or 12:7).

  b. Yes. Again, the pairs of 60° angles assure that the triangles will be similar. How would you determine the scale factor for the chosen triangles?

  c. No. One triangle might have angles 90°, 45°, 45°; the other 90°, 30°, 60°.

  d. Yes. Every pair of corresponding angles has 90°, and because all of the sides of each square have the same length, the equal ratios for similarity will be assured.

  e. No, even though the corresponding angles all have the same size. Give an example to show that the ratios of corresponding sides will not necessarily all be equal.

  f. No. Sketch a couple, avoiding regular hexagons.

  g. Yes. Corresponding angles will have the same sizes, and because all the sides of each n-gon have the same length, the ratios of lengths of corresponding sides will all be equal.

29. Measure your drawings. For example, the woolly mammoth is about 7 m from tip of tail to tusks' end, and about 4.2 m tall. This termite is about 0.8 cm long.

30. a. For example, $\frac{x'}{y'} = \frac{rx}{ry} = \frac{x}{y}$ *and* $\frac{x''}{y''} = \frac{sx}{sy} = \frac{x}{y}$.

  b. These ratios are all equal.

  c. These ratios are also all equal. In trigonometry, the ratios are related to the angle C in the right triangle and given names like "sine $\angle C$."

20.2 More About Similar Figures

2. A size change like that in the section shows the relative sizes.

3. The triangles in one pair are *not* similar.

4. b. A "tricky" part is seeing the correspondence after you have established similarity because the two triangles share an angle, giving a second pair of the same size along with the 114° angles. It may be helpful to redraw the triangles separately, with one triangle reoriented and the shared angles marked. $k = 5.6$ cm, and $n = 5.4 - 5.1 = 0.3$ cm

  c. The right triangles also have same-sized angles where the lines cross, so they are similar. $p \approx 6.4$ mi; $q \approx 6.4$ mi.

  d. 30 ft

  e. Part (a), $(1.5)^2 = 2.25$; part (c), $(1.6)^2 = 2.56$

   f. Treat the pond like the tree in part (d). From some location a convenient distance from one side of the pond (and perpendicular to the line segment showing the distance across the pond), sight to see the other side of the pond, and make a convenient right triangle like the small one in part (d).

5. a. $2\frac{1}{4}$

   b. A rectangle, because size changes keep angles the same size.

   c. 4 cm by $6\frac{2}{3}$ cm

   d. $26\frac{2}{3}$ cm² and 135 cm². The second is $\left(2\frac{1}{4}\right)^2$ times the first.

   e. Each could have been answered differently, because the 4 cm might have referred to the longer side and hence correspond to the 15 cm side rather than the 9 cm one.

6. $x = 45$ cm, using a scale factor of 1.5 (or $\frac{2}{3}$, depending on your viewpoint)

7. a. Ask about the sizes of two angles in the remote triangle, and check them against the angle sizes in your triangle.

   b. Unless the quadrilaterals are special, you would have to find out about the sizes of 3 of the angles (why not 4?) and the lengths of the four sides, for each quadrilateral. If the angles can be paired so that their sizes are equal, then you would have to check the ratios of the lengths of the paired sides.

20.3 Size Changes in Space Figures

1. This exercise is important, because it requires that you summarize some of the major relationships for similar polyhedra, and they reinforce the relationships for similar 2D shapes.

Corresponding lengths: New length = scale factor × old length. Or, the ratios $\frac{\text{new length}}{\text{original length}}$ are all equal to the same value, the scale factor.

Corresponding angles: New angle size = original angle size.

Corresponding areas: New area = (scale factor)^2 × original area.

Corresponding volumes: New volume = (scale factor)^3 × original volume.

2. b. 1.5

3. Shapes b and d are similar, with scale factor 2 (or $\frac{1}{2}$, depending on your view of the *original*); shapes b and e are similar, with scale factor $1\frac{1}{2}$ (or $\frac{2}{3}$); and shapes d and e are similar, with scale factor $\frac{3}{4}$ (or $1\frac{1}{3}$).

4. Shapes b, d, f, and g are congruent (and therefore similar), and shapes b, d, f, and g are similar to shape a.   **h.** $2^3 = 8$, because the shapes are similar.

5. b. Because 36 = 12 × 3, 84 = 12 × 7, and 96 = 12 × 8 and all the corresponding angles are right angles, the prism in b is similar to the given one. Alternatively, we could say that each of the ratios 36:3, 84:7, and 96:8 is equal to 12:1 or 12 (and the corresponding angles are all equal), so the prisms are similar.

     There are three others that are definitely "Yes" and one "Well, probably, taking rounding into account."

   j. Yes. The scale factor is about 4.14.

6. **a.** 12 feet x 12 inches per foot = (scale factor) x 8 inches, ... , scale factor = 18. You might also get $\frac{1}{18}$ by using a different viewpoint as to the original figure, and the latter way is probably more common: "A $\frac{1}{18}$ scale model."

8. With a scale factor of $\frac{1}{30}$, the height in the scale model should be $\frac{1}{30}$ × 40 inches, so the son is correct (the roommate probably subtracted 30 inches). The other dimensions should be $1\frac{1}{5}$ inches for the length and $\frac{2}{3}$ inch for the width.

9. **a.** 8   **b.** 27
   c. Yes, because...
   d. From the theory, one is $\left(1\frac{1}{2}\right)^2 = 2\frac{1}{4}$ times as large as the other.
   e. The ratio of the volumes is 27 : 8, but $\frac{27}{8} = \frac{3^3}{2^3} = \left(\frac{3}{2}\right)^3$, the cube of the scale factor.

10. **a.** Yes, with scale factor...
    b. Yes. The two scale factors are reciprocals, or multiplicative inverses.
    c. Yes, X and Z are similar. It is tricky to keep track of *new* and *original*, but using Z as the original and X as the final, the scale factor is (s.f. from Z to Y) × (s.f. from Y to X). Try a specific example to see how the product of the two scale factors enters in.

11. **c.** The ratio of the two should be the square of your scale factor.
    d. The ratio of the two should be the cube of your scale factor.

13. *Twice as large* could refer to lengths, or to areas, or to volumes, and the three of these are related by different powers of 2.

14. **a.** 8.8 cm by 13.2 cm by 22 cm   **b.** 3 cm by 4.5 cm by 7.5 cm

15. The new surface area is 803.5 cm^2 (the surface area of the original is 62 cm^2).
    The new volume is 1399.68 cm^3 (the volume of the original is 30 cm^3); the new dimensions are 7.2 cm by 10.8 cm by 18 cm.

16. It is *not* 40; recall how *volumes* of similar figures are related.

17. No. If the scale factor were 0, then the image of every point would be the center.

18. **a.** Yes. All the angles are 90° and every ratio of the lengths of edges is 5:8.
    b. Yes. All the angles are 90° and every ratio of the lengths of edges is *m:n*.
    c. No. Their angles need not be equal, nor do the ratios of lengths have to be the same.
    d. No. Give an example.
    e. No. Although the ratios of the lengths of edges are all equal to 1:3, there is no assurance that the angles in the rhomboidal prism are 90°, as in the cube.

20. Use the same pattern as the given net so that the angles are the same, but multiply each segment in the net by your scale factor.

21. "Each cubic centimeter becomes a 4 cm by 4 cm by 4 cm cube in the enlargement, so each original cubic centimeter is now 4^3 cubic centimeters."

22. **a.** 25,600 cm^2
    b. 204,800 cm^3

23. a. 3 (or $\frac{1}{3}$) The ratio of the volumes, 810:30, is 27, and that is the cube of the scale factor.

    b. $3^2 = 9$ (or $(\frac{1}{3})^2 = \frac{1}{9}$)

26. Under the assumption that your shape is similar to that of the Statue of Liberty, your answers might be about 4 ft 6 in. for the statue's nose and 3 ft for its width of mouth.

Answers for Chapter 21

21.1 Planar Curves and Constructions

1. a. NT   **b.** AT   **c.** ST   **d.** AT
    e. AT   **f.** AT   **g.** AT

4. a. Any line through the center will give a reflection symmetry, and any size rotation with center of rotation at the center of the circle will give a rotational symmetry.

    b. There are many reflection symmetries (all the lines of reflection will be parallel) and many rotational symmetries (all 180°, but with different centers).

    c. "Flattening out" a piece of a sphere leads to some distortion.

5. Your sketches should show the appropriate part of the circle or the circular region.

    a. $\frac{1}{4}$ **b.** $\frac{3}{4}$ **c.** $\frac{1}{3}$

    d. Because the whole circle has 360°, 80° would be $\frac{80}{360}$, or $\frac{2}{9}$, of the circumference.

    e. $\frac{1}{2}$ **f.** $\frac{1}{8}$ **g.** $\frac{3}{8}$ **h.** $\frac{1}{6}$

6. a. 84°   **b.** 42°   **c.** 42°   **d.** 42°   **e.** 96°   **f.** 180°   **g.** 90°   **h.** 90°   **i.** 90°

7. The angle at A is the inscribed angle, intercepting the $d°$ arc. Triangle ABC is isosceles because of the radii, so the angles at A and B are equal. The size of the central angle = 2 × the size of the inscribed angle. Or, the size of the inscribed angle is half that of the central angle.

8. You may check your work by measuring.

9. a. You can get the midpoint of a segment by constructing the perpendicular bisector of the segment.

11. Your eyes can usually tell you whether your work is all right.

12. a. Because the two distances are from the same radius, they are equal.

    b. All the points appear to lie on the perpendicular bisector of segment AB.

    c. The center will be where two perpendicular bisectors of chords intersect. The radius can then be found by measuring from the center to any point on the arc (about 4 cm here). Notice that you can use any three points of the arc to find the center of the circle.

    d. Because concentric circles share the same center, the perpendicular bisectors of chords from the different arcs will meet at the common center of the circles.

13. a. *Hint*: 45 = half of 90   **b.** *Hint*: 135 = 90 + 45
    c–d. *Hint*: $\frac{3}{4} = \frac{1}{2} + \frac{1}{4}$, and $\frac{1}{4}$ is half of a half; $\frac{3}{4} = \frac{1}{2} + \frac{1}{4}$

    e. Bisect the given segment to get half of the segment. Bisect one of the half segments to obtain quarters. Bisect the quarter closest to the half mark to get eighths. Then a half segment with an eighth segment will be $\frac{5}{8}$ of the original segment.

14. a. Suppose a vandal or a malicious drunk came by.

    b. Yes. The same idea works with any regular polygon.

15. You may check your accuracy by measuring the central angle and comparing that to the $360°$ for the whole circular region.

16. *Hint*: See Learning Exercise 5.

18. a. Usually just a visual check will do.

19. Using A as center, draw a circle with radius AB. Using B as center, draw a circle with radius AB. Either of the two points in which the circles intersect can be used for C.

21. a. Yes (SAS, or side-angle-side)

    b. Not necessarily, but they are similar

    c. Yes (SSS, or side-side-side)

    d. Yes, the third angle in GHI makes ASA (angle-side-angle) with Triangle 7.

21.2 Curved Surfaces

1. a. NT   **b.** AT   **c.** AT (but sometimes just 1)

    d. AT (but sometimes just 1 nontrivial one)

    e. AT   **f.** AT   **g.** AT

2. a. right circular cylinder   **b.** right circular cylinders

    c. right circular cone   **d.** right circular cone

    e. oblique cone   **f.** right circular cylinder

3. a. Using the line through the centers of the bases as axis, there are infinitely many rotational symmetries. With every line along a diameter of a cross-section halfway down as axis, there are $180°$ and $360°$ rotational symmetries as well. Any plane perpendicular to the bases and passing through the centers of the bases will give a reflection symmetry, along with the plane parallel to the bases and halfway down the cylinder.

    b. Do you see infinitely many rotational symmetries and infinitely many reflection symmetries? If not, reread the answer for part (b).

    c. Any line (or plane) through the center of the sphere will give a rotational (or reflection) symmetry.

4. c. "Flattening out" a piece of a sphere leads to some distortion.

6. e. Not possible—every two great circles on a sphere will intersect.

8. a. If the layers are the same thickness, the whole cylinder would hold $22\frac{2}{3}$ cups.

    b. 66 ml (*Hint*: How much will $\frac{1}{4}$ of the cylinder hold? $\frac{4}{4}$?)

9. a. The larger sphere has diameter with length twice the diameter of the smaller sphere.

10. a. Circles or ellipses, if the resulting cylinder is a circular cylinder.

    b. Two of the open curves may be of different types, if the cutting plane is or is not parallel to some position of the generating lines.

Answers for Chapter 22

22.1 Some Types of Rigid Motions

2. **a.** B reflection, C translation, D rotation, E rotation, F translation
   b. Each is congruent to shape A, because it is the image of A for a rigid motion.

3. **a.** translation (unless you focus on the wheels only)   **b.** rotation
   c. translation (if the slide is straight)   **d.** rotation
   e. rotation   **f.** rotation (either as it turns, or as the door opens)

4.

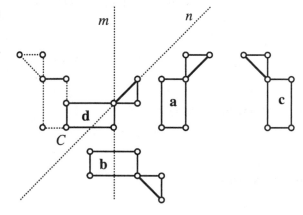

   e. Each is congruent to the original, because each is the image of the original for some rigid motion.

5. **a.** Translations leave the orientation unchanged.
   b. Rotations leave the orientation unchanged.
   c. Reflections change the orientation.

7. There are at least 14. Decision-making likely involves all of the rigid motions.

22.2 Finding Images for Rigid Motions

1-2. Visual checks usually reveal whether images have been located correctly. Rotation images are the most difficult for many people.

4.

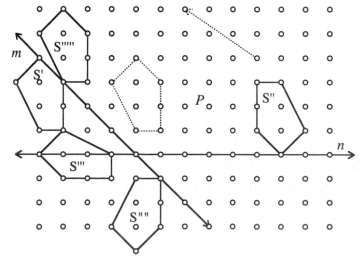

5.

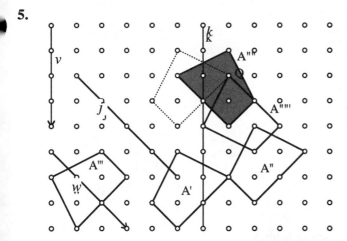

6.

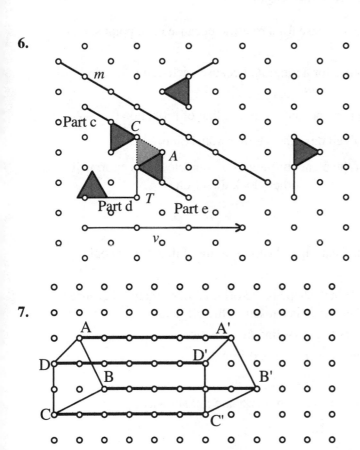

7.

Each of the segments is 6 spaces long. (And each is directed toward the east.)

8. a.   The segments are not all the same length. Points farther from the center have to "travel" farther than do points closer to the center.

b.

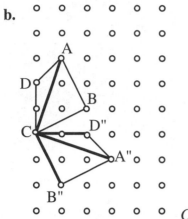

CA and $\overline{CA}$" have the same length,

as do $\overline{CB}$ and $\overline{CB}$", and $\overline{CD}$ and $\overline{CD}$". This makes sense for a rotation because each point should stay its distance from the center, C.

c. Each of the angles is 90°. This result makes sense for a rotation, because each point "travels" through the same angle.

9. The segments can have different lengths, but each is perpendicular to the line of reflection.

10. a, d, and g all give the same translation. c, e, f, and j all describe another translation.

11. c and d will have the same effect on every point of the plane; turning 180° one clock direction will end a shape up in exactly the same place as will 180° in the other clock direction.

22.3 A Closer Look at Rigid Motions

1. Again, your eyes usually tell you whether the result is all right, keeping in mind that most people have more trouble with rotations.

2. a. The vector should *end* at the figure to the left. Which shape is the original does matter, because the direction of the vector is opposite if the other figure is chosen as the original.

   b. For a reflection, either shape as the original gives the same line of reflection.

   c. The clock direction of the angle depends on which shape is the original.

   d. Notice that this reflection is one of the lines of symmetry.

3. a. reflection in line *m* (see the following diagram; construction marks are not shown)

   b. translation with vector *v*

   c. reflection in line *n*

   d. rotation, center D, angle about 120° counterclockwise

   e. rotation, center E, angle 180°

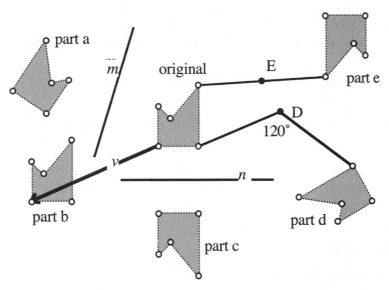

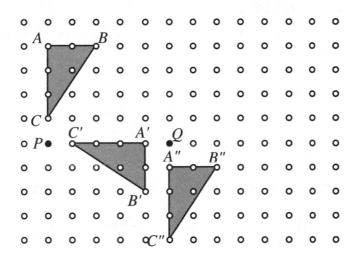

4. a. Every point on line k is a fixed point. **b.** There are no fixed points.

   c-d. There is one fixed point, namely... **e.** Every point is a fixed point, for the 360° rotation.

5. a-b.

   c. A translation...

6. a. Line n itself   **b.** Ray $\overrightarrow{BC}$; ray $\overrightarrow{BA}$

22.4 Composition of Rigid Motions

1. Lines k and m are perpendicular to the direction of the translation (and therefore are parallel) and are 1.5 cm apart. Note that 1.5 cm is one-half the 3 cm.

2. a. translation, 1.2 cm east   **b.** translation, 3 cm southwest

   c. translation....   **d.** rotation....

   e. rotation...   **f.** rotation...

   g. rotation....   **h.** reflection in a different line through T

   i. glide-reflection

3. a. A glide-reflection changes the orientation of a figure.

   b. Translations and rotations do not change the orientation of a figure, but reflections and glide-reflections do.

   c. The image will be congruent to the original, because each of the motions making up a glide-reflection gives a figure congruent to its original.

4. a. a translation or a rotation (Each of the originals keeps the orientation the same, so their composition will also.)

   b. a translation or a rotation

   c. a translation or a rotation

   d. a single reflection or a glide-reflection

   e. even: translation or rotation; odd: reflection or glide-reflection

   f. a reflection or a glide-reflection, because...

5. b. The line of reflection appears to pass through the midpoints of the segments.

6. a. In general, yes. For example, ...(try two reflections)

   b. Order does not matter for the two motions defining a glide-reflection. (That is why the definition demands that the line of reflection and the vector of the translation be parallel.)

7. a. rotation, because the orientations are the same, and a translation won't work. (You may also have just "eye-balled" it.)

   b. reflection, because...

   c. translation, because...

   d. reflection, because...

   e. glide-reflection, because...

8. Q'R'S'T' by a glide-reflection; Q"R"S"T" by a rotation.

9. a. Your two lines of reflection should be perpendicular to the line of the vector, and half the vector's length apart.

   b. Your two lines of reflection should intersect at the center of the rotation; the angle they make will be half the size of the angle of the rotation.

   c. Perhaps surprisingly, there are many possibilities in each case.

11. Any rigid motion is one of these: reflection, translation, rotation, or glide-reflection. Each translation/rotation can be achieved by the composition of two reflections (Exercises 9-10), and a glide-reflection can be achieved by the composition of three reflections (two for the translation, plus the separate reflection of the glide-reflection).

12. a. 1 or 3 reflections   **b.** 2 reflections

13. a. glide-reflection   **b.** translation   **c.** glide-reflection   **d.** rotation

   e. rotation or translation, depending on the type of tuner (dial or lever)

   f. rotation or translation, depending on the type of thermostat

14. No

15. The rigid "motion" that leaves every point in the same place; this is a legitimate isometry, even though there is no net change of position for any point.

16. The composition will be a single reflection. The line of reflection will be parallel to the other lines. If the original lines are, from the left, x units and y units apart, with $x > y$ and the composition is done starting at the right, then the composition line will be y units to the right of the third line of reflection (or x units to the left of the first line of reflection).

22.5 Transformations and Earlier Topics

1. **a.** There are many translation symmetries, as well as many reflection symmetries. Describe several of the translation symmetries.

   b. There are many translation symmetries, as well as many rotational, reflection, and glide-reflection symmetries.

2. Only one of the statements is true in each part.

3. **a.** (two, yes, two) reflection symmetries, (two) rotational symmetries (counting the $360°$ rotation)

   b. (only one) reflection symmetry

   c. reflection, rotational, translation, glide-reflection

   d. (one) reflection symmetry

5. **a.** There are several different translation symmetries, as well as reflection and rotational symmetries. There are also glide-reflection symmetries.

6. *Hint*: What is the size of the third angle in each triangle?

7. The image will be congruent to the original shape.

8. **a.** Yes, just use the reverse of the rigid motion.

   b. Yes, use a $360°$ rotation.

   c. Yes, use the composition of the two rigid motions.

9. **a.** Yes,…

   b. Yes, use a scale factor of 1.

   c. Yes,…

11. **a.** Each of the triangles is similar to each of the others. Any will tessellate the plane.

   b. The shape has 6 reflection symmetries and 6 rotational symmetries. It will tessellate the plane (assume the inner white pieces are filled with some color).

   c. The shape has 6 rotational symmetries, but no reflection symmetries.

   d. It is likely to have translation symmetries, and perhaps other sorts. It will tessellate the plane.

Answers for Chapter 23

23.1 Key Ideas of Measurement

1. **a.** length   **b.** volume, although weight could conceivably be used

   c. temperature   **d.** weight

   j. Your ideas, besides student achievement?

2. (Other correct answers are possible.)

   a. yards, feet, inches, centimeters (!), millimeters (!!)

   b. milliliters, or ounces if weight is used

   c. degrees Fahrenheit or degrees Celsius

   d. grams or ounces

   e. square centimeters or square inches

   f. meters per second or yards per second

   g. minutes

   h. square meters or square yards

   i. square meters or square yards

   j. students' scores on tests or students' later success rate or…

3. a. temperature, height

   b. height, weight, mathematics achievement

   c. running speed, walking speed, respiration rate—all of which involve measuring other quantities as well

4. a. barometric pressure

   b. population density

   c. area

5. c. "One person's junk is another person's treasure," so the unit would have different values depending on who was using it.

   d. You have probably read about perception experiments in which people's judgments of relative temperature were vastly influenced when one finger was in hot water, as compared to when the finger was in cold water.

   e. The actual amount in a *pinch* likely varies from person to person.

   f. Different people, or even the same person at a more thirsty time, likely would have differently sized *sips*.

6. a. Real-life length measurements cannot be 100% exact.

7. a. Show segments as short as $6\frac{1}{2}$ units and up to $7\frac{1}{2}$ units.

8. b. 161.75 pounds $\leq$ a possible weight $<$ 162.25 pounds

   c. 128.25 pounds $\leq$ a possible weight $<$ 128.75 pounds

9. a. $x > 2000$ because it would take more than 2000 raisins to weigh 2000 pounds.

   b. $x < 2000$ because a raisin's weight is smaller than a pound.

   c. $x > 2000$ because…

   d. $x < 2000$ because…

10. a. The ap unit is larger than the ag, because it takes fewer aps to equal 150 ags.

    b. The ba unit is larger than the bo, because… (*Hint*: Recall that $1.31 \times 10^3 = 1310$.)

11. Weigh yourself holding the puppy, and then…

12. a. $8\frac{1}{2}$ units, by counting repetitions of the unit; "cutting" the region into individual and part units and totaling them

b. 8 units, by...　　　　　　　　*Hint* for exact reasoning:

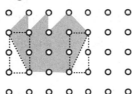

c. $6\frac{1}{2}$ units, by...

d. 4 units, by...

e. $2\frac{1}{8}$ new units, because...; 2 new units because...; $1\frac{5}{8}$ new units because...

13. Probably $8 \times \$2.89 = \$23.12$, because some leftover pieces from a section would be too short to be useful elsewhere.

14. a. $17\frac{1}{8}$ inches

c. $5\frac{5}{8} + 7\frac{13}{16} + 3\frac{1}{4} = 16\frac{11}{16}$ inches

d. Just under $5\frac{7}{8} + 7\frac{15}{16} + 3\frac{3}{4} = 17\frac{9}{16}$ inches

e. From $16\frac{11}{16}$ inches to just under $17\frac{9}{16}$ inches (whereas the part (a) length would incorrectly imply the more narrow range of possible lengths between $17\frac{1}{16}$ inches and $17\frac{3}{16}$ inches).

16. a. 0.763　　　　　　**b.** 270

c. 1.9　　　　　　　　**d.** 46.2

17. a. 1300 ms　　　　　　**b.** 143×10^{-9} s $= 1.43 \times 10^{-7}$ s

c. 0.500 s or 0.5 s　　　　**d.** 2.5×10^{-3} s

18. a. 0.1532 kg　　　　　**b.** 3400 mg

19. a. 80 km　　　　　　**b.** 15 cm

20. 1

22. Correct: only parts (a) and (d). *Hints*: The calculations are done as though the relationships are base ten relationships, but 1 hour = 60 minutes, not 100; 1 pound = 16 ounces, not 10; 1 gallon = 4 quarts, not 10.

23. Rather than what appears to be a random collection of terms, as in the given list, the metric system uses prefixes with a basic term for all of its units of a particular type.

24. a. 16

b. In order, starting with mouthful: $\frac{1}{64}, \frac{1}{32}, \frac{1}{16}, \frac{1}{8}, \frac{1}{4}, \frac{1}{2}, 1, 2, 4, 8, 16, 32, 64, 128, 256, 512, 1024$

c. Units are related by powers of the same number. 2 is used instead of 10.

25. About $0.9144018 - 0.9144 \approx 0.0000018$ meter shorter

23.2 Length and Angle Size

1. Recall that measurements are not exact, so answers close to those given likely reflect a correct approach. (Production processes also can change lengths slightly.)

a. ≈ 31.2 cm　　　　　　**b.** ≈ 10.5 cm

c. ≈ 10.6 cm　　　　　　**d.** A: about 20 cm; B: 2 faces each—about 14.4 cm, 18.2 cm, 15.4 cm

2. Measurements are approximate.

3. Any segment with length ≥ 6.25 cm but < 6.5 cm would fit the conditions.

4. Try doing these mentally, if you did them with paper-pencil.

    a. $3\frac{3}{4}$ inches   **b.** $3\frac{3}{8}$ inches   **c.** $3\frac{9}{16}$ inches

6. **h.** Just under 2.5 cm, if you do not have a quarter handy.

    i. Almost 28 cm

    j. About 99 cm, or about 1 m

7. Remember that the sides have to fit together to make a polygon: 1 cm, 1 cm, 1 cm, and 21 cm would be impossible. The complete answers are not given here.

    a. Try to be systematic, possibly this way: 6-6-6-6; 5-6-6-7; 4-6-6-8; 5-6-6-7; 4-6-6-8; 3-6-6-9; 2-6-6-10; 1-6-6-11.

    b. 1, 11, 1, 11 cm; 2, 10, 2, 10 cm; 3, 9, 3, 9 cm; 4, 8, 4, 8 cm; 5, 7, 5, 7 cm; 6, 6, 6, 6 cm. Notice how much easier the problem is with a rectangle, because the opposite sides must be the same length.

8. Experiment, gathering and organizing the data from several simpler, specific values for n (for example, $n = 1$, $n = 2$, $n = 3$, etc.), and look for a pattern.

9. **a.** By measuring the distance of the line segment perpendicular to the line(s) from the point to the line or from one parallel line to the other.

    b. No, so long as the distance is measured along a perpendicular.

10. The distance between the top and bottom parallel sides.

11. Ancient Greeks used this idea: The perimeter (and area) of the circle should be between the perimeters (and areas) of the outer and inner polygons.

12. **a.** 1200 m   **b.** 530 cm

    e. 3.35 cm + 4.25 cm = 7.6 cm. Remember that "3.4 cm" implies the measurement is accurate to the nearest tenth-centimeter.

13. 4 and a little more, using a 2 cm unit; somewhat under 9, using a 1 cm unit; just under 18, using a 0.5 cm unit. The 0.5 cm fits very closely, so an estimate of just under 9 cm should be a good estimate.

14. **a.** About 90°   **b.** About 60°   **c.** About 145°

    d. right angle a (or close to it), acute angle b, obtuse angle c. No straight angle is shown; are you clear about what a straight angle would look like?

16. **a.** 270°   **b.** 35/60, or 7/12, of 360° is 210°   **c.** 30°

    g. 618°   **h.** 8640°

17. 21 600 minutes, so 1 296 000 seconds. One second would then be $\frac{1}{1296000}$ of a full turn.

18. **a.** 17° 43' 37"   **b.** 46° 28' 43"

19. *Hint*: 360 ÷ 15 =...

20. 25 000 ÷ 360 = ...

21. Remember to check your drawings by measuring with a protractor.

22. **a.** $y = 180 - x$, so then ? $= 180 - y = 180 - (180 - x) = 180 - 180 + x = x$.

23. a. *c,z; a,x; d,y*

   b. No

   c. Corresponding angles of parallel lines appear to be the same size.

   d. The other pair of alternate interior angles is *c*, *x*. If lines are parallel, the alternate interior angles are the same size.

25. a. *Hint*: What are the sizes of the other angles at vertex A, in terms of *z* and *y*?

   b. 69°   **c.** 49°   **d.** 60° 38'

   e. 80° and 80°; 20° and 140°   **f.** 90°

26. *a=y; b=z; c=x*   *d=z; e=w; f=y; g=x*

27. a. Because the *n* angles total ... and they are all equal in size, each is ...

   b. Your table should show these results: 3---60°; 4---90°; 5---108°; 6---120°; 7---$128\frac{4}{7}$°; 8---135°; 9---140°; 10---144°; 11---$147\frac{3}{11}$°; 12---150°. Notice that the angle sizes are getting larger. How do you know that they will never equal 180°?

   c. The sizes get larger and larger, but less than 180°.

   d. *Hint*: $(n-2)180 = 4500$

   e. 16

28. a-b. Focus on what must happen at a given vertex, and apply Learning Exercise 27(b).

29. a. If it were 360°, it would be flat. (If it were more than 360°, it would not be convex.)

   b. What polygons give (same-sized) angles that will total less than 360° at a vertex? See Learning Exercise 27(b) and be sure to see whether there is more than one possibility for a given polygon.

   c. *Hint*: See Learning Exercise 27(b) again.

30. The 1080 refers to the number of degrees in the turn the athlete can make when she/he is in air. So a 1080 refers to 3 full turns. Excellent athletes can do 720s and 900s as well.

31. 65° 35' (*Hint*: 120.25° = 120° + how many minutes?)

32. Look at 90° arcs on circles of quite different sizes.

34. a. 120°, 90°, 72°, . . .

   b. *Hint*: See part (a).

35. a. 120°   **b.** 55°   **c.** *p + q* degrees

36. The conventional way is to measure the angle formed by the two perpendiculars to the edge of the dihedral angle, at the same point on the edge and with one in each plane making the dihedral angle.

37. *Hint*: Look at lots of multiples of 19.

38. a. Additive comparison: The 100-yd dash is 8.56 m (or 9.36 yd) shorter than the 100-m dash.

   Multiplicative comparison: 100 yd:100 m = 0.9144:1, or

   100 m:100 yd = 1:0.9144 = 1.0936:1

   The mile run is about 109 meters (or about 120 yd) longer than the 1500-m run. The ratio 1760 yd:1500 m would most likely be given with the units the same. 1760 yd:1640 yd = ..., or 1609:1500.

41. b. Although you can make definite assertions about the angles, you can say only that the ratios of lengths of corresponding sides will be equal; you do not know the value of that ratio.

42. a. 400

   b. 0.009° (This is not a temperature, even though you may know that the Celsius temperature scale was once called the centigrade scale.)

43. 117 cm

44. a. The endpoints give a square. Each angle intercepts half the circle and so has size 90°. Rotate 90° to see that the sides have the same length.

   b. A regular hexagon. Joining the points to the center of the circle shows 6 connected equilateral triangles, so each side of the hexagon has the same length, and the angle at each vertex is 120°.

   c. Octagon: Bisect the central angles in part (a); 12-gon: Bisect the central angles in part (b).

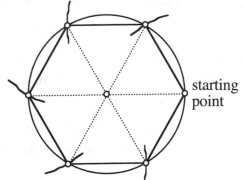

starting point

Answers for Chapter 24

24.1 Area and Surface Area

1. a. $3\frac{1}{6}$ hexagonal regions; $6\frac{1}{3}$ trapezoidal regions; $9\frac{1}{2}$ rhombus regions

   b. $3\frac{1}{3}$ hexagonal regions; $6\frac{2}{3}$ trapezoidal regions; 10 rhombus regions

2. a. 24 rhombus regions, because...

3. Here are possibilities, if you cannot think of any: nail of little finger for square centimeter, VW Beetle door for square meter, floor of an ordinary classroom (10 m by 10 m, or roughly 30^+ ft. by 30^+ ft.)

4. c. Varies, perhaps 1 are, more likely in square meters

   d. Varies, square meters likely unit

   e. Varies, might be in dm^2 or m^2, depending on size

5. a. $20 > x$, because if the measurements are equal, then it will take more of the smaller units to give an area equal to x of the larger units (or, …it will take fewer of the larger units to make an area equal to 20 of the smaller units).

   b. $20 > x$, because…   **e.** $y > x$, because…

   f. $x > y$, because…   **h.** $\frac{8}{3}$ Qs make 1 R. $\frac{3}{8}$ R s make 1 Q.

   i. $\frac{3.7}{2.4}$, or $\frac{37}{24}$, or $1\frac{13}{24}$ blobs make 1 glob. $\frac{24}{37}$ glob makes 1 blob.

6. a. 64 of Beth's unit, $10\frac{2}{3}$ of Cai's unit   **b.** $2\frac{3}{8}$ of Al's unit, $1\frac{7}{12}$ of Cai's unit

7. a. Your sketch should confirm, for example, that there are 144 square inches in 1 square foot. Hence, 1 square inch is $\frac{1}{144}$ of a square foot.

   b. ...9 sq. ft in a square yard; $\frac{1}{9}$ sq. yd makes a square foot

   c. *Hint*: There are 1760 yards in 1 mile.

8. 640 acres in a square mile, perhaps from a dictionary or from $\frac{5280 \times 5280}{43,560}$

9. a. 230   **b.** 0.45

10. 10 m

11. a. $\approx$ 26 units   **b.** $\approx$ 13 units

12. a. 19 units   **b.** *Hint*: "Surround" the triangle with a rectangle. 10.5 units

   c. "Cut off" a slice from the left end and put it on the right end. 25 units

   d. 26 units   **e.** 26 units   **f.** 195 units

13. a. Find the areas of one of the 8 lateral faces, multiply that by 8, and add twice the area of one of the bases. What might be an efficient way to find the area of a base?

   c. Find the area of one face and multiply that by 8.

14. b. 82 units

16. No. The second one has area 16 square meters.

18. First region: around 13 cm^2; second region: around 9.5 cm^2

19. a. The different sizes are $\frac{1}{4}$ (region I), $\frac{1}{8}$ (regions III, IV, V), and $\frac{1}{16}$ (region II). Cutting out the pieces and moving them around should convince you.

   b. $11\frac{3}{4}$ area units (I), $5\frac{7}{8}$ area units (III, IV, V), and $2\frac{15}{16}$ area units (II).

   c. $1\frac{1}{6}$ area units (I), $\frac{7}{12}$ area unit (III, IV, V), and $\frac{7}{24}$ area unit (II).

20. $\approx$ 20 units. "Cutting" the region into pieces, getting an approximate measurement of each piece, and then totaling is one method.

21. a. Ollie is incorrect, because... (*Hint*: Learning Exercise 7(b).)

   b. 270 dm^2, 27000 cm^2, 2.7 m^2...

22. The original 64 squares now seem to fill 65 squares! This strange result would violate the cutting-up key idea. The secret is that the apparent diagonal of the rectangle is really a very thin but long region, with area 1 square region.

23. Your sketch should show that the original square centimeter now occupies 25 square centimeters.

24. a. 24 010 cm^2, because areas are related by the square of the scale factor. SA(larger) $= 7^2 \bullet 490$

   c. Not necessarily, because the pyramids are not similar (4:6 $\neq$ 6:8).

25. The scale factor is either 2 or $\frac{1}{2}$, depending on which region is the original, because the ratio of the two areas (4, say) is the square of the scale factor.

26. a. Add the lengths of the three sides of the rectangle, and half the circumference of the circle.

   b. Subtract half the area of the circular region from the area of the rectangular region.

27. Your work should show that figures with the same perimeter may not have the same area.

28. Each is incorrect, usually because of the inappropriateness of the unit for the quantity.

24.2 Volume

1. The units given here are possible, but others can be defended. The important thing is that the units be of the correct kind and not too large or small. Units like km or cm^2 for the area of a lake are either not appropriate (km is for length) or sensible (cm^2 is too small).

   a. volume, km^3 (possibly m^3)   **b.** area, km^2 **c.** length, m or dam

   g. angle size, degrees   **h.** volume, m^3 **i.** length, m

   j. volume, m^3 **k.** volume, km^3 **l.** area, m^2 or dam^2

   m. length, m   **n.** area

2. If you are stuck, here are some ideas: a portion of your little finger ($1 cm^3$, 1 mL), some plastic soda containers ($1 dm^3$, 1 L), a box for a large washing machine ($1 m^3$)

4.   **a.** About 250 mL or $250 cm^3$ **b.** About a liter (slightly less)

   c. About $\frac{1}{3}$ liter   **d.** Perhaps about $300 m^3$

5. The usual piece of paper is about 28 cm by 21.5 cm, allowing only 2 dm across and 2 dm down. So the net would not fit.

7. These are important for classroom work. For part (a), to see the 1000 cubic centimeters in a cubic decimeter, show the 10 cubic centimeters in 1 row, then the 100 in the 10 rows in one layer, then the 1000 in the 10 layers.

   b. 1000   **c.** 1000 ($1 L = 1 dm^3$)   **d.** 1 000 000

9.   **a.** 10 times, 100 times, 1000 times

10. **a.** 3280   **b.** 32.8

   a. Your drawings should suggest that 1 cubic foot = 1728 cubic inches; 1 cubic yard = 27 cubic feet; OR 1 cubic inch = $\frac{1}{1728}$ cubic feet; 1 cubic foot = $\frac{1}{27}$ cubic yard.

   b. 7.48 (often rounded to 7.5)   **c.** About 325,830

13. Key to the second question: Your answer to, "Does *anything* include idealizations that exist just in the mind?"

14. **a.** Surface area = 150 square regions; volume = 108 cubic regions

   c. S. A. = 160 sq. regions; volume = 105 cu. regions

   d. 108 mL, 222 mL, 105 mL, respectively ($1 mL = 1 cm^3$)

   e. No ($1 L = 1000 mL$ or $1000 cm^3$)

15. 1 gram, 1 gram

16. Most have surface area 18 square regions.

17. **a.** Count by rows. 42 cubic regions; 40 cubic regions

   b. 42 square regions; 40 square regions

   c. The first (30 stories, each 42 cubic regions = 1260 cubic regions vs. 31 stories, each 40 cubic regions = 1240 cubic regions)

18. Six cubic regions in each layer, 5 layers = 30 cubic regions. Some additional partial cubic regions would be needed to fill in the rest—estimate 2 per layer. 40 cubic regions. Key ideas: measurements are approximate; thinking of a region in pieces, getting the measurement of each piece, and then adding those measurements to get the measurement of the whole thing.

19. a. $13\frac{1}{2}$ **b.** $1\frac{2}{3}$ **c.** $\frac{1}{2}$ **h.** $9\frac{1}{3}$

    i. $\frac{3}{4}$ **j.** $\frac{2}{3}$ **k.** 48   **l.** $\frac{3}{16}$

20. a. Congruent shapes have the same measurements, so S.A. = 32 square regions and volume = 12 cubic regions for the first shape, and S.A. = 34 square regions, volume = 9 cubic regions for the second shape.

    b. Surface area of the hidden, larger version of the first shape = 800 square regions; volume = 1500 cubes.

21. a. 20 800 cm^2; 192 000 cm^3

    c. 53 248 cm^2; 786 432 cm^3

    d. 6292 cm2; 31 944 cm^3

Answers for Chapter 25

25.1 Circumference, Area, and Surface Area Formulas

2. **a.** 5π cm, or 15.7 cm

    b. 320π km, or 1004.8 km, or 1005 km. (So this is about 1005 × 1000 × 100 cm, or about 1.005×10^8 cm.)

    c. The radius is about 3 cm, so $C = 6\pi$ cm, or 18.8 cm, or about 19 cm.

3. 3981 miles; 7962 miles (often referred to as 4000 miles and 8000 miles). *Note*: Our Earth is not a perfect sphere but is often treated as such.

4. **a.** $\frac{22}{7} \approx 3.1428571$, so...   **b.** 0.038 cm

    c. The radius of the orbit is 200 miles more than the Earth's radius, or about 4181 miles. Then the difference from the calculations with the two approximations of π is 13.3 miles, which might be important if there are people on the satellite. (How does the answer differ if you use 4000 miles as the radius? Are you surprised?)

6. 31.8 cm, or 32 cm

8. **a.** "Let me draw a parallelogram on graph paper. Check it out."

    b. "Remember how we put two triangles together to make a parallelogram. Then to find the area of one triangle we had to take half the area of the parallelogram."

9. **a.** 12.16 cm^2 **b.** 76.5 cm^2 **c.** 54 cm^2

10. Create a parallelogram region, and see how it is related to the triangular region.

11. Make sure that your heights make right angles with the sides. In the right triangle, d is the altitude for side e, and vice versa. Two of the heights for the obtuse triangle are outside the triangle, and the sides i and g must be extended to see the heights (but one would use just g and i as the bases, not the extensions).

12. It should not matter, but actual measurements may be off enough to make the calculated areas seem to be different. You should get the same area no matter which side you choose as base.

13. Each way should give an area of 24 square regions.

14. Each of the triangles has the same area, $7\frac{1}{2}$ units, even though the triangles may appear to the eye to have different areas. Because parallel lines are the same distance apart no matter where you measure it, the heights of all the triangles are the same (and the base is the same for each of them).

15. So long as the height is measured between the lines the bases are on, it does not matter where so long as it is measured along a perpendicular.

16. **a.** 8.99 cm^2

    c.   Cut each of the bases into 4 equal segments, and join them. (It will not be visually obvious; check with the formula.)

17. **a.**   62 square inches

18. **i.**   shape a: 15 cm^2

    shape c: 29.75 cm^2

    shape e: $4.5\pi + 9$, or about 23.14 cm^2

    shape g: $12 + 9\pi$, or about 40.27 cm^2

    ii. shape i. Area $= mj + \frac{1}{2}(m + n)(k - j)$

    shape j. Area $= \frac{1}{2}(pq + rs)$

    shape k. *Hint:* Sketch in the rest of two opposite semicircles; then the radius $= \frac{1}{4}t$. Area $=$ Area (two whole circular regions) $+$ square region $= \ldots = \frac{\pi+2}{8}t^2$

    shape l. Area $= v(w - \frac{v}{2}) + \frac{1}{2}\pi(\frac{v}{2})^2 = \ldots$

    iii. For shapes a, b, and i, the "slant" sides cannot be predicted at this time. (If you remember the Pythagorean theorem and if the shape is symmetric, as it appears to be, you can make progress.)

    Perimeters: c—22.3 cm; d—12 cm; e and f—6π cm;

             g—$10 + 3\pi$ cm; h—$18 + 2\pi$ cm

    Shape j: Perimeter $= p + q + r + s$

    Shape k: Perimeter $= \pi t$

    Shape l: Perimeter $= v + 2(w - \frac{v}{2}) + \pi\frac{v}{2} = \ldots$

19. **a.**   What are the areas of the two pizzas? (Assume that they have the same thickness.) The larger pizza is cheaper by the square inch. If you were surprised by the answer, put the smaller pizza on top of the larger one and look at a slice of each with the same central angle.

    b.   No, the larger one costs about 15.1¢ per square inch, but the smaller costs only about 13.7¢ per square inch.

20. a. 12.96 cm^2

  b. 1 cm^2 for the first grid; 0.25 cm^2 for the second

  c. The second grid should give a better estimate, unless you are a fantastic estimator!

21. a. 48π or 150.8 cm^2

  b. 13.842π or 43.43 cm^2

  e. This time, consider $\frac{\text{actual length of arc}}{\text{whole circumference}}$, or $\frac{\text{actual length of arc}}{2\pi r}$. Multiply that fraction by the area of the
    whole circle, and continuing: $\frac{\text{actual length of arc}}{2\pi r} \times \pi r^2 = \frac{\text{actual length of arc}}{2} \cdot r$, or $\frac{1}{2}$(length of arc) $\cdot\ r$.
    If the length of the arc is labeled s, $A(\text{sector}) = \frac{1}{2}sr$, with a pleasing resemblance to the formula for
    the area of a triangle.

  f. 24 + 8π or 49.13 cm

  g. 20 + 16π or 70.27 cm (for part (c))

22. In the first figure, assuming that the side of the square is s units long (= the diameter of the circular
   region), the percent uncovered = 100% – the percent covered = $100\% - \frac{(\frac{s}{2})^2\pi}{s^2} = 100\% - \frac{\pi}{4} \approx 21.5\%$.
   In the second figure, ...

23. a. SA ≈ 200,000,000 or 2 × 10^8 sq. miles.

24. a. Because the globes are similar, the ratio of their surface areas will be the square of the
    scale factor: $\left(\frac{16}{12}\right)^2 = \left(\frac{4}{3}\right)^2 = \frac{16}{9} \approx 1.78$. The larger globe has 1.78 times as much area as the
    smaller one does.

  b. smaller: 576π sq. in.; larger: 1024π sq. in. (Does this check with part (a)?)

25. a. 592 cm^2

  c. $22\frac{1}{3}$ ft^2, or 3216 in^2

  d. $2xy + 2xz + 2yz$, or $2(xy + xz + yz)$

26. 2880 cm^2

27. The estimate could be improved by using narrower rectangles.

28. Look at the units that would result; neither the product nor the sum of four lengths would give square
   units.

29. a. 22.5 cm^2 **b.** 156.25%   **c.** 56.25% (Why not 25%?)

30. Recall that the scale factor affects each length measurement. See what happens to the original length
   and the original width, so when you multiply the two new lengths, each involves a scale factor, giving (scale factor)^2 times the product of the original lengths. The areas of triangular regions are multiplied by k^2 also, because each of the two length measurements in the formula introduces a factor of k.

31. a. See the right triangles?   **b.** Rhombuses and squares, because...

32. If you get stuck, look at $\frac{\text{\# dots on}}{2}$ + # dots inside, which is close to the correct number. The final result
   that does give the area is called Pick's formula.

33. a. See the parallelogram region? How is its area related to the area of the triangle?

b. See the "short" rectangular region? What is its area?

35. a. A triangle

b. A(triangle as special "trapezoid") $= \frac{1}{2}(0+b)h = \frac{1}{2}bh$

36. b. "Cut" the general triangle into two right triangles.

37. A(sphere) = area of the cylinder's curved surface (without the two bases of the cylinder)

25.2 Volume Formulas

1. In which ones are all the layers identical in volume?

2. b. 105, if the 2 cm cubes can be cut

3. Measurements can vary somewhat, and the production process may have changed measurements used in calculating the answers. If your answer is in the neighborhood of the listed answers, you were likely correct in your reasoning.

a. For B = about 3.1 cm^2, 1000 such pieces would need about 1860 cm^3 of plastic.

b. With B = 2.9 cm^2 (or thereabouts—don't forget the holes), the volume of plastic needed for 1000 such pieces would be 1740 cm^3.

c. With B = about 9.3 cm^2, 1000 pieces would need 5580 cm^3 of plastic.

d. The key idea about the measurement of the whole equaling the sum of the measurements of its parts

4. a. The same.

b. The top-bottom way gives a a radius of $\frac{11}{2\pi}$ and a volume about 81.8 cubic inches, whereas the side-side way gives radius of $\frac{8.5}{2\pi}$ and a volume about 63.2 cubic inches. So the top-bottom way gives 18.6 cubic inches more, or is about 130% as large as the side-side.

c. You can find another example of shapes having the same surface area but different volumes, but it takes some work. *Hint*: Examine the surface area of a 1 by 1 by 5 right rectangular prism and find a shape made with 6 cubes having the same surface area.

6. Again, measurements can vary somewhat and the production process may alter the original dimensions, so if your answers are somewhat close to the ones here, you were probably thinking all right.

a. 13.4 cm^3

8. a. 8" ball, volume $= \frac{256\pi}{3} \approx 268.1$ in^3;

16" ball, volume $= \frac{2048\pi}{3} \approx 2144.7$ in^3

b. The areas are 64π in^2 and 256π in^2, so the costs of the plastic are about \$0.39 and \$1.56 (don't forget to change the square inches into square feet).

c. Because the spheres are similar, the ratio of the volumes is $\left(\frac{1}{2}\right)^3$ or 1:8, and the ratio of the areas is $\left(\frac{1}{2}\right)^2$ or 1:4.

9. a. $\pi 8^2 \cdot 12 + \frac{1}{3}\pi 8^2 \cdot 3 \approx 2613.8$ ft^3

   b. Because 2150.42 cu. in. ÷ 1728 cu. in. per cu. ft, 1 bushel ≈ 1.24 cu. ft. So the silo will hold about 2613.8 ÷ 1.24, or 2108 bushels. Notice that the calculations would be simpler in the metric system.

10. a. $S.A. = 4\pi$ m^2; $V = \frac{4\pi}{3}$ m^3

   c. $\approx 3.45 \times 10^{17}$ cubic miles

   d. about 1,277,000, using the rounded answers in parts (b) and (c)

11. a. 2 to 1   **b.** 2 to 3

12. a-b. No, they are not congruent, but they have the same volume.

   c. $\sqrt[3]{\frac{6}{\pi}} \approx 1.24$, so about $1\frac{1}{4}$ inches

13. a. $\frac{2}{3}$ (Compare with Learning Exercise 11(b).)

   b. $1 - \frac{\pi}{6} \approx 47.6\%$

14. The sphere, by about 2.4 cm (its radius is about 6.2 cm).

15. $r = 3$ cm for the original sphere. $r = 0.005$ cm for the small spheres. The number x of small spheres can be found from $36\pi = x \cdot \frac{4}{3}\pi(0.005)^3$, which gives that there are 2.16×10^8 small spheres. These will have a total surface area of $2.16 \cdot 10^8 \cdot 4\pi(0.005)^2$, or 21600π cm^2. The ratio of the surface areas, all smaller spheres to original sphere, is $\frac{21600\pi}{36\pi} = \frac{600}{1}$, giving considerably more surface for burning. (A similar principle holds for melting ice: Broken-up ice from a block will melt faster than the block would.)

16. a. $\frac{4}{3}\pi\left(\frac{1}{6}\right)^2 \approx 0.016$ cubic miles

   b. $\dfrac{\text{later volume}}{\text{earlier volume}} \approx 0.027$, so the later volume is only 2.7% of the earlier volume, quite an error. (But even the smaller asteroid could cause immense damage.)

17. b. "Cut" shape K into rectangular and triangular prisms and pyramids. Find the volume of each of those, and add them.

18. a. $V = 72\pi + 18\pi = 90\pi$, about 282.7 cm^3;
       $SA = 9\pi$ (the bottom) $+ (\pi 6)8 + 18\pi$, about 235.6 cm^2

   c. $V = \pi r^2(h - r) + \frac{2}{3}\pi r^3$

   d. $V = kmn + \frac{1}{3}mnh$

   e. $V = \pi r^2 h$, and $SA = 2\pi r^2 + 2\pi rh$. For the surface area, did you account for both bases, and did you notice that a net for a right circular cylinder includes a rectangle?

19. The volume of a **cube** with edges x units long is x^3 cubic units.

20. a. 384 cm^2 **b.** SA(cube) $= 6s^2$

   c. 512 cm^3 **d.** V(cube) $= s^3$

e. As measurements, the area and volume cannot be equal of course, because area and volume are completely different characteristics. The second question comes down to whether $6s^2 = s^3$ has any *numerical* solutions, and it does: $s = 6$ and the trivial (for here) $s = 0$.

21. Recall that the scale factor multiplies each length measurement, so in the formulas...

22. a. $V = \frac{\pi}{6}d^3$ (The relationship between the diameter and the radius is so simple that most people do not memorize this formula.)

    b. $V = \frac{2}{3}\pi r^3$

    c. $A = \pi d^2$

    d. $A = \frac{1}{2}\pi d^2$ (for just the curved part; add $\pi(\frac{d}{2})^2$ if you included the planar part)

23. Without more restrictions on the shape of the dog house, there is no definite answer.

24. a. $...x^2 + 2xy + y^2$ **c.** $...x^2 + xy$ **d.** $... x^2 + 5x + 6$

25. There are no "right" answers, but it is surprising that some progress can be made, using estimations.

Answers for Chapter 26

26.1 The Pythagorean Theorem

1. a. $p^2 + q^2 = r^2$

2. Do not have either a or b equal to 0, and you will have a counterexample.

3. a. perimeter = 60 cm, area = 150 cm^2

    b. $35 + \sqrt{175}$ cm, or 48.2 cm; $7.5\sqrt{175}$ cm^2, or 99.2 cm^2

    d. $10 + \sqrt{50}$ cm, or 17.1 cm; 12.5 cm^2

    g. 90 in.; 270 in^2 **h.** 20 m; 15 m^2

4. a. 14.1 cm   **b.** $\sqrt{2s^2}$, or $s\sqrt{2}$, cm   **d.** $\sqrt{m^2 + n^2}$ cm

6. a. $\sqrt{x^2 + y^2 + z^2}$ **b.** No, but a 4-foot one would, just barely.

    c. $e\sqrt{3}$ units

7. Consider a right triangle with legs 22 ft and $\frac{x}{4}$ ft, and hypotenuse x.

8. More than $70.

9. Volume = $28\sqrt{42} \approx 181$ cm^3; surface area = $84 + 6\sqrt{91} + 14\sqrt{51} \approx 241.2$ cm^2

10. a. 4.5π cm^2, 8π cm^2, 12.5π cm^2. The sum of the areas on the legs equals the area on the hypotenuse, just as in the Pythagorean theorem!

    b. The area of the semicircular region on the hypotenuse is equal to the sum of the areas of the semicircular regions on the legs. Because $a^2 + b^2 = c^2$ from the right triangle, $\frac{1}{2}\pi(\frac{a}{2})^2 + \frac{1}{2}\pi(\frac{b}{2})^2 = \frac{\pi}{8}(a^2 + b^2) = \frac{\pi}{8}c^2$, and $\frac{\pi}{8}c^2$ is also what you get from $\frac{1}{2}\pi(\frac{c}{2})^2$.

11. **a.** The height of an equilateral triangle in terms of the length s of its sides is derived in the narrative, $h = \frac{s\sqrt{3}}{2}$.

b. 10.83 cm^2, 62.35 cm^2, 73.18 cm^2. Once again, the sum of the areas on the legs $(10.83 + 62.35)$ is equal to the area on the hypotenuse.

c. The justification is like that in Exercise 10 (but with the triangle area formula, of course).

12. How do you know that $\angle PVQ$ is a right angle? If you are stuck, it may be because you need $(a+b)(a+b) = a^2 + 2ab + b^2$.

13. Parts (b), (c), and one other part give Pythagorean triples. Do you see how they are related to the triple 3, 4, 5?

e. Yes, with an algebraic justification. This fact is useful for a teacher, as in part (f).

14. **a.** $\sqrt{20}$ units

b. $\overline{QR}$, 2 units; $\overline{ST}$, $\sqrt{20}$ units; $\overline{UV}$, $\sqrt{32}$ units; $\overline{WX}$, $\sqrt{20}$ units; $\overline{YZ}$, 10 units

c. Find the algebraic difference in the first coordinates and in the second coordinates; then...

15. One statement in each pair is false.

16. **a.** $A = 270$ sq. units

b. Because $15^2 + 36^2 = 225 + 1296 = 1521$, and because $39^2 = 1521$ also, the measurements give a right triangle. The area, from $A = \frac{1}{2}bh = \frac{1}{2}36 \cdot 15 = 270$, agrees with the result from part (a).

17. For the 6 rows with 6 dots in each row, 20 is not correct; there are only 19! (Which one is missing?) This problem is another example to show that patterns cannot be trusted 100%.

18. **a.** $p = 10 + 2\sqrt{10}$ units $\qquad\qquad A = 15$ square units

d. $p = 4\sqrt{5}$ units $\qquad\qquad A = 4$

19. *Suggestion:* Use the Pythagorean theorem for the heights of the triangles and of the pyramid.

a. A drawing helps to see that the altitude of each triangle is 2 cm $(1.5^2 + h^2 = 2.5^2)$ and the height x for the pyramid is about 1.3 cm $(1.5^2 + x^2 = 2^2)$. So, $SA = 3^2 + 4(\frac{1}{2} \cdot 3 \cdot 2) = 21$ cm^2, and $V = \frac{1}{3}Bh \approx \frac{1}{3} \cdot 3^2 \cdot 1.3 = 3.9$ cm^3.

20. **a.** Assume that the ground covered is a circular region, that the pile has lots of rotational symmetries, and that the pile will be shaped like a cone.

b. 16π, or about 50.3 m^3

c. Filling one sandbox to the top will take 0.675 m^3, so the pile will fill $16\pi \div 0.675$ sandboxes, about 74.

21. **a.** Make a drawing. Where is a right triangle?

b. An 80° angle cuts off what part of the whole circumference? That length is the circumference of the base of the cone; now what is the radius? The height? The volume?

22. One way: How are areas of similar shapes related?

23. Values are in feet. P to A: $\sqrt{300} + 2 \approx 19.3$; P to B: $\sqrt{200} + 2 \approx 16.1$;

P to C: $\sqrt{2100} + 2 \approx 47.8$; P to D: $\sqrt{1400} + 2 \approx 39.4$. Total ≈ 122.6 ft.

24. Use a key idea of measurement and Learning Exercise 11(a).

25. The volumes of cubes with edges equal to legs a and b and hypotenuse c of a right triangle are related by the given equation.

26. *Hint*: Place one of the boards across the corner of the canal to make an isosceles right triangle.

28. Stuck? Does the Pythagorean theorem help?

29. In order: $\sqrt{2}, \sqrt{3}, \sqrt{4}, \sqrt{5}, \ldots$

26.2 Some Other Kinds of Measurements

4. **a.** 97.5 ms, up to 98.5 ms   **b.** 149.5 m, up to 150.5 m   **c.** 1.415 L, up to 1.425 L

5. If, say, your measuring container is smaller than a container of liquid, you can remove amounts with your measuring container, keeping a record of each amount and then adding these amounts when the large container is empty.

6. These might give examples: costs of lettuce, breathing rates, gasoline mileage rates, and so on.

8. Rather than what appears to be a random collection of terms, the metric system uses prefixes with a basic term for all of its units of a particular type.

10. **a.** Slightly under 3.3   **b.** About 3.2
    c. About 41 mph   **d.** About .328

11. **a.** Slightly under 26.1   **b.** About 24.8
    c. About 22.2   **d.** About 81 kg or 178 lb
    e. About 8.7 kg or 19 lb, at least

12. **a.** One way: Showing on the drug number line that $\frac{1}{4}$ is $\frac{1}{3}$ of $\frac{3}{4}$, so $\frac{1}{4}$ g should use $\frac{1}{3}$ of 12 mL, or 4 mL, on the water number line.

    b. So 1 g, or 4 one-fourths, should take 4 times as much, 16 mL

    c. $1\frac{1}{2}$ g

    d. Each 4 mL uses $\frac{1}{4}$ g, so 20 mL would use $\frac{5}{4}$, or $1\frac{1}{4}$, g.

    e. $\frac{3}{8}$ g

13. **a.** Because 100 Celsius degrees match 180 Fahrenheit degrees, the Celsius degree is larger: $1\,C^\circ = 1.8\,F^\circ$

    b. 20° C would be $\frac{20}{100}$, or $\frac{1}{5}$ of the way from 0° C to 100° C. The corresponding Fahrenheit temperature should then be $\frac{1}{5}$ of the way from 32° F to 212° F, or $\frac{1}{5}$ of 180, or 36°. Starting from 32° gives a temperature of 68° F.

    c. Reasoning as in part (b), $^-40^\circ$ C corresponds to a temperature $\frac{2}{5}$ of 180, or 72°, below 32° F. $^-40^\circ$ F (This is the only temperature at which the two scales give the same reading.)

14. **a.** km/s, because a kilometer is longer than a meter

    b. km/s, because 1 km per sec = 3600 km per hour

    c. m/s, because 1 m/s = 3600 m/h = 3.6 km/h

    d. yard/s, because 1 yd/s = 3600 yd/h and there are only 1760 yards in a mile.

15. a. $\frac{1}{25}$ gallon per mile (the 25 miles per gallon means 25 miles per 1 gallon)

b. About 9.1 kilometers per liter

16. a. 10 m/s

b. 36 km/h (if the runner could run that fast for an hour)

c. The runner's rate is 10 meters for every second.

d. The runner's rate is 36 km for every hour (if …)

17. a. 10 yd/s   **b.**   About 20.45 mi/h

c. Metric (Learning Exercise 16) is easier, because the calculations are easier.

18. a. Using the cost per pound as a criterion, rather than the total cost, Danyell's was most expensive ($7.20 versus $6.99 per lb for Amy's, $6.79 per lb for Bea's, $6.40 per lb for Conchita's).

b. The average for the amounts actually bought is about $6.862 ($42.72 for 6.225 lb), but the average of the four costs per pound is $6.845 ($27.38 ÷ 4).

19. a. The total cost was $130, or $32.50/blouse.

b. Your meal was roughly $10 of the total $70, so you could argue that you should pay only $10. Splitting the $70 evenly would mean you would pay $14.

c. Although $2.29 is the average of the $1.99 and $2.59, you bought more of the $2.59 bags, giving a total cost of $29.88 for the 12 bags, or an average of $2.49 per bag.

20. For example, the cost per pound, the rate of eating, the cost per day per cow.

a. $22\frac{3}{4}$ ¢ per day per cow

b. 24¢ per day per cow

21. $\dfrac{20}{3\times10^6\,km/s\cdot3600s/h\cdot24h/day\cdot365day/yr\cdot1500yr}\times360°\approx$

$5.07\times10^{-14} = 0.0000000000000507°$

22. With 8000 miles as the diameter of Earth and a world population of 6 billion,

$\dfrac{6\times10^9}{0.29\times4\pi(4000)^2}\approx 103$ people per square mile.

23. a. For example, ounces/serving size, # servings/container, calories/serving

b. 495 calories

c. 10 000 mg (because 1% must have 100 mg)

d. No, there are 3 grams of each. Comparing the 5% and 10% rates does not make sense, because they are based on different values.

e. $6\frac{1}{4}$ servings ÷ 4.5 servings/box, or $1\frac{7}{18}$ boxes

24. a. $6\frac{1}{4}$ cups powdered sugar, $6\frac{1}{4}$ cups molasses, $2\frac{11}{32}$ (about $2\frac{1}{3}$) teaspoons each of salt and soda, $16\frac{13}{32}$ cups flour,… 1200 square inches, or $8\frac{1}{3}$ square feet.

b. $\frac{1}{4}$ cup sugar, $\frac{1}{4}$ cup molasses, $\frac{3}{32}$ tsp. each of salt and soda, $\frac{21}{32}$ cup flour,… (What would be approximations for the latter two?).

c. For example, 16 bars per recipe, different amounts of ingredients per recipe or per 16 bars.

25. About 55.9 miles per hour (475 miles traveled in 8.5 hours). (Why is the average larger than 55 mi/h?)

26. If the number of children were distributed evenly over all the families, each family would have 2.6 children (a sharing-equally division of the total number of children by the number of families).

27. **a.** $1\frac{1}{2}$ days

 b. 6 days. There are different analyses possible. Here is one, using the compound unit, painter-day: It takes 6 painter-days to paint 1 house, so it will take 120 painter-days to paint 20 houses, which will take 20 painters 6 days.

 c. $14\frac{7}{12}$ days

Appendix A

A Review of Some Rules

Courses for preservice elementary school teachers usually assume competence with whole number, fraction, and decimal arithmetic (addition, subtraction, multiplication, and division) and a previous exposure to elementary algebra. The courses themselves often focus on *why* the particular calculational procedures work rather than how to do them.

Experience shows that some students, however, are quite rusty with some of the *rules* (and there are a lot of them!). If you are such a student, these pages offer a quick review of a few topics, without any explanation of why the rules give correct answers, or even what addition, subtraction, multiplication, and division mean. You should not use a calculator for any calculation, to assure yourself that your basic facts and techniques with whole numbers are still in good working order. Here are the areas reviewed; sample from them as you need, or as your instructor suggests:

1. Fractions (including mixed numbers)

2. Decimals

3. Fraction, Decimal, and Percent Conversions

4. Solving a Proportion

5. Whole-number and Negative Exponents

6. Order of Operations

Final answers are given at the end.

A.1 | Fractions (Including Mixed Numbers)

Equal (or Equivalent) Fractions

RULE: Multiply or divide the numerator and denominator by the same number (not zero) to get an equal fraction. (Terms: $\dfrac{\text{numerator}}{\text{denominator}}$)

EXAMPLES: $\dfrac{2}{3} = \dfrac{2 \cdot 7}{3 \cdot 7} = \dfrac{14}{21}$ $\dfrac{60}{72} = \dfrac{60 \div 2}{72 \div 2} = \dfrac{30}{36} = \dfrac{30 \div 3}{36 \div 3} = \dfrac{10}{12} = \dfrac{5}{6}$

$\dfrac{4\frac{1}{2}}{7} = \dfrac{4\frac{1}{2} \times 2}{7 \times 2} = \dfrac{9}{14}$ $\dfrac{17}{40} = \dfrac{2\frac{1}{2} \times 17}{2\frac{1}{2} \times 40} = \dfrac{42\frac{1}{2}}{100}$

PRACTICE:

1.1. Simplify as much as possible.

a. $\dfrac{126}{35}$ b. $\dfrac{96}{100}$ c. $\dfrac{42}{56}$ d. $\dfrac{196}{240}$ e. $\dfrac{168}{64}$ f. $\dfrac{72}{216}$ g. $\dfrac{7\frac{1}{3}}{10}$

h. $\dfrac{248}{120}$ i. $\dfrac{28}{36}$ j. $\dfrac{5.2}{10}$ k. $\dfrac{588}{1000}$ l. $\dfrac{\frac{3}{4}}{9}$ m. $\dfrac{7\frac{1}{2}}{100}$ n. $\dfrac{384}{512}$

1.2. Write a fraction equal to the given fraction, but with the designated numerator or denominator. (This skill is needed for adding or subtracting fractions.)

   EXAMPLE: Write a fraction equal to $\dfrac{5}{16}$, but with the denominator 96. To get a denominator of 96, one must multiply by 6 (from $96 \div 16$, thinking "What times 16 will give 96?"). So multiply numerator and denominator by 6: $\dfrac{5 \times 6}{16 \times 6} = \dfrac{30}{96}$

a. $\dfrac{9}{10}$, with denominator 70   b. $\dfrac{2}{3}$, with denominator 36

c. $\dfrac{8}{15}$, with denominator 180   d. $\dfrac{9}{11}$, with numerator 99

e. $\dfrac{3}{8}$, with numerator 27   f. $\dfrac{84}{96}$, with denominator 56 (Hint: simplify first)

1.3. In a and b, write ten fractions equal to the given fraction.

a. $\dfrac{3}{12}$ b. $\dfrac{8}{7}$

1.4. Do any of your fractions in 1.3 have a smaller or greater value than the original fraction in each case?

Rewriting Fractions Greater Than One as Mixed Numbers, and Vice Versa

RULE: To change a fraction greater than 1 to a mixed (or whole) number, divide the numerator by the denominator. If the fraction can be simplified first, the division involves smaller numbers.

EXAMPLES: $\dfrac{13}{5} = 13 \div 5 = 2\dfrac{3}{5}$ $\dfrac{100}{12} = 100 \div 12 = 8\dfrac{1}{3}$ $\dfrac{368}{23} = 368 \div 23 = 16$

PRACTICE:

1.5.   Write each as a mixed (or whole) number.

   a. $\dfrac{493}{72}$ **b.** $\dfrac{15}{8}$ **c.** $\dfrac{52}{16}$ **d.** $\dfrac{1000}{15}$

   e. $\dfrac{2400}{128}$ **f.** $\dfrac{96}{9}$ **g.** $\dfrac{360}{28}$ **h.** $\dfrac{1010}{12}$

RULE: To change a mixed number to a fraction, multiply the denominator by the whole number, add the product to the numerator, and write the sum over the denominator. A whole number can be written as a fraction in many ways.

EXAMPLES: $4\dfrac{2}{3} = \dfrac{4 \cdot 3 + 2}{3} = \dfrac{14}{3}$ $7\dfrac{5}{8} = \dfrac{7 \cdot 8 + 5}{8} = \dfrac{61}{8}$

   $9 = \dfrac{9}{1} = \dfrac{18}{2} = \dfrac{27}{3} = \dfrac{144}{16} = \cdots$

PRACTICE:

1.6.   Write each as a fraction.

   a. $7\dfrac{1}{2}$ **b.** $19\dfrac{1}{3}$ **c.** $52\dfrac{7}{8}$ **d.** 17 **e.** $11\dfrac{9}{10}$

Adding or Subtracting Fractions and Mixed Numbers

RULE: If the fractions have the same denominator, then add/subtract the numerators, writing that answer over the original denominator. If the fractions do not have the same denominator, then replace them with equal fractions that do have a common denominator and proceed as in the first sentence. The common denominator need not be the <u>least</u> common denominator, but a least common denominator keeps the numbers smaller. It is customary to simplify the answer.

   If a mixed number is involved, there are two ways to proceed. The first way is to change each mixed number to a fraction first. The second way is to deal with the fraction parts and the whole number parts separately, perhaps re-naming the first mixed number if necessary to do the fraction subtraction.

EXAMPLES: $\dfrac{5}{14} + \dfrac{3}{14} - \dfrac{2}{14} = \dfrac{5 + 3 - 2}{14} = \dfrac{6}{14} = \dfrac{3}{7}$

   $\dfrac{2}{3} + \dfrac{5}{6} - \dfrac{7}{12} = \dfrac{48}{72} + \dfrac{60}{72} - \dfrac{42}{72} = \dfrac{48 + 60 - 42}{72} = \dfrac{66}{72} = \dfrac{11}{12}$

One way, with mixed numbers:	A second way, with mixed numbers:
$12\frac{1}{4} - 6\frac{7}{8} = \frac{49}{4} - \frac{55}{8} = \frac{98}{8} - \frac{55}{8} = \frac{98-55}{8} = \frac{43}{8} = 5\frac{3}{8}$	$12\frac{1}{4} = 11\frac{5}{4} = 11\frac{10}{8}$ $\underline{-6\frac{7}{8} = -6\frac{7}{8} = -6\frac{7}{8}}$ $\qquad\qquad\qquad 5\frac{3}{8}$

PRACTICE:

1.7. Give the answers in simplest form (if the answer is a fraction greater than 1, give the mixed number).

a. $\dfrac{9}{16} - \dfrac{5}{12} + \dfrac{17}{24}$

b. $\frac{2}{3} + 6\frac{7}{8} + 2\frac{1}{2} - \frac{5}{4}$

c. $\frac{19}{36} + 2\frac{2}{3} - 1\frac{17}{18}$

d. $120\frac{1}{5} - 3\frac{7}{10} + 2\frac{1}{10}$

e. $600 - 60\frac{2}{7}$

f. $3\frac{1}{3} + 1\frac{5}{6} - \frac{3}{4}$

Multiplying Fractions (and Mixed Numbers)

RULE: To multiply two fractions, write the product (that is, the result of multiplication) of the numerators over the product of the denominators. It is customary to simplify the answer. Mixed numbers should be changed to fractions before multiplying.

EXAMPLES: $\dfrac{2}{3} \times \dfrac{7}{8} = \dfrac{2 \times 7}{3 \times 8} = \dfrac{14}{24} = \dfrac{7}{12}$ $\qquad 2\frac{1}{2} \times 3\dfrac{9}{10} = \dfrac{5}{2} \times \dfrac{39}{10} = \dfrac{195}{20} = \dfrac{39}{4} = 9\dfrac{3}{4}$

$$\dfrac{2}{3} \times 24 \times \dfrac{15}{16} = \left(\dfrac{2}{3} \times \dfrac{24}{1}\right) \times \dfrac{15}{16} = \dfrac{48}{3} \times \dfrac{15}{16} = \dfrac{16}{1} \times \dfrac{15}{16} = \dfrac{16 \times 15}{1 \times 16} = 1$$

PRACTICE:

1.8. Find the products (multiply).

a. $\dfrac{3}{4} \times \dfrac{7}{8}$

b. $\dfrac{5}{8} \times 120$

c. $\dfrac{2}{3} \times \dfrac{5}{2} \times \dfrac{9}{8}$

d. $3\frac{1}{3} \times 92$

e. $5\frac{1}{12} \times 7\frac{1}{5}$

f. $\dfrac{11}{12} \times \dfrac{2}{3} \times \dfrac{4}{5} \times \dfrac{10}{11}$

Dividing Fractions

RULE: To divide by a fraction, invert the fraction and multiply. If mixed numbers are involved, change them to fractions first.

EXAMPLES: $7 \div \dfrac{2}{3} = \dfrac{7}{1} \times \dfrac{3}{2} = \dfrac{21}{2} = 10\frac{1}{2}$ $\qquad \dfrac{9}{10} \div \dfrac{3}{5} = \dfrac{9}{10} \times \dfrac{5}{3} = \dfrac{45}{30} = 1\frac{1}{2}$

$$4\frac{1}{4} \div 2\frac{1}{2} = \dfrac{17}{4} \div \dfrac{5}{2} = \dfrac{17}{4} \times \dfrac{2}{5} = \dfrac{34}{20} = 1\frac{7}{10}$$

PRACTICE:

1.9. Find the quotients (divide).

a. $\dfrac{3}{4} \div \dfrac{1}{2}$

b. $\dfrac{1}{2} \div \dfrac{3}{4}$

c. $\dfrac{21}{32} \div \dfrac{1}{8}$

d. $21\frac{1}{4} \div 3$

e. $11 \div \dfrac{2}{3}$

f. $\dfrac{49}{1000} \div 3\frac{1}{2}$

A.2 | Decimals

Equal Decimals

RULE: Annexing zeros to the last digit to the right of the decimal point gives an equal decimal. Removing zeros on the right end of a decimal gives an equal decimal.

EXAMPLES: $0.4 = 0.40 = 0.400000$ $2.073 = 2.07300$ $4 = 4.0$ $8.750 = 8.75$
$0.08 = 0.080$ $73.200 = 73.2$ $19.00 = 19$

PRACTICE:

2.1. Write two decimals that are equal to each given number.

    a. 435.06   **b.** 1.4   **c.** 927.0400   **d.** 17   **e.** 0.680

Adding and Subtracting Decimals

RULE: Write in vertical form, with the decimal points aligned. Then add or subtract as though they were whole numbers, aligning the decimal point in the answer with the other decimal points.

EXAMPLES: $34.2 - 7.6 \rightarrow$

$$
\begin{array}{r}
34.2 \\
- 7.6 \\
\hline
26.6
\end{array}
$$

$200 - 63.08 \rightarrow$

$$
\begin{array}{r}
200.00 \\
- 63.08 \\
\hline
136.92
\end{array}
$$

PRACTICE (Notice that you can make up exercises, do them, and then check with a calculator.)

2.2. Calculate by hand.

    a. $0.05 + 1.9$ **b.** $175.3 - 11.94$ **c.** $68.3 + 4 + 19.84 - 72.756$

Multiplying Decimals

RULE: To multiply two decimals, multiply as though they were whole numbers, count the total number of decimal places in the numbers being multiplied (the factors), and then place the decimal point that many places from the right end of the answer.

EXAMPLES: $0.2 \times 0.49 \rightarrow 2 \times 49 = 98$, 3 total decimal places in 0.2 and 0.49 $\rightarrow 0.098$
$1.52 \times 0.075 \rightarrow 152 \times 75 = 11{,}400$, 5 total dec. places $\rightarrow 0.11400 = 0.114$

PRACTICE (Notice that you can make up exercises, do them, and then check with a calculator; keep in mind that calculators usually do not show unnecessary zeros.)

2.3. Find the products.

    a. 0.2×0.3 **b.** 4.8×75 **c.** 12.39×0.14 **d.** 19.88×4.23

Dividing Decimals

Terms and notation: Dividend ÷ divisor = quotient; in working form,

$$\frac{\text{quotient}}{\text{divisor} \,)\, \text{dividend}}$$

RULE: To divide two decimals, move the decimal point in the divisor to make the divisor a whole number, and move the decimal point the same number of places in the dividend (you may have to annex 0s). Do the division as though the numbers were whole numbers, keeping digits carefully aligned, and put the decimal point in the answer (the quotient) right above its new location in the dividend.

EXAMPLES: $11.2 \div 0.28 \rightarrow 1120 \div 28 = 40$ $11.256 \div 0.28 \rightarrow 1125.6 \div 28 = 40.2$

$336.4 \div 2.32 \rightarrow 33640 \div 232 = 145$ $0.69336 \div 9.63 \rightarrow 69.336 \div 963 = 0.072$

$100 \div 6.3 \rightarrow 1000 \div 63 = $ approximately 15.873016

PRACTICE (Again notice that you can make up exercises, do them, and then check with a calculator.)

2.4.   Find the quotients. If there does not seem to be an exact answer, give the quotient to six decimal places.

 a. $120 \div 2.5$ **b.** $36.344 \div 15.4$ **c.** $3.6344 \div 15.4$ **d.** $3.782 \div 0.0775$

 e. $14 \div 200$ **f.** $27 \div 0.04$ **g.** $0.008 \div 0.2$

A.3 | Fraction, Decimal, and Percent Conversions

You likely know that $\frac{1}{4} = 0.25 = 25\%$. These three forms—fraction, decimal, and percent—are "dialects" for the same number. Viewed as dialects that require "translation," there are six "translations," as indicated in the drawing below. You should be able to start with any form and "translate" into the other two forms.

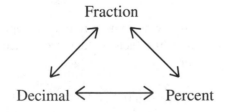

Fraction to Decimal

RULE: Divide the numerator by the denominator. Annex a decimal point and zeros as needed. Many times the quotient (the answer) is not exact, but the last decimal place given is possibly rounded, depending on the value in the next place.

EXAMPLES: $\frac{7}{16} = 7 \div 16 = \ldots = 0.4375$ $\frac{9}{11} = 9 \div 11 = \ldots = 0.8181818181 \ldots$ *(forever)*

PRACTICE:

3.1.   Write each fraction as a decimal. If the decimal appears to go on forever, give eight decimal places.

   a. $\frac{3}{8}$ **b.** $\frac{1}{16}$ **c.** $\frac{3}{16}$ **d.** $\frac{1}{7}$ **e.** $\frac{2}{7}$ **f.** $\frac{1}{9}$ **g.** $\frac{7}{9}$ **h.** $\frac{1}{12}$

   i. $\frac{1}{6}$ **j.** $\frac{12}{7}$ **k.** $\frac{1}{25}$ **l.** $\frac{27}{25}$ **m.** $\frac{22}{7}$ **n.** $\frac{1}{13}$

Decimal to Fraction

RULE: Write a fraction that has as numerator the same digits as the decimal but no decimal point, and a denominator that suggests the smallest place value in the decimal (e.g., if the smallest place value is hundred**th**s, write 100 in the denominator). The place values, going to the right from the decimal point, are tenths, hundredths, thousandths, ten-thousandths, hundred-thousandths, millionths, etc. Many times the resulting fraction can be simplified.

EXAMPLES: $1.35 = \frac{135}{100}$ (The smallest place value is hundredths, so use denominator 100.)

   And, if desired, $\frac{135}{100} = \frac{27}{20} = 1\frac{7}{20}$

   $0.7421 = \frac{7421}{10,000}$ $2.1674932 = \frac{21,674,932}{10,000,000}$ (which can be simplified)

PRACTICE:

3.2.   Write a fraction and then simplify it as much as possible.

   a. 3.75   **b.** 0.092   **c.** 0.0004   **d.** 4.68

Decimal to Percent

RULE: Move the decimal point two places to the right, and put the % sign on the end. You may have to annex a zero or two to the original number. You do not usually write the decimal point in the percent expression unless there are more digits to the right.

EXAMPLES: $1.07 = 107\%$ $0.2 = 20\%$ $3 = 300\%$ $1.5 = 150\%$ $0.0067 = 0.67\%$

PRACTICE:

3.3.   Write each as a percent.

   a. 4.25   **b.** 3.146   **c.** 1   **d.** 0.62   **e.** 0.045   **f.** 0.00003

Percent to Decimal

RULE: Move the decimal point two places to the left, and remove the % sign. You may have to insert one or more zeros.

EXAMPLES: $34\% = 0.34$ $110\% = 1.1$ $7.75\% = 0.0775$ $0.12\% = 0.0012$

PRACTICE:

3.4. Write each percent as a decimal.

   a. 88%   **b.** 33.3%   **c.** 105%   **d.** 1.5%   **e.** 500%   **f.** 5.5%

Fraction to Percent

RULE: Change the fraction to a decimal, as above, and then change the decimal to a percent, as above.

EXAMPLES: $\dfrac{5}{6} = 0.8333\ldots = 83.333\ldots\%$ $\dfrac{33}{40} = 0.825 = 82.5\%$ $\dfrac{15}{8} = 1.875 = 187.5\%$

PRACTICE:

3.5. Write each fraction as a percent.

   a. $\dfrac{8}{5}$ **b.** $\dfrac{5}{8}$ **c.** $\dfrac{17}{20}$ **d.** $\dfrac{952}{1140}$ **e.** $\dfrac{113}{125}$ **f.** $\dfrac{140}{32}$

Percent to Fraction

RULE: Write the percent as a decimal, as above, and then write the decimal as a fraction, as above. The fraction often can be simplified.

EXAMPLES: $32.5\% = 0.325 = \dfrac{325}{1000}\ (=\dfrac{13}{40})$ $0.72\% = 0.0072 = \dfrac{72}{10,000}\ (=\dfrac{9}{1250})$

PRACTICE:

3.6. Write each percent as a fraction. Simplify the fraction if you need practice.

   a. 40%   **b.** $66\tfrac{2}{3}\%$ **c.** 165%   **d.** 11.5%   **e.** 0.25%

MIXED PRACTICE:

3.7. Write each of the given fractions, decimals, or percents in the other two forms.

   a. $\dfrac{9}{10}$ **b.** 2.3   **c.** 56%   **d.** $\dfrac{18}{15}$ **e.** 0.8   **f.** 1.58%

A.4 | Solving a Proportion

A proportion is an equation like $\frac{24}{36} = \frac{2}{3}$ (and occasionally as 24:36 = 2:3). Notice that $24 \times 3 = 72$ and $36 \times 2 = 72$, so $24 \times 3 = 36 \times 2$. In $\frac{24}{36} = \frac{2}{3}$ if you draw a line from the 24 to the 3, and from the 36 to the 2, you make an X-shaped "cross." This "cross-multiplying" gives $24 \times 3 = 36 \times 2$.

RULE: To solve a proportion, cross-multiply and solve the resulting equation. The unknown value can be in any position in the proportion.

EXAMPLE: Solve $\frac{18}{45} = \frac{28}{x}$. Cross-multiply to get $18x = 45 \times 28$, or $18x = 1260$. Then divide both sides of the equation to get $x = 70$.

PRACTICE:

4.1. Cross-multiply to solve each proportion.

    a. $\frac{48}{100} = \frac{x}{75}$ **b.** $\frac{x}{100} = \frac{16}{75}$ **c.** $\frac{15}{38} = \frac{9}{x}$ **d.** $\frac{25.2}{x} = \frac{18}{35}$

A.5 | Whole-Number and Negative Exponents

Exponents are used a lot in mathematics, because they provide an excellent shorthand for a repeated multiplication. For example, expressions like x^3 for $x \cdot x \cdot x$ or 2^5 for $2 \cdot 2 \cdot 2 \cdot 2 \cdot 2$ obviously save time. When there is no exponent visible, it is understood to be 1, if needed. There are several rules for working with exponents, and the rules lead to definitions for exponents that are 0 or negative and do not fit the repeated multiplication idea.

Further definitions: $x^0 = 1$, for any value of x different from 0.

                        $x^{-n} = \frac{1}{x^n}$, for n any whole number and any x not 0.

Think of the exponents in the following rules as whole numbers.

RULES: **a.** $x^m x^n = x^{m+n}$ **EXAMPLES:** $x^3 x^4 = x^{3+4} = x^7$; $10^3 \cdot 10^2 = 10^5$

          b. $(x^m)^n = x^{mn}$ **EXAMPLES:** $(x^4)^5 = x^{4 \cdot 5} = x^{20}$; $(10^2)^3 = 10^6$

          c. $(xy)^n = x^n y^n$ **EXAMPLE:** $(3y)^2 = 3^2 y^2 = 9y^2$

          d. $\dfrac{x^m}{x^n} = x^{m-n}$ **EXAMPLE:** $\dfrac{y^8}{y^2} = y^{8-2} = y^6$; $\dfrac{10^5}{10^3} = 10^{5-3} = 10^2$

PRACTICE:

5.1. Use the rules to write the following as simply as you can. The 10 could be any number, so you can make up variations easily.

a. $10^6 \cdot 10^6$ **b.** $(10^6)^6$ **c.** $10^2 \cdot 10^3$ **d.** $(10^2)^3$ **e.** $\dfrac{10^{12}}{10^3}$

f. $b^4 \cdot b^3$ **g.** $(b^4)^3$ **h.** $b^{-2}b^3$ **i.** $(b^{-2})^3$ **j.** $\dfrac{b^6}{b^3}$

k. $\dfrac{(3x)^5}{3x^2}$ **l.** $\dfrac{(2xy)^3}{(3y)^2}$ **m.** $(1.4 \times 10^4) \cdot (3 \times 10^{-3})$

n. $(2 \times 10^5) \cdot (3.2 \times 10^3)$

A.6 | Order of Operations

To avoid lots of parentheses, there is a commonly accepted convention on how to calculate something like, $3 + 4 \times 5$. (Parentheses are allowed, of course, for complete clarity.) $3 + 4 \times 5 = 23$, not 35, by the convention. Sometimes in informal work, spacing makes clear the intent: $3 + 4 \times 5$.

RULE: First do the work inside any grouping symbols, like parentheses or the terms in a fraction, then attend to any exponents. Next do the multiplications and divisions as you encounter them, from left to right. Finally, do the additions and subtractions as you encounter them, from left to right. (Mnemonic: Please Excuse My Dear Aunt Sally)

EXAMPLE: Evaluate $7 + 4 \times 600 \div 5 - 6 \times (2 + 3)^2$. Following the rule, and doing just one step at a time in this example, the expression $= 7 + 4 \times 600 \div 5 - 6 \times 5^2 = 7 + 4 \times 600 \div 5 - 6 \times 25$ $= 7 + 2400 \div 5 - 6 \times 25 = 7 + 480 - 150 = 487 - 150 = 337$.

EXAMPLE: Evaluate $5x^2 - 3(x - 4)^2$ when $x = 6$. Substituting and following the rule, the expression $=$ $5 \times 6^2 - 3 \times (6 - 4)^2 = 5 \times 6^2 - 3 \times 2^2 = 5 \times 36 - 3 \times 4 = 180 - 12 = 168$.

PRACTICE:

6.1. Evaluate each of the following:

a. $3 \times 10^2 + 5 \times 10 + 2$ **b.** $417 - 2(10 - 3)^2$ **c.** $\frac{5}{9} \times (212 - 32)$

d. $\frac{3+15}{6}$ **e.** $\frac{1}{2} + \frac{1}{2}(5 - 2)^2$

6.2. Evaluate the expressions.

a. $2x^3 - 7x - (10 - 2)$, when $x = 3$ **b.** $25x - (x + 2)(x - 3)^2$, when $x = 5$

c. $\frac{16+3x}{2}$, when $x = 3$ **d.** $\frac{2x^2 + 18}{9}$, when $x = 6$

Appendix A Answers

A.1 Fractions (Including Mixed Numbers)

1.1. **a.** $\dfrac{18}{5}$ **b.** $\dfrac{24}{25}$ **c.** $\dfrac{3}{4}$ **d.** $\dfrac{49}{60}$ **e.** $\dfrac{21}{8}$ **f.** $\dfrac{1}{3}$ **g.** $\dfrac{11}{15}$ **h.** $\dfrac{31}{15}$ **i.** $\dfrac{7}{9}$

  j. $\dfrac{13}{25}$ **k.** $\dfrac{147}{250}$ **l.** $\dfrac{3}{36} = \dfrac{1}{12}$ **m.** $\dfrac{3}{40}$ **n.** $\dfrac{3}{4}$

1.2. **a.** $\dfrac{63}{70}$ **b.** $\dfrac{24}{36}$ **c.** $\dfrac{96}{180}$ **d.** $\dfrac{99}{121}$ **e.** $\dfrac{27}{72}$ **f.** $\dfrac{49}{56}$

1.3. **a.** $\dfrac{3}{12} = \dfrac{3 \times 2}{12 \times 2} = \dfrac{6}{24}; or \dfrac{3}{12} = \dfrac{3 \times 3}{12 \times 3} = \dfrac{9}{36}; similarly = \dfrac{12}{48} = \dfrac{15}{60} = ...;$

  $also \dfrac{1}{4} = \dfrac{2}{8} = \dfrac{3}{12} = \dfrac{4}{16}$. There are many other possibilities.

  b. $Similarly, \dfrac{8}{7} = \dfrac{16}{14} = \dfrac{24}{21} = \dfrac{32}{28} = ... = \dfrac{800}{700}$

1.4. None should be greater than, or less than, the given fraction. This question is to make certain that you realize that your answers are indeed <u>equal</u> to the given fraction (and to each other).

1.5. **a.** $6\frac{61}{72}$ **b.** $1\frac{7}{8}$ **c.** $3\frac{1}{4}$ (It is customary to simplify the fraction.)

  d. $66\frac{2}{3}$ **e.** $18\frac{3}{4}$ **f.** $10\frac{2}{3}$ **g.** $12\frac{6}{7}$ **h.** $84\frac{1}{6}$

1.6. **a.** $\dfrac{15}{2}$ **b.** $\dfrac{58}{3}$ **c.** $\dfrac{423}{8}$ **d.** $\dfrac{17}{1}$ **e.** $\dfrac{119}{10}$

1.7. **a.** $\frac{41}{48}$ **b.** $8\frac{19}{24}$ **c.** $1\frac{1}{4}$ **d.** $118\frac{3}{5}$ **e.** $539\frac{5}{7}$ **f.** $4\frac{5}{12}$

1.8. **a.** $\frac{21}{32}$ **b.** 75 **c.** $\frac{45}{24} = 1\frac{7}{8}$ **d.** $306\frac{2}{3}$ **e.** $36\frac{3}{5}$ **f.** $\frac{4}{9}$

  g. 3 **h.** $737\frac{1}{2}$

1.9. **a.** $1\frac{1}{2}$ **b.** $\frac{2}{3}$ **c.** $5\frac{1}{4}$ **d.** $7\frac{1}{12}$ **e.** $16\frac{1}{2}$ **f.** $\dfrac{7}{500}$

A.2 Decimals

2.1. **a.** E.g., 435.060 and 435.0600 **b.** E.g., 1.40 and 1.4000
  c. E.g., 927.04 and 927.040 and 927.04000 **d.** E.g., 17.00 and 17.000
  e. E.g., 0.68 and 0.6800

2.2. **a.** 1.95 **b.** 163.36 **c.** 19.384

2.3. **a.** 0.06 **b.** 360 **c.** 1.7346 **d.** 84.0924

2.4. **a.** 48 **b.** 2.36 **c.** 0.236 **d.** 48.8 **e.** 0.07 **f.** 675 **g.** 0.04

A.3 Fraction, Decimal, and Percent Conversions

3.1. Some of the answers here are given to more than eight decimal places.
  a. 0.375 (The initial zero is often written to alert one so that the decimal point is not overlooked.)
  b. 0.0625   **c.** 0.1875   **d.** 0.142857142857142857... (forever)
  e. 0.285714285714285714... (forever)   **f.** 0.111111... (forever)   **g.** 0.777... (forever)
  h. 0.0833333...(forever)   **i.** 0.166666... (forever)   **j.** 1.714285714285...   **k.** 0.04
  l. 1.08   **m.** 3.142857142857... (forever)   **n.** 0.076923076923...

3.2.   **a.** $\dfrac{15}{4} = 3\frac{3}{4}$ **b.** $\dfrac{92}{1000} = \dfrac{23}{250}$ **c.** $\dfrac{4}{10,000} = \dfrac{1}{2500}$ **d.** $\dfrac{468}{100} = \dfrac{117}{25} = 4\dfrac{17}{25}$

3.3.   **a.** 425%   **b.** 314.6%   **c.** 100%   **d.** 62%   **e.** 4.5%   **f.** 0.003%

3.4.   **a.** 0.88   **b.** 0.333   **c.** 1.05   **d.** 0.015   **e.** 5   **f.** 0.055

3.5.   **a.** $1.6 = 160\%$ **b.** $0.625 = 62.5\%$ **c.** $0.85 = 85\%$
  d. $\dfrac{952}{1140} \approx 0.8350877 = 83.50877\%$ **e.** $0.904 = 90.4\%$ **f.** $4.375 = 437.5\%$

3.6.   **a.** $0.40 = ... = \dfrac{2}{5}$ **b.** $0.66\frac{2}{3} = \dfrac{66\frac{2}{3}}{100} = ... = \dfrac{2}{3}$ **c.** $1.65 = \dfrac{165}{100} = \dfrac{33}{20} = 1\dfrac{13}{20}$

  d. $0.115 = \dfrac{115}{1000} = \dfrac{23}{200}$ **e.** $0.0025 = \dfrac{25}{10,000} = \dfrac{1}{400}$

3.7.   **a.** 0.9, 90%   **b.** $\dfrac{23}{10} = 2\dfrac{3}{10}$, 230%   **c.** 0.56, $\dfrac{56}{100} = \dfrac{14}{25}$

  d. 1.2, 120%   **e.** 80%, $\dfrac{8}{10} = \dfrac{4}{5}$ **f.** 0.0158, $\dfrac{158}{10,000} = \dfrac{79}{5000}$

A.4 Solving a Proportion

4.1.   **a.** Equation from cross-multiplying: $48 \times 75 = 100x$, or $3600 = 100x$.
  Divide both sides by 100; $36 = x$.   **b.** $21\frac{1}{3}$ **c.** $22\frac{4}{5}$ **d.** 49

A.5 Whole-Number and Negative Exponents

5.1.   **a.** 10^{12} (not 100^{12})   **b.** 10^{36} **c.** 10^5 **d.** 10^6 **e.** 10^9
  f. b^7 **g.** b^{12} **h.** b^1 or just b **i.** b^{-6} **j.** b^3

  k. $3^4 x^3$ or $81x^3$ **l.** $\dfrac{8x^3 y}{9}$ **m.** 4.2×10^1 (scientific notation), or 42

  n. 6.5×10^8 (scientific notation), or 640000000

A.6 Order of Operations

6.1.   **a.** 352   **b.** 319   **c.** 100   **d.** 3   **e.** 5

6.2.   **a.** 25   **b.** 97   **c.** $12\frac{1}{2}$ **d.** 10

Appendix B

Video Clips Illustrating Children's Mathematical Thinking

The six video clips associated with *Reconcepualizing Mathematics: Reasoning About Numbers and Quantities* were developed during a federally funded project at San Diego State University called *Integrating Mathematics and Pedagogy (IMAP)*. The clips are all from interviews with elementary school children. All of the teachers and students involved with the making of these videos have given their permission for the video clips to be used to help teachers better understand students' reasoning about, and understanding of, a variety of mathematical topics. As a viewer of these clips, we ask that you, in turn, respect these students and their teachers. Thus, if a student does not understand a topic, neither the student nor their teacher should be regarded in a negative fashion. There are many reasons why what you see in these clips could have come about, and you will be asked to explore some of these reasons. The purpose of each interview was to assess student knowledge, not to teach. To view the video clips, see http://sdmp-server.sdsu.edu/nickerson.

Although you may encounter some similar types of activities in a mathematics methods course, these videos are included with this mathematics content material because we have learned from experience that many prospective teachers come to view their own mathematics learning differently after watching these children. It will become clear to you that you will need to have a deep understanding of mathematics if you are to successfully teach children such as those you see here. We hope that seeing these children will motivate you to take seriously the study of the mathematics of elementary school.

Video Clip 1: Strategies

In this clip there are three first graders being asked to add and subtract small numbers. Strategies children often use for adding, in a relative order of sophistication, include (a) counting all, using manipulatives of some sort (in this case small blocks); (b) starting with the first number and then counting on in some fashion, such as using fingers; (c) counting on from the larger addend rather than the first addend; (d) compensating by using a known fact to produce a new fact. Counting with manipulatives such as in (a) also has different levels. Children sometimes try to count without moving the objects, and thus count too many or too few. To subtract, children use similar strategies, using manipulatives, counting on fingers, or using known facts to arrive at a new answer.

QUESTIONS FOR REFLECTION AND DISCUSSION

1. In the first interview, a girl is asked to take 5 objects away from 14 objects, and then 6 from 14. Describe the counting strategies she used. Were there any surprises here? If you were helping her, what problem would you give her next, and why?

2. The second girl is asked to add 7 to 4. How did she do this? Notice how she tapped her head when starting from 7. Her teacher taught students to "Put the big number in your head, then count on." Do you think this child actually undertook the process she describes here? Or was she just trying to help the interviewers understand how to do the problem?

3. How would you describe the strategy used by the boy in the third part of this clip? How did he decompose one of the numbers? What problem would you give him next to solve for you and why?

4. These children do not yet appear to know their basic addition and subtraction facts. Are any of them ready to learn them? As a teacher or parent, do you think that children should think about problems like these before being asked to develop instant recall of facts?

Video Clip 2: Javier

Javier, a fifth-grade Limited English Proficient student, uses mental strategies to multiply 6 times 12 and 12 times 12. Before viewing the Javier video clip, tell how you could mentally find 6×12 and 12×12.

Questions for Reflection and Discussion

1. In each case, Javier appears to first do the problem mentally, then explains his reasoning to the interviewer. In each case, do you think his explanations matched his answers?

2. Were you surprised by his strategy for finding 12×12? Why or why not? How did Javier display good number sense?

3. Use the distributive property, as Javier did, to find 8×15 and 16×15.

4. Javier is learning English. Does he explain his thinking clearly to the interviewer?

Video Clip 3: Rachel

The purpose of this clip is to contrast the effectiveness of teaching only procedural rules with teaching for understanding. Doing so is difficult because one cannot select and video a "bad teacher" to be shown in this type of forum. We therefore asked a teacher who does teach for understanding to first teach a lesson (in this case changing mixed numbers to improper fractions and vice versa) very procedurally, and then to teach the lesson about a month later in a way that focused on understanding. Rachel, a student in this class, is interviewed twice, once after each lesson.

Questions for Reflection and Discussion

1. In the first 50 seconds of the video clip, the teacher describes how she taught the first lesson. Do you think this type of teaching is typical of most teachers? How does this match up with your own introduction to work with fractions in elementary school?

2. Rachel is interviewed after this lesson. She is asked to change $\frac{9}{5}$ to a mixed number. She does not appear to be clear about what to do. Why did this happen, do you suppose?

3. The teacher is then interviewed about the second lesson she taught. What do you think she did differently?

4. Rachel is interviewed after the second lesson and asked to change $3\frac{3}{8}$ to an improper fraction. She begins by trying to apply the rule. What goes wrong here?

5. Rachel immediately tries to make a drawing to explain her reasoning. What happens then, and why? How does her drawing help her?

6. Many times teachers teach a lesson procedurally first because they have a lot of content to cover before standardized testing. They then go back and try to supply reasons for the procedures they've taught. Would you have any suggestions for these teachers about the advisability of this strategy of ordering lessons?

Video Clip 4: Ally

Ally is a fifth grader whose teacher has been teaching fractions to her class. This clip is an excerpt from a much longer clip in which the interviewer first tried to diagnose what Ally knew about fractions, next he taught a lesson based on what was learned about Ally's knowledge of fractions, and finally he assessed what Ally had learned from the lesson. You are seeing only some of the first part of the interview with Ally followed by an interview of her teacher. Ally is a student at a school that has regularly had very high standardized text scores.

Notice how the interviewer gives Ally opportunities to work and tell about how she reasoned, without interrupting her or giving any indication about whether she was correct or not.

Ally is first asked to compare the following pairs of fractions by circling the larger fraction in each pair:

$\frac{1}{6}$ and $\frac{1}{3}$ 1 and $\frac{4}{3}$ $\frac{3}{6}$ and $\frac{1}{2}$ $\frac{1}{7}$ and $\frac{2}{7}$ $\frac{3}{10}$ and $\frac{1}{2}$

She is also asked to change $1\frac{1}{3}$ to an improper fraction and $\frac{13}{6}$ to a mixed number.

Before viewing the video clip, do each of the above problems.

QUESTIONS FOR REFLECTION AND DISCUSSION

1. If possible, stop the video and compare the fractions that Ally is being asked to compare.

2. For each of the pairs of fractions Ally was asked to compare, describe how Ally reasoned about the pair.

3. What was the interviewer thinking when he chose a new pair of fractions for Ally to compare?

4. How well do you think Ally understands what a mixed number is? Why do you say this?

5. What did you learn about Ally from her teacher? Were you surprised about how much the teacher knew about Ally, and probably the other thirty-some students in the class?

6. Why did students in this teacher's class think multiplication and division of fractions was easier than adding and subtracting fractions?

7. If you were asked to tutor Ally, where would you begin, and why?

Video Clip 5: Felisha

During the summer after second grade, Felisha and three other students were given opportunities to explore basic fraction concepts over several days with a skilled teacher. In a post interview, Felisha was asked to add two simple fractions, $\frac{3}{4}$ and $\frac{1}{2}$, even though addition of fractions had not been taught during the prior sessions. She works silently for a few minutes before being asked about her reasoning.

QUESTIONS FOR REFLECTION AND DISCUSSION

1. Knowing that this child had not had any instruction on adding fractions, what knowledge do you think she did possess to undertake this work?

2. Was her explanation clear? Correct?

3. Were her drawings sufficient for solving this problem?

4. What problem would you pose next to Felisha? Why?

5. Do you think students can solve a lot of problems even though they've not been taught procedures for doing so? Why or why not?

Video Clip 6: Elliot

Elliot, a sixth-grade student, solves two division-of-fractions problems using his understanding of division. Before viewing this video clip, do the following division problems: $1 \div \frac{1}{3}$ and $1\frac{1}{2} \div \frac{1}{3}$.

QUESTIONS FOR REFLECTION AND DISCUSSION

1. Describe Elliot's reasoning for the first problem. Are his drawings correct? Are they the drawings you would use? Do you think Elliot has a good understanding of division? Why or why not?

2. Do you think Elliot has a good understanding of fractions? Why do you say that?

3. Is your answer the same as Elliot's for the second problem? What went wrong? (Hint: Attend to the last comment by Elliot. Was he thinking of the referent unit for the answer, or the referent unit 1? What was confusing here?)

4. How do you think you could help Elliot understand his error?

Appendix *C*

Supplementary Learning Exercises with Answers for Parts I and II

Available at <u>www.whfreeman.com/sowderpreview</u>

Appendix D

Masters for Base Materials and Pattern Blocks

Masters are included in Appendix G on page APP-25.

Appendix E

Supplementary Learning Exercises with Answers for Part III

Available at www.whfreeman.com/sowderpreview

Appendix F

Using a Protractor to Measure Angle Size

One tool for measuring angle size is called the **protractor**. Different kinds of protractors are available, but a common type of protractor is partially illustrated below. One complication is that this protractor has two scales going from 0 to 180, so you must be attentive to which scale you are using. In this drawing, the scale marks are 5 degrees apart and only a few are labeled; on an actual protractor the marks may be 1 degree or even ½ degree apart. Notice also that an important location, marked here by a point (but sometimes by an arrowhead), is halfway between the two 0 marks. The vertex of the angle to be measured *must* be at this point.

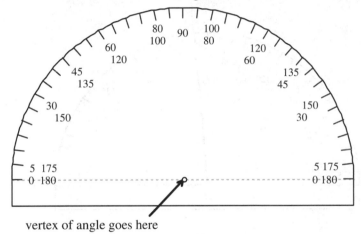

vertex of angle goes here

To measure an angle, say angle *ABC* as shown below, place the protractor so that the vertex of the angle, *B* for this angle, is at the special point. Align the protractor so that one side (side *CB* here) of the angle goes through a 0 point on one of the scales. The other side of the angle gives the size of the angle, which is about 52° here. Be sure to read the measure on the same scale containing your 0 point.

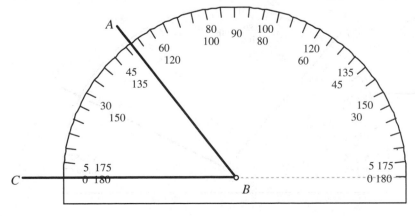

Angle *DEF* has size about 133°. Notice that side *EF* had to be extended so that the scale marking could be read. Such extensions are common, especially when using a large protractor.

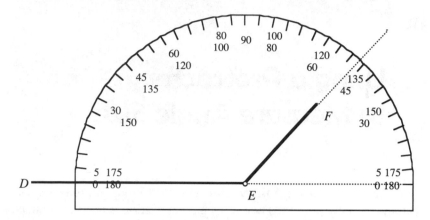

The inner scale is also useful, as in finding that angle *GHI* has size about 85°. Notice that both sides of the angle had to be extended to align one side with 0 and then to read the angle size.

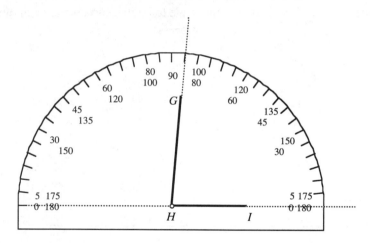

If you are careful to use the same scale for both readings, you can subtract scale readings to find an angle size, as in finding the size of angle *JKL* shown below. (Notice that the vertex of the angle still has to be at the special point.) Using the outer scale, the angle size is about 154 – 50 = 104°; using the inner scale instead, the angle size is about 130 – 26 = 104°.

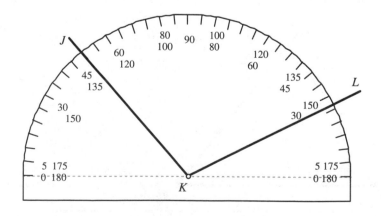

Appendix *G*

Masters for Base Materials, Pattern Blocks, Dot Paper, and Nets

The following pages contain masters for these materials.

1. **Two-dimensional materials for homework in bases two, four, five** (two sheets), **and ten**

2. **Pattern Block patterns**   The first four shapes are quite useful with fraction work, but the square and the thin rhombus do not have easy rational relationships to the first four (they are good for geometry, however). The 3D blocks have one-inch sides.

   a.   (Regular) hexagons (colored yellow in a common 3D version)

   b.   (Isosceles) trapezoids (red)

   c.   "Fat" rhombuses (blue)

   d.   (Equilateral) triangles (grccn)

   e.   Squares (orange)

   f.   "Thin" rhombuses (natural wood)

3. **Dot Paper**   Two pages of each of the isometric dot paper and the square dot paper are included. You may wish to photocopy a page when you need dot paper.

4. **Nets**   Patterns A through O give 3D shapes when they are cut out and taped. The shapes are mentioned often in Part III, so for greater durability you may wish to copy these pages onto a heavier paper, such as card stock.

SOME BASE
TWO PIECES

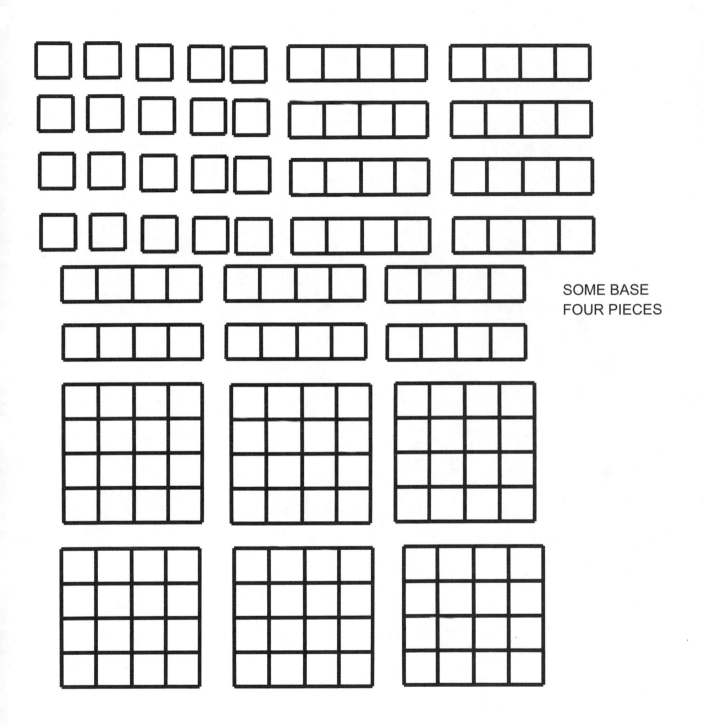

SOME BASE
FOUR PIECES

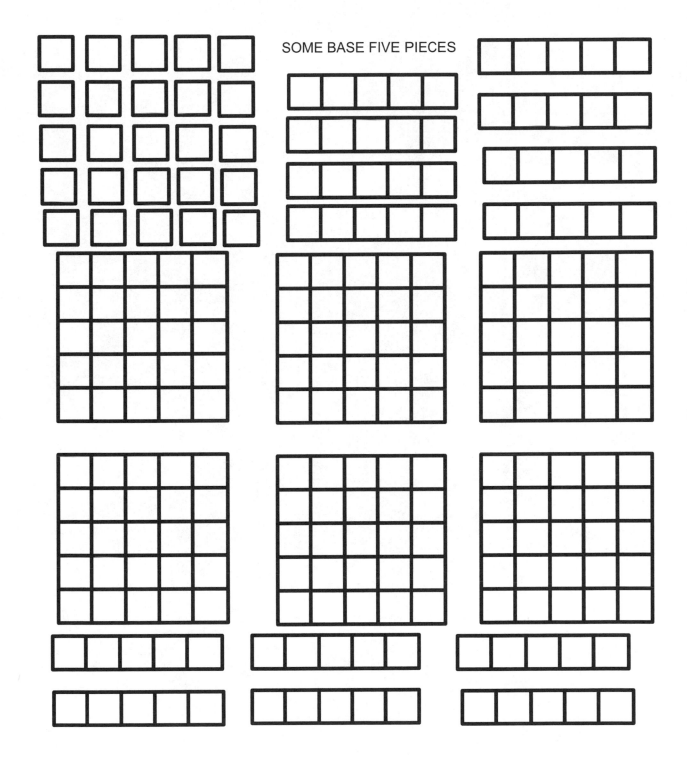

SOME BASE FIVE PIECES

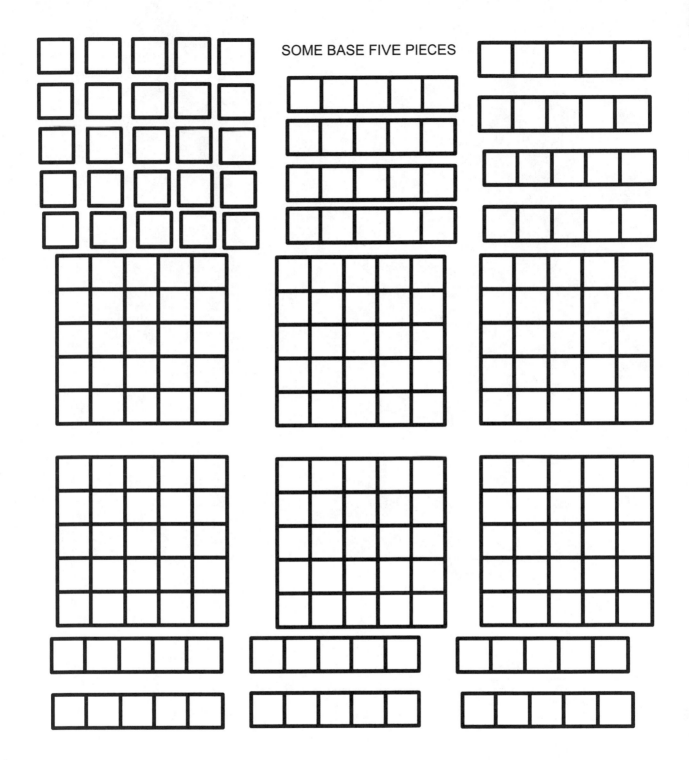

SOME BASE FIVE PIECES

SOME BASE TEN PIECES
(not based on centimeters)

Pattern Block Hexagons (yellow)

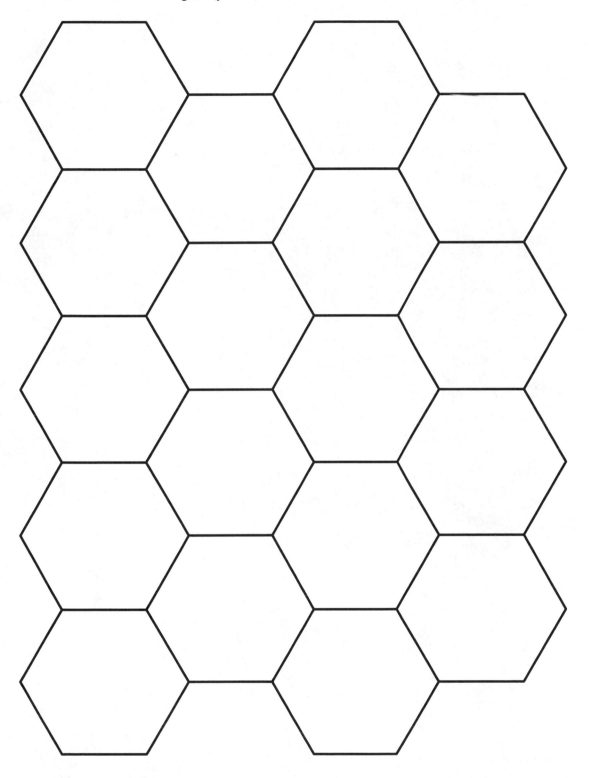

Pattern Block Trapezoids (red)

Pattern Block "Fat" Rhombuses (blue)

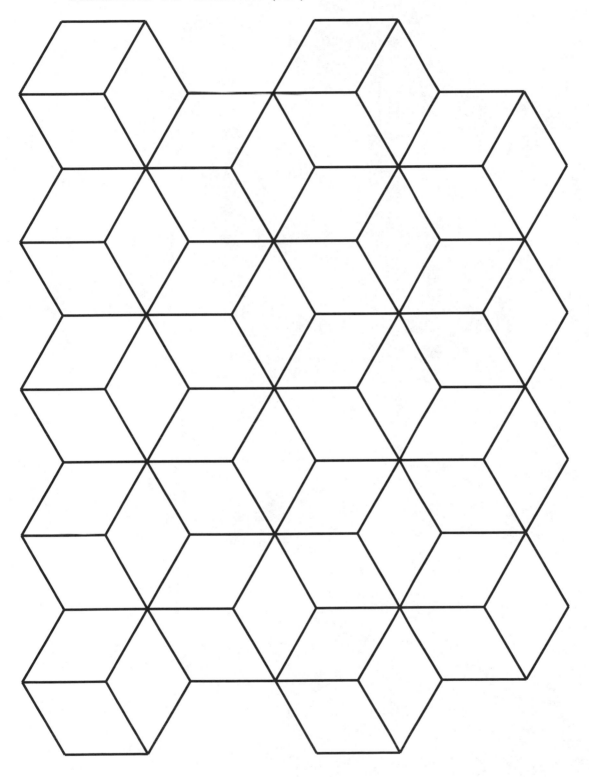

Pattern Block Triangles (green)

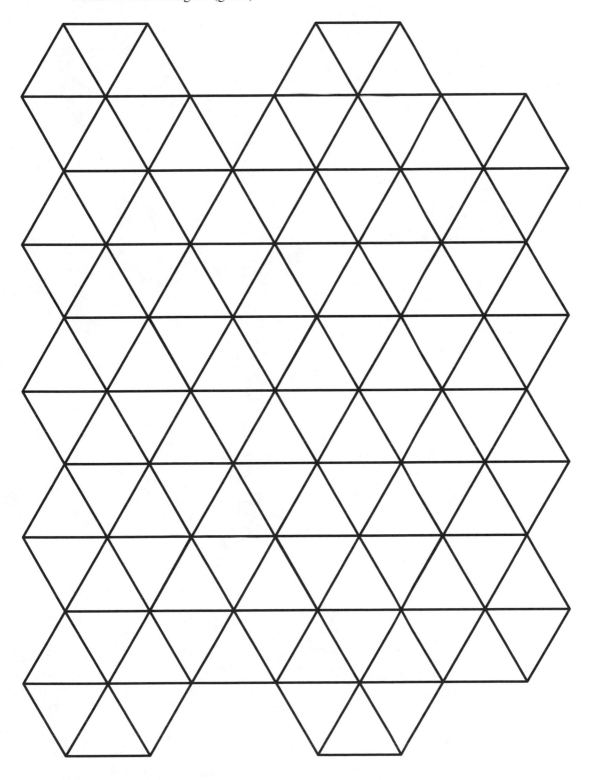

Pattern Block Squares (orange; not useful in most fraction work)

"Thin" rhombuses (natural wood color; not particularly useful with most fraction work)

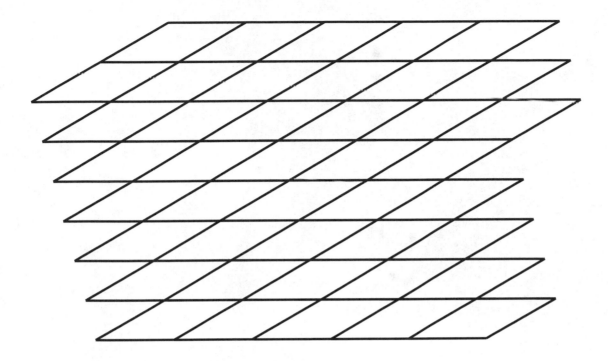

Isometric Dot Paper

Square Dot Paper